THE
Shtetl

THE

Shtetl

TRANSLATED AND EDITED BY
JOACHIM NEUGROSCHEL

RICHARD MAREK PUBLISHERS
NEW YORK

Library of Congress Cataloging in Publication Data

Main entry under title:

The Shtetl.

    Collection of Yiddish tales depicting Jewish life in
the shtetls in Eastern Europe.
    1. Yiddish fiction—Europe—Translations into English.
2. English fiction—Translations from Yiddish.
I. Neugroschel, Joachim.
PJ5191.E8S5   839'.09'301   79-13624
ISBN 0-399-90033-0

Case and book designed by Lynn Hollyn and Associates

PRINTED IN THE UNITED STATES OF AMERICA

Second Impression

CONTENTS

INTRODUCTION
MIRROR MAZE

MIRROR MAZE

Shtetl *is Yiddish for "small town." The word has passed
sentimentally into English, describing the small towns where Jews lived in
Eastern Europe for centuries. In fact, nostalgia has made the shtetl the
symbol of Ashkenazi civilization. Historians and sociologists have somewhat gone along with this synthetic memory, leaving us with a simplified,
often stereotyped image of a relatively serene, self-contained world,
troubled only by a foreign politics generally summed up in pogroms and
survival.*

*Obviously, the reality and the complexity of the shtetl, or rather the
shtetls, were far more confusing and interesting. First of all, we have to
think in plurals, we have to talk about shtetls, many, many shtetls.*

*Of course, certain essential Jewish features were recurrent throughout
Eastern Europe. Most important, there was the nuclear religion and its
overlay of habits, customs, and traditions, completely ruling the lives of
Jews as individuals and as a collective—or collectives. There was the
community structure, socializing, protecting, domineering, with its own
survival as one of its chief functions. There were the two symbiotic
languages: Yiddish, mainly, but not only, for secular life, Hebrew, mainly
for religion and for certain other forms of communication, as in business.
And there was the omnipresent Christian world, with its laws, pressures,
hostility, friendliness, its commercial and economic relations, and its
myriad other energies that were part of an intricate cultural enmeshing
with Jews.*

*But despite the features common to all Eastern European Jews, no two
shtetls were truly alike. The personal and public dynamics, the interrela-*

tions with non-Jews, the climate, the economics, the politics, even the dialect of Yiddish and the pronunciation of Hebrew varied sufficiently to form sharp differences, often contradictions—a crazy quilt through time and space. For we are speaking of an enormous geographical area, and we are speaking of centuries of Jewish history.

The most exciting mirror of Jewish life (or lives) in the shtetls was the absorbing literature created mainly in Yiddish and Hebrew, and then to some extent in Gentile languages like Polish and Russian. But if we speak of mirrors, then we have to imagine the mirrors in the fun house of an amusement park. Each mirror distorts in a different way, focusing on a different image. And if we chance to see a more "objective" mirror, say "realistic" fiction or documented historiography, we find that it warps reality in its own peculiar way—any mirror will at least exchange left and right, disorienting us in the universe of our experience.

In this collection of Yiddish tales about the shtetls, I have tried to show the variety and diversity of Jewish life in Eastern Europe from the religious roots of the late middle ages to World War II and the destruction of the shtetl world. Like imaginative literature anywhere, these tales had an infinity of goals. The authors meant to instruct, entertain, attack, flatter, inquire, analyze, moralize, laud, preach, reform, restore, amuse, divert, ridicule, destroy, depict. . . . The list is endless. Common to all of them is a reflection of certain aspects of shtetl life, and at the very least the author's personal shtetl experiences—refracted through later experiences and emotions. But books change with every reader. And a mirror, of course, usually reflects the observer. Need it be said that this literary array of the Jewish past tells us almost as much about our own present, about most people in most places.

The collection is divided into chronological sections, paralleling Jewish history in Eastern Europe, showing how the literary shtetl developed from a backdrop to the object and substance of both satirical and sentimental treatments, of negative, affectionate, and even indifferent approaches. Not even historiography can honestly testify to so-called "accuracy" of description. True accuracy can at best be found in the tone, style, language, attitude, and psychological space of each writer. For we learned long ago that the reality of literature lies in its own creativity, just as its truth lies in spiritual revelation, and in what Aristotle called its "universality."

The shtetls achieved "universal" realities in one of the most stimulating phases of Jewish literature—a diminishing microcosm of which is presented here. This literature, in turn, was a major creative legacy of shtetl life, a profound and inexhaustible gift to the future. The nineteenth century brought the disruption of shtetl life. The twentieth century brought its destruction and the end of a civilization. The people of the shtetl took up permanent abode in the literature created about them. They were like Rilke's flamingos: They entered one by one into imagination.

PART ONE

THE RELIGIOUS ROOTS
THE CREATION OF THE WORLD
AND THE DESTRUCTION OF THE WORLD

The core of Jewish life has always been its religion. Likewise, the life of shtetl Jews revolved around religious customs and traditions, and a historical awareness going back to Talmudic and Biblical times. The best bridge between the pre-Ashkenazi past and the shtetl reality is *Tsene Rene,* the so-called women's Bible in Yiddish. Jacob ben Isaac Ashkenazi composed this adaptation of the Pentateuch, the Haftorat, and the Five Scrolls in the sixteenth century. Although printed in Germany, it quickly spread to Eastern Europe; and so far, there have been two hundred and ten editions. The author retold the Biblical stories, interweaving his narrative with explanations, interpretations, anecdotes from various exegetical sources. According to the frontispiece, this Yiddish retelling was "designed to enable men and women . . . to understand the word of God in simple language." But since women were barred from learning Hebrew and studying the holy texts, the Yiddish Bible became more properly theirs, and formed a spiritual basis in their lives.

The Jewish religion was churned to its depths by Hassidism, a popular mystical movement launched in the eighteenth century. Appealing to the masses, making religion more accessible to them than scholarly erudition could, it became a major energy in Jewish life. Hagiographic stories about its founder, Israel ben Eliezer Baal Shem Tov (the Master of the Good Name) (c. 1700–1760) were gathered in 1814–1815 by Dov Ber ben Shmuel of Linits. The collection was titled: *In Praise of the Baal Shem Tov.*

1

It distorted the historical personage, creating a supernatural world of magical feats and deeds, although the historical references are certainly rooted in actual events. This enchanted world, with salvation and solution for every calamity that happened to Jews, was a universe of wishful thinking, ruled by a charismatic leader who was endowed with superhuman powers, providing an endless optimism for a highly vulnerable community.

A somewhat similar embodiment of wishful thinking was the Prophet Elijah, who became just about the most popular character in Jewish folklore. Known affectionately in Yiddish as Eli ha-Novi (*novi* being Hebrew for "prophet"), he was an expression of social protest, heeding the cries of the wretched and unfortunate against the oppressive elements *within* the Jewish communities. Disguised as a beggar, a poor man, or even a Gentile peasant, he invariably brought solace and comfort to the sick, the poor, the despairing. But the social criticism in the stories was tempered by the literary optimism of the happy endings.

A different kind of optimism, wrapped in convoluted, messianic allegories, permeated the tales of Rabbi Nakhman of Bratslev (1772–1811). A great-grandson of the Baal Shem Tov, he left an oral tradition of at least thirteen eerie, puzzling tales, which were set down by his son-in-law Nathan and published in a Hebrew/Yiddish edition in 1815. Unlike the multitude of Hassidic stories, which generally praise the supernatural feats of the rebbes, these tales of Nakhman's are more in a fairy-tale tradition of princes, princesses, enchanted castles, magicians, demons, magical voyages, mysterious forests, and the like. The rabbi as story-teller enters and creates Yiddish literature, hinting at mystical energies and eschatological forces. While the section from *Tsene Rene* describes the creation of the world, Rabbi Nakhman's *A Tale of a Lame Man*, inspired by the First Psalm, provides a hopelessly intricate enigma, whose messianic solution points to the end of the world and the ultimate salvation of virtue. ✿

TSENE RENE: THE CREATION
JACOB BEN ISAAC ASHKENAZI

B'REYSHES BORO ELOHIM ES HASHOMAIM
V'ES HAORETS. . . . IN THE BEGINNING, GOD CREATED
THE HEAVENS AND THE EARTH. . . .

In the first creation of heaven and earth, the earth was waste
and wild, and God's Throne of Glory hovered in the air over the
water.

Now why does the Torah begin with *B*, ב, *beys,* the second
letter of the Hebrew alphabet? To show that just as ב, beys, has
three sides that are closed and a fourth that is open, so too is the
universe. God Blessed Be He closed three sides, but on the
northern side, He did not make any heaven. Also, perhaps
because *beys, B,* is the first letter of *brokha* (blessing). Whereas א,
aleph, the first letter of the Hebrew alphabet, is also the first letter
of ארור *(orur),* meaning curse. That is why God began with
the *B*.

So the *aleph* flew up to God Blessed Be He and said: "Start the
Torah with me, for I am the first letter of the alphabet."

God answered: "I am going to give the Ten Commandments
on Mount Sinai, and I shall begin them with *aleph.*"

Now the Torah begins with the word *B'REYSHES*, IN THE
BEGINNING, to teach us that the world was created for the sake
of the Torah, of which it is written in Proverbs 8:22: "God
created me in the beginning of His way, before His works of old."

Rabbi Isaac asks: "Why does the Torah describe how God
created the world? After all, the Torah is all duties and precepts,

3

and it should have begun with duties and precepts. But then the seven nations of Canaan would have told the Children of Israel: 'You are thieves. You are stealing our earth *(erets)*, the land *(erets)* of Israel, from us.' The Children of Israel could then reply: 'God Blessed Be His Name created the earth *(erets)*. First he gave it to you, and today he wants to give it to us.' "

Our sages have said: "God created the world for three things: For the Torah, which is called the Beginning of the Way. And for the offerings that were offered up in the Temple, which is called the First Temple, because it was created first, in the Beginning, before the world. And for the tithes, which are the first, the beginning, of the grain."

And because the Torah speaks of the Temple, it also tells us how the Temple will be destroyed. That is why it says: THE EARTH WAS WASTE AND WILD. The earth will be laid waste. For the Shekhina, the Divine Radiance, will turn from us in the Destruction. And that is why it says: AND THE SPIRIT OF GOD HOVERED OVER THE FACE OF THE WATER. This tells us that even when we are in exile, the Torah will not be turned from us. And that is why it says: AND GOD SAID: LET THERE BE LIGHT. This shows us that after the Exile, God will make Zion bright and will send us the Messiah. For it is written in Isaiah 60:1: ARISE AND SHINE UPON US FOR THY LIGHT IS COME.

GOD SAID: LET THERE BE A LIGHT AND LET THERE BE A LIGHT. He created two lights, the sun and the moon, to light the world. And He created one more light, for the righteous, when the Messiah comes. This light is very great. And because the world has not deserved such a great light, God has kept it hidden for the righteous.

Rabbi Simeon says that the word LIGHT *(UR)* appears five times in this opening portion of Genesis, for the five books of the Torah, because the Torah is like a light:

The first time, LET THERE BE LIGHT, is for Genesis. Because with that light, God created the world. The second time, AND THERE WAS LIGHT, for Exodus, which tells how the Children of Israel left the Egyptian Exile, from darkness to light. For with salvation, it is written (Exodus 10:23): ALL THE

CHILDREN OF ISRAEL HAD LIGHT IN THEIR DWELL-INGS. The third time: AND GOD SAW THE LIGHT THAT IT WAS GOOD. That is for Leviticus, where He speaks about the offerings: A man had to repent when sacrificing, and thus he saw the light. The fourth time, it says: GOD DIVIDED THE LIGHT FROM THE DARKNESS. That is for Numbers. There it is written that the Children of Israel were divided from their evil deeds. And the Temple went with them through the desert and shone upon them. The fifth time, it says: AND GOD CALLED THE LIGHT DAY. That is for Deuteronomy, which contains only laws and duties. They light up like a light.

And that shows us that there are five lights. One light is the one with which the world was created. The second light is Salvation, which is like a light. The third light is when a man repents, and he sees the light. The fourth light is the Temple. The fifth light is the Torah and the laws. And the verse LET THERE BE LIGHT teaches us that God created the world with light. For as soon as God said LET THERE BE LIGHT, the world began to be created.

Now the letters in the word YIHI (LET THERE BE) have a total numerical value of twenty-five. This shows that the world was created on the twenty-fifth day of Elul, the last month of the year. For the Talmud says that Adam the First Man was created on Rosh Hashanah (the first of the year). And that was already the sixth day of the Six Days of Creation.

Now everything else was created before Adam, so that man would not be haughty. He should remember that the beasts and cattle were created before him. Another reason why Adam was created after all creatures was so that he would find everything prepared for him.

AND GOD CALLED THE LIGHT DAY AND THE DARK-NESS HE CALLED NIGHT AND IT WAS EVENING AND IT WAS MORNING THE FIRST DAY.

AND GOD SAID LET THE HEAVENS GROW STRONG. On that first day, the heavens were weak. So God shouted at them. The second day, they grew strong from God's shout.

AMID THE WATERS: The heavens (SHOMAÏM) made a separation in the waters (MAÏM), for above the heavens there are

5

waters just like on the earth. And the waters are as high above the heavens as the heavens are far from the earth. And the waters above the heavens hang in the air by God's bidding.

And the lower waters warred with the higher waters and said: "Why should we be below, on the earth. We want to be above too, over the earth." So God promised the water on the earth that there should be no offering on the altar without salt. And the salt comes from the water that is on the earth.

On all days, it is written: IT WAS GOOD. But on the second day, it is not written: IT WAS GOOD. That is because the creation of the second day was not quite done. And a thing that is not done is not good. For the creation of the water was not finished on the second day. It was only on the third day that God Blessed Be He finished creating the water. That is why on the third day, IT WAS GOOD appears twice. Once, when the waters were fully created, and a second time, because the creation of the earth was finished on the third day.

Now some sages say: Hell was created on the second day, and that is why IT WAS GOOD does not appear on the second day. And some say: War began on the second day, when the waters began warring. That is why IT WAS GOOD does not appear on the second day, for nothing good comes of war. For that is why Hell was already created on the second day. For the man who wages war will fall down to hell, which is what happened to Corah.

In the Talmud, Rabbah Bar Bar Hannah says that he was once traveling through the desert when a merchant came to him and said: "I will show you where Corah sank into the earth." He saw that the earth was cloven and smoke was pouring forth. So he took a spear, wrapped some wool around the tip, and thrust the spear into the cleft. The wool was burnt up by the fire that was in the cleft. So he put his ear to the cleft and he heard them shouting: "Moses is Truth and his Torah is Truth, and we are liars." And every thirty days, the fire in hell is turned over for them so that they may suffer more and keep shouting: "Moses is Truth and his Torah is Truth, and we are liars." Hence, all men should be warned not to wage war.

Also, some sages say that no trade should be started on a

Monday, the second day, for it is not written on that day: IT WAS GOOD. And as of Monday, there was war all the time. And on the third day, we find war. God bade the earth bring forth trees, and they should have a taste like the fruits. But the earth did not do so. On the fourth day, there was also war. The moon said: "Why must the sun shine as brightly as the moon itself." It wanted to shine more brightly. So God made it smaller, along with its light. On the sixth day, Adam sinned and was driven from the Garden of Eden. So we can see that war began with the second day.

LET THE WATERS GATHER.

On the third day, God said: "Let all the waters gather in one place, and let the earth come forth." And so all the waters soon gathered in one place, and that was the Great Sea.

And God said: "Let the earth bring forth trees and let them have a taste like the fruits." But the earth did not do so. Therefore, it was cursed along with Adam.

LET THERE BE LIGHTS!

On the fourth day, God said: "Let there be lights in the heavens." For light was already created on the first day. But the lights were not hung in the heavens until the fourth day. God hung up the sun and the moon, and the constellations and the stars. And the lights were to be signs. If the sun is beaten, that is a sign for those who serve the sun that God shall send destruction to them and when the moon is beaten, that is a sign that God is angry at the Children of Israel because they are not good. For the Children of Israel count by the moon.

And the sun and the moon were signs when to pray. In the morning, the sun is a sign to put on prayer thongs and say morning prayers. And at night, when the stars come up, it is time to say evening prayers.

And the sun and the moon were given so that we may know when to have holy days. For we reckon all holy days by the moon. Also, we are to know from the sun and the moon when it is day or night and we are to know when the year comes to an end.

Rabbi Azariah says:

"The sun was not created to shine alone, for God said: 'There will be men who see the sun as a god if only the sun shines.' That is why God created the moon, so that they would not see the sun as a god."

And the sun and the moon were equally great with their light. But the moon said: "Why should we both shine equally? Let me shine alone." So God said to the moon: "Since you want to be haughty and want to shine alone, you have to become small."

The Bkhai writes: "For the sacrifice of the new month, the sacrifice is more for God than for all other sacrifices. This is because God created the sun and the moon equally with their light. But the moon, it has its light from the sun, for the moon itself is black, but it shines from the sun. For the moon said to God: 'Lord of the Universe, have you no power to let me shine myself, without the sun? I am useful to the world, like the sun, and people will say, God forbid, that you had no power to make my own light.' Thereupon God grew angry at the moon and said: 'Do you want to teach me what to do?' And he said to the moon: 'Because you spoke against me, your light, even what you have from the sun, must be lessened.' And the moon said: 'Because I spoke amiss, I have to lessen my light.' And God said to the moon: 'I know why I created your light to come from the sun. And because you spoke amiss, my Children of Israel are to make an offering at the start of every month when the moon shows itself and renews itself.' "

And the sun was to shine in the day and the moon at night. And if the light of the moon were the same as the light of the sun, men would not know when it is day and when it is night. And they would work in the nighttime as in the daytime, and they would have no rest, and they would soon die of hard work. That was why God said: "People have to know when it is day and when it is night, so that they may rest at night from their work and doings." God also said: "They must have the night to study Torah, for people are silent at night, so they can study."

And God showed that when a man repents, God accepts his penance, as we find with the moon.

And God bade that an offering be offered up at the start of the month, when the moon renews itself. For God said: "Make an offering for what I did to the moon." And that is why it is written for the offering of the new month: "An offering to God, that is to say, for God's sake."

LET THE WATERS ABOUND.

On the fifth day, God said: "Let the waters abound, and let there be a living body, and birds that have wings, and also the great Leviathan." And the Holy Blessed Be His Name did bless the fishes more than other creatures because all people catch the fishes, for they belong to no man, they have no owners. Therefore did God bless them, so they might abound even if many of them were caught. Nor do the beasts have masters, they belong to no man, they have no owners, and people catch many of them. Yet the Holy Blessed Be He wrote no blessing for the beasts, for the serpent was also a beast. And the Holy Blessed Be He wanted to curse her. Therefore He wrote no blessing for any beast, so that the serpent would not be blest.

Now the verse says: THE BIG FISHES. For there are big fishes that are many leagues long, as the Talmud says, and Rabbah Bar Bar Hannah says: "The sea cast forth a big fish, and from one eye they made three hundred barrels of fat. And a year later, I came back, and they were sawing huge beams from the fish's bones." Rabbah Bar Bar Hannah also says: "Once we came to the middle of the sea, when we saw a very big fish, and his back loomed out of the water, and sand was on his back. So we left the ship and built a fire on the fish's back to cook, for we thought it was a mountain. When the fire grew big and the fish felt the fire, he turned over, and if the ship had not been near, we would all have drowned."

The Bkhai writes: "Because God blest the fishes, they survived the Flood, for all things were doomed in the Flood. Only the fishes survived."

LET US MAKE MAN. . . .

On the sixth day, God said to the angels: "Let us create a man." God thus taught us that a man should not be proud, he should consult with other people and seek their advice when he wishes to do something. Even if they are lowlier people than he is, he should ask them. And that was why God said to the angels: "Let us create a man." In truth, however, no one helped Him, God alone created man, as it is written: AND GOD CREATED MAN. This means that God alone created man. For God said that if there is no shape on earth like the angels in heaven, then there will be envy in Creation. So God created the same on earth as the

9

angels in heaven, with a mind and with a shape. That is man on the earth. And God said that man shall rule over the fishes in the sea and over the birds that fly under heaven and over the beasts and cattle that are on the earth.

The Bkhai writes that since the verse says AND GOD BLEST THEM AND SAID TO THEM BE FRUITFUL AND MULTIPLY, those were two blessings for man. One blessing was that his food and drink be blest in his body, for the body grows weak every day, and with food he makes it sound again. And the humors in man grow dry for two reasons. One reason is that man has much heat, which dries his humors and moisture. The other reason is that the wind blows upon man and dries his humors. So eating and drinking make his humors moist again. That is why God gave his blessing. So that the food would spread in man's body, through all parts, and make good what he loses every day in his humors, not more and not less, so that he may remain sound.

And the other blessing, BE FRUITFUL AND MULTIPLY, is so that man may cleave to his wife and have children to serve God and to know his Creator.

And God said that man should eat the fruits and all that on earth is sown. But the beasts and birds and cattle should eat no fruits, not even what is sown, but only grass. However, man was not allowed to eat the flesh of any creature, for the beasts and cattle also have living souls. And even though they are not quite equal to man, there is dignity in their souls. But after the Flood, the beasts and birds and cattle spoiled their ways. So after the Flood God said that man may eat flesh. For Noah was a righteous man in the days of the Flood and through his merits some of every creature survived in the Ark. That was why God said to Noah: "You may eat flesh. For the soul of a man was created only to study Torah and to grasp the strength of God and to do his laws."

The Midrash Rabbah in the Sidrah Rabbi Simeon says that when God wanted to create man, the angels gathered together. Some of them said he should not be created because he would be full of falsehood. And some said he should be created for he would be righteous and charitable. Some said he should not be created for he had no peace in him and liked to wage war. What did God do? He took Truth and hurled it down from heaven to earth. For God said: "Man is better than you all, for you each have a mind and a good spirit and you have no evil spirit. Hence you must always be pious. But man on earth has an evil spirit, who talks him into doing evil; and if he is pious, that is more of a wonder than for you angels. And since you say he is full of falsehood and will wage war and will sin, therefore will I let him die. He will be afraid of death and will be pious. And I will take back his holy soul and I will purge it in hell and it will come back to its first place under the Throne of Glory, and I will not lose it."

Therefore, Rabbi Simeon says: "God hurled Truth down from heaven because Truth in Hebrew, *emet,* is spelled: *aleph mem tov. Aleph* is the first letter of *arun,* meaning coffin. *Mem* is the first leter of *mitah,* meaning bier. *Tov* is the first letter of *takhrikhim,* meaning shroud. This means: Man must die and he is put into a shroud, in the coffin, in the grave, and he is carried to the grave on a bier. That is why God said man would be pious, because he has to die. He would therefore not be haughty."

And our sages have said about that: "It is a great boon." This means that death is very good for man. For the righteous man has the right life after his death. He comes under the Throne of Glory.

The verse (in Psalms) says about that: DEAR TO GOD'S EYES IS THE DEATH OF HIS PIOUS. This means that God would not even have created the pious if it were not for death. For even the pious man must sin. And through death he atones and then he comes to his rest.

Then the angels said to God: "Lord of the Universe, why do you wish to shame your ornament and your likeness and cast him upon the earth? He will be doomed. That is: Man was created in God's form and likeness, and you want to ruin his form and kill it. Keep your likeness above, in heaven." God answered: THROUGH TRUTH FROM THE EARTH. Truth means: coffin, bier, shroud. When man dies, he rises again from earth to heaven. And as the Talmud says: "Three have a share in man: father, mother, and God."—"And as soon as a man dies," says God, "you, father and mother, take your shares, and I want to take my share. That is the soul. My likeness shall come back to me."

Rabbi Honah says that the angels fought with one another. Some said man should be created and some said no. But God went and created man and said to the angels: "Why are you fighting? I have already settled the fight. There is a parable about a great lord who had much wealth and property, and much good wine. But he had no guest. So what good was his property if he could not show his wealth and honor? Likewise, there are many creatures in the world. But if man does not exist, who would know the glory and strength of God?"

THE SIXTH DAY. . . .

The Torah uses an extra letter, ה , *hey*, the fifth letter of the alphabet, for the creation of man, because God set one condition: that the Children of Israel receive the Torah, which is made up of five books. If they study the Torah, then the world will survive. The extra *hey* shows us that everything was created in fives, everything on that condition. On the first day, five lights were created. On the second day, five heavens. And *water* is written five times on the second day. On the third day, five kinds of plants were created from the earth. On the fourth day, there were five kinds of light: the sun and the moon, and the constellations, and the stars, and the day shines too. On the fifth day, God created all living things, and they have five ways of moving: some walk on two legs, some on four legs, and some crawl on their bellies, and some fly, and some swim. On the sixth day, God created man, and his soul has five names in Hebrew: *nefesh, ruakh, neshamah, yikhrah, khai.*

Now it is certain that man was created with more changes than all other living creatures. For in all other creatures there is no war, but there is war in man's body. For when he wishes to do good, the evil spirit comes and tries to stop him. And when he wishes to do evil, then the good spirit comes and tries to stop him. Thus, he has war in his body all his days.

Now why did God create him with war and not with peace? God did it for man's sake so that he would have the power to do what he wishes. However, the beasts and cattle have an evil spirit, but no good spirit. Hence, their nature is for evil: to eat well, to drink well, and to give in to all good lusts. Even the angels have no might to do as they will for they are full of understanding and goodness. So they have to be good. And because no creature in the world has the might to do what it will, God wanted to create a creature that *would* have might to do as it will. Man is thus equal to God. Just as God has might to do what He will, so too has man. God lets him do as he will, and before he ate of the Tree of Knowledge, he had might to do his will. But his nature was for good and not for evil. And as soon as he ate of the Tree of Knowledge, he began to do evil and good. That is why the tree is called the Tree of the Knowledge of Good and Evil. This means that he who eats of the tree has the intelligence to do good and evil. And so God did not say LET US CREATE IN OUR LIKENESS for any other creature. Only for man does the Torah say: LET US CREATE MAN IN OUR LIKENESS. Which means that man would have might to do as he will. Just as I have might to do what I will, and for man's sake the Torah has written for man: AND GOD CREATED MAN IN HIS OWN LIKENESS, IN GOD'S LIKENESS DID GOD CREATE HIM. And that is why the angels wanted to sing the praises of Adam the First Man and wanted to serve him. For they heard from God that man has might to do what he will, like God.

Now what did God do? He cast a sleep upon Adam and showed the angels that they were better than Adam. For even though man has might to do as he will, then nevertheless, sleep comes over him, and he can do no evil and no good. However, the angels never sleep and they can always do as they will. That is why the angels are called "the Wakeful," for they are always awake. And that is why the beasts and cattle were created on the sixth day, and man too, so that if man were pious, then he would be better than all beasts and cattle, and if he were not pious, then he would be worse than all beasts and cattle, for he has intelligence to do good but would do evil.

AND GOD ENDED ALL HIS WORKS ON THE SEVENTH DAY.

Now the Hebrew word for ENDED also means DESIRED. This means that on the seventh day, God desired that all the things which he had created in the six days remain forever as they were.

AND GOD BLEST . . . AND SANCTIFIED. God blest the Sabbath so that man would have one more soul than during the week. And that is why when the Sabbath goes away, we speak a blessing over spices, because our Sabbath soul has gone away.

AND HE SANCTIFIED.

God sanctified the Sabbath and did no work on that day.

AND HE RESTED ON THE SEVENTH DAY FROM ALL THE WORKS HE HAD DONE AND CREATED.

That means that the six days are for the six thousand years that the world will exist. On the first day, God created light. That is for the first thousand years, when Adam lived. He was the light of the world, he recognized his Creator. On the second day, God created the heavens and made a separation between the waters. That was for the second thousand years, when Noah was separated from the evil people who lived in his times, and they were drowned in the Flood. And that too is why IT WAS GOOD was not written on the second day. For the Flood was for the second day. On the third day, the earth was seen, and all trees and fruits did grow. That is for the third thousand years, when Abraham was born, and his children received the Torah and the precepts, which are like the fruits of the world. On the fourth day, two lights were created, a great one and a small one. That was for the fourth thousand years, when there were two temples. One shone greatly upon Israel, and one less. On the fifth day, the birds and the fishes in the water were created. That was for the fifth thousand years. On the sixth day, man was created. That is for the sixth thousand years, when the Messiah will come. And just as Adam was created in God's likeness, so too was the Messiah anointed by God, and the spirit of God will be upon him. And we rest on the Sabbath because we will have our rest in the days of the Messiah. The Midrash Rabbah writes in the Sidrah: "God blest the Sabbath, so that we would honor it with good food, and thus will God make man rich."

Rabbi Khai bar Aba says: "Once I stayed with a householder in the city of Lurkia. A silver table was brought in, and it took sixteen men to carry it, and on it were all the things created on the Six Days of Creation. And a child was sitting in the middle of the table and it was shouting: THE EARTH IS THE LORD'S

AND THE FULLNESS THEREOF. And the child was shouting these words so that the master of the house would not be haughty. So I asked him: 'What have you done to deserve such riches?' And he replied: 'I was a butcher, and whenever I had a good head of cattle, I saved it for the Sabbath. As of Sunday, I saved everything for the Sabbath.' So I said to him: 'I know very well that this is why God gives good luck and blessings. If a man honors the Sabbath and the holy days, God will make him rich in this world and He will give him a good reward in the next world.'"

It is written: "Once upon a time, a prince sent his servant to buy fish on the eve of Yom Kippur. The servant came to the fisherman. Then a Jewish tailor came, and they bid for a fish and the Jew bought it for twelve ducats and took it away. And so the servant left without any fish. His master was angry at him for not bringing back any fish. The servant replied: 'A Jewish tailor outbid me, he bought the fish for twelve ducats.' So the prince sent for the tailor and asked him: 'Why did you outbid my servant?' The tailor replied: 'How can I help buying fish and all sorts of good food? Tomorrow we have a day which God told us to sanctify, and we hope that He will forgive our sins, which we have committed all through the year. How can I help but be merry?' The prince replied: 'You are right.' So the tailor went home and split open the fish and found a pearl inside, from which he was able to live for the rest of his life."

Rabbi Eleazar says about Rabbi Yossi: "God blest the Sabbath with a good fragrance because food on the Sabbath tastes better than during the week."

Rabbi Yehudah Hanassi gave a banquet for Emperor Antoninus on the Sabbath and he served him cold food, and it tasted very good. Then Rabbi Yehudah gave another banquet for the emperor during the week and served him hot food. The emperor said to the rabbi: "Give me the cold food. It tasted better." So the rabbi said: "This food needs spices." The emperor said: "I have enough spices among my treasures." To which the rabbi said: "The spices are the Sabbath. That day is blest with a good fragrance."

Tinius Rufus asked Rabbi Akibah why the Sabbath is better than the other days of the week. Rabbi Akibah replied: "Why are you greater than other men?" Tinius Rufus replied: "The king made me great and wants me to be honored." Rabbi Akibah replied: "God likewise wants the Sabbath to be honored more than other days." So Tinius Rufus said to Rabbi Akibah: "How can you prove that the Sabbath is better than other days and that God ordained it thus?" Rabbi Akibah replied: "The river Sambatyon shows this to be true. For it casts out stones all through the week. But on the Sabbath, it rests." To which Tinius Rufus said: "The man who wants to tell a lie will offer proof from far away, where no people have ever been, so that no man can refute him. That is what you have done. You offer me proof with the river Sambatyon, where no one has been. Could that be a lie?" So Rabbi Akibah said to him: "Try and use magic to bring a dead man back from the dead on the Sabbath." He tried, but the dead man would not come back on the Sabbath. During the week, however, he *would* come back. And Rabbi Akibah then offered further proof that the Sabbath was greater than all the other days.

Some sages say: "The Sabbath is blest because it has no friend. Sunday has a friend: Monday. Tuesday has Wednesday. And Thursday has Friday. But the Sabbath has no friend." Rabbi Samuel bar Nakhman says: "The Sabbath is blest and cannot be put off on another day, the way a holy day is put off, and Yom Kippur is sometimes put off so that it will not fall on a Friday or Sunday. For if a man dies, the corpse will have to lie for two days, Friday and Saturday, or Saturday and Sunday. But the Sabbath is never put off."

So the Sabbath said to God: "Why don't I have a friend?" And God said to the Sabbath: "Israel will be your friend." And so, when the Children of Israel came to Mount Sinai, the Sabbath said for God: HONOR THE SEVENTH DAY, THE SABBATH. This means: "Remember you promised me that Israel will rest in me and will be my friend."

TALES OF THE BAAL SHEM TOV
ANONYMOUS

TSADDIKS WHO ARE PRIVILEGED TO RECEIVE THE LIGHT OF THE TORAH CAN SEE FROM ONE END OF THE WORLD TO THE OTHER

I.

There were two rich brothers who lived in Kamenke. One was named Jonah and the other Borukh. They each sent out a shipment of bulls, but then they heard that soldiers had taken Jonah's bulls. Borukh was afraid that they might have taken away his bulls too. So he sent Joseph of Kamenke to the Baal Shem Tov to find out if that had happened. Jonah also went to the Baal Shem Tov.

When the Baal Shem Tov set about washing before his meal, he asked Jonah to wash as well. After blessing the bread, the Baal Shem Tov said: "Why didn't they tell me when they started out on the road, I would have watched out for them." The Baal Shem Tov opened a holy book, gazed inside for a moment, and then closed it again. He said: "I see that Borukh's bulls are safe. They were not stolen." Jonah asked him: "Is that written in the book?" The Baal Shem Tov replied: "It is written in the Torah that when the Good Lord created the first day, one could look through it from one end of the world to the other. But God knew that there would be evil people in the world. Therefore he hid the light, so

17

that no one could look from one end of the world to the other, for evil things would come of it if evil people could look from one end of the world to the other end. It is written that the Good Lord hid the light, and it is not written that the Good Lord took away the light. Hence, the light must be in the world, but it is hidden from people. Where did he hide the light? Did he dig a hole in the earth and hide the light in the hole? You should know that God hid the light in the Torah. The man who is privileged to receive the light that is hidden in the Torah can also see from one end of the world to the other today. And when the Torah says that God hid the light for the tsaddiks for the future, when the Messiah comes, it means the tsaddiks who live in each generation. Do you think that this is all I saw? Why I could see things that were happening in Amsterdam."

And what he said was true. The bulls were not taken away.

II.

Once, the Baal Shem Tov had to go away during the day. But it was the time for blessing the new moon, so he waited until night. The wagon was all prepared, and the Baal Shem Tov went to bless the new moon. One of his followers went with him. He did not leave him for even a second. When they still weren't very far from the wagon, the man wanted to look back. But the Baal Shem Tov wouldn't let him look back, because a man who had nothing for the Sabbath was stealing the bridle. That was why the Baal Shem Tov wouldn't let his follower look back, so that the needy person could steal the bridle. After the benediction for the new moon, the drayman shouted: "Who stole the bridle?!" The Baal Shem Tov said: "Don't shout, here's some money, redeem the bridle from the man with whom it was pawned."

III.

One day, the Baal Shem Tov traveled to Satinov.

Upon nearing the town, he saw a great light inside the town. So he halted. The light shone upon a woman. When the Baal Shem Tov entered the town, he was welcomed by friends. The Baal Shem Tov said: "You ought to be ashamed of yourselves. I saw a light on a woman in this town, but not on a man. Tell me, do you know her, do you know about this woman?" His friends said: "That must be pious Rebecca." The Baal Shem Tov wanted to send for her, but his friends said: "You needn't send for her. She will certainly come to you for alms, for she does good deeds."

The next morning, after prayers, the Baal Shem Tov saw her coming. He said: "She has decided to get forty guldens from me. You shall see how I act towards her." She came and said: "There are poor people and sick people here. I ask you to give me decent alms." The Baal Shem Tov gave her a small coin. She didn't say a word, but she acted as if she wouldn't take it. So he gave her another small coin, but she wouldn't take that either. So he said to her: "Who made you an administrator so that you could steal alms?"

Rebecca didn't hear that at all for she held herself low and humble like earth. And she wouldn't go away from him until he had given her forty guldens. In the evening, she came again and said: "There is a healer here, he is dangerously ill. Pray for him, you people." The Baal Shem Tov said: "A fornicator will pass away." She said: "Who says that this is so?" The Baal Shem Tov said to the people who were in the room: "Am I telling the truth?" They said: "Yes." She said: "Did they see that the healer should be judged? And besides, the healer is a very ignorant man, he doesn't know the harshness of the sin at all. If he knew the harshness of the sin, he would certainly never have done it." The Baal Shem Tov said that he had heard the divine accusation against the healer, and that he had deliberately talked the divine accuser into letting Rebecca plead for the sick man. Her pleading was accepted, and the healer became well again.

And whenever the woman went to her husband's grave, she would tap on the stone and say: "Hershel, Hershel, go to the Throne of Glory and pray for your children so that they may be poor and needy, and thus never leave the path of God." Once, her two sons, Isaac and Joseph, visited her for the Sabbath to

19

fulfill the commandment to honor their mother. And they arrived on Thursday. The townsfolk came to welcome them. And a great love arose between them, for they realized they were friends. On Friday morning, the day before Sabbath, Rebecca prepared breakfast, she served it and she told them: "My children, I want to ask you to do something for me." They said: "Whatever you ask us to do, we will certainly do." So she said to them: "Swear to me that you will do my will." They said: "We are amazed that you could even suspect that we would not do your will." She said: "I will most likely ask so much of you that I am afraid you will not obey me." The sons begged her not to make them swear, and they assured her that they would certainly obey her. So she said: "I ask you to go away from here today, right away, and not celebrate the Sabbath in my home, for the Good Lord gave me children to be my pride and joy in the next world, not in this world." The sons said to her: "The townsfolk will not let us go away when they find out." But she said: "Send the wagons out behind the town and I will lead you out from behind, so that the townsfolk will not see you." And they did so and went away on the eve of Sabbath.

Thus we can see that the Baal Shem Tov was right about the light on her, for where else in the world can we find such a pious woman?

WHY THE BAAL SHEM TOV LAUGHED

Once, the Baal Shem Tov was in a wagon with several people. On the way, they came into a woods. In the middle of the woods, the Baal Shem Tov began laughing. When they asked him why he was laughing, he told them:

"When I was still living in the village, the people once needed rain, and so I prayed for rain. Now there was a witch in the village, and she worked a spell to keep away the rain. But my prayer and my fervor destroyed her spell. The witch had a demon with her, and the demon told her that I had destroyed her spell. So the witch went to my mother and said to her: 'Tell your son to leave me in peace, otherwise I will cast a spell on him.' My mother thought that I was having a fight with the witch about liquor in connection with my tavern. So my mother said to me: 'Don't fight with her, she is a witch.' I said: 'Don't be afraid of her.' I went about my business. The witch came to my mother again and warned her again. When the witch saw that I ignored her, she sent her demon to hurt me. When the demon came, he had to stand far away from me, four cubits from me. He didn't have the power to come within four cubits of me. Then I said to him: 'If you had the nerve to come to me, then you can go and hurt the witch. You are to drag her out through a pane in a small window.' The demon immediately did so. And to punish him for coming to me at her command, I imprisoned him in a place which I selected in the woods. And today, we passed the place, and that was why I laughed so hard." ❁

TALES OF THE PROPHET ELIJAH

ANONYMOUS

THE PROPHET ELIJAH AND THE WATER-CARRIER

Once there was a Jew, a water-carrier, and he was very poor. He was so poor that he didn't have a crust of bread in his home.

Once he was walking along the street, very hungry, walking and walking, and he kept walking until he went astray in a forest. Meanwhile, the night came. It became darker and darker and soon it was pitch-black.

The Jew stood in the middle of the forest, bewildered, frightened, when all at once, as he stood there, he saw seven fires. And the seven fires came nearer and nearer to him. They were seven brigands dressed in red.

And the brigands said to him: "If you become a brigand, we'll let you live, but if you don't, then you'll die on the spot."

The Jew became even more confused and didn't know what to say.

As he stood there, trembling, a man suddenly appeared, he looked like a brigand, and he said to the other brigands:

"Brothers, why don't we go over there! See those rich merchants driving by? Let's attack them!"

The brigands left the poor Jew and went after the rich merchants.

23

The water-carrier almost fainted. The new brigand came over, motioned to him, and led him over hill and dale until he brought him out of the forest.

Meanwhile, the day had started dawning. The water-carrier looked around—and lo, they were in the marketplace of a town.

The poor water-carrier kept weeping because he thought the brigand was taking him somewhere to kill him.

There was not a soul in the marketplace, but far in the distance a wealthy nobleman was approaching.

The brigand took the water-carrier to the nobleman and he said to him: "Your lordship, you can rely on this Jew, he will do everything you need."

"Fine," answered the nobleman. "I need to have a palace built on this square by a certain day. And if the palace is built one day earlier, then I will pay four times the price. And if it is two days earlier, then I will pay eight times the price."

The brigand was really the prophet Elijah in disguise.

Elijah asked:

"And what if the palace is ready tomorrow?"

The nobleman replied: "Then I will pay one tenth of my entire fortune."

And the nobleman left, promising to come back the next day.

Elijah told the Jew to lie down and go to sleep.

And nine hundred angels descended and they built the palace in one day.

And when the palace was ready, Elijah took the key, placed it by the Jew's head, and disappeared.

And the next day, when the nobleman came and found the palace, which had been built that night, he gave the Jew so much money that he had enough for the rest of his life.

THE PROPHET ELIJAH HEALS THE SICK

In a village, there lived a family: a father, a mother, and a son. The father was a poor tailor, he earned little and they lived poorly. The son helped a bit, and the mother did house-work. One day, she fell ill and she lay in bed for a long time. There was no doctor. Once, in the middle of the day, an old man walked in and he asked them:

"Who is sick here? I will cure him."

The father answered: "I have nothing to pay you with."

The old man answered: "I will wait for the money."

The father said: "I don't have a penny to my name."

The old man gave them a medicine and promptly vanished. The woman recovered. At night, when their son went to bed on the oven, he found a sack of gold. From then on, they lived in wealth. They realized that the old man was the prophet Elijah.

A SWAMP THAT WAS IN A VILLAGE

Once there was a village, and there was a swamp in the village. And the swamp could never be drained, and it caused a great deal of hardship for the Jews because they couldn't get across. And if they built a bridge, it never stood for more than a few days.

One summer, there was a terrible heat, and a very old Jew came along, and he wanted to get across the swamp. He was the prophet Elijah.

On the other side, people were standing and watching. When the old man was about to set foot on the bridge, they shouted: "Hey you, don't walk on the bridge, don't walk on the bridge, or else you'll fall in!" For this was the third day, and they were afraid that the bridge might fall.

The old man shouted across to them: "Don't be afraid, I'll make sure that the bridge has a long life."

The people kept shouting, telling him not to go across, but he paid no heed, and he began to walk across. When he reached the middle of the bridge, he turned and went back.

The Jews stood and watched, they feared he might fall in, God forbid, and now they saw him walking back and forth across the first half of the bridge several times.

Then he took out a handkerchief and spread it out on the second half of the bridge and went across.

When they saw this, they realized that it was no ordinary matter and that the man must be a great man.

The Jews wouldn't let him leave and they asked him for a salvation. And he answered: "I did bring you a salvation, because you will be able to walk and drive across the bridge, and the bridge will have a long life. And those two houses over there" (he pointed at two houses) "will stand for a long time, no evil eye will have power over them."

As the Jews looked over towards the two houses, Elijah disappeared.

HOW THE PROPHET ELIJAH TURNED AN EVIL WEALTHY MAN INTO A HORSE

Once there was a rich villager, and he was to marry off a daughter. When the evening of the wedding came, the guests started gathering, and then an old man came in, a poor man, and he stood at the door, he wanted them to give him something.

When the rich man saw him, he began shouting: "What does that beggar want? Why has he come here now?" And they began shouting at the Jew, telling him to leave. The beggar answered: "You're having a wedding, I want to taste a bit of it too." But they wouldn't give him anything at all, and the rich man even shouted at his servants to throw the beggar out.

"Who will throw him out?" the rich man said to the boy who served him. "Why don't you throw out the beggar?" So the boy went over to the old Jew and asked him to leave. But the beggar refused to move, and the boy didn't have the heart to throw out such an old man.

26

The host saw that the boy wouldn't obey him, so he walked over to the window, opened it, and called in the doorkeeper, and he told him to throw out the beggar. When the doorkeeper went over to the old man and tried to throw him out, a huge fear came over the doorkeeper, and he couldn't throw out the old man.

The rich man thought that the doorkeeper didn't want to throw him out either, so he walked over to him and said: "You don't want to do it, but I will throw him out." And he went over and·took the old man by his collar and threw him out.

As the rich man dragged him out of the courtyard, the old Jew pulled out a cloth, waved it in his face, and turned him into a horse, and then he mounted the horse and rode away.

He kept riding until he came to a small town. The horse was nicely fattened, just as the rich man had been, with a fat belly and a fat neck. That's what the horse was like, a fattened creature, huge and heavy. And the old man rode on it.

Then he saw a poor man driving a little horse. The horse was lean and scraggy and it was hauling a wagon of bricks. And the poor man beat it and whipped it to make it pull, but it couldn't pull the wagon.

So the old man asked him: "Tell me, brother Jew, why are you beating the horse, why are you lashing it so hard?" The poor man answered: "My dear friend, what should I do? One man wants a wagonload of clay, another man wants a wagonload of bricks, and if the horse won't move, then I have nothing to feed my wife and children." So the old man said: "Why don't you feed it better? It would do a better job of hauling!" The poor man said: "I don't have so much, it doesn't earn enough for me." So the old man said: "You know what, I want to make a deal with you: I'll give you my horse, the fat, the better horse, and you'll give me your scraggy little horse. You'll feed only hay to my horse, and it will eat the hay because it's a strong horse, and it will have the strength to haul. But you ought to know that I'll give it to you for only a year. I will come to you in a year, I will give you the scraggy little horse back and you will give me my horse."

The poor Jew agreed and he was overjoyed and thanked him. And the old man blessed him and wished him luck and hoped that he would become rich and earn a great deal. The poor man

27

harnessed the horse, and it could haul twice as much as his own horse. So he earned three times as much with this horse and things went well for him, thank God, and he became rich.

Well, things don't happen as quickly as we can talk about them. The year went by. The old Jew came with the scraggy horse. When he came, he left it at the door, and it walked in by itself. And he went into the house, the man's home, and he was living in a different place, a lovely place, everything was changed.

The children said: "Papa, an old man has come in and he's calling you." The father came into the room and asked the old man to sit down. The old man said: "I don't have the time to sit here, I've come for my horse." The father said: "All right, old man, for the great favor that you did me—I'll get it." He went right to the stable, took the horse, and gave it to him, and they traded again. But the horse no longer had such a fat belly and such a fat neck.

Before mounting his horse, the old Jew said good-bye to the man and he blessed him and his wife and his little children and then he mounted the horse and rode away.

Where did he ride? He rode to the place from which the horse had come, the villager's house. He arrived there, took the horse and tied it up by the gate and then he went inside. He went into the house, into the kitchen, but no one was there, only two children were standing there and they looked at him. He asked them: "Where is your father? Where is your mother?" But the children didn't want to answer, they simply ran into the other room and said: "Mama dear, you know what, the old man has come, the one who tricked Papa." The mother looked at them. "What are you talking about?" She came into the kitchen and looked at the old man. He said: "My dear lady, why are you looking at me like that?" She said: "My dear friend, why shouldn't I look at you? The children say such foolish things. A misfortune struck us. We were celebrating a wedding, and an old man came in to ask for something, but we had no time for him, and he was asked to go away and come again another time. The house was full of guests. But he didn't want to go away, so my husband went and took him out, and he hasn't come back here since that day. My children have remained fatherless."

While she spoke, the children ran into the courtyard, they saw a horse standing at the gate, and just as all children, upon seeing a horse, go over to it, look at it, and play with it, they looked at it and saw something like tears pouring from its eyes—because the horse recognized them, but it couldn't talk. The children ran back into the house and said: "Oh, Mama, there's a horse standing outside and it's crying." — "A horse crying? It must be a crazy horse!" exclaimed the mother. "Go on with you! A crying horse? Don't be silly! You have more reason to cry than the horse! If only I knew where my husband was and whether he's dead or alive!" And she went to give the old man some food—she was already afraid.

"My dear friend," she said to the old man. "What should I do? I would give away half our fortune just to know what's happened to my husband. It's even worse than when a man dies: At least then you know that he's dead and you bury him. But I don't even know what's become of him!"

The old man said: "My dear woman, would you recognize your husband?"

"Oh," she said, "old man, what do you mean: Would I recognize my husband? What wife wouldn't recognize her husband? I've lived with my husband for so many years, how could I possibly *not* recognize him? May God only help me see him again—oh, how I would recognize him!" The old man said: "Come outside with me and I'll see whether you recognize your husband."

So she went out with him. When she reached the gate with him, she looked, and there was a horse standing there. She said: "Old man, why are you showing me a horse? Was my husband a horse?" The old man said: "He behaved worse than a horse, for a horse is a horse, and he was a human being, yet he behaved like a horse. But do you recognize your husband?" And she said: "But you're showing me a horse!" So the old man went over and took out his cloth and waved it over the horse, and a man was standing there.

The woman saw this, and she fainted at the sight of what happened at that moment. They barely revived her. Then they were overcome with joy. Her husband wanted to have the old Jew stay, he wanted to give him great gifts. But the old man wished ιim well: "From now on, make sure that you are never a horse again." And he blessed them, and wished them luck, and hoped they would know how to behave towards others. And he didn't want to take anything from them, they were about to turn around and celebrate, but they didn't know what had become of the old man.

And that old man was the prophet Elijah. ❧

A TALE OF A LAME MAN
RABBI NAKHMAN OF BRATSLEV

Once upon a time there was a wise man.

Before his death, he called his children and his family and told them that they ought to water trees: "You can ply other trades as well. But you ought to make sure that you always water trees."

Then the wise man died, leaving his children.

Now he had one son, who could not walk. The son could stand, but he could not walk. So his brothers took care of all his needs. And they gave him so much that he always had something left over.

Little by little, he gathered everything that was left over beyond his needs until he accumulated a great deal of money.

And this son, who could not walk, thought to himself: "Why should I take money from them? I'd be better off having some kind of trade."

And since he could not walk, he decided to hire a wagon and a trustworthy man and a driver and travel to Leipzig, where he would do business even though he could not walk.

When the other members of the family heard this idea, they liked it very much.

They also said: "Why should we give him money? It would be better if he went into some kind of trade."

And they even lent him some money so that he could do business.

And so he began.

He hired a wagon and a trustworthy assistant and a driver, and he drove off and came to an inn.

His assistant said that they should spend the night here.
But the young man did not want to.
No matter how much they pleaded, he would not give in.
So they drove away from there.
As they drove on, they got lost in a forest.
Suddenly, they were attacked by highwaymen.

And this is the story of how the highwaymen had become highwaymen:

Once a famine was raging.
And a man came into the town and cried out: Anyone who wanted to eat should come to him.
And many people came to him.
He did everything cunningly, and if he realized that certain people would be useless to him, he sent them away.
He told one man:
"You can be an artisan."
And he told another:
"You can work in a mill."
And he picked out intelligent young men and took them into the forest.
And there he talked them into becoming highwaymen: "There are roads running from here to Leipzig and Breslau and other places, and there are always merchants driving by. We can rob them and get money."
That was how the highwayman, who had come to the town, talked them into becoming highwaymen.

And now these highwaymen attacked the son who could not walk and his servants, that is, the assistant and the driver.
The assistant and the driver were able to run away, and they escaped.
The son, however, remained in the wagon.
The highwaymen came over and asked him: "Why are you sitting?"
He answered: "I can't walk." So they took away his money box and the horses.

32

And he remained in the wagon.

The assistant and the driver, who had run away, decided that since they had started with landowners, why should they return home? They might end up in chains. They would be better off remaining there, in the place they had escaped to, they could be an assistant and a driver.

And the son, who could not walk and had remained in the wagon, ate whatever was left of the food he had taken from home, the dry bread. But when it was gone and he had nothing left to eat, he reflected: "What can I do?" And he threw himself off the wagon to eat grass.

And he slept alone out there every night.

He was terror-stricken.

And the terror sapped his strength.

And now he couldn't even stand, he could only crawl.

And he would eat the grass all around him.

And so long as he could reach the grass around him and eat it, he would keep eating it.

And when the grass around him was gone, he crept further on and ate there.

And thus he kept eating the grass for a time.

Once he came to an herb and he had never eaten anything like it before.

He liked the herb very much.

So he decided to pull it out by the roots.

Under the roots, there was a diamond.

And the diamond was rectangular.

And each side of the diamond had a different virtue.

And on one side of the diamond, it was written that whoever held it on that side would be carried to the place where day and night come together, that is, where the sun and the moon come together.

And the diamond carried him there, and he arrived at the place where day and night come together.

He looked around and he saw that he was in the place where the sun and the moon come together.

He could hear the sun and the moon conversing.

33

The sun was lamenting to the moon: "There is a tree that has many branches and fruits and leaves.

"And every branch and every fruit and every leaf has a special virtue.

"This one has a virtue for bearing children, that one has a virtue for business.

"One can heal a certain illness, and another can heal another illness.

"Each bit of the tree is good for something else. And the tree has to be watered.

"If it is watered, it will have all its virtues.

"But not only don't I water the tree, I shine upon it, which makes it dry out."

The moon said to the sun:

"You worry about things beyond you. I want to tell you my problem: I have a thousand mountains.

"And around the thousand mountains there are a thousand more mountains.

"And that is the place of the demons.

"And the demons have legs like chickens.

"And they have no strength in their legs.

"So they take strength from my legs.

"And that's why I have no strength in my legs.

"And I even had a dust, which is a remedy for my legs.

"But a wind came along and carried it away."

The sun said to the moon:

"Is that what you're worried about. I can tell you a remedy:

"There is a road.

"And many roads branch off from that road.

"One road is the road of saints.

"And when a saint travels that road, the dust of that road is shaken under each step he takes.

"Every time he takes a step, he picks up that dust.

"And there is a road of heretics.

"And when a heretic travels that road, the dust of that road is shaken under each step he takes.

"And there is a road of madmen. And when a madman travels that road, the dust is shaken under his feet.

"And thus there are many roads.

"And there is a road of saints who suffer: They are led in chains by the landowners and they have no strength in their legs. If the dust of that road is shaken under them, they *will* have strength in their legs.

"Thus, you should go there. For there is a lot of dust there, and you will have a remedy for your legs."

The sun said all that to the moon.

And the young man, who had no strength in his legs, heard it all.

Then he looked at the other side of the diamond.

He saw that on this side it was written that whoever held the diamond on this side would be carried to the road from which many roads branched off, that is to say, the road that the sun had described to the moon.

So he held the diamond on this side.

And his legs were on the road whose dust is a remedy for legs.

And he was instantly healed.

He walked along and took up the dust from all roads, and he tied up each dust in a separate packet.

Now the dust of the road of saints was also tied up in a separate packet; and that was how each dust from each of the other roads was tied up.

He made up packets of each dust and he took all these packets along.

And he made up his mind and went to the forest where he had been waylaid.

And when he got there, he chose a tall tree that was close to the road from which the highwaymen went out to rob people.

And he took the dust of saints and the dust of madmen and mixed them together and shook the mixture on the road.

And he climbed up the tree and perched there to see what would happen.

He then saw the highwaymen coming along the road.

Those were the highwaymen whose chief had sent them out to rob.

And when they arrived at that road, the instant they stepped on the dust, they turned into saints.

They began shouting about the years they had spent robbing and killing so many people.

But since there was dust of madmen in the mixture, they turned into mad saints.

They began arguing with one another.

One man said: "It was your fault that we killed people."

And the other said: "It was your fault."

And they argued and fought until they all killed one another.

Then the chief sent out other highwaymen.

And the same thing happened to them: They all killed one another.

And the same thing happened each time.

Until they were all killed.

Until the young man, who once had no strength in his legs, and who was now perching in the tree, realized that none of the highwaymen were left. Only the chief of the highwaymen, who had talked them into becoming highwaymen, and one other.

So the young man climbed back down the tree, cleared the dust from the road, and shook the pure dust of saints, and then he climbed up the tree again and perched there.

And the chief of the highwaymen, who had sent out all his highwaymen, and they had all killed one another, he was very surprised that he had sent them all out and none had come back.

He made up his mind and went out himself with the one remaining highwayman.

And as soon as he came to the road where the son had shaken the dust of saints, he turned into a saint and began shouting at the other that he had killed so many people and robbed so much.

He made strenuous efforts at penance and greatly repented what he had done.

And when the son, who was sitting in the tree, saw that the chief was so remorseful and was doing such great penance, he climbed down from the tree.

When the highwayman saw another human being, he screamed at him: "How miserable I am, for I have done such terrible things. Help me! Give me a penance to do."

The son replied: "Give me back the money box you stole from me."

For the highwaymen had always written down every theft they had committed as well as the name of the victim.

The chief replied: "I'll give it back to you right away. I'll even give you all the stolen treasures that I have, but give me a penance."

The son said: "Your penance will merely be to go into the town and shout and tell the people: 'I am the man who called out back then and made many highwaymen and robbed and murdered so many people.' That will be your penance."

And the highwayman gave him all the treasures and went to the town with him and did what the son had told him to do.

There, in town, he was condemned to be hanged for killing so many people, so that others might learn a lesson.

Then the son, who once had no strength in his feet, made up his mind to go to the two thousand mountains and see what was happening there.

When he arrived, he stopped at a distance from the two thousand mountains.

He saw that there were millions upon millions of families of demons. For they were fruitful and multiplied and had offspring like human beings, and there were very many of them.

And the son saw their king, who sat on a throne, and no mortal man born of a woman ever sits on such a throne.

And he heard the demons telling about their pranks.

One demon told that he had injured a child.

Another told that he had injured a man's arm.

And another told that he had injured a man's leg.

And there were further pranks just like those.

Meanwhile, the son saw that a father and mother were walking and weeping.

And someone asked them:

"Why are you weeping?"

They answered that they had a son who would go away at a certain time and come back at a certain time. But now, a great deal of time had passed and he still had not come back.

And all three of them, the father and the mother and the son, were all demons.

The parents were brought to the king.

The king ordered that messengers be sent throughout the world to find the son.

And when the parents left the king, they met a demon who had traveled with their son, that is to say, the demon they met was a friend of their son's and had traveled with him. But when they met him now, he was alone.

And he also asked them:

"Why are you weeping?"

And they told him why.

Whereupon he said to them:

"Let me tell you a story. We had a small island in the ocean, and that was our place. But then the king who owned the island came and wanted to build palaces there.

"And he laid a foundation.

"Your son suggested that we injure him.

"So we went and took away the king's strength.

"The king consulted doctors, but they couldn't help him.

"So he began consulting wizards.

"Now there was one wizard who did not know my family, so he couldn't do anything to me. But he did know your son's family, so he caught him and he is torturing him horribly."

He was brought to the king—the demon telling this story.

And he told his story to the king too.

The king said:

"Give that king his strength back."

The demon replied:

"One of our demons had no strength, and so we gave him the king's strength."

The king said:

"Have them take away his strength and give the strength back to the king."

He was told: "The demon who was given the king's strength has turned into a cloud."

The king ordered them to call the cloud and bring it here.

So they sent a messenger to the cloud.

Now the young man, who once had no strength in his legs, and had come here and seen all these things—he made up his mind: "Let me go and see how these demons can become clouds."

He followed the messenger and came to the city where the cloud was.

The messenger asked the cityfolk: "Why is there a cloud like that in the city?"

They replied:

"There is never any cloud here in the city. A cloud has only been covering the city for a while now."

And the messenger came and called to the cloud.

And the cloud went away from there.

And the young man, who once had no strength in his legs, made up his mind: He would follow them and listen to what they said.

And he heard the messenger ask the cloud: "Why is it you became a cloud?"

And the cloud answered:

"Let me tell you a story."

THE CLOUD'S STORY

Once upon a time there was a wise man.

And the emperor of the land was a great heretic.

And he turned the entire land into heretics.

So the wise man went and called together his entire family and said to them:

"You can see that the emperor is a great heretic. He has turned the entire land into heretics. He has even turned some of our family into heretics. Let us therefore go into the desert so that we can remain with our faith in God Blessed Be He."

His family agreed.

And the wise man spoke a NAME, that is to say, he pronounced one of the many names of the Good Lord Blessed Be He—and he soon brought them to the desert by saying that NAME.

But he didn't like the desert.

So he spoke another NAME—

And they were brought to another desert.

But he didn't like that desert either.

So he spoke another NAME.

And he brought them to still another desert.

And this desert he did like.

In this desert, they were close to the two thousand mountains.

The wise man went and executed a circle, that is to say, he made a ring around the mountains so no one could get to them.

And there is a tree, and if that tree were watered, then nothing would remain of us demons.

That is why our fellow demons always dig night and day to keep any water from getting to the tree.

The other asked him:

"Why do we have to stand here day and night digging? If we dig just once to keep the water from coming, isn't that enough?"

He answered:

"There are orators among us, sham speakers.

"And these speakers go and cause fights between the king and another king.

"And these fights lead to wars.

"And the wars lead to earthquakes.

"And the earth around the ditch around the tree falls in.

"And so water can get to the tree.

"That is why we always have to stand here digging."

And if a king is enthroned over us demons, we play all sorts of pranks for him and have a wonderful time.

One demon jokes about hurting a baby and about the woman in childbed grieving over it.

And the next one plays other pranks.

And thus they play all kinds of pranks.

And when the king is in a good mood, he strolls about with the princes of the realm and he tries to tear out the tree.

For if the tree didn't exist, we would be very happy.

And the king gathers all his strength to pull out the tree.

But whenever he comes to the tree, the tree utters a loud scream.

And the king is terror-stricken.

He has to turn back.

Now once we had a new king.

And the demons all played wild pranks for him.

And he was in a very good mood.

So he gathered all his courage and he wanted to tear out the entire tree.

He went strolling with his princes, and he really gathered all his courage, and he went to tear out the tree.

And just as he came to the tree, the tree uttered a great shriek at him.

The king was terror-stricken.

He turned around.

And he was furious as he went back.

Then he looked and saw people sitting there.

These were the wise man and his people.

The king sent his servants to hurt them.

And when the wise man's family saw them, they were terribly frightened.

But the wise man told them:

"Don't be afraid."

And when the demons arrived, they could not get close to them because of the circle around them.

So the king sent other messsengers.

But they could not get close to them either.

The king was furious and he went out himself.

But he could not get close to them either.

So he asked the old man to let him come in to them.

The old man said:

"Since you've asked me, I *will* let you in. But it's not proper for a king to come alone, so I'll let you come in with one other."

And the old man opened a tiny door for them.

They entered.

Then he closed the circle again.

The king said to the old man:

"How do you come to settle in my territory?"

The old man said:

"Why is this your territory? It's my territory."

The king said to the old man:

"Aren't you afraid of me at all?"

The old man said:

"No."

The king said again:

"You're not afraid?"

And he instantly stretched out into the air.

He became very tall, as tall as the sky, and was about to devour him.

But the old man said:

"I'm still not afraid of you. But if I like, you'll be afraid of me."

And he went and prayed a bit.

And there were great clouds and great thunderbolts.

And the thunderbolts killed all of them.

They killed all his princes of the realm, and only the king remained, and the man who had come into the circle with him.

The king begged the old man to make the thundering stop.

The thundering stopped.

The king spoke and he said to the old man:

"Since you are such a man, I will give you a book of all the families of the demons. For there are miracle-workers who know only about one family: and they don't even know the entire family. So I'll give you a book containing all the families, for they are all registered with the king. Everyone who is born is registered with the king."

The king sent the demon remaining with him for the book.

Thus, the old man had done right in letting him in with one other, for whom else could he have sent for the book?

The demon brought back the book.

The old man opened the book and he saw that it contained millions upon millions of demon families.

The king promised the old man that they would never harm any of the old man's family.

And he asked him to bring him the portraits of his entire family.

He said that when a child was born into the family, they should instantly bring him the child's portrait so that they would not harm any of the old man's family.

When the time came for the old man to leave the world, he called his children and told them his will and said:

"I am leaving you this book. And you can see that I am able to use it in a holy manner, and yet I do not use it, I have faith in the Good Lord, and you should not use the book either. Even if one of you is able to use it in a holy manner, he should still not use it, he should have faith in the Good Lord."

Then the wise man died.

And the book was handed down and came to his grandson.

And this grandson was able to use the book in a holy manner. But he had faith in the Good Lord, and so he did not use the book, just as the old man had willed.

And the orators, that is to say, the instigators among the demons, tried to instigate the old man's grandson: "Since you have grown daughters whom you can't support or marry off, then make use of the book."

And he did not realize they were talking to him. He thought his heart was talking to him.

So he went to his grandfather's grave.

And he asked him:

"You willed that we should not use the book, that we should have faith in the Good Lord. But now my heart is telling me that I should use the book."

His dead grandfather answered:

"Even though you can use it in a holy manner, it is better for you to have faith in the Good Lord. You should not use the book. The Good Lord will help you."

And the grandson did as his grandfather willed.

One day, the king of the country where the grandson lived became ill. The king called in doctors, but they could not find any cure because of the great heat that was raging there. The heat kept the remedies from working.

The king issued an edict, saying that Jews should pray for him.

So our king, the king of the demons, said: "The grandson is able to use the book in a holy manner, yet he does not use it, so we ought to do him a favor."

And he told me to become a cloud so that the king would be

43

cured by the remedies he had already taken and by the remedies he would still take.

And the grandson knew nothing about it.

And that is why I became a cloud.

And that was the story that the cloud told the messenger.

And the young man who once had no strength in his legs—he followed them and he heard the entire story.

And the demon, the one who had turned into a cloud, was brought to the king.

And the king ordered that his strength be taken and returned to the king whose strength they had taken because he had built on their territory.

So they took away the demon's strength.

And then the son of the demons, that is, the weeping parents, returned.

And he came home wracked and without strength. For he had been terribly tortured.

And he was very angry at the wizard who had inflicted such torments on him there.

He told his children and his family that they should always lie in wait for that wizard.

Now among the demons, there are orators, that is to say, instigators, and they went and informed the wizard that the demons were lying in wait for him and that he should be careful.

The wizard had cunning designs. He also called in other wizards who knew other demon families so that he could be careful with them.

The demon son and his family were very angry at the orators for telling the wizard the secret.

One day they went to the guards of the king of the son's family with those of the orators.

The children of the son's family went and made an accusation against the orators.

So the king had the orators killed.

The other orators were very angry.

So they went and created sedition among all kings.

And famine and illness raged among the demons, and pestilence and devastation, and there was warfare among all kings.

And all this created an earthquake.

And the whole earth collapsed.

And the tree was watered utterly.

Nothing was left of the demons.

They became nothing.

Amen.

The enigma of this tale refers to the First Psalm:

Happy the man
Who never walked in the counsel of the evil
Nor stood on the road of the sinners,
Nor sat in the seat of the scorners.
His only delight is the Law of the Lord,
And he thinks of His Law all day and all night.
He will be
Like a tree, planted by ditches of water,
That gives its fruit in its season,
And its leaf will not wither:
And all that he does will prosper.

The evil are otherwise!
They are like chaff that the wind wafts away.
Thus the evil will not endure the judgment,
Nor the sinners in the congregation of the saintly.
For God knows the road of the saintly:
And the road of the evil shall be doomed.

The road of the saintly refers to the roads that have the dust that is scattered under the steps of the saints. The tree refers to the tree above because all its fruits and leaves have their virtues. And if you ponder, you will find your own allusions.

45

Happy the man who never walked, because he once was not able to walk. *Nor stood*, because then he could not even stand. *Nor . . . the seat of the scornful*, that is to say, the scornful demons who play pranks. *The evil are . . . like chaff that the wind wafts away*—that is the wind that carries off the dust from the roads.

And all these things refer only to the universe, and he has illuminated our eyes a little so that we may understand a little of what the words refer to.

All these words are concealed for oblivion. For all these tales are beyond human understanding, and they are hidden from the eyes of all living creatures.

Whoever has eyes, let him see. And whoever has
a heart, let him understand what
is happening in the
world. ❁

PART TWO
THE JEWISH ENLIGHTENMENT

The nineteenth-century Jewish Enlightenment, *Haskalah* in Hebrew, was partly aimed at what the Enlighteners saw as dead tradition, superstition, backwardness. They held up the shtetl as the locale and symbol of these horrors, and assaulted it ruthlessly for what they regarded as its stranglehold on Jewish progress. In earlier writings, the shtetl was simply a backdrop, a matter of course—because that was where Jews lived. But now the shtetl became the object, the subject matter, the endless target of Haskalah criticism, especially satire. The vehemence of the attacks, the vitriol of the satire, though perhaps justified in part, distorted the shtetl out of all proportion. And often, the Enlighteners completely disregarded the Gentile pressures on Jews. The two novels and the short story in this section are prime examples of the Jewish Haskalah.

Aksenfeld's *The Headband* is vicious and unflinching. Despite little peeps of hope here and there, it crushes shtetl life under caricaturing pessimism. Even the few sympathetic characters among the shtetl Jews are rendered defective by the parody and by the exposure of a basic materialistic nominalism in Jewish life, where wealth is prized more highly than spiritual values.

Peretz's "A Woman's Fury" exemplifies one of the Haskalah's pet peeves: the Jewish treatment of women. Drumming along in a claustrophobic present tense, squeezing the character into an overcrowded space, that slowly shrinks down to the suicidal hook at the precise center of the room, the story attacks the inability of the religion to deal with the human needs of women. Historical studies reveal that the situation of women was even worse than depicted in these Enlightened diatribes.

The issue of how accurately fiction mirrors reality is put to an extreme test in the novels of Mendele Moykher-Sforim, particularly in the one presented here: *The Travels of Benjamin the Third*. Dwelling on the yearning of Jews to escape the shtetl and also to achieve the utopian and messianic goal of the Holy Land, the author offers us a picaresque account of an attempt at realization. Mendele gives his satirical knife a further twist with the sexual ambiguity of the characters, letting Sender, a hen-pecked husband nicknamed the Housewife, act out a role traditionally assigned to women. In a mixture of scorn and sympathy, the author dwells on the metaphorical power of rivers as stations in the pilgrimage. And this metaphor betrays the almost anti-realistic caricature of the fiction. Many of the shtetls were actually located on broad, lovely rivers, and yet most Yiddish writers, like Mendele, focusing on the static aspects of Jewish life and the ugly features of the shtetl, tended to depict tiny, filthy rivulets, perennial eyesores that ultimately acquired an aura of loving nostalgia as in Reyzen's "The Creek" (p. 281). The further Benjamin and Sender get from their shtetl, the broader and more attractive the rivers appear, with the ultimate fantasy river beckoning at their utopian destination: the Sambatyon, the Sabbath river, hence the river of ultimate salvation.

THE HEADBAND
YISROEL AKSENFELD

I

Anyone familiar with our Russian Poland knows what Jews mean by a small *shtetl*, a little town.

A small shtetl has a few small cabins, and a fair every other Sunday. The Jews deal in liquor, grain, burlap, or tar. Usually, there's one man striving to be a Hassidic rebbe.

A *shtot*, on the other hand, a town, contains several hundred wooden homes (that's what they call a house: a *home*) and a row of brick shops. There are: a very rich man (a parvenu), several well-to-do storekeepers, a few dealers in fields, hareskins, wax, honey, some big money-lenders, who use cash belonging either to the rich man, going halves on the profits, or to the tenant farmers and tenant innkeepers in the surrounding area. Such a town has a Polish landowner (the *porits*) with his manor. He owns the town and some ten villages, this entire district being known as a *shlisl*. Some prominent Jew, who is held in esteem at the manor, leases the entire town or even the entire district. Such a town also has a Jewish VIP, who is a big shot with the district police chief. Such a town has an intriguer, who is always litigating with the town and the Jewish community administration, even on the level of the provincial government. In such a town, the landowner tries to get a Hassidic rebbe to take up residence, because if Jews come to him from all over, you can sell them vodka, ale, and mead. All these goods belong to the landowner, and so up goes his income.

49

Such a town has a winehouse keeper, a watchmaker, and a doctor, a past cantor and a present cantor, a broker, a madman, and an abandoned wife (an *agunah*), community beadles, and a caterer. Such a town has a tailors' association, a burial association, a Talmud association, and a free-loan association. Such a town has various kinds of synagogues: a *shul* (mainly for the Sabbath and holidays) a *bes-medresh* (the house of study, for everyday use), and sometimes even a *klaizl* (a smaller house of worship) or a *shtibl* (a small Hassidic synagogue). God forbid that anyone should accidently blurt out the wrong word and call the town a *shtetl!* He'll instantly be branded as the local smartass or madman.

A town is called a *big town* if there are a couple of thousand householders and a few brick buildings aside from the wooden homes. This is a horse of a different color. Here, everyone boasts that he greeted someone from the next street because he mistook him for an out-of-towner. After all: In such a big town like this, how can you tell if a stranger is a local? There are tons of people whom you don't know from Adam.

The story we are going to read took place in two towns: One town is Mezhbezh and the other town cannot be mentioned by name. So we will call it Nosuchville. The two towns are forty miles apart.

In a town like Nosuchville, who isn't doing well? Only the bes-medresh beadle, the shul beadle or the community beadles aren't so well off, because ever since the Hassidim came along, the Cold Shul has remained empty. At Rosh Hashanah (New Year's) and Yom Kippur (Day of Atonement), the tenant farmers come from the countryside with their wives and children to pray in the shul. But the rest of the year, you'll hardly ever see the *minyan,* the quorum of ten men, there. They have to rely on the "ten idlers," the ten pious men maintained by a congregation to ensure a minyan. Hence, the standing joke: "Who goes to shul? The rain, because the roof is full of holes." But no worshipers go to the shul.

All the rich Jews pray in the bes-medresh because it's warm in the winter. When peasants get together for a talk, they go to the tavern. There they chatter and babble over vodka. But Jews won't go to a tavern for drinks and conversation, so the best place for them is a synagogue. All day long, young men and boys sit in the bes-medresh, they study a bit and the rest of the time they talk. The whole town gathers there for prayers, and they also talk. Some people talk while they pray or pray while they talk, the rest talk business, all kinds of business, they exchange news and gossip, and they scarcely pray a word or two—all this in the bes-medresh.

The bes-medresh beadle is the right sort of beadle because all the householders are his masters: when it comes to Hanukkah money, Purim money, and the collection bowl on the eve of Yom Kippur, they give him more than they give the shul beadle. And when the householders go on a trip or come back, he's always sure to get something.

And then there are the community beadles, they go around asking for alms, the victims curse the living daylights out of them and hate their guts. Which leaves the beadles impoverished and degraded all their lives.

Aaron, the town beadle, had a room in the bes-medresh, and there he lived with his wife Sarah. In addition, Sarah worked as a nurse for women in childbirth, she would bring back cakes and quarters of roast capon, whole jars of butter and flasks of liquor. While tending the new mother, Sarah did not forget her husband and her daughter Sheyntse, she let them enjoy the good things too.

Aaron the Beadle was no ignoramus in religion: Occasionally, he said the Sabbath afternoon prayer and he could also manage the beginning of prayers on Rosh Hashanah and Yom Kippur. Once, in Yampelye, he had been a Talmud instructor, but an eye disease had forced him to give up teaching, so he had become the bes-medresh beadle in Nosuchville. When he greeted people on the holidays, they always gave him a large chunk of cake—and on Purim, gingerbread with some fried poppy.

Now Aaron and Sarah had a very beautiful daughter named Sheyntse, and she had just turned fourteen when our story begins, in the year 5572 (or, according to the Christian calendar, the winter of 1812–1813).

The daughter of a beadle, a bes-medresh beadle, who lives in the bes-medresh with her father and mother, sees nothing but

51

men and boys, young husbands or teachers, who sometimes come to summon her mother: "Hurry up, Sarah, they need you!" She also saw men in the bes-medresh on winter days, when they interrupted their studies to ask for a drink of water, and her mother would snap: "Aha! The Torah's blazing in you, so you have to guzzle up all my water. For the three and a half goddamn ducats that Aaron gets every goddamn week, he has to throw in his goddamn water."

Risking another "goddamn!" they guzzled the water.

As for women or girls, Sheyntse never saw any, but in the summer, girls would gather in the anteroom of the shul to teach one another how to dance. Sheyntse would also join in, learning how to dance, playing jacks, and singing songs.

Sheyntse was envious of the rich girls here, who showed one another their penmanship models on lined paper and boasted that they could already pray and read. It made her cry, and she begged her father and mother to teach her how to write and pray and read.

She was an only child, and when she refused to eat—whether it was cake or roast capon that her mother gave her—and only wept and wept, begging them to let her study the things that other girls could do, her parents had to give in, and they promised: "Of course, Sheyntse darling, sweetheart, just eat, tomorrow morning, first thing, we'll hire Mikhel the Belfer to tutor you. You'll know more than any of the other girls." (The *belfer* is the teacher's assistant, the one who brings the little boys and girls to the *heder*, the school, and back home again.)

Now Aaron the Beadle was not a poor man. He had money, and his wife Sarah had her own little stash tucked away. So the next morning, before prayers, they called in Mikhel and they hired him wholesale for all three things, praying, reading, and writing, for fifteen guldens.

II

Mikhel was head belfer for Shloyme Beshekhes, the best teacher of young children (the *dardeke-melamed*). He was nicknamed Mikhel Gravestone, because he always walked bolt upright, keeping his head high instead of sticking it forward the way other people do. Mikhel had a lovely penmanship and he studied the Pentateuch with the finest group. That was why he enjoyed the esteem of Shloyme Beshekhes, the teacher. Shloyme paid him twenty silver guldens a semester plus belfer money for every child, which added up to something like twenty guldens more per semester. Mikhel took his meals with the householders, rotating month after month.

Mikhel Gravestone, Mikhel the Belfer, earned another twenty silver guldens each semester teaching girls how to write. The rich daughters were tutored in reading and praying by Shloyme Beshekhes, but Mikhel was paid extra to teach them penmanship.

Mikhel the Belfer also knew a little of the Muscovite language, and so the Jews would ask him to read a ticket for them: "Please, Mikhel, just glance at it, would you, and tell me how long it's good for." You don't pay a single kopek for a favor like that, you don't even say "thank you," because Mikhel's news was almost always bad: "Uh, oh! Your ticket expired a long time ago."

Mikhel could also do arithmetic. But that's a pretty useless skill, because the Jews in such a town have a standing joke, which always cracks them up: "Oh boy! Where can I ever get the money that I could count up with circles and dashes! The guys doing arithmetic always say: 'Five, take away eight, take away, take away.' In the end, there ain't a kopek in sight, hahaha!"

Mikhel Gravestone, a handsome boy of twenty or so, with curly earlocks that were always crisp from being shampooed in beer, with whole pointed shoes, stockings made of thread down to the middle and cotton below, linen breeches with yellow ribbons, a blue taffeta *arbe-kanfes* (ritual undergarment), a collar at his throat, a gaberdine with hooks (no straps), tightly girded in a black belt, a high fur hat, and a clean velveteen skullcap. All this was known as: Mikhel the Belfer.

During the summer (before the winter in which our story begins), Sheyntse learned how to pray and read and write a lot better than all the other girls, and Mikhel received his fifteen silver guldens.

The beadle and his wife groaned at shelling out the cash, but they were delighted that their only child was so interested and that she could pray and read fluently plus write all the model epistles by heart and very well to boot.

III

Shloyme Beshekhes the teacher was no fool, he knew that Mikhel the Belfer was keeping his school afloat, and that as soon as he got married, he'd be the greatest teacher (you have to marry if you want to be a teacher; so long as you're a bachelor, you can only be an assistant). As a result, some time ago, Shloyme had offered Mikhel Gravestone a partnership on condition that if he married he was not to start his own school; the heder was based on their equal partnership, except that Shloyme had two rubles more.

Mikhel Gravestone accepted, but only on condition that Shloyme Beshekhes agree to act as marriage-broker and get Aaron the Beadle's daughter for Mikhel.

Shloyme kept his part of the bargain and told Aaron the Beadle and Sarah the beadle's wife that this would be an excellent match.

"Just look at Mikhel, absolutely, why, he dresses like a king, absolutely, he's got a spare gaberdine, and he's got at least three hundred guldens saved up, and besides, he's a very practical fellow, he puts by every kopek he makes, and the rich men in town are absolutely mad about him. He knows all about their tax dealings, absolutely, because he writes all their documents, yes, absolutely. Even Meyer Tsippes, the government supplier, always asks him to read his government contracts, absolutely, the ones on stamped paper, and he also reads the town leaseholder's receipts in Polish and he can tell you the name of every landowner and when the money's due. Oh my, if God had considered me worthy to have a daughter, then I would grab a man like Mikhel, absolutely, what a son-in-law! His learning is priceless, absolutely. He can read the weekly section of the Bible with the greatest scholars, absolutely, as though he were reeling off a single verse. And if you like, I'll tell you another secret:

Mikhel has a marvelous voice: if he wraps the prayer shawl around his head, he'll make a fantastic prayer leader, they'll lick their fingers, absolutely, when they hear him pray! Just do what I, Shloyme Beshekhes, tell you, absolutely, give him your daughter's hand, and do it right away. Why, Aaron, you know what it says in the Torah: 'Lest another come first!' So say yes and mazeltov, absolutely!"

When Shloyme came to talk about the match, they had told Sheyntse: "Just step into the chamber, darling, for a moment, would you." (How far is it from the beadle's room to the chamber? Closer than from the stove to the oven.) A partition of thin boards couldn't prevent the girl from overhearing every word that Shloyme Beshekhes spoke.

Sarah, the beadle's wife, said that she liked the match. She would offer a dowry of two hundred guldens, she had a hundred guldens, which she could pay out, one by one, if you please and right away at that, and the town could help out. If you please.

"Cat got your tongue, Aaron? Your healthy, wealthy householders—if you please. Just bring them some cake—won't they chip in a hundred guldens together, if you please? Are you worried about clothes? The Good Lord will provide, and if worst comes to worst, if you please, I'll give her my own feathers, and my own bedding, if you please. And the wedding, if you please, should take place right after the holidays!"

Aaron the Beadle snapped at her:

"A woman has long hair and short brains. Y' know, you're forgetting that Sheyntse has to have a headband, y' know, isn't that right? We can give them room and board, y' know, but a headband, that's the most important thing, y' know. What do you say, Shloyme?"

Sheyntse burst out of the chamber in tears:

"I wanna big headband! What are you gonna do? Stick a veil on me like a peasant and leave out the headband? No, no, and no again!"

Sarah the beadle's wife sided with Shloyme and pointed her finger at Aaron:

"Do you see what he's done, Shloyme? When did she ever see a headband, if you please? Would she have ever known by herself

55

what a headband is, if you please? He has to come and start in—
and she thinks that if you don't get a headband, you have to wear
a veil, if you please!"

Sheyntse retorted: "Of course I've seen headbands. You think
I'm blind or something? When those rich women go and kiss the
Torah on the Feast of the Torah, they wear a headband. The
poor women don't have headbands, and they look like something
the cat dragged in. I wanna have a big headband, like Gabriel's
wife, Gittel, with big pearls and diamonds. Why not?"

"Hahaha!" laughed Sarah. "Don't be silly, if you please! Gittel's
headband must have cost at least ten thousand rubles."

Shloyme Beshekhes brought forth a learned council:

"Do you know what you should do, absolutely? Do what
Abraham said: 'I am a stranger and a sojourner with you.'
Borrow some of the dowry to buy a headband, so it will be both a
stranger and a sojourner, absolutely. Ha, now Shimen the
Magnate is utterly impoverished now, absolutely. He has sold his
home and all he's got left is the headband, his wife's, absolutely.
Of course she doesn't want to sell it, but she must be willing to
borrow money on it, absolutely. Their boy is my pupil but they
can't afford to pay me, absolutely, he's an awfully bright lad, he
is, absolutely, but the poor thing walks around in rags. Ha, a fine
piece of advice, don't you think, absolutely."

Whether or not she agreed with the advice, Sarah was delighted at the prospect of having her daughter wear Shimen the
Magnate's wife's headband. Sarah cried:

"Oh, what a God we have! That Yente-Pessye thought she had
God in the palm of her hand, if you please, she always used to say
so charmingly: 'What do those filthy beadles' wives want from
me?' Oh, my, what do the goyim say? 'Give not, bark not!' Well,
you won't be so hoity-toity anymore, my dear, if you please!
Today, the 'filthy beadle's wife' will have the glory of seeing her
daughter wear Yente-Pessye's headband to synagogue, if you
please! Cat got your tongue, Aaron? Make up your mind, why,
after all, a marriage is made in heaven, if you please!"

Aaron, with his dripping eyes, glanced at his wife Sarah and at
Sheyntse, and he saw that both of them wanted the marriage.
Waving his hand, he said:

"Well, Shloyme, y' know, if it's fated to be, then go to it."

Shloyme went to it with a will, the engagement contract was drawn up and the wedding was slated for the first of Adar (early March), mazel-tov!

Sheyntse had no concept of money, and so she didn't understand that if you have a dowry of two hundred rubles and you lend only some of it on a headband, then the headband probably won't be as big as Gittel's. Meanwhile, right after the engagement contract was signed, Sheyntse hung up a small mirror in the chamber to view herself in the big headband after the wedding. But for now, she was a bride-to-be.

Sarah the beadle's wife was elated. For once, she could be the mother of a bride; for once, people would be saying "mazel-tov!" to her, instead of her saying it to everyone else. And what sweet revenge: Yente-Pessye's headband would come to her Sheyntse, the daughter of the "filthy beadle's wife" would be wearing it, and the thought of revenge made Sarah swell with pride.

Aaron the Beadle had a good head on his shoulders, and when the wealthy men in town said: "Mazel-tov, Aaron!" he replied instead of thanking them:

"Mazel-tov to *you, you're* the ones who are giving the wedding, so I have to be congratulating *you,* y' know. I'll be coming around to collect money for the dowry, y' know, and the clothes."

The bridegroom, Mikhel the Belfer, was smart enough to be delighted when he saw that Beautiful Sheyntse had become even more beautiful and was growing more and more beautiful by the day. He really loved Sheyntse, and after the engagement contract was signed, she began loving her Mikhel too. In a shtetl like—oops! pardon me, that was a slip of the tongue—in a *town* like Nosuchville, a man and his fiancée aren't supposed to talk a lot. But on the pretext of wanting to teach her arithmetic ("Who knows, it might come in handy some time!" said Aaron the Beadle), Mikhel came over every day. Whether they did any arithmetic, nobody knows—but they did chat as behooves an intelligent bridegroom and a beautiful bride.

IV

In the town of Nosuchville, on the Tenth of Tebeth (the fast commemorating the first siege of Jerusalem), in the winter of the year 5572—or 1812 according to the Christian calendar—there arose a turmoil. From one end of town to the other, old and young, men and women, and even little girls were dashing about as though a house were on fire. They hurried, they scurried, they overtook one another. Some ran in silence, and some were talking and clicking and clucking their tongues.

"It just can't be! What a scoundrel! What a scoundrel! A thing like that just can't happen in any town!"

"It had to happen in Nosuchville! How loathsome—Heaven preserve us!"

"Our town's been afflicted! It's fate!"

"What a scoundrel! What a scoundrel! May the Good Lord preserve and protect us!"

"Hurry up! Faster! Let's hear what that swine has to say for himself!"

"They oughta whip him and throw him out of town!"

"I wanna get a good look at that scoundrel and that blasphemous mug of his!"

"Let him suffer all the horrible things that the town could suffer!"

"What a town, I swear! To think that such horrible things can happen here too!"

"What a sinner! In olden times, such an evil man would have been stoned!"

All these comments were blurted out by a dozen Jews at the same time, in one breath, or half a breath, as they panted along.

Suddenly, there were shouts from all sides:

"There he is! There he is! Look, they're taking him away!"

"Great! Great! His hands are tied. Two community beadles. . . . Great, that's just what a scoundrel like him deserves!"

"That'll teach the swine to eat on a fastday. And Mikhel Gravestone thought they wouldn't catch him."

"No, goddammit! It's better to get rid of you, Mikhel Gravestone, than make the whole town suffer and make pregnant woman go through agonies. God forbid!"

"As long as it's out in the open, it won't hurt the town!"

"Look at him walking along, straight up, just like a gravestone. . . . They oughtta put up a gravestone for him as soon as possible!"

"A gravestone? The hell with him! Over my dead body! A scoundrel like that can be buried behind a fence, far, far away from the cemetery!"

These words were spoken by several other people, very quickly; but they weren't running, because, after all, the beadles and Mikhel weren't running. With his hands tied, Mikhel Gravestone was taken into the Community Office, accompanied by the townsfolk.

Three community officers were sitting there. (A community officer is known as a *kagalnye* in Russian, and the Jews in the shtetls use the old Hebrew term *parnes-khadoshim,* the monthly leader.)

Tevye Bilenkis, a lanky, scrawny man, with a long red beard. Even though his lips were pale, his face was ablaze, perhaps because of the wintry cold outside. The Community Office was hot, sultry, and people were mobbing it. Avremel Velis, a small, roly-poly man in a shabby kaftan, with a sparse gray little beard and two nasty, ugly eyes. And Itsik the Stammerer, a man in his fifties, with a very long beard divided in half, almost in two separate beards, and with elflocks in both earlocks; medium height, wearing a long, quilted vest that was girded with a remnant from a belt.

The three men sat around a table: Tevye at the head, and the two others at the sides.

The two beadles, bringing Mikhel Gravestone into the room, pushed him to the table.

"Get over there, kid! Eating on the Tenth of Tebeth, huh?! Well, we've done you the honor of bringing you here to the community elders—long life to them—and they'll do you even more honors."

The crowd in the office roared with mirth for several minutes.

They all fell silent when they saw Tevye open his mouth. But Tevye quipped:

59

"You swine! Why did you have to do it on a fastday? Why couldn't you do it some other day so we could have a mug of good mead?"

At first, the two other elders didn't get the joke, it was only a minute later that Itsik the Stammerer burst into guffaws:

"I-i-i-if the b-b-b-boy h-h-h-hadn't eaten on a f-f-f-fastday then the e-e-e-e-elders w-w-w-wouldn't 've ea-ea-eaten, huh . . . ?"

The crowd laughed, but the dreadful stammering ruined everything. Avremel Velis tugged on his little beard and said with an earnest scowl:

"What? Are we supposed to buy him a drink, God forbid? We'll have our drinks tonight, after sunset, by God! He didn't feel like waiting, by God, well, by God, we *will* wait, by God!"

Mikhel was in the throes of misery, but he managed to speak:

"You're right, I committed a great sin. But we Jews have our Shulhan Aruk, and it tells us the punishment for every sin. I'm no scholar, but I do know that a sin like this doesn't deserve bound hands or bloodshed, maybe—"

Mikhel would have gone on talking, but Tevye Bilenkis screamed in fury:

"Mind your manners, you lout! Huh! You miscreant! Huh! I'll teach you some respect, huh!"

Avremel Velis finished up the judgment and began with a "God forbid!":

"We'll send the boy with the two beadles to Rabbi N., by God. The rebbe's son can't leave Nosuchville without making some money, God forbid, because the town is so humiliated today. Rabbi N. has just made some money, by God. Well? Hah? Well, the rebbe's son could go away in a bad mood, God forbid, from Nosuchville, God forbid. Let's have the boy put down ten guldens for a drink, by God, and don't forget the beadles, God forbid, he has to give them half a gulden apiece. Well, c'mon, you scoundrel, pay up, ten guldens for us, and half a gulden for each beadle. Beadles, take him to the rebbe's son, by God, and tell Rabbi N. that the community elders said he ought to come to terms with the scoundrel. Hah! The rabbi's son mustn't go away in a bad mood, God forbid, without money, God forbid, from Nosuchville, God forbid!"

Before Itsik could stutter and before Tevye could say "huh!"

Avremel strode over to Mikhel, by God! Mikhel stood there, truly like a gravestone, with bound hands. Avremel undid the ropes and ordered him to cough up the ten guldens.

Mikhel took out some money and handed ten guldens to the community elder and one silver gulden to the beadles. He was sensible enough to slip ten kopeks to the rabbinical court beadle Yekhezkel so that he would leave his hands untied and take him through the back streets. Mikhel made sure that the other beadle, Leyb, who was blind in one eye, didn't notice the payment. Yekhezkel got his drift.

Thus ended the session of the community elders, and the two beadles, Yekhezkel and Leyb, grabbed Mikhel on each side and took him, with his hands unbound, through a back street, hurrying him to Rabbi N.

The townsfolk were tired after such a long fast; standing outdoors in the winter didn't agree with some of them, it was freezing cold. So about fifty people hurried over to the inn where Rabbi N. was staying. Whether or not they liked the community elders' sentence, they were glad that something had happened and that something was still happening in Nosuchville.

V

Rabbi N., the rabbi's son, who had come to Nosuchville to make money, knew nothing of the Talmud or the talmudic literature. Since his father was a scholar, the son hadn't wanted to study in his boyhood, and so he knew absolutely nothing, poor man. And he knew even less about the Cabala. Now a Hassidic rebbe's son has heard enough chatting since his childhood to at least spout some wisdom at a Sabbath repast, but Rabbi N. couldn't even do that. You can lead a horse to water but you can't make it drink. Despite his deficiencies, he was still the rabbi's son. That was all. He didn't have the talent to become anything else, or he didn't want to work very hard. He felt it wouldn't do to work for someone else or become a village merchant. Even though our Talmud says: "It is better to flay a carcass in the street than to ask for charity." But that's one homily

Jews like to ignore. And so the rabbi's son traveled about from town to town, from shtetl to shtetl: "Give him money, he's the rabbi's son!"

The rabbi did something that other Hassidic rabbis do. He lied and told falsehoods in a different way. He prophesized no miracles—he told stories. He had bagloads and sackloads of tales about his grandfather, strange tales that weren't in *In Praise of the Baal Shem Tov*. This was a collection gathered by a slaughterer from all the liars in his generation, stories about the Baal Shem Tov and the rebbe, which were printed before Rabbi N. had begun spinning his yarns. He told the biggest whoppers with earnest, pious grimaces as though they were God's own truth and had really happened.

There were some twenty-odd tales, which he kept telling and retailing everywhere and anywhere, over and over again, over and over. When the flock of Hassids get together to hear the stories, that's the time when young husbands try to join the Hassidic ranks themselves. While the older Hassids know the stories from having heard them a dozen times from Rabbi N., they're a novelty for the young pups. They make crazy grimaces, whether they understand the stories or not, whether the stories are probable or not, believable or not, the Baal Shem Tov's grandson has told the stories, and so they must be true, and God forbid that anyone shouldn't swallow them whole—that man could only be a heretic.

However, the Hassidic flock and the young men never give any money, or if they do hand in a small coin, it's never enough for Rabbi N. So he carries his tales to the rich Jews, hoping to unload his wares and make more cash. Some of these rich men give him money just to get him out of the house and avoid listening to his disgusting stories. Some have to suffer through them, after which they fork something over.

Late one night in Kameniets, the rabbi was carrying on in the home of a rich Jew named Moyshe Blank. The host had already given him a few rubles. But Rabbi N. kept telling story after story. It was already midnight, everyone wanted to slip off to bed, but the rabbi wouldn't stop. Finally, a clever soul said:

"Well, apparently you haven't heard about *this* story?"

"What, what? What story?" asked the rabbi. He thought he

would have a new lie, some new tale about the Baal Shem Tov. Just what the doctor ordered.

"Tell me, what kind of a story is it, my friend?"

"You don't know it, rabbi?" said the clever mocker. "You don't know the story about the grandfather and the grandmother, and the little children, and the bear who came and let out a fart that blasted down the door? That's a miracle too, don't you know!"

The entire company burst into such uproarious laughter that the rabbi took to his heels. That was how Moyshe Blank got rid of him.

Now that we know who and what the rabbi was, we can understand that the community elder, with his elflocks and his God-forbid's, had done the right thing when he sent Mikhel Gravestone, who had eaten on a fastday, to the rabbi's son, the Great Rabbi's grandson: the town would save money since it wouldn't have to give the rabbi anything, and the rabbi would get money from that scoundrel, that infidel!

Where was the rabbi staying? With Shmerel, the son of Tevye, the community elder; Shmerel had an inn, where Jews would stay, but he wasn't exactly making barrels of money from Jews who passed through Nosuchville. He was also the son-in-law of Itsik the Stutterer. That was why both community elders went along with Avremel Velis (a cousin of Itsik's wife) when he suggested that they send Mikhel over to the inn for his punishment.

Before the two beadles, Yekhezkel and Leyb, arrived with Mikhel, some of the townsfolk had beaten them to the inn with the breathless tiding that they were bringing that scoundrel, and they told the rabbi in so many words that Avremel Velis had said the community was sending the culprit to him so that he could earn some cash.

It takes no time to understand that the rabbi understood that he had to take money. But he was such an ignoramus that he didn't know what the penalty was for the sin of eating on a fastday. He *had* heard that the Tenth of Tebeth may be one of the Four Fasts, the *Arbe Taneysim,* but, like all ignoramuses, he confused the Hebrew word *arbe* (four) with the Yiddish word *harbe* (hard) and always spoke about the "hard an' fasts," and he now felt he would have to stick up for them hard and fast. He

63

had to show that he was more pious than the entire community, and so he decided on drastic measures, especially since the culprit was supposed to have money. He would have to put on a big show with lots of grimaces and gestures to give the culprit a good scare.

The rabbi was a scrawny little mannikin in a white skullcap, an old puce gros-de-Tours coat without a belt. His long ritual undergarment stuck out. He was at the head of the long plain wooden table, sitting on a calico cushion on an oaken bench. A copy of the *Zohar* lay open in front of him. He was peering into the book, but it was all double Dutch to him, he was totally at sea, he didn't have the foggiest notion of what it said.

After all, since the entire *Zohar* is written in some weird goyish language (and not our Holy Tongue, Yiddish), some language like Chaldean, it's very, very hard to figure out what the words mean in Yiddish. Furthermore, whoever wrote it deliberately twisted all the terms around so that not everyone could get the meaning. If an ordinary Jew wants to check this out, then I, the person writing this tale, will say only one thing about the *Zohar*, and you'll have to admit I'm right. For instance: The *Zohar* calls Wisdom "father" and Understanding "mother," because, with Intelligence, one can invent one thing from another. The *Zohar* even refers to them as "male" and "female." Well, so if a man doesn't know about all these wild distortions, how in the world can he tell that "male and female" means "Wisdom and Understanding"?

From that one example, you can imagine what the rest is like. Hassids call the *Book of Zohar* the *Holy Zohar* or the *Cabala*, because it makes everyone equally holy. If the Hassidic rabbi peers into a *Zohar* or "recites" from it, no one can possibly contradict him. If he had a Talmud in front of him or some other Jewish book, someone might up and ask: "Rabbi, you say you know what's happening even in heaven. Well, so explain this line in the Talmud or this gloss. You can't? Well, then you're a bald-faced liar."

Whether the *Zohar* was open or shut made no difference to Rabbi N. But keeping it open was useful for the hanky-panky, and so the rabbi moaned and peered into it. He was an expert moaner.

64

The room turned silent when Mikhel entered. The two beadles shoved him over to Rabbi N. and halted at a distance. Everyone gawked at the rabbi, wondering what the Great Rabbi's grandson and the rabbi's son would say and do.

Rabbi N. closed the *Zohar* and pretended to look past Mikhel. He asked the beadles:

"Why have you brought this villain to me? My grandfather and my father carried the entire world on their shoulders long enough."

Yekhezkel trudged up, and Leyb, the one-eyed beadle, stood behind him.

"Rabbi, nothing like this, rabbi, has ever happened in Nosuchville, nothing like this. The community elders had a session, the community elders—quit shoving, you blind bastard, I can do my own talking, I can—thank God," he said to Leyb. "Well, anyway, rabbi, the elders said, the elders, that there was now a great Hassidic rabbi, a great one, in Nosuchville—Leyb, I'll punch you so hard that your other eye'll zoom right out, your other eye. . . . The elders, rabbi, the elders, they want you to sentence him, you. . . . Drive him out of town and stop the marriage with Aaron the Beadle's girl. . . . Leyb, I'm telling you again, I'm telling you: Quit shoving! I can do my own talking, I can, thank goodness. I've got a silver tongue, I do. . . . And kick him out of the school where he works as a belfer, kick him out."

Yekhezkel couldn't even go on because the rabbi grabbed his own earlocks with both hands and stood up with a horribly pious screech:

"What?! Such an evil scoundrel in a school where little Jewish children are learning? Oh, God, oh Lord of the Universe, have pity on little Jewish children. Such a scoundrel should teach your little Jewish children? No! No! I won't have it! A thousand times no! Oh God, oh God! A pious Jew's daughter should give her hand to such a criminal, such an infidel? No, no, I won't have it! A thousand times no! I won't have it! No, no, a thousand times no!"

The rabbi would have waxed even wrother and ordered Mikhel kicked out of town if the money hadn't popped into his mind. He observed a minute of silence and gaped at his victim.

Mikhel was smart enough to catch his drift promptly; he

reached for his money pouch, which was slung around his neck, showed it to the rabbi (as though to say: "Here's what you're after, rabbi!"), and murmured:

"Rabbi, the beadle hasn't told you the truth. The community elders, long may they live, sent me here to ask you to let me pay a fine. I've suffered enough shame and disgrace for my sin. Just tell me how much of a fine I have to pay you, rabbi. I've spent eight years drudging for my few pennies, and I gave the elders ten guldens for drinks. Have pity on me, rabbi: Tell me, how much of a fine do I have to pay you?"

Mikhel said his piece stoutly and quickly, in two minutes.

The rabbi didn't have time to think it over, and so, with a huge, heavy, pious moan, he sat down again on his bench and let go of his earlocks. Another moan and another moan. Then the rabbi said:

"Blackguard! You will pay a sum equal to the numerical value of the Hebrew letters of your name. That is the number of guldens that you will give me, the Great Rabbi's grandson. Do you hear, you blackguard!"

Shmerel the innkeeper grabbed a piece of chalk and did some figuring, then he said:

"Exactly one hundred guldens!" And he turned to Mikhel: "Cough up, boy, and don't make faces. You'll get yours, by God. You're lucky your name isn't worth more. If it were Nathan, you'd have to pay five hundred guldens. Since your name's Mikhel, you only have to fork over one hundred, damn your luck!"

Mikhel saw that the rabbi was looking hard at his pouch and was ready to grab the hundred guldens, so the young teacher began pleading pitifully:

"Rabbi, please make it half-guldens, like the money we give at Purim to redeem souls, that's half-guldens. I swear, I had to drudge so hard for my—"

The rabbi hit the ceiling:

"Pay the full amount, you blackguard, just as Shmerel worked it out, and pay immediately. If not, then I'll—"

Mikhel saw the game was up. A rabbi like this one preferred money to mercy. With a bitter heart, the ex-belfer counted the guldens into Shmerel's hand, deliberately clinking each coin in turn. He had once heard that when you're buying a cartload of lumber from simple-minded peasants, you can increase your bargaining power by clinking the coins. And so he counted out only ninety guldens. Then he looked at the rabbi.

"Rabbi! The ten guldens for the community elders, long may they live—you won't take that, will you? Why, they did send the fine your way, didn't they, rabbi?"

The clinking had worked, and the rabbi held his tongue. Shmerel took the ninety guldens and not a kopek more.

But to add a trimming to the whole affair, the rabbi said with a pious grimace:

"For six months, he is not to be summoned up to read the Torah in synagogue and he is not to participate in ushering in the new moon, do you hear, gentlemen?"

Poor Mikhel trudged away with a heavy heart and a light pouch. It was getting late, and on a fastday, Jews see the evening stars (which end the day) quite early; indeed, some call them the liquor stars, because once the stars are out, you can have a drink. At any rate, the crowd dispersed.

The rabbi had made a mint. He wouldn't rake in that much even in four different towns. And so right after supper, he had the wagon hitched and he drove off to tell more lies and more whoppers. He wouldn't have another such windfall that soon.

The town of Nosuchville talked and tattled about the Mikhel Gravestone affair for weeks and weeks. Quips and jokes flew back and forth about how Mikhel had broken the fast and the rabbi had broken the bank.

Aaron the Beadle tore up the engagement contract.

Shloyme Beshekhes hired another assistant.

And as for what became of Mikhel, we'll find out later.

VI

Not far from Nosuchville, just a few miles from town, Dovid Smik had leased a large village named Nimyevke, which belonged to the nobleman of Nosuchville.

Dovid Smik had an only daughter, and she was married. His son-in-law, a good boy named Zainvil, was the grandson of the Preacher of Ostro, and he cost Dovid Smik a pretty penny; all he did was study the holy books all the livelong day. Dovid Smik also had an only son named Naphtali, a pock-marked boy of about fifteen, who was a fool and an utter ignoramus in religious matters, he didn't even know how to pray.

Dovid Smik employed tutors and even a belfer, but Naphtali had no desire to study the holy books. Perhaps if he had been beaten and forced, he might have put his nose to the grindstone. But Dovid Smik's wife Braine-Dobrish was pretty much the manager of the estate. People said that Dovid Smik's fortune of one hundred thousand rubles was all her doing. If it weren't for her, he wouldn't have dealt in oxen and he couldn't even have tied his own shoelaces—she had lifted him up by his bootstraps. And when it came to their son, the mother wouldn't let him do a lick of work. He was the apple of her eye, her darling only son.

As Naphtali grew older and loafed around with all the crippled kids (the healthy farm children work for the Polish landowner, only the cripples are idle), he had a good situation with the military whenever a company of soldiers came to the village. He accompanied them early in the morning when they went to drill outside the village, he watched as each soldier in turn was taught to pronounce the names of the Tsar and the Tsarina and all their children and the commander-in-chief, so that they learned them by heart. And they were also taught how to clean their rifles and polish the buttons on their uniforms. Naphtali was everywhere.

He was wild about the drummers. He would bring bottles of vodka from home and swap them for the privilege of beating the drums with the drumsticks. The officers and all the troops knew him by name, and he did all kinds of services for them.

Zainvil, Dovid Smik's son-in-law, saw that Naphtali wasn't even around on the Sabbath for prayers or for meals. Where was he? With the soldiers. When he came home later, his mother gave him food, and then he promptly ran back to see the soldiers getting haircuts.

Before afternoon prayers on the Sabbath, Zainvil made a point of walking through the village, and he spotted Naphtali strolling along with two peasant girls and an officer's orderly, very busy for the company captain; Naphtali didn't look sober and appeared to be saying wicked things to the girls. He was so absorbed and his head was so full of vodka, that he didn't see his brother-in-law. Furthermore, Zainvil sighted a flask of vodka sticking out of Naphtali's pocket, and a Jew is not allowed to carry anything on the Sabbath inside a village.

That night, Zainvil asked his father-in-law Dovid Smik, his mother-in-law Braine-Dobrish, and his wife Beyltse to come to his room, where he was sitting and studying. Zainvil then told the three of them what he had seen Naphtali doing that Sabbath, and he spoke so eloquently and so tearfully that his wife and even his mother-in-law began weeping. Dovid Smik, his father-in-law, argued that it was all his wife's fault.

Zainvil was smart and scholarly enough to realize that accusations like "It's your fault, it's all your fault!" were no remedy for the plague; Braine-Dobrish could beat her head with both fists as much as she liked, it would not change Naphtali one iota. The next thing they knew, his wife Beyltse, who was expecting, fainted dead away, and they had an awful time bringing her to.

When things had quieted down a bit, Zainvil asked his in-laws to sit down next to Beyltse, whom they had laid out on Zainvil's bed.

"Now listen," said Zainvil with a cheerful expression. "I have a plan to save your son, but you have to promise you'll do what I tell you right away."

The mother-in-law pounced upon Zainvil, hugging him and pleading:

"Yesh, I shwear, you've alwaysh been a good boy, for goodnesh' shake. Ashk your Talmud what we should do, for goodnesh' shake. I'll give you my headband, the big one, for goodnesh' shake, shave me; oh pity the poor mother, oh, the poor mother, for goodnesh' shake, oh me!"

"It's fine that you want to give away your headband. But not to me. I don't want it!" said Zainvil. "You should give your headband to your son, and you should also give your son six hundred rubles for a dowry, and I'll go to town early in the morning. Last Thursday, I learned that Aaron the Beadle has a very beautiful daughter. You heard about the rabbi ordering him to tear up the engagement contract? Now the girl is no longer engaged, well, so why can't she marry Naphtali? Of course, my grandfather would not have been honored by becoming in-laws with Aaron the Beadle, but rather than letting him become in-laws with some peasant—God forbid—we have to arrange this marriage—" Braine-Dobrish tried to say something. "I beg you, mother-in-law, please hear me out first. Now if it's not clear to you why this marriage requires such a large dowry and such a large headband, I must tell you that the townspeople weren't born yesterday. They have eyes and ears, they know more about our Naphtali's carryings-on than you realize. They've heard a lot more than I've seen. Any townsman who gets a look at Naphtali is quite aware of what's in him. Aaron the Beadle also wants a son-in-law who can study the holy books—at least a smidgen. And even if the girl *is* a beadle's daughter, she wants an attractive husband. I made a point of looking at her some time ago when I went into town to light anniversary candles. She's a beauty, she's very attractive, and I've been told she's no fool. It struck me even then that she might be the best cure for Naphtali. For her sake, he could turn into a mannerly person," (Dovid Smik nodded his head) "but she was already engaged to Mikhel. Now that the marriage has been cancelled, we have to say immediately that six thousand rubles plus your large headband would be a fine treat" (Dovid Smik nodded his head) "and Aaron the Beadle and his wife, as well as the girl, will nod their heads, just as my father-in-law is nodding his. . . ."

"For goodnesh' shake, my boy, you have to go to town with ush, I'll do everything you shay. Beyltshe, darling, you mind the tavern, for goodnesh' shake, we'll be gone for three or four daysh, sho give the cowhandsh millet and flour and a flashk of vodka each, right, Dovid?" (Dovid Smik nodded his head.)

Zainvil shook his head:

"No, I tell you, we have to arrange the match and celebrate the wedding right away. We can't put it off for any reason what-soever. Beyltse can stay at home, I'll stay in town with you just long enough to work out the marriage, you'll have the wedding without me. I can't leave Beyltse alone for a whole week when she's close to her time. We mustn't delay the marriage. You're an intelligent woman, mother-in-law, you have to understand that with a marriage like this, you have to have the ceremony quickly. You can use the pretext that you have no time to wait, you have to take care of some oxen, and you can't leave the village now. I'll formulate the excuse in some polished way so that it will sound good. . . ." (Dovid Smik nodded his head.) "I've still got a big chore to do. Beyltse will have to help me make our Naphtali feel like going. He won't want to leave his Muscovites. Beyltse has to praise the beautiful girl whom we're getting for him, and I'll tell him that for such a wonderful match we have to go to town immediately so that nobody else will grab her away. Well, do you all agree? Tell me."

"For goodnesh' shake, long may you live, my Zhainvil darling. But he ishn't here yet, for goodnesh' shake, I'll have to shend the shuperintendent after him. Oh, pity the poor mother, for goodnesh' shake! Oh the poor mother! Ha, what do you shay, Dovid? He shtill ishn't here."

Beyltse exclaimed:

"Quiet! I hear his voice outside."

Naphtali walked in, wearing a striped silk coat and a fur hat. However, pieces of the coat had been torn out, and the hat was smeared with mud. He was accompanied by a drunken soldier, who kept tugging and grabbing at him. If the soldier hadn't been drinking, Naphtali wouldn't have been able to escape, but since the man was drunk out of his mind, Naphtali had managed to drag him all the way home.

"Oh, for goodnesh' shake, pity the poor mother! Oh, Naphtali, what doesh the Mushcovite want from you?" Braine-Dobrish asked her one and only son. "Oh, pity the poor mother!"

Naphtali wasn't quite sober himself, but his annoyance and embarrassment at having the soldier tearing and ripping out pieces of his coat, and right in front of his brother-in-law (whom he respected more than his parents) sobered him up. He said shame-facedly:

"I don't know what the drunkard wantsh. He shaysh I shtole a brash button of hish, and it cosht a gulden. May God shtrike me dead if I took it! He'sh been beating me and trying to drag me to

71

the sheargeant. He'sh been pulling me and tearing my coat for an hour now!"

Zainvil instantly had an idea. He said:

"Mother-in-law, give the drunken Muscovite a gulden. Is it poor Naphtali's fault if some drunkard starts harassing him with slander? His coat's an old coat anyway, it's a shame he has to wear it. You'll be making fine new clothes for him, won't you, when he becomes engaged tomorrow—God willing? Take off the torn coat, Naphtali dear. Goodness, it's not right for a rich man's darling son to carry on with a drunken Muscovite, especially when he's about to sign an engagement contract tomorrow."

Dovid Smik nodded his head from afar to Zainvil, making sure that Naphtali didn't notice. His nodding meant: "Very smart!" And he went into the tavern with Braine-Dobrish, dragging along the soldier. Zainvil remained in the room with Beyltse and Naphtali.

Beyltse pulled Naphtali aside while Zainvil sat down at the table, burying his nose in a holy book; he pretended not to hear or know what the brother and sister were saying. She was talking away at Naphtali with all her strength, and Naphtali kept retorting:

"Beyltshe, Beltyshe, it can't be, you're not telling me the truth, Beyltshe, it'sh a lie. If she'sh that beautiful, what'sh she doing in Noshuchville?"

Beyltse talked and talked, and then she said in a loud voice:

"Ashk him, if you don't believe me, ashk Zhainvil. Hey, Zhainvil, aren't they arranging a match for him with a beautiful girl?"

Zainvil strode over to Naphtali and stroked him:

"Oh me, oh my! A boy like Naphtali, the son of such a wealthy man, with six hundred rubles dowry, and the boy's mother wants to give her son's bride her headband, the big headband—why shouldn't the beautiful girl marry him? If Naphtali asks me, I'll go to town with him. His parents will go in a separate britska. And I'll see to it that the marriage is arranged, and that the wedding takes place right away. But you can't come, Beyltse, because you're fighting with him. Well, Naphtali, do you want to ask me along?"

"Ashk you?" said Naphtali. "If you like. But she can't come, she'll only shay nashty thingsh to the bride. The hell with her, she can shtay here! Right?"

"When we're in town," replied Zainvil, "the first thing tomorrow morning, God willing, we'll order two new coats and also a silk jacket."

"And new pantsh, yellow pantsh," said Naphtali. "With good buttonsh, exshpensive buttonsh. . . ."

"Of course," Zainvil said with an earnest mien. "The tailor's life won't be worth a kopek if he doesn't make yellow trousers and a yellow *arbe-kanfes*, just as behooves a rich man's only son when he gets married."

"And brand-new morocco shoesh, pointed shoesh, right, Zhainvil? For a wedding, the groom getsh pointed shoesh with hobble-nailsh, morocco leather, right, Zhainvil?" said Naphtali.

"Now go to bed, Naphtali, we have to get up at the crack of dawn and drive to town. As soon as we're there, I'll order some morocco-leather shoes for you. And the shoemaker had better watch out, he's got to make fine shoes for you in the latest style. And Beyltse, you'd better not say a word. Do you know why, Naphtali? Tell us."

"Becaushe the mishe are gonna eat up her blousheh, she'sh pregnant," said Naphtali.

"Dear boy," Zainvil stroked. "You really ought to say: Because we won't take her to the engagement or to the wedding. She can stay here, right?"

Naphtali laughed:

"Let her shtay in Nimyeveke. We'll go to the wedding in Noshuchville. You'll take me along, right Zhainvil?"

Zainvil cleverly arranged everything. For money, Tevye Bilenkis, the community elder, and his son Shmerel Tevyes promptly acted as matchmakers.

Aaron the Beadle and his wife, together with their daughter Sheyntse, beautiful Sheyntse, went to Shmerel Tevyes' inn, where the bridegroom-to-be was staying with his parents. And Zainvil was bustling on all fronts: with tailors, shopkeepers, and shoemakers. He ordered jackets and yellow trousers and morocco-leather shoes for Naphtali. But only on one condition: that they all sew night and day and have everything ready by Tuesday.

Sheyntse took just one look at the big headband and saw that it was bigger than Gittel's. The headband would be hers, and she would wear it. The bridegroom could be deaf and dumb for all she cared, she didn't give him a second thought when she gazed at the big, rich, beautiful headband. Aaron the Beadle and Sarah felt just fine and dandy: Sheyntse had struck it rich. Furthermore, Naphtali was the only child of a sound father who was worth something like a hundred thousand rubles. Besides, Zainvil would have made even an uglier bridegroom look good.

Naphtali kept going back for yet another look at beautiful Sheyntse, he still couldn't believe that this beautiful girl was about to be his fiancée and, very soon, his wife. He chewed his lips and murmured to his mother:

"Oh boy, Mama, ish she ever good-looking, oh boy, what'sh her name, Mama, the beauty? C'mon, tell me, Mama, what'sh her name, tell me!"

Since it was winter, night fell very early. In Shmerel Tevyes' inn, they were saying the evening prayers: Shmerel's wife and her mother had two causes for celebrating: their husbands were earning money as matchmakers, and the bridegroom's family was going to throw an engagement dinner right here in the inn, and especially, as Zainvil said: "Let there be a wedding right away!"

Aaron the Beadle was not going to give the rich wedding. Well, then who? It was going to be celebrated right here, in the inn, where the boy's parents were staying. Braine-Dobrish was going to pay for a fabulous wedding. At a feast like that, another batch of money would be earned.

For the engagement party, Shmerel prepared all the necessary paraphernalia: a cantor and a shul beadle, pen and ink, and two sheets of paper, as well as crockery to be broken.

Zainvil and Aaron the Beadle had agreed to deposit the dowry with the town magnate Gabriel Gittels (*she* was known as Gittel Gabriels and *he* was known as Gabriel Gittels; being nouveau riche, he had no parents or parents-in-law to be named after). Since the six thousand rubles were to be left with him, Tevye also brought him along to the engagement party.

Nobody cared about the bride-to-be or the groom-to-be. All

that counted was: the in-laws and the dowry and the engagement and the wedding. Since more was being given than Aaron the Beadle could ever have imagined, everyone was in high spirits. If anyone had asked Sheyntse: "Do you want to be engaged to Naphtali and marry him, as you see him?"—she might have replied: "No! He's a moron and a creep! I don't want him or his money or his big headband!" But since no one asked her. . . .

And there was a hubbub, a merry hubbub. They lit candles in the chandelier, they threw a tablecloth on the table, they put out the huge three-branched candle-holder with three high candles, bottles of liquor were standing in readiness, and plates of preserves lay next to them. People kept arriving every minute, more and more, rubles piled up on the table. And someone called Aaron and his wife and their daughter to the table. Who called them? Gabriel Gittels himself. He personally called them:

"Observe, if you please, that the father of the groom, Dovid, and his son-in-law and his wife Braine-Dobrish are giving me six thousand rubles, gold rubles, on deposit. The money is to remain in my hands for a year until both sides are willing to take the money for their children" (he glanced at Sheyntse and at Naphtali when Zainvil pointed at him) "I mean you, the bride-and-groom-to-be, this is your money, these six thousand rubles. Are you satisfied? Well, then mazel-tov, may God give you luck and happiness!"

He acted as though he were waiting for an answer. . . .

A booming of thunder: the pots were smashed on the floor, and there were shouts on all sides:

"Mazel-tov!"

"Mazel-tov!"

It was deafening.

Hershel, the famous Jewish prankster and jester, had once explained why musicians play at weddings: "It's like a military recruitment: the fiddle sings, a bottle of vodka stands on the table, and everyone dances. If a man happens to come by, the whole bash will make him insist he wants to join the army. If it weren't for the fiddle and the dancing and the bottle of vodka, then only a lunatic would sign up. In exactly the same way, no one would want to get married. So they have to have musicians playing and they have to dance and make a merry clamor—and people jump right in and get married."

In Sheyntse's case, it was really only the hubbub and the cheery mazel-tov's that got her engaged. The big headband cast the first spell and the tumult did the rest to make her a bride, Naphtali's bride.

The engagement contract was drawn up and signed. A rather decent supper was served. Zainvil asked his mother-in-law to slip ten gold ducats into Naphtali's hands. Then Zainvil and Naphtali walked over to the beautiful girl, to Sheyntse, the bride-to-be, and Zainvil told Naphtali to give her the money, while Zainvil said:

"Sheyntse, our bride, your intended husband Naphtali is giving you this gift. Mazel-tov to both of you. I may not be able to attend the wedding because my wife is about to have a baby, if you please," (he took three guldens out of his pocket) "but I would like you have these three guldens as my wedding present. You, Aaron, my new in-law," he said to Aaron the Beadle, who was standing with his wife next to Sheyntse, "you're a good Jew, you won't forget to call my name out in the list of wedding presents, will you?"

"Take it, Sheyntse, go ahead, don't be bashful," said Sarah. "It's all yours, praise the Lord, yours and your husband's."

Around midnight, the guests went home.

The previous night, Aaron the Beadle, his wife Sarah, and Sheyntse would never have dreamt what good fortune this night would bring them: "Gold rubles all at once, and such rich in-laws. Sheyntse's luck must be high in heaven, right . . . ?"

Throughout Nosuchville, from one end of town to the other, in the tiniest corners, everyone was talking about the marriage, the great fortune, and how lucky the girl was:

"She's gonna be covered with gold, she's being gilded!"

"Who's the loony who suggested Aaron's girl of all people?"

"A rich guy like Dovid Smik! Who wouldn't have leaped at the chance? A pile of gold for the dowry, plus Braine-Dobrish's big headband! Why, gracious me, Gabriel Gittels would have jumped at the opportunity for his daughter."

"What's the world coming to! Dovid Smik's an ignoramus! He's a jackass. A beadle's got a pretty daughter, and he thinks she's a good match. But she, she, she, that lousy bitch Braine-Dobrish. *She* runs the world. Where did *she* ever get such a crazy idea?"

"You'd better ask that smart Zainvil! Why, he's a gem, a scholar, a pious man. People say he took the boy by the hand and led him to the beadle's daughter."

"Hahahaha! Who can figure people out? Who knows . . . ? It's better not to say anything."

"What can you do?"

All these comments and all these questions, as we know, were not difficult. Zainvil knew the answers. But he preferred to leave the questions unanswered rather than owning up to the bitter truth that Naphtali wasn't even good enough for a peasant girl, but if they got him such a beautiful wife and they had the couple live with them forever and ever, then Naphtali would settle down and mend his ways because she would keep him at home.

On Tuesday, when the tailor delivered the jackets, plus yellow trousers with buttons, and pointed morocco-leather shoes, attractive ones, plus a sable hat; and a mirror and manufactured stockings and hair nets and yellow hair ribbons and a gold-brocade bodice as gifts for the bride—everything was ready, and Zainvil prepared to drive back to the village. He asked Tevye Bilenkis and Shmerel Tevyes to look after the wedding, the ceremony was to take place on Friday. He asked his parents-in-law to go along with Tevye and Shmerel in everything as though they were Zainvil himself. Dovid Smik nodded his head and murmured (it was the first time anyone had heard a word out of him):

"A luminoush bride, a hideoush groom, don't you know."

Braine-Dobrish added:

"Godshpeed, for goodnesh' shake, I'm marrying off my only shon, for goodnesh' shake. Thank you for everything, Zhainvil. Lishen, the farmhandsh can take care of the okshen, for goodnesh' shake. I'll take your advishe, Zhainvil, I won't shpare any ekshpenshesh, jusht ash you shay, for goodnesh' shake."

Zainvil went to Aaron the Beadle to say good-bye, as an in-law ought to do, and he even bade a fond and friendly farewell to Sarah:

"Have a good time and enjoy yourselves. On Sunday, God willing, when you and the happy couple come out to visit us in Nimyevke, we'll have a real celebration. Be well."

"Be well, Zainvil."

He gave the bride a gold ducat as a going-away present and spoke some cheerful words:

"You won't have to worry about anything, thank the Lord. As the wife of the only son, and with all that wealth, you'll be well off."

Aaron the Beadle and his wife and Sheyntse overwhelmed him with their fondest wishes for his wife's safe delivery.

"God be with you both!"

"Godspeed!"

VII

On Thursday, the pre-wedding feast took place. There was dancing and carousing in Nosuchville. That same day, Dovid Smik gave a meal for poor people. If you give poor people food and money, they wish you the very best.

On Friday, the wedding took place. People danced like there was no tomorrow. "Mazel-tov! Mazel-tov!" from all sides. But the big banquet was put off for Saturday night because Sabbath is Sabbath. Tevye and Shmerel made all the preparations. They couldn't perform the ritual ceremony of leading the bride and groom to bed because the wedding came so unexpectedly: "We *are* Jews after all. . . ."

On Saturday night, no sooner had they ushered out the Sabbath than Zainvil came rushing to town, driving the life out of his horses—he burst in and exchanged whispers with his parents-in-law, scowling all the while.

The three of them emerged from the alcove where they had been whispering, they were at a loss what to do: Should they ask Tevye, the community elder, or someone else, someone more experienced—they needed advice. All three of them were sad and in a dither.

Who should come in but the chief of police while a squad

leader and soldiers surrounded Shmerel's house. There were guards at every door and no one was allowed to leave.

The police chief grabbed Naphtali, ordering three soldiers to watch him and two squad leaders to get his belongings.

"What's happening? What's this all about?"

The police chief was quietly taking money from Braine-Dobrish and promising to help. But he had to drag Naphtali along.

Faint, swoon, wring your hands, oh me, oh my, oh goodness, oh God—Naphtali was dragged away with all his belongings. Where? Some people said to the city, others to the province capital, straight to Zhitomir, and perhaps to Kameniets. Some people said back to the village.

A turmoil. A tumult. A whispering, a chattering. No one knew what was what.

"Nosuchville is a city."

"Anything can happen in Nosuchville."

"The city has something new every day."

That night, Zainvil and his father-in-law drove back to the village. Braine-Dobrish, along with Tevye Bilenkis, the community elder, got into a rented wagon. They headed for the city. Once there, they would see, perhaps they would have to go further.

The biggest secret of all comes out after nine months: a woman has a baby after carrying the secret all that time. The secret of Naphtali's arrest came out the next day; they learned the reason from Zachariah, who was buddy-buddy with the police chief. But the police chief told him only after the soldiers had taken Naphtali away.

Naphtali was in the habit of visiting the captain of the division stationed in Nimyevke, he was there all the time and he performed all sorts of services. Four weeks ago, the regimental priest had been a guest in the captain's home and had begun talking to Naphtali, trying to convert him to Christianity. Naphtali had agreed to get baptized, but only on condition that he would become a drummer. Very good. The priest asked the captain's chancellery to prepare the proper document. Naphtali more or less wrote his name in Jewish letters. The priest had two officers sign as witnesses. A further document was prepared, in which Naphtali requested permission to serve the Tsar as a drummer. He more or less signed that document too in Jewish letters. Both petitions had to be sent on to the proper agencies. Until they got word, said the priest, the entire matter should be kept a secret. He told the division captain to make sure that Naphtali didn't run away.

For three weeks, the captain saw Naphtali in his home and with the drummers every day, he was learning how to play the drum. It was only in the fourth week, on Tuesday, that the captain began asking: "Where's Naphtali keeping himself? Why don't we see him? Where is our Naphtali?"

He found out that Naphtali was getting married in Nosuchville. So he drove off to get the police chief, who was going through the villages, grabbing smugglers or taking care of other business. The captain finally caught up with him on Friday evening, he gave him the documents and described the entire matter to him. Two knotty problems at once: baptism and military service. A police chief can only make short shrift of them. He took off for Nosuchville on the spot, arriving before Zainvil could do anything. One hour earlier, they might have gotten Naphtali across the border. But Zainvil had learned about the matter only that evening in the village. He drove his horses as fast as he could. But alas, the police chief got to Naphtali first.

Sheyntse was both a maiden and a married woman! Whose wife? A drummer's. They refused to give her the dowry. But what about the big, beautiful, expensive headband, which she wore throughout the Sabbath? Did that belong to her now? Well, keep reading.

God punisheth with one hand, and He blesseth with the other. All the running around and heavy bribing didn't help. Naphtali was baptized and he became a soldier, a *drummer*. The only effect of the money was to have Naphtali assigned to a different regiment. There was one stationed forty miles away. And that's where Naphtali was sent.

Beyltse had a safe delivery, thank heaven. It was a boy, and he was named after the Preacher of Ostro.

But there's an old saying: It's the child that gets married, not

80

the parents. Out of sight, out of mind. In Nimyevke, they forgot all about Naphtali.

Sheyntse, however, *had* gotten married—to the drummer, to Naphtali the convert. She threw herself on her bed and wept bitterly: She—she had to get divorced from the drummer.

Aaron the Beadle procured letters from the community elders to all the elders of the towns where they said the regiment was billeted, and where Naphtali the convert was serving as drummer. Sheyntse gave her few rubles to her father for expenses; he was to go off and obtain the divorce after Purim.

Poor Aaron the Beadle, alas (people love saying "alas!"), had to drive through the post-Purim slush and mire until he found Naphtali, whose name was Ritsko now. He was stationed near a little town called Mishelovke.

Kind-hearted Jews in Mishelovke offered to help Aaron. As soon as they gave the priest of Mishelovke a gold ducat, he said: "Yes, he has to divorce his accursed Jewish wife."

When the division officers asked Ritsko the Drummer what had happened, he told them about the big headband and the hundred gold rubles that he had given Sheyntse. The officers instructed him to say: "Yes, I'll grant her a divorce, but she has to return the headband and the hundred rubles."

Aaron the Beadle drove back fifty miles and got the headband and the hundred rubles. Aaron was a simple man, and he had an idea: "Maybe I'll take along a smaller headband." How much can a swinish head like his grasp? He won't be able to tell the difference—so long as it's a headband." But he was afraid the convert might have made some mark in his mother's headband, and he'd be so angry he wouldn't agree to the divorce no matter what. So Aaron the Beadle decided to take the real headband, as it was. If he could manage to give Naphtali a smaller one, he could find it in that little town, in Mishelovke, couldn't he?

Aaron was right! Naphtali knew his mother's headband very well, and when Aaron tried to palm off a different one, Naphtali spewed the filthiest military curse and said he had made a mark in his mother's headband.

So Aaron had to bring the big headband to the Jewish religious judge in Mishelovke (there is no real rabbi in any Russian-Polish town in these times; ever since the Hassidic rebbes have become all the rage, one such rebbe controls several towns). The division captain likewise came to the Jewish judge. The headband, said Naphtali, had a mark:

"At Rosh Hashanah, in town, I stole three pearls before my mother put it on to wear in synagogue."

Aaron did give him the hundred rubles, almost as a ransom, to pay for the divorce, which Naphtali, or Ritsko the Drummer, then sent to Sheyntse by messenger.

Aaron the Beadle came home three days before Passover, embittered and worn out from traveling, and Sarah wept when she saw him.

The messenger gave Sheyntse the bill of divorcement right away, in front of the Jewish judge of Nosuchville, and the town had something to gossip about all through Passover.

VIII

Mikhel the Belfer stood like a gravestone—is that what you think? No indeed. Mikhel had become a lively broker in Nosuchville, hustling and bustling on all sides, and little by little, he started making money.

In Jewish towns, a broker is held in contempt, although a wee bit less than the dog-catcher. Why is a broker held in contempt? Because there's a popular saying: "It's not the work that degrades the man, but the man that degrades the work." A broker is really very necessary for a landowner who comes into a town or village to buy something or to order clothes from a tailor or to sell grain from his estates. After all, he doesn't know where to go, whom to negotiate with, and so on and so forth. If a local man guides the stranger and serves him loyally, he certainly deserves to be paid for his troubles and to be thanked for all the good things he's done.

In Germany and in all the great countries of the wide world, they call such a broker a "commissioner" or something even more respectable. But the brokers in Jewish towns are put down as drunkards, hoodlums, highway robbers. They have no intention of serving the stranger honestly—no, all they want to do is cheat him. They tell lies by the ton for a few pennies. The broker holds himself in contempt because he does the filthiest chores for a gulden and he even permits the landowner's servant to spit in his face, so long as he treats him to a glass of vodka afterwards.

Why is this so? Perhaps because most Polish landowners (one cannot say *all* landowners, there *are* a few better ones) are so full of themselves, each one thinks *he* is the cream of the human race. For' him, a peasant is on a par with a horse, an ox, a cow. Peasants were created to drudge for the landowner. Since Jews are not his serfs, he regards them as instruments existing only for the landowner's sake. Of course, when the landowner reluctantly needs a favor from the rich Jew, a cash loan, he treats him like a cobbler: He has to have him because he needs boots; once he gets the boots, the cobbler is a cobbler, and that's that. And all the more so his innkeeper and his shopkeeper, the Jew, whom the arrogant landowner despises more than a stray dog: He derides him, pokes fun at him, hits him and slaps him whenever he feels like it. Cursing and berating are simply customary. "You thieving Jew, you Jewish sonovabitch!" is the same as "Sir." A Jewish broker connected to a Polish landowner hears even coarser language: "Swine! Get the hell out of here!" A tug on a sidelock or a beard is a jest. And when the Pole pays the Jew for his hard work, he hurls the gulden on the ground: "Take it, bastard!" To put up with that kind of treatment, a man truly has to be a footpad, a drunkard, a hoodlum.

Our Russian aristocrats are quite a different breed. The Pole's overweening pride, the Pole's arrogance is never found in a Russian. When a Russian gets to know a Jew and deals with him a couple of times, he calls him "brother" or "little brother." Even a broker. If he serves him loyally, the Russian gets to love him. Yes indeed, love him. Especially when he becomes acquainted with a Jewish merchant after doing business with him for a while: then even the greatest Russian becomes friends with the Jew. Yes indeed: friends.

Meshl, the old broker in Nosuchville, was useful only for Polish landowners. He was somewhat fluent in Polish and was always despised in town. A poor man all his life, he drank, and as he got on in years, he was usually more drunk than sober. Oddly enough, Meshl the Broker only liked Poles. He couldn't stand Russians. He would have put his life on the line for a Pole. He used only the foulest curses for Russians, and he couldn't speak a word of their language. Mikhel Gravestone worked only for Russian officers, which didn't bother Meshl, the old broker, one bit. Meshl derided him and the Russians together.

The time in which Mikhel became a broker was a period of war, Napoleon and his French army had invaded the Tsarist Empire. Russian officers were traveling back and forth through Nosuchville. An active guy, a handsome guy, an intelligent guy, Mikhel did a fine job of serving all the officers, earning money from and around them every day. By working for them, he got to speak Russian fluently. He could also write a bit of Russian and do bookkeeping. Altogether, he was an excellent broker.

When the Russian general stopped in Nosuchville, Mikhel presented him a written account of all the things he had bought for him. The general was delighted and gave Mikhel a twenty-five-ruble note.

"Here you are, brother. I'm very satisfied with you."

A major, who stopped off, a prince named Kanianov, also gave Mikhel a twenty-five-ruble note plus a fine britska because he drove off in the stagecoach. The next day, Mikhel sold the britska for one hundred rubles to another officer, who needed it.

That's how things went, and they went very well for Mikhel. All the shopkeepers needed Mikhel's good graces and cajoled him to come with the officers and buy from them. Mikhel was no longer nicknamed Mikhel the Belfer or Mikhel Gravestone, and certainly not Mikhel the Broker, God forbid! Now he was known as Mikhel the Muscovite. Sometimes Mikhel would go shopping alone, without officers, carrying thousands of rubles in cash, to buy from the storekeepers. Because of the officers, they addressed him as Mr. Mikhel:

"Mr. Mikhel, do come in, why don't you."

Mikhel the Muscovite would visit Gabriel Gittels, the great magnate, in order to change banknotes. Gabriel would say:

"Have a seat, Mr. Mikhel! Gittel, serve us some vodka and cake. Help yourself, Mr. Mikhel. Upon my word, you're quite a businessman. It should only happen to me. . . ."

Once, while changing money, Mikhel took a fifty-ruble note from Gabriel Gittels. Along with what the officer gave him:

"Here you are, brother, for your trouble."

During the summer, Mikhel dressed well and he had as much as a thousand rubles cash in his pocket.

It was only in the fall, before Rosh Hashanah that an officer named Khlyebov, a military broker, passed through Nosuchville. He was en route to the Russian headquarters, where he was to become an inspector in the provisions storehouse. He was very impressed with Mikhel's qualities and he talked him into coming along, he promised he would send business his way. Now almost all the Russian officers had been sent off to battle against Napoleon in Germany. So fewer and fewer of them were passing back and forth through town. Considering the situation, Mikhel accepted Commissioner Khlyebov's proposal and accompanied him to the headquarters of the army.

"So long, Nosuchville!"

IX

Nosuchville is a town where anything can happen. As of the Ninth of Ab (which commemorates the destruction of the first and second temples), every nook and cranny of town is filled with tumult and turmoil—from Markel's saloon. Markel pours liquor like there was no tomorrow. You can drink good, strong mead in Markel's place, you can drink good distilled vodka in Markel's place, you can drink March ale in Markel's place. Jews and peasants, even landowners, come to imbibe in Markel's saloon. There was talk that Markel was planning to open a wine garden on the Jewish holidays. For Sukkoth, the Feast of Tabernacles, he wanted to turn one of the traditional wooden tabernacles into a large house, as a wine garden for the landowners.

Suddenly, a rumor went through town: a poltergeist had moved into Markel's cellar. His customers began staying away. Who wants to have a run-in with a poltergeist, a demon, an

85

unclean thing? Jews and Christians told all kinds of stories about Markel's cellar: you could hear rattling chains and sudden guffaws and an uproar that made your hair stand on end.

Some people said that a servant of Markel's had been injured. While going to tap mead, he had been so frightened that his mouth had gone askew, and they had taken him to a healer. Some people said Markel himself had tried to take on the poltergeist and had gone down to the cellar for beer. But the poltergeist had thrown buckets at his head, almost killing him, and Markel barely clambered out alive. People added that he had twisted a finger, and had been unable to move one leg since that time.

"The thing is so foul," said the women, "that you can smell the horrible stench ten houses away. Just the other day, the miller's wife had to throw out her entire Sabbath stew because it stank of devil's dung."

"The same thing happened in Bosivke once, they had to vacate the house, and it was left abandoned. A wonderful place, with everything—they had to get rid of it. You only live once, y' know."

Shmerel Tevyes, an ardent Hassid, accompanied by two young men, also Hassids, went to visit old Markel the Innkeeper. The poor man was a bundle of misery.

"Good evening, Markel. Why are you sitting there so gloomy. Don't you know that if you're gloomy, that's worse than the thing itself. Act cheerful, just act cheerful, and the thing won't have any power. Act cheerful, Markel. We Hassids have come to wish you good evening. Well, cat got your tongue?"

"It's the other way around with me," sighed Markel the Innkeeper. "During the day, there's nothing here. Absolutely nothing. It's deathly still, just as God commanded. But when night comes, there's banging, rattling, laughing, things get thrown around, and you take your life in your hands even if you keep your distance."

"Do you know why we've come to you, Markel?" said Shmerel in chorus with the two young Hassids. "You're a good Jew, but you hang out too much with the old Cossacks and the ruffians. You have no faith in the sages, you don't believe in the miracles of the rebbes. That's why the devil has power over you and your house."

Markel always hit the roof when people said anything against his place, and he angrily retorted:

"You're a Hassid, and something much, much worse happened in your place: A convert got married—to a Jewish girl. Well, c'mon? Was that your fault?"

"You lunatic! Do you think we came to fight with you? Honestly!" Shmerel and the two young Hassids laughed. "Just look at him, the old Rationalist! We're gonna do you a favor. We're gonna give you some advice. If you pay the rebbe, you can get rid of that trouble in your cellar, honestly."

Markel tried to talk, but he couldn't get a word in edgewise. All three men crowded in on him with wild gestures and Hassidic grimaces:

"You may not believe in other rebbes, but this tsaddik, long may he live, is not a rebbe, he's a saint, honestly. Listen: Rabbi X., long live the memory of that righteous man, was really like a Moses, and the whole world said that Rabbi X., honestly, was a loftier soul than Rabbi Y. Well, just before he died, Rabbi X. passed his leadership down to our tsaddik. He came all the way from Jassi, even though, honestly, Jassi didn't want to let him go for love or money. Imagine all the things and feats and miracles they saw him perform every day in Jassi." (A pious Hassidic sigh.) "May God grant us the privilege of seeing just his under-under-stool in paradise—that would be enough of a reward for us. What did he always say, the rebbe: 'Thou canst not enter paradise in clodhoppers.' You have to work hard and go to the rebbe first, that's obvious. After all, the rebbe is also a rabbi. Markel, do you know why they call him the Faithful Rebbe?"

"I know," said old Markel. "Because at first he was a rabbi in a shtetl, then he became a Hassid and moved to Moldavia, among the roughnecks."

"Hahaha!" all three of them guffawed. "You lunatic! You moron! You idiot! You old Rationalist! You don't know anything, you can't even pray right. Hahaha! You can't even say a Hebrew word! *Shtetl! Rebbe!* Any kid can say that! You ought to be ashamed of yourself! The Great Rebbe, may he rest in peace, was more intelligent than Markel the Innkeeper of Nosuchville. Didn't he say: 'How much does the word *tsaddik* add up to'? Come on! Tell us! Well? Ninety? Like the Jewish letter *tsaddik* which indicates the number 90? Right. Markel, you fool, keep going. What is ninety? A *tsaddik*, right? Because he is the true tsaddik of his generation, honestly. That was why the rebbe, may he rest in peace, said we should only call him the 'Miracle-Worker.' Ha. Right? His eyes could see things that our blind eyes couldn't see. He could see so much further, higher. Honestly, we saw how he passed on his leadership in Mezhbezh. No one understood what their meeting meant, honestly. Just look at all the warfare now. They're the only ones who know, and nothing can happen without them. People ask them if there should be a war. Without them, no king is crowned, not for love or money, honestly. Hey, hey, Markel!" Shmerel Tevyes heaved a sigh, and the other two Hassids scratched their heads and hung on his lips with a crazy grimace. "Hey, hey! Whatever the rebbes do in their synagogues, kings and princes have to obey them. Just the other day, an abandoned wife came to the tsaddik. She'd been traveling for years and years, looking for her husband. She'd called upon all the Hassidic rebbes, and none of them could help her, honestly. Moyshe was present when the tsaddik laughed and took the woman into the kitchen. His wife has been lying senseless for years now, honestly. There was a vat of water standing in the kitchen, and the healer was taking a bath in it. 'Woman, place thy hand into the water,' the rebbe said to the woman. She stuck in her hand and pulled out a skullcap. 'Go and seek the head for that skullcap,' he told her, 'this skullcap belongs to thy husband.' The whole town was in a dither, honestly, because of that miracle. And you, you old graybeard, Markel! You refuse to go to the miracle-worker about your cellar? You ought to be ashamed of yourself, you old fool, you lunatic, you madman, you simpleton!"

The old saloon-keeper tried to ask a question, he wanted to understand what the three men were telling him. The stories about the miracles didn't sound all that kosher. But he couldn't get a word in edgewise, Shmerel was heatedly talking away at him:

"Now, before Elul (September) creeps up on you, you can get

rid of your problem in a minute, honestly. When Elul comes, you could give a thousand guldens, honestly, and they wouldn't let you in to see the rebbe for love or money. He's got the whole world on his back. Elul! That's no chickenshit! All the rebbes have their eye on the Tsaddik of the Generation, you have no reason to doubt our word. We don't want your approval, honestly, and he certainly doesn't need it. . . . Just the other day, some Litvaks came from far, far off, maybe four or five hundred miles away, honestly. 'Rebbe,' they said, 'rebbe, we can only come to you!' He quickly guessed what they wanted and told them to go home. If you want to take our advice, Markel, that's fine, if not, then they'll tear down your house. . . . God forbid it should bring harm to the town, honestly."

The whole chatter wouldn't have touched the old Rationalist. But Markel was in a bad mood because of all the business he had lost. He felt no better after the last "honestly" and the threat of having his place demolished. The poor man was absolutely flabbergasted.

The next day, the saloon-keeper, old Markel, drove off to Mezhbezh with Shmerel Tevyes. The rebbe's fee was the numerical equivalent of the Hebrew letters in Markel's name: three hundred eighty-one guldens. The miracle-worker gave him an old copy of the *Zohar* to hang up on his cellar door, and he said:

"For thirty years, I have seen the Sublime Lights in this *Book of Zohar,* and I know that all the foul demons will have no might, especially. . . ." He began brooding and staring at Markel: ". . . because a Jew needs his business, poor man, and even more so a good, decent Jew. . . ."

Markel stopped being a Rationalist after that journey. He arrived home one day before the first of Elul. Shmerel took old Markel to the bathhouse before they hung the old *Zohar* on the cellar door, honestly.

The whole town of Nosuchville came running to hear the amazing story from Markel's own lips when slap dab on the Ides of Elul, the rebbe's prediction came true: "At mid-Elul, the thing will stop in thy cellar, and thou shalt do better commerce than ever before."

An even greater miracle than any other was the fact that the ancient *Zohar*, the dear *Holy Zohar*, which the rebbe had been studying for thirty years, yes indeed, thirty years in a row, and in which he had seen all the souls that he had brought to rest and saved from Gehenna—that very *Zohar* vanished from the cellar door where they had hung it (people elbowed one another with dumbstruck expressions) and it had come back into the hands of the miracle-worker, simply straight back to him, honestly. . . .

We mustn't ask a lot of questions. Markel, once a stout Rationalist, became a Hassid, he carried on with Hassidic grimaces and with glassy eyes more thumpingly than a native Hassid, and he told the others the story. Well, how could anyone doubt him?

Customers once again drank ale, mead, and distilled vodka in Markel's saloon.

A miracle. Right?

X

Zainvil of Nimyevke, Dovid Smik's son-in-law, came to Nosuchville during the week before Rosh Hashanah and he too went over to old Markel's saloon to learn more about the miracle, which Shmerel Tevyes had amply described to him.

Even though he had already heard about it in the village, Zainvil then went to see the great miracle-worker in Mezhbezh at Rosh Hashanah.

Nosuchville is a town. Without scandals, apparently, no town can survive. There was another scandal, a terrible scandal.

Two days after Rosh Hashanah, Sheyntse vanished. No one knew what had happened: She disappeared some time between day and night. She was gone for one day, for two days, for three days—she was gone, simply gone.

Aaron the Beadle and his wife Sarah looked for her day and night.

"It's like hunting a needle in a haystack," Aaron was told. "It's just no use. You'd be better off if both of you, or just you alone, Aaron, went to the tsaddik. You'll find people you know there, they'll take you in to the rebbe. He's worked much bigger miracles than finding a young woman. Just ask him—it'll be fine."

90

Aaron the Beadle and his wife Sarah were distraught about having to leave the Yom Kippur bowl. That's something they looked forward to all year long. So they decided that Sarah would travel alone, together with some young wives who wanted to have children.

Privately, Aaron the Beadle and his wife were kind of suspicious of Zainvil because they thought he had stared very hard at Sheyntse during the dark betrothal when he had brought that scoundrel Naphtali and the ten gold ducats over to her. Furthermore, Zainvil himself had given her three ducats so eagerly and, furthermore, he had conversed with her much too long. Sarah recalled what Zainvil had told Sheyntse when he came to say good-bye: "You won't have to worry about anything!" That sounded more like a man talking about himself, to get Sheyntse for himself. Furthermore, neighbors claimed that on the day Sheyntse had vanished, they had seen some young man talking to her in a corner of the back alley.

Even though Zainvil had actually gone to see the rebbe in Mezhbezh on Rosh Hashanah together with all the Hassids, he might very well have sneaked back right after the holiday and carried her off. What could Zainvil have done with her? Hard to say. They hit upon an answer: A man that rich would rent an apartment for Sheyntse in another village, so that he could visit her any time.

The first thing they did was to go over to Shmerel Tevyes' inn, where Dovid Smik and Braine-Dobrish were celebrating Rosh Hashanah. Perhaps they could get a lead. They learned that the day after Rosh Hashanah, Zainvil had indeed returned from Mezhbezh and spent the night in Shmerel's inn. At the crack of dawn, right after prayers, he drove off to the village. He was to come to town for Yom Kippur with his parents-in-law, Beyltse, and the baby.

Hearing all those things, the beadle and his wife decided to confide them to the miracle-worker, and he would be sure to judge that Zainvil must return Sheyntse secretly.

"But for God's sake!" Aaron said to his wife. "Mum's the word! Don't tell anyone, y' know, that you're gonna tell the secret to the tsaddik."

Sarah understood and put her finger on her lips to show that

91

she would tell the secret only to the tsaddik. And off she drove.

XI

Sarah the beadle's wife returned from Mezhbezh two days after Yom Kippur. All the women, even Gittel Gabriels, the richest woman in town, dashed over to hear what Sarah had to tell and what she had managed to do about Sheyntse. The men were afraid to crowd with the women into the beadle's small room in the bes-medresh, but every husband told his wife to come out right away and tell him what Sarah told her.

Outside, in front of the bes-medresh, a large crowd gathered, waiting for the women to come out. Waiting is no fun, but waiting and waiting for an hour and even more than an hour is awful. Some of the men cursed their absent wives, some scolded—but they didn't dare leave.

"What's taking them so long?" ten men asked at once.

"You know women!" a half dozen householders replied. "They can never stop talking! They're talking about veils and pins and carrot stew."

But actually, it wasn't the women's fault. Sarah the beadle's wife felt she had to tell them how she had traveled with a bitter heart, how a wheel had smashed and she had met women returning from a cemetery, how a cloudburst had come and all three women had been forced to huddle under a horse blanket and had gotten soaked anyway, down to their undergarments, if you'll pardon the expression, and how they had run into a crazy woman, who was being taken to a healer, can you imagine, and how she heard about the rebbe's miracles along the way.

That was why it took so long to get to the point:

"If you please, a woman, upon my word, what do they say, a woman can't, if you please, push in among householders, if you please. Men and women are there from all over the world, if you please, but one woman, long may she live, gave me a piece of advice: 'You know what, lady? Slip the *gabai*, the rebbe's administrator, some money, and he'll take you all the way up to the rebbe.' Well, so what do I do? I show the gabai a nice, large ruble, but I don't put it in his hand, if you please, and after looking at the ruble, he led me all the way to the tsaddik, right into his alcove, if you please, and when I was already inside, I handed the gabai a five-kopek piece."

All the women burst into guffaws:

"Hahahahaha!"

"I'm laughing, but my laughter turned to tears," said Sarah. "Aaron, move the pot over on the stove. I don't want the little bit of broth to run out, if you please. I had to pay thirteen kopeks, if you please, for a ritual rooster, a tiny thing. Here it would only cost ten. . . . Let me forget my sorrows, but not my words. When I got to the tsaddik, he instantly knew exactly what I wanted." The women craned their necks in amazement. "He asked me about every last detail, and he moaned like a woman having a baby, if you please. . . . Aaron, you know about that, don't you? . . . And so I told the tsaddik everything that came to my mind, that's what I told him. And he—just listen—he gave me such a look that I practically passed out, if you please. . . ."

All the women shook their heads.

"May my life in heaven be as wonderful as that tsaddik. 'Sarah,' he said to me, so plainly, with such good words. 'Sarah, journey home and make thee a huge candle of white wax, a candle that can burn for two days and two nights. That will be good.' And he also blessed me, if you please. I put down the silver ruble and I went away, if you please. May all the things that I wished him come true!"

Gittel Gabriels blurted out:

"Well, did you make the candle, the big white wax candle?"

Aaron called out:

"Y'know, it's been burning in the bes-medresh for two hours already. Why, that's the reason she went in the first place. . . . Sarah, go to the stove. This is no fastday, y' know."

The women left, and each wife told her husband the story she had heard from Sarah, but added a few lies as trimming. The candle was burning for now, that was already half a miracle. The other half would come tomorrow—Sheyntse would be found.

Naturally, when the men realized what the big, fat, white wax candle meant, they all ran to have a look. Well, what did they see?

93

A burning candle. The women envied the householders, the men: they were allowed to see the white wax candle burning. Women are not permitted to enter a bes-medresh. What can they see there, after all? But still, they wanted to see it with their own eyes. Maybe that's how it is with other small things in the great world, people absolutely want to see with their own eyes.

Aaron the Beadle tended the white wax candle better than a candle for the anniversary of a death. The white candle was not to go out, God forbid. The miracle-worker had said the candle was to burn, and the burning would help them find Sheyntse. So it had to be tended.

XII

Nosuchville is a town. In Nosuchville, anything can happen.

That Yom Kippur, Dovid Smik and his wife Braine-Dobrish, and their only daughter Beyltse, and the baby she was nursing, and Zainvil were in town. Because of the fastday and the mob in the women's section of the synagogue (it was also a very hot day, although, as Jews say, even a fish trembles in the water during the Days of Awe; and Beyltse, who was very delicate, was nursing a child, and the holy day required weeping), Beyltse fainted dead away during the closing services. They had a terrible time bringing her to Shmerel Tevyes' inn (where the family was staying) and reviving her.

If they had called the landowner's physician, he would certainly have given her something. But they didn't call him because it often happens that a woman faints in synagogue, she generally recovers and by nightfall she's eating cold chicken (the fowl killed in the Yom Kippur ritual) and hard pears with more gusto than anyone else, and it does her no harm at all.

Beyltse, however, became sick, very sick. The next day, she was worse, dangerously ill. When they finally brought the physician the night after Yom Kippur, he said: "It looks bad." He had some medicines, but Beyltse couldn't take them because her throat was closed up. Not even a drop of water could get through. It was bad, very bad, very, very bad.

The day before the Feast of Tabernacles, Beyltse died, at noon.

What misery, what misery! How dreadful the parents felt, how dark were their lives! Their only son had converted to Christianity, and their only daughter, that fine girl, had died.

How dreadful Zainvil felt! He had loved Beyltse, and she had loved him, that is to say, they had both loved one another. Beyltse was smart, good, and pious, and she was also a very beautiful young woman. A rib had been torn out of poor Zainvil's body. It pained him even more to know how awful, how dreadful the miserable parents felt. For all their wealth, they were very, very unhappy. They had had two children: That scoundrel had converted to Christianity. A shame, a disgrace, a sorrow, but they could endure it because they had Beyltse and a new grandson, a darling boy, and they also looked upon Zainvil as their own child. Now, all at once, their only daughter had died. A dreadful tragedy for a father and mother! Their only daughter had been snatched away.

Zainvil, the good, smart, pious scholar Zainvil, understood all that in the midst of mourning his dear wife, and so, in front of all the mourners, at the side of Beyltse's body, he promised his in-laws that he would never take another wife under any circumstances and that he would never leave them, he and his child, the little boy, would stay with them forever, and they would be as their children, all their lives.

Well, of course, on the one hand, when the wound is still open to the eyes, the only daughter is lying on the ground with her feet towards the door, covered with a black cloth, it's not right to talk about never marrying again, never taking another wife. And on the other hand, how can a young man of eighteen, like Zainvil, promise never to take another wife? But for the moment, it was a somber consolation for the parents as they sat on the ground, mourning the death of their one and only daughter. Rather than becoming even more miserable in their great misery, they welcomed such words from the good boy, from the grandson of the Preacher of Ostro, they were very glad to hear that he didn't want to leave them.

95

Both of them, Braine-Dobrish with her broken heart, with her sad, bitter thoughts, and even Dovid Smik, who scarcely ever spoke, hugged and kissed their good, smart, pious son-in-law Zainvil for his words.

Women stood around, crying and crying at the dreadful laments that Braine-Dobrish, for goodnesh' shake, was sobbing and weeping for her one and only daughter. At every word that the suffering, agonizing mother brought forth over the corpse, the women let out a heart-rending wail. The keening went on for about an hour. Braine-Dobrish kept grieving and talking, and the women wept along with her.

Then, when Zainvil promised to remain with them and his little boy, his motherless baby, and the parents-in-law threw their arms around him and showered him with kisses ("Do you hear, Beyltshe, what your Zhainvil ish shaying to ush? In front of all the townshfolk, for goodnesh' shake . . .?"), all the women burst into a flood of tears.

Suddenly, they heard a racket outside. Aaron and Sarah were arguing with the beadles. And when a few women ran out to see what all the commotion was about, the mourners inside the house could hear Sarah's voice:

"Make him give me back my child! The candle burnt up, if you please, right when Beyltse died. Cat got your tongue, Aaron? Shout: 'You kidnapper! Give us back our Sheyntse!' The tsaddik, the miracle-worker, he had his reasons when he said: 'After two days and two nights, when the candle has burnt down, that will be right, they will give thee Sheyntse again. . . .' "

Aaron the Beadle had to shout because Sarah told him to:

"Y'know, the candle burnt down the very moment when his wife died. . . ."

Tevye and Shmerel Tevyes, together with several members of the burial society, came dashing over to rebuke Sarah and her husband.

Meanwhile, the crowd, waiting outside for the funeral to begin, started mobbing the door where the beadle's wife was standing and screaming. The pushing and shoving were so bad that some people almost suffocated. No one knew what Sarah and Aaron had to yell about, and so everyone squeezed in even more.

"I'll shout out the secret, yes, I, Sarah, the beadle's wife, if you please, I'll shout it to high heaven! Aaron! Shout! Make him give us back our Sheyntse! Make him tell us where she is and we'll go and get her! Ha, the candle showed the truth, if you please. . . ."
She was screaming at the top of her lungs and struggling with the beadles, fighting like a madwoman to get inside. "Let me at him! Let me get my hands on Zainvil. Make him give me back my Sheyntse. He's got her, he and no one else. . . ."
Zainvil, in the midst of his great distress, heard his name being yelled, he came over to the door and asked:
"Did somebody call me?"
Tevye and Shmerel squealed and shrieked:
"Tie the woman up. She's off her rocker!"
Sarah screamed even louder:
"Yes, yes, the candle burnt down. I'm not off my rocker. . . ."
Spotting Zainvil, she grabbed him with both hands:
"Swear to me, if you please, on the corpse, that you will return my Sheyntse, the tsaddik said so, if you please. . . ."
Zainvil assumed that the woman had gone crazy in her grief. With tearful eyes, he walked back to his dead wife.
The town beadles grabbed Sarah's arms and dragged her home. Meanwhile Tevye Bilenkis and Shmerel Tevyes tried to make Aaron the Beadle realize that it was stupid and terribly wrong to suspect a man like Zainvil, and they said some harsh things to him:
"If you or your wife so much as dare to say a bad word against the grandson of the Preacher of Ostro, that dear man Zainvil, then tomorrow you'll no longer be beadle of the bes-medresh."
That brought Aaron to his senses, and he quietly stole away.
Sarah, as she was being dragged home, screamed across the entire marketplace:
"Why did I spend all that money traveling? Why did I pay the rebbe a ruble? Why did I buy three pounds of white wax? If he doesn't know, why is he trying to cheat me? Why's he talking about miracles? Why do so many people pile in to see him?"
You can scream your heart out, Sarah! He won't pay you back your travel expenses, your ruble, or what the candle cost you. You're not the first and you won't be the last. People want to be

cheated and they'll always find someone who knows how to pull the wool over their eyes and fleece them for it.

Beyltse was given a proper funeral that night. The seven days of mourning began on the Feast of Tabernacles, but Jews are not allowed to grieve as much during a holiday. So when the feast was over, Dovid Smik, Braine-Dobrish, and Zainvil, together with the little baby and a wetnurse, drove back to Nimyevke, to grieve there and try to find solace in the fact that the little boy had Beyltse's face.

XIII

That's enough out of Nosuchville. It's time to see what's happening with Mikhel—Mikhel the ex-belfer, Mikhel Gravestone, and then Mikhel the Muscovite.

We saw that three days before Rosh Hashanah, Mikhel left Nosuchville with the Russian officer Commissioner Khlyebov and drove to the Russian headquarters.

Khlyebov and Mikhel (from now on, we'll talk about him without any nickname, just plain Mikhel) arrived in Breslau two days after the Feast of Tabernacles. Breslau is a big German city in Prussia.

In Breslau, Khlyebov called upon the Russian commander, Major Redrikov, who gave him a document from the Commissioner-General of the Tsarist army, making Khlyebov inspector at the Russian provisions storehouse of Breslau. He was to supply flour, cereal, biscuits, oats, and hay to all the Russian regiments passing through Breslau and to all the Russian troops stationed in the city.

Khlyebov was taken care of. But Mikhel couldn't have much to do for him. The inspector had no business to throw Mikhel's way. However, since he had taken Mikhel away from his home, he was concerned about him. Besides, Mikhel was a perfect stranger in Germany, he knew nobody there, he couldn't even speak German. Though every Jew at home, in Polish provinces, thinks: "Ah, if the landowner talks German, I'll be able to tell him everything." The moment that Jew gets to Germany, he hears the language, but they might as well be speaking in tongues. He catches a few words that sound almost like Yiddish; but he doesn't understand what the German wants or what the German means.

Khlyebov was a good egg! He cudgeled his brains until he hit on a way to help Mikhel. Khlyebov had lots of Jewish friends who were contractors and suppliers, they had come from Russia with the Tsarist army to do business, and some of them happened to be in Breslau. A few had contracts from the military commission to provide everything to the soldiers in Russian hospitals, and with prices for every item. That too was a big business. Others had contracts for transportation. That too was a big business.

Khlyebov took his friend Mikhel from one contractor to another, asking each to employ Mikhel. He praised Mikhel and guaranteed that he was an honest, loyal man, who could be relied on in every way and entrusted with money.

Who wouldn't do a favor for a friend like Commissioner Khlyebov? A man like him could come in very handy some time. Oxman, a supplier for the Breslau Hospital, hired Mikhel for his staff, Mikhel would have to be near him all the time and in his lodgings. Not as a servant, for in Germany you don't have to take your servants when you travel; in hotels the domestics serve you better than a dozen of your own menials (that's incomprehensible for us in the Russian-Polish towns, where, with all the inns, they don't know the meaning of the words *service* and *guest*). No, Oxman took Mikhel along to purchase the supplies for the hospital. Oxman had a German employee, a man from Breslau, but he didn't feel that he was all that trustworthy, so he had Mikhel join him to buy the goods they needed.

When a young man comes to Germany from a Russian-Polish town, and especially to a big city like Breslau—how dazed he is at first.

Mikhel had once traveled from Nosuchville to Berditchev, accompanying a bridegroom to his wedding. A wealthy man in Nosuchville had taken the bright young belfer along to serve him, and had paid him eight silver ducats, plus a bonus of six silver ducats.

What had Mikhel seen in the big town of Berditchev? Ten

99

Nosuchville mudholes together, fifteen times as many bedraggled women and bespattered men as in Nosuchville, thirty-eight times as many paupers yanking at your coattails, forty times as many horse-drawn wagons. A shoving, a dashing, a chasing, one man scolding, one man beating, ten people arguing, five people shouting: "How ya doin'? What are ya up to?" No one's got time. One man runs afoul of a wheel, which rips away half of his kaftan; on the other side, somebody says to him: "Mazel-tov!" Tin alms-boxes clatter: "Charity delivereth from death!" and women dance over to a bride with challahs and musicians across the street. Jews with tall bamboo canes demand money for various charities, while a dozen men race past, yelling: "Stop thief! There he is! . . ."

Then all at once, Mikhel saw Breslau. A city with no mudholes, no bedraggled people, everyone dressed like a lord, clean and lovely. Even the stairs leading to large buildings are scoured, and none of the shopkeepers yells: "Come on in! What are you buying?!"

Even more miracles. Supposedly, ten thousand Jews live in Breslau, and Mikhel hadn't seen a single one—like a Jew in Nosuchville or in Berditchev—until he inquired and found out that the Jews also dressed like lords. He thought to himself: "How can Jews be lords? How is it possible? When he went to synagogue on the Sabbath and heard and saw the worshipers, he went over to look into the daily prayerbook that each man held in front of him as he stood praying. It was the same kind of praying as back home, but this was no Sephardic, no Hassidic prayerbook, by God; it began with: "How good. . . ." A man stood at the lectern, but he didn't carry on like a lunatic. Each worshiper stood in his place, calm, quiet, praying earnestly, and yet they were all Jews. The women were dressed like ladies, and they said "Good Sabbath!" to one another.

The next day was Sunday. Mikhel saw thousands of German men and women, old and young, in fine, festive clothes, strolling out of the town. Where were they heading? Not to a bes-medresh because there was no filthy bes-medresh in Breslau. Nor to perform *tashlekh*, the rite in which men shake out their pockets into a stream to wash away all their sins for the new year. Were they going to greet the governor or a newly arriving ruler?

Mikhel caught sight of Avrom Zaks, the man at whose home he had eaten the Sabbath meal, and he too was dressed like an aristocrat, as was his wife. Like everyone else, they were walking out of the town, so Mikhel strode over to them and asked:

"Where is everyone going?"

"Come along, Mr. Pole," said the man. "You can treat us!"

Although he didn't understand what Zaks meant, Mikhel followed at their heels, until they came to a long, vast garden. All the lords and ladies, and even the children, were entering through the gate. Mikhel heard some of the older Jews, the ones he had seen praying so earnestly in synagogue, call it: "Liebich's Gorten." (They used the Yiddish word for garden.) The young couple he was walking with said to him in German:

"Well, Mr. Pole, here is the garden. Would you like to treat us?"

Mikhel saw that what the older Jews called a *gorten* (which was Yiddish), the younger ones called a *Garten* (which was German). "A garden," he thought to himself. "What do I need a garden for? Corn, cucumbers, and beets, or maybe cherries, sour cherries, or pears, plums, or apples?" But he nodded his head:

"Yes. . . ."

"Or would you rather not? . . ."

The man with whom he had eaten the Sabbath meal pulled him along and winked at his wife, who also tugged him inside.

Mikhel entered through the beautiful gates of the garden, along with all the lords and ladies, and he removed his hat. (He had put away his *spodek*, his high fur headpiece, on coming to Breslau and had purchased a hat.) The man and his wife laughed and pointed out that all the men were wearing their hats, so that Mikhel could keep his on.

Here, in the garden, in Liebich's Garden, Mikhel saw that there were no beets and no corn, not even plums or pears. But what *did* the garden have? In front, there was a huge square, with all sorts of beautiful plants, autumnal vegetation. Further on, there were small and large trees, very beautiful, in either rows or circles. And in between the trees, there were small tables and chairs. So many of these tables were already occupied by ladies and gentlemen.

101

Some of them, Mikhel saw, were sipping coffee and paying only half a gulden to the waiter who brought the tray with the cups, the coffeepot, a small pitcher of milk, and sugar. At other tables, ladies and gentlemen were sitting with their children, they were drinking beer from lovely glasses and paying even less.

"God, it's so cheap!" thought Mikhel to himself. "In Nosuchville, even a glass of stale mead costs more than that."

"Okay, over here," said Mikhel to the small waiters who were carrying around coffee or beer. "Hey, waiter! Bring coffee and beer!"

The waiter didn't seem to understand what Mikhel said, but he did catch the two words: "Coffee, beer!" And he saw Mikhel pointing to the table where the couple was sitting. A minute later, the German waiter in the green jacket strode over, with a tray containing coffee, milk, sugar, and cups on one arm, and a tray containing a corked bottle of beer and glasses on his other arm. He swiftly put everything down on the table and pulled out the cork, saying:

"Here you are!"

He was already off and bringing orders to another table. Several such small, green-clad waiters were hurrying about, carrying trays of refreshments to the patrons. There were perhaps twenty fine, dextrous waiters. In the middle of the garden stood a platform, something like the kind from which the Torah is read in synagogue (if you'll excuse the blasphemous comparison). There were some twenty men on the platform, playing violins and flutes and other instruments, and so effectively that the music could be heard all the way across the garden.

Mikhel couldn't believe that no wedding was being celebrated. And he couldn't figure out why the musicians were playing and no one was dancing.

Mikhel saw that Avrom Zaks and his wife were drinking coffee, so he helped himself to the beer. It was cold and delicious, a lot tastier than the March ale he had drunk at the wedding in Berditchev. When the waiter noticed they were done, he said only one word:

"Geld!" (Money.)

Mikhel put down a Polish gulden and received a few coins as

change. The waiter cleared the table and hurried off.

The musicians kept playing different pieces, but they always played them beautifully. However, no one was dancing. "These Germans are meshugge!" Mikhel thought to himself.

Avrom Zaks and his lovely wife went for a stroll through the garden. One of the musicians came towards them with a tray. There was a sheet of music paper on it. Avrom Zaks motioned to Mikhel to put his change from the gulden on the tray. The musician thanked him and went on. Other people likewise gave him money. Some gave him nothing and waved their hands. That was all right too.

Mikhel couldn't get over all these great wonders. Just think! For one Polish gulden, he was in Paradise among gentlemen and such lovely, radiant ladies! He had drunk beer and treated Avrom Zaks and his lovely wife to coffee. He was listening to musicians, and they were playing a thousand times better than Yitsikel Livak in Nosuchville. He strolled about in Paradise for two whole hours. And it all cost only one Polish gulden. That was what life was all about, wasn't it! "Back home, the people live like pigs!" said Mikhel to himself.

Sunday evening, Commissioner Khlyebov had gotten Oxman the contractor to hire Mikhel. On Monday morning, Mikhel entered Oxman's two big, lovely rooms at the inn. One room was a chamber with a lovely clean bed and bedding in shiny-white slipcovers. Next to the bed stood a small table with a large porcelain basin, a porcelain jug filled with water, a bar of soap, and a comb, and next to it a clean white towel. There were also a couple of chairs in the chamber. The other room was more spacious, it had a large mirror, a bureau, a lovely sofa, and six fine chairs. A big, lovely table, plus a small ecritoire with paper, ink, and a quill lying on it. In front of the two rooms there was something like a vestibule, containing boots and brushes. Here you hung up your coat or jacket before entering.

When Mikhel arrived in Oxman's quarters on Monday morning, he found him writing. Mikhel saw an attractive chambermaid bring in a tray of coffee, milk, and sugar and say: "Good morning!" Oxman put away his writing utensils and, as he began sipping his coffee, he motioned to his bed in the other room. The

103

lovely young chambermaid hurried out and then returned a minute later, carrying a basket of fresh white linen, and changed the linen on Oxman's bed. She put the used linen in her basket. She also picked up the coffee tray, curtseyed, and asked:

"Will there be anything else, Herr Oxman?"

Mikhel gaped in amazement:

"How fast, how promptly everything gets done, and how respectful the people are!"

Oxman could appreciate that a Jew from a Russian-Polish shtetl would be flabbergasted at all these things or else believe that Oxman was paying a hundred ducats a day. He said to Mikhel:

"Would you like coffee? Why don't you order some?"

Mikhel replied:

"No, thank you. Karp Semyonovitch wouldn't let me go without having me drink some tea first."

It was only now that Oxman said: "No, Caroline, the gentleman is not having coffee."

The girl left.

"Mikhel," Oxman said when she was gone, "you must be wondering how much I pay for these rooms, isn't that so? Well, these beautiful rooms, with the bed, and with fresh white linen every week, with all the chairs and tables, and all these marvelous things you see, and . . . there's even a key hanging there, for a very clean toilet, if you'll excuse me. I pay only eight good groschens, that's two Polish guldens a day. Which adds up to nine rubles a month. I've got an apartment that I needn't be ashamed of, and I can receive corporals and even generals here. For my business I have to have attractive lodgings, and I can't be bothered with carrying bed linen around when I travel. You have to pay more for freight than for your own fare. And the chambermaid serves twenty guests in the inn, each in his rooms. When I go out to take care of my business, I leave the key with the maid, and she sweeps and cleans the place till it glistens like gold. I can leave money here uncounted, and not a kopek will be missing. When I come back, my key is hanging downstairs with the innkeeper. I pay half a Polish gulden for coffee, and anything a guest may need is written on a board" (he pointed to a board hanging on the wall) "along with the price. So I can keep my own account of what I get from the innkeeper and what I owe him. And the innkeeper is very amenable. Germans are good at figures. Who knows how long it will take our abominable little towns in Russian Poland to start doing business in this way and keeping accounts like this! We'll have to wait a long, long time."

Mikhel shook his head.

"No. It'll never happen back home, I can tell you. Unless all the Jews in Russian Poland are forced to spend a couple of years over here, then they might learn from the example. If someone were to come here and then go back and tell them about it, they wouldn't believe him and they'd make fun of him."

"Making fun of people like that," replied Oxman, "is something our Jews have learned from those awful Hassids and their con men, the Hassidic rebbes and tsaddiks. They've made Jews so arrogant. You don't realize, Mikhel, that the Talmud praises Jews for three virtues: modesty, compassion, and charity. It says: 'Those who are modest are compassionate and charitable.' As for the first quality, the Hassids have given the lie to Jewish modesty. They're pushy and arrogant! They never address an elderly Jew politely as 'Reb' (Mister). With those louts, it's always: 'Hey you! Shmuel!' That's how they talk to an old gentleman of eighty. Except for their rebbe, they care about nothing. Compassion or charity for anyone who's not a Hassid is something they regard as sinful. That's why before Hassids and the plague of Hassidic rebbes spread among Jews, you could tell them: 'Brothers, what you're doing isn't right. Look at older countries and learn finer ways, more intelligent customs, and a method of livelihood. It costs less and it makes for a better life.' They understood and they went along with it. Little by little, they got rid of old windows with curtains and other nonsense. And they heeded the advice. The arrogant Hassids poke fun at everything and everybody. They have to be absolutely ignorant and incapable, and the rebbes even say quite plainly: All that counts is being a Hassid and believing that the rebbe has one foot here on earth and the other foot above the angels' heads so that he can reach the button on God's trousers. That's all a Jew should be able to do, everything else is crap! This is the worst misfortune for the Jews

105

in Russian Poland. Jews get more and more crippled every day, they can't even learn how to read and write Yiddish, they're simply arrogant. Why can't Rabbi R. even sign his own name— doesn't he make a mint? Thousands of silver rubles come pouring into his home. 'Well, here you are!' says every Hassid. . . . Mikhel, the silly Jews are going to make us forget our sick soldiers. Come to the hospital with me and I'll introduce you to the German. You'll always go shopping with him and buy everything that's needed for the hospital. And I'll introduce you to the man to whom you have to deliver all your purchases. Every evening, you're to give him a bill for all the things you've bought.

"I'll take Khlyebov's word that you're an honest man. I don't really trust my German. I'll pay you two hundred rubles a month. Try and buy cheap so that I can compare with the prices the German has been handing me. If you can get me better prices, then you can be sure that I'll reward you over and above your salary. Let's go!"

Mikhel had listened carefully to everything. He was even more astonished at finding a man who regarded the rebbes as ignorant and arrogant liars and anything but what he always heard in Nosuchville.

He went out with Oxman, and on the way he mulled over everything that Oxman had said. At the hospital, Mikhel understood all his tasks and he became a fine steward.

XIV

A bright and capable young man like Mikhel was a great boon to Oxman's business. Ten days later, he started making all the purchases himself, without the German. He didn't speak German very well, he still didn't have the hang of it; but when he had to make his purchases, he knew the names of the items. Money has the virtue of making the Germans understand when you want to buy something, even if your German is poor.

Oxman grew fond of Mikhel and often asked him to his lodgings when he had visitors, other contractors, in the evening, to have tea and talk about all sorts of things.

Mikhel had already gone to the theater with Oxman several

times, and Oxman had explained each play to him.

Mikhel saw that Oxman was a good man, who wanted him to understand, and so he said:

"It *is* very beautiful, it *is* very intelligent, and everything's done very cleverly. And it *is* enjoyable. But if you don't mind my asking, I'd like to know: What use is the theater with all its make-believe?"

"It's good that you've asked me, Mikhel!" said Oxman. "Think about the six plays you've seen with me, and tell me if you don't feel that each one has a moral for us. A character is rich, he's a baron, and he uses so much intelligence and money to get a poor man away from his virtuous daughter and even drive him out of his home. Do you remember the baron? Well, what happens in the end? The baron loses all his wealth and becomes a cripple. While the poor man's good, virtuous, beautiful girl marries a count and the man himself becomes happy. Do you recall, Mikhel?"

"I certainly do!" said Mikhel. "I remember that all the plays are like that. Yes indeed. In the end, the just man always becomes known, and the villain is killed, or else his evil doings are exposed and he is put to shame."

"Well," said Oxman, "then the theater is more useful than a preacher's moral sermonizing. Here, in the theater, you enjoy the 'make-believe,' as you call it, Mikhel, but in the process, moral lessons are smuggled into the hearts of the people watching and listening. The play demonstrates that it's best to be honest and to follow the example of good people. On the other hand, it also demonstrates that a proud man, an evil man, a debaucher may appear to be successful for a while, but in the end he comes to shame and woe. Not everyone wants to listen to a preacher, and even if you do listen to him you'll forget his sermon and his good words an hour later. But at a play, the audience pays strict attention and listens carefully to each word, so that it sticks in their minds. I'll bet you remember every play we've seen!"

"That's right," said Mikhel. "I'll show you at home: I've jotted down the names of all the plays in Yiddish. All I need is the title, and even back in Nosuchville I'll be able to go through every play from start to finish."

"I'm delighted that you're recording the names," laughed

107

Oxman. "But do you think that the basic device of the theater comes from the jesters, what you call 'make-believe'? Back home, in that dark place, the shtetl, the wedding jesters disguise themselves and make believe. Children may dress up as soldiers, but if you see them, you won't think that military strategy comes from little children. No, Mikhel. The man who first dealt with the essence of theater was Aristotle, and even the simplest Jews talk about being 'as smart as Aristotle.' He lived thousands of years ago and he was versed in all the wisdoms of the world. And he said: 'A theater is a classroom where people learn how to be good and pious and honest. Theater is the school of virtue.' So now, Mikhel, you know what use theater is, don't you?"

"I really have to thank you, Mr. Oxman," said Mikhel. "I've learned many things that I didn't know before. In our shtetls, the Jews live like simple animals. If it weren't for one thing that draws my heart back home, I certainly wouldn't travel back into the darkness, as you put it—not to mention the liars and the Hassidic rebbes with their make-believe and the way they turn people into liars, windbags, and cripples. Those poor, poor Jews—how pitiful they are! It tears my heart apart. . . ."

And thus both men, Oxman and Mikhel, went home from the theater. . . .

XV

A few days later, after this conversation about the theater, all the Russian contractors in Breslau assembled in Oxman's apartment. Not to talk business. It's only in the shtetl that there is no respect and people come into your home to see what you're writing or to whom you're talking and to ferret out your secrets. In Germany, our Russian contractors learned manners: When a man is counting money at a table, you stand away from the table, and if he's writing something, don't go near him under any circumstances, so that you won't seem to be prying. Well, the contractors got together. In the evening, after doing their business during the day, they wanted to chat a bit about matters of the world.

Mikhel sat there too, because Oxman called him in whenever he had company so that the young man could meet better people than he found in Nosuchville. To people who didn't know Mikhel, Oxman said, in the German manner:

"This is my Mikhel, an honest, virtuous young man from Russian Poland. He only emerged recently from the darkness of the shtetl. I want him to gather experience and get to know people in the wide world, not just Hassids or men who are intelligent but misguided. When he goes back home, even if he doesn't have a lot of money, then I'd like him at least to be able to say: 'You misguided people! The things they tell you are lies and falsehoods!' "

That was what Oxman said each time. Now this evening, when all the Russian contractors gathered in his apartment, Oxman recommended Mikhel with the same or similar words.

Being an intelligent young man, Mikhel had already acquired good manners and he bowed to each man, saying to Oxman:

"Thank you very much for your kind words."

Not like some Jew in Russian Poland instantly calling each man a friend or a good friend. How does acquaintanceship turn into friendship? Mikhel already knew the difference between the two.

The contractors, Gershon Margosin, Moyshe Davidson, Yankel Hailperin, Chaim Kroin, Shloyme Blumenfeld, Avrom Lande, were all highly capable men, experienced contractors, they were well-known throughout the country, they came from a fine background, were wealthy, some very wealthy, some less so, but in their business they were all intelligent and enlightened people, who had known, even back home, that the plague of Hassidism was a catastrophe for Jews, especially since here in Germany they saw young Jewish men with fine qualities, they saw Jewish children studying and mastering languages and all kinds of subjects, so that one could not help but respect such children.

The contractors had a lot to talk about, considering the great difference between their own children at home and the children here.

One man's son-in-law and son were both Hassids and hovered in the rebbe's home day and night, they didn't even learn how to read Yiddish, much less write it.

109

Another man sighed. He had two boys, and they had good, sound minds. But he couldn't find anyone to teach them Hebrew, not to mention Russian or German—God forbid, a child was not alllowed to study those languages, it could only go to those cripples, the Hassidic teachers. A teacher named Pinhas the Hunchback had only a smattering of scholarship and only an inkling of the Talmud, but he was highly respected by the Hassidic rebbe: a dear, marvelous man! The rebbe said that half the world patted him on his hunched back. "What's he going to tell my children? He'll tell them about the miracles performed by the Hassidic rebbes, each lie bigger than the other, each bit of nonsense worse than the last. Young kids believe anything: 'Goodness! The teacher, that dear marvelous man, told us, so it must be true. . . .' "

Gershon Margosin began to speak:

"Gentlemen, let me talk frankly: I gave up long ago on our Jews back home. Nothing can help them. Why, I've been to Tulczin, where the highly praised Hassidic rebbe did something shameful, very shameful to Leyzertse, the wealthiest man in Tulczin—a learned Jew and a very honest man to boot. Well, so Leyzertse went to Count Potocki. As you know, in Russian Poland, the Polish landowner polices the town. And Leyzertse complained bitterly to the count. Potocki didn't realize that a rebbe is practically a demigod to the Hassids. His honest merchant was dearer to him because there was no greater or more honest businessman in town. So Count Potocki sent out his bailiffs and his commissioner. At Purim, they drove the miracle-worker, the demigod, out of Tulczin. He and his wife and his children—they were all kicked out right at Purim. Well, gentlemen, you probably think that the Hassids said: 'You, rebbe, you miracle-worker, you've lucked out. They've simply chased you away from town like goodness knows what! You're no divine wonder!' But nothing of the sort, goodness knows! They kept right on believing, they kept right on traveling to him for miracles, they kept right on paying him his fees. More and more people went to see him in Bratslev, a few miles from Tulczin, and especially when he moved to Mezhbezh. I ask you, gentlemen, can such people, who deny everything that common sense tells

110

us, can such people get any better? Assuming a man is a fool, you can say: 'I'll teach him some common sense.' But if people are smart, very smart, and yet want to destroy common sense by force and care only for nonsense—how can you help them in any way? That was why David Friedländer in Berlin answered our minister when he was asked how Russia could enlighten her Jews like the Jews in Germany. Friedländer, that wise man, wrote back: 'What? A great man, a minister, thinks that the Russian Jews can be helped like the German Jews? No, the two kinds of Jews are utterly different. In Germany, there was no lack of scholarly Jews, but they had to be enlightened, they had to be shown that it's not enough to study the Talmud, you have to master other subjects and languages as well, and this was demonstrated with the help of the Talmud. That's why the German Jews began learning everything you must know to get along in the world. But the Jews in Russia are altogether different. Your Hassids, without the Talmud and without all the commentators, simply claim: A Jew mustn't know any worldly subjects, even being able to write is impious, even Hebrew is impious—the minute a Jew learns anything, he is branded a heretic. A Jew, says a rebbe, mustn't hear anything but the rebbe's obscure doctrines, God forbid, or his soul might be damaged. You can see for yourself, Herr Minister, whether the two kinds of Jews are at all similar.' "

Davidson let out a booming laugh.

"Do you know what that's like? A peasant's notion of hell. You put the peasant in a tub of vodka and someone holds him by the hair and prevents him from drinking even a drop of the vodka. And the rebbes hold the Jews by their earlocks, God forbid, and prevent them from learning or studying anything."

"We are the peasants," said Avrom Lande. "We have to have talented, educated Jews, young men who know a great deal and who would like our children to know a great deal as well. But those destroying angels, the rebbes, hold us by our hair and won't let us. I agree with Mr. Margosin that there's no remedy for such a plague. What do you think, Hailperin, what do you think, Kroin, and you Blumenfeld? Unless we send our children to Germany."

111

Everyone chimed in:

"That's right. That's right. Just send them here."

After these comments, Oxman said:

"Tell me, you intelligent people, do you really feel that would be humane? You can send your own children here. But should hundreds of thousands of Jewish children be forced? No, that's horrible! I think we can help them all, but with an easier remedy. You don't feel they can be helped, do you? But I tell you, just making fun of the Hassidic rebbes is enough to get rid of them. For instance, let me tell you what I did in a small town.—I think its name was Cholmecz.

"When I was en route here, it was wintertime, and all the fine French and German armies in Russia were dropping like straw because of the great cold. Travelers had to stop for the night very early. Now there was this Jew from Zhitomir traveling with me, his name was Lippe—after I tell you this story, remind me to tell you about Lippe Levit of Zhitomir and the false headband. Anyway, before we came to the inn at Cholmecz, I told Lippe:

" 'Listen, don't say anything. I want to show these Jews how easy it is to make fools of them. Just promise me not to utter a word for two whole hours.'

"Lippe didn't know what I was planning, but he did promise not to utter a single word for two hours.

"When we entered the main room of the inn, they were just lighting a candle. I quickly put on my robe and my sable hat and stood at the wall to say my evening prayers. I started doing what Hassidic rebbes do—I clapped and moaned and groaned all through my prayers, and let out all sorts of weird sounds and weird pious noises:

" 'Oh, Father, oh Father, ooh, aah, ech, dear Father, oh me, oh my!'

"By the time I finished, a dozen Jews were already standing around me. They held out their hands and twisted their faces: 'Sholom Aleichem.' I replied: 'Aleichem Sholom.' With a crazy Hassidic grimace. Then I walked over to the table and sat down at the head, and poured out some Hassidic Cabala and Torah— their chatterbox Torah comes off the cuff, and off the collar. And I kept throwing in a 'bim-bam!' or two. And: 'Dearest

Father.' And an Aramaic phrase or two and 'ha-pa, bim-bam! . . .' It went flowingly. The room filled up. It got so crowded you could hardly breathe. They licked their fingers over my teachings. I carried on about the Ten Spherot, the Attributes, I spouted things from the *Zohar*, I bragged and boasted about myself.

" 'How beautiful! A delight! A wonder! A sheer miracle!' said those who understood anything. The others, who either didn't hear or didn't grasp a single word, thought I could hear their whispers:

" 'A great rebbe!'

" 'A saint!'

" 'A wondrous man!'

" 'How learned he is in the Torah!'

" 'The Divine Radiance illuminates him!'

"If I had kept on chattering for another half hour with my false faces, people would have started bringing me money. Women with blind girls were already jamming around me. Then Lippe, that gross fellow, burst into guffaws:

" 'You idiots! He's making fools of you. You know who this is? This is Oxman, a contractor. Hahahaha! . . . .'

"They might not have believed him, but I blurted out:

" 'Look how easy it is to fool you. There wasn't one true word in the whole Hassidic Cabala that I was spouting here. I really pulled the wool over your eyes. And that's how rebbes trick you all the time. The rebbe praises himself, and you believe him. He lies, and you give him money for his lies. Now let me tell you the truth. King Solomon wrote in Proverbs: "The gullible man believeth every word." The great sage did not say that about a fool, for a fool does not believe everything. In fact, we Jews have a saying: "A fool is hard to fool." Solomon's proverb refers to the man who falls for anything. You, my brethren in Russian Poland, you're nobody's fools. And only a fool would mistake you for fools. But *what* are you? You're credulous, you're gullible, you're easily taken in. . . .'

"What do you think, gentlemen? Several people in that big crowd took me aside and thanked me for my performance and for my last words:

113

" 'You've done a good deed and you've done a lot of people a big favor in many ways. Nowadays so many young men are being recruited by the Lubavitcher Hassids. Your joke will pull the rug out from under the recruiter's feet.'

"Understand me correctly, gentlemen. You have to fight fire with fire, you have to use their own weapons against them, their pointless, uneducated biblical nonsense, their false laughter, their twisted grimaces. You have to ridicule them so that simple people will laugh at them in the streets. That's the only way to destroy their prestige. Furthermore, we have to ask the Tsar to issue a ukase compelling all Jews to learn how to read and write. If Jews read the excellent works by modern young Russian authors, we'd have a whole different life. Jews would drive out the Hassids and their rebbes with sticks. God willing, I hope that happens within fifty years throughout Russian Poland, with consolations and salvations for Jews in all the shtetls."

No one enjoyed Oxman's story or laughed as much as Mikhel did.

Gershon Margosin wouldn't pass up the chance. He said:

"We won't leave you, Oxman, until you tell us about Lippe Levit, because I know that man. He's a broker, a bad egg. How did *you* ever meet him? How can you travel with someone like that. I'd really like to know!"

XVI

It was already late at night. The next morning, Oxman would have to make sure that all the food supplies reached the hospital kitchens so that the staff would be able to cook for the sick soldiers. It was therefore agreed that the company would get together in a week at Gershon Margosin's home, and there Oxman would tell the story about Lippe Levit and the false headband.

Exactly seven days later, in the evening, Mikhel reminded Oxman that it was time to go to Margosin.

"Yes, you're right. I did promise. Come along with me, Mikhel."

The two of them arrived at Margosin's home, where they

found the entire group of contractors all waiting to hear Oxman's story. They begged him to start right away.

Oxman asked:

"How do you know the story is worth hearing? Why are you so anxious for me to tell it on the spot? My dear colleagues, don't you realize a man is not always prepared to tell a story, especially if it's treated as an obligation."

Gershon Margosin replied:

"My dear Oxman, you, in turn, don't realize that I heard something about this matter in Kalisz when our Tsar had a conference there with the King of Prussia. I've got my audience on tenterhooks with what I've told them so far. But we all realize that the main part is missing. That's why we're all pleading with you to tell us the whole thing, exactly as it happened."

"If that's the case," said Oxman, "I'll have to tell you, especially for your sake, Mr. Margosin, since you asked me how I ever came to travel with a bad egg like Lippe Levit, the broker of Zhitomir. This is what happened."

OXMAN'S STORY

It began during the great cold waves in the winter of 1812–1813, which seemed to come almost deliberately in honor of the French.

On the Christian New Year, I arrived in Czernigov, intending to continue to army headquarters. If you remember the story of Wise Hans, his saying was: "When do all contractors get together? In hell and at military headquarters." All the suppliers were going to headquarters for business, and so I went too. But it was very dangerous traveling in that terrible weather, and so I had to stay a while in Czernigov until it got a bit less cold. Besides, there was no way of knowing where the headquarters were because Tsar Alexander, Field Marshal Kutuzov, and the entire army never lingered anywhere. They kept marching and marching towards Germany, to drive Napoleon and the remnants of his army all the way across Germany's borders. And so I stayed on in the Lithuanian town of Czernigov.

There was only one house in town where Jews could stay, it belonged to a man named Aizl, and he took in lodgers. So I drove over.

How awful I felt upon arriving when I saw that Aizl had only one room, and fifteen guests were lying in it. They all slept on the floor like cows in a barn. I asked Aizl's wife, a filthy woman, whether she couldn't give me a private room.

"We ain' got none. We did have one, but it's taken by Mr. Lippe, the big contractor."

She said that to me right by the door to the room. Lippe opened the door when he heard me say:

"My name is Oxman, I'll have to find a private room somewhere else."

"Oh, Mr. Oxman?" said Lippe charmingly. "I'd be delighted to share my room with Mr. Oxman. Do come in. I've got this whole room to myself. It'll be fine with me, that's the kind of tenant I'd like."

I'd never heard of him, I didn't know who the great contractor Lippe was. I had never even heard his name. But he knew me and he was doing me a big favor.

Lippe's servant ran to get my bed linen and my belongings. I found myself in a large, clean room, very warm and well lit.

There was a samovar standing on the table and a chest with plates and a tea service. The old-time Russian contractors never traveled without the three S's: a servant, a suitcase, and a samovar. I thought to myself: Lippe must really be an old-time contractor. I felt good coming in from the cold. Hot tea with a bottle of rum: I could soon warm up, couldn't I?

I saw that a shopkeeper had brought over a large cone of sugar, plus two more bottles of rum and a pound of tea. He held a written bill in his hand and probably wanted to be paid. Lippe told him:

"Come back tomorrow."

As we drank our tea, Lippe said to me:

"You don't know me because you're still very young. I knew both your father and your mother" (Lippe mentioned them by name) "and they knew me very well. Your mother is no longer with us, and your father lives in Uman, isn't that so?"

Even though I didn't know him, these various indications made me believe that Lippe was truly one of the old-time big contractors with the three *S*'s.

The two of us ate in Lippe's warm, clean room, where I spent the entire day. As did Lippe. He said he had been held up by the great cold waves. He had important business, in partnership with a man named Leyzer Dilon of Nezvizh. Dilon had remained at the headquarters, but Lippe had had to come here for a few days. He was going to wait until the cold weather got a bit less severe. He had his transportation. A sleigh, with three horses eating oats and ready to speed off. As night came, Lippe asked me if I'd like to go to the bath with him.

"I'd be glad to," I replied. Especially since Aizl, the landlord, came in and respectfully announced:

"The bath is ready, they say."

So the landlord, Lippe, and I went out. The bathhouse was only a few streets away. It was dark inside, an awful place to undress, but I was already there, so I had to take my clothes off.

All at once, in the dark bathhouse, I was terrified to see—you probably won't believe me, just as I couldn't believe my own eyes: Russians, male and female, stark-naked, were bathing together, right there in the bathhouse. . . .

I ran away and pulled on my clothes, then I dashed back to the room.

There were Jews from Berditchev there, and I angrily asked them:

"What's this business anyway? Men bathing together with women!"

"Yes, that's the way it is here. We're used to it already," the guests answered.

"Used to it?! A fine thing! It's disgusting!" I snapped, and stormed into my room.

There I saw that my bed linen and my belongings were scattered about. I asked the servant:

"Who threw my things around?"

The servant replied:

"My master, Mr. Levit, told me to take out a shirt and trousers and a pair of stockings with a few other things and bring them to the bathhouse, and I gave them to him there. You didn't see me because it was so dark."

Now it can happen that a man may run out of clean linen and be forced to borrow from someone else. But why hadn't Mr. Lippe asked me? That was one thing. Then I began peering around carefully. All I could see in the large room was the suitcase, the large cone of sugar, and the bottles of rum. There was absolutely nothing else. Lippe's coat also served him as his dressing gown. Even the bed was nothing but straw. It had a Russian featherbed, new and white, and a filthy pillow from the landlady, with Russian eagles embroidered on it. The featherbed must have been supplied by a local shopkeeper against the promise of being paid tomorrow. The suitcase probably too, just like the sugar and the rum.

I went to bed. I didn't hear Lippe come home. When I got up in the morning, people were drinking tea, and Lippe had gone off somewhere.

The landlord and his wife, together with the servant, came in to ask me something. I won't bother imitating their Lithuanian Yiddish and their gestures and grimaces, I'll just tell you everything in our Yiddish. What did they ask me?

"Mr. Levit, the great contractor, has a headband with very large pearls. He wants ten thousand rubles for it. I, Aizl, want to buy the headband for my wife, and I'll give him three thousand rubles in bank notes on the spot. I want to pay the shopkeepers three hundred rubles for what Mr. Levit owes them. Plus room and board for him and his servant and his driver for four weeks, plus hay and oats for his horse, and there'll be a fifth week—that makes another three hundred rubles. And I'll give him an IOU for the rest, to be paid in six months. With such a big contractor, it's no problem waiting till I get the money, I've got a post station with forty horses. Things are a bit tough now, I can't give him any cash. We saw that he paid you his respects and took you into his room. So I'm asking you to get him to do us the favor. You'd be doing a good deed."

The servant then said:

"Mr. Levit only hired me here, and I've already lent him a hundred rubles of my own money because he said it would only

118

be for a few days. But now I have to send the money to my wife in Kiev. I'll travel along with him, but I have to send something to my wife so she won't starve to death. He's giving me a big salary, fifty rubles a month. But meanwhile, my wife needs money, she does. If you can get him to sell the headband, he'd have enough cash to pay me back my hundred rubles."

"What about the horses?" I asked the servant.

"The horses belong to a drayman. He was hired by Mr. Levit. The horses are eating oats at the drayman's expense, and the drayman is charging twenty-five rubles a week for waiting—and sixty a week for driving. He's been waiting here three weeks already. It's too cold to travel."

I promised them I would talk to Mr. Levit about these matters.

If Lippe had a headband to sell for ten thousand rubles, he must be a wealthy man. When the landlord and his wife said that the headband with the big pearls was worth ten thousand rubles, I assumed they had called in an expert or were experts themselves. There's an old saying: "Ten locks are better than one impoverishment." If Lippe had something worth ten thousand rubles, that is to say, one thousand ducats, then he had to be rich.

Yet shopping on credit, borrowing a hundred rubles from his servant—that was the way of the old-time contractors. We, the new generation of contractors, hate that sort of thing, just as we don't like to put on someone else's shirt without asking. But one point bothered me: Why was he carrying a headband around to sell? I didn't understand at all, but perhaps I would find out later. . . .

"Well, gentlemen?" Oxman asked his audience. "Did I calculate properly?"

They all laughed and said:

"Gershon Margosin ruined it for us, we already know that it's a story about a false headband. But please go on and tell us the rest."

The cold abated somewhat, and things were looking better. We

119

could move on to the headquarters. So I asked Lippe:

"Are you traveling alone? If you allow me to accompany you, I'll give you a hundred rubles to drop me off at the headquarters."

"No problem at all!" replied Lippe. "A hundred rubles is fine, but I need them right away. If you like, give me the money now."

I gave Lippe the hundred rubles and made out a Russian receipt for the amount, stipulating that it was payment for his taking me to the military headquarters. Lippe signed the receipt.

Handing him the money, I told him what the landlord and his wife had said to me about the headband.

Lippe explained why he couldn't sell the headband in Czernigov under any circumstances.

"Imagine, I have such extensive dealings with my partner Leyzer Dilon, and I need money right now because that scoundrel promised to send me a hundred thousand rubles here, and he still hasn't done it. I took along my wife's headband because I was afraid—and indeed I was right—that Dilon might not send me the money, and this way, willing or not, I could at least sell the headband to pay for my expenses until I reached the headquarters. And you can see, Oxman, that so many Berditchev Jews have come here to Czernigov, almost to spite me. Now how far is it from Zhitomir to Berditchev? Only a few miles, and soon all of Zhitomir will know that Lippe Levit has sold his wife's headband. My wife will be very upset, and I'll be extremely embarrassed. That's why I don't want to sell the headband here under any circumstances. Now you may wonder where I'll get the cash for my expenses. Well, there's something I can do."

I listened in silence, believing everything he said.

Three days later, we made preparations to depart. I told Aizl and his wife what Lippe had said to me.

The landlord and the landlady replied:

"Mr. Levit is right, the Berditchev Jews were already talking about him. And if he sells his wife's headband, the news would soon get to Zhitomir."

You're probably wondering what Lippe wanted to do. Just wait a bit. The landlord and his wife, together with Lippe, came to me

120

and asked me to set up a document. They told me what to write and I wrote it:

"A Jewish document: Write, long may you live, that Lippe Levit, long may he live, owes us fifteen hundred rubles, that is the account."

They calculated once again:

"Five hundred rubles cash, five hundred rubles for the shopkeepers, five hundred rubles for room and board—oh how funny, I forget the overcoat, one hundred rubles for a new overcoat. That makes sixteen hundred rubles, write it down. With the condition that if Lippe Levit doesn't send us the money from Nezvizh, then the headband becomes our property at that price. Please write it down, long may you live."

I wrote it all down and handed them the document.

"Wonderful, long may you live!" the landlord and his wife said to me.

I assumed that Lippe was giving them the headband as collateral. And you would all have assumed the same thing, wouldn't you?

I was even more horror-struck than when I'd seen the naked old Russian women. They were leaving the headband with Lippe, long may he live. The document was enough. "A fine safeguard," I thought to myself.

Very early the next morning, we boarded the fine sleigh with the three good horses and drove off to Nezvizh.

En route, Lippe spent money like water, which is what they say about those spendthrifts, the old-time contractors. Lippe also played cards if he found a willing group, even at an inn; he would spend two days in a shtetl if there was a group of card-players.

We arrived in Nezvizh. Lippe asked me to come with him to Leyzer Dilon's wife to find out about his partner's dealings. She ought to know.

Leyzer Dilon, as I found out in Nezvizh, and Zundl Sonnenberg, a man from Grodno, had become deputies for all the Jewish communities to Tsar Alexander's headquarters. (The story of their experiences is something I'll tell you another time.

121

It's worth writing a whole book about them. And sooner or later, it will be written.)

Lippe and I entered Leyzer Dilon's home, and he said to Dilon's wife:

"Have you received any letters from Leyzer? You should have gotten money and letters from him long ago concerning our partnership. The cold weather kept me in one town for several weeks. My partner must have thought I froze to death somewhere or other, perhaps he took over my share, hahaha. . . . But I'm alive, Lippe Levit is alive and has come to settle accounts. Meanwhile, I need a few thousand rubles for expenses. . . ."

Leyzer Dilon's wife had never seen Lippe or known anything about him. She ordered her servant to bring in some coffee, as is fitting and proper when such a rich woman has guests, especially when one is her husband's partner. But she did not give him any money.

"I'm only a woman," she said. "I don't meddle in my husband's business dealings. I have my own drapery business here, and I take care of it myself. Please don't be offended, but I can't give you any money on my husband's account."

Naturally, that was all we went away with. That is to say, coffee and good words, but no money.

In my heart, I could and had to believe that Lippe was Dilon's partner, and the proof was that he had even told Dilon's wife the very same thing.

But meanwhile, Lippe didn't have a kopek for further travel expenses. I began feeling nervous, because my hundred rubles were also spent.

The next day, Lippe came with a new driver named Zisl, a man from Nezvizh. He was well off, and his wagon had four horses. Since the frost had let up quite a bit, said Lippe, he preferred going on with a wagon rather than a sleigh.

Lippe hired Zisl the drayman for fifteen silver rubles a week in cash, plus expenses for him and the horses. That would add up to quite a bit for Lippe, but. . . .

The new drayman was to lend Lippe a thousand rubles in banknotes—but this involved something which had to be kept a secret, even from me, which was why I had to leave the room for a couple of minutes.

However, I could peer between the boards of the wall and find out the secret. The servant lit a candle, and Lippe, using the wax drippings, sealed a piece of paper in which he had wrapped the headband.

If it had remained a secret from me, then it would have made no difference. But they called me back into the room to set up a new document, a fine document.

"Write this down for me, long may you live," the drayman said: "Mr. Levit says that you can write better, so it makes no sense for him to go to so much trouble. After all, the document is my only proof."

So I acted as scribe for Lippe and Zisl the drayman.

Lippe dictated and I wrote out what he was to pay the man for his services and the expenses for the horses and himself. Everything on Lippe's account. He also owed him the thousand rubles cash, which he had to return as soon as they got to the headquarters. By way of security, Zisl took a pearl headband, sealed with Lippe's seal (his name wasn't on it, only the imprint of a steel signet, the kind you buy in Russian shops, with an engraved bird or something else). Zisl was to keep the headband and return it unopened to Mr. Levit as soon as the debt was paid: the salary, the expenses, and the loan of one thousand rubles cash. The drayman kept one copy of the document and Lippe the other copy.

Lippe now had money! He paid off the sleigh driver for both of us, he returned the hundred rubles to his servant and gave him his salary, but fired him for telling me that Lippe owed him the money. And so off we drove in a fine wagon with four fine horses.

I don't want to tell you what happened en route since it's getting late. To make a long story short: Three days after Purim, 1813, we arrived in Kalisz, on the Prussian border. The town itself was Polish, it belonged to the Duchy of Warsaw, which at that time was occupied by the Russian army. The Tsar had set up a Russian governor, Count Polin, in Warsaw.

123

Zisl the drayman had a brother-in-law named Zalman Sakir in Tsar Alexander's headquarters. This man supplied everything that was necessary for the Tsar's kitchen. Naturally, as soon as the horses were unhitched, Zisl went to see his brother-in-law. Neither Lippe nor I knew where the drayman was going.

And now comes the real story. Just let me rest a bit. . . .

But everyone shouted:

"No, no! Don't leave us in suspense, just when it's getting exciting. No, no, Oxman. You have to finish the story. Stop torturing us. . . ."

So Oxman went on.

I asked Lippe whether he would go over to Leyzer Dilon right away, because I myself wanted to look around a bit and see if I could find any acquaintances among the commissioners or any sort of business.

Lippe, as I noticed, was in no big hurry. He was nervous, a little pensive. He dressed and went off.

I went off too and I did, in fact, run into people I knew, they wanted to take me to the intendant general's chief commissioner Nevakhovitch. I spent something like an hour talking to them.

All at once, Zisl the drayman came dashing up to me with a tearful face, he pulled me into a street, weeping all the while:

"You've slaughtered me, me and my wife and kids, slaughtered me. . . ."

"What's wrong? What are you talking about?" I asked.

Zisl pulled the sealed paper out of his shirt and held it up to me. Weeping, he blurted out:

"Look, just look. These ain't real pearls. They're phony, they're strung together to make them look like a headband . . . to cheat people. . . ."

Zisl tore off a few of the pearls and chewed them up.

"I went to my brother-in-law, Zalman Sakir," Zisl whined, "you know, he's a supplier for the Tsar's kitchen, but he wasn't in his room. He only came back half an hour later and he was laughing, he told me about a man named Lippe Levit, who went to see Leyzer Dilon, but Dilon wouldn't even shake his hand, he gave him two hard slaps with his right hand—two hard slaps. And he screamed furiously: 'You thief! They kicked you out of the Moscow headquarters because you tried to rob Tikhonov the paymaster! You dog! You dared to tell my wife in Nezvizh that we're partners!? My wife wrote me a letter. You scoundrel, you thief! Tikhonov is here. I'm going to tell him that his broker, who tried to rob him, is back again! Hey, Cossacks!' Since he's a deputy for the Jewish communities, he and Zundl Sonnenberg got two Cossacks to accompany them at all times. When he screamed: 'Cossacks, tie up the thief!' they nearly did tie him up. But Lippe was too smart for them, he ran away. That's what my brother-in-law told me and he laughed, he laughed when he told it to me. And I told him that I brought that very same Mr. Lippe here in my wagon and I told him about the thousand rubles I lent him, but I said: 'I've got collateral, a pearl headband.' Zalman opened the paper it was wrapped in. Oh, God help me and my wife and my poor little children! Zalman just laughed out loud: 'Why, these aren't pearls!' he said. 'This is an imitation, these are artificial pearls.' And to test them, he chewed one pearl. So we're gonna wipe him and you out, the two of us, that's why I'm here. Give me my money, you robbers! Why do you want to slaughter me and my wife and kids!"

Can you imagine, gentlemen? I had a bitter taste in my mouth. My blood ran cold.

I thought quickly. I was in terrible danger. For instance, Zalman Sakir and his brother-in-law could go to General Ertel, the police superintendent at army headquarters, and bring charges against two Russian-Polish Jews, me and Lippe. They could say that we had robbed the drayman of a thousand rubles cash plus his salary and expenses, giving him a false headband with false pearls as collateral. Before you could say Jack Robinson, Ertel, that cruel man, would clap me and Lippe in chains, both of us, and send us home in chains to be tried. A fine business for me! I was going to make a killing at army headquarters!

125

The listeners clicked their tongues:

"That's right. It could have happened. Well, Oxman, what *did* you do? Tell us. We can see that they didn't put you in chains. You must have done something intelligent. You didn't have a thousand rubles in your pocket to give the drayman," they all said.

"No, my friends," replied Oxman. "I barely had enough to cover my expenses. Only my wits helped me."

I instantly asked the drayman:

"What do you want from me, you evil man? You know you're Lippe's drayman, and Lippe was my drayman. Look, I have exactly the same kind of document from him as you do. It says he's supposed to take me right up to the headquarters. But I want to tell you something else—Lippe could argue just the opposite about you, drayman; he could say that you stole his headband with the real pearls and replaced it with a false headband and false pearls. The proof is that you broke all his seals. You know that he's got a document just like yours, Zisl. He'll tell you: 'Scoundrel! Thief! You've stolen my headband, and it's worth ten thousand rubles! . . .' "

The drayman stood there, dazed, thunderstruck.

"Tell me what I can do!" he started pleading.

"Well, since you're talking like a decent man, I'll give you some good advice. You ought to save yourself from this great danger, so that they won't think you're a thief. You can see for yourself that Lippe could send you to Siberia for robbing him of ten thousand rubles. You broke his seals, which is the same as robbing his strongbox. But since I feel sorry for your wife and children, I'll give you some advice. Go home to your horses and wait in the stable while I go to my lodgings from another direction, okay?"

The drayman did as I said. I came to my lodgings and there I found our Mr. Lippe in the worst state imaginable—may it happen to all scoundrels!

He assumed I didn't know how Leyzer Dilon had received him, and I didn't let on what I'd heard. I motioned to Zisl to follow me. Pointing at him, I laughed and asked Lippe amiably:

126

"What does this scoundrel want anyway? At the very outset, he wants you to give him money and he keeps saying: 'My collateral!' The scoundrel has no manners! Come here, you! Make up your mind! Mr. Lippe, just settle accounts with him, figure out how much you owe him and give him an IOU for a couple of days." I spoke more softly now to Lippe, but I let the drayman overhear me: "And take back the collateral. Why should he hold on to it now that we're at headquarters!"

Lippe was more than willing to take the false trinket off his hands, and the drayman said:

"If that's what Mr. Lippe wants, long may he live, then I can wait four more days. It's not worth it. If he says four days, then that's all right. . . ."

I quickly told him to summon the innkeeper so that he could make out an IOU in German, as is customary in Kalisz.

Lippe made his reckoning and found that he owed the drayman one thousand three hundred and eighty rubles. This was converted into Prussian talers, and an IOU for four days was set up. Our Lippe promptly signed. The German innkeeper and another man signed as witnesses. I deliberately left the room to avoid being present.

Both Lippe and the drayman were delighted. Zisl felt as if an angel were playing with him: Lippe was taking back his "crown jewels" and not making any fuss about the appearance of the package. All the seals were broken, but Lippe asked no questions, he didn't even look. Knowing how much trouble he was in, he got rid of the danger of going to Siberia: He grabbed the headband and went over to the oven, where a fire was blazing, he placed the sacrifice on the altar and burnt it to ashes.

And that, my friends, was how my wits got me out of a bad fix. Half an hour later, while Lippe was in his room, I packed up my belongings and moved to a different street, where I lodged with a Jew. When Lippe saw me packing my bags to bring them to a wagon, he asked:

"What's this? Are you leaving?"

And now, as the saying goes, I poured out my bile on him. I gave him two powerful smacks and made it clear to him that I knew all about Leyzer Dilon's slaps and his reasons for the way he received Lippe, and that I had found out about the false headband that very day. I settled my own account with that scoundrel and gave him what he deserved.

That same day, Lippe fled Kalisz on foot. Not because he was worried 'bout his IOU, but because, as I was told, Leyzer Dilon was looking for him with Cossacks. Lippe had probably heard they were coming after him, and so, as the Polish Jews phrase it, he "made feet."

"Well," said Oxman. "Now I've finished the story of the false headband. So let me go home. I've got to get up early tomorrow morning."

"Good night, good night!" they said to one another, and they all left after thanking Oxman for the long, fine, interesting story.

On the way back, Mikhel said to Oxman:

"I understood the entire story, but a man like me doesn't know there are false pearls that look like real ones."

Oxman laughed:

"Lippe Levit wouldn't get very far in your Nosuchville. That was why he had to buy his false pearls in the boutiques of Berditchev. That's where all the Polish aristocrats go shopping. Here in Breslau the German women also buy false pearls and wear them the way our peasant women wear beads. . . ."

XVII

Since chapter sixteen was too long, chapter seventeen will be very short.

Mikhel had a fine life in Oxman's employ. He had good food and a good salary. Furthermore, the merchants, whose goods he bought for the hospital, always gave him presents—money, a watch, a silk handkerchief. He also learned a little German and he heard so many good things from Oxman and the people who came to see Oxman or whom Oxman visited. Mikhel became experienced in supplying hospitals. Everything succeeded for him. But his luck didn't hold out. All at once, the commissioner general issued a document ordering all the hospitalized soldiers to be moved to the Duchy of Warsaw—to save the Tsar the expense of hospitals. In Breslau, the Tsar had to pay for them himself. But in the Duchy of Warsaw, the ducal treasury would bear the costs.

Oxman terminated his dealings and had to go and find some other kind of business at the military headquarters.

Mikhel didn't want to travel there and so he took six weeks' salary. Oxman also made him a gift of one hundred Prussian talers for his loyalty. In a short time, Mikhel had earned more than one thousand talers for Oxman. So he certainly deserved a bonus.

On the eighteenth of November, 1813, Mikhel took a stage-coach together with a relative of Khlyebov's, who was being sent from the headquarters to Kiev. Khlyebov had asked his relative to take Mikhel back to his home for free.

If we take a quick look, Mikhel was very happy. Within a single year, the former belfer, broker, the little Jew of Nosuchville, had become a mature, responsible, enlightened man, he was dressed like a lord, he had several thousand rubles and a fine watch with a watchchain. And even more: He knew a bit about the contracting business. He had had his own experience in a hospital, and he had heard and seen the dealings of other contractors. So he felt wonderful as he traveled home.

Going by coach, Mikhel very quickly reached Zwohil across the Russian border.

Khlyebov's relative went off to Kiev, and Mikhel continued towards his destination.

XVIII

MEZHBEZH, ON THE SABBATH OF HANUKKAH

A few years ago, Lipinsky, a petty nobleman from a little Polish shtetl near Mohilov, came to a Russian town, where there was a merchant who knew Lipinsky from home. When the merchant heard the brokers and all the others flocking around Lipinsky and calling him a count, the merchant furiously snapped in Polish:

"What? I know Lipinsky very well in our home town, and he's anything but a count, he's not even a count's behind."

To which one of the aristocratic flatterers, an adjutant of Lipinsky's, replied in Polish:

"Lord Lipinsky is a traveling count."

The merchant burst into roars of laughter and translated the reply into Russian and Yiddish so that everyone could understand:

"Hahaha! Laugh, gentlemen! What a riot! Hahaha! This gentleman says that at home Lipinsky is just a plain, ordinary nobleman, but when he travels, he's a count."

They all roared.

This little anecdote about Lipinsky will help us understand what we are now going to read about Mezhbezh.

Mezhbezh is an old Jewish town in Poland. It has long been a commercial town. Many great businessmen, wholesalers in all kinds of goods and products, great magnates, financiers, and bankers can be found in Mezhbezh. It is also a town quite full of Talmudic scholars: several great scholars as well as burghers who can study the holy texts.

However, Mezhbezh was also the first breeding ground of the Hassidic plague in Poland some fifty years ago. For that was where Rabbi Israel Baal Shem Tov, the founder of Hassidism, once lived—he was the first Hassidic wonder-worker, miracle-maker, almost like Mohammed among the Arabs and Turks, except that Mohammed was also a great warrior. Still, the better half of Mohammed's book, the Koran, is full of Hassidic chattering, what the Hassidic rebbes call "Torah" (learning, wisdom). But even though the Baal Shem Tov came from Mezhbezh and lived in Mezhbezh, you won't find the slightest trace of Hassidism there today, in 1813, unlike other towns, which are crawling with Hassidism.

It would appear that the same could be said about the Baal Shem Tov as about Lipinsky. He was not taken very seriously in Mezhbezh. But throughout Poland, the little brokers and all the Jews clustering around him called him: Rabbi Israel Baal Shem Tov, the Traveling Count. The reason why Hassidism spread all over the land can be found in my pamphlet *The Book of Hassidim*. What is pertinent to our story, however, is the fact that after the founder of Hassidism passed away, no great Hassidic rebbe lived in Mezhbezh until his grandson Borukh. This grandson was driven out of Tulczin and then hung around in Bratslev for something like a year; next, he migrated to Mezhbezh, where he finally died in 1810.

Before his death, a man who had once been an obscure rabbi in a Polish shtetl came to Mezhbezh. This little rabbi did what a lot of other rabbis and preachers did in the shtetls: He had an idea. Why should he torment himself giving sermons with explanations from the Talmud and interpretations from Moses Maimonides? And for only ten ducats a week at that? He would do better to jump on the Hassidic bandwagon and officiate at Hassidic Sabbath meals, with obscure sayings and bogus Cabala and secret doctrines—which went trippingly off the tongue and for which he could rake in a lot of fees. A man could earn a much better living that way. You can get a thousand rubles in just one hour from the donors. And every day, there are more and more donors.

But back to the anecdote. At home in the shtetl, like the petty nobleman Lipinsky, he couldn't be more than a petty rabbi. The trick was to become a traveling count! So the little rabbi went off to Jassi, Moldavia. There, in a city of ignorant fools, a city of Jews who were almost as stupid as the peasants, the Hassidic plague was only just starting to creep in. And there the little rabbi became a Great Rabbi, a great tsaddik and wonder-worker, a great Hassidic Rebbe. The Jews in Moldavia, those ignorant fools, are great mayvens in all these things. Actually, whatever they know about the Cabala and about fees for the rebbes stems from Moses Maimonides' tome on the Jewish calendar. Hassids, the Hassids of Moldavia, praised the great tsaddik to the skies twenty-four hours a day, and he began raking in piles of money.

Now this Great Rabbi, this rebbe, knew very well that he didn't know a thing. He reflected that the other rebbe was the Baal Shem Tov's grandson, after all, and didn't live among the Moldavian ignoramuses, and yet they praised him to the skies. So that man simply *must* know something. Now if the rebbe wanted to go to Mezhbezh, he needn't take along any travel money. After all, there were Jews living along the way, and they would donate

131

money on all sides. Well, so off he went with pomp and circumstance, in a carriage drawn by four horses. And Hassidic paupers followed in small covered wagons. They didn't have a kopek, but all along the road, Jews gave them alms since they were with the tsaddik.

The "traveling count" with all his camp followers arrived in Mezhbezh and went to the home of the rebbe there.

"The Great Rabbi himself has come to Rabbi Borukh!" The news spread to all the Hassids in Poland.

Anyone who knew Rabbi Borukh realized that this visit must gladden his heart. Rabbi Borukh was a proud and haughty man, and he also had a sharp tongue. (Like a man who was called a "strong face"; he failed to understand that this was a literal rendering of a Hebrew expression meaning "arrogant.") Once, Rabbi Borukh said to the Rebbe of Shpole, who was known as the "Grandfather of Shpole": "Why do people call you 'Grandfather'? They ought to call you 'Grandmother'!" He always ran other rebbes into the ground just so that Hassids would acclaim him as the greatest rebbe and ignore all the other wonder-workers. The Grandfather of Shpole gave him an answer that was smarter·than the stupid and arrogant question:

"The only thing *you* have to show for yourself is *your* grandfather." By whom he meant the Baal Shem Tov.

And now his pride was fed by the visit of the great rebbe, who was coming to him from so far away, all the way from Jassi, which meant that he, Rabbi Borukh, was the greatest rebbe of them all.

We can easily imagine what the Rebbe of Jassi (people had started calling him that) got out of his visit in Mezhbezh: "You know nothing, and I know nothing—except how to lie and make money. Those things are useful, and I can waggle my tongue and wiggle my hands, which is something that both of us know how to do."

When Rabbi Borukh died about six months later, the Rebbe of Jassi realized he could grab the dead man's place in Mezhbezh because he knew everything that Rabbi Borukh had known.

So in 1813 he moved to Mezhbezh, where he made more money than in Jassi. There they compute in Turkish ducats (so-called *lyeves*, each *lyeve* being worth half a ruble) and in rubles.

The reader should also know that at Rosh Hashanah a rebbe

132

has many guests from other towns. The Sabbath of Hanukkah comes soon after Rosh Hashanah, and there are few visitors except for tenant farmers who have to discuss their leases with the landowners before the Christian New Year. One landowner wants to raise the rent, another wants a new tenant. So the Hassidic farmers go and consult the rebbe about these and other crucial matters. A woman and her son-in-law ask the rebbe to settle some conflict between them, or a tenant farmer arranges a match with a follower of the rebbe—none of these problems can be resolved without the rebbe. These guests come on the Sabbath of Hanukkah. But the rebbe certainly loses no money entertaining. On the contrary, he earns rubles on these occasions too.

On the Sabbath of Hanukkah, who should come to the Rebbe of Mezhbezh but Dovid Smik and his wife Braine-Dobrish and their son-in-law Zainvil. The three of them had donated two hundred rubles on the eve of Sabbath because they wanted Zainvil to remarry after all. He was a young man, and Tevye Bilenkis was offering him a match, Gabriel Gittels' daughter. Gabriel Gittels and Tevye Bilenkis were visiting the tsaddik to see whether Gabriel Gittels should allow his daughter to marry Zainvil and spend the rest of her days in that family so that Zainvil's son and their future children would think that she was Zainvil's first wife Beyltse. Gabriel Gittels had to promise the rebbe that he would never say: "I want my daughter and my son-in-law with me in Nosuchville."

It worked. The rebbe told Gabriel Gittels to make his promise, but he also wanted Dovid Smik to promise (otherwise no one would have paid any attention to that silent man, and Braine-Dobrish couldn't promise anything because, for goodnesh' shake, she was a woman—Lord help us) that the children to come would share the inheritance equally with Beyltse's son. Dovid Smik promised. And the documents were accordingly drawn up. Gabriel Gittels gave the rebbe fifty rubles, and Velvele the Expert got a gold ducat for writing out the documents.

Another couple from Nosuchville came to see the rebbe: Aaron the Beadle and his wife Sarah. You see, after Beyltse's death, as you recall, Sarah had attacked Zainvil (who was the grandson of the Preacher of Ostro, after all) and Aaron had helped her.

133

Furthermore, Sarah had said horrible things about the rebbe all over town. And so, during Sukkoth, the community elders had a meeting and decided to fire Aaron. Even though Aaron and his wife drove out to Nimyevke and made up with Zainvil, the elders nevertheless threw Aaron out of the beadle's apartment and planned to take Shloyme Beshekhes, the poor heder teacher, instead. The only thing that Aaron and Sarah could do was go to Mezhbezh on the Sabbath of Hanukkah, especially since Tevye Bilenkis, the community elder, had also gone there. They wanted to ask the tsaddik to make Tevye rehire his bes-medresh beadle.

Now Aaron wouldn't have gotten anywhere, because Bilenkis not only told the tsaddik what Sarah had screamed about him in the streets of Nosuchville, but he also added a few insults. Luckily for Aaron and Sarah, Zainvil was also there, and he asked the rebbe to help the beadle. Tevye had to go along with Zainvil because he wanted to get his large matchmaking fee from him.

It worked. The tsaddik said: "Aaron regrets what he has done. Besides, the Good Lord has punished Sarah, her daughter has vanished." (Oh, that was earlier, you say? Well, in such cases, our Hassidim speak of the "rebbe's eye"!) He told Tevye to rehire Aaron, and Tevye agreed. Aaron was beadle again, but the community elders mustn't go thirsty, so Aaron would have to treat them to a pail of mead when he got home.

On the eve of the Sabbath of Hanukkah, Aaron and Sarah were overjoyed by Tevye's promise, but they remained in Mezhbezh for the Sabbath. They would go home on Sunday, God willing, and head straight back to their apartment in the bes-medresh as before.

A few tenant farmers, who had been asked for large raises by the landowners, were too done on Friday and they paid the rebbe their fees. They also slipped a few rubles to the scribe, Velvele the Expert, and he wrote the farmer's name and his mother's name on a *kvitl*, the slip you hand a Hassidic rebbe—you only write the mother's name, not the father's. The scribe added the land-owner's name and the landowner's mother's name. Thus, the farmers were assured that everything would turn out all right, the landowner would change into an utterly different person. Only a single shopkeeper and his wife arrived in Mezhbezh very late on Friday; the Sabbath begins at sundown, and so they had to stay over till the next night, since Jews are not allowed to travel on the Sabbath. Then, a dear guest came for the Sabbath, an emissary from the Holy Land, collecting money for a worthy cause. His name was Fishl and he had an assistant. Fishl stayed in the rebbe's home. He had important references from Avrom Kalisker, a Hassidic rebbe in Palestine, who explained that Fishl was a marvelous man, greatly admired by Rabbi Avrom Kalisker, and hence an excellent emissary for the Holy Land.

This emissary, a small, dark, pock-marked Jew in his fifties, very fat, with a long, thick, tangled beard, two short, thin earlocks, and a white skullcap peering out from under a white kerchief that was wrapped around his head like a turban, wore a long robe sewn in the Turkish fashion, with many small decorative buttons and a wide blue woolen belt. On his feet, he had yellow Turkish slippers and stockings that were also of yellow leather. His voice sounded like the noise made by rubbing a sack of walnuts. The Holy Land emissary spoke the Holy Tongue, but it wasn't our sort of Hebrew, the vowels were utterly different. Which is why he sounded so peculiar when he was called up to read the Torah in synagogue, where he asked for blessings: first on Rabbi Avrom Kalisker, then on the local tsaddik, and finally on other rebbes, whom the worshipers all knew.

The emissary's assistant, a very handsome boy of about twenty, also wore semi-Turkish garb, though he came from Poland.

At the Sabbath dinner, the Holy Land emissary sat right next to the rebbe. His chair was almost at the head of the table, facing the wall, but his gaze was riveted on the rebbe. The same thing happened at the meal ushering out the Sabbath. Making pious grimaces, he hung on the tsaddik's every word. Perhaps because he didn't understand the rebbe's teachings, which were expounded in our Yiddish, the emissary sat there with a gaping mouth so that the words of wisdom might fly in.

A great company was present at this meal. Adding up the numerical value of the Hebrew letters in HANUKKAH and connecting the various syllables with various other words and with still further words and Biblical verses, and vice versa, the rebbe proved beyond a shadow of a doubt that this holiday and

135

holy day was both holy and a day and wholly a holiday, and that the Jews were wholly holy for holding such a wholly holy holiday. And Hanukkah was *eight* days long because Jews always *ate* on Hanukkah, and therefore it was wholly holy for Jews to eat on this wholly holy holiday, and on all wholly holy days of this wholly holy holiday and holy day.

These sublime cabalistic doctrines and these obscure teachings were accompanied by Jewish sighs and moans. For such an audience, the less you understand, the more sublime the teachings.

"Sheer delight!" said the rebbe's followers.

XIX

Mezhbezh was truly a large town. Mezhbezh had a madman, not a native, but he'd been there for three years, so he was known as the Madman of Mezhbezh: People called him Obadiah the Madman. How he ever got here in the first place— nobody knew. He never spoke to anyone and kept to himself all day in some vacant house. But as soon as night fell, he ran around with a long stick and a broken pail, shouting:

"I, Obadiah, shout: Watch out for fire! Save yourselves!"

Suddenly, he would dash into a house, screaming and snuffing all the candles. And he even threw water on the fire in the stove. He worked so fast, in an instant. No sooner did the people look around than wow!, he was done and gone, like lightning. Sometimes, if he spotted a crust of bread on a table or stove, he grabbed it. He probably lived on these chance finds. In both winter and summer, he wore a fur coat with a piece of rope as a belt, a fur cap with lappets on his head, and old, worn-out shoes on his feet. Such were his clothes. The clothes he always ran around in. Pious wives, feeling sorry for him, would grab Obadiah the Madman, yank him indoors, and put a new shirt on him or a pair of new shoes. He would remain silent as they dressed him, never replying to all the things they said to him, and then off he scurried, shouting:

"I, Obadiah, shout: Watch out for fire! Save yourselves!"

Obadiah would do the same thing on Friday evening, he would dash into a home, put out the Sabbath candles, and grab a few handfuls of challah, shouting all the while: "Watch out for fire! Save yourselves!" And then scurry off. That was why Jews drew the chains on their front doors every Friday evening: "Here comes Obadiah!"

In the rebbe's house, however, there was no chain on the door because out-of-town guests went in and out. So one man was usually stationed outside to keep Obadiah the Madman at bay. But it didn't always work. Obadiah might suddenly dash into the house and snuff all the Sabbath candles. The Hassidim remained in the dark until someone brought an old peasant woman to light the candles again, since Jews cannot perform any work on the Sabbath. There was a standing joke in town: If someone accidentally put out a candle, someone else would say: "Aha! You're Obadiah the Madman!"

Hassidim in Mezhbezh and elsewhere kept talking so much about Obadiah the Madman because the tsaddik had explained that Obadiah was the reincarnation of a great Rationalist of long ago, whose Rationalism had driven him to burn up a copy of the holy *Zohar*. His divine punishment was to return to earth as Obadiah the Madman. And that was why he ran around, snuffing all the candles. Some of the rebbe's intimates whispered that the rebbe had actually confided in them what Obadiah's name had really been, who the soul was, what great Rationalist the soul had belonged to. The name was murmured only in secret (it was an open secret, but when Hassidim whisper something and make a mysterious gesture and scratch their heads: "Why bother saying it aloud?"—that's what Hassidim call a secret). They said it was the soul of Yankev Emdin. That's what Hassidim call a miracle. Because for the gullible, everything that the rebbe says is Truth. If the rebbe says that he heard what the feather duster told the broom last night, they take it for sheer gospel. They may be smart, very smart, but they give in to this fancy, which turns their minds upside down. And it all makes sense to them; in fact, anybody who doesn't believe it is crazy or evil, a heretic.

In Mezhbezh, there was an *agunah* (an abandoned wife), named Pini, who kept a stand in the marketplace. She sold boiled

137

peas, stewed hard pears, fried almonds, and cookies. For Purim, honey puffs (perhaps they have a different name in other towns); and in summer, boiled corn on the cob, egg cakes (you don't have to wash yourself for that), and poppy-seed cakes. Anything you needed just to nosh on, you could get from Pini. Her nickname was "Pini the Agunah" or simply "The Agunah." If neighbors in the marketplace got into a fight with her, they would yell: "Foreigner!" at her because she was born in Berditchev. She had come to Mezhbezh some eighteen years ago, saying she was looking for her runaway husband, and then she stayed on because it was already winter. Evil tongues whispered that Pini didn't actually have a husband, she had remained an old maid against her will.

But Pini was really a decent, virtuous woman in her late forties. She tilted her head to one side and worked very hard. She plied her trade summer and winter. And she never asked anyone for a handout, God forbid; on the contrary, she had given money for the weddings of orphans and bought winter fur coats for poor boys. Her little house was in a back street. "When you're alone, your soul is pure," she used to say. That was why she never took in any lodgers. As God gives, if she had anything, she ate; if not, if sales were bad, then a dry crust of bread was enough. When she left for the marketplace in the morning, with her trough of goodies, she would lock up her little house. And when she came home at night, she would heat the stove and do all the cooking for the next day. Sometimes an acquaintance would buy her a piece of meat at the butcher's or some innards.

If anyone went about collecting alms in town, he knew that Pini the Agunah would never refuse to drop a few kopeks, and sometimes even more, into the alms box.

Pini's almonds were praised even by the young Polish lords. Pini was famous for them in Mezhbezh. She was known in every corner of town.

Now there's one person whose name we only mentioned in passing: Velvele the Expert. You ought to know that Velvele was about forty years old, he was tall, handsome, and he had a red beard and red earlocks. From the way he looked today, you could tell that he must have once been a very attractive young man.

And there was a good reason why he was nicknamed Velvele the Expert: He was a fine student of the holy texts and he could read and write very well. He could also do arithmetic. Furthermore, he could pray beautifully at the lectern and blow a *shofar* (ram's horn) better than anyone else at Rosh Hashanah, he was renowned far and wide for this talent. Velvele was also a connoisseur of jewelry. The rebbe's grandsons and their wives dealt in pearls and headbands, and they would always ask Velvele's opinion. They relied completely on his appraisals. In this way, Velvele would sometimes earn himself a fee. He was also a marriage broker. And when the rebbe's scribe, Leybele Hodes, had no time, Velvele would come over and earn money from the guests by writing their names on kvitls, which were then inserted in the rebbe's prayer book. That was why Velvele was an intimate of the rebbe's, just about as close as anyone could be. Velvele was born in Constantine, but he lived in Mezhbezh with his third wife, a native of the town.

XX

THE EVENING OF THE SABBATH OF HANUKKAH, AT THE HOME OF THE REBBE OF MEZHBEZH

After the rebbe had expounded his teachings at the meal ushering out the Sabbath, after the closing ceremony, after the blessing of the Hanukkah candles, after the Hanukkah candles had burnt out, they put the big menorah with the silver clock plus two high silver candleholders with burning candles on the table. The guests went home. After all, everyone had to bless their own Hanukkah candles. Very few people remained with the rebbe.

The rebbe sat at the head of the table. Next to him sat the Holy Land emissary. Behind the table, by the wall, sat one of the rebbe's sons, a young man. (For many years now, the rebbe's wife had been an invalid. Some people said she couldn't move her arms or legs. That's why she's never mentioned here. The poor woman lay in sorrow, while the men lived in pleasure.) The grandsons and their wives sat in the alcove talking to the emissary's assistant. Several Hassidim, close friends of the rebbe, were wandering about the main room.

In walked an old and simple Jew named Peysakh, who owned an inn in Mezhbezh. He was accompanied by a very handsome young man, dressed in fine, rich clothing, the very latest fashion, an expensive coat with an attractive silk belt, and—a lively touch—a black silk "kerchief" around his neck—that was the humorous nickname for a cravat; boots with waxed points, squeaking like crunchy snow when you walk through it; a fine sable hat on his head; a very, very sparse beard and short, curly earlocks; and a red silk handkerchief peering out of the side pocket.

Peysakh walked over to the rebbe like a man in a hurry:

"Rebbe, this is Yekhiel the Contractor." Then, softly, so that not everyone could hear: "A very wealthy man." Then out loud again: "He's staying with me. Ha. How do you like my guests, ha? They asked me to bring them here. Well, ha, that's why I'm an innkeeper, ha? As you know, rebbe, I represent the kosher meat tax, so I have to check out the butcher shops, ha, what do you say, Rebbe, ha?" Then he laughed: "I'm leaving you, my honored guest in good hands here, ha, I am, Mr. Yekhiel, ha? Good night to you!"

And off he went.

During these words, the rebbe had already held out his hand in welcome. Then all the others, even the Holy Land emissary, shook hands with the wealthy newcomer, Yekhiel the Contractor.

Yekhiel didn't wait to be asked to sit. He took a chair and sat down next to the rebbe. Then he stood up again, removed a gold ducat from a lovely pouch, and deposited it on the table in front of the miracle-worker, saying:

"A gold ducat for a whole week is a sign that the week will be golden." He laughed: "And I want you to help me have children. I want to be a father."

The rebbe also laughed:

"You probably know that old biblical saying: 'It is not good that a *coin* should be alone.'"

The older Hassids in the room, as well as a few more, who had come in one by one, enjoyed the rebbe's little joke, and they pulled some Hassidic faces:

"Oooh! How marvelous! Oh what sheer delight!"

Yekhiel replied:

"I agree with the Good Lord. 'It is not good that a man should be alone.' That's why I've come to Mezhbezh."

"I'm only joking," said the rebbe when he saw that no further ducats was forthcoming. "Now tell me, dear friend, is your wife here too?"

"Now, now," replied Yekhiel the Contractor. "If I had a wife, I could have children without paying your fee. But I am a man alone."

The Hassidim standing around laughed:

"Hahaha! What an answer! What a nimble mind! What a wonderful, miraculous answer!"

The rebbe asked:

"Tell me, dear friend, how can a Jew settle down without a wife?"

"Settle down?" replied Yekhiel the Contractor. "I'm always on my feet, I'm always on the move because of my business dealings. That's why I want to find a wife here in Mezhbezh, and right away to boot. Yessir!"

The rebbe couldn't tell whether the young man was joking or making fun of him. He couldn't very well lose his temper—a gold ducat was lying on the table. So he made up his mind and assumed an earnest mien:

"Call over Velvele. He's a brilliant matchmaker. What a marvelous man, he can arrange all kinds of marriages."

One of the Hassidim dashed off; and three minutes later, Velvele the Expert came in.

But Yekhiel hadn't even waited; he said to the rebbe:

"I don't even need a matchmaker. What's the old saying? 'Blessed are the hands that do their own taking.' "

Because of the Hassidim in the room, the rebbe would have preferred to hit the roof. Yekhiel was talking to him with no respect whatsoever. That could destroy his prestige as a rebbe. But the gold ducat was lying there. So he laughed and said:

"Rabbi X., long live the memory of that righteous man, used to

141

say to such jokesters: 'You are . . . you are a marvelous person. . . .' "

The Hassids perked up their ears and peered at the contractor. Yekhiel laughed:

"If one of you goes and summons Pini, I'll pay you for your trouble. Tell her to come here immediately with Frumma." He turned to the rebbe. "I'll perform my miracle for you, right here, in your home, without a marriage broker, and we'll have a wedding that will please both God and man."

A young boy, a Hassid, ran to get Pini.

Meanwhile, Velvele arrived. The Hassidim whispered to him. While they were telling him about Yekhiel the Contractor—in burst Obadiah the Madman, shouting: "Watch out for fire! Save yourselves!"

At this point, the emissary's assistant walked in from the alcove with a candle in his hand.

Obadiah saw the young assistant and ground to a halt. He didn't snuff the candles, he didn't keep shouting. Instead, he threw his arms around the assistant, laughing and crying, and leaping joyfully:

"Yossele, my Yossele, oh my Yossele!"

Then he fainted dead away.

"Father! Don't faint! Please. Have pity, don't faint, father, please, have pity!"

All the people in the room did their best to revive the Madman. Velvele the Expert once again showed his expertise. He could revive a person better than anyone else. He went to the kitchen and got a pail of cold water, and he splashed and poured it on Obadiah until he revived him.

How sad and miserable all the Hassids felt, as did Velvele the Expert, and also the rebbe, when the emissary's assistant told his story:

"Three years ago, there was that huge fire in Shargorod, and it spread to our home. Father was always studying at the besmedresh day and night. His nickname in Shargorod was Obadiah the Pious. My mother, may she rest in peace, was a woman of valor, she ran the tavern and the inn. She supported us. At twilight, when the hay in the attic caught fire, my mother, may she rest in peace, died amid the flames, in the vestibule, by the gate. I was pulled out through a window and taken far away, outside the town, where a lot of the people were stranded. My poor father was so absorbed in his holy text that he was one of the last to realize the town was burning. The next day they told me that when he ran over and saw that our home had burnt down and my mother was dead, he assumed that I, his only child, had also perished. The grief drove him mad and he ran away from Shargorod. Until today, no one was able to track down Obadiah the Pious. . . ." He hugged and kissed his silent, gaping father. "Oh, father dear! Come home! Let's both go home. We still have our lot. The landowner gave all the townsfolk free wood to rebuild their houses. And you'll certainly be given wood. And the rich Jews will give you money to live in Shargorod again. They still know what sort of a man you are. And I have some money too, not much, but enough to tide us over till we have a home again. You'll come back with me, won't you, Father?"

Obadiah kissed him as he wept, wept as he kissed him, for several minutes. Then, peering around, he said: "It's winter."

Yekhiel the Contractor took out a gold ducat and gave it to Obadiah:

"Take this for now. And you, young man, come and see me. I'm staying in Peysakh's place. I want to give you a coat and a plain jacket for your father, so that he can go home with you. He won't have to wander through the world anymore as a reincarnation."

Yekhiel had probably heard the Hassidim repeat what the rebbe had said about Obadiah the Madman being the reincarnation of a Rationalist.

XXI

Throughout the story of Obadiah, the rebbe never stirred once. Perhaps he was confused because his lie was exposed: This was no reincarnation, as he had told all the Hassidim—and Velvele the Expert had heard it from his own lips. Or perhaps because a man who likes to receive hates to give,

143

and in this case, people should have been reaching into their pockets. The rebbe felt it was better to be off in the higher spheres and peruse the kvitls lying before him on the table.

Velvele the Expert sensed that the rebbe would have liked them to take Obadiah far, far away from there. And Velvele realized he would thereby mount greatly in the rebbe's esteem. Which would be very useful to his livelihood. So Velvele said to the emissary's assistant and his father, Obadiah:

"Listen to me. It's not proper to stay here and trouble the rebbe. Just come into the alcove with me and meet the rebbe's grandchildren. They're marvelous. They'll take care of you."

And Velvele pulled the weak old man along, and Yossele followed them. In a flash, the rebbe's room was cleared again: No Obadiah in sight; they were in the alcove. And whatever went on in the alcove—nobody knew.

When Velvele returned, he looked at the rebbe, who was lost in thought. Velvele could tell that the rebbe was delighted with his quick thinking. But the Expert was disturbed at seeing Yekhiel. The rich contractor was scrutinizing everything carefully. Velvele went over to him and spoke softly, with earnest Hassidic grimaces:

"You're a sensible man. You must understand that a Tsaddik of the Generation has to carry the whole world on his shoulders, by God. Does he have the strength to bear all the sorrows of mankind, by God? He drudges, he asks: 'What do people want from me? They won't even allow me to study my holy texts, to serve God. Go to other tsaddiks, there are other rebbes in the world. . . .' As we know, he is the most modest of men. He tells people: 'Go, go! I don't know what you want from me! Why are you all after me? There are great tsaddiks in the world. Go to them!' "

Yekhiel the Contractor burst into loud laughter:

"Hahahaha! When a grinder doesn't want people to bring him knives to sharpen, he doesn't put his grindstone out for all to see. If a man doesn't want to have a lot of rowdy drunken peasants around, he doesn't lease a tavern. If a tailor wants to give up tailoring, he sells his tools and doesn't take measures. I think that if your rebbe wants to be pious and devote himself to the holy texts, then he can take measures to do so—rather than taking money. C'mon, you look like an intelligent man, but you're treating me like a fool. A fool? For God's sake! How can you try to tell me such lies? Go on! I know about the whole swindle!"

No one knows whether the rebbe heard what Yekhiel said. The Holy Land emissary seemed to be mute. Everything that was happening, everything that was spoken was in plain Yiddish after all—which he didn't understand, after all. He turned around only twice, when his assistant was talking to his father. Even fainting, he seemed to think, was in plain Yiddish, so he had made no effort to help revive Obadiah. Moreover, when he saw that the rebbe didn't lift a finger, he felt it wouldn't do for him to lift one either. He sat and just stared and stared at the rebbe. That was the proper thing to do, he felt, for a Jew from Jerusalem.

Velvele didn't care at all for Yekhiel's comments. He was confused by this man, who had come to the rebbe with a ducat and who was spending ducats left and right. He had just given Obadiah the Madman a ducat, which meant that he must be very rich. Yet he was making fun of the rebbe and using a harsh word: swindle. If only Pini would come! She was deliberately late. Besides, Velvele knew that Pini was an agunah. He himself had written letters for her to any number of towns where rumors had placed her husband. And just who was Frumma anyway? Velvele simply didn't understand. Meanwhile, Yekhiel the Contractor sat on a chair and scrutinized every detail. . . . "Well," thought Velvele the Expert, "Pini'll be here soon, and we'll see what the guy wants." Velvele was also upset that Yekhiel, the rich man, the contractor, from whom they should have and could have gotten a nice tidy sum, happened to be present during Obadiah's story. Yekhiel had heard that the rebbe considered Obadiah a reincarnation. Was that why he was staring and smiling? Velvele was extremely upset.

Velvele felt even worse—Velvele, the Expert, who was so esteemed by, so close to, the rebbe—when suddenly they heard a scream.

The scream came from the other side of the door, probably from the inkeepers who had arrived in Mezhbezh late Friday

145

evening—there was a woman's voice and a man's voice. They were arguing with the rebbe's adjutants, who allowed no one to enter without paying. The man's voice was plain:

"If I don't have it in my pocket to give him, you won't let us in?"

The woman's voice screamed in anger:

"What?! Is the rebbe an aristocrat or something? A lackey won't let you in to see the landowner. But how can a Jew keep you away from a tsaddik who works miracles?! You should be ashamed of yourself, you should! We've driven eighty miles for his miracles!"

But the adjutant still wouldn't let them in!

"Goddamn it! I'm gonna scream your dirty beard off! Are you a policeman or something, you filthy rat! They kick us out of our job and he—"

The woman's scream and all her words were reeled off in one minute, in a flash, in a single breath, like the names of Haman's ten sons during the reading of the Book of Esther at Purim. Every word was audible inside the house.

The rebbe stirred in his meditation and motioned to Velvele to open the door and let in the screaming woman.

But Velvele the Expert couldn't budge, he was too upset by the woman's screams. Not because he was embarrassed in front of Yekhiel the Contractor—no, there was another reason. We'll hear about that later on.

Since Velvele the Expert didn't budge, another Hassid went and opened the door. In strode a big, broad man wearing a long, quilted jacket of blue nankeen with a striped peasant belt, gross calf-leather shoes, thick felt stockings, and a foxfur cap with lappets. He had never had a beard, but there were two long plaits hanging down over his armpits—those were earlocks. Although in his fifties, he was strong and healthy, as you could tell by his face, an honest-to-goodness innkeeper.

His wife had once been beautiful, she was a tall woman in her thirties, but hard work had taken its toll. She was wearing a tiny headband, worth perhaps two hundred guldens, with a veil but no net; she also had a jacket of the same nankeen as her husband's, lined with white hareskin, an old, red gros-de-Tours

146

bodice, and a trimmed apron. And this innkeeper's wife could scream so loud and talk a blue streak.

Here, inside the house, they both held their peace upon viewing the table with the large silver menorah and the large silver candlesticks, and the rebbe, sitting at the head of the table, a handsome, gray-haired man with a long beard, as well as a Jew from Jerusalem, wearing a turban. The innkeeper and his wife hadn't often seen such a sight, and they halted there, dumbstruck. The innkeeper finally took a few steps towards the table. The rebbe, and then the emissary, greeted him.

The woman stood at a distance, listening to her husband ask the rebbe for miracles. In case he lacked a word, she would put in hers.

The man's name was Tordes Leykhevker (the village where he had his tavern was probably Leykhevke), and he started telling the rebbe that he had been running his tavern for twenty years . . . and now they wanted to rent it to someone else. . . . Velvele the Expert stood there averting his face so that the innkeeper's wife couldn't see him. He would much have preferred to leave, but because of Pini—she ought to be coming any minute—he had to wait.

Yekhiel the Contractor saw that Velvele the Expert was on pins and needles, so he walked over and asked him:

"Well, who is right? Don't you think *I* am? This man wants his drunkards, he wants his peasants. That's why he's been running a tavern for twenty years."

Menye-Rasye, the innkeeper's wife, had sharp ears. She heard Yekhiel as he laughed: "A tavern for twenty years." Springing over to the table like a wild beast, she screamed:

"What, rebbe, you hold your tongue when that scoundrel says he wants to lease our tavern to someone else? The landowner actually said: 'A debauched person wants to rent from me. . . .' What? Do you intend to hold your tongue, rebbe?"

Tordes heard his wife's chatter and thought that Yekhiel the Contractor was the man who wanted his tavern. So he started screaming along with her.

"Rebbe, you have to excommunicate him! Can you imagine! Robbing a Jew of his livelihood? You rat, you scoundrel, you

147

heretic! Excommunicate him! Excommunicate him! Rebbe! Ex-communicate that heretic! Don't ever let him back on his feet again! Not in this world and not in the next! Excommunicate him!"

Yekhiel the Contractor saw that he was in a tough spot. Whether or not the rebbe would excommunicate him, the two wild beasts could pounce upon him and beat him. Gathering his wits, he drew the couple's attention to Velvele the Expert:

"On the contrary, I've taken your side, my dear friends."

Tordes made Velvele whirl around like a stick, with his face towards him and his wife, and then Tordes screamed:

"Thank you! And please excuse me, dear friend. I thought it was you. You rat, is that you?! Goddamn your hide! Trying to rob me of my living! Excommunicate him, Rebbe. For God's sake, excommunicate the bastard!"

His wife, Menye-Rasye, instantly recognized Velvele the Expert and she began screaming again. She grabbed his coattail on one side, and Tordes thrust his hand in Velvele's belt on the other side. Velvele couldn't wriggle free.

"You traitor!" screamed Menye-Rasye. "You traitor! Why do you think I divorced him, Rebbe? I gave him everything I had, I was left pregnant, because he wanted to convert to Christianity. All of Kosznetin knows the story! You impoverished me, you traitor. God alone knows the truth! I had so much property, Rebbe. . . ." She burst into tears. "My father died, may he rest in peace. I had to give away my child, my wonderful baby, and then I married Tordes just to have a crust of bread, oh Lord! And now that traitor wants to take away my tavern!? Oh, God! How can you let such a traitor live?!"

While she screamed, Tordes screamed too:

"Rebbe, he's *already* excommunicated. My wife told me that this traitor already went to the priest. That means he's absolutely excommunicated. He stayed with the priest for four weeks. Hahaha!"

The rebbe wouldn't hear the bitter, shameful words that his esteemed follower, Velvele the Expert, had to endure. So he called over one of the other Hassids.

"Isser, please take this man and his wife into the alcove and

148

make them understand that Velvele has no designs whatsoever on their tavern. Tell them to leave him in peace and to write down what they want in the alcove."

Isser had long been striving to become one of the rebbe's right-hand men. He was delighted that the rebbe was asking him to do this. He grabbed Tordes and Menye-Rasye and pulled them into the alcove:

"You're making a terrible mistake. Velvele is a local house-holder. Just come with me, the rebbe wants to bestow a boon upon you. Have faith! If the rebbe says so, then no one will take away your tavern, no matter what."

Tordes and Menye-Rasye took Isser's words at face value. They left Velvele, who was in an awful state, and they trudged into the alcove with Isser.

How useful was Isser in getting the complaints down on paper, and convincing the innkeeper and his wife that the rebbe, by peering at their written names, would make their business remain with them, and that no one would take away their tavern, no matter what? Who knows! But we do know how someone can talk simple, unlettered people into believing such things: If a man is worried, fearful, anxious, then the poor creature wants to save himself. Well, and if someone comes along and tells him: *"I can help you,"* then the poor creature forgets to reflect: "Could he be lying?" All he knows for sure is that he feels terrible. And if the would-be helper is a man who talks to God and whom thousands of people call "rebbe," "tsaddik," "miracle-worker," then his words ring true.

Anybody can imagine what Velvele felt like, even though the innkeeper and his wife had left him. He couldn't even walk away, no. He was in a daze, he couldn't move.

XXII

Still, no matter how awful Velvele may have felt, he was delighted at the sound of Pini's voice from the other side of the door.

A candle was burning near the rebbe's adjutant, who was not

supposed to let anyone in without a fee. All along the way, from Pini's home to the rebbe's home, she and Frumma walked in darkness. The night was so cloudy, that you couldn't make out another person. Suddenly, in the light of the rebbe's home, Pini saw that Frumma, who had left her home as a *girl*, with a red ribbon in her braid, had changed into a *young wife* on the way: She was wearing a huge headband.

"It's magic! It's a spell! She's enchanted!" cried Pini. "I'm scared to touch you. You've suddenly turned into a wife. . . . I have to spit three times, and I've got to touch the mezuzah. All year long, I've been dreaming. . . ."

Yekhiel the Contractor knew what Pini was talking about. He laughed and opened the door himself and said to Pini:

"Don't scream, don't curse. Come in and you'll soon find out that it's neither magic nor any kind of spell."

Pini entered the house with a very beautiful young wife in a huge headband. When a woman enters the home of a Hassidic rebbe, she is not supposed to say "good evening."

The rebbe's grandsons came out of the alcove and paused at the threshold to look at the beautiful young woman as well as the huge headband. They stood there transfixed, gawking and gaping.

At that moment, Yossele, Obadiah's son, also came out of the alcove. Until now, he and his father had been sitting in there because the sick old man (madness is a disease like any other) still didn't have the strength to walk. And besides, the two of them didn't know where to go. Yesterday, they had found a place for the young man, but no one was willing to put up the old, poor, sick father. Earlier, when Obadiah was the Madman, he had lived in all the vacant houses. But now that he was Mr. Obadiah, a sick, pious Jew from another town, he could not live in a vacant house. Here, in the rebbe's home, no one would pity him. On the contrary, the grandsons and their wives made it clear to Yossele that he had to take his sick father away.

"This is not a charity hospital for a sick Jew," they told the son.

Yossele had an idea: "That good contractor, the one who felt sorry for my father and gave him a gold ducat, and told me to come to him. He's staying in Peysakh's inn, he wants to give

Father a jacket and a coat. He's such a good person, I'll ask him if he can take Father in for a couple of days until we can rent a wagon to go home." With a face exciting pity, Yossele walked over to Yekhiel the Contractor and whispered to him. Yekhiel replied:

"Yes. Take your father to my room immediately, and tell them I said it was all right."

Yossele was overjoyed and wanted to kiss Yekhiel's hand. Yekhiel wouldn't let him, he pushed him away.

"Go on with you, don't be silly! Just take your father and don't drive me crazy. There's something else I have to do here."

Yossele walked over to the Holy Land emissary. He saw that the man was bending over with his face on his hands. Yossele began speaking to the man in our Hebrew. Not very fluently, but he had always spoken to him in the Holy Tongue:

"Rabbi, I am going with my father. I will not come to the Rabbi tonight."

The emissary might not have turned his face up—for a reason that we will soon learn. But Yossele gave the man a yank when he spoke to him:

The emissary turned around, glaring at his assistant.

At that moment, Pini was standing opposite the emissary. Upon seeing his face, she yelled, throwing everyone else into a panic:

"Fishl! Is that you!? You lousy rat! You've wasted so many years of my life, you dirty swine!" Pini ran to the rebbe, weeping, sobbing, screaming: "He's up and changed into a Turk! How many times have I troubled you, rebbe, and Velvele wrote letters for me. He ran out on me, the pig, and he must have taken another wife somewhere. Rebbe, if you keep this a secret, it's the end of the world!" She turned to the emissary. "You criminal! Cat got your tongue? You robber! you murderer! If you didn't want to live with me, then you should have gotten a divorce—we *are* Jews after all. The whole town knows I was desperate for a livelihood and lying in the cold and working my fingers to the bone so I wouldn't have to depend on anyone else, God forbid! It was in Berditchev, rebbe, he was younger, of course, but with that same disgusting face, and my father was a good Jew, and that

151

Fishl, he took me away from him, he was an assistant cantor, he was. 'He's a belfer,' that's what my father said. 'A decent boy. Marry him!' A year later, he got hold of the dowry, five hundred guldens, goddamn it, and he impoverished my father, he did, may he rest in peace. And my mother had a big headband, she did, and he stole it and ran away and we never heard from him again. My poor mother, may she rest in peace, died that very same year from worrying so much and from all my crying day and night. You killer! If you'd only sent me a divorce for my money, I could have gotten another husband. But now," she wept, "I'm an old woman. Who'd be crazy enough to marry me? I'm gonna die like a dog out in the cold!" She turned to Yekhiel the Contractor. "Long may you live for sending for me. Just let me get even with that Turk or Tartar! You really have a Tartar's heart, you assassin!"

Screaming and weeping at the same time is something a fishwife has down pat. The rebbe felt awful. This was his third setback of the night: Obadiah was not the reincarnation of a Rationalist; Velvele the Expert, his close follower, was a convert to Christianity; and the Holy Land emissary, who was sitting right next to him, that dear man from Jerusalem, he was nothing but a belfer from Berditchev, a thief who had run away from his wife, and the important letters from the Holy Land were probably forged. What a disgusting turn of events, what an awful setback!

They had quickly gotten rid of Obadiah. They had also gotten rid of Velvele's first wife. But goddamm it: "How are we gonna get rid of the belfer?" the miracle-worker wondered to himself.

Yossele, the son of Obadiah the Pious, asked the entire company a question, like a boy from Shargorod:

"Why did he force me to break my back talking Hebrew all the time? A man from Berditchev ought to know plain Yiddish."

They all laughed, even though they would much have preferred not to laugh.

And Fishl, the belfer from Berditchev, the thief, what did he do while Pini screamed and wept? He held his tongue, like a fish.

It was Pini who answered Yossele's question:

"You know, when Fishl was a young man in Berditchev, he could disguise himself as a beggar or a priest at weddings. He

152

could also play Ahasuerus in Purim skits, all the actors would learn from him. Yes, yes, Rebbe," she turned to the miracle-worker, "the whole town knew him. He was as sly as a fox!"

Everyone laughed again.

The rebbe called over Velvele the Expert and said to him so that Pini could hear:

"Velvele, my dear friend, and Isser, my dear friend, please take Fishl to your home and let him spend the night. Tomorrow, God willing, you shall take him to the Jewish judges, and they will judge him according to the Laws of our Holy Torah" (he heaved a Hassidic, rabbinical, piously pitiful moan). "Both of you, go with him!"

Velvele hated to leave without learning what would happen with Yekhiel the Contractor; but since the rebbe had ordered him (even though his first wife had testified that he was a convert), Velvele, the rebbe's "dear friend," still had grace in the miracle-worker's eyes, and so he diligently grabbed Fishl, the bogus Jerusalemite. Issir, likewise the rebbe's "dear friend," also grabbed the fat emissary to take him away. Pini was delighted that the rebbe had asked two virtuous Hassidic men to guard that murderous thief. He'd be taken care of tomorrow. Her murderer must have money, she thought, and she was going to take back her dowry and every single ruble for her mother's headband.

All that remained now was to settle the matter for which she had been called: Yekhiel and Frumma.

XXIII

The rebbe himself wanted to know what was going on with Yekhiel the Contractor. He had heard as clearly as anyone else when Pini had yelled from the other side of the door: "It's magic! It's a spell! . . . You've suddenly turned into a young woman." The girl who had changed into a woman was not enchanted by any stretch of the imagination. On the contrary, she was cheerful and radiant, and she was wearing a huge headband. There must be something to her. And even though a

153

rebbe may not speak his thoughts, he is human, after all, he wanted to know what such a rich woman had to do with a poor market vendor.

The Hassidim could still hear the innkeeper and his wife in the alcove, but they would probably leave soon. Meanwhile, the room was quiet. The Hassidim stopped where they were, gaping to see what would happen. The rebbe's grandsons were at the threshold of the alcove, gawking at the radiant young woman with the huge headband, they were thankful to the Good Lord that they were rid of the fat Jerusalemite. They would be hearing and seeing fine things.

Yekhiel the Contractor did not wait for the rebbe to begin. He eagerly walked over to the table:

"The start of the week didn't quite work out for me. Rebbe, what you took for pure gold was fool's gold. But let's forget about that, and let's talk about my miracle. I meant this woman. I wish to marry her. And I want the wedding to take place here in your home, tonight."

"No!" cried Pini, clutching her head with both hands. "No, rebbe, I don't want to sell my soul. Oh, God help me, rebbe! A brother can't marry his sister! The world will collapse! How can this be? Oh, help me, God! A brother and sister?! No! It can't be! It can't! How can you allow it, rebbe, God forbid!"

All eyes were glued on Yekhiel the Contractor and the beautiful woman. It wasn't proper for a brother to marry his own sister.

Yekhiel the Contractor laughed:

"Hahahaha! Don't clutch your head and don't yell. You already called her a witch for nothing. I promised you'd understand the transformation very soon. Just keep silent for a few minutes and I'll explain everything."

And he stared at the rebbe:

"You know that our Father Abraham was once in a terrible predicament and he had to say that his wife Sarah was his sister. Right? Now three months ago, I told this good woman that my bride-to-be was my sister. I had to bring my fiancée here secretly for a reason that I'll tell you in a few minutes. In Mezhbezh, I deliberately chose Pini the Agunah, as she is called, because she

154

lives all alone in her house, no one ever visits her. I paid six months' board for my fiancée—fifty rubles cash on the spot. That was enough, right? The poor woman needed all that money for her business. But I did insist on one condition: She was never to send my bride-to-be anywhere. I wanted to make sure that no one ever saw her and that no one ever found out that she was in Mezhbezh. . . . Thank you very much, Pini, you are a good and honest woman! I want to give you a present for taking care of my fiancée and keeping the secret better than any Hassidim. You can see that the Good Lord has rewarded you. We helped you find your husband." (Yekhiel had to say that to get in a dig at the Hassidim.) "Furthermore, Pini, my fiancée dressed as a girl for the same reason that I pretended she was my sister. So that no one would realize she was in Mezhbezh. Her braid was false, it belonged to a bride, who cut it off. My fiancée was married once, so she is permitted to wear a wig, right, rebbe? It's in the Talmud. My fiancée was married. . . ." All the onlookers gaped in amazement.

The rebbe answered:

"Yes, it's in the section on what a wife may wear on the Sabbath. But Jews don't follow it. However, in retrospect, it's not a great sin. Well, Yekhiel? . . ."

Yekhiel the Contractor went on:

"There's something else you have to know, Pini. My fiancée's name isn't Frumma. You'll find out her real name later on. But because she's virtuous and pious (*frum* in Yiddish), I gave her the name Frumma. . . ."

The onlookers simply couldn't believe their ears. Even the innkeeper and his wife pushed their way over to the threshold to hear this curious story.

Yekhiel the Contractor walked over to the rebbe's adjutant, who was sitting outside the door. He had fallen asleep. From inside the house, they could hear the contractor wake him up by giving him money:

"Here you are. This is something you like. . . . But you've got to run an errand for me quickly. Take a lantern." He softly listed a few people, some by name. "Wake them up if they're asleep. Bring all of them here to the rebbe along with all the parapher-

155

nalia. Hurry up, and if you can get all these people and all the stuff here within fifteen minutes, I'll give you four more silver guldens. Get going! Hurry up! And get them here quickly!"

Inside the house, they saw that the money-man had already left, and Yekhiel came back indoors.

During that time, Pini, who was delighted that the rich contractor had praised her, said:

"It's too bad, rebbe. The woman's name could just as well be Frumma, for she's as quiet and decent as a dove. I never heard a peep out of her. She never left the house as long as she lived with me, except late Friday night. When Yekhiel came to my home with new clothes for her, the two of them went outside and spoke together. I saw all the clothes, but I didn't know about the headband. Maybe she hid her jewelry." The beautiful young woman smiled. "It was only on the way over here that she took off her braid in the darkness and put on the veil and the headband. I swear, what a business!" The beautiful young woman smiled again. "Now I realize why you took so long to get dressed, something like an hour. . . ."

The young woman laughed modestly.

Yekhiel the Contractor came back into the house and walked over to the rebbe:

"Now, Pini, that decent woman, has said that we are brother and sister. But I have said that I was only pretending, like our Father Abraham, when I told her a few months ago that this woman was my sister. You do not know me, rebbe. This is the first time I've ever come to your home. That's why I've sent your men to gather witnesses. People that you, rebbe, and the other people here already know. These witnesses will tell you who this woman is. Then you'll see that she's not my sister." He turned to Pini. "And you, Pini, wait a bit, and you'll know the truth and you'll be able to attend our wedding."

Everyone heard what he said and they were amazed. Even Tordes and his wife Menye-Rasye remained spellbound until the end.

Yekhiel the Contractor went on:

"There's one favor I want to ask you, rebbe. When the witnesses arrive, I want to go into the alcove for a few minutes, and I want you to say that it's all right. Meanwhile, please ask Pini, that honest woman, and my bride to sit down. The witnesses may not come all that soon."

He didn't wait for the rebbe to invite them. He pulled over two chairs, and Pini and the beautiful young woman sat down.

Although Mezhbezh is a big town, it's not as big as Saint Petersburg. The money-man was already back, panting and gasping, he ran over to Yekhiel and whispered—quite audibly—into his ear:

"Only two were gone after the Sabbath. The rest will be here in a couple of minutes, together with all the stuff."

XXIV

When the witnesses could be heard arriving, Yekhiel the Contractor slipped into the alcove, and the beautiful young woman stood up from her chair. Her heart was pounding. She was very nervous.

In walked Aaron the Beadle of Nosuchville, together with his wife Sarah. Upon seeing the young woman, they fell upon her and she threw her arms around them. They shouted cheerfully and wept for joy.

"Sheyntse, it's you!" they shouted.

"Daddy, Mommy!" she shouted.

"Our Sheyntse!" they shouted in cheerful and tearful voices.

She sobbed:

"Yes, Daddy, Mommy!"

"You're really here, in the rebbe's home? We've really got you here, where the rebbe said I shouldn't worry?" shouted Sarah.

A kissing, a hugging, a joy. A merriment. It lasted for several minutes.

They all saw how glad the rebbe was that this meeting was regarded as a miracle. At least he had *this* for the night and all his setbacks.

Suddenly, the innkeeper's wife Menye-Rasye burst in:

"What?! Is that you, Sarah? Why, I gave you my beautiful girl. Her name was Sheyntse. I've been looking for you all over the

157

district, you criminal! Give me back my child! Tordes, cat got your tongue? This is Sarah, I've been looking for her. . . ."

Everyone was silent, paralyzed. Aaron the Beadle and Sarah his wife were as dumb as stone. So was the rebbe.

Tordes, the brawny innkeeper, lifted his brawny arm to strike Sarah. He was ready to kill her. Luckily, Yekhiel the Contractor came leaping from the alcove. He was no weakling himself. Pulling them apart, he snapped:

"Don't shout, don't fight. There's a man sitting here," he pointed to the rebbe, "he'll hear what you have to say. We're all Jews after all, we'll listen to everything. Come now. What's the use of fighting and shouting. Just say what's on your mind."

Tordes the Innkeeper lowered his arm. But his wife kept weeping and yelling bitterly to the rebbe. It was heart-rending.

"Rebbe, when I divorced that scoundrel Velvele, I was pregnant, as I told you before. My poor father, may he rest in peace, died when I had my baby, may he intercede for me. My father, may he rest in peace, was Shneur, the tax-collector of Kosznetin. Cat got your tongue, Tordes? I don't have the strength. . . ."

Tordes the Innkeeper told the rest of the story:

"Do you understand, rebbe, the girl was named Sheyntse, after her grandfather Shneur, may he rest in peace, that's right. My wife, Menye-Rasye, didn't nurse the girl. . . ."

Having rested a bit, Menye-Rasye could take up her shouting again, she wrung her hands and let out a torrent of tears:

"They took everything because Father had so many debts. My mother lived on, poor, without a crust of bread. When she went to a rabbinical court, they said—Tordes, you tell them, you're a man. . . ."

Tordes took up the thread: "They said Menye-Rasye could marry me because my first wife committed suicide. . . ."

"The child, rebbe," Menye-Rasye shouted and wept, "a woman took her by way of doing a good deed. Sarah, she was also from Kosznetin. She promised she would return my baby in two years. I married Tordes, and he also took in my mother. But she died in a year because she missed the beautiful child so much. . . ."

She wept and sobbed and couldn't go on. So Tordes continued:

"My wife didn't have a child for two, three, four, five years, and she began longing for the baby. Look for Sarah, look for Sarah—but she was gone. I hitched up a horse and rode around asking after Sarah's whereabouts. She was gone, and so was the child. 'No hide nor hair of them,' as the peasant says."

Menye-Rasye spoke again, wringing her hands and weeping:

"A peasant's saying is like a biblical verse: 'There's no use crying over spilt milk.' "

The company started laughing at her proverb.

"I don't want to talk to the tsaddik anymore. . . ."

She fell upon Sheyntse, the beautiful young woman, kissing and hugging her:

"My child, I carried you under my heart, I am your mother. My darling, my love, my life, kiss me, my Sheyntse. . . ." She fainted dead away, plopping full-length on the floor.

Meanwhile, other people began arriving: Tevye Bilenkis, Gabriel Gittels, Zainvil, and a Jewish judge, and a cantor, and two beadles, and several other Jews. The newcomers were talking about what had happened so far and what was happening now.

As Velvele the Expert had done earlier, Yekhiel the Contractor sprinkled water on Menye-Rasye until she came to.

Aaron the Beadle and his wife Sarah walked over to the rebbe.

"Yes, that's absolutely true. Sheyntse is her daughter," said Aaron.

"It's true, rebbe, if you please. I took the child from her, from Menye-Rasye, yes, this beautiful woman here, Sheyntse!" said Sarah. "We left Kosznetin and then Yampelye. My husband Aaron became the bes-medresh beadle in Nosuchville. We loved the child. And we brought her up. We thought of her as our own daughter, if you please. Why, rebbe, you know, if you please, how I bothered you when she vanished. And you, rebbe, you worked a miracle, if you please, we've found her again in your home. My husband and I both forgot that she was someone else's child, if you please. Our Sheyntse, if you please, really became *our* Sheyntse. . . ."

During the commotion, during the yelling and weeping and fainting, Yekhiel the Contractor had hidden his face so that those who had come after Aaron and his wife couldn't see him. Not even Aaron and Sarah had noticed him. Now, after the tumult of

159

arousing the innkeeper's wife, when Tordes had helped him get Menye-Rasye back on her feet, Yekhiel saw that the rebbe was at a loss to reach a verdict between Menye-Rasye and Sarah. So Yekhiel turned to the company:

"Good evening to you, Tevye, our dear community elder! Good evening to you, Zainvil! Good evening to you, Gabriel Gittels! Good evening to you, Aaron and Sarah! I am Mikhel!"

He turned to the tsaddik: "Rebbe, Mikhel is the Yiddish equivalent for the Hebrew name Yekhiel, right? So I didn't lie, did I?"

They were all dumbstruck. The people of Nosuchville cried:

"Mikhel! For God's sake! Mikhel! For God's sake! What are you doing here?"

Mikhel (or Yekhiel the Contractor, it's all the same now) spoke to the rebbe eagerly:

"Rebbe, so long as this girl or woman (you can ask Aaron's wife and she'll tell you that Sheyntse can be called either a girl or a woman)—so long as she has no one to turn to, both women can fight over her. Perhaps Aaron's wife could win, because a mother who gives away a newborn baby and then remarries may lose the right to be called 'mother.' After all, Aaron's wife did bring up Sheyntse, she saw her through chicken pox and measles. They can call Sheyntse their child. I never heard the word 'child' from them. They had me teach Sheyntse how to read and write. They arranged a marriage between her and me. I was her proper bridegroom. Then, because of a foolish matter and Rabbi N.'s swindle, they broke up the engagement. They forced Sheyntse to marry someone else against God and His commandment."

He turned to Zainvil:

"You, Zainvil, you did everything in your power to have Aaron and his wife marry her off to—I won't say whom. But Aaron and his wife were concerned about providing for her by getting her married. Sheyntse cost them a lot of money, and they had a lot of trouble with her like any devoted parents. If she had remained with her real mother and Tordes at the inn, she would certainly never have become the Sheyntse she is today. On the other hand, Aaron and Sarah committed a great wrong. They should have told her: 'You are not our own child, you have a mother, Menye-Rasye, the daughter of Shneur the Tax Collector in Kosznetin.'

Who knows, Sheyntse could have unwittingly married a brother, God forbid—which Pini thought she was about to do." (A glance at Pini.) "Right, Pini? Perhaps Sheyntse's father" (a glance at Sheyntse), "Velvele the Expert has a son. Sheyntse could very easily have gotten his son for a husband. Do you understand, Aaron, do you understand, Sarah, what might have happened, God forbid? Merely because you never told Sheyntse who she really is! Right, rebbe?"

The tsaddik stared glassy-eyed. Everyone looked at him.

"The Good Lord protects Jews from unwitting sins, that's why Velvele has no children, and that's why Menye-Rasye has no children. 'The Torah and God are one,' says the *Holy Zohar*. The Good Lord wrote in the Holy Torah that a brother may not marry his sister. Well, that could really have been the stumbling block, as you have said, Yekhiel-Mikhel. God Blessed Be He preserved the Torah by not letting Velvele or Menye-Rasye have any children."

Everyone listened and felt that this was well put. Mikhel laughed and jeered:

"Hahahaha! . . . Zainvil knows his sacred texts, rebbe. He can tell you a thing or two—since I haven't studied the Talmud for a long time. He can tell you when a brother and sister did marry unwittingly. Besides, it's not the least bit fair that Velvele and Tordes should have no children just because Aaron and his wife committed a sin and never told Sheyntse about her real father and mother. God is not such a wrongdoer. Not on your life! . . . But let's forget about that. There are two sides already, and now I'm the third side. I want to marry Sheyntse. For the moment, she belongs to no one. I've offered the best verdict, right, Menye-Rasye, right, Sarah?"

The rebbe had a sour taste in his mouth. And all the Hassidim in the room might have gotten into a bitter fight with Yekhiel the Contractor, who was now known as Yekhiel-Mikhel of Nosuchville. But the contractor was looking at them the way Jews look at cats and just laughing away. Nor had he exhibited any ignorance of Judaism. And then there was the huge headband that Sheyntse was wearing. . . . Yekhiel-Mikhel must be very rich. So they held their tongues.

"Do you remember," said Mikhel to Gabriel Gittels, "that

Markel the Innkeeper had a poltergeist in his cellar last year? That was me. Sheyntse used to meet me there. . . ." He laughed. "We had no place else to meet, to talk. . . . Hahahaha! I rattled a horse fetter, and people were too scared to come down into the cellar. So nobody saw us."

He turned to Sheyntse:

"Where did you put the old *Zohar*? I asked you to bring the book that hung over the cellar door. Around mid-Elul, we stopped meeting, so I hid the *Zohar*. . . ."

These words created a quiet disturbance, a whispering, a shrugging of shoulders among the people who knew about Markel's poltergeist.

The rebbe knew that he had given Markel the old *Zohar*. The Nosuchvillers had thought that a great miracle had occurred. But Mikhel was wise enough not to mention the rebbe's name, so the disturbance didn't get out of hand.

Sheyntse answered Mikhel's question.

"I've still got the book. Why don't we give it back? We don't need someone else's book."

This was the first time Sheyntse said anything, and her words were so sharp that she might have caused a greater disturbance if it hadn't been for the huge headband that the beautiful young woman was wearing.

Gabriel Gittels deliberately tried to change the subject; he asked:

"Tell us, Mikhel, you witnessed the wars in Germany. Did you earn any money, thank the Lord? All the Nosuchvillers are wondering." He turned to the tsaddik: "Rebbe, I tell you, he's a marvelous man! We used to call him 'Mikhel the Muscovite' because he was useful for the greatest generals. Today he could probably be useful even for the French. . . . Listen, Mikhel, are you going to come and exchange money with me again. The rates are different now. Tell me, did you ever see Napoleon? People say he's a wild creature! Ha, Tevye, you're a fan of Napoleon's, aren't you?"

Tevye let out a Hassidic giggle:

"Hehehe! I'm no fan of his anymore, huh. He gave money to Mikhel, huh, and he didn't even send *me* a French watch, huh. . . ."

Everyone laughed at Tevye's bon mot.

XXV

Zainvil likewise saw the huge headband and heard his future father-in-law, Gabriel Gittels, flattering and praising Mikhel in front of the tsaddik. Even Tevye Bilenkis' bon mot indicated that Mikhel had struck oil with the French and was now a rich man. So Zainvil had to flatter him a bit too. He said to Mikhel:

"Please don't be disappointed, Mikhel, if my present father-in-law Dovid Smik and his wife don't attend your wedding. When the Sabbath was over, they had to drive off to Nimyevke. No one is at home, and so they had to hurry."

Mikhel replied in a loud voice, making sure that everyone could hear:

"On the contrary, Zainvil, I owe you an apology for the trouble I caused you with Sarah. It was a silly female notion of hers. She's not even stupid, but this time she made a fool of herself."

They all surrounded Mikhel, a circle of Hassidim. And even Tordes and his wife Menye-Rasye listened. At the head of the table, the rebbe, although pretending to study the *Zohar*, was listening to every word that Mikhel uttered:

"Sarah didn't realize what I had done. Even though I left Nosuchville three days before Rosh Hashanah, I asked Khlyebov to wait for me for five days a few miles outside of town, and I drove back at night. Sheyntse, my fiancée, knew where I'd be waiting in town for her. She came out to me, and we made her up to look like an unmarried woman, and then we took the night coach for Mezhbezh, where I left her with this decent woman." (He pointed to Pini.) "I said she was my sister. Pini took care of my 'sister' until, with God's help, I came back safe and sound, just as we had prayed. Meanwhile, the Nosuchville fools paid a rebbe and burned a candle for forty-eight hours. . . . Hahaha! Sarah was foolish enough to attack you for nothing. Sheyntse was in Mezhbezh while they were hunting for her high and low. We can thank the Lord that *my* miracle helped Sheyntse find her real parents."

He turned to the tsaddik:

"Rebbe, I think it would only be fair to send for Velvele. He *is* Sheyntse's father, after all."

The rebbe reflected for a moment and then said to one of the young Hassidim:

"Lemele, my dear friend, go and summon Velvele. But tell him to have someone else guard Fishl."

The young Hassid was radiant at receiving the tsaddik's orders. He said:

"If there's no one else, then *I* will stand guard. I will make sure that Velvele comes here."

Lemele took off.

Gabriel Gittels asked:

"What are we waiting for? Let's start the wedding. Put up the canopy. How about it, Mikhel?"

For Hassidim, disorder is order. One man says something, the next man issues a command, and someone else understands and obeys. That's how things get done, and Mikhel knew it very well.

He laughed:

"Hahaha! Gabriel, do you know who my attendants will be?" He pointed to the innkeeper and his wife and to Aaron and his wife. "These two couples. Sheyntse's real mother and Sarah, who acted like a devoted mother to her for fifteen years. Right, Aaron? Right, Tordes? Why don't you be our attendants, just as you are!"

Turning to the judge and the cantor, Mikhel took out the beautiful pouch:

"How much should I pay you? Here are two gold ducats. Start the wedding, raise the canopy. And you beadles, I'll pay you handsomely if you perform the wedding quickly—I've got a ring here."

The beadles set up the four poles for the canopy. The cantor quickly wrote the marriage contract in the alcove. The judge assumed he would be performing the ceremony and he adjusted his fur hat.

Mikhel nudged Gabriel Gittels and Zainvil, and the three of them went up to the rebbe:

"If you perform the ceremony for our Mikhel of Nosuchville," said Gabriel, "we'll know that you respect our town."

"By God!" said Zainvil. "Since the Good Lord has arranged for this to happen in your home, it is your Jewish duty. Who else is a shield for our generation?"

Meanwhile, Velvele the Expert came back. The rebbe said:

"It is written in our Talmud: 'Where a penitent doth stand, not even a perfect saint can stand.' Penitents have a higher place in paradise than the saints. Now who is going to find a place in your inn, Velvele? God Blessed Be He has forgiven you for your past conversion, for which you atoned by becoming a Hassid. And now He has sent a very rich man to you as your son-in-law, and thus perhaps you will not need guests. These people want me to perform the ceremony. This is your daughter, Velvele. You have proably heard what has now clearly come out, namely, that the woman who is to marry the wealthy Yekhiel-Mikhel is not Aaron's daughter. The Good Lord is the Reason of all Reasons. We are his Hassids, his pious and loyal followers, every day, every minute of the day. Tonight, during the Sabbath repast, you certainly did not realize, poor man, that you were about to become a father and a father-in-law."

Velvele's wounds instantly healed when he saw that everyone heard how high he stood in the rebbe's esteem. But deep down, he understood that the rebbe was only flattering him for some other reason—because he knew that Velvele's son-in-law, the contractor, was very, very rich. Velvele was quite upset by this, as we shall soon hear from his own lips.

But for the moment, he enjoyed himself. And the Hassidim had heard that he stood higher in the rebbe's esteem than before, so none of them would dare to rebuke him for his past sins. A situation like that is explained by a Hassidic quip: "Jews say you can never tell what a man's tomorrow will be like. But I say you can't even tell what his today is like."

They raised the canopy and the wedding began. The attendants did a good job of it. The rebbe performed the ceremony with utmost fervor. The cantor read out the contract. Mikhel placed the ring on Sheyntse's finger. Everything was done according to the traditional order.

"Mazel-tov, mazel-tov! Mazel-tov, mazel-tov!" Mikhel married Sheyntse.

When Mikhel departed, saying, "Good night to you, rebbe!"

the rebbe thought that Mikhel would probably bring him twenty gold ducats the next day. Even though the boy had cut him to the quick with his sharp words, money heals all wounds.

Velvele the Expert, Mikhel's father-in-law, accompanied the newlyweds. And so did Pini. Tordes and Menye-Rasye were overjoyed. They were also going to Nosuchville. They hugged and kissed Sheyntse, and she kissed her mother a hundred times until they finally left. Aaron the Beadle and his wife Sarah also followed at a distance.

Gabriel and Zainvil went to their lodgings, planning to leave early in the morning.

"We'll be seeing you soon, God willing, in Nosuchville probably," the two of them said to the newlyweds, bidding them goodbye.

When Velvele had gotten all the others out, he told Pini to escort Sheyntse:

"Take my daughter to Peysakh. I'll come right away with Mikhel. We have to discuss something. Go, my new daughter."

Pini left with Sheyntse. Velvele and Mikhel followed at a distance so as not to be heard. Velvele hugged and kissed Mikhel, saying:

"People call me 'Velvele the Expert.' But I'm no expert compared with you, Mikhel. The old have to learn from the young. There's a story about one rebbe's follower speaking to another rebbe's follower. He said: 'My rebbe won ten thousand guldens in the lottery even though he never bought a ticket.' The other Hassid said that his rebbe had drunk ten thousand cups of Hungarian wine at the first Passover seder and remained dead sober. The first man cried: 'What?! Ten thousand cups? How is that possible?' To which the other Hassid replied: 'What about winning ten thousand guldens without buying a lottery ticket? If you forget about the ten thousand guldens, then I'll forget about the ten thousand cups.' Which means both of them were lying. . . . It's a simple anecdote, a very simple one. But it's applicable now, Mikhel. I'm something of a mayven, I could tell right off that the headband is made of false pearls. . . . Right, Mikhel? We're even now. You're my son-in-law, Mikhel the Expert. . . ."

Mikhel hugged and kissed his father-in-law, laughing and saying:

"I'm really glad you're being open with me, and I'll treat you like a father, I'll tell you the whole story, just to prove that I'm no swindler, God forbid.

"You probably know about my original betrothal to Sheyntse and you also know that Rabbi N. tried to get on the good side of the Nosuchville klutzes by telling them to tear up my engagement contract. And you also know about Sheyntse's marriage to the drummer. Sheyntse loved me and certainly didn't want to swap me for a country bumpkin—drummer or not. But a big headband is so important to a young Jewish girl that if a stray dog had six strings of pearls with spikes like a horse's collar to wear on the head, she'd marry him on the spot. They turned Sheyntse's head with the big headband, and so she agreed to the match. But then, when it fell apart, Sheyntse realized that a headband is no help and she had to give it back just to get rid of him. She was left with a bitter desire: A big headband is great, but a fine husband with a big headband to boot—that is true happiness. However, I love Sheyntse so much that when I began earning money from Russian officers, I promised her, in Markel's cellar—you know, when your rebbe had Markel hang up the *Zohar* to scare away the poltergeist—I promised Sheyntse I would go to the Tsarist headquarters, make a lot of money, and buy her a big headband, only it would be a lot bigger than the one she had to give back to Naphtali the Drummer. To tell you the truth, if I hadn't loved Sheyntse so passionately and if I hadn't been so eager to get home, I could have eventually made a lot of money at the headquarters. But I missed her so much and I wanted to get home so badly. And in that short time, I didn't earn a great deal. Now how could I pay a thousand ducats for Sheyntse's headband when I didn't have enough money? No one knew about my anguish, I kept it to myself. You can't tell another person about a thing like that. He'd merely laugh and make fun of it for being so silly. But the whole problem kept me awake at night. I was ready to give up the ghost. But then I was hired by a hospital supplier in Breslau, and he told other contractors a story about a scoundrel named Lippe Levit, who cheated a householder in

167

Czernigov of fifteen hundred rubles, and a drayman of thirteen hundred rubles. He used collateral, a headband with false pearls. I enjoyed the story more than anyone else did. I, a Jew from Nosuchville, had never known that there was such a thing as false pearls. And I thought to myself: 'That's the balm for all the wounds in my heart. I can make my Sheyntse a nice big headband for very little money.' And that's what I did. And I didn't have to hunt for any more business. The small sum I already had was enough for me. I took the stagecoach home and made my—today she's also your—Sheyntse happy. She'll never know the truth, and none of our Jews can tell the difference between real and phony pearls."

"Yes indeed, my wise expert!" said Velvele. "What you've done is ingenious. You got what you wanted with a phony headband. Now why do you carry on about Hassidic rebbes fooling people? People want to be fooled. Are they experts, after all? Are they Mikhels? Tell me."

"Don't be offended, father-in-law, but how can you compare my brainstorm to the lies, falsehoods, and deceptions practiced by the Hassidic rebbes?" rejoined Mikhel. "When it comes to wordly things, when people are only after money or silly ornaments or other wasteful things, then they deserve to be punished, we ought to fool them. There are lots of fine countries in the world where the women don't have pearl-encrusted horse collars on their heads. The richest women there may have millions at their disposal, but they'll just spend four guldens for a coif of white percale. It's only these lunatics, these wives of poor Jews in Poland, who've talked themselves into thinking that a woman without a pearl collar on her head is less than human. . . . It's a scandal and a shame to see a poor, miserable woman sitting by a sick child or her feeble husband, wearing her pearl collar and weeping, going to a funeral and grieving for the dead person, and actually wearing that pearl headband, wringing her hands and sobbing. It's disgusting, it's nauseating! A Polish lord can make fun of Jews and laugh at them because his own wife, his lady, spends two guldens on a çoif, while his Jewish tavern-keeper's better half—or should I say worse half?—like your ex-wife, no matter how poor and filthy she may be, she'll always wear a headband. . . . And there are so many other silly and crazy things like that. So it's no sin to make fools of people like that. Don't forget what Fredrick the Great, that wise King of Prussia, said: 'I won't levy any tax on ryebread, because people have to eat it just to stay alive. But if you want to eat cake and drink wine and coffee, then you'll have to pay taxes on them.' Now tell me, father-in-law, how can you compare these things to what the rebbes, the so-called tsaddiks, do? These poor people come to the Hassidic rabbi, looking for truth and piety, ethics and God's words. It's dismal to remember what Isaiah cried: 'Your leaders mislead you.' Isaiah meant those Jews who drive in carriages, take money, eat and drink, sybarites, who claim to be leaders, and who are false Jews, liars, swindlers, they tell Jews to do all sorts of foolish things and lead them up the garden path and into the mire, making them cripples, ignoramuses, ruffians. You don't have to know anything, so long as you're a Hassid and applaud— that's enough. Well, for people like that, I can only say that the entire Chapter of Reprehensions and all the curses in the world aren't enough for all those swindlers. Right? You're not saying anything. . . . Among the benefits I got from the false headband, the greatest is that it allowed me to say things that cut your rebbe through and through. He'd never heard such comments from anybody. He was ready to have me kicked out the door. There were Hassidic ruffians all prepared to do it. But the big headband made him think I'm a Rothschild. So he held his tongue and so did they. Hahaha! I'm laughing, and you should laugh too. He thinks I'm going to bring him piles of ducats tomorrow. He's not getting a single kopek! I gave him one ducat just to dazzle him. After all, my wedding did take place in his home, right?"

Velvele the Expert began hugging and kissing Mikhel:

"You deserve a thousand kisses just for getting the tsaddik to perform the wedding ceremony. You're really on the ball. And do you know what else I want to say? This headband will bring you the greatest trust and faith in Nosuchville. I'm a mayven, I know people. They're all going to suck up to you, they're all going to think you're fabulously rich. They'll bring money into your home. I won't have to worry about you, thank the Lord. The prestige and credit will actually make you rich. I don't have any children. Believe me, Mikhel, I'm disgusted. I know all about the tsaddik, but I have to dance along with the rest of them for my livelihood. If God Blessed Be He helps you to strike it rich, then I'll join you when I get old. I'm no shlimazel, I can be useful to you."

Mikhel returned his father-in-law's kiss and gave him his hand: "Here's my hand on it. If I have any kind of livelihood, I'll come and get you myself from that master liar. You'll live a good life with us. Now we have to hurry. Our near and dear are waiting for us. My Sheyntse must be frozen." The two men caught up with Sheyntse and the others. "I'm sorry. It's not fair of us to keep you waiting so long in the cold. But we had to talk about something, it was very urgent, because Sheyntse and I have to leave by morning. Right, Sheyntse?"

At that moment, when they were about to enter the house, they heard a yelling from Lemele, the young Hassid, and old Isser:

"Grab him! He's getting away! The Holy Land bastard! . . ."

The two men whom the tsaddik had told to guard Fishl, Pini's long-vanished husband, the bogus Jerusalemite, had apparently drifted off to sleep, and Fishl, that sturdy man, had run away. The door was chained inside, and Fishl had very quietly undone the chain and would easily have stolen off. But, to his great misfortune, the broad Turkish pantaloons had caught in the pole wedged in the door. When Fishl gave his pantaloons a strong yank, the pole and the door collapsed because the door had no hinges, and the jambs had been broken for over a year.

The clattering awoke the two guards, but the bird had already flown the coop. Well, off they dashed after him. But Fishl ran faster despite the Turkish slippers. That was why they were shouting: "Grab him! Catch him! He's getting away, the Holy Land bastard! . . ."

Mikhel knew that the Hassidic shlimazels all wore slippers, so they'd never catch Fishl. Taking Tordes along, Mikhel ran after Fishl, and they really ran!

Poor Pini screamed:

"Oh God, oh God! I'll be an agunah forever, a poor, miserable agunah! The filthy bastard's gonna get away again! . . ."

170

She kept screaming these words, louder and louder, a hundred times.

But Mikhel, panting and gasping, returned, dragging Fishl along. Tordes also helped, yanking on the fat culprit.

They brought him to Peysakh's house. Everyone was laughing, they were rolling in mirth. What was going on?

Before dashing out of Isser's home, Fishl had unwound his turban and wrapped the white cloth around his neck. Then he had covered his Turkish coat with an old kaftan of Isser's, girding it with a towel. That was how he was dressed when they pulled him into Peysakh's home.

Yossele and Obadiah had been sitting in a corner, waiting for Mikhel. Upon his arrival, Yossele walked over to him, he told Mikhel that the thief had cash in a belt, money he had gathered from all the Jewish towns for Holy Land charities.

Fine, fine. They unbuckled the money belt and counted the cash on the table. Four hundred and six gold ducats and six hundred rubles in bills, plus about a hundred silver guldens.

Obadiah, sick, pious Obadiah, trudged over to the table. While everyone remained silent, he said;

"Gentlemen, Holy Land alms must be sent to the Holy Land, but if we find any other money, we have to give it to his wife. I think that would be the only just way."

Everyone agreed:

"That's fair, that's fair."

Mikhel asked Fishl:

"Listen, do you have some kind of memo book or list of how much Holy Land money you collected? Tell me, otherwise I'll hit you!"

"Yes!" The donkey opened his mouth to speak for the first time. "Yes, I have a list, the administrators in every town wrote down what they gave. The list has three hundred twenty ducats. The rest is mine."

Velvele the Expert also did his share. They read and they calculated. It was correct: Only three hundred twenty ducats was registered. Mikhel told Isser and his father-in-law Velvele to hold on to the money and make sure it got to the Holy Land. The rest he gave to Pini, the ducats, the banknotes, and the silver guldens:

171

"Here you are, Pini, for your dowry, your mother's headband, and for alimony. I want to say something else to you, Pini, which I think would be only fair. You ought to share some of the money with poor, sick Obadiah. Right, gentlemen?"

Pini raised both her arms to God:

"You are good, oh Lord! You wait a long time, but you pay properly. Here are ten ducats for you, Obadiah!" She put the money in his hands. "And you, Yekhiel, I mean Mikhel, I want to thank you. May God bless you and your good, pious wife and grant you the best of luck. May you grow old in wealth and honor. Amen!"

A WOMAN'S FURY

YITZIK LEYB PERETZ

The tiny room is gloomy and dingy, and all four walls are weeping over the squalor. . . . Up on the dilapidated ceiling, there is a hook—an orphan bereft of its lamp. The huge, peeling oven, its loins girded with coarse sackcloth, stands hunched over in a corner, gazing at its lifeless neighbor, the black, empty stove. A pot with a scorched edge is sprawling upside down on the hob, and off to the side lies a broken spoon, RIP. The tin hero died a noble death: in the battle against dry, stubborn, leftover buckwheat.

The room is packed with furniture: there is a canopy bed with tattered curtains; the bedding, ungraced by linen, peers through the holes with red, feathery eyes; there is a cradle, revealing the big yellowish head of a sleeping baby. There is a tin-lined chest with an open padlock (and most likely containing no great riches); there is also a table with three chairs, the wood, once painted red, is dark and dirty now. . . . And if we add a bucket, a garbage can, a barrel of water, a poker, and a peel, you will understand why the two-by-four cabin is bursting at the seams.

And yet, it also has: a male and a female.

She, a woman just past her prime, is sitting on the chest, which is stuffed in between the canopy bed and the cradle.

To her right, the lone window, small and moldy; to her left, the table. While knitting a stocking, she rocks the cradle with one foot and listens to him, at the table, studying the Talmud, crooning the words in a lamenting tone. While chanting, he shifts about,

173

restless, fidgety, nervous. He either swallows the words, drawls them out, reels them off, or gulps them down; some he stresses and dwells on lovingly, some he rattles off as though pouring peas out of a bag. And he never rests for an instant; now he pulls out a handkerchief that used to be red and whole, wipes his nose, and mops the sweat off his face and brow; next, he drops the handkerchief in his lap and starts twirling his sidelocks, tugging his pointed little beard with its touches of gray. . . . A hair comes out, and he hides it in the holy book, and begins slapping his knees. His hands touch the handkerchief, grab it, and stick a corner of it into his mouth; he bites down on it, crosses and then alternately recrosses his legs.

All the while, his pale forehead breaks into lines and creases, up and down and across, and a tiny *T* emerges above his nose. The folds of skin almost cover up the long eyebrows. All at once, apparently feeling a pang in his heart, he beats his right fist against the left side of his chest. . . . Abruptly he tilts his head to the left, closes off his left nostril with a finger, and turns his right nostril into an artificial fountain, swings his head over to the right, and the fountain spurts out of the left nostril! . . . In between, he inhales a pinch of snuff, sways back and forth more briskly, his voice rings out, the chair creaks, and the table groans!

The child sleeps through everything, it is accustomed to the background music.

And she, the prematurely shrunken wife, sits and beams at her husband. Her eyes are fixed on him; her ears never miss a single sound from his lips. . . . Every so often, she sighs: If only, she muses, he were as fit for this life as for the afterlife, then things would be bright and lovely for her in this world too. . . .

"Oh well," she consoles herself, "that would be asking too much. Not everyone is destined to have the best of both worlds."

She listens. . . . Her shrunken face keeps changing: she is nervous too.

Only a moment ago, she was beaming with pleasure, taking such pride in his learning. . . . Now it strikes her that today is Thursday and she has no money for the Sabbath. And the heavenly light upon her face grows dimmer and dimmer until the smile fades totally. . . . Then she glances through the moldy window, peers at the sun (it must be late by now and she hasn't cooked a thing), and the knitting needles freeze in her hands. A dark shadow has drawn across her face. She looks at the baby; it's tossing and turning now, it will soon wake up. There isn't a drop of milk in the house for the sick child. And the shadow has already grown into a cloud. The knitting needles start quivering, quaking. . . .

And when she remembers that Passover is coming . . . that her earrings and the Sabbath candlesticks are at the pawnbroker's, that the chest is empty and the ceiling lamp has been sold—then the needles begin dancing murderously! The cloud over her face turns dark blue, heavy. And the small gray eyes, barely visible under the headcloth, flash like lightning.

He is still sitting there, chanting away; unaware that a storm is brewing, that the danger is nearing . . . that she has dropped the stocking and her needles and begun cracking her emaciated fingers, that her forehead is all wrinkled with pain. One eye closes and the other eye looks daggers at him, the husband, the scholar, so piercingly, that if he saw it, his blood would run cold; but he fails to see her blue lips shivering, her chin trembling, her teeth chattering, as she holds back with all her strength to keep from erupting. . . . He fails to notice that the thunder is about to boom out, that the tiniest spark could make it burst from her mouth.

And he provides the spark:

Crooning a talmudic phrase, he then translates it: "From this we can deduce—" He is about to say: ". . . three things," but the word "deduce" is enough: Her bitter heart pounces upon it, the word falls like a spark in gunpowder.

Her self-control explodes. The unfortunate word has opened all the locked gates, torn away all the bolts. Raging, foaming at the mouth, she leaps at her husband, waving her nails in his face.

"Deduce!? Did you say 'deduce'!? I'll deduce *you*, by God!" she shrieks, hoarse with anger. "I'll deduce *you*, by God! Yes, yes!" she hisses, like a serpent. "Passover's coming . . . today's Thursday . . . the baby's sick . . . not a drop of milk! Ha!"

She gasps for breath, her sunken chest heaves up and down, her eyes blaze.

175

He is petrified. Blanching, he jumps up from the chair. Breathless with terror, he backs towards the door.

They stand face to face, staring at one another. His eyes are glassy with fear, hers are burning with anger. . . . He quickly realizes that her fury has paralyzed her tongue and her hands. His eyes keep getting smaller and smaller; he sticks one corner of the handkerchief in his mouth, moves a bit further back, takes a deep breath, and murmurs:

"Listen, woman . . . do you realize what it means to profane the holy writings, to prevent your husband from studying the Talmud? Huh! All you care about is bread and butter. Huh! Who feeds the tiniest sparrow? It all comes from not believing in God! You're filled with the Evil Spirit. You care only about *this* world. . . . Foolish woman! Wicked woman! Not letting your husband study the Talmud! You'll go straight to hell!"

Her failure to answer spurs him on! Her face turns paler and paler, she trembles more and more violently, and the harder she trembles and the paler she becomes—the more quickly and firmly he speaks:

"Hell! Fire! Hang you by your tongue. The Highest Judgment: the Four Death Penalties."

She can't speak, her face is chalky.

He senses he is doing wrong, he shouldn't be hurting her like this, he's being dishonest; but he can't stop now. All the bad things in him come gushing out, he can't pull back.

"Do you know what that means?" His voice turns into a sinister thunder: "Stoning—they'll fling you into a pit and pelt you with stones! Burning—" he continues, astonished at his own audacity, "burning—they'll pour a spoonful of boiling molten lead into your innards! Slaying with a sword—they'll take a sword and slice your head off . . . like this!" And he draws his fingers across his neck. And finally: "Strangling—they'll choke you, choke you, do you hear! Do you understand? For keeping a man from studying! For profaning the Talmud!"

His heart is already aching with pity for his victim. But this is the first time he's ever won. The thought intoxicates him! What a stupid woman! He never thought he could terrorize her so easily.

"That's what happens when you profane the Holy Writings!"

176

he finally exclaims. But then he breaks off; after all, she might come to her senses and grab a broom! He jumps back to the table, closes the talmudic tome, and dashes out. . . .

"I'm going to synagogue!" he calls in a softer voice, banging the door behind him.

The yelling and the slamming have awoken the sickly child. It slowly raises its heavy lids. The waxen face twists, and the swollen nose starts whistling. But she remains motionless, raging, transfixed, oblivious of the child's voice.

"Ha!" a hoarse sound finally struggles out of her constricted chest. "So . . . not this world, not the next world. . . . Hang, he says, strangle, he says, burning pitch, lead, he says. Profaning the Talmud!

"Nothing . . . nothing for *me*," her wretched heart sobs, "here, hunger, no clothes . . . no Sabbath candlesticks . . . nothing . . . the child starving . . . not a drop of milk . . . and in the next world—hanging . . . hanging by the tongue . . . for profaning the Talmud—he says.

"Hanging. . . . Ha! Ha! Ha!" these sounds choke out of her despairing voice. "Hanging, yes, but down here! Right away! What's the difference! Why wait?"

The child starts crying louder, but she still doesn't hear it.

"A rope! A rope!" she shrieks, beside herself, her eyes wildly scouring every nook and cranny for a rope. "Where can I get a rope? At least he won't find me here! Just let me out of this hell! Let him know what it's like! Let him be a mother! It's over with me, I'm an angel of death. Let me just put an end to it! An end to it! A rope!"

And the last word struggles out of her throat like a call for help at a fire.

She remembers that there is a rope around somewhere . . . yes, under the oven . . . they were supposed to bind up the oven for the winter, it must be underneath. . . .

She runs over and finds the rope: What joy, she has found the treasure. She looks up at the ceiling, the hook is there. . . . All she has to do is get on the table.

Up she goes.

But from that height she sees the frightened, weakened child sitting up, leaning out of the cradle, trying to escape! It's about to tumble over.

"Mommy!" the sounds barely emerge from the weak throat.

Now a new anger takes hold of her.

She throws away the rope, jumps down, runs over to the child, and pushes it back down on the pillow, screaming:

"Bastard! Won't even let me hang myself! Can't even hang myself in peace! It wants to suck again! You can suck poison from my breast! Poison!

"C'mon, you greedy hog, c'mon!" she screams in one gasp, and stuffs her emaciated breast into the child's mouth:

"C'mon, suck it, bite it!"

THE TRAVELS OF BENJAMIN THE THIRD

MENDELE MOYKHER-SFORIM

Mendele Moykher-Sforim (the Book Peddler) says: "Praised be the Creator who marks the course of the spheres in the heavens above and the course of all His creatures on the earth below. Not even a blade of grass can creep out from the ground unless an angel strike it and say: 'Grow now! Come forth!' And how much more so a human being, he most certainly has an angel who strikes him and says: 'Come, come, come forth!' And even more so, our fine people, our praiseworthy little Jews. No fool can blurt out a word among us Jews, no moron can give advice, no ignoramus can become a Hassid, no ruffian an enlightened gentleman—unless he be struck by his angel, who thereby goads him to become what he becomes. The angels also strike our paupers, saying: 'Grow, ye paupers, beggars, schnorrers, rag-pickers, native poor, nouveau poor, open, hidden: Sprout, grow, like grass, like nettles! Go, ye sons of Israel, go—go a-begging! . . .' "

But that's all neither here nor there. The point is, gentlemen, I want to tell you about one of our brethren, who traveled to faraway climes, thereby becoming famous.

A year ago, all the English and German gazettes were bursting with the wonderful journey that Benjamin, a Polish Jew, had taken to the Eastern lands. "Just imagine," they exclaimed in wonder, "just imagine, a Jew, a Polish Jew, without weapons, without machines, with only a bag over his shoulder and a sack of prayer paraphernalia under his arm—managing to get to those regions, which world-famous English travelers were unable to reach! One can only assume that non-human forces were at work here, the human mind cannot grasp such matters, for such matters are simply mindless. But in any event, and in any case, mankind is indebted to Benjamin for the great marvels and miracles which he has revealed and which have utterly revised the map of the world. Benjamin rightfully deserves the medal awarded to him by the Geographical Society. . . ."

The Jewish newspapers eagerly swooped upon these testimonials and couldn't stop talking about them all last summer, as anyone who follows those papers knows so well. They added up all the sages who have ever appeared among Jews, from Adam down to the present, in order to demonstrate what intelligent people the Jews are. They also drew up a list of Jewish travelers in all ages from Benjamin the First, seven hundred years ago, and Benjamin the Second, down to the whole crew of globetrotters wandering about in our climes today. And in order to magnify the importance of our present-day Benjamin, the newspapers thumbed their noses and snapped their fingers, as Jews are wont to do, at all those other journeys, saying that the whole gang of modern travelers were nothing but common panhandlers who didn't know a mountain from a molehill, and all their so-called travels were nothing but door-to-door begging: They all looked like monkeys compared with the present-day Benjamin, Benjamin the Third, the true and authentic traveler. In regard to him and the tomes indited about him, they quoted that well-known biblical verse: "There is something new under the sun." Which means, in our plain Yiddish, that the sun is shining upon a new Jewish hero. "Blessed and showered with diamonds," they all unanimously exulted, "be he who takes this precious treasure, Benjamin's travels, now available in all foreign languages, and translated it into the Holy Tongue as well, so that Jews, poor things, may also taste the honey dripping from the Jewish beehive and may delight and rejoice therein."

And I, Mendele, whose intention has always been to be as useful as I can to our Jews, I could not restrain myself, and I said: "Before the Jewish authors, whose little finger is thicker than my loins, before the Jewish authors get around to publishing their tomes on Benjamin's voyage in Hebrew, I will, in the meantime, try to put out at least a digest in plain Yiddish. I have girded my loins like a hero and, old and weak as I am—may you be spared— I have made every effort to pull forth from the great treasure trove such gems as would be of interest to the Children of Israel, and to retell them freely, in my own style."

And I felt someone striking me from above with these words:

"Awake, Mendele, and creep out from behind the stove! Go forth and take up handfuls of fragrant herbs from Benjamin's treasure trove and prepare succulent dishes for thy brethren, to their liking."

And so, with God's help, I crept forth and prepared a tasty repast, which I will now set down before you. Eat, gentlemen, and hearty appetites!

I

WHO BENJAMIN IS, WHERE HE'S FROM, AND HOW HE WAS SUDDENLY OVERCOME BY WANDERLUST

"All my days," writes Benjamin the Third (he starts his book off in Hebrew but is kind enough to explain everything in Yiddish), *"All my days did I dwell in Moochville,* I mean, I spent my whole life in Moochville until my great voyage. I was born there, I was raised there, and there I married *the wife of my bosom,* my missus, *that pious spouse,* Zelda—*long may she live!"*

Moochville is a tiny, jerkwater shtetl, far from the highway, and so cut off from the rest of the world that if ever anyone happens to come driving in, the townsfolk open their doors and windows to gawk and gape at the newcomer. Neighbors, peering through open windows, ask one another: "Ha! Now just who could that be? Now just where did he pop up from out of a clear blue sky? What's he after anyway? Doesn't he have something up his sleeve? It just doesn't look kosher. You don't just up and come like that. There's more here than meets the eye, we'll have to get to the bottom of this. . . ."

And they all want to show how smart they are, how worldly,

and they spout conjectures off the tops of their heads, as rich as rubbish. Old folks tell tales and fables about wayfarers who arrived here in such and such a year. Comedians crack jokes, not quite on-color. The men stroke their beards and smirk, the older women scold the comedians just for fun, rebuking and laughing at once. Young wives peep up askance from their lowered eyes, holding their hands on their mouths and choking with mirth. The discussion about this issue rolls from home to home like a snowball, growing bigger and bigger until it rolls into the synagogue and behind the stove, the place to which all discussions about all issues come rolling—domestic secrets, the politics of Istanbul, the Sultan, the Austrian Kaiser, high finance, Rothschild's fortune compared with the wealth of the great aristocrats and the other magnates, as well as rumors about persecutions and about the Red Jews (the Ten Lost Tribes of Israel), and so on and so forth. And all these things are taken up in due order by a special committee of honorable and venerable Jews, who sit there all the livelong day until the wee hours of the night, abandoning wives and children and devoting themselves to all these matters, completely dedicating themselves, simply out of pure idealism, charging nothing for their efforts, not asking one kopek for their toil.

The issues often proceed from this committee, on to the bathhouse, up to the top bench, where they are resolved once and for all at a plenary meeting of the town burghers, and their decisions are so firm and abiding that all the kings of East and West could stand on their heads and wave their feet—and they wouldn't accomplish a thing. The Turk has had quite a few close shaves at top-bench plenary sessions. If several worthy householders hadn't stood up for him, then goodness knows where he'd be today. Once, poor Rothschild nearly lost about ten or fifteen million rubles here. But God came to his rescue a couple of weeks later. Everybody on the top bench was, well "high," the place was jumping, the whisk brooms were going full swing—and all at once they granted him a clear profit of some one hundred fifty million rubles!

Most of the townspeople here in Moochville are terribly poor and horribly needy (may you be spared), but it must be said that they are cheerful paupers and merry beggars, bursting with faith and hope, if not charity. Should you, for instance, happen to ask a Moochville Jew how he earns his living, he'll stand there flustered, unable to answer. But then, a little later, he'll gather his wits and reply in all innocence: "Me, earn a living? Me? Why, there is a God, you know, and he doesn't abandon his creatures, he helps, and he's sure to keep on helping, you know."

"But just what do you do? Do you have some kind of a trade or a business?"

"Praise the Lord, Blessed Be His Name! As you see me here, I have a gift from God, a precious instrument, a singing voice, I'm a cantor on high holidays in this area, I perform circumcisions, and I do occasional work rolling holes in matzos—I'm a whiz at it—and every so often I arrange a marriage, yes indeed! As you see me here, I have a seat in the synagogue. Furthermore—but this is strictly between you, me, and the lamp post—I have a little shop, where I can skim off a bit of cream, I own a goat that gives a lot of milk (knock on wood), and then not too far from here I've got a rich relative, whom I can also squeeze in bad times. And besides all these things, you know, the Good Lord watches over us like a father, and Jews are the merciful and the sons of the merciful, you know (knock on wood). . . .".

Furthermore, you have to credit the Moochvillers for being content with what God gives them and not being very fussy, Heaven forfend, when it comes to clothes and food. If the Sabbath kaftan, for instance, is shabby, grimy, sleazy, a little muddy and not so tidy, who cares, so long as it's satin and it shines. Now here and there the naked skin peeps out as through a sieve. But so what? What's the difference? Who's going to look? What about heels? Is that any worse than worn-out heels? Aren't heels human skin and flesh? . . .

A hunk of bread and potato soup—if you can get some—make a fine lunch. Not to mention a roll and pot roast on Friday—if only you can afford them—why, that's a royal treat, there's probably nothing better in the whole wide world. If these Jews were told about other dishes besides fish soup, roast, and carrot- or parsnip-stew, they'd think it highly peculiar and they would crack jokes and crack up, and split their sides as though the men

183

telling them this were stupid and cracked and trying to make fools of them, to pull their legs and the wool over their eyes, claiming a cow had jumped over the moon and laid an egg.

A piece of carob on the Fifteenth of Shebat (Arbor Day)—now there's a fruit for you, sheer bliss! The sight of it conjures up the Holy Land. The Moochvillers turn their eyes to heaven and moan: "Oh. . . . Lead us erect into our land, Merciful Father, our very own land, where the goats eat carob! . . ."

Once, somebody happened to bring a date into town—can you imagine—and you should have seen the way they came running to feast their eyes. Somebody else opened a Bible and demonstrated that *tamar* (date), was to be found in Scriptures: "Just think, the date, this very date, right here, comes from the Holy Land! . . ." Looking at the date, they were whisked away to the Holy Land. There they crossed the Jordan: There was the cave where our Patriarchs and Matriarchs are buried, there was Mother Rachel's tomb, there was the Wailing Wall. Now they were bathing in the hot springs of Tiberias, climbing up the Mount of Olives, gorging themselves on carob and dates, stuffing their pockets with Holy Land soil. "Ahhh!" they moaned, and tears welled up in everybody's eyes.

"At that time," says Benjamin, "all of Moochville, big as it is, was in the Holy Land. People spoke fervently about the Messiah, it was already afternoon on God's Friday. The new police commissioner, who had only arrived a short while back, was running things with an iron hand. He had torn the skullcaps off a few heads, shorn an earlock, seized a couple of poor men without passports in a side street one night, and arrested a goat for eating a newly thatched roof. And he was the reason why the committee behind the stove kept talking about the 'Turkish Sultan,' by which of course they meant the Tsar. How much longer would the guardian angel of 'Ishmael' stay in power? They launched into their usual discussion about the Ten Lost Tribes and how happily they lived in those faraway lands, in glory, grandeur, and wealth. They pulled out the Red Jews, the Sons of Moses, with tall tales about their strength and what not. Naturally, Eldad the Danite also danced in their midst. Those days were mainly responsible for the voyage I undertook afterwards."

184

Benjamin used to be like a chick in its egg, or a worm in horse radish, or a pig in a poke. He thought that the world ended on the other side of Moochville. Life couldn't be sweeter or better than here.

"I believed," says Benjamin at some point, "that no one could be richer than our tenant farmer. What a house, and what furnishings: four brass candle-holders, a six-armed chandelier topped by an eagle, two pareve copper pots and about five copper pans, a cupboard full of pewter plates, and, of course, about a dozen spoons of German silver, two goblets of real silver, a spice box, a menorah, a turnip clock in a double case, and a heavy string of artificial pearls, no less than two cows, plus a heifer about to calve, two Sabbath gaberdines, and so many other wonderful things.

"I believed there was no sage like Aizik-Dovid the son of Aaron-Yossel. Just think, people say that when he was young he actually dabbled in *fractions*. With a little more luck, he could have become a minister of state. Who, I wondered, could possibly look more majestic or speak more gracefully than our Khaikel the Stutterer? Or who could be so skilled in healing, a physician making the dead come alive, as our barber-surgeon, who, according to rumor, mastered the art of medicine from a Gypsy descendant of the Egyptian sorcerers."

In short, life in his little shtetl was fine and dandy for Benjamin. He did live in poverty, he and his wife and children wore rags and tatters, to be sure. But did Adam and his wife in paradise know anything like shame for going naked and bare-foot?

However, the wondrous fables about the Red Jews and the Ten Lost Tribes went deep into his heart, and from that time on he felt too confined in the town, he was drawn far, far, to distant places. He felt his heart pulling away, just as little children clutch out for the moon. At first blush, you may wonder what all those things had to do with it: a date, a police commissioner, a skullcap, an earlock, a poor Jew arrested in a side street late at night, a goat and a thatched roof. Yet the whole kit and kaboodle spawned a great change in Benjamin so that ultimately he blessed mankind with his renowned voyage. In the world, one often sees how big

185

things come from little things—very big things at that! Thus, the farmer sowed his wheat and rye, which the miller ground, and some of it went into the distillery and became liquor, and some of the flour got into the hands of Gittel, the tavernkeeper, and she leavened it, kneaded it, rolled it, and made knishes, in addition to which the Phoenicians discovered how to make glass thousands of years ago, and thus came cups and beakers. Now all these little things led to those carousers in a lot of towns, those infamous, those fine, feathered creatures. . . .

It could be that Benjamin had a spark of a globetrotter in him. But the spark would have died if the circumstances of the day and the tales of olden times had not puffed it up. And even if the spark had not dimmed out fully, Benjamin, but for those circumstances, would have had so little strength, that ultimately he would only have become a water-carrier or, at best, a drayman.

In my time, I've met a lot of draymen and carters who, I swear it, would have been able to become such travelers, like those who wander about today among Jews. . . . But that's all neither here nor there.

From then on, Benjamin eagerly devoted himself to Rabbah Bar Bar Hannah's sea voyages and desert travels. He also stumbled upon the book *Eldad the Danite*, the opus *The Travels of Benjamin*, by the explorer who journeyed to the ends of the earth seven hundred years ago, and the tome *In Praise of Jerusalem* with appendices, and the volume *Image of the World*, which, in seven tiny pages, contains all the Seven Wisdoms and relates amazing and miraculous things from the four corners of the earth and about its wild and wooly creatures. These books opened Benjamin's eyes and simply transformed him into a different person.

"Those wonderful stories," says Benjamin in his book, "got me so excited, 'Oh my! Oh my!' I so ofted shouted in my enthusiasm. 'If God would only help me see even one one-hundredth of all that with my own eyes!' My mind traveled far, far away. . . ."

From that time on, Moochville became too narrow for him. He made up his mind to do anything he could to get out, just like a chick starting to peck and creep its way out of the egg into the bright world.

HOW BENJAMIN BECOMES A MARTYR
AND ZELDA AN ABANDONED WIFE

By nature, our Benjamin the Traveler was lily-livered. At night, he was afraid to leave the house, and he wouldn't have slept alone in a room for any amount of money in the world. Going away a bit from the town simply meant risking his life, for who knows what could happen—God forbid! And he was scared to death of even the tiniest puppy.

"Once," Benjamin tells us, "once—I remember it as though it were yesterday—it was a sweltering day in the month of Tammuz (July), and our rabbi, together with one of his disciples, went to have a dip in the creek outside of town. I and a few other boys, friends of mine, followed the rabbi with great respect, we were certain we could rely on the rabbi and not have anything bad happen to us (God willing) and return home safe and sound. Why, that's no small potatoes—a rabbi, whom all the world respects. And who's second to none! And whose honorific titles alone cover an entire page! . . .

"Now the rabbi, our protector, strode far ahead of us with great dignity, and while he was undressing, along came a peasant and sicked his dog on him. Our protector, half dead with fear, zoomed away, clutching (if you'll pardon me) his unbuttoned trousers in one hand and his round plush hat in the other. We boys were flabbergasted. For if the Leviathan is caught on a fishhook, then what should the poor minnows in the mud do? We girded our loins and, as swift as stags, we ran headlong, screaming for help, shouting woefully, until we reached town, breathless, at top speed, with our hero. There was a tumult, a crowd, a clamor: 'Fire! Murder! Massacre!' No one knew what was happening!"

When Benjamin decided to travel to faraway lands, he resolved, first of all, to grow strong and cast off his fear. He forced himself to walk alone outside the town, even though it told on his health, for the terror made the poor man shed a lot of weight. His new behavior at home and in synagogue, his pale, dreamy face, and his absences outside of town for many hours, came as something of a surprise to everyone. Tongues wagged, and he was soon the talk of the shtetl.

Some people said: "He must be crazy, he's out of his mind. First of all," so they reasoned, "Benjamin was always a bit of a simpleton, he's got a screw loose in his head. Secondly, Mooch-ville hasn't had a town lunatic for years, and we Jews have a tradition—How does it go in Hebrew: *Every town hath its sage and its lunatic.* . . . Especially now, in this great heat! Why it's perfectly clear: He's insane."

Others, however (led by Aizik-Dovid the son of Aaron-Yossel and Sarah-Zlatte) shrugged, shrugged, and shrugged again: "Now, it's true that Benjamin is something of a simpleton, indeed quite a simpleton at that. Yet that doesn't necessarily lead to the conclusion that he has actually gone insane. For even assuming he *has,* the question remains: Why precisely now and not earlier? After all, two years ago and also last summer, the heat waves were far worse. Now you may argue that, according to the traditional saying, Moochville is no worse than other towns; so then the questions remains: Why haven't we had a lunatic for several years? What do we do with the traditional saying?

"Well, as for that tradition, the answer would appear to be— our river. We have a rule, you know, that since time immemorial, our river has unerringly taken one person every year, and yet nevertheless, it has not taken a victim for several years now! On the contrary, during these past few years it has shrunken so greatly that in some places one can actually cross it without wetting one's toes. . . . But as for Benjamin? . . . Well, the question is still moot. . . ."

Most people, however, including the women, said: "He must be carrying on with demons . . . with the devil. . . . Why else would he be wandering around in the dead of night, in the darkness? Why else would he be traipsing off for hours at a time? Why else would he be sleeping alone in the pantry?" Even Zelda, his very own wife, said that she could hear a knocking in the pantry at night, a banging, as if someone were walking about in there. . . .

This conversation, as usual, rolled off behind the stove, and from there to the council on the top bench. No conclusion about Benjamin was reached. However, there was general agreement about forming a committee of several pious and prominent men, including the scribe, and they would visit all the homes in proper order, according to the register, and inspect and investigate every mezuzah. And since the council regarded this matter as a community issue, for the benefit of the town, they resolved that to subsidize the expenses that such a committee would entail, they would raise the tax on kosher meat. . . .

There's an old saying in Moochville: "No matter what you talk about, it ends in death, and no matter what you discuss at a meeting, it ends with a higher meat tax." And indeed, that's virtually a law of nature, it can't be anything else. Nor does logic permit us to think otherwise, for it is written: "The end of a man is death, and the end of a Jew is—taxes!" Death and taxes are two laws of nature that we cannot abolish. Thus did the Eternal create the world, and the way He created it is good, this is the way it has to be. Only heretics would question it. . . .

A short time later, Benjamin had an experience that brought him renown.

One hot day in summer, around twelve noon, when the sun was broiling, he walked out of town and came deeper and deeper into a forest, about three or four miles. In his pocket, he had his books, without which he wouldn't move an inch. He sat down in the woods, leaning against a tree, and was lost in thought. He had a great deal to think about. His mind soon drifted off to those lands at the ends of the earth. He trudged over mountains, through valleys, across deserts, and to all the places that were in his books. He followed in the footsteps of Alexander the Great, Eldad the Danite, and others. He saw the terrifying dragon, the lindworm, serpents, lizards, and all kinds of vermin and reptiles. He traveled all the way to the Red Jews and conversed with the Sons of Moses. Then he came to and back, safe and sound, and wondered just how and when he would finally undertake his voyage.

Meanwhile, as he was musing, night fell. He stood up,

stretched his legs, and started for home. He walked and walked, but he was still in the woods. He slogged along for an hour, for two, three, four hours, no edge or end in sight. He roamed deeper into the woods, where it was so dark that he couldn't see beyond the tip of his nose. All at once, a stormy wind swept up and a pelting rain came down. There was lightning and thunder, and the trees roared fearfully! Benjamin stopped, drenched to the skin, his teeth chattered with cold, wetness, and great dread. He imagined a bear would pounce on him, a lion, a leopard would tear him to pieces. There was the matool, which, according to *Image of the World*, is a huge towering monster with two long arms that can hurl down an elephant. Benjamin was terrified, poor thing, and he was starving to boot, he had eaten nothing all day but a buckwheat cake. In his great affliction, he began to say his evening prayer, and he prayed fervently, with all his heart.

God helped, and the dawn came. Our Benjamin went on rambling about aimlessly, he plodded and plodded until he finally managed to reach a narrow path. He trudged along this path for an hour or so until he suddenly heard a man's voice in the distance. Instead of feeling joy, he was all a-tremble (it shouldn't happen to our worst enemies). All he could think of was: brigands! He was so scared that he breathlessly doubled back. But then he promptly had second thoughts: "C'mon, Benjamin! You want to wander so far over seas and deserts teeming and crawling with horrible vermin, beasts of prey, and wild savages, and here you're scared at the very thought of bumping into a brigand! Oh my, Benjamin! You should really be ashamed of yourself, I swear! Did Alexander the Great of Macedonia run away like you? Did Alexander despair, like you, when he flew through the air on his eagle's back, and there was no meat left on the tip of the spear, the meat that the eagle nibbled at and flew higher to get at? No! Alexander the Great did *not* run away! Alexander the Great cut out a chunk of his own flesh and stuck it on the spear! Courage, Benjamin, take heart! God only wants to test you. If you pass the test, you'll do well and fare well! You'll be a valiant man and you'll deserve the privilege of having His Holy Name make your wish come true about reaching the Sons of Moses and talking to them about the Jews here at home. You can tell them every last detail about our Jews here, what they do and how they live. If you just overcome this ordeal and go back to where the voice came from, you'll conquer all fears and terrors. You'll be a wonderful person, a blessing, a paragon among the Children of Israel, and you'll bring honor upon all Moochville. Moochville and Macedonia—both cities will be equally famous throughout the world because of Alexander of Moochville and Benjamin of Macedonia! . . ."

Our Benjamin really did turn back and he strode as courageously and confidently as a hero, until he saw before him: the brigand! It was a farmer riding on a wagon, which was filled with sacks and drawn by a pair of oxen.

"*Dobry dyen!* Good day!" said Benjamin in Ukrainian, as he drew nearer, his voice suddenly changing—it had everything in it, wailing and pleading, as if to say: "Okay, do whatever you like with me!" And imploring: "Help, have pity on me, on my wife and children, the poor things!"

After speaking, or rather shouting and weeping his *dobry dyen,* Benjamin remained speechless, as if strangled. His head whirled, his eyes darkened, his legs buckled, and he fell down lifeless.

When he opened his eyes and came to, he found himself sprawling on a big sack of potatoes in the wagon and covered with a thick, coarse coat. At his head lay a trussed-up rooster, who glared at him askance with one eye and scratched him with his claws. At his feet, there were baskets of young garlic, onions, and other vegetables, and apparently eggs, for the chaff they were buried in kept flying into his face and covering his eyes. The farmer sat there, calmly smoking his pipe and calling "sop, heita, sop!" to the oxen every moment. The oxen barely stirred, and the wheels creaked wildly, each in a different voice.

Together, they melded into an ear-shattering creak-concert. The rooster didn't seem to care much for the creaking either, because every time the wheels turned, letting out a long, shrill squeal, the rooster dug his nails into Benjamin and emitted such a quick, angry cockadoodledoo that a muffled rattling came from his throat for a few seconds afterwards. Benjamin felt numb in every limb and he lay there dazed for a long, long time. He had gone through so much: terror, hunger, rain, and cold! He imagined a Turk had captured him in the desert and was carrying him off somewhere to sell him into slavery. "If only," thought Benjamin, "if only he sells me to a Jew, then at least there'll be some hope for me. But if I end up with a Gentile prince or even, God forbid, a princess, then I'll be doomed forever." The story of Joseph and Potiphar's wife flashed through his mind, and he felt so miserable that he let out a heavy groan.

Upon hearing Benjamin's groan, the farmer turned around, then shifted closer to him, and asked in Ukrainian:

"Well, my li'l Jew, how are ya? Feelin' better?"

Benjamin's head had cleared a bit and he remembered everything that had happened to him. But still, he found his predicament very serious. He didn't know a word of the farmer's language, so what could he do? How could he answer him? How could he inquire and find out exactly where the man was taking him?

Benjamin tried to sit up. But it was no use. His legs ached horribly.

"Ya feelin' better?" the farmer asked again, and in the same breath he shouted at his oxen: "Sop, heita, sop!"

"Betta, yes, legs, legs, oh, oh!" poor Benjamin tried to speak the goyish language as best he could and pointed at his legs.

"Where ya from, my little Jew?"

"Wheyafrom?!" Benjamin repeated in a cantorial warble. "Me, Ben, Benjamin, from Moochville."

"Oh, so you're from Moochville? Then why did you glare at me like I was crazy?! Well, maybe *you're* crazy, goddamn it! Sop, heita, sop!"

"Me, you see, tell you at start, me Benjamin, from Moochville!" answered Benjamin with a woebegone face, raising his arms and pleading: "In Moochville, wife, give schnapps, shabbes roll, and thank you good."

The farmer apparently got Benjamin's drift.

"Okay, little Jew!" he cried, sat down in his seat facing the oxen and called: "Sop, heita!"

A couple of hours later, the wagon rumbled into the marketplace of Moochville. Women and men crowded around with various questions.

One man yelled: "Hey, whattaya want for the rooster? For the onions?"

Another asked: "Ya got eggs, potatoes?"

A question shot out of the crowd: "Listen, did you see a Jew on the way here? One of our people, Benjamin, has been missing since yesterday!"

And before the farmer even had a chance to reply, the women swarmed all over his wagon like locusts, pulled away the coat, and then shouted in unison:

"Benjamin! . . . He's here! Tsippe-Kroina, Bathsheba-Braindl, run straight over to Zelda, tell her the good news! Her lost husband's been found! She's not abandoned after all!"

There was a tumult, more people came running, all Moochville was on the move, everybody and his uncle dashed over to look at Benjamin. They showered him with comments, questions, jokes, they said they'd been hunting for him, searching for him all day and night, they'd already decided that he was martyred and his wife abandoned.

Suddenly, in the midst of the hubbub, his wife came running up, weeping. She wrung her hands at the sight of her one and only sprawling there pale and lifeless, unable to move a limb. The poor woman didn't know what to do: Should she curse him, pour out her heavy, bitter heart to him, or should she show him her joy, her delight that God had assisted her, her, the abandoned wife?

A few minutes later, Benjamin, lying on the sack of potatoes, was taken home across the marketplace in a grand parade. All the people of Moochville, young and old, paid homage to him, no one needed to be asked twice, and they escorted him, shouting and yelling: "Martyr! Martyr! Martyr!"

From that moment on, the name "Martyr" remained with Benjamin forever. He was known as Benjamin the Martyr and his wife as Zelda the Widow.

The town healer visited Benjamin that very same day and helped with all possible remedies. He applied leeches and

193

cupping glasses, shaved the patient's head, and told him, upon leaving, that after all these remedies he would recover, God willing, and would be able to go to synagogue the very next day—if he had the strength—and thank the Good Lord for escaping death.

III

HOW BENJAMIN HITCHED UP WITH SENDER THE HOUSEWIFE

This ordeal, which was so harrowing for Benjamin, which caused so much grief for his wife and so much gossip in town, behind the stove, and on the top bench, should—one might think—have forever dislodged Benjamin's plan of traveling to distant places. But far from it! In a pig's eye! The plan was lodged more firmly than ever before. From that point on, Benjamin felt great esteem for himself as an experienced man who has gone through a great deal in his life. He appreciated himself tenfold for his strength and bravery in enduring so many trials and vanquishing his cowardice. He began seeing himself as a hero, a philosopher, an initiate in all the Seven Wisdoms (or as much of them as is contained in *Image of the World*), a wise man who had read more than his fill of such books and knew what was happening all over the earth. He began to understand himself now and pity himself—that he, a man like him, poor thing, should be like a rose among thorns. Where? In Moochville, some backwater town, among ignorant people, who grasp nothing, know nothing about their own lives! The jokes and rumors circulating about him were what really egged him on to travel. He yearned to get out of Moochville as quickly as possible. "If only I can do it," he kept thinking, "If only I can travel there, far away, and come back safe and sound with salvations and consolations for Jews, respected and renowned throughout the world, then all Moochville will realize who Benjamin is, and what a great man he is! . . ."

Meanwhile, only minor obstacles kept Benjamin from his journey. First of all, where could he get the money? He never had a kopek in his pocket. He always sat idly in synagogue, and his missus was a "woman of valor," the breadwinner, for she owned a little stand, which she had put up soon after they had moved from her parents' home. But, I ask you, how much was the little shop really worth? If she hadn't knitted socks, if she hadn't plucked feathers in winter till late at night, if she hadn't rendered fat to sell at Passover, if she hadn't gotten occasional bargains on market days from friendly peasants—then they wouldn't have had enough to keep body and soul together.

Should Benjamin pawn any of the household belongings? But what was there really? A couple of brass candlesticks, which Zelda had inherited from her parents. She used them for the Sabbath candles, was forever polishing them, and enjoyed them so much. She had no jewelry except for a silver ring set with a pearl from her mother's headband, and she kept the ring locked up, wearing it only for major celebrations and on congratulatory visits. Should Benjamin sell any of his own clothes? But all he owned was a satin gaberdine for the Sabbath, which he still had from his wedding, it was worn and tattered in front and in back, and the yellow lining showed through in places. True, he also had a sheepskin overcoat—if one could call it that, for want of a better name! The collar wasn't even lined. At the wedding, his father (long may he live!) had said don't spare the collar, make it long and generous, and line it for now on top with a piece of lining left over from the overcoat; and he had promised that once the rest of the dowry was paid, he would line the entire coat and trim the collar with squirrel fur. But the rest of the dowry had never come, and so the coat and the collar remained as they were to this very day. . . .

In addition to the money problem, Benjamin just didn't know how to get away from his home.

Could he discuss the journey with his wife and tell her everything in detail? God forbid and heaven forfend! She would scream and rage and weep and plead and she would certainly think he'd lost his mind, for how can a woman be smart enough to understand such matters? A wife may be a "woman of valor," but she's still a mere woman for all that. The lowliest man has

195

more intelligence in his little finger than the finest and smartest female could ever possibly have in her head. . . .

Should he sneak off without saying good-bye? That would be slightly unpleasant, the kind of thing a Litvak Jew might do. Then again, should he just remain home and forget about traveling? That was absolutely impossible. It was nothing less than suicide.

The journey had become second nature for Benjamin, like praying three times daily. And so he had to keep thinking about the journey at every moment of the day. And he couldn't shake it off even when he slept, he kept dreaming about it all night long. It took root deep in his heart and grabbed hold of his eyes and ears so that he no longer saw or heard the things in front of him, he could see and hear only what was happening far, far away, in those distant lands. Often, while talking with someone, he would suddenly throw in: India, Sambatyon, Antikuda, lindworm, dragon, donkey, mule, carob, manna, Turk, Tartar, brigand, and similar words.

The journey *had* to be taken, but what about the obstacles? Benjamin was all at sea. He felt he needed someone to talk to about the whole thing.

And there dwelt a man in the city of Moochville and his name was called Sender—he was named after his great-grandfather—*and this Sender was of a simple mind*—that is to say, he was plain, unlearned, sort of ignorant. In the synagogue, his pew was behind the pulpit, and that alone was the best sign that he didn't belong to the Moochville elite, the upper crust, the cream. When the men talked in synagogue or elsewhere, he would usually listen quietly like an outsider. If ever he did put in a word, it would provoke great mirth. Not because it was particularly witty or original, but simply because any word from his lips made people laugh, even though the poor man said it quite naively, not intending to make anyone laugh. On the contrary: When people laughed, his eyes would gape and he wondered why they were laughing. He never resented the mirth, for he was humble and good-natured, like a gentle cow, and he didn't even realize there was anything to resent. If somebody was laughing, well, okay, let him laugh, so long as he enjoyed it.

Still, we have to admit that Sender's comments occasionally harbored a bright idea, even though he didn't realize it and was speaking quite naively. People liked to play jokes on him. On the Ninth of Ab, the fast for the destruction of the Temple, Jews like to throw burrs at each other, and most of the burrs got ensnarled in his earlocks. During the night of the Great Hosanna, the seventh day of the Feast of Tabernacles, when everyone stays awake, most of the pillows that were thrown around landed on his head. In contrast, he received the smallest share of buckwheat crackers and liquor on religious occasions or liquor simply for no special occasion.

In short, Sender was the scapegoat any place and any time. Now, by nature, Sender wasn't opinionated, like other people. If a man said one thing, that was all right with Sender. He would let the man have his way, not to belittle his own way so that the other man would belittle his own way for Sender's way. Sender just simply went along with him, that was all.

"Why should I care?" he would say. "Why should I worry? If you say so, then it's okay, it's fine with me."

Among boys, Sender was a boy. He would often hang around with them, talk to them, play with them, and enjoy himself. When he was with them, Sender was truly a docile animal, he allowed the children to come up and ride him and scratch him under the chin. The pranksters would climb on his head and pull his beard. Sometimes passers-by would be annoyed at this and shout:

"Mind your manners, you scoundrels! Have respect for an adult, a man with a beard! Why are you pulling his beard out!?"

"It's all right, it's all right," Sender would say. "I don't mind. I don't care. So let them scratch me."

Poor Sender's home life was no bed of roses. His wife wore the breeches, and he had a terrible, horrible time with her. She ruled with a reign of terror and occasional punches, and the poor wretch had to put up with it. Just before a holiday, she would tie a cloth around his beard and make him whitewash the house. He would peel potatoes for her, roll and slice noodles, stuff the gefilte fish, bring in firewood, put it in the stove, and light the fire—just like a housewife. That was why people nicknamed him Sender the Housewife.

197

Now it was this man, Sender the Housewife, whom our Benjamin selected to pour out his heart to; Sender would help him figure things out. What was the reason? Why Sender of all people? Well, Benjamin had always been fond of him. There was a lot he liked about him, they felt the same way about a number of things, and Benjamin often had a wonderful time talking to him. Perhaps Benjamin also counted on the fact that Sender never insisted on getting his way: Sender would accept Benhamin's idea and go along with everything he said. And if Sender were ever to dig in his heels on any points, well, then Benjamin would win him over with God's help and with his own glib tongue.

And it came to pass that when Benjamin did come unto Sender, he did find him in the act of removing the exteriors of tubers—Sender was peeling potatoes—on the dairy bench. One cheek was blazing red and his left eye was swollen blue with a scratch underneath as though fingernails had torn his face. He sat there, numb, dismal, gloomy, like a young wife whose husband has deserted her and vanished overseas, or at least slapped her face. . . .

Sender's wife was not at home.

"Good morning, Sender! Why are you so gloomy?" asked Benjamin, entering and pointing at Sender's cheek? "Is she at it again? Where is your lady Cossack?"

"At the market."

"Great!" Benjamin almost shouted for joy. "Put down your potatoes, old friend, and come into the alcove with me. No one's there, right? I don't need any chaperon with you now, I want to tell you what's on my mind. I can't hold back anymore, I'm seething inside. Hurry, Sender, hurry! She might come and ruin everything before we're done!"

"Fine with me! You want me to hurry, so I'll hurry. It's okay with me!" exclaimed Sender and hurried into the alcove.

"Sender," Benjamin started off, "tell me, do you know what's beyond Moochville?"

"Sure, I know. Pickafite Inn. You can get a good glass of vodka there!"

"Don't be an idiot. I mean further on, a lot further."

"Further than Pickafite Inn?" Sender exclaimed in surprise.

"Further? I don't know. Do you know, Benjamin?"

"Do I know? How can you ask! Do I ever know! That's where the world begins," Benjamin said ecstatically, like Columbus discovering America.

"But where is 'there'?"

"There, there," Benjamin was ablaze. "The dragon! The lindworm!"

"The lindworm that Solomon used to cut the stones for the Temple?" Sender asked timidly.

"Yes, Sender, yes, yes. In the Holy Land. In those places. . . . Would you like to go there?"

"Would you?"

"What a question! I *do* want to go there, and soon I *will* be there!"

"I'm envious, Benjamin. You'll be eating carob and dates to your heart's content. Oh me!"

"You can eat them too, Sender. You have as much right to be in the Holy Land as me."

"I do have the right. But how can we get there? The Turk's in the Holy Land."

"There's a way, Sender, there's a way. Listen, do you know anything about the Red Jews?"

"I've heard enough stories about them behind the stove. But I don't know exactly where they live or how to get to them. If I knew, I'd probably tell you. Why not? It's okay with me."

"Ha! And *I* know, you see," Benjamin said proudly, drawing *In Praise of Jerusalem* out of his pocket. "Just look at what's written here. I'll read it to you:

" 'When I arriv'd in Bruti,' that's what it says, 'I found four Jews from Babylon. I spoke with one of them, who understood the Holy Tongue and whose Name was Rabbi Moses, and he told me very true Stories about the River Sambatyon, which he had heard from Ishmaelites who had seen it, and there, he said, dwelt the Sons of Moses.'

"And it goes on: 'According to what the Head of the Jewish Community told me: Some thirty years ago, a Man of the Tribe of Simeon had stay'd with him and he told him that there were four Tribes where he dwelt. One of them was the Tribe of

199

Issachar, and they only study the Torah, and a Man of this Tribe is King over all the Tribes!'

"Now listen to what it says in this book, *The Travels of Benjamin:* 'From there it is a Journey of a Score of Days to the Nisbon Mountains, which are on the River Gozan. And in the Nisbon Mountains dwell four Tribes: the Tribe of Dan, the Tribe of Zebulun, the Tribe of Asher, and the Tribe of Naphtali. They have Countries and Cities in the Mountains. On one side, they are encompass'd by the River Gozan. They are not afflicted with the Yoke of the Nations, only a King rules over them, and his Name is Joseph Amarekla ha-Levi. And they have a Covenant with the infidel Turks.' Besides that, there are so many things recorded about the Rachiabites in the land of Tema, they have a Jewish king and they fast and always pray to God for the Exiles of Israel. Well, what do you think, Sender? What would they say, old friend, if they suddenly saw me, their brother Benjamin of Moochville, coming to visit them? Ha, what do you think?"

"They'd be absolutely thrilled, I tell you, Benjamin. What a guest! What a welcome guest! Everyone will invite you home for a meal. Probably even King Amarekla himself. Give them all my best regards. If I could, I swear, I would go along with you myself."

"Ha!" said Benjamin, ablaze with a new thought that popped into his head. "Ha! Sender, my old friend! What if you *did* go with me on the journey? Don't be a fool, I swear, it's the chance of a lifetime. I'm going alone and I'll take you too. It'll be more fun if I have someone with me, Sender. And if I become king there—stranger things have happened—I swear I'll make you viceroy. Let's shake on it. . . . Why should you sit here, you poor man, and go through the worst sufferings of Exile because of your wife—that shrew. Just take a look at your cheek, Sender. You have a dark and dismal life with her. C'mon, Sender, travel with me. You won't regret it, I promise you."

"Well," said Sender, "if that's what you want, that's what I'll do. And as for her? Why, I'd be an idiot telling her where I'm off to."

"Sender, my dearest friend, let me kiss you," cried Benjamin, overjoyed, and he lovingly threw his arms around Sender the Housewife. "Friend of my bosom, with just one word you've solved a dilemma, a big dilemma. I agree with you: As for her? I mean *my* wife: Who cares! But there's one other problem? Where are we going to get the money?"

"Money? Do you want to buy new clothes or turn your coat? Listen, if you want my opinion, it's really not necessary. In fact, on the road, it's better to wear old clothes. Once we're there, we'll probably get beautiful new coats."

"Yes, that's true. Once I'm there, my worries'll be over. But while we're traveling, we'll need money just for food."

"What do you mean, for food, Benjamin? Are you gonna take along a whole kitchen? What for? Aren't there taverns and homes along the way?"

"I don't understand what you mean, Sender," cried Benjamin puzzled.

"I mean," Sender answered naively, "as long as there are homes, we can go begging. What do all other Jews do? Nowadays, some Jews go begging to other houses, and then those people go begging to still other houses. That's the way it is with Jews. . . . Just an interest-free loan. . . ."

"Dammit, you're right," said Benjamin joyfully. "You've opened my eyes. If that's the way it is, then, thank the Lord, I'm totally prepared and I've got everything I need. We can leave tomorrow, at the crack of dawn, when the town's still asleep. It's no good wasting time, dammit. Do you agree?"

"If you wanna go tomorrow, then it's okay with me. I don't care."

"So listen, Sender. Tomorrow, at the crack of dawn, I'm going to sneak out of the house, very quietly. I'll wait for you by the abandoned windmill. Don't forget, Sender, tomorrow morning, at the crack of dawn, you're to come out there. Don't forget," Benjamin repeated and started for the door.

"Wait a moment, Benjamin, just wait!" said Sender, rummaging in the breast pocket of his jacket. He finally fished out an old, sweaty piece of leather, bound crisscross with strings and some twenty knots. "Look, Benjamin! I managed to save this money behind my wife's back all the years we've been married. It'll be useful for us at the start, won't it?"

"Sender, you deserve to be hugged and kissed a thousand

times!" Benjamin shouted, grabbing hold of Sender the House-wife.

"Goddamn your eyes! Just look at the love birds! Hugging and kissing, and there's a goat in the house eating up the potatoes! May the worms eat your body!" screeched a voice.

The screeching voice was Sender's better half. She stood there, blazing with fury, one hand pointing at the goat and the other hand beckoning to Sender. With his head hanging, Sender very, very slowly inched over to her like a naughty child about to be whipped.

"Be strong, friend of my bosom, this is the last time. . . . Just don't forget tomorrow," Benjamin whispered into Sender's ear and stole out like a kitten.

IV

HOW BENJAMIN AND SENDER LEAVE MOOCHVILLE

Early the next morning, before the shepherd had even gathered the herd, our Benjamin was already standing, bright-eyed and bushy-tailed, near the windmill, with a bundle under his arm. The bundle contained all the things that were necessary for the journey: a prayer shawl and prayer thongs, the prayer book *Path of Life*, a copy of *A Law unto Israel*, a Psalter, and all the volumes without which he could not stir, like a craftsman without his tools. His Sabbath gaberdine was also tucked inside—after all, clothes make the man, and you have to keep up appearances. His pocket contained fourteen and a half kopeks, which he had filched from under his wife's pillow before sneaking off.

In short, he had everything he needed—thank the Lord—and was all set to go.

Meanwhile, the sun was rising beautifully, her radiant face staring down at the world. A single glance of hers delighted and exhilarated everything. Trees and grass smiled sweetly before the large tears of nightly dew fully dried, just the way little children burst into cheerful laughter at the sight of a glittering toy, though still weeping, though tears as big as beans swell in their eyes. The birds in the fields soared through the air, playing and warbling around Benjamin as though saying:

"Come on, let's sing and rejoice and gladden that fine man by the windmill. That's Benjamin himself, that's Benjamin of Moochville, the Alexander the Great of our time. He is leaving his native soil, abandoning his wife and children, going forth on a mission, to wander and wander. That is the great Benjamin, who has left his tent like the sun, and, like a hero, is looking forward to the road with his bundle under his arm! He is strong as a leopard, light as an eagle, to do the will of our Father in Heaven. Sing and play, one and all: Trililili, trill, trill! Rejoice, sing, and delight his heart! . . ."

Benjamin was truly glad at heart. He thought to himself: "Why, I'm the happiest man in the world. There's nothing I lack (knock on wood!). There's nothing I need. I've taken care of my wife, God be praised. She's got a little business of her own. And I'm a free bird, just like the birds in the meadows here. The whole world lies open before me. With my skill, with my courage, and with my knowledge of the Seven Wisdoms, there's no way I could get lost. Besides, I'm a Jew, I have faith in God. Aside from all their virtues, Jews live their lives with faith in God, and God brings them through."

Benjamin felt so wonderful that his mouth opened, and, in a lovely falsetto, he began singing the march of "Melekh Elion." His voice blended with the warbling of the birds, the humming of the flies, the chirping of the crickets, and the concert wafted up to the Good Lord's Throne of Glory high in the seventh heaven!

Meanwhile, a good deal of time wore on, and Sender didn't show up. This began to worry Benjamin and it destroyed his good mood. He looked in all directions, he peered his eyes out. But it was useless. He heard nothing, saw nothing, there was no sign of Sender!

Could that shrew of his have forced some chore upon him? But it was too early for that, all Moochville was sound asleep. Housewives don't start peeling potatoes till later on, they don't begin preparing lunch until they've nagged and argued with their husbands, given the kids a good licking, and hung out the laundry to dry. . . .

Our Benjamin was at a loss what to do, he felt unhappy, terribly unhappy. Should he return home? Not on your life! What a terrible idea! Alexander the Great burnt the bridge when he crossed to India so that he wouldn't be able to turn back. Should he start off without Sender? No, that was unthinkable, really unthinkable! He greatly needed Sender. Since joining up with him, he felt that the world had become brighter. Going off without Sender would have been strange and unnatural, like a ship without a helm, a state without a prime minister.

Suddenly, far in the distance, there appeared something like a human shape. It looked like Sender and yet it wasn't, it seemed to be a woman in a calico dress and a kerchief.

Benjamin felt a stab in his heart, he almost dropped dead, he turned pale as a ghost. He thought it was his wife walking along—not, not walking, but running, dashing. Soon she'd come hurrying up, pounce upon him furiously, pour out her heavy, bitter heart, and drag him home, nagging and yammering.

"God alone knows," writes Benjamin himself, "what terrors, what horrors I endured at that moment. I would rather have encountered a hundred dragons than my wife. For a dragon bites only the body, the flesh, whereas a wrathful woman chews and chomps the soul. But God Praised Be His Name did strengthen me, I mustered my courage and fled, I hid behind the windmill and peered out like a lion waiting for his prey."

A few minutes later, Benjamin sprang out from his hiding place, leaping and shrieking like a lunatic.

"Sender! For God's sake!"

It was Sender trudging along in a calico bathrobe, with a greasy kerchief around his cheeks. His eyes were black and surrounded by scratches. He held a stick in one hand and a large bundle over his shoulders. But for Benjamin, he was the loveliest creature in the world, like a ravishing bride in the eyes of the groom.

Benjamin describes his joy at that moment as follows: "Even as a hind that yearneth for springs of water, even as a thirsty man who findeth in the desert living, gushing water that runneth from the peak of a rock, thus did my yearning body rejoice at the

204

sight of Sender, my promised one, my faithful companion."

"What's wrong, Sender? Why've you kept me waiting so long?"

"Goodness, I went to your home," replied Sender naively. "By the time I arrived there and by the time I managed to wake your Zelda, it got pretty late."

"You woke Zelda?!" shouted Benjamin in a strange and utterly different voice. "You lunatic! Why in the world did you do that?"

"What do you mean why?" exclaimed Sender in surprise. "Why? Because first I knocked on your pantry door, and you didn't answer, so I began knocking on the front door, knock, knock, knock! Well, and then Zelda got up, scared to death, and I asked for you."

"Sender, we're sunk! You've cooked our goose! Why, Zelda's gonna come running after us, and she'll—"

"Oh, don't worry, Benjamin! She told me to go to hell! She was so furious at me, as though I'd robbed her cooky jar or something! 'You and that husband of mine can go straight to hell, goddamn you!' That's what she said, and she slammed the door. I was so confused that I stood there for a long time. But then I remembered about the windmill, and I figured you must be there already. That's probably why your wife said: 'You and that husband of mine can go straight to hell!' It stands to reason—she probably saw that you were gone."

"What, Sender?! She saw I was gone? Maybe she followed you! Maybe she's coming!"

"God forbid, Benjamin! She just drew the chain. And before I left, I knocked again and I asked: 'Hey Zelda, do you want me to tell your husband anything, or do you have anything you want me to give him? Huh?' But she didn't say a word. She must sleep like a log (knock on wood) and she was probably dead to the world. Well, so I said: 'Zelda, you're sleeping, so sleep, and pleasant dreams. So long, Zelda!' I said and I went away."

Sender's last words resuscitated Benjamin like drops of medicine. He started breathing freely and panting as though a weight had dropped from his heart. His face shone and his eyes blazed with sheer joy.

"And now, Sender," he let out a wild yell. "Put your right foot forward!"

At that moment, in a pool off to the side, the frogs began

croaking, as though saying farewell to our friends and striking up a march for them. Moochville frogs croak very loudly in their moldy mud. They are as world-renowned as the bedbugs and cockroaches of Dnieprovitz.

V

WHAT HAPPENS TO OUR FRIENDS AT THE VERY START

Our friends strode off and tramped at a smart pace, as though tearing loose from a chain or being driven by a whip. Their broad coattails billowing in the wind made them look like a ship scudding along with full sails. I'm sure there are stagecoach drivers in our part of the country who wish their horses were as swift as our wayfarers, by God! Crows and ravens, strolling about on the ground, respectfully moved aside and flew in all directions for fear of the two-legged creatures that were dashing along with such diligence and enthusiasm.

No pen could possibly describe how happy, how utterly happy they were. They were so wildly delighted, so deeply contented—with themselves and with the whole world.

Sender looked jubilant about escaping from his wife's hands and leaving such a harsh and bitter life. Yesterday had been especially harsh and bitter for the poor man, a day of sorrows and sufferings that had left a trail of bruises on his body, that had stormily uprooted a mass of hairs from his beard, and that had openly left a black seal on both eyes. May all you henpecked husbands be spared the dismal reproof that poor Sender had gotten from his missus yesterday morning.

For quite a while, our friends ran on, breathless and silent, never exchanging a word. They were very hot, and big beads of sweat emerged on their faces. Sender had to stop every so often, gasping like a goose.

"Faster, Sender, faster!" Benjamin kept heartening him and eagerly dashing ahead, like a hero who has girded his loins and is coursing to battle with his bow and arrow.

"Oh please, Benjamin, have pity on my soul!" pleaded Sender. "I don't have the strength to keep up with you. You're running like a stag in the mountains and like a billy goat in front of the herd."

"Faster, Sender, faster!" Benjamin kept shouting and leaping on, proud of his skill. "Why, Sender, I could keep running and running till the ends of the earth!"

"But Benjamin, what's your rush?" asked Sender. "Believe me, we won't miss anything. If we arrive a day or even several days later, it won't matter much. The world isn't coming to an end. This is still the sixth millenium, and so far as I know, the world is supposed to exist until the seventh millenium. That's centuries away!"

"Faster, Sender, faster! We can't waste time. The sooner we get out of here, the better. Make an effort, Sender, push yourself. Don't worry. Once we arrive, you can stretch your legs, you'll breathe and live like a prince."

"You're so right, Benjamin. You want me to go faster—that's fine with me. I don't care. You've talked me into it. But what about my legs? What can I do with my legs?"

Benjamin had no choice. For Sender's sake, he had to slow down.

When the sun came out of her case and was nicely heating and broiling with her luminous beams, our wanderers dropped down by a wayside grove. They lay there, sweating like mad, huffing and puffing with heaving sides. The sweat burnt Sender's bruises, and the pain was like the pricking of needles.

After a rest, the first thing they did was to take out their prayer shawls and prayer thongs and say their prayers. Benjamin rocked vehemently and prayed ardently, for which he indeed deserved a glass of vodka, but where could he get any out here? He would have liked at least a piece of bread. He was faint with hunger, his stomach was growling after that sturdy hike, he could have gobbled up the entire world, and yet, the devil take it, he didn't even have a crust of bread on him. He peered all around, cracked his knuckles, yawned, scratched himself, smacked his lips, said "well, well" several times, stroked and tugged his earlocks and his beard, then scratched himself again, said "well" again, and then, after mulling a bit, he reached into his bundle, pulled out a tiny volume the size of a prayer book, and read while humming a Pentecostal chant, the "Akdamut."

"Sender!" Benjamin broke off in the middle. "Do you know what I'm crooning? And do you know why I'm crooning it with this melody?"

"You must be hungry," Sender replied naively.

"What does that have to do with the price of eggs?" Benjamin protested. "But if I *were* hungry, then what?"

"Well, that's why you're singing," replied Sender. "You know what the goyim say: 'When does the Jew sing? When he's hungry!' If you feel like singing, Benjamin, then sing, sing to your heart's content. Meanwhile, I'll get busy."

Sender reached into his bundle and pulled out a bag.

"Oh, c'mon! You don't understand, you don't see why I'm doing it," said Benjamin. "My dear, foolish Sender, let me explain the reason."

But meanwhile, Sender went on with what he was doing and slowly, slowly he untied the bag. When Benjamin looked, sheer joy poured through his two hundred forty-eight parts. The bag was filled with all kinds of goodies—bread, pieces of challah left over from the Sabbath, cucumbers, radishes, onions, and garlic! Sender had thought of everything, like a good housewife, and Benjamin thought the world of him, thought more of him than before. His heart surged because God Blessed Be His Name had granted him such a dear companion for the journey. "Sender was sent to me by God," said Benjamin to himself, "like manna to the Children of Israel in the desert."

When they had refreshed themselves, Sender wrapped up the few leftovers and packed them in his sack, commenting:

"This bit of food will come in handy again, and the sack a thousand times over, throughout our lives. We'll use it to go begging, God willing. Don't worry, the Good Lord will provide."

Remember the wonderful tablecloth in the fairy tale? You command: "Tablecloth, tablecloth, give me food! Give me this, give me that!" And the tablecloth gives. Now for us Jews, this wonderful and miraculous tablecloth is the beggar's bag. Many, very many Jews nourish themselves all their lives with miraculous ease from the beggar's bag, which they then pass on to their children and children's children. The bag is always the same in essence, but in different classes it gets different forms and names. Among the common people, it's simply a beggar's bag, a plain canvas sack. Further up the ladder, it assumes all kinds of shapes: a chest, a tax container, a religious office, a fraternal order, an alms box, a community chest, a free-loan society, a writer who's a windbag, and so on and so forth. Yet they're all nothing but bags, beggar's bags, genuine Jewish beggar's bags! . . .

"Sender!" cried Benjamin, fortified by Sender's words. "The two of us are a marriage made in heaven, we're like a body and its soul. *You* take care of the material things, like food and drink on the journey, and *I'll* take care of spiritual matters. I'll ask you once again, Sender: Do you know why I was singing "Akdamut"? I had a definite goal in mind. I'm making sure now that when the Good Lord brings us safe and sound to the Sons of Moses, we'll be able to speak to them and have a good talk. They sort of speak Aramaic there, but mostly the "Akdamut" tongue. It's my opinion that Eldad the Danite, who traveled from there to our land, was the author of the "Akdamut" chant. Why, *'vesh-oroyes shuso'* means: 'I start to speak.' Remember, Sender, here in these foreign countries, we can get along with our language, with Yiddish. But there, they certainly don't know a word of Yiddish."

"Well, in these matters, I'll rely totally on you," Sender murmured submissively. "You're a learned man and you study your books. You certainly know what you're doing and where you're going. Why, I didn't even ask you if we're going the right way. You go, that's okay with me, go and I'll follow you, like a mule after a donkey."

Benjamin was delighted by Sender's great faith in his wisdom. He saw himself as a captain steering his vessel across the briny deep. But that didn't prevent him from realizing that he didn't have the vaguest notion where they were. Maybe they had lost their way and were wandering. While he was mulling, God sent a peasant to them on a wagon with a tower of hay.

"Sender," said Benjamin, "it wouldn't do any harm to ask the goy for directions. Why don't you ask him, for curiosity's sake. Here, outside the Holy Land, you're better at the coarse peasant language. After all, your missus used to take you along to market very often."

209

Sender got up, trudged over to the peasant very cere-moniously, and said the following:

"Good day. Tell me, my good man, which is the road to the Holy Land?"

"What?!" the peasant, taken aback, glowered at Sender. "Holes? Holes? What are you talking about?"

"No, no!" Benjamin couldn't hold back, and he butted in from his distance. "Not holes! Not holes! God forbid! No, the Holy Land! Sender, repeat it very precisely. He's got a peasant head. Tell him clearly, Sender, clearly!"

"Which is the road to the Holy Land?" Sender repeated very clearly.

"The devil knows what Jews want! Stop banging my head! This is the road to Leechville, not the holiday, not the holiday!" cried the peasant, mimicking them. Then he spat and tooled off.

Our friends trudged on again.

Benjamin had pains in his calves, his feet felt as if they'd been sliced off (may God preserve you!). But the poor man shrugged, screwed up his courage, and mustered his last ounce of strength. And since it was hard for him (may Jews be spared!) to keep up a fast, even stride, he tried to hop along. Of course, this wasn't his previous snappy march. It was agonizing, but he did what he had to do and kept moving, for after all—what else could he have done? Lie down on the road? It shouldn't happen to our worst enemies! What good would that do? Besides, how can a Jew lie down, just like that, in the middle of the road? It would only upset Sender and delay the trip, God forbid! So on they plodded, and they plodded all the livelong day, until God brought them safe and sound to Leechville, where they could spend the night.

When they trudged into the Leechville inn, the first thing Benjamin did was to throw himself into a corner and stretch out full length, in order to rest his legs and catch up on his breathing.

Sender, like a veteran housewife, went off to take care of domestic matters and negotiate about supper.

The innkeeper scrutinized Sender from top to bottom, he could tell from Sender's getup that this wasn't the usual sort of person who normally passed through here. He greeted him and asked him what his name was and where he came from, to which

Sender naively replied that his name was Sender, that he was sort of a Holy Land Jew, in the employment of Mr. Benjamin, who had the honor of lying right there in the corner. The innkeeper made a pious face, mulled for an instant, and then asked Sender to have a seat.

Now let's leave the princess (i.e. Sender), talking with the innkeeper, and let's return to the prince (i.e. Benjamin) to see what he was up to.

Our Benjamin, having collapsed in the corner, lay there like a rock, dead to the world. The veins in his legs were bursting, the blood surged, roiled, nipped, as though battalions of army ants were scurrying around, biting and pricking. His temples throbbed and banged like hammers. There was a dull roaring in his ears, and it kept stopping with a long, loud blare like a trumpet, or a sharp zoom like a rocket taking off. Every time a rocket spluttered from his head, his eyes blazed up with a myriad of fireworks: yellow, green, blue, white, red, crimson, and more and more colors, endless, unremitting. A moment later, the fireworks would go out, it got dark in his eyes, and his ears roared again like a windmill.

After lying there dazed for quite a while, Benjamin heard the ringing of bells far in the distance, coming closer and closer, louder and clearer, and suddenly there was a creaking and scraping, like a wagon halting by the gate. The air was filled sky-high with a chaos of voices, as though an entire shtetl had gathered there for an important meeting, shrill, falsetto, rumbling voices, thick, hoarse, rattling voices, there was no telling any whys or wherefores. When cats in heat assemble on the rooftops, we know they're cats and we know what they've come for and what their caterwauling means, even though we don't speak a word of felinese. But here it was hard to grasp what the people were shouting and what they wanted, for the hubbub was filled with laughing and groaning and sighing and whispering and squealing and the sound of a peasant, and a sweet honeyed tone, and coughing and nose-blowing and banging and hitting. Now how in the world could anyone understand what it all was and what it all meant? Soon the door crashed open and a gang of people burst and tumbled into the room.

211

Benjamin huddled deeper and deeper into his corner.

Meanwhile the room became very bright from a large number of candles burning in Sabbath holders. Some of these brass holders were clogged with stubs, and the candles were stuck on them and tottering. Some holders had holes that were too big, wide, and not deep enough, and the candles leaned askew and had clumps of drippings underneath.

At the end of a long oaken table sat a group of musicians tuning and warming up their instruments. The fiddler was fiddling around with his fiddle, tickling it with his finger, and each string went "zim, zim, zim" in its own voice as though saying: "Okay, you can tickle us, but we're all set, so long as there's no problem with your bow." He grabbed the bow, stroked it, and held it ready to play. The flutist was chatting softly with his flute, which was softly whispering to him, and the cymbalist did a slow run on his cymbal. Only the blind drummer sat there with his fur cap lowered over his eyes as he tried to catch forty winks.

Near the musicians, a strange figure was standing on a chair, and no sooner had he spoken a word than everyone roared. Even children, crowding at the windows and staring into the room, laughed wildly and made faces. Then the strange figure shouted: "Behold! In honor of the parents of the bride and groom and in honor of the host and in honor of the guests gathered here, strike up a lively tune, a merry tune!" And the musicians let loose on their instruments, merry, lively, and men and women joined hands and danced in a circle, hippity-hop!

The whole room moved, even bedbugs and cockroaches scuttled out of the cracks and all over the walls.

One of the dancers fell on top of Benjamin in the corner. The dancer eyed his face and then shouted:

"Aha! Benjamin! I've found him, by God, that lowdown skunk! He's here! He's here!"

The shout brought other people running over. Benjamin recognized all kinds of fine folk from Moochville, including the rabbi.

As one man they shouted:

"Benjamin, come and dance! Benjamin, come and dance!"

"I just can't, I swear!" pleaded Benjamin. "I can't move a muscle!"

"Don't worry, don't worry!" they replied. "C'mon! C'mon! You'll manage! There's nothing to it! Get moving, you jackass, get moving! Just wait, we're gonna tell everything!"

"Zelda!" screamed Benjamin in one breath. "Please don't tell Zelda, please, I beg you!"

"Move, you jackass!" they shouted. "Move! Get on your feet, you jackass!"

"Have pity, fellow Jews!" begged Benjamin. "I just can't, I swear, I can't move now. There's a reason why I can't. It's a secret, and I'll tell it to the rabbi."

And as he threw his arms around the rabbi in order to whisper the secret into his ear, he felt a sudden, terrible kick in his ribs. It was so awful that he reeled as though getting a whiff of horseradish, leaped up, rubbed his eyes, and saw that the room was quite dark, the moon was shining in through the windows, he was lying next to a little donkey, hugging it hard with both arms.

What was going on? Where did a donkey suddenly come from? Had Benjamin given birth? How could that be? Even assuming that Benjamin was something of a jackass, tenfold, a hundred fold, he was nevertheless a two-legged jackass, and who has ever seen or heard of a two-legged jackass giving birth to a donkey? True, there are a lot of donkeys, jackasses, and mules among us, and most of them actually in refined homes. But those are merely jackasses in human guise. The majority are very beautiful and have beautiful faces and dimples, but the donkey that Benjamin was hugging and clutching was a real donkey. And just where— that is the question—did it come from? A wonder, a miracle. It must have fallen from the sky! . . .

No, my friends! Do not put your faith in heavenly donkeys. Of all our jackasses, not a single one has ever been sent from on high. It wasn't as miraculous as you think. You needn't marvel at the donkey or indite an exegesis upon it. It was very simple, and as plain as the nose on its face. This is what happened:

When Benjamin collapsed in the corner, more dead than alive, he was so worn out that he didn't notice a donkey lying there. With his blood coursing, he fell asleep, and he dreamt the entire wedding with the parents and the musicians. He was terribly fidgety, he kept tossing and turning in the corner. And when he threw his arms around the rabbi of Moochville in his dream, he

213

actually embraced the Leechville innkeeper's donkey and whispered the secret of the journey into its ear. But the donkey would have none of it, the poor creature couldn't stand being hugged and choked like that. It thrust out its hoof, kicked Benjamin's thigh, and Benjamin awoke.

Upon awakening, Benjamin was still holding on to the donkey with both arms, stunned and bewildered. It was only after a moment that he pushed the donkey away, jumped up terrified, and rushed off. The donkey, for its part, as soon as it was released from strange hands, also sprang up and took off, banging violently into Benjamin, so that both of them fell on a big tub of water and crashed fearfully to the ground!

Alarmed by the crash, Sender and the innkeeper, holding a candle, came running in from the other room and then stopped in their tracks, horrified!

If a bard had gazed at Benjamin and the little donkey, he would have crooned:

So tender and so loving,
From heart to heart,
In the corner and the puddle
They did not part!

However, the innkeeper and Sender were ordinary mortals, and not bards, and so they promptly did pull the tender and the loving hearts apart. The donkey was sent to its mother with caustic words about its gross comportment. And Benjamin was taken from his immersion to a special room, where he was laid out on a few handfuls of straw with a pillow at his head.

VI

BENJAMIN GETS SLAPPED

After being drenched by a whole tub of cold water, Benjamin's limbs finally thawed a bit during the immersion night, and upon awakening in the morning, he felt fresher and stronger. He plainly saw a finger of Providence in the nocturnal affair with the donkey, which had brought him relief for his aches and pains. He thereby proved to Sender how unjust the sinful man is who laments about some misfortune and fails to understand that fortune may come from misfortune and good from bad. He explained that the Lord can use any of his creatures as a messenger, even a donkey; that a physician can sometimes even be an ass; and that a mosquito can sometimes actually bite into your brain, pester you, and stick in your craw. As evidence, there was the story of the gnat that God had sent to torment Titus for destroying the Temple, in olden, olden times. Benjamin's nightly encounter was now a good omen that his journey had begun at a propitious time and that he, God willing, would succeed in making his wishes come true.

"A water-carrier who passes by with full pails has been a good sign since time immemorial—so imagine what a huge, brimming tub can do," Sender chimed in agreeably.

But because Benjamin's legs were still aching, and because the handfuls of straw were so soft to lie on, he remained in Leechville for the rest of the day. He was like a ship at sea, which has foundered on a sandbar, and there is no good wind to drive it away.

Early the next day, Benjamin got up from his straw and resumed his journey.

For a good while, Benjamin trudged along, grim, brooding, never uttering a word. All at once, he smacked his forehead and stopped dead in his tracks, deeply troubled. It was only a few minutes later that he opened his mouth, heaved a sigh, and said:

"Oh, Sender, I forgot something!"

"What did you forget? What did you forget?" exclaimed Sender and grabbed the pack.

"At home, Sender. I forgot it at home!"

"Oh, Benjamin! What are you saying!" said Sender. "I thought we'd taken everything people might need on a trip: We can't complain—we've got a bag, and a prayer shawl, prayer thongs, and the daily prayer books, and we've got Sabbath coats too. . . . Why, thank goodness, we've taken along everything. What's missing? What could we possibly have forgotten?"

"The thing that I've forgotten, Sender, is vital and crucial, it's a

215

matter of life and death. Let's hope that everything goes right. But if—God forbid and heaven forfend and the Good Lord protect us and save us from harm—if, well . . . something, uh . . . diabolical happens on the way, then we'll feel the great value of the precious thing that I've forgotten. I was in such a hurry to get out of the house that I forgot to recite the magic formula I found in an ancient tome, it was based on a very archaic manuscript. You have to recite the incantation before a journey, when you're leaving home, at the town limits. And it's guaranteed to protect you against all dangers and awful occurrences while you're traveling—that's what I forgot!"

"Do you want to turn around?" Sender asked naively.

"Are you crazy? Have you gone nuts?" shouted Benjamin, and the blood dashed to his face. "Turn around?! Go home?! After all this trouble and getting so far, you want us to head back?! Why, and what about the people we know? What in the world will people say?!"

"Who cares about people, Benjamin!" exclaimed Sender. "Did people ask you to take a trip? Did they sign a contract with you and give you money for expenses, so that you could go wandering?"

"How brilliant!" said Benjamin sarcastically. "And what about Alexander the Great? Did the world ask him to go to India and fight a war there? And what about all our Jewish wanderers? Did the world ask them to go roving about from place to place?"

"How should I know?" Sender answered with a smile. "For all I care, they could have stayed at home, by God! They'd all be better off if they *had*. Oh me, oh my, Alexander the Great. You had everything you needed at home. Stay put, live in peace, and rub your belly. Why on earth did you need India? 'There's no place like home and the grass is always greener!' That's an old goyish saying, and people say that an old saying is practically as good as a talmudic verse—if you'll pardon my mentioning them in the same breath. I'm even more amazed at our Jews. After all, they of all people should abide by the Talmud, and stay at home and go about their business. What's the use of wandering all over, roaming and rambling like some confused bigshot? Never having any fun, never enjoying life, and wearing out your boots for nothing? As sure as I'm a Jew, Benjamin! If ever I ran into a person like that, I would tell him that old saying right on the spot—I mean that talmudic proverb, if you'll excuse my mentioning them in the same breath."

Our friends kept fighting and bickering. Sender kept bringing up arguments and Benjamin kept showing him that he was a fool and didn't have the slightest inkling about such matters.

Sender was like a horse who has always served his master faithfully, going through fire and water for him, when all at once something comes over him out of nowhere, an obsession, he gets pigheaded, rears up on his hind legs, refuses to budge, no matter what's done to him, no matter what tortures are inflicted on him. And while Benjamin didn't whip Sender for his stubbornness, he did give him a good tongue-lashing, he overwhelmed him with a flood of words, until he got Sender as soft as dough, the same good horse as before. Sender perked up his ears at Benjamin's words, which cudgeled his brain, and finally, as was his wont, he said:

"Well, if that's what you want, it's okay with me. Why should I care?"

When Benjamin was done with Sender, they started down the road again, and after following various paths and bypaths, they arrived in Snoresville more dead than alive. Snoresville was the first big city that our wayfarers had ever seen in their lives. So no wonder they gawked at the straight cobblestone streets and at the huge, tall buildings—gawked their eyes out. They practically tiptoed over the sidewalks, lifting their feet rather gingerly as though trying not to step too hard on the smooth stones, trying not to damage them—God forbid! Feet that don't lead such good lives with their owners in the small shtetls, and that are never handled with kid gloves! Small-town feet, alas, never knowing a floor, even in their homes, alas, creeping through mud and mire like hogs—their owners sticking them deep down, hurrying them along, straight from the shoulder, without further ado—such feet must really get as wobbly as drunkards when they suddenly feel a stone pavement underfoot, and out of sheer courtesy they just have to hop, skip, and jump a bit, not knowing where to put themselves for a time. You can instantly recognize feet that are

217

fresh from a small town when they pass over the cobblestones of big cities.

Our friends from Moochville lurched along with heavy hearts, making way humbly for everybody who came by. Sender would grab Benjamin's coattail and pull him to the side. At times, he even performed a quiet little dance with someone who was heading towards him. The man walked straight on and barged into Sender, who by stepping aside only cut him off. The man stepped to the right, but our Sender had already done the same and was standing there all set. Both of them veered to the left and then to the right again, until the man was able to sashay around him. One man, in no mood to dance with Sender, merely threw him aside so violently that his teeth almost fell out.

Everything was new for our friends, everyone seemed to be pointing at them, the droshkies were screeching, the coaches were rumbling, the doors stood with their noses in the air, glaring proudly with their glass panes, and the people scowled, and everything and everyone shouted after them: "Have respect, you yokels! Have respect, you bumpkins! Respect! Respect! . . ."

"Listen, Benjamin," said Sender after throwing back his head and gaping reverently at the buildings. "You know what? I think we're in Istanbul."

"Come on! Don't be such a fool! How could this be Istanbul!" retorted Benjamin, acting like a native son of Istanbul. "Why Istanbul has five hundred times five hundred streets, you fool, and every street has five hundred times five hundred buildings that are fifteen or twenty or even thirty stories high, and there are five hundred times five hundred people living in every building! And you think that's all? Just wait, you fool, just wait! Istanbul also has small streets, Jewish districts, tents, water closets, ravines, and plains—as the sand on the sea!"

"Oh me, oh my!" exclaimed Sender in amazement. "Why, a big city like that must be terrifying! But please tell me, Benjamin, where do all those big cities come from? Why do people jam together like that in one place, lying on top of one another, as though the world were small and there were no land left! There must be some reason why people leave the earth to soar up to heaven, to the high, high windows. Is it because a person's soul comes from heaven originally, so that the poor thing is drawn up, up, and he yearns to spread his wings and only be up there? What do your philosophers say to that, Benjamin? Haven't you found some talk about that somewhere in your philosophy books?"

"In philosophy," said Benjamin with a profound look on his face, "there is great controversy on that very matter. Once, I even dealt with it myself, by the stove in synagogue, and I expounded the talmudic passage about the ten measures of poverty that were sent down into the world, 'nine to Babylon, and one to the rest of the world'—And I explained the verse in Genesis: 'And the earth was filled with violence.' But let me clarify it for you according to our teachings. After all, Sender, you did study the Torah. Now, the Torah says that the early generations of our forebears lived in tents, but by the age of the Tower of Babel, all people had gathered in one place, and they started making bricks and building a city with buildings that reached to the sky. But right in the middle of their work, an awful confusion began, a hubbub, no one understood anyone else, and the whole business went haywire. Luckily, God worked a miracle and scattered them apart, and so people started living again, breathing freer, and the world was restored. Only the sin of the Tower of Babel didn't stop altogether. From that time on, our sinful nature has made people crowd together and suffocate together and build high buildings, make a name for themselves, and fly to heaven. 'Why do you stick to me like a burr?' said Abraham to Lot. 'Why should your people fight with mine over a piece of soil? You've got the whole world open to you, after all. Go wherever you like and leave me in peace.' "

But before Benjamin could finish, there was a loud scream from a coachman, driving towards our friends from behind and almost smashing them with the pole.

"You assholes!" shouted the coachman as he lashed at them. "Goddamn it! Why the hell are you crawling along like crabs and hogging the road! You creeps! You assholes!"

Our poor terrified friends ran for their lives, they scurried off in different directions like poisoned mice.

As he ran, Sender stumbled and crashed down full-length on

219

the ground. Benjamin was in such a hurry that he smashed into a basket of eggs carried by a poultry woman. The eggs burst open and all hell broke loose, and a big mouth, a fire, a scream exploded. The owner of the scrambled eggs inundated Benjamin in a flood of curses. She threatened to punch him or had already punched him, she would have given anything to grab his hair—in short, Benjamin got more than his share until he managed to struggle out of her clutches and escape into a back street, where Sender soon joined him.

"Now that's the big city for you!" said Sender, wiping the sweat off his face with his coattail. "Don't walk here, don't stand there, don't stop to rest—and the hell with all of them!"

"It all goes back to the Tower of Babel," said Benjamin, panting like a goose. "All these things you see here, they all go back to the Tower of Babel, with its evil confusion, its tumult, and that generation's theft and robbery and murder!"

"The hell with all of them," said Sender, waving the city away. "C'mon Benjamin, let's go and rest a while! You look pretty awful, your cheek is blazing. That bitch can go straight to hell! Please wipe your face. . . . Just look. . . . That bitch smeared egg yolk all over you!"

VII

HOW BENJAMIN CAUSES AN UPHEAVAL IN POLITICS

One of the small synagogues in Snoresville was up in arms about the Crimean War, which was going full blast then. The stove bench split into several factions, each with its own chairman and its own political direction. Khaikel the Thinker and his followers overwhelmingly supported Aunt Vicki (Queen Victoria), they would analyze her in detail and demonstrate her cunning and ingenuity.

Khaikel had once been something of a clockmaker, he had a

knack for perforating matzos, no one could build a hut for Sukkoth the way he could, out of a noodle board, shovel, dairy bench, tsholent board, and broken chicken cage, which were not assembled that skillfully in any other Sukkoth hut. So whenever the conversation turned to machines, people were in awe of him, saying: "That's Khaikel's department. Khaikel knows all about that."

Khaikel always told marvelous tales about English machines, and people's hair simply stood on end when they listened to him, and if anybody ever interrupted with a question, asking what made them work, Khaikel would briefly and simply explain that it was a kind of spring, and he would smile such a dear smile, as though he had solved an intricate dilemma and opened up that man's eyes. In a word, Khaikel's spring explained everything— the clock, the telegraph, the music box, and any other invention in the world. However, Isaac the Literalist was never satisfied with Khaikel's spring, he viewed it as some kind of heresy, and he would jeer:

"Soon Khaikel will be saying that a golem and other miracles like it are also caused by a spring. . . . No, no, Khaikel! All that stuff is, well, nothing could be plainer, if you'll excuse my saying so—all that stuff is nonsense, it's pure crap!"

And because Khaikel the Thinker was crazy about Aunt Vicki, Isaac the Literalist, his relentless opponent in everything, stuck fast to Aunt Russia, defending her with all his might and main. Each contender moved heaven and earth to win over the other groups. Khaikel had already practically gotten on the right path with Shmuel Carob, the head of Uncle Ishmael's party (the Turks) and halfway come to terms with Beryl Frenchie, an ardent fan of Napoleon's. But then Isaac pulled a fast one and formed an alliance with Tevye Walz, the Austrian Kaiser's man. Dispatches came pouring in on all sides, everyone issued bulletins, there was a wild hubbub, and the synagogue quaked and rocked.

It was at this very point, during the great commotion, that our friends arrived in Snoresville and chose this very synagogue to stay in.

Sender, with his compliant personality, was not headstrong in

221

political matters either, and he let everyone have his way: "If that's what you want," he would say, "then I don't care, it's okay with me." And so he became very popular and everybody liked him. From the instant they said hello, the men agreed that Sender didn't have a nasty bone in his body, that he was a simple, straightforward fellow without a trace of obstinacy. Now if Sender was on friendly terms with one and all, and never at loggerheads with anybody, Benjamin was more critical, and at the very start, he liked Shmuel Carob best of all, he got closer and closer to him until they became bosom buddies. Benjamin revealed his travel plan to Shmuel, who liked the idea very much. Shmuel talked about it to Khaikel, and Khaikel mulled and mulled, and even though the matter was a bit hard for him, it did finally lodge in his head. He promptly took it up in a session with Beryl Frenchie and Tevye Waltz, and they were all flabbergasted.

"Benjamin," they said, "doesn't really look like an ordinary person. He's sort of not all there, his head's in the clouds. When he talks, it's hard to understand what he means. Sometimes he's lost in thought, his eyes get glassy, he smiles. His behavior, his gestures are so weird. It all goes to show that he's really far, far away, on a very different level from us, he's not just anybody, there's something odd about him, there's more here than meets the eye, who knows, maybe Benjamin isn't Benjamin at all. Anything is possible! . . ."

One day, when Benjamin and Sender trudged into the synagogue, the place was in a dreadful uproar. Our politicians were in a heated debate with Isaac the Literalist, who was yelling at the top of his lungs, drowning out everyone else.

"Just look at what it says in Joseph," Isaac was shouting, as he pointed his finger at a passage in a book. "Joseph says that Alexander the Great wanted to reach the children of Jonadab ben Rekhab, and he got as far as the Mountains of Darkness, but then he and his heroes couldn't go any further, their legs sank into the mud over their knees. The sun never shines there, and so the ground is very swampy. Now do you understand? Alexander the Great, Alexander of Macedonia, who flew on an eagle and who soared as high as the gates of paradise—he couldn't get across the Mountains of Darkness. So how could your man do it, a shmuck like him?! And nothing can help him, not even Khaikel with all his springs!"

"You dumbass!" bellowed Khaikel, poking Isaac with his thumb. "Where the hell are your eyes? Just keep looking at what it says further on. It says: 'Alexander the Great heard the Birds speak Greek. And one Bird spake unto him: "Thine Efforts are to no Avail, because thou wishest to enter God's Mansion and the Mansion of His Servants, the Sons of Abraham, Isaac, and Jacob!" ' Now do you understand, you dumbass, why Alexander the Great couldn't get across the mountains?"

"But what will you do, my big thinker, if the other school of thought turns out to be right and the Ten Lost Tribes and Red Jews or the Sons of Moses actually live somewhere by the land of Prester John?! Well, could your shmuck please find the land of Prester John somewhere?! In a pig's eye!"

"Oh, c'mon, Isaac. That's baloney! I swear, that's absolute baloney!"

"Wait, just wait, my fine feathered thinker! There's also such a thing as a Sambatyon River! And don't forget, it hurls out rocks all week long! What's he going to do with that? Let's just assume, for argument's sake, that he makes it through the Mountains of Darkness, and that he finds the land of Prester John. But now he comes to the Sambatyon, and whoah! It's raining rocks. You can't get a foothold. Not even your Aunt Vicki can help him there, even if she stands on her head and wiggles her toes!"

"Aha! So now you're attacking Aunt Vicki! How low can a man sink?!"

"That's no way to act, Isaac—making fun of the Crown for no reason," Beryl Frenchie resentfully poked in his nose. "We're talking about Benjamin, you know. You can insult *him* till you're blue in the face, but please keep your hands off the Crown!"

"Why should we insult Benjamin?" cried Tevye Waltz. "Benjamin seems to be on the right track, he might bring salvation for Jews."

"Oh, Tevye, Tevye Waltz!" lamented Isaac, angrily shaking his head. "Why, I would never have expected you, of all people, to side with them and make such a big deal of Benjamin. What do you see in him anyway?"

"Just listen to that man talk! 'What do you see in him anyway?' " Shmuel Carob mimicked nastily. "Have you gone crazy, Isaac, or what? His absentmindedness, his confusion, the way he stares, the way he talks, the way he acts—it all shows very well who he is, I tell you. The face is the best mirror. If all those things aren't evidence for you, then I don't know what you mean by a human being! Why, here he comes himself. Just look at him, please, and tell me you're not crazy, tell me you haven't lost your mind. . . . You can see his cheek is burning, and there are three yellow stripes running across his face like the letter *shin!* Well, Isaac, what do you say to that?"

Isaac strode over to Benjamin, sized him up from head to foot, spat out, barely missing his face and then stormed away.

This debate over Benjamin altered the political alignment radically. Shmuel Carob and Beryl Frenchie joined forces with Khaikel, Aunt Vickie sent a thousand large vessels out to sea, with wild, terrifying machines, Uncle Ishmael crossed the river Prut, and Napoleon bombarded Sevastopol! Tevye Waltz couldn't make up his mind, he wavered back and forth, he twisted his tongue, he didn't really know where he was from one moment to the next. And Isaac the Literalist remained all alone, at sea, shipwrecked. The poor man worked with might and main until he nearly burst out of his skin. Just imagine: One individual against a whole mob! That's why he was so resentful of Benjamin. From that moment on, he always kept attacking him and did everything he could to make his life miserable.

"As God is my witness," says Benjamin at one point in his book, "I never meddled in politics. First of all, what good is it? Secondly, what does it have to do with Jews? For all I care, it could go one way or the other, it's all the same to me. My Sender didn't get mixed up in such nonsense either, I swear, and yet Isaac would never give me a moment's peace, he pestered me day and night. Sometimes he'd poke me from behind with a feather, or quietly throw a pillow at me, or hurl my shoe somewhere, so that I had to beat my brains out looking for it. When I fell asleep at night, he would get a straw and tickle the soles of my feet, so that I jumped up. Or else he would light a paper cone and puff smoke in my face. I would awaken, scared out of my wits, in spells of whooping cough, for maybe an hour—because of the smoke. As though I were at fault for what the three parties did in tandem."

VIII

HOW OUR FRIENDS WENT BEGGING

Most of the day, our friends were busy earning a living. They paid visits to the homes in Snoresville, and soon made such a name for themselves that people pointed their fingers at them and met them with a quip or a smile. Anyone else would have gotten a swollen head from such honors and made a big to-do about them everywhere in the world (knock on wood!), boasting about how entranced people were at the sheer sight of him, how they lapped up every mere word of his, how they smiled when they welcomed him in or escorted him out. However, our friends were simple people and made light of such tributes. Benjamin was absorbed in his own affairs, and all that Sender worried about was whether the bag was full and whether there were a few kopeks in his pocket for expenses. Give with a smile, give with a frown—a Jew doesn't care how you give, so long as you give.

Today is Purim, tomorrow it's past!
Give us a penny and kick us in the ass!

That's the well-known Jewish ditty, and it describes Jewish simplicity, Jewish meekness so accurately, and Sender often hummed it to himself softly as they trudged along their way.

"Good morning to you and yours!" Sender would say upon entering a home, dragging Benjamin along by his coattail. Then he would push him ahead, telling him in a whisper not to be

225

embarrassed and then respectfully stationing himself to the side.

In this way, our friends once entered a home where they found a young man jabbering at the householder. From what they could make out, it seemed as if the young man was telling about the importance of some matter that was making him a great sensation. He appeared to be singing his own praises, showing papers, and demanding something. His prey was making faces, arguing, and doing his best to escape the young man's clutches. The householder pounced on our friends like a drowning man grabbing a straw. He dashed over, hoping they had come on some urgent matter that would free him from the young man's urgency. But no sooner had he heard who they were and what they wanted than he stopped in his tracks, confused, astonished, like a man plagued by sudden misfortune on all sides.

"Here you have some more travelers!" the householder exclaimed to the young man, after pulling himself together. "These men are also travelers, you see! Just what the doctor ordered: travelers! On my expense account!"

The young man and our friends stared at one another.

"Listen," whispered Sender to Benjamin, tugging at his coattail. "Maybe this young man is also wandering there. . . . He might get there earlier and pull a fast one on us—God forbid!"

"Are you all in cahoots?" the householder asked.

"God forbid and heaven forfend!" Sender and Benjamin shouted in harmony. "We're traveling alone. All alone!"

"Well, Godspeed alone! But as far as I'm concerned, you're one gang," said the householder, producing a coin from his pocket.

"Ooh! Give it to us, please. Oh please, give it to us!" begged Sender, stretching out his hand. "We'll give the young man his share. C'mon, young man, we'll give it to you. We've got change."

All at once, the kitchen door flew open and a shrill, horrible voice came thundering out:

"That's him! That's him! The one next to the skinny little guy. Both of them were running around at that time. I recognized him, that fine fellow, by his face, and his yellow beard—oh, I'd like to pull out every last hair of it! Oh, God in heaven: Tear his filthy little heart out, roll it in the dirt! Kill him! Make the marrow gush out of his slimy bones! GUSH OUT!"

"C'mon, Benjamin. Let's get out of here!" cried Sender, yanking Benjamin by his coattail. "Damn her to hell, the bitch! She's still carrying on about her broken eggs!"

IX

HOW ANCESTRAL MERIT CAME TO THE AID OF OUR FRIENDS

Sighs and moans escape us when we read about the great and renowned geniuses, who, poor creatures, suffered so deeply at the hands of mankind, for whom they sacrificed their days and years and whom they blessed with very useful things that their minds came up with. The world is a child who's tied to his mother's apron strings, afraid to budge even an inch from her; who likes all the old silly stories told by nannies and grannies over and over again, a hundred times a day; who thinks that there's nothing finer than his toys, and that they contain all the wisdom there could be. And when the school assistant comes to take him to school, to teach him something, he screams bloody murder. Man likes the kind of life he's used to, and anything new strikes him as utterly wild and off the wall, he rants and raves and curses, and dumps on the person who thought it up. It's only later on, after the new thing has been born and settled in and clearly shown how useful it is, that people latch on to it, enjoy it, and completely forget the poor man who invented it in the sweat of his brow. We can be thankful if the world at least says a prayer for him after his death and puts up a gravestone. Today, in America, millions of people live happily and breathe freely. Yet when Columbus hit upon the idea of discovering the new continent, the poor fellow went through a harrowing ordeal, the world thought he was crazy and made fun of him.

The same thing happened to our Benjamin of Moochville. The moment they clapped eyes on him, people thought he was loony, and the instant they heard him talk about his journey, they split their sides laughing, they played jokes on him, everyone took

227

turns making a fool of him. Fortunately, it didn't get through to him, much less get to him. Otherwise, he would have been terribly upset, fallen ill—God forbid!—and given up the whole trip in disgust!

We will pass over many of the little tricks that were played on Benjamin, so that no eternal blot may fall upon our escutcheon, so that our names shall not go down with shame and disgrace in history for future generations. Instead, let us avert our eyes from all those things and get back to our story.

"In Snoresville," says Benjamin, "there is a large community of Jews—may they be fruitful and multiply. Yet, as to who they are, what kind of people they may be, and where they originally come from—you can ask them all you like, it's no use, they don't even know themselves. All they do know, as handed down from their fathers, grandfathers, and great-great-grandfathers, is that they're descended from Jews. And to judge by some of their customs, their attire, their language, their commerce, and so forth, they apparently must be Jews, but straggling away and flocking together from various tribes, for no one seems to care about anyone else. For instance, if one man should happen to fall, then another will not help him up, even if the man (it should not happen to your worst enemy) drops dead and gives up the ghost right then and there. . . .

"Some of them are proficient at telling rather than making fortunes, they know the science of the hand, they can read palms, that is to say, they live on handouts and hand-me-downs, which they then palm off on others. They also know other trades, like sheep-shearing and gardening: It is amazing to watch them pulling the wool over someone's eyes or leading him up the garden path—like nobody's business! And the Good Lord has endowed them with a special gift for loftiness—they can tell a tall story, so quietly and with such eloquent gestures as to make tears come to your eyes and knock your breath away. . . . It is said that, apparently, they descend from the rabble that joined the children of Israel when they left Egypt.

"On the whole," says Benjamin, "the inhabitants are honest folk, good people, they would always welcome me with a smile and appeared to enjoy talking to me. One could plainly see that they had a good time with me. I hope with all my heart that God and the world may be as happy with them everlastingly. Amen.

"It is astonishing to note," Benjamin goes on, "that in this region one can sometimes encounter people who look something like pigs. One can see this trait at first blush. Some observers claim they are like that by nature, whereas others ascribe it to the environment." Benjamin refuses to pass a verdict, that is a matter for scholars, they can investigate the problem and explain to us exactly what it signifies. "But whatever the reason may be," says Benjamin, "wherever the answer may lie, the fact itself is nothing new in the world. Even old Mattithiah Delecarti, who lived long, long ago, writes the following in his book *Image of the World:*

" 'In Britannia, there is a Nation of People who have Tails in Back like Animals, there are also Women as tall and large as Giants, and they are cover'd with Pig's Hair like Swine. In Gaul, there appear'd a Nation with Horns. In those Mountains, there are crooked Women, and the more crooked a Woman, the more beautiful she is consider'd. Just as nowadays, one can encounter in our Climes, very many Women who look crooked, very plainly crooked from behind (if you'll pardon my saying so), with a long Tail, that dangles and drags after them on the Ground. "What has been," says the Preacher, "will be, and there is nothing new under the Sun!" '

"Snoresville," Benjamin continued, "is large, with lovely buildings, long thoroughfares. When viewed for the first time, they look as if they were alive, they seethe and roar. But later on, when one grows a bit accustomed to them, one realizes that, basically, the town is nothing but a larger version of Moochville. The inhabitants eat, go to bed, get up at the same time every day. Time is calculated there according to meals—for instance, from breakfast to lunch, and from lunch to supper, for breakfast, lunch, and supper are the three wayside stations of their lives, and people look forward to reaching food as soon as possible and doing something after spending time doing nothing in a deserted steppe. It is said that the air of Snoresville makes people lazy, sleepy, and shiftless. If by some chance a man with courage shows up, a man with ambition to do something, then before you know it, the town takes away both his courage and his ambition, and the

229

only aspiration he has left is to eat, to sleep, and to get up in order to eat and sleep some more."

Benjamin saw the offices of the small-town tax-collectors and attorneys. In leaving home, they had shown a lot more strength and courage than necessary. "One has to travel," they urged people and prevailed upon them. "One has to travel, try to work, organize money for certain community necessities and for other municipal matters." Even though their efforts, their labor, their activities are altogether useless, like a fifth wheel on a wagon, because there's a tax estimate, and everything is done completely without their help. However, they had such great ambition, such wanderlust, that they accepted public funds for their wives and children and for expenses and then took off in a propitious moment. Coming to Snoresville, they soon lost their great desire, alas—so much for their dexterity and efficiency! They settled down in their offices, lazy, shiftless, only eating, drinking, and sleeping, as though a spell had been cast upon them. In this condition, those poor men live their days and years, the public sends them everything they ask for, money and more money, and they just sit there all the time, yawning, eating, sleeping, poor things, like enchanted princes, and it's simply impossible to tear them away from there—no wonder-rabbi and no healer could do it.

Benjamin was seized with a passionate desire to meet the renowned scholars and writers of Snoresville. After all, he himself was something of a learned man, a thinker, he liked to stick his nose into a book and he knew what a Jewish philosophical tome was, the kind that gave these people their knowledge, their inklings of the Seven Wisdoms. Now how could he possibly come here and not have any contact with his sort of people?! Besides, he wanted to talk to them about his journey, such men would understand him after all and appreciate his true value. He hoped they would give him letters of recommendation, praising him to the skies. After all, they liked to write testimonials for trivial things, for all sorts of bagatelles. So for such a thing, for such an important matter, their pens would gallop away like horses.

But no matter which of those scholars Benjamin visited, the

man was always eating or sleeping! Once he did manage to find one—a great writer, an international celebrity—he was leaning on a bedstead in a separate room.

"Good morning!"

"Good morning to you! What's up?"

"Oh, well, I just wanted to chat a bit!"

Things went back and forth, the whole business was a bit flat. The celebrity was dull, dreary, he hardly moved his lips, he looked as if he had one foot in the grave, he could barely hold his eyes open. Benjamin tried to keep him awake, he talked away at him as best he could, but to no avail. The man was as cold as ice. Eventually, he did sort of come to, he yawned and called in his wife:

"When are we eating, already?" he asked her and stretched his limbs with a hearty yawn. "Let's eat already," he said. "I want to lie down and catch forty winks. . . ."

All in all, Snoresville is a fine bedroom, everything sleeps peacefully there: learning, commerce, banking, jurisprudence. One can do one's best to arouse them, but to no avail. Even when a few people get together, their tongues soon become still, they sit there, yawning and gaping at one another like golems, and the whole crew falls asleep. It's only when supper is served that any of them stirs a limb, they grow lively, they munch away with gusto, eat up—and good night! They go home to sleep. . . .

Our Benjamin ultimately experienced the same apathy. All he finally did in Snoresville was to eat and sleep, and all his wanderlust simply droused away. He was in great danger of foundering there, like a ship in the Pacific, and snoring away his whole life. But fortunately for him and for mankind, something happened, like a tempest, violently driving him out and sending him on his way.

Isaac the Literalist hated Benjamin more and more each day. Now, he was gnawing into Benjamin like a tick, arguing and arguing with him about his journey, taunting him in every way: Hair would grow on Isaac's palm before Benjamin ever reached the Sambatyon, and he'd get to see his own ears before he ever laid eyes on the Red Jews. But Benjamin wouldn't let anyone stick a thumb in his soup or spit in his kasha. He countered that there

231

was a Creator in the universe, who never abandons those who believe in Him. They would see: God willing, and with God's help, he would reach his destination—let his enemies burst!—and as Benjamin argued, his blood came to a boil, he blazed with passion, and in the middle of the debate he would shout: "Dragon, lindworm, donkey, mule, etc.!" Which meant: "Bark all you like! I'm already far, far away, I'm in the desert, striding, striding, striding! . . ."

Isaac would spit three times and say: "He's got bats in his belfry and bees in his bonnet, we ought to take him to a doctor." Things eventually came to such a pass that the moment Benjamin stepped outdoors, the guttersnipes began charging after him, throwing rocks, as though he were a madman, they cheered and yelled: "Dragon! Lindworm!"

One evening, when Benjamin and Sender were walking along the street, the horde pounced on them like locusts and harassed them so dreadfully that they had to flee through the back streets. In one of those narrow alleys, they scurried uphill and started across a long, narrow footbridge over a brook, and right in the middle of the plank, they barged into someone coming from the opposite end. There was no possible way of squeezing past him without jumping down and cracking their skulls or at least breaking a leg. However, these parts were rather crucial to our friends. Without a skull or a leg, there would have been no way for them to continue their journey. So Benjamin and Sender stopped short, crestfallen.

"Ahhhh! Good day to you, Benjamin!" the man coming towards them said both angrily and cheerfully at once. "A nice coincidence, I swear! Just the man I was looking for!"

"Good day to you, Aizik-Dovid, good day!" Benjamin mumbled in a strange, bewildered voice.

The man was none other than Aizik-Dovid, the sage of Moochville.

"A fine pair you are!" Aizik-Dovid chided them. "Sneaking away from home, just like that, without so much as a by-your-leave! And for what, for whom? Who knows? Everything has to have its order, its natural logic, it does. How can you just steal away and abandon your poor wives, without ceremony, practically making them widows! How can you do that?! But fine, let's leave that aside, I won't ask you anymore. But just tell me once again: How could you do it, how could you do it? And what are you doing here anyway? That goes for you too Sender, you too. That's right, I can see you hiding behind him, I can. Your wife's going to give it to you, yessir, she'll roll out the red carpet for you, she will! She's so furious she's ready to tear you to shreds like a herring, to shreds. But her intuition told her you must be here, yessir, her intuition, your wife's, and she absolutely insisted on coming here, she did, your wife, she absolutely insisted on coming along with me, she did."

"Ha! There he is!" screeched a woman behind Aizik-Dovid.

Sender recognized his missus. He turned deathly pale, he was paralyzed with fear. His head whirled so fast that he grabbed Benjamin's coattail with both hands to keep from toppling off the bridge. He felt as if his wife had already seized him, as if her slaps and punches were hailing down upon him.

"Just look at them, those fine gentlemen! Oh, may God strike you dead, both of you! Oh, where is he—may his name be blotted out!? Just let me get my hands on him, let me at him, I'll show him what kind of a God we have!"

Sender's wife screamed and she tried to shove Aizik-Dovid out of the way.

"Please," begged Aizik-Dovid. "No shouting, no noise! Just take your time. You've waited so long, just wait a wee bit longer. You're not an abandoned wife anymore, with God's help, you're no longer a widow. And then again, how does the old saying go? Hmm? It's the same old story, a woman is a woman, she is. No matter how smart she may be, she's still a woman, she is, yessir. Let us investigate the matter from another point of view. Thus, why the uproar? It's merely anger: He ran away just like that, for what, for whom? Everything has to have its order, it does, do you understand me? But if things are as they are, then the question is: Why bother shouting? The answer to that, however, please forgive me, I'm talking to you like a son. The answer is: A woman is a woman, if you'll excuse my saying so."

Aizik-Dovid was only just getting warmed up. As was his custom, he wanted to investigate from still another point of view,

233

and then yet another one, seasoning with a bit of pepper and onion. But both ends of the footbridge were crowding up with people who had been coming all the while. From a distance, they were furious that these folks had stopped to chat there, of all places, indifferent to the rest of the world, allowing no one to pass.

The bridge was so narrow that two people couldn't squeeze by one another. The pedestrians on one end always had to wait until those on the other end had crossed over. As a result, Sender's wife and Aizik-Dovid had to back up to the other end of the bridge, from which they had come in the first place, and Sender and Benjamin also had to back up to their end, and it was only now that the group at their end could start crossing the bridge.

"Sender, why in the world are we just standing here and waiting?" exclaimed Benjamin, who came to his wits first. "Why are we just standing here like a boy who's had one end of a string tied to a tooth and the other end to a table leg? Dammit, we've got time to save ourselves."

"You're right, as sure as I'm a Jew!" said Sender cheerfully, like a man wriggling out of a tight spot. "Quick, Benjamin, quick, if you don't want me to fall into her hands. That's not a mere footbridge! Ancestral merit has come to our aid!"

Our heroes scuttled away, and a few minutes later they were at the other end of town. They didn't hang around for long. Grabbing their bundles, they bade farewell to Snoresville.

X

HOORAY, RED JEWS!

"Hey! Giddyap!" came a hoarse voice from a wagon that nearly ran down two women standing in the middle of the road, the liveliest in Dumbsville. Both women held sacks of food under their arms—meat, radishes, onions, garlic, and they were whispering confidences to one another, pouring out their hearts so loudly that you could hear them miles away.

The women scrambled for their lives to opposite sides of the street, and stood there, resuming their dialogue, shouting back and forth over wagons, droshkies, carts, vans, drays of lumber, which were rolling past, one after the other, in a long, long train, making it impossible for anyone to cross the street for quite a while.

"Khasye-Beyle! Are you gonna go tonight—to the fortune-teller? I'll be there with my husband. . . . Your husband's coming too, he asked me to tell you it's gonna be a fun evening. C'mon, don't be a party-pooper. You'll have a great time. Well, are you gonna come?"

"My mistress—may she burn in hell—she wants me to leaven bread today and grind the grits. I'll try to get out of it and come. But, Dobrish, mum's the word, don't tell a soul."

"Don't worry, Khasye-Beyle, don't worry! Your mistress won't croak if she has to munch an hour later. She wants to feed her face? Well, let her eat worms, the bitch! Oh, I nearly forgot. Don't sift the flour so much. The miller's wife isn't too happy with your bran. How much do you have left over from shopping?"

"Bastard! Grab him! Grab the bastard! What's he doing! Goddamn grabby bastard! The devil grab you!"

"What's going on, Khasye-Beyle? Why are you shouting?"

"A pickpocket, Dobrish! He almost carried away my bag of food. It's lucky I looked around in time."

"Hey, look, Khasye-Beyle! What's that crowd over there? There must be another fire. That makes the second fire today. There might be a few more by evening."

"I don't hear any bells, Dobrish! If there's a fire, they always ring the bells!"

"Hey, there's the agent's wife. I'll ask her. Simme-Dvosye! What's all the excitement over there?"

"I don't know, for goodness' sake! Maybe Nakhmah-Gisse knows. Hey, Nakhmah-Gisse! What's that crowd over there, darling? Your ducks are quacking so loud that a body can't hear herself think. Hodel just had a baby today, she'll take some of your ducks. Do you have chickens too? Nice, fat ducks. You couldn't buy eggs today for love or money. What's all that commotion over there?"

235

"How should I know? Something about Red Jews. I heard someone yelling something like: 'Red Jews!' "

"What? Red Jews have come here? Oh dear me! We've got to go and have a look!" all of them screamed at once and bustled over to the mob.

"Hooray for the dragon! Hooray for the lindworm! Hooray for the Red Jews!" a gang of kids was screaming in the crowd.

These Red Jews—were our friends Benjamin and Sender, who had arrived in Dumbsville a short while after the footbridge caper, making a name for themselves within a few weeks here. There were a number of pious Jews, who were simply mad about them, as they were about the shoemaker who had worked miracles in Dumbsville, thereby revealing himself to be a hidden saint, a lamed-vovnik.

Toltse and Treyne, two pious elderly women, were in the habit, as everyone knows, of donning their Sabbath best every evening, their silk jackets and their pearl-encrusted headbands, and strolling out of town to meet the Messiah. Now it was these pious crones who were fortunate enough to encounter our friends on the other side of the town gate one evening, just as they were arriving from Snoresville, and to escort them into Dumbsville at a propitious hour. The instant the two silk jackets met them, they knew everything, they knew whom God had blessed them with. Toltse and Treyne exchanged astonished looks and nudged one another: "Well, Treyne?" "Well, Toltse?" they whispered. "Didn't we sense right away that these were no ordinary mortals?" Toltse and Treyne were absolutely entranced with our friends, they were positively rejuvenated, their hearts were overjoyed at hearing about the journey, they gazed at their God-sent heroes and kept nudging one another and exchanging smiles: "Well, Treyne?" "Well Toltse?" Toltse darned their socks, Treyne patched their shirts, sewed on laces, and both women were terribly happy, delirious, as in the days when they were young brides. In short, our wanderers found esteem and sympathy in Dumbsville. It's only in a place like Dumbsville that such people can be appreciated and their true worth understood.

Come to Dumbsville, all you Jews! Why vegetate, you children of Israel, you fine people, why idle your time away and come to

236

nothing behind the stove in little towns?! Go to Dumbsville, for heaven's sake. You'll find your own kind of people there, your Toltses are waiting for you there, your Treynes and your pious souls, you can grow there, you can be saved there, you can be popular there, you can be respected there, you can be renowned there—and really start living! . . .

Come to Dumbsville, goddamn it, and for God's sake! . . .

This is how our Benjamin describes the town of Dumbsville:

"When you arrive in Dumbsville by way of the Snoresville Road, you first have to jump across a mud puddle, then a second one further on, and then, just a bit further on, a third one, the very biggest, the meeting place, if you will pardon me, of the sewers and household slops, which bring along all sorts of goodies. Every day has its own delicacies, its own specialties, with all kinds of colors and all sorts of smells appropriate to the individual article and thus making it very easy to guess the day of the week. If, for example, there are yellow streams of sand, with which housewives scrub their floors, and if they have fish scales floating in them, poultry claws, chicken heads, a bit of hair with charred pieces of hooves—then you've got all the evidence: today is Friday, grab a birch broom, if you please, and a wooden pail and hurry to the bathhouse. If, on the other hand, the puddle receives eggshells, onion skins, radish parings, liver sinews, herring tails, and big sucked-out marrowbones—well, then, good Sabbath to you, fellow Jews! And may the Sabbath dinner agree with you! If however, the gutters barely move, if all they have is pieces of charred buckwheat dragging along, bits of dry dough, a shredded rag, a worn-out whisk broom, then you know that today is Sunday. The water drayman still hasn't brought any water, housewives have barely managed to squeeze a last drop of water from the barrel in order to more or less rinse at least the Sabbath cauldron and the earthen pots. And likewise, on every other day of the week, each puddle has its own special look, its special shape, and its special smell.

"And once you have gotten safely across this mud, gentlemen, then you will pass a large hill of garbage, the ruins of a burnt-down house. On top of the garbage, there normally stands a cow, like a preacher giving a sermon, peacefully chewing her cud,

237

moving her jaws, and gazing foolishly at the whole mob of Jews scurrying around below like madmen, with all kinds of sticks, canes, and umbrellas. Every so often, the cow snorts, or lets out a bovine moan, as though sighing and groaning, as it were, over this mob, and over her own awful luck, poor thing, at having fallen into Jewish hands. . . .

"Having managed to get across the hill, you keep on going straight, always straight. You may possibly—God forbid and heaven forfend—stub your toe on one of the sharp cobblestones scattered about helter-skelter, and you may even—may the Good Lord spare you—trip and fall. If so, please pick yourself up if you can, and then keep walking and walking, so long as you have not broken your leg—knock on wood—until you come to a square of sorts. There, on that square, you will find the essence of Dumbsville.

"Now if it makes sense to call Snoresville Road the *stomach* of Dumbsville, then one can justifiably say that this square is its *heart,* beating day and night, its vital blood, its very life. There you find stores, little shops, stands, and the well-known fence places, where artisans sell off their leftovers: pieces of cloth, ribbons, borders, velvet, and shreds of fur. The square teems and crawls and swarms, a dense throng of Jews shoving, pushing, and getting knocked, poor things, by wagons and coaches. (Physicians state that if one dissects a Jew of Dumbsville, one usually finds a wagon pole in his body. But one cannot bank on Dumbsville physicians; healers play a much greater role.) There, one can always hear a shouting: 'Hot buckwheat cakes, Jews! Get your hot buckwheat pudding, garlic, onions, c'mon Jews!' The shouting comes from raggedy boys, who wander about, yelling in a strange singsong. There, you can say a quick prayer in the evening, people usher in the new moon with loud voices, shouting to every passer-by: 'Good evening, cousin!' There, porters stand about, with thick ropes entwined around their bodies, army veterans in old boots and threadbare overcoats, old-clothes dealers peddling all kinds of breeches, kaftans, undershirts, and all manner of rags. Right in the midst stands the Christian watchman, chomping away on a piece of challah, which he gets for snuffing the candles on the Sabbath. And, like a Jew eating carefully prepared

238

matzos (if you will pardon my mentioning them in the same breath), he makes sure, as he bites into it, that no crumb falls on the ground, God forbid. Pickpockets roam about, plying their craft. All at once, an unwashed girl with messy, disheveled hair jumps out from nowhere, bellowing for alms in a screaking voice, grabbing your coattail, shouting, sobbing, weeping, as though you were murdering her and stealing her money. A gang of yelling urchins chases a lunatic, who sings tearful ditties, half-Yiddish, half-Polish, and wears a crushed cap on his head. There, a young man stands with some kind of box, the Jews peer through a peephole, while he glibly reels off his customary megillah: 'This is London, the Pope is riding in red hose, and all the people are doffing their hats to him! Now you see Napoleon and his Frenchies battling with the Prussians, and the Prussians are scurrying in all directions like German measles! And now, a woman is riding with the Sultan in a carriage, the Grand Vizier is holding the whip and driving the horses. The horses have panicked, the carriage has overturned, the poor Sultan has tumbled out, he's had a bad fall, and the woman is trying to make her getaway! Well, that's it, you've had enough for half a kopek.'

"There, women sit in long files, with troughs chock-full of garlic, cucumbers, cherries, gooseberries, currants, Holy Land apples, Kol Nidre pears, and all kinds of other things. Off to the side, an old hunched booth crouches on stilts like chicken feet, without a door or windows; according to what the old, old people say, this booth once housed a sentry, and the whole town came running to gape and gawk at the miracle of the booth and the soldier. Next to the old booth, which Dumbsville is as proud of as if it were a fortress, sits Dvossye the market woman, completely surrounded by troughs, under a small roof covered with moldy planks, rotten straw and rush mats and resting on four bent and crooked poles. Dvossye always has her huge fire pot; in winter she squats on it, like a brood hen on eggs, all day long, taking it out from underneath every so often in order to puff on the coals or pluck a baked potato from the ashes.

"Of those Jews—so goes an old legend here—of those Jews whom King Solomon sent out on vessels to Ophir, to look for gold and all manner of foreign wares, many, for a variety of reasons, settled there. In the course of time, they established great shops and businesses in India, with all kinds of precious goods; they received loans and commissions from the Germans there, and luck was with them for a long time. But then, their fortune changed, the merchants went bankrupt and had to escape. Some of them vanished in the desert, some managed to get safely across the border, found vessels, and sailed up the Puddlemudd River, which in those days flowed right into the sea. Thus, they sailed and sailed, until all at once a dreadful tempest arose, the waves towered to the sky and smashed the vessels, hurling the passengers ashore. And there they built them a city, and they did call its name Dumbsville.

"The archeologists, who, in their great wisdom, can make a nutmeg kernel out of nothing, have done a thorough interpretation of that legend, concluding with myriad subtleties, as is their wont, that it contains some measure of truth. The evidence they offer is:

"Firstly: the outlandish architectural style of the dwellings, which is rather ancient, as though dating from thousands of years ago, when people were living in tents and huddling in caves. There are numerous houses in Dumbsville that truly look like caves, and many like Tartar tents. Their appearance, the way they stand, makes them all seem at loggerheads with one another. You stand bending in, so then I, out of spite, will stand bending out. You stand athwart, so then I'll stand topsy-turvy. You want a stoop outside—and I a ladder. The man who needs it is perfectly capable of climbing. And if your patched-up roof soars aloft, well then I'll just keep mine swerving downward. Perfect in spite of you! And if you don't like it, then don't look. . . . In short, all this points to ancient, ancient times.

"Secondly: the customs of the inhabitants. Even today, one can still find customs deriving from the heathens among whom they dwelt in earlier times. Writing and accounting are not common there, so that all community affairs and all the business of the fraternal orders are pursued without bookkeeping, and the leaders are never accountable to anyone.

"Thirdly: the castes. The people here are divided into different castes as the Hindus once were. For instance, there is the caste of

Grabbers, the upper crust, who rule high-handedly. Then there is the caste of supporters, the protectors, who go through thick and thin for the Grabbers, fighting and battling their enemies, in exchange for which they receive certain salaries and free meat. There is also the caste of Cozeners, the glib dupers, who can also slip out of anything. The latter, in turn, are subdivided into: Bankrupts (secular men with a say in commerce) and Hypocrites (religious men with a say in the synagogue). The caste of Mute-Stupid-Craven-Paupers, the poor common folk, who submit completely to all the other castes and quake in their boots at the mere sight of them.

"And fourthly: the coin that was once unearthed during the digging of a drainage ditch. One side of the coin was well-worn, one could just dimly make out something like a piece of apron on a stick and, underneath, something resembling a small trough, with heads peeping out. The other side of the coin was almost smooth, but a closer look revealed letters in an old-fashioned Hebrew script: *YASHLAG VANAF,* meaning 'potash and branch.' Scholars cudgeled their brains over this inscription and put all sorts of constructions upon it, each interpreting it in his own way. Some of the scholars claimed that the letters at the beginning and end of *YASHLAG* were not really letters, but remnants of ornaments that had been rubbed away by time, so that the engraving actually read *AYSHEL* (tree) *VANAF* (and branch), which referred to the stick and apron. Other scholars offered a completely different explanation, thereby making a great stir in the world, until someone came along with open eyes, analyzing the letters as the initials of Hebrew words meaning: Jews from Ophir (i.e. India) who came here (i.e. Dumbsville) and settled on the Puddlemudd River. The stick with the apron and the trough with the heads signified a boat with sails and passengers. This selfsame scholar indited a very voluminous tome on this subject, wherein he offers a suggestion to his audience, to wit, that the town should clean up the river and, by so doing, it will be sure to unearth a multitude of ancient artifacts, which would shed light on the investigation of the Jews of Dumbsville. However, the inhabitants of this town are loathe to clean up the mud, they say that what olden times have done away with must remain where it

241

is. let no human eye peer into hidden matters. . . .

"In the town itself, there are some thirty or forty mud holes including the swampy fields. They are connected by caverns with the depths of the Puddlemudd River, and at certain times of the year, especially in the spring, towards Passover, they swell and spill over dreadfully, flooding the streets with such a deep, sleazy slime that even when very tall people slosh through it, their hats are bespattered.

"On dark nights, Dumbsville is lit by a single small lantern, which is guarded by two watchmen. Nevertheless, people do trip and fall at night, hurting themselves badly, and robberies are also very frequent, despite the sentries. Ergo: One must conclude that one cannot rely on anything, one cannot guard against everything. What will be, will be. Useless is man's wisdom and futile are his best-laid plans. Hence," says Benjamin, "we must close our eyes and always walk at random, trusting in God, hoping that He will bid His angels watch over us and carry us in their hands. Not even the tiniest sparrow can fall without His knowing it. Can one," asks Benjamin, "put one's prayer shawl and prayer thongs in a safer place than on a shelf in the synagogue, as I did? Nevertheless, God did not wish to keep His eye on them, and so the pouch was stolen from there along with all our other belongings!"

XI

MIRACLES UPON MIRACLES ON THE PUDDLEMUDD RIVER

When our heroes first set eyes on the Puddlemudd River, they were absolutely flabbergasted. They had never seen such a river before in all their lives. Sender said that this must be the biggest river in the whole wide world. He simply couldn't grasp anything bigger. A river like that was no chickenshit—it was perhaps a hundred times larger than Moochville's river. But Sender was a simple fellow, Moochville was all he had ever known, he couldn't really read, and so for him, everything that was like nothing in Moochville was a miracle and could not be surpassed by anything else in the world. Benjamin, however, was much better read than Sender, and, in perusing his philosophical tomes, he had gotten a nip, as it were, of the Seven Wisdoms, and knew something of the appearance of the nether paradise, the wild and outlandish creatures in India, and all kinds of similar things. Now whenever Benjamin got his first sight of something new, he too would be amazed at heart, but he would smile and make a superior face, as though to say: "Oh well, how trivial. That's nothing compared to other things that exist. . . ." He proved to Sender that the Puddlemudd was mere slime, if you'll excuse me, pure crap, next to the Jordan, which was many times larger. Why, the Wild Ox, which the pious will feast upon when the Messiah comes, could lap up the Puddlemudd in one slurp. And the word 'Jordan' makes this apparent, for the meaning, after all, is: 'more than,' something huge, something enormous, a torrent, a flood!

"Do you know what I'm thinking, Sender?" Benjamin once said after standing deeply absorbed in the Puddlemudd. "I'm thinking that we could travel from here down the river."

"Oh, for God's sake, Benjamin!" cried Sender in terror. "Just remember that our own river claims a person every year. Goodness only knows how many victims this river must claim every year. Have pity on our lives, Benjamin, and on your wife and children!"

"Have faith, Sender, have faith! Faith in God is Jewish. It was faith in God that helped Jacob cross the Jordan with his staff. It's with faith in God that Jews open up big stores. Everything you see here is pure faith. Even stairs and ceilings, and a lot of big houses, rest only on faith. . . ."

"But why do you want to travel by water, of all things," asked Sender, "if we can do the same thing on dry land?"

"I have a lot of reasons," answered Benjamin. "First of all, I think the water route would be shorter and faster. We have to make sure we get there as fast as possible. The earlier, the better. Why? That's for me to know, that's my business! It bothers me, Sender, it bothers me terribly, it frazzles my brain, I wish I were

243

there right now, I wish it with all my heart and soul. If I could, I would fly there through the air like a bird. . . . Second of all, when Benjamin of Tudela began his journey, he first sailed down the river Ebro—which is plainly written in his book. If he traveled by water long ago instead of by land, then that must be the right thing, he must have known what he was doing, he was as smart as any of us, by God! Benjamin was one of our ancient scholars, he lived long before us, and so we have to listen to him unquestioningly. . . ."

"If that's so," said Sender, "then it's okay with me. As sure as I'm a Jew, Benjamin! Not only on the river. Even if Benjamin of Tudela had ridden on a poker, we wouldn't have to give it a second thought, we would simply get on a poker and fly away—"

"And third of all," Benjamin broke in, "it wouldn't hurt us any to get used to traveling by water, before we put out to sea later on. Why, I would even say that before we leave Dumbsville, it wouldn't be such a bad idea just to try out the water and take a short trip on the river. Look over there, do you see that guy standing there with the little boat? Why don't we slip him a few kopeks and ask him to take us on a little boat ride."

A few minutes later, our wanderers courageously clambered into a boat and started out across the Puddlemudd. At first, they were petrified. Sender's head whirled and his arms and legs were quaking. Now, right now, it was about to capsize, he thought to himself, and he would plunge down to the bottom of the river, his life would end, his spouse would remain abandoned forever. But then he felt a little better.

"Don't worry, Sender," Benjamin comforted him when they came ashore, "don't worry if you feel dizzy and lousy. That's seasickness, everyone gets it the first time they go sailing. You'll see, the second time, you'll feel better—you won't feel a thing."

From then on, our heroes took frequent boat rides on the river, and they had a wonderful time. They became so tough that they figured it would be child's play to sail across the ocean.

With Sender as his interpreter, Benjamin would converse with the boatman, showering him with questions; for instance: "Sender, just ask the captain how many miles it is till the ocean? Ask him if there are any islands along the way? What kind of people live there? Are there any Jews living among them? Who do they pay taxes to, and do they know anything about the Diaspora?" Or, for example: "Sender, just for curiosity's sake, ask him about the Nisbon Mountains and the infidels. Does he know anything about the Ten Lost Tribes? Who knows, maybe he's heard something!" Benjamin kept telling Sender to ask the boatman more and more questions like that.

Now the little bit of peasant language that Sender had learned when going to market with his wife was not sufficient for such lofty matters. Haggling over eggs, onions, potatoes—that much he could just barely manage to do. But discussing learned subjects with a ship's captain—that was simply out of the question. It was heartbreaking to see poor Sender torturing himself in such a conversation, he would speak with his arms and legs, work himself ragged, and sweat blood, so that God Himself would be moved to pity. The captain would spit, argue, and glare at him askance, and Benjamin would harass him, jostle him, and hang on his every word on the other side.

"He . . . Red . . . Jews!" Sender would squeeze out the words, pointing at Benjamin.

"Oh, I know red-haired Jews . . . Leyb, Shmuel, rich Jews." That was the kind of answer that Sender would normally receive from his captain.

"No, no Leyb, no! He ask for Red Jews, there . . . there . . . how do you say . . . Nisbon Mountains."

"Nisbon? A Jew named Nisbon?"

"Tell him they're mountains, Sender," Benjamin would scream. "Just tell him they're mountains. Use sign language."

Sender held up his arms to depict a mountain and shouted: "High, very, very!"

"Phooey!" the captain would spit out, curse Sender, and tell him to go to hell.

Benjamin recounts marvelous things, sheer wonders, about his travels on the Puddlemudd—miracles that caused a stir in the world. We will offer only a selection here:

Once, when sailing down the Puddlemudd, Benjamin saw a very large patch in the middle of the river, it was covered with green, a dazzling green. He thought it was an island overgrown with grass and fragrant herbs. Just as he stuck out one leg and was about to hop on to the island, the captain yelled, grabbed him from behind, and threw him back into the vessel with all his strength, so that Benjamin lay stunned for a while on the bottom of the boat. All he could hear was a seething and roaring around the boat, as though it were grappling with something and struggling along. And later, when Benjamin came to, the captain told him that he had been in great danger of drowning in the greenery, because it wasn't an island, as he had thought, it was the blossoms that bloom on the river surface every year.

"But I," Benjamin writes, "would not be convinced that that was blossoming vegetation. To be sure, it did have a fragrance, but I have never heard in all my life or read in any of my books that water can blossom. If it did blossom, then it would have to bear some sort of fruit, over which one could say a benediction: 'Blessed Be He who createth the fruit of the water!' But no such benediction exists! I am of the opinion that the green phenomenon was the gigantic oceanic fish, the khileyno, of which there is a very lovely description in the book *Image of the World,* to wit: 'The gigantic Fish covereth it Self with Grass and Earth until it doth look like a big Island, and sometimes those who sail the Ocean believe that it is a lovely Mountain, they set Foot upon it, do what they have to do, cook Victuals, and when the Fish feeleth the Heat of the Fire, it diveth down into the Depths, and all the People who have camped on the Fish are drown'd.' And that is also iron-clad evidence for those scholars who believe that the Jews of Dumbsville originated in India. Sailing from India and then up the Puddlemudd in olden times, they brought along the khileyno, whose native habitat is India and whose instinct is to chase after vessels."

Once, when Benjamin peered into the river, he saw some kind of creatures deep in the water, they looked just like women. "Long before that day," writes Benjamin, "I had read in the books that mermaids live in water, and the author of *Image of the World* testifies as follows: 'A Sea-Nymph's Head, Body, and Breasts look like those of a Maiden, and she singeth very beautifully, and she is known as a *Shreyno.'* Old, venerable people, whose words we can believe, have told me that they themselves viewed such mermaids among traveling performers, who, after a theatrical presentation, usually exhibited them to all and sundry for a few pennies. But today I saw some with my own eyes. I pointed the maidens out with great astonishment to the captain, but he pointed at some washerwomen who were doing laundry on the shore. I pointed down to the water, and he pointed up to the shore. And since neither of us could understand the other's language, he did not know what I was showing him, and I did not know what he was showing me, and so I was unable to get any precise information from him about the mermaids."

Not far from shore, near the town, Benjamin spied an area where the water was very dense, in places it was rigid like meat jelly, and in some places it was even denser. It was this water that the water-carriers brought to the householders. In their homes, the thick jelly is diluted with plain water in the barrel, and they use it for cooking all their food.

"I myself," writes Benjamin, "partook of food that was cooked in such water. May the flesh of the Leviathan be as tasty in paradise, for this food had a divine flavor. A pot roast prepared with such water is a royal treat. I stuffed my pockets with that water and told Sender to pack some of it, for it could be highly useful in our further travels across oceans and deserts."

One afternoon, our heroes were wandering along, merry and cheerful, not far from town, they were laughing, joking, exchanging glances, and enjoying themselves thoroughly. They were like a loving couple right after the wedding, strolling freely across the green grass and drinking in one another's every word, every look. Now why were our heroes in such a wonderful mood? What made them so wildly overjoyed that they jumped, hummed, and acted like utter lunatics? The reason, my friends, was this: They had made up their minds to leave Dumbsville the next day (knock on wood) and, at a propitious hour, to sail to their destination. . . .

Now as they frolicked along, a wagon suddenly came rattling up with two Jews, one driving and the other lolling to the side, his cap pushed back and a straw in his mouth—excellent signs that a Jewish head is thinking up a trick or two and mulling very hard.

The two Jews gazed at our two cheerful friends, they examined

247

them from head to foot and then struck up a conversation with them. The first question was the usual one: "Where do you come from?" Then: "What are your names?" And after that, the remaining list of questions that Jews normally ask upon first meeting. That was all our friends needed; they opened their mouths and blurted out everything that was on their minds. What they had in their lungs rolled over their tongues—as we say. The two men grinned at one another, whispered to one another, and the man with the tilted cap and the straw in his mouth said: "Oh well, never mind, it'll be okay. At worst, it'll cost a bit more. . . ."

"You know what?" the men finally said. "Our town really ought to have the same privilege of welcoming two such fine men as yourselves. We would very much like to ask you to do us the honor of joining us in our wagon, if you please. Don't stand on ceremony. We guarantee that our people will welcome you with food, drink, and anything else we can."

"We'd really like to very much, honestly," replied Benjamin. "But we've made up our minds to leave tomorrow by way of the river (knock on wood)."

"Don't be offended," said the Jews, "but your plan doesn't really hold water. The Puddlemudd? Some river! If you'll pardon my saying so, it's a pisshole, a pile of crap, a smelly swamp, a moldy, putrid slime. *Our* town has the Dnieper, which flows right into the sea. From there, God willing, you'll reach your destination, quickly and speedily. Don't be headstrong, by God. C'mon, hop aboard!"

"What do you think, Sender?" cried Benjamin. "Let's do them the favor and go with them."

"What do I care!" replied Sender. "If you want to go with them, then let's go."

And a few moments later, our heroes were sitting in the wagon, elated and honored at being invited by the two Jews and looking forward to greater glory. The ride was a very merry one. The Jews kept a sharp eye on them and practically waited on them hand and foot, plying them with food and drink like a woman in childbed. Never in their lives had our friends even dreamt of anything like this.

The next evening, they arrived in Dnieprovitz safe and sound. The two Jews drove up to an inn with them and treated them to a fine dinner.

"You must be tired and sleepy after such a long trip," said the Jews. "You'd probably be better off going to bed early. Tomorrow, God willing, you'll wake up bright-eyed and bushy-tailed, and then we'll take you around to meet some important people. We'll throw in a good word for you, and if they take you in, they'll supply you with everything you need, and you'll be able to go on your distant journey promptly and quickly. So good night!"

"Good night to you!" our friends answered. They recited their evening prayers, rubbed their bellies a bit, yawned, scratched themselves, as people do, and went to sleep in the finest of spirits.

XII

OUR FRIENDS ARE INDEED TAKEN IN

"Oh, my God, just let me confess my sins!" Sender screamed in his sleep, in a bizarre, frightened voice, waking up Benjamin.

Scared out of his wits, Benjamin leaped up, dashed some water on his hands, and ran over to see what was wrong.

Outside, the day was just dawning, and there was silence everywhere, all you could hear was the snores of the people in the room, each one snoring in his own way: one man twanging like a banjo, another blaring like a trumpet, another sotto voce, still another drawing higher and higher, three levels high, then letting out with a twist, a rebuke, like someone asking a knotty question, and he drummed with his cheeks. The result was a snore concert, each nose playing to beat the band, celebrating the renowned bedbugs of Dnieprovitz, who were heartily dining on the sleepers and drinking their blood—Jewish blood!

Dnieprovitz had pastured its bedbugs, its man-eaters, for a long time in that dreadful inn, that awful, out-of-the-way Jewish tavern. If there was a bedbug in any neighborhood, it would

249

crawl there, to put the bite on Jews, to suck and sip Jewish blood. . . . Any Jew coming to Dnieprovitz was prepared to donate a little blood, knowing there was no way to wriggle out of it. So bite, just bite, you Dnieprovitz wit, stink, just stink, you little bedbug, write, just write your bloody signs and keep on going, go straight to hell.

"Why are you screaming, Sender?" Benjamin asked, upon reaching him. "A bedbug must have bitten you. It's awful how many bedbugs there are here, they didn't let me sleep a wink all night. I only just dozed off a little while ago."

"C'mon, c'mon, let's get out of here!" Sender shouted, still dazed.

"For God's sake, Sender! What are you saying? So a bedbug bites you. What's the difference? A bug's a bug, and you're a human being. . . ."

A bewildered Sender gaped at Benjamin for a few minutes. Then he rubbed his eyes and moaned:

"Oooh! I had a horrible dream. I hope none of it comes true."

"Oh, c'mon! The things that people dream!" said Benjamin. "I dreamt last night that a dragon rushed up to me, glared right into my eyes, and asked: 'Are you Benjamin of Moochville? Please be so good as to come with me, we're going there, there, Alexander the Great is standing there with his army and he is dying to meet you.' I started off, and the dragon ran on ahead, with me at his heels. 'You're running lightning-fast, God protect you. I can't keep up,' I heard someone shouting behind me. I turned around and saw Alexander the Great. 'Your Majesty,' I cried, grabbed his hand, and squeezed and squeezed it. But then suddenly my nose was filled with a horrible stench, it made me sick. I woke up and in my hand I felt a squashed-up bedbug. . . ." Benjamin spat. "Well, by God, just spit three times, Sender, and forget your dream. What did you dream, anyway?"

Sender dutifully spat three times, and then narrated his dream:

"I dreamt I was just walking down the street for a long, long time. All at once, someone grabbed me from behind and stuffed me into a sack, and he carried me along in the sack, and carried me and carried me, until we arrived somewhere or other. I could feel him untying the sack, he punched me really hard, so hard that two of my teeth fell out. 'That's just a down payment,' I heard him say. 'I'll settle with you in full later on.' I looked up, my wife was standing there in breeches, she was furious, her eyes were blazing like the devil and she was foaming at the mouth. 'Just you wait, just wait, my darling,' she said with a nasty laugh, 'I'll get the poker and show you what kind of a God we have.' As she went over to get the poker, I took off like the dickens, I ran and ran, and I didn't stop running, until I reached some kind of tavern. Inside, it was dark, eerie, not a soul to be seen. I lay down in a corner, shut my eyes, and dozed off. While I was sleeping, my grandfather, Reb Sender, may he rest in peace, came over to me, very gloomy, his eyes were filled with tears, and he said: 'Sender, my child, don't sleep, for the love of God, Sender, get up, get up, Sender, Sender, get away from here! Get away, Sender, just go anywhere you can. You're in danger!' I wanted to get up, but I couldn't move, it was as if someone were holding me tight. I felt my head and there was some kind of woman's coif on it. Ha, ha, I wasn't Sender, I was—a woman, if you please, no sign of a beard, I had a woman's jacket on, and my belly, my belly, I had a horrible stomachache—may all Jews be spared! 'Don't worry!' someone shouted, 'the first baby's always the hardest.' 'Oh, please, please!' I screamed. 'I just don't have the strength, I'm passing out.' 'A punch in the back of the neck is a good remedy. That'll arouse you,' said the man, and he really whacked me a few times. 'This is for before, this is for now, and this is for later,' he snapped, turning around and then vanishing. I lay there in sheer agony, just lay and lay, until, with God's help, I pulled myself up with all my strength and got to my feet. I dashed over to the door, it was locked. I banged and banged and banged, but it was no use. Suddenly the door flew open and I stuck out one foot. But robbers jumped on me and dragged me off to a cave. There they took out a knife and wanted to slaughter me. Just as they held the knife to my throat, I screamed: 'Help! Let me confess my sins first!' Well, that was my dream, Benjamin. I just hope it turns out well."

"Spit three times, Sender," Benjamin advised him, "and forget all about your dream. By the way, if you like, you can get up, it's already daylight. Just recite a few psalms."

Sender got up with a sigh, rinsed his hands, put on his coat and

251

took out his Yiddish Psalter. The book opened to the Tenth Psalm, and Sender began crooning in a gloomy melody:

Why, oh Lord, do you stand far away,
Concealing yourself on a troubled day?

The melody became sadder and more poignant with these verses:

He lurks in some hiding place
And kills the innocent apace.
His eyes go back and forth, forth and back,
And he glares at the poor man in his shack.
He lurks like a lion in his den,
And then he pounces upon poor men.
He crouches and waits until he can get
The poor man in his dreadful net.

By the time Sender was done, it was broad daylight, all the people in the room had already gotten up. A samovar as big as a cauldron was seething on the table, and people were drinking tea. Benjamin and Sender were each given a glass of hot tea. They felt refreshed and cheerful.

The room, which had been a dormitory, and then a teahouse, all at once became a synagogue. Sleeves were rolled up, naked Jewish arms were bared: hairy, smooth, skinny, fat, dark, white, gray, in all colors and shapes. Each worshiper slipped into a prayer shawl and prayer thongs and began to pray.

Our two strangers prayed for all they were worth, they lamented, they twisted their faces and bodies, they flattered and cozened, like truly broken Jews. They kept arguing with the Good Lord: "Oh, father, oh father!" and they kept praying longer than anyone else. After prayers, they poured themselves a glass of strong vodka, took a sip, and let it melt in their mouths so that bright-red currants emerged on their noses. Then they said to the other people: "L'chaim! L'chaim!" And they wished that the Good Lord would take pity on Jews everywhere, alas! And they rolled their eyes, heaved a quiet sigh, and bottoms up.

Which showed that they were no ordinary, common run of Jews, but pious, devout, and distinguished Jews.

Meanwhile, one of these distinguished Jews went off to town, remaining there for a couple of hours. When he came back, his friend looked into his face, which was absolutely aglow, and both men were very pleased. They had the table set, went out to wash, after first inspecting the vessel, as behooves pious, distinguished Jews. They also asked our friends to wash up and sit down with them for breakfast, if they pleased. At the table, they were very cheerful, they praised the innkeeper's wife for her good food, and were absolutely delighted with her. They began talking, they discussed the condition of Jews, saying it was high time that Jews, poor things, should be raised up. Why should such a nation, such a wonderful nation, alas, suffer so terribly? They sang the praises of the Jewish people, they lauded Jewish braininess to the skies.

"Is there anything that Jews can't do?" All the great inventions in the world, the telegraph, the railroad, and what not, they had all been thought up by Jews long, long ago. But that was nothing. The important thing was something else—the innermost core, the essence, the Jewish essence, that was the important thing. . . .

Then they attacked the heretics with a vengeance, the modern style of scholars, they cursed them with bell, book, and candle, they spat their lungs out at them and their new-fangled schools, where the students went bareheaded and studied profane books.

"Soon a section of the Talmud will be worth a kopek, and writing a secular petition will be worth a ruble. Oh, what's the world coming to! What a world, what a world! By God! . . ."

They kept on in that vein, eventually turning to the subject of our heroes' journey.

"May the Good Lord," they said, "show you His grace and fulfill all our wishes for you."

Benjamin was in seventh heaven after this benediction. Besides he was a bit, well, how can we put it, he was "tipsy," he opened his mouth and talked a blue streak.

"You know what, dear friends!" the Jews said lazily after getting up from the table. "Why don't we do the simple things, like plain, ordinary Jews, just as our forebears always did? After our journey, we should go to the bathhouse to steam our bodies.

253

You can trim your hair or your beards there, that'll make new men out of you, by God! And after the bathhouse, we'll attend to our business. That'll be the best thing, the simplest thing. It's not very modern perhaps. The heretics don't think too much of the bathhouse. We're not 'edjicated,' so let's do what our ancestors always did, long, long ago."

No Jew can turn down a bathhouse. What a tavern means to peasants and a pond to geese and ducks, that's what a bathhouse means a hundred degrees more to a Jew. No other nation could possibly feel the delight that Jews feel in a bathhouse. The bath is closely knit to his religion, his innermost feelings, and his family life. No Jewish soul can be talked into leaving heaven to enter any womb, it can't be enticed or persuaded by anything except a bath. That is the head agency, the central office between heaven and earth. Before a Jew is born, before a single limb of his even wiggles, they know about him in this office, from the bathkeeper and his wife to the woman administering the ablutions to women. A Jew can't truly feel his oversoul, the second soul that he gets on Sabbath and holidays, if he doesn't first have a bath. Otherwise he feels old and stale, not fresh and crisp. Just look at a Jew coming from the bathhouse on a Friday, he's blossoming, he's years younger, the spark of Jewishness burns in him and shines from his eyes. All his senses are fresher, more acute, the fragrance of the gefilte fish, of the steaming carrot stew, wafts into his nostrils like incense, his nose sniffs, smells, and delights. There is a singing in his heart, he croons a concert, he warbles the Song of Songs like a nightingale, coddles himself like a child, blazes, burns, and is half in the other world. . . . A Jew enters the bathhouse as if he were entering a fatherland, a realm of freedom, where all people have the same rights, where anyone is free to reach a high level—to clamber up to the top bench, revive his gloomy soul, relax his bones for even an hour, and cast away his burden of cares and worries. That's what the bathhouse means to Jews!

Which is why our friends were so happy at the idea of going to the bathhouse. They didn't have to be asked twice, and a few minutes later, they were walking along with the two fine Jews.

Our friends pictured the normal kind of bathhouse that's

found in Jewish towns. A dark, grimy building, far off at the foot of a mountain, with narrow, broken, inaccessible steps leading into it. However, the men took them to a lovely three-story building smack dab in the middle of town and said: "That's the bathhouse." Our friends gaped and gawked in surprise.

"You two are really a scream," the men laughed. "Come on in, why don't you, and you'll find something even more beautiful."

Upon entering the vestibule, our friends were dazzled by the painted floor and the spreading carpets. They felt as if they had stepped into the enchanted palace of *The Bovve Book* or *The Thousand and One Nights,* and soon princesses would come to welcome them. They would have a wonderful time and live like there was no tomorrow. But instead of a princess, a soldier with medallions came over and politely asked them to undress.

"Why don't you take your clothes off," the two fine Jews interpreted for them. "Meanwhile we'll go inside and pay for the tickets. Don't worry, you'll be taken in nicely, you'll really sweat!"

When our friends had stripped, they took their things along in order, as the custom is, to pick out the lice. Not having a dozen shirts in their wardrobe, they would wear one shirt for several weeks. Naturally, our poor friends itched by now, and delousing was absolutely crucial. But the soldier took their belongings and led our friends into another room. The room was furnished with chairs, and well-dressed gentlemen were sitting in armchairs around a long table. Our friends looked all over the place and they scratched their heads: Where was there a stone to pour water on, and where could they sweat here?

"Is this the Jewish bath?" Sender asked in the goyish language after Benjamin jostled him and told him to speak right up.

One of the gentlemen at the table walked over to them, looked at our naked friends, who were scrawny and scraggy, poor things, all skin and bones, with not an ounce of flesh upon them. The gentleman asked them something or other in the Muscovite tongue:

"Hey, what's he saying, Sender?" asked Benjamin.

"How should I know? I don't understand a word!" Sender replied with a shrug. "What kind of a language is that supposed to be anyway! He keeps saying something like: ticket, ticket."

255

"Oh, you fool," exclaimed Benjamin. "Don't you understand? That's the owner, he wants to see our tickets. In this kind of bathhouse, people need tickets. Tell him that the two Jews paid for our tickets."

"Already, gentlemen . . . Jews paid ticket. . . ." Sender stammered and stopped all at once as though he were choking, unable to finish what he wanted to say.

"Ticket, gentleman . . . paid . . . Jews. . . ." Benjamin squeezed out in his own way, explaining and clarifying the matter, tersely and precisely.

The gentleman who had gone over to our friends waved his hand and took them into a further room, where they assumed they would finally have a good sweat. . . .

After a while, when Benjamin and Sender were let out into the street, they were unrecognizable, the poor things had changed so drastically: clean-shaven, no beards, no earlocks, their eyes twisted and glassy, huge, cold beads of sweat on their foreheads, a gloom, a dark fog over their faces. Cramped up, huddling, their bodies quaking, and soldiers all around them.

A black, dismal cloud oozed across the sky. Lightning suddenly lit up the convoy. Then thunder boomed, so horribly that everyone trembled. A storm wind arose, billows of dust swept by like ghosts, snatching up garbage, straw, leaves, shreds of paper, everything together dancing a wild, lunatic dance, whirling, swirling, higher and higher. . . . The herd in the meadow ran nervously, roaring and bellowing, as if a pack of starving wolves were after them. The world was filled with wind and lightning and thunder, as if the Lord were furious at the sinful earth and everything upon it. He grabbed His head, His wrathful eyes shot out lightning, He screamed and shouted: "Oh! Oh!" in His thunderous voice. Finally a dreadful thunderbolt smashed through the universe, huge raindrops came trickling down like tears, they were mixed with beads of agonizing sweat and bloody tears from our poor, unhappy friends. . . .

Alas, Benjamin and Sender didn't realize that the desert wasn't the least bit dangerous, with its dreadful creatures, its lizards, dragons, and carnivores. The greatest danger was right here, in our lands. The time when our friends were wandering was the bad, the bitter, the dreadful time—the time when one Jew tried to catch the other and:

He lurked like a lion inside his lair
To pounce upon men without passports there.

To hand him over as a substitute, as a scapegoat for his own or someone else's children, for military service. Alas, our poor friends didn't realize that they had already reached the desert, that they were living among wild animals and predatory beasts. And that the two fine, pious Jews were worms, lindworms!

XIII

OUR POOR TRAVELERS HAVE BECOME SOLDIERS

Everyone can imagine what an awful situation our poor, miserable friends were in, how dark and bitter it was. We can spare ourselves the trouble of describing it.

At first, they were totally bewildered, they didn't have the least idea of what was happening. Everything was alien to them, the barracks, the soldiers, the language, and all the things they were ordered to do. The military coats hung on them like sacks, looking like women's jackets, and their caps, if you could call them that, loomed almost like kerchiefs on their heads. All in all, our friends almost seemed to be in costume: two Jews had disguised themselves to make fun of the army, mimicking soldiers and very freely showing how foolish they all were along with the whole military business. Pity the poor rifle that wound up with our friends. In their hands, it didn't appear like itself at all, it was as awkward as a poker in the hands of a man floundering in a kitchen. In drills, they pulled off such funny tricks with their hands and feet that the whole thing became a pure comedy.

Naturally, they were not starved for beatings. But what trouble is there in the world that a human being cannot get accustomed to? Not only man, but other creatures as well can get habituated to anything. Is there any creature freer than a bird? Yet when it's captured and put in a cage, it gradually settles in, it regains its appetite, starts picking at seeds, it hops about and warbles cheerful ditties, as though it had the entire world, with all its fields and forests, right there in the narrow cage. Our Sender took his situation more and more in stride. He would look hard at the soldiers drilling and then try to imitate everything they did in his own way. It was a joy to watch Sender repeating the exercises over and over again, standing up straight as a ramrod, pulling his head high, puffing his cheeks out like a hero, swinging his legs and marching and strutting like a turkey ruffling its feathers, he would wheel about, wheel about, and eventually entangle his legs and crash to the ground. In contrast, Benjamin simply couldn't get used to these things. By his very nature, he was a bird of passage, a wanderer, the kind of bird that flies off at the end of summer to spend the winter far away, in warm regions. The call of its migratory instinct is so powerful that if such a bird is kept in a cage then, come autumn, its life is miserable, it won't eat, it won't drink, it climbs up the walls, hunting for a crack to escape through. The journey to those faraway places, which ate into Benjamin's mind like a termite, which had become second nature for him, which had made him abandon his wife and children—that journey never gave him any peace, it bored, it bit into his brain, it seethed in him and kept shouting: "Benjamin, get going, get going!"

Meanwhile, the winter wore on and our poor Benjamin had a dreadful time of it.

One fine spring day, after Passover, when Sender was drilling away all by himself, Benjamin came over and said:

"I swear, Sender, you're really a child! You fool around and you play pranks like some kid in the street! What's the fun of it, I ask you. Remember, you've got a wife, thank the Lord, and besides you're a Jew. So why are you wasting your time with such nonsense and putting all your energy into it. What's the difference whether you do an 'about-face'—as they call it—with your left foot or your right foot? Who cares?"

"I don't know," replied Sender. "They order 'about face!' so I about face. That's fine with me. What do I care!"

"And what about our voyage? Tell me, have you forgotten all about it? For goodness' sake, our voyage to those faraway places. . . . Lindworm, mule, dragon!" Benjamin got all heated up.

"Hup, two, three, four!" exclaimed Sender, raising his legs.

"The hell with you and your marching, Sender! For God's sake, you should be ashamed of yourself. You child! Why don't you tell me when we're going on our journey?"

"We could leave right away, for all I care!" Sender replied. "As long as they let us go!"

"What do we need them for, and why do they need us!" cried Benjamin. "Why, Sender, as sure as we're Jews, tell me, if the enemy comes, God forbid, could two guys like us fend him off? You can tell him: 'Go away, or else I'll go bang-bang!,' and if you tell him that a thousand times, is he going to pay any attention? Not on your life! He'll pounce upon you, and you can thank your lucky stars if you escape with your skin. For goodness' sake, take my word for it, we're absolutely useless here, they'd love to get rid of us. I once heard the company commander say that we're a pain in the ass, and if it were up to him, he'd have sent us to the devil long ago. And when you come right down to it, what good are we to them, really? I tell you, Sender, quite openly, the whole thing was wrong from the very start, this is no marriage made in heaven. We're no good for them and they're no good for us. The Jews who put us in their hands must have told them that we were great heroes and that we knew everything there is to know about military strategy. Why, it's not our fault if those Jews played a trick on them. And they played a dirty trick on us too. We only came here to get some money and then travel on. No one said anything about military strategy. I'm ready to swear on a stack of Bibles that I didn't say a single word about that. They can't just kidnap us like that, it's simply not fair. Why, that's scandalous! In short, it's not the army's fault that we were tricked, and it's not our fault that the army was tricked. It's all the fault of the Jews, the liars, the rats who defrauded both sides. The Jews, Sender, the Jews, they're responsible for everything, it's all their fault, you

259

can't blame anyone else, only the Jews, I tell you, the Jews!"

"Well, so what do you want us to do, Benjamin?" asked Sender.

"I want us to continue our journey," said Benjamin. "The marriage is off, we're free again! I don't think anyone can keep us here or stop us from leaving, we've got the law and justice on our side. And if you're scared that they'll try to prevent us, then there's a very simple remedy: We can sneak away. It's no one's business but our own, nobody has to know. We don't have to say good-bye to anyone."

"I think so too, saying good-bye is useless," said Sender. "After all, we left home a year ago and we didn't say 'go to hell' to anyone, not even our wives and kids!"

From that moment on, our friends began thinking about their journey again and forging plans to escape. Benjamin's blood was seething, he was terribly nervous, he wandered about as excited as a hen wanting to brood on her eggs in spring. He was so absorbed in his thoughts that he never heard or saw what was going on all around him. If an officer happened to pass by, Benjamin didn't salute, so the officer punched him in the back of his neck, and Benjamin didn't even make a face, as though it weren't meant for him. When the officer barked out orders during exercises, they went in one ear and out the other. Benjamin was as oblivious as some Jews in synagogue. All he could think about was the journey, and his mind soared far, far away!

Late one night, when all the soldiers in the barracks were fast asleep, Benjamin tiptoed over to Sender's bed.

"Sender, are you ready?" Benjamin whispered.

Sender nodded, seized hold of Benjamin's coattail, and the two of them stole out into the courtyard as silently as mice.

A warm breeze was wafting outdoors, tatters of black and brownish-blue clouds were drifting through the sky, one after the other, as though thousands of draymen were driving wagons full of goods, dashing so as not to arrive a day after the fair. The moon, like an overseer, followed this long caravan, sticking its head out for a minute to see what was happening and then concealing itself for a long time, snuggling up under its cloudy tarpaulin, which looked as black as pitch.

Our friends sneaked through the darkness of the courtyard, quietly reaching the fence. They clambered up a heap of wood, from which they could easily get over the fence. All at once, Sender jumped and whispered:

"Oh, my God, Benjamin! I forgot our sack! Should I go back and get it?"

"God forbid!" said Benjamin. "That would be awful. If God helps a man, he'll help him with a sack too."

"Now I remember," said Sender, "what my grandfather, God rest his soul, warned me in my dream: 'Get up, Sender,' he said, and run away from here wherever you can!' May his merits help us out now, he was as good a Jew as can be and a straightforward man. Grandmother, God rest her soul, always used to say—"

But before Sender could finish saying what his grandmother always used to say about his grandfather, they heard a shout— from a soldier who was standing watch off to the side.

Our friends hugged the fence with bated breath, they lay there silently, they didn't stir, they looked like two large, old rags. A bit later, when it was quiet and calm again, the two rags showed signs of life and slowly descended from the fence. They crawled on their hands and knees, slowly edging further and further, until God helped them avoid the sentry and slink into an alley. Our friends got to their feet, paused a moment to catch their breath, and looked at one another with bright, joyful eyes.

"Grandmother, God rest her soul, used to say," Sender started talking, "that Grandfather, God rest his soul, thought all his life about going to the Holy Land. Just before dying, he sat up and said: 'If I was not fit in God's eyes to go to the Holy Land, then I have faith that one of my children will get there.' My heart tells me now that he meant me. May the Almighty hear my prayers!"

But Sender's prayers were heard by someone else! No sooner had he uttered his wish than all at once someone asked them in the Muscovite language: "Who goes there?" And upon receiving no answer, the man strode over and asked again.

Unfortunately, the moon stuck out its head from behind a dark patch of clouds and shone upon our poor friends, who stood there speechless and deathly pale, in front of their officer, while

261

he furiously waved his arms around, yelling, screaming, cursing them soundly.

A few minutes later, our friends were sitting in the guardhouse!

There are no words to describe the horrible sufferings of our friends as they wasted away behind bars. The poor things lost a mass of weight, they were total wrecks. Sender could at least sleep, and while sleeping, he could at least be numb to the dreadful suffering for a few hours, he had yet another good dream. His grandfather often came to him and joked with him, he would never come empty-handed: once he brought a bow and arrow, another time a sword or a Purim noisemaker, he would pinch his grandson's cheek, smile at him, and say: "Here are some toys for you, my child! Play with them, my boy, go bang-bang-bang, Sender! . . ." And once he brought a Hanukkah dreydel and sat down to spin it with his darling little grandson. Sender whirled and whirled and whirled, and then he won, and he got a kopek from his grandfather. . . . A good dream is a fine thing. Isn't the world a dream? But Benjamin didn't have that solace, he couldn't fall asleep. He was in a state of total confusion and his blood boiled like a cauldron. He gazed through the window and saw the sun shining delightfully, the green grass shooting and sprouting, trees blossoming beautifully, people walking, hurrying back and forth, and birds soaring through the heavens. Now was the right time to travel. But he was sitting there locked up, unable to start out on his journey. He was so miserable that he would hop, grab his head, scurry about in a daze, scream, and yell bitterly: "Oh God, oh God! What did I ever do to them? Oh God, oh God! What do they have against me? . . ."

XIV

THE WEDDING'S OFF, WE'RE FREE AGAIN!

A few days after the arrest of our friends, a court-martial convened, and a large number of officers, including the general and the colonel, sat there in full dress, while two soldiers with drooping heads stood by the side door, looking for all the world like mice that have been fished out of a jar of sour milk. The officers gaped at the soldiers, scrutinized them from top to bottom, then talked among themselves and exchanged fleeting grins.

"Listen Sender," one soldier muttered to the other while the officers conversed among themselves. "Even if it kills me, I've got to tell them the whole truth. Or else I'll explode!"

"Go ahead, Benjamin, tell them the truth," said the other soldier. "If that's what you want, then it's okay with me. What do I care."

"You are the men who sneaked out of the barracks late at night?" the general snapped. "Do you know the penalty for that?"

"Oh well, *bozhe moy,*" said Benjamin speaking randomly, half in Yiddish, half in Russian, and he talked so fervently, that Khaikel the Stutterer, the orator of Moochville, would have crawled six feet under.

The general turned away, laughing, he waved his hand, and the colonel began speaking in his place.

"You committed a grave offence and you can expect a very severe punishment for such a crime."

"Your highness," Benjamin blurted out. "Grabbing people in broad daylight and selling them like chickens in the marketplace—that's permitted; and when those poor people try to save themselves, that's called a crime! If that's the way things are, then the world is lawless, and I swear I don't understand what 'permitted' and 'not permitted' mean! But nevertheless, let's ask the people here, let them say who the guilty party is. For instance, what if someone captured you somewhere on the road and shoved you into a sack. Would you, God forbid, be guilty of a crime if you did all you could to get out of the sack? I tell you plainly: We were forced from the very beginning, we were taken in. The guilty ones are the Jews! Who knows what nonsense they filled your heads with! We swear to you—speak up, Sender, speak up! Why are you standing there like a golem? Trust in God and tell the truth, don't be afraid, speak together with me! We swear to you that we knew absolutely nothing about military strategy, we don't know anything about it, and we don't want to know anything about it. We have wives, thank the Lord, and we have future plans of our own, and we absolutely can't have anything to do with such stuff, our minds just couldn't take them in. So why do you need us? I think you ought to get rid of us yourselves."

Benjamin had hit the nail on the head. The military had been wishing to get rid of them long ago. When the superior officers had looked at our friends, at the way they dressed, the way they acted, the way they talked, the way they marched, they soon realized what kind of creatures they were dealing with, and they roared with laughter any number of times. The intention of this officers' council was to interrogate our friends and try to see whom they were dealing with. Benjamin and Sender were interrogated and, praise the Lord, they passed the examination with flying colors, even better than they wished, so that all the officers laughed and had a rollicking good time.

"Well, doctor?" the general finally asked an officer, who had been questioning our friends for a long time.

The doctor placed his finger on his forehead and shook his head as though to say: There's a screw loose here!

After the officers had conferred and then written something, the upshot was that our friends were released from the military.

"Go away," they were told, "go away, Godspeed!"

Benjamin very cordially took his leave with a bow and began striding off.

Sender raised his legs like a soldier and marched right after him. ❧

PART THREE
TRADITION AND MODERNISM

In the late nineteenth and the early twentieth century, Yiddish writers continued what was basically a genre tradition, recording and illuminating everyday Jewish life in the shtetl, but, of course, selecting and omitting. For even though they often claimed to be "historians," dealing with types rather than individuals, more concerned with the collective than with individuals, they nevertheless, and obviously, created literature rather than historiography. The shtetl tended to be stereotyped in this fiction, largely in the negative, but at times lovingly.

The attempts at a quasi-historical recording of life are exemplified in Sholom Aleichem's novel *Stempeniu.* While attacking the Yiddish pulp writers and depicting a highly moral romance in an everyday Jewish milieu, he aimed for realism by imaginatively using the jargon of Jewish musicians in his dialogues. This jargon was so specialized that he had to provide translation footnotes for his audience. An English equivalent, used to render the jargon here, is the lingo of contemporary American rock musicians, who, in our culture, have the same erotic outsider appeal of these itinerant Jewish musicians. (The latter, however, were an accepted component in shtetl life rather than superstars of a youth culture.)

Stempeniu has an ethical resolution, promoting the traditional structure of courtship and marriage. Although critical, Sholom Aleichem is nowhere as negative as the Haskalah about the way

Jewish husbands treated their wives. From a modern viewpoint, Rachel's final acceptance of marriage and materialism, though hardly as drastic as that of Stempeniu's wife, may be a rather dismal end. But for some contemporary thinking, it was good for herself and the collective.

The decay of the courtship ritual (which Sholom Aleichem later described in the Tevye stories) was at the core of evolution in Jewish life. And Dovid Bergelson depicted it with *fin-de-siècle* pessimism in *Joseph Shorr*. Reduced to the virtues of property and propriety, which none of his young urban contemporaries take seriously, the title character, a non-hero, embodies (upper-class) small-town traditionalism, which the modern age was undermining. This impressionistic novella also exposes the gap between shtetl and city Jews and between conventional, materialistic parents and the iconoclastic, metropolitan younger generation with its uprooted cosmopolitanism.

A more nostalgic picture of shtetl life at the turn of the century can be found in the hundreds of pastel sketches by Avrom Reyzen. Generally showing types rather than individuals, and using a delicate, lyrical language, he produced a low-key and loving *comédie humaine* of Jewish life (both in Eastern Europe and the New World). "The Dog" is a rather bizarre exception for him, since he seldom dwelt openly on horror.

A writer who focused almost exclusively on violence was Lamed Shapiro. His stories explore the psychology of both Gentile murderers and Jewish victims, especially in regard to the issue of Jewish response and self-defense, a question that he examined but could never fully resolve.

Amid the realism, soi-disant, of Yiddish fiction, there has always been a tradition of fantasy, even in modern times, when writers have competed with constant new editions of older fairy tales, legends, and romances, from the medieval *Mayse Book* to Yiddish versions of *The Arabian Nights*. Weissenberg's satirical "A Tale of a Goat" attacks superstition and provincialism with

266

Haskalah acid and yet poetic charm, leaving the characters in an endless waiting for a "stranger," presumably the Messiah.

This Messianic yearning, of course, infused Jewish life—and now in various new forms, both religious and political, e.g. socialism, Zionism, and the like. But while the shtetl may have been assailed as static, backward, and rooted in superstition, as Weissenberg shows it to be, it nevertheless remained a tenacious social organization, despite the breakup of traditions, despite industrialization, despite large migration to big cities and foreign countries. It was not modernism that destroyed the shtetl.

THE CONVERT

DOVID BERGELSON

There were rumors that Moyshe-Leyb Yanashov's daughter, the convert, was back in the country, with her husband, the justice of the peace. The rumors had begun right after Passover.

A Jewish beggar was walking from one village to the next. He was as pensive as his day of poverty after the charitable week of Passover: He couldn't tell whether his begging would bring in anything.

And on the road, which was hidden in the green depths of tilled fields, he suddenly saw a wagon coming his way, heaped with furniture as tall as a house, tables and chairs with their legs jutting out towards the lofty blue sky of early summer, and rocking so slowly as if to tell that they were being brought from far away . . . off to the justice of the peace . . . straight to the justice of the peace.

And then here they were, the convert, and her husband, the justice of the peace.

More than two weeks had passed since they moved into the small manor house in the neighboring administrative village. Near the kitchen door, they kept a large number of turkeys, chickens, and geese; they never socialized with anyone and they commanded respect.

Now the spreading orchards in the village were in blossom. Trees were standing about like white brides, wistful, mournful, the air could not produce the slightest breeze to stir their

269

branches, and, just before twilight, a Jewish merchant came driving through the village in his own britska. His coachman sat in front, urging on the horses. The merchant gazed over at the justice's attractive manor and saw the convert with her longish, beautiful, slightly weary face, which looked stubborn and was still demanding something from the entire county. There, among the different fowls, she wore summer clothes. She asked the coachman something as he came driving up, then she walked far over to the fenced-in courtyard, which was full of the lowing of the calf, a yelling from the kitchen, and the smell of a milch cow, and there was silence all around. From the remote end of the village came the brief tolling of the church bell, the bass. It was urging the Jew on. It was calling to a tardy Christian wagon in some green valley far away, and kept repeating incessantly:

"It's almost over, it's almost over, the strange, quiet Christian holiday."

People were saying that the young justice of the peace was kind and decent to everyone.

He would always find a way of getting two hostile peasants to reach a compromise, or of gently reprimanding a drunk. Close to sundown, he would stroll through the village, handing out candy and laughing at the peasant children, who were sitting in dirty shirts with their bare buttocks in the middle of the road, measuring the dust with their fists.

"Gophers!" he shouted to them.

The children concealed their embarrassed faces in their sleeves. But then they ran after him until the distant riverbank. There they stopped and watched him escaping from them as he sat down in his new white boat and skillfully rowed towards the overgrown neck of the river:

"Gophers!"

Fiery golden threads were running from under his oars. So many setting suns were shredded, and the pieces sank into the depths of the river. The justice reached the peasants who were squaring logs for the old, ruinous bridge. The air smelled of fresh oak, of chips, wet spices, and a silent summer evening. Soon a frog would be sticking out its head and croaking at the pale moon; a stork would be standing on one foot, clapping out a bony story to the thickening evening; and the justice would be sitting near the peasants for a long time, talking about the overgrown meadow. In his opinion, they were ultimately going to draw the river water over there and make the sluices stronger and deeper.

The convert with her earnest, longish face was even more of a recluse than in her youth, and she would never drive to the village.

She loved her husband. Perhaps that was why she would often put on the white knitted dress that revealed her full, clear throat and made her look broader at her waist and her breasts. At dusk, when he went off to the village, she would walk by herself outside near the fence, and she looked so patient, as if constantly thinking about his having the right to go away for a long while. . . .

She couldn't say anything to him about it. . . .

Her voice was sad and wistful. Whenever she spoke, you couldn't tell which was sadder, her black eyes, her longish face, or her voice. And her voice was nearly always scolding her husband at lunch:

"Kolye, you're not eating!"

Some Jews once overheard her when they were called as witnesses in regard to a fistfight between peasants and were waiting for the justice at lunchtime, out in the hall. Her voice seemed maternal, protective. The Jews felt so strange, as if just noticing once more that they had been sitting without hats for a long time; they smiled and winked at one another:

"Looks like she really loves the goy, huh?"

And sometimes, from the inner rooms, a strange, tidy little creature came running out, a wee four-year-old, whose eyes were even bigger and blacker than his mother's, his small mouth was chewing, and he had a dimple in his left cheek. Each time, he would stop at the door and give the Jews such a curious look of surprise, as if they, the whole community, all Jews from near and far, were related to him on his mother's side. One of the smiling

271

Jews even began teasing him with his finger, motioned to him with his wrinkled forehead, his nose, and his entire smiling face, and he mumbled in Yiddish:

"Come here, you little bugger, come here. . . ."

But the little creature was frighted by these motions. He heard his mother's voice from the inner rooms, and hurried back with a thumping heart, pounding his feet loudly and running quickly, as if terror-stricken.✿

THE DOG

AVROM REYZEN

No one knew where he came from. One bright summer morning, the men in the old synagogue noticed a newcomer in the gang of kids. He was about fifteen, in rags and tatters, with unkempt hair under his cap and scratches all over his face.

"A new duck!" said Khone, who had caught sight of him upon coming early to prayers, and he ogled him wryly: "Who are you?"

"My parents' child!" the kid retorted sarcastically, scratching himself all over.

"Ugh!" said Khone, spitting on the ground and heading for his pew.

The kids accepted him without giving him any trouble at first. But when they started hazing him, he straightway knocked them down. Getsl, the barley-woman's son, earnestly exclaimed:

"You're pretty tough, all right!"

"Like a soldier!" agreed Feyvl-Kulye.

The others came over to take a close and respectful look at the newcomer.

"Ya ain't from aroun' here, are ya?" asked Getsl.

"Nope!" he replied in a dry, standoffish tone.

"Where ya from?"

"Kletsk."

"A bunch of robbers!" someone threw in.

"They're more honest than the people around here," the newcomer angrily snapped back.

273

"Ya got any folks?" asked someone else.

"Nope!"

"Whatta ya gonna do here?"

"I'm gonna stand my ground!" he answered proudly, like a grown-up, winking his eye.

That was all that the kids could get out of him at first.

Later on, after a few weeks, when he got to know Getsl a bit better and had taken a few drags on Getsl's cigarette, the kid began to tell them his story:

"I walked here. . . ."

"All the way from Kletsk?" the gang was startled.

"It was nothing," he boasted. "Gimme another drag, Getsl," and he held out his hand.

Getsl, not trusting the cigarette out of his own hand, put it in the kid's mouth himself; the newcomer puffed with all his might.

"Some drag!" Getsl made a face. "You've smoked up the whole cigarette."

"So what! When I get cigarettes, I'll share 'em with you. I ain't selfish."

"Ain' no one more generous than beggars!" someone quipped.

"I'll tell ya why I ran away," the newcomer continued his biography: "When my ol' man died—"

"Ya got a mother?" someone interrupted.

"I already told ya I don't. . . . She died when she had me. When my ol' man died, this neighbor, a shoemaker, took me up and says to me:

" 'Okay, Hatskl . . . it's over—' "

"Your name's Hatskl?" they interrupted.

"Hatskl," he answered quietly, as though embarrassed by his name.

" 'It's over,' says the shoemaker to me, 'No more loafin'. Time you grew up. I'm gonna take ya in, and you're gonna become a shoemaker. . . .' But I didn' wanna, goddamn it! Who wants to sit around a whole day bangin' nails! It would kill me. 'Why work?' I says to myself. 'It's best to live free.' As for eatin' . . .? I wouldn' mind workin' just a li'l bit: say, four hours a day—"

"Four hours a day is still too much," Getsl broke in. "An hour a day's enough. I help my ma grind the barley one hour a day. That's all I'm up to."

"But the shoemaker wanted me to sit and work all day long. Whenever I goofed off a li'l, he beat my ass. It really pissed me. Like, I don't mind if the guys in town mess aroun' with me. I sock them, they sock me, we're even. But I couldn' hit the shoemaker back, he was as skinny as a greyhound, I coulda knocked him out with my li'l finger. Whenever he'd lay his skinny fists on me, I felt like puking. . . . But it never hurt."

"I woulda let him have it straight in the kisser, and so hard he wouldna had the strength to hit anyone," said Getsl scornfully.

"I did somethin' much better. I ripped off a coupla boots from him and ran away."

"Where're the boots?"

"Sold. I got two rubles for them," Hatskl boasted.

"But ya ain' got no passport."

"I don' need no passport. I come from around here. This is where my ol' man useta get his passport."

"Ya got any relatives here?"

"Relatives?" he shrugged. "Maybe, only I don' know 'em."

"Fuck relatives!" Getsl cursed. "My ma's got relatives here, and they won' even let her in the house."

"They must be rich."

"Very rich," Getsl was all worked up. "One of them, Yankl Hatshes, must be worth about ten thousand rubles. He lends money on interest."

"A relative like that is good to rip off!" said Hatskl with a smirk.

"He can go to hell!" replied Getsl with a wave of his hand.

When the guys got better acquainted, they found out that Hatskl was a thoroughgoing prankster. They particularly enjoyed his barking like a dog.

"Hatskl, why don'tcha bark a li'l?" Getsl would ask him.

"Bow-wow-wow!" Hatskl would start barking, and the guys would split their sides laughing.

"Just like a dog!" they praised him.

"Back in Kletsk, I scared everybody at night," Hatskl said

275

laughing. "This rich guy, Leybe Wolfs, got so scared he fell over when I started barkin' at him one night."

"Punks," the guys laughed.

"Bow-wow-wow!" Hatskl showed how he had barked.

And the guys came up with a nickname for him: "The Dog." Gradually, his real name was forgotten, and "Dog" became his normal, natural handle.

And he didn't mind at all. On the contrary, he even liked the fact that the name set him apart from everyone else, from all the people he didn't much care for. It kept him from having any contact with any other human beings, except for his buddies, the gang of kids. The name put him at liberty to run around, to go hungry, and to sleep wherever he could. If the beadle threw him out of the anteroom of the synagogue, he could spend the night on the porch of the women's section, just like a dog. And at times, barking, he would actually forget he was human. He would play his canine role with a vengeance, deeply, viciously, murderously, as though he were about to tear someone to shreds.

Once Getsl called him over to his mother's place:

"Hey Dog, wanna earn some money?"

"Yeah!" replied the Dog lukewarmly.

"Come over and help us turn the stones for the barley, and Ma'll give ya five kopeks."

The Dog hesitated and finally started out. On the way, he barked:

"Bow-wow-wow!"

"You're goin' to work. Whatcha barkin' for?" asked Getsl.

"Don' feel like goin'," the Dog said lazily.

"You're a real dog!" Getsl reproved him. "You'll starve to death, like a dog."

"Better than workin'. . . . Bow-wow!"

Entering Getsl's home, the Dog shot a scornful look at the huge stick attached to two flour-covered stones, and he started scratching himself.

"So this is your fine feathered friend . . ." the barley-woman grimaced, "a respectable man if ever I saw one!"

"Bow-wow!" barked the Dog, laughing wildly.

"None a your crazy tricks now," snapped the widow. "If you

wanna help turn the stones, then fine. If not, good-bye!"

The Dog began turning the stones, every so often barking to himself.

"What'sa matter? Does he have a dybbuk or somethin'!" The barley-woman was frightened. "All he does is bark."

"Bow-wow!" The Dog burst into angry barking. "I'm sick of turnin', gimme my money."

"You think you can earn five kopeks that quickly! You dog!" snapped Getsl's mother. "Ya gotta turn for a whole day!"

"Over your dead body!" yelled the Dog, running off without his pay.

"It's better to be a dog than to turn the stones for a whole day," he spit as he walked along, and started barking. . . .

And thus the Dog spent two homeless years in the town, running around the synagogue yard, in the streets, and through the open countryside. Out there, he felt better than anywhere else; he would do his canine tricks, walking on his hands, and barking and barking. . . . He felt as though he were a real, free dog out there and as though the whole world were his. But whenever he got really hungry, he would angrily look around the vast, open meadow and see there was nothing there but grass, and he would start to bark, and, standing up erect, he would run back to town and go looking for food. . . .

"Ain'tcha ever gonna stop?" Getsl once asked when the Dog had burst out barking.

"Never!" yelled the Dog. "When I bark, I forget all my troubles. . . . You think I don' mind goin' aroun' in rags, like I was crazy . . .? Uhn-uhn! Sometimes I feel like tearin' the whole world t' pieces, and that's when I get a hankerin' to bark, you see?"

"Then go ta hell, you Dog!" Getsl cursed. "As long as ya keep barkin', you'll never have anythin'. People won't take ya in their homes."

"Fuck 'em, an' fuck their homes! I need 'em like a hole in the head!"

"You'll die like a dog! You'll see," Getsl was trying to scare him.

277

"Makes no difference whether you're a dog or a human!" the Dog philosophized. "I like dogs better 'n people. Fuck people!" he spit out.

One day, in the synagogue yard, Getsl came over to the Dog and laughing, said to him:

"You know what, Dog? Tomorrow they're poisonin' all the stray dogs."

"Drop dead!" the Dog replied.

"I swear it's true!" Getsl assured him.

"What're they poisonin' 'em for?" the Dog asked earnestly.

"Why not!" answered Getsl. "It's the law, ownerless dogs've gotta be poisoned. . . ."

"Who cares if they run around?" the Dog asked.

"We don't need 'em."

The Dog started brooding. Finally, he asked:

"How do they poison 'em?"

"They chop up hamburgers and put poison inside. When they throw the meat to them, they grab it and eat it up."

"Real hamburgers?" the Dog interrupted.

"Sure 'nuff. Real, delicious hamburgers. If you like, you can taste one. You probably never ate a hamburger like that in your whole life."

"Go fuck yaself!" the Dog yelled, and turned pale.

"They're gonna give you one of those hamburgers, you're a dog too, ya know!" Getsl laughed.

Instead of answering, the Dog socked Getsl and ran off.

Night came on. It was cold and dark in the anteroom of the synagogue, where the Dog was spending the night. He was lying with open eyes, brooding. He was in a turmoil over the news that Getsl had brought him that day. He was frightened.

"Why am I scared?" He tried to calm himself. "I'm not a real dog, no one's gonna throw me a poisoned hamburger."

But it didn't help. He felt that in the morning he would get up hungry, unable to hold himself back, and, along with all the hungry dogs, he would pick up a hamburger and gulp it down, poison and all.

"Bow-wow!" he started barking.

But now he was frightened by his own bark. He had to stop

being a dog, he decided. "It's better to be human. . . ."

"But how do you start livin' like a human bein'?" he wondered. "I'm so ragged, I'm so cut off, I never talked to people. I hate them and they hate me.

"Fuck them!" he cursed, and started barking again.

The sleepless night made him even hungrier the next day. He had never been so hungry in all his life.

"They're throwin' hamburgers to the dogs today," kept flashing through his mind all morning.

And barking furiously, he ran off to the marketplace. . . .✿

THE CREEK

AVROM REYZEN

Even the biggest patriots in town had to admit, with sorrow in their hearts, that the town did not have a river. And that the creek which it did have was no river. Since a Jew can be divorced only near a river, they had to strain things a bit to make our creek valid. After all, its trickle of water did move on and off. Some of the local patriots cited geographical evidence to prove that the creek had a major source, it might very likely be a branch of the Nieman. And we had all heard of the Nieman, we knew of its world-wide fame as a river. No mean thing the Nieman. Why it might even flow into the Great Sea.

But no one believed that the family tree of our creek really went back to the Nieman. And how could we? Its water was so shallow that in the summer, three-year-olds could toddle across it, and even the most overprotective mother didn't feel she had to warn her pet: "Careful, darling, you'll drown—God forbid!" On the contrary, the child was safer in the creek than ashore. The land all around was pitted, and the small fry were always tumbling all over the place.

The creek did have one bridge, but only for show. The bridge itself looked quite respectable, it even had two railings, just like a bridge across a genuine river. With all the trimmings.

People would laugh: "What good is the bridge if the river's not a river . . . ?"

And all year long, the river was shamefaced, shamefaced and a laughingstock. The local wags gave it a nickname: The Deep Blue Sea.

281

Even at the Jewish New Year, when the Jews gather at a stream to "empty all the sins" out of their pockets, you could always count on somebody cracking a joke at the creek's expense:

"What's it gonna do with all those sins?"

And someone else would answer: "The river's not a river, and the sins aren't sins. . . ."

And the creek itself seemed to feel how small and trivial it was, the bit of water that it did have flowed in a long strip, so quietly that you couldn't hear the least splashing or swishing. It was sometimes really painful to look at it, and there were moments when it would have seemed better to die outright than to lead such a life, better to run dry altogether.

And there were actually times when the creek, on a bright July day, after a few weeks of great heat, did run dry without leaving any trace of itself. And some of its friends had aching hearts, especially the schoolboys, and the bridge really looked like a headstone on a grave. . . .

True, after a few days of rain, it would rise from the dead, but so small and narrow, and the water so turbid and silent.

And the creek remained deathly still!

However, there were days in the year, when the little creek was fully restored, it would mount and swell, and grow wider and deeper, and, even more surprising, it would become proud and gush noisily and tumultuously.

On such a day, it was a joy to look at the river. Especially for those who knew what it was like the rest of the year.

They would look at it in great astonishment, unable to believe their eyes. Was this the little creek that was known ironically as the Deep Blue Sea and that had never once raised its voice above a whisper?

And people came running to marvel at it.

This was one of the finest days in the life of the creek and the shtetl Jews.

It was spring, during the lovely time of Passover. The Jews, provided with matzos and all sorts of good food for eight days, lacked only a bit of entertainment.

For, by Passover, the days are long, and there aren't enough prayers to fill them. After lunch, a Jew won't sit down and recite the psalms. The young sun calls him out of doors.

And he heads for the river.

It was as though the creek had chosen to reveal its wonders at Passover.

For, if it had been a miracle for the sea to part and allow the Jews to cross it on dry land, then how much more of a miracle, perhaps, for the creek, which was dry all year round, to suddenly turn into a sea!

"A real sea!" said the Jews in amazement, staring at the water which tossed and gushed and splashed on all sides and would soon reach the home of Aaron the blacksmith.

"The river's gonna carry off his house!" said someone, terrified, yet in awe.

But, if the truth must be told, such worries were groundless. One year, when the creek did overflow, it only got as far as the foundations.

And a lot of people were eager for the river to engulf the house altogether. . . . No one really had anything against Aaron the blacksmith, and they would hardly have let him drown, God forbid! They would have rescued him along with his wife and children; he could count on it! . . .

But, as I've said, nothing of the sort ever happened, and deep down, people regretted it. . . .

If the creek had only done something wild, something cruel!

Now one year, the townsfolk did have a happy Passover: The river washed away the bridge, and the bridge floated along on its back like a chip of wood. . . .

The whole shtetl came running, all and sundry, everybody.

And for once, they were really frightened by the river:

"It looks dangerous! It's rebelling!"

And this time, even the rabbi, who never leaves his home except for synagogue, came to look at the great miracle.

He didn't come alone of course, he was accompanied by the community leader, his beadle, and his son-in-law.

"Make way, the rabbi's coming," said the beadle irately.

The people instantly drew back, and the rabbi waddled

through, pausing a good distance from the water.

"To go any further would be perilous!" he said in fright.

The son-in-law, being younger, was anxious to get right up close, but since he was still living with the rabbi, he felt it wouldn't be proper.

"Why in the world is the river running wild this year?" the rabbi finally asked, upon recovering from his initial shock. "What's the meaning of this?"

"It's quite simple," said the community leader, "there was a heavy snowfall this year. . . ."

"Ah . . . snow . . ." the rabbi nodded thoughtfully, "that's why . . . a heavy snowfall . . . aha . . . tut-tut-tut . . . such a flood. . . ."

"Rabbi, come closer!" suggested a worthy burgher.

"No, this is far enough, far enough!" said the rabbi, begging off.

And watching the water gush and gurgle on all sides, he piously murmured:

"How great are your wonders, oh Lord!"

And he started back.

A bit later, the authorities came, if you'll pardon my mentioning it—the police commissioner, escorted by the town constable and two gendarmes.

On an ordinary weekday, the crowd would have scattered at once, it's wiser not to get too close to the authorities. . . . But today, with Passover, they were so excited that they stayed.

Some of the men thought of doffing their hats, and did so. . . .

And the commissioner had a sense of *politesse*, and responded courteously in Russian:

"Excuse me, gentlemen, may we pass through. . . ."

And if the commissioner was polite, then the constable, who was looking forward to getting matzos from the Jews, was doubly and triply polite, and called out even more courteously in Russian:

"Dear friends, do let His Honor pass through."

The Jews were curious to know what the commissioner would do.

And one of the more audacious ones went over to him, with his hat in his hands, and said:

"It's a bad business, the bridge has flown away."

And the Jews cocked their ears and heard the commissioner saying very courteously as he slapped the audacious fellow on the shoulders:

"Vsyo ispravim. . . ."

And the Jews translated it into Yiddish:

"It's gonna be okay."

And the whole town was blissful. . . . The creek had run wild! It had turned into a sea! ❧

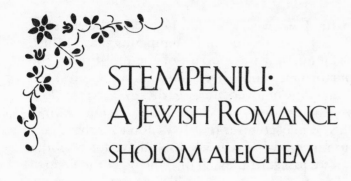

STEMPENIU: A JEWISH ROMANCE

SHOLOM ALEICHEM

STEMPENIU'S ESCUTCHEON

Stempeniu. That was a sort of nickname he inherited from his father. His dad, may he rest in peace, was a musician, he was known as Beryl the Bassist or Beryl of Stempeni, a village in the area of Mazepevke. He played the bass and he was also a good wedding Jester, a fine rhymester, a crafty prankster, he disguised himself as a beggar at all weddings, twisted his eyes, danced like a bear, mimicked a woman in labor yelling "Oh God, oh God, I swear on a stack of Bibles it'll never happen again! . . ." Or else he let out a stream of water in the middle of a room so that all the men rolled up their coattails and the women lifted their skirts. Or else he hung some sort of rubbish on the mother-in-law's apron, and he played further tricks and hoaxes galore.

They had been musicians for generations. Beryl the Bassist or Beryl of Stempeni, as we know, played the bass. Beryl's father, Shmulik the Trumpeter, had played the trumpet. His grandfather, Faivish the Cymbalist, had played the cymbals, and his great-grandfather, Ephraim the Violist. . . . In short, Stempeniu came from a long line of musicians, and he wasn't the least bit ashamed (unlike many Jewish craftsmen, who, just between you and me, are ashamed of what they are). And no wonder: The name he made for himself in Mazepevke, the renown he acquired throughout the world—those were no mean accomplishments. Now *there* was a musician for you!

It was an honor for Jews everywhere to hear Nissi Belzer sing, Godik the Wedding Jester recite, and Stempeniu play. Which goes to show that Stempeniu was no run-of-the-mill fiddler, no garden-variety performer, and there must have been solid reasons for the fame he enjoyed among the great. Jews love music and have an ear for song—which even our enemies cannot deny. . . . Though you may counter that Jews don't get that many chances to listen to music—what reasons do we have for celebrating? How often can we just start playing or dancing at the drop of a hat? But, say what you like, we are still mayvens, experts on singing, playing, and everything else. Why, if a cantor should come to town, we all go running for tickets, and having musicians at a wedding is a downright obligation for us, we would give a bag of borsht just to hear the band playing as the happy couple begin to sip the golden broth—not a merry ditty, of course, a merry one comes later. The company sits about in great respect, the musicians play a doleful tune, a mournful, plaintive dirge. The fiddle weeps, and the rest of the band accompanies it very sorrowfully. The audience is seized with melancholy, and everyone feels grief, a pleasant grief, but still a grief. Each guest becomes wistful, lowers his head, and, rubbing his finger on his plate or kneading balls from the fresh challah, he drifts off in his own thoughts, his own sad thoughts, for each guest must have his own worries, and trouble is one thing a Jew doesn't go borrowing. And so, the gloomy playing and the dismal thinking fuse into one, and every moan of the violin touches the hearts of the wedding guests and finds an echo there. Any heart, especially a Jewish heart is a fiddle: You squeeze the strings and you draw forth all kinds of songs, mostly sad and gloomy songs. . . . All you need is the right musician, a master violinist, the kind of master that Stempeniu was.

Oh, what a master he was! He would grab the violin and apply the bow, just one stroke, nothing more, and the violin had already begun to speak. And how do you think it spoke? Why, with words, with a tongue, like a living human being—if you'll forgive my mentioning them in the same breath. It spoke, pleaded, crooned tearfully, in a Jewish mode, with a force, a scream from the depths of the heart, the soul. Stempeniu would lean his head to one side, the long, black shock of hair flowing across his wide shoulders, his eyes, his black, burning eyes, peering upward, and his lovely radiant face would suddenly turn as pale as death. Another minute—and no more Stempeniu! All you could see was a hand flying up and down, up and down, and you could hear all kinds of sounds, and all sorts of singing came pouring out, dark, melancholy, cutting to the quick, piercing the soul, shattering the mind. The audience was fainting, languishing, perishing in every limb. Hearts filled up, they overflowed, and tears came to all eyes. Jews sighed, Jews moaned, Jews wept. And Stempeniu? Who cared about Stempeniu? Not even Stempeniu knew where he was. He did what he had to do, he fiddled, and that was that! And when he stopped playing, he threw down the violin and put his hand to his heart. And his eyes burnt like Sabbath candles, and his beautiful face shone in ecstasy. The listeners awoke as though from sleep, a sad but sweet sleep, and they gave voice to their enthusiasm, all of them at once. They oohed, they aahed, they mmmmed, they lauded, they were beside themselves, they couldn't stop praising him.

"Ooh, Stempeniu! Ah, Stempeniu!"

And the women? What can I tell you about the women? I doubt very much whether they shed as many tears on the Day of Atonement as they did for Stempeniu's music. You mustn't even weep as much for the Destruction of the Temple as the women wept during Stempeniu's playing.

"If only God will let me have Stempeniu for my youngest daughter's wedding! Oh, Lord, oh Lord!"

And thus the women made their wishes, wiped their red, swollen eyes, blew what was left in their noses, and, while they made their wishes, their strings of pearls and gold earrings, and rings, and brooches, and necklaces, and all the other Jewish baubles twinkled and glittered and sparkled.

And then there were the girls, the young ladies. They were shackled to the earth, like mannequins, gaping at Stempeniu and his violin, not stirring a limb, not batting an eyelash, but somewhere, inside their corsets, hearts were fluttering, and concealed sighs kept escaping. . . .

289

STEMPENIU AND HIS BAND

The sensation made by Stempeniu and his band when they came to a little town, the turmoil they aroused, simply cannot be described.

"Hey look! There's a four-horse wagon coming round from behind the mills. It must be the in-laws!"

"Nope! It's the musicians. That's Stempeniu and his gang!"

"What? Stempeniu? Stempeniu's here already? Now that'll be a merry wedding for Haym ben-Tsion—damn his eyes!"

Jewish wives blushed. Jewish girls set about combing their hair and weaving their long braids. Boys rolled their pants up to their thighs and ran to welcome Stempeniu. And even grown men, bearded husbands, let out smiles, which meant they were thrilled that Stempeniu had come to play at Haym ben-Tsion's wedding. Fine! Why not? Why should they care? It wasn't costing *them* any money, was it?

By the time the wagon fetched up at the inn, the street was chock-full of people. Everyone was curious to catch a look at Stempeniu and his gang, and so they stood there for a moment.

"Just look at them shoving!" everyone yelled, and shoved to the front, as Jews are wont to do. "Just look at him elbowing his way, he wants to be the first! What's there to look at? Haven't you ever seen musicians before?"

That's what each Jew said, pushing his way up to the wagon, while the musicians emerged one by one.

The first to step down was Yokel the Bassist (who played the contrabass), a nasty man with a squashed nose and with wads of cotton in his ears. Next came Leybush with his clarinet, a drowsy mannikin with thick lips. He was followed by Haykel Hump, *the* Haykel Hump, the hunchbacked wedding jester. Then out jumped a man with a tangle of black hair and with hair all over like a wild man from the desert, and terrifying bushy eyebrows. That was Shneyer-Meyer the back-up fiddler. A couple of boys came leaping after him, ferocious-looking creatures with swollen cheeks, blackened eyes, dreadful buckteeth the size of shovels. These were the apprentices, who were still working for nothing, but later, in time, they might turn into respectable musicians. Last but not least, who should come rolling out on crooked bowlegs, but red-haired Mekhtshi the Drummer, with a drum that was twice his size. His face was beginning to sprout a beard, a reddish growth, but only on one side, the right side, while the other half of his face, the left side, was naked, as barren as a steppe. Mekhtshi the Drummer, you must know, had first married at thirty, and rumor had it that his wife was a hermaphrodite. . . .

The town scamps had probably spread the news that Stempeniu was coming with his band. Every so often, a schoolboy sneaked in and gave the drum a bop or twanged the *G*-string of the contrabass. The boy got a whack in the nape of his neck from Yokel the nasty bassist. And little by little, the street began boiling and bubbling, for the bridegroom had also arrived in town with dozens of young men who had driven out to meet him on the other side of the mills. *And the town of Yampeli did shout and was glad.*

And: like Yampeli, like Stristsh, and all the other little Jewish towns that had the privilege of having Stempeniu at a wedding, and that's how it was in Mazepevke, where Stempeniu made his home. In short, the whole world was in a turmoil over Stempeniu!

STEMPENIU'S PREPARATIONS

What was all the excitement about in Mazepevke? Haym ben-Tsion Glock was marrying off his youngest daughter, his fledgling, Rivke. So why not celebrate and rejoice with him? His wedding was the place to be. After all, he was, so they say, one of the richest men in town. Everybody and his uncle would be there. Some for friendship, some for envy, some for duty, some to show off their wives' pearls, earrings, or the new necklace

291

brought back from the county fair; but more than anything—for Stempeniu. In short, *everyone* attended the festivities! All of Mazepevke rejoiced at Rivke's wedding. Not to mention Isaak-Naphtali and his wife and children, for Isaak-Naphtali was Haym ben-Tsion's partner in the store and in the mill, as well as a distant relation, that is to say, Isaak-Naphtali's wife Dvosse-Malke was sort of distantly related to Rivke's mother, a cousin once removed on her mother's side.

No wonder Dvosse-Malke was veiled and bedizened like a genuine member of the family. She bustled around and didn't do anything, but she waved her arms and shouted and made a racket as though she *were* doing something. And her beautiful daughter-in-law, Rachel, stood next to the bride, bedecked and bejeweled like a princess, her big blue eyes shone like two big diamonds and her red cheeks glowed like two blossoming roses. Her one hand held the bride's loosened hair, which the women, copiously weeping, had unbraided for the veiling ceremony. And her other hand stroked her white throat. And she never noticed two black burning eyes staring at her all the while. . . .

The servants scurried about like chickens without heads. The in-laws were clamoring: "Oh God! Oh God! It's time for the veiling! How long can we torment the children, they've been fasting for a whole summer's day already!" Everyone shouted: "It's time! It's time!" But no one did anything. Isaak-Naphtali wandered about in a velvet cap, his hands behind his back like a preacher, and Dvosse-Malke was raising the roof. The other relatives on both sides were dashing past one another, sticking out their hands as though they wanted to do something but couldn't get anything to do.

"Well, why aren't they doing anything?" asked the groom's family.

"Why aren't they starting to do something?" answered the bride's family.

"Have you ever seen the like before? Making children starve that long!" shouted the groom's family.

"Have you ever heard the like before? Making children starve this long?" shouted the bride's family.

"Why's everyone chasing back and forth?"

"What's all this running around anyway?"

"Everyone's running, everyone's making a racket, and they're not even budging! A fine state of affairs!"

"Just running and raising a racket—and no one's willing to do anything!"

"Hasn't there been enough talk already? It's time for action! There's a limit to everything!"

"C'mon already! Stop all the talking! Let's get going! Isn't there a limit?!"

"Where are the musicians?" asked the groom's family.

"The musicians! Where are they?" answered the bride's family.

And the musicians were busy getting ready. They polished the bows, they tuned the instruments. Yokel the Bassist yanked a boy along by the ear, warning him softly: "You little bastard, I'll teach you to pluck strings!" Mekhtshi the Drummer scratched the bristly half of his face, not deigning to glance at anyone. Haykel the Jester was talking to an acquaintance, a teacher, he took a pinch of snuff from him with two fingers and poured out a cascade of jokes. And the other musicians, the boys with swollen cheeks and buckteeth like shovels, stood around Stempeniu, discussing an important matter with him in their jargon:

"Who's the chick next to the frau-to-be?" asked Stempeniu in musician's lingo, staring at lovely Rachel. "Hey, Rakhmiel!" he said to one of the swollen-cheeked apprentices. "Go and check her out, but snappy, man, snappy!"

Rakhmiel quickly came back with a clear answer: "That's no chick, man, she's already hitched. Dig, she's Isaak-Naphtali's daughter-in-law, and she comes from Skvirre. That's her ol' man over there. The one with the velvet cap!"

"You're too much, baby!" said Stempeniu cheerily. "You checked it out that fast? Man, she is really dynamite! A righteous chick! Dig those eyes!"

"If you like," the swollen-cheeked boy asked Stempeniu, "I'll go and rap with her. . . ."

"Go to hell!" replied Stempeniu. "No one asked you to be my go-between, dig! I'll do my own rappin' with her!"

"Hey man!" cried Shneyer-Meyer in their jargon. "Just throw those big black eyes of yours out from the fiddle. Pull some Jewish guts out of those strings! . . ."

293

Stempeniu picked up his fiddle, nodded to the others, and they got their instruments ready.

STEMPENIU'S VIOLIN

Now, the bride, with loosened hair, was seated in the center of the room, and the girls and women formed a circle around her, and with God's help, Stempeniu began to play.

Ah, how hard it is for my pen to describe what Stempeniu did! This was no scraping, no mere playing. It was like a religious service, a divine labor, with a lofty feeling, a noble spirit! Stempeniu stood opposite the bride and played a sermon on his violin, a long, lovely sermon, a poignant sermon about the bride's free and happy life until now, about her maidenhood, and about the dark, bitter life in store for her, later, later. Gone was her girlhood! Her head was covered, her long, beautiful hair was out of sight, forever and ever. . . . No more joy! Farewell, youth. Now you're a married woman! . . . How bleak and cheerless— may God forgive me! . . .

That was what came from Stempeniu's fiddle. All the wives understood the wordless sermon, all the wives felt it. They felt it and wept for it with bitter tears.

"How long did *I* sit like that?" a young wife thought, swallowing her tears. "How long did *I* sit like that, with loose, undone braids, and I thought that angels were playing with me, that I was the happiest girl in the world. And now, ah, now! . . ."

"Oh, God," prayed an old woman, the mother of grown daughters. "Oh God, bring my poor daughter her intended, very, very soon, and with better luck than I had, and with a better life than I have with my husband—may God forgive me! . . ."

Such were the thoughts of the wives, and Stempeniu did his job. He played for all he was worth, and the violin spoke. Stempeniu drew forth a doleful melody, and the band backed him up. The people grew still, the noise vanished, the turmoil was gone. Everyone, everyone wanted to hear Stempeniu. The

294

men fell to brooding, the women held their tongues, boys and girls climbed up on benches and tables—everyone wanted to hear Stempeniu.

"Quiet, everyone. Hush! Shush!"

And Stempeniu melted and flowed like wax on the fiddle: That was all that could be heard. A hand flew up and down: That was all that could be seen. And they could hear all kinds of sounds, and it struck every heart, it pierced every soul, it cut to the quick. The audience was dying, its strength was waning, its flesh was perishing. The hearts filled and overflowed, and tears came to their eyes. Jews sighed, Jews moaned, Jews wept. . . .

And Stempeniu? Who cared about Stempeniu? No one even saw him, no one could see Stempeniu, no one could see a fiddle. They only heard sweet sounds, divine singing, which filled the entire room. . . . And beautiful Rachel, who had never heard Stempeniu play before, Rachel, who had known that there *was* such a person as Stempeniu, but had never heard such playing before, Rachel stood and listened to the magical singing, to the rare sounds—and she couldn't understand what was happening to her. Something pulled at her heart, something caressed her soul, but what it was—she couldn't understand. She raised her eyes towards where the sweet sounds were pouring from, and she saw two wonderful black eyes, burning eyes, looking straight at her and piercing her like spears, like sharp spears. The wonderful black burning eyes stared at her and beckoned to her and spoke with her. Rachel wanted to drop her eyes again—and couldn't.

"So that's Stempeniu?"

Such were Rachel's thoughts when the veiling ceremony was over and the relatives began to think about leading the bride to the canopy.

"Where are the candles?" asked the groom's family.

"The candles? Where are they?" answered the bride's family.

And the same old hubbub resumed. Everyone ran and no one knew where. They jostled, they shoved, they trod on corns, they tore dresses, they sweated, they cursed the waiters and the beadles, who in turn cursed the families, and the in-laws argued with one another—it was, God be praised, a lively affair!

In the stampede away from the canopy, Stempeniu left the band, re-emerged among the women, right there, next to Isaak-Naphtali's daughter-in-law, beautiful Rachel. He murmured a few words, smiling, and tossing his lovely black curls. Rachel blushed, lowered her eyes to the ground, and replied to only every tenth word. It wasn't proper talking to a musician, and in front of all those people to boot! . . .

STEMPENIU'S FIRST MEETING
WITH RACHEL

People tell so many different stories about Stempeniu. They say he hobnobbed with wizards and with all the demons, and if he wanted to take a bride away from a groom, he knew a special sort of incantation, all he had to do was give her a look, the right kind of look—and the girl was done for, Lord preserve us! A lot of mothers knew about it, and they kept a sharp eye on their unmarried daughters. When the girls talked to Stempeniu, there was always an older sister at their side, an aunt, a sister-in-law, or some married woman. . . . True, that was no compliment for our hero, but so what? What did that have to do with the price of eggs? It was no skin off Stempeniu's—nose, heaven forbid. Everyone knew that Stempeniu was a fine scoundrel. So what of it? No one was about to marry their daughter off to him, by God, and Stempeniu remained Stempeniu.

Blessed are you, Jewish wives, who have husbands, and blessed are the men who've given you such a precious gift—freedom. And pity the poor girls who are chained and shackled, guarded and protected until they're led to the wedding canopy—and only then do the girls become women, unshackled, free, happy wives. . . .

Rachel, being a married woman, had no reason to run away from Stempeniu when he walked towards her with his fiddle under his arm and a smile upon his lips. Why was she afraid? Who should she hide from? Her father-in-law Isaak-Naphtali was absorbed in the wedding: He was strolling about with his hands behind his back, watching over the waiters, to make sure they stepped lively. And her mother-in-law Dvosse-Malke was so preoccupied, that if someone had taken the veil from her head, she wouldn't have noticed. Running by, Dvosse-Malke did stop to see what Stempeniu was doing with her daughter-in-law. But she quickly thought to herself: "Who cares? It's nothing. Their business. Forget it!" And she hurried on to order the waitresses to step lively. Isaak-Naphtali and Dvosse-Malke were excellent commanders. The servants dashed about like lunatics, the in-laws on both sides made a tumult as is customary, the guests had washed their hands and were beginning to stake out places on the long benches flanking the long tables, where fresh rolls had already been put out, a whole string of them. All at once, an uproar: There was no water left in the kneading trough.

"Where are we gonna get water?" asked the groom's family.

"Water? Where are we gonna get it?" answered the bride's family.

"Water!" screamed Dvosse-Malke, slightly hoarse.

"Water! Water!" Isaak-Naphtali seconded her screams, pulled up his coattails, and imagined he was doing something.

This new panic gave Stempeniu a chance to talk a bit more with Rachel, who was grave and somewhat reflective. Her lovely blue eyes gazed far, far into the distance, not at Stempeniu, and her ears heard him talking for a long, long time.

And talking was something Stempeniu could really do. He had the gift of the gab—that rascal! His words spun round and round a person, like the words of a demon, and he stared into the eyes. . . . The eyes? What am I saying? The heart. Deep, deep into the heart.

Stempeniu talked, and Rachel listened, and the noise of the wedding company was so overwhelming that no one could hear this conversation except for the last few words.

"So that's your Moyshe-Mendel?" Stempeniu asked her, glancing at a young man who was holding the lapel of a Jewish coat and arguing away at that lapel with body and soul, with might and main.

"That's him," replied Rachel, stepping aside as if offended.

297

Rachel, her feelings bruised, didn't even look towards the corner where the musicians were sitting. Stempeniu hung around her for a long time, but it didn't help. One can actually say that she got tired of him, sick and tired—of that Stempeniu with his arrogant eyes and his ways. . . . "Ugh! It's shameful, scandalous for a Jewish woman to be anywhere near him. . . ."

Such were Rachel's thoughts as she walked back to the bride, ready to forget that there was such a person as Stempeniu. But . . . wait! What was that sudden commotion? Stempeniu was playing a sorrowful melody again, and the group was backing him up. Gone was the clamor, gone the uproar! Men fell to brooding, women held their tongues, boys and girls clambered up on the benches and tables—everyone wanted to hear Stempeniu.

Isaak-Naphtali leaned his head to one side, listening with a knowledgeable air. Dvosse-Malke, bound up in a silk cloth and holding a plate in her hand, stood transfixed where she was, and even the waiters with tucked-up coattails and the waitresses with turned-up skirts likewise remained where they were, spellbound, in the middle of the room. And Stempeniu's violin melted into such a plaintive, poignant melody that the entire company held its breath, dying, simply dying . . . lifeless people! . . . Hearts filled, overflowed, tears came to the eyes. Jews sighed, Jews moaned, Jews wept. And Stempeniu? . . . Who cared about Stempeniu? No one saw him, no one saw any Stempeniu, no one saw any fiddle. They heard the sweet tones, the divine chant that filled the room. . . . And beautiful Rachel, who had never heard Stempeniu play before, stood and listened to the magical singing, to the rare sounds—and couldn't understand what was happening. Something pulled at her heart, something caressed her, but what it was—she didn't understand. She looked up to where the wondrous melodies were coming from, and her eyes met two wonderful black burning eyes gazing straight at her, piercing her through like two spears. . . . Rachel lowered her head and saw the wonderful black burning eyes, Rachel looked every which way—and kept seeing those wonderful black burning eyes. . . .

AFTER THE WEDDING SUPPER

The wedding supper had been over for some time now, it was long past the "Hooray" melodies, past the presentation of wedding gifts, past the bride's "chastity dance"—the company was reveling, everyone tipped the band for a dance and did a cheerful jig. Yontel the slaughterer performed a kazatska, and opposite him the mother-in-law herself was letting go with lots of pluck and belly (pardon me!), and the entire crowd was clapping to accompany Yontel, who didn't even notice that he was dancing with a woman, and he squatted up and down like a daredevil, and opposite him, the mother-in-law was hippity-hopping with her arms akimbo, and grinning at Yontel, with a broad grin across her broad face like the moon at midmonth. . . .

Things got even wilder after that. Men were dancing in just their (excuse the expression) breeches. Isaak-Naphtali had already removed his coat, he stood there in his broad, white shirtsleeves. They had nudged and noodged him until he finally agreed to take off his coat, and someone cocked a cap on his head down to his nose—and everyone laughed at him with drunken eyes, and his own son Moyshe-Mendel, Rachel's husband, dragged him by one sleeve into the round.

"Use your legs! Use your legs!" shouted Moyshe-Mendel, jumping up to the ceiling.

The musicians were already playing alone, without Stempeniu. They were totally letting go by now. One of the swollen-cheeked buck-toothed boys was leading. Shneyer-Meyer, the second fiddler, with the black tangle of hair, was dozing. Yokel the Bassist was asleep. Only the younger men were concertizing to beat the band, and most of all poor Mekhtshi the Drummer. He was thrashing away as if his life depended on it. His red hair hung down to the drum, and all you could see was his shoulders heaving and his bow legs stamping. And Stempeniu? Stempeniu was wandering among the young wives, and especially around Rachel.

"Mother-in-law, do let's go home." said Rachel to Dvosse-

Malke, who stood there, watching Isaak-Naphtali in his white sleeves and his cap.

"C'mon, dear!" replied Dvosse-Malke. "Tomorrow's market day, we've got to get some rest. Just look at them carrying on!"

And Dvosse-Malke left with Rachel.

The edge of the dark-blue sky began turning lighter, more radiant. Dawn was coming. A rooster crowed. And ten others responded. From far, far away came the barking of a dog. All homes, even the farmhouses, were still shut. Only Hersh-Ber the slaughterer's light was on. Hersh-Ber always got up an hour before dawn to study the Talmud.

"Now, Rachel, wasn't Gnessi's daughter something? Did you get a load of her getup??"

But Rachel didn't answer. She was lost in her own thoughts. Who could tell what and whom she was thinking about? . . .

"Mother-in-law!" said Rachel all at once. "That was the first time I ever heard Stempeniu play."

"C'mon, child! The first time indeed!" replied her mother-in-law. "What about that evening at Leybtsi's place? And at Nekhemiah's home? And at Sarah's home? And at the rebbe's?"

"I don't recall," answered Rachel. "I only heard about him a lot, but I never saw him."

"Well, obviously. . . . At that time, you were just. . . . Well, what were you? A baby chick when Stempeniu played at the rebbe's daughter's wedding in Skvirre. Oh, was that a wedding! May the Good Lord bring such weddings to all my loved ones. What a wedding! Just imagine, I was expecting at the time, I was carrying Yossel, and I was, let me see, I was in my sixth—no, no, my *eighth* month. . . . Why, where ever are you going, Rachel? We're home, and you're wandering off to Gnessi's place! Goodness gracious me! Hahaha!"

"Oh dear," replied Rachel, peering all around. "A fine thing!! Really! Hahaha!"

And the two laughing women entered their home to lie down for a few hours, for tomorrow Mazepevke was having a huge market day, practically a county fair.

RACHEL CAN'T FALL ASLEEP

How awful! Rachel couldn't sleep! She tossed and turned, she covered herself and uncovered herself—but sleep wouldn't come! No matter how hard she tried not to think about him, about Stempeniu, I mean—he kept popping up in front of her, the devil only knows how and when! She squeezed her eyes shut as tight as she could—and saw his wonderful black burning eyes, which stared straight at her, beckoned to her, called to her. . . . "Oh, get rid of him!" she thought. "If only Moyshe-Mendel were here!" She opened her eyes and saw Stempeniu with his fiddle, and she thought she could still hear the rare and beautiful playing. . . . "Oh, what music, oh . . . ! No wonder people tell such fantastic stories about him!" And Rachel remembered all the lovely tales she had heard about him in Skvirre, during her schooldays, when she was learning how to write from Mottl Shpraiz, the girl's scribe. Back then, her girl friends had told her stories about how Stempeniu had once taken a bride away from a groom, and the bride died of shame, and they set up a black wedding canopy by her grave. And once Stempeniu had gotten back at a girl for calling him a lecher. . . . And once Stempeniu had played at an aristocratic wedding, in a count's home. And the count's daughter, a great beauty, had fallen for him and had said: Come what may, even death itself, she just had to have Stempeniu. . . . And when the count heard this, he tried to talk Stempeniu into it, at first with threats, then cajolingly, and at last he promised him three whole villages if he would convert and take the daughter for his wife. But Stempeniu replied in French (he knew German and French) that even if the count offered him a torrent of ducats, he wouldn't take a single drop of baptismal water for love or money. (And that was why he was so greatly respected by all pious Jews, even the Rebbe.) And when the count's daughter heard what he said, she threw herself fully dressed into the river. . . . And there were so many wondrous tales that made your flesh crawl. . . .

Rachel also recollected what her girl friends had told her about

301

Stempeniu's having a bottle of "love potion." "Love, dove, heavens above!" thought Rachel, remembering all those pretty stories. "You can keep your love! My Moyshe-Mendel loves me without any potion. And do I love him? Do I love Moyshe-Mendel?"

And Rachel turned over, with her face to the wall, and thought hard about all these things. This was the first time she had ever had such a thought: "Oh, it's all a bunch of nonsense. What's this love-dove business anyway? I certainly don't hate him!"

And honestly, why should she hate him? Moyshe-Mendel wasn't bad-looking, thank goodness. A wee bit modern, he tucked his earlocks up out of sight, he read newspapers, he liked to drink a glass of wine, crack a joke, have some fun with young people—but he was a fine young man. True, he was a bit of a stranger to his wife, he hardly ever exchanged two words with her, he would mumble something and then zip off to synagogue or to the market. And he never sat down, to speak, to talk to his wife, just like that, for fun, the way people do. Not on your life, he was like a wild doe.

Before her marriage, Rachel would never have expected that, poor thing! When she got engaged, it seemed as if everyone envied her for her husband—what a wonderful man (he was so handsome)! There was no one like him in all the world! How happy she would be! . . . And now? Now she saw that all her girl friends were leading fine lives. One, who had moved to a large city with her husband, wrote her the most incredible letters. And another was already mistress of her own home. And even Hannah-Mirel, who had moved heaven and earth to get a husband and finally married a widower with five children—well, she was happy now too. And Rachel? . . . Ahh, she had nothing to boast about. Locked up all week like a bird in a cage. Eating, drinking, sleeping! Her father-in-law and mother-in-law wouldn't let her breathe: Rachel, Rachel, day and night. And Moyshe-Mendel with his ways, his spare words, as though she were some sort of—goodness knows what! Shush! Someone was knocking at the door. That might be Moyshe-Mendel. Her mother-in-law went to open.

"Moyshe-Mendel!"

"What's up?"

"Is that you, Moyshe-Mendel?" his mother asked.

"Oh, what dancing, goddamn it! Brrrr!" her son replied.

"What are you chattering about?" his mother went on. "Get undressed and go to bed!"

"Goddamn it! What drinking, that Beryl-Menashe, hahaha!"

"For goodness' sake, Moyshe-Mendel! What are you blabbering about?" Dvosse-Malke said to him, striking a match.

"Can't you see he's as drunk as a lord, mother-in-law?" said Rachel. "Light a candle over there, please, he'll break every bone in his body!"

"Hey, goddamn it, give me another glass!"

Jibbering to himself, Moyshe-Mendel collapsed on his bed and quickly fell asleep with a dreadful snore. Dvosse-Malke also went to sleep. Her little children had been sleeping for some time now. Every corner of the house was filled with hissing and whistling. Everyone slept soundly, only Rachel couldn't doze off. No matter how hard she strained, sleep just wouldn't come! . . . The moon shone in through a window, and a long white beam fell on the bed, where Moyshe-Mendel was sprawled with his face up, his mouth open, his eyes gaping, his neck twisted, and his adam's apple, a sharp knob, jutting out of his throat—he was hideous to look at.

Rachel didn't want to look—but look she did. Moyshe-Mendel had never seemed so ugly to her as now, on this night. And, willy-nilly, she compared him with someone else, with that rascal Stempeniu. . . . Was this the same Moyshe-Mendel as once? The bridegroom with his lovely white face, his sweet smile, with his merry eyes, his straight posture, with his gait, with his graceful manners, his sparkling jokes? Was this the same Moyshe-Mendel? . . .

And Rachel, willy-nilly, compared him once again with someone else, with Stempeniu. . . .

Go away, go away, you dark thoughts, stop tormenting a Jewish woman!

THE VEILING LUNCH

The next morning, Hiene, the beadle's wife, came to tell Dvosse-Malke that the mother-in-law, the bridegroom, the bride, and all the in-laws were inviting them to the veiling lunch, the ceremonial meal at which the bride dons the *sheytel,* the marriage wig. Rachel had already put on her sheytel and she was all dressed up in the latest fashion (by Dovid Mekhanik, the ladies' tailor): a sky-blue frock with white lace trimming and very broad sleeves, which were being worn in Mazepevke, always a few years behind in the fashions. On her head, a blue silk openwork kerchief, revealing the entire wig and the braids. . . . But false braids. Rachel had put away her own blond hair long, long ago, concealed it forever, for all time! A few strings of pearls around her neck, on her white, lovely throat, a large golden necklace, a brooch, bracelets, rings, eardrops—all the Jewish jewelry, all the Jewish wealth.

Rachel, all decked out, in her room, where Moyshe-Mendel was still lying in the same position as last night, with his jutting adam's apple and his gaping mouth, and snoring endlessly.

"Oh, what a difference there is between the two Moyshe-Mendels, I mean, between Moyshe-Mendel, the man I was engaged to, and Moyshe-Mendel, the man I'm married to. *That* Moyshe-Mendel was so charming, his eyes glowed like candles, his voice was as sweet as honey, his gestures were all so pleasant, so dear! And this Moyshe-Mendel? He's so long and skinny and round-shouldered and he's got a red beard sprouting. Where did he get that goat's beard?"

And, willy-nilly, she kept picturing that scoundrel who hadn't let her sleep all night long—what an awful thing! "It's my own fault," thought Rachel, "it's all my own fault. Imagine running into a calamity like Stempeniu! What sort of woman stops and talks to a musician? It's disgraceful. And what would people say if they saw me talking to him? It's lucky there was such a commotion. And what would Moyshe-Mendel have said? . . ."

And with a smile, Rachel walked over to Moyshe-Mendel's bed and leaned over him and spoke his name. Moyshe-Mendel opened his gray eyes and stared for a long time and couldn't fathom what he saw before him.

"Moyshe-Mendel!" said Rachel, bending over him fully. "Moyshe-Mendel! Don't you recognize me?! Goodness, the way you're looking at me! Don't you care for me like this?"

"Lemme alone, I wanna sleep!" And with these words, Moyshe-Mendel turned to the wall and burst into a ferocious snore.

"The mother-in-law and the happy couple and all the kith and kin would like you to come to the veiling meal!"

It was Hiene, the beadle's wife, calling out as she stuck her head in the door. But when she saw Rachel standing over her husband's head, she swiftly withdrew.

Rachel met the bride before she even donned her wig. The two friends hugged and kissed, and instantly launched into an ardent conversation, the way two young wives always do.

The company was gathering little by little, and the waiters and waitresses were covering the tables with all sorts of goodies: with cakes and preserves, with gingerbread, and almond bagels, and every kind of strudel. Yesterday's beadles and yesterday's paupers were already here. The father-in-law, Haym ben-Tsion, had washed his hair and donned a velvet cap, and the mother-in-law had already shouted herself hoarse, but she still kept managing and ordering, sending one person here, another there, and screaming with her last ounce of strength:

"You're driving me to my grave, God help me! You put a platter of cake and preserves where you ought to put a bottle of vodka and glasses! Oh, *veyz mir!* Oh, my heart, my heart! What's the use of all my sacrifices! What's the use of having a wedding! You spend a fortune, and in the end—what's the use! Not even the musicians are here! There's no way out but suicide!"

"Quiet! Silence!" yelled Haym ben-Tsion, the father-in-law. "Why are you making such a racket? You're not helping matters any! She does nothing and she shrieks! What are you shrieking for anyway? Haven't you ever married off a child before? Is this the first time? Just look at her, she's rattling! The whole town's invited, and all the relatives, and she just runs around and screeches! What's wrong with you anyway!"

305

"Who's screeching, you lunatic! Who's screeching?"

"I should know who's screeching? Why don't you tell me?!"

"I'm not screeching! *You're* screeching."

"I'm screeching? Bullshit! It's the other way around!"

"You're screeching now, Haym ben-Tsion! What's come over you?"

"A grand good morning to the happy father-in-law and the mother-in-law, to the groom and the bride to all the kith and all the kin on both sides, and to all the dear friends. Now play a *vivat* for all you're worth!"

With this vociferous proclamation from Haykel the Jester, the musicians took up their instruments, and the wedding became a wedding again! The guests wiped their hands on their coattails, pushed up their sleeves, and after washing, they sat down at the table for the veiling lunch. And now Stempeniu took his violin and repeated all of yesterday's tricks with a few extras thrown in, plus two or three new pieces, while the audience gaped awestruck, in sheer ecstasy. All eyes were glued on him, on Stempeniu, only Rachel wouldn't look toward that corner—but still she saw him, but still she felt him watching her. . . . It was only when Stempeniu put down his violin and the company was in an uproar—it was only then that Rachel raised her blue eyes and saw . . . Stempeniu.

"What do you think of him?" the bride asked her after not saying a word the whole time.

"Who?" said Rachel innocently.

"Stempeniu! Isn't he a miracle-worker?"

Rachel didn't answer. She felt the blood rushing to her face. The bride noticed and asked:

"Are you hot, Rachel? Tell me, are you hot?"

"Yes, hot. Awfully hot. I'm going to step out for a minute to cool off," Rachel answered.

She left the table and at every step she encountered a servant, who gave her the right of way with great respect—not for her, but for her silken attire. Still, she couldn't get to the door that quickly. First of all, she would have to walk past the musicians, who were feasting their eyes on her, telling one another in their jargon: "Dig the groovy chick! Yummy-scrumptious! . . ."

And when her eyes met Stempeniu's, her heart began pounding, such as she had never felt it pound before. She blushed more furiously and she felt a dreadful heat in her face, like a person next to a burning house. On top of all her troubles, whom should she run into but the father-in-law, Haym ben-Tsion, almost by the door, and now a new turmoil started. Haym ben-Tsion was a pious man and he was terrified of women. The encounter was sudden. Haym ben-Tsion ought really to have backed away as is customary. But, the devil take it, he stepped to the right, and since Rachel was moving to the right, they nearly collided, missing each other by a gnat's eyelash. Haym ben-Tsion had an idea: He jumped to the left. Unfortunately, Rachel had the same idea and also swerved to the left. Haym ben-Tsion realized he had to step to the right quickly, but by the time he shifted, Rachel was standing face to face with him, almost as if to spite him—and God knows how long they would have kept dancing like that, if, to their good fortune, the hoarse mother-in-law hadn't come lumbering over to argue with her husband in their normal way. Rachel used the opportunity to slip outside and cool off from the dreadful heat.

RACHEL'S BIOGRAPHY AND HAIA-ETEL'S ROMANCE

But the outdoors was even hotter. It was a day in July. The sun stood at its zenith, roasting and broiling mercilessly. On the wooden or thatched roofs of Mazepevke, it poured out thousands of rays, that trembled and hovered, like the waves of a river. Schoolboys say: "The *Shekhinah* (Divine Presence) is resting."

Rachel stood facing the market. It was vast and deserted. The shops with red curtains were open, and the women sat on rectangular stools, knitting stockings at a fearful speed. Troughs of berries, cookies, shortbread stood by their sides, and a goat kept sneaking up with a hankering to cause trouble, only the women wouldn't let her. Far, far away, a pair of oxen were trudging along, dragging a huge wagon filled with sheaves of grain and sending up an enormous swirl of powder. Behind it walked a little peasant boy, barefoot, with a big, warm hat, a bag, and a long whip; and a dog was running after him, with a lolling tongue.

Rachel stood there, gazing at the humdrum scene, and compared it with her sky-blue silk dress, with the pearls, bracelets, eardrops, rings—and she felt alien to the surroundings, to the whole of nature, she felt betwixt and between, neither a market vendor nor a countess—simply a Jewish woman, a daughter of Israel, that was all, she had a husband, she lived with her in-laws, never doing a lick of work, and her husband was either in synagogue or at the market, walking about with his cane and cracking jokes.

Now, standing there, close to nature, Rachel, for the first time ever, began thinking about her life, about who she was, and a new thought passed through her mind, she was lacking something— she didn't know what, but something was lacking, something was missing. . . .

Rachel was a simple Jewish woman, devoid of tricks or dodges. In a word, what we call a "daughter of Israel." Growing up among a lot of children, she was nothing special to her parents in Skvirre: "A daughter, so what? Let her grow up as best she can. . . ." And so that she wouldn't wander about in front of them, and so that they might have one less child underfoot, they whisked her off to Hebrew school with her brothers. Then, when she got a bit older, they sent her to Mottl Shpraiz, the tutor for girls, and he taught her how to write. There, Rachel had her girl friends, of course, younger and older, but she liked hanging around the older girls, she liked hearing them tell stories, lovely, wondrous tales. And the girls, in turn, liked Rachel for her singing, her lovely singing.

"Sing for us, Rachel, darling! C'mon, sing! There are no boys around!"

Rachel was ashamed of singing in front of boys and adults, and her friends even told her it wasn't right to sing for big boys, a girl mustn't do that. . . .

"C'mon, Rachel. Sing! Just look at her! She has to be coaxed!"

And Rachel obeyed the big girls and crooned a song, a Yiddish ditty, in her soft, delicate voice.

On the mountain stood a dove,
And she so sadly did hum:
Where oh where is my sweet love?
To me he cannot come. . . .

Rachel sang the song with great feeling, as though she understood the word "love." The others, however—I mean the older girls—did seem to understand, for they would sigh and grieve and, occasionally, shed a tear. . . .

They loved hearing Rachel sing these songs, and the one who enjoyed it most was Haia-Etel, a very beautiful girl, an orphan. She was not unusual. Her life story was that of many Jewish girls, and it can be reeled off as quickly as a blessing. Here it is:

Once, and not so long ago, there were two brothers in the town of Skvirre, one was named Aaron and the other Leyb. Aaron died while still young, and his wife died soon after, leaving their daughter Haia-Etel. Her uncle Leyb felt sorry for her and took her into his home along with her inheritance. But Uncle Leyb didn't act very decently towards the orphan, he kept the inheritance (some three thousand rubles supposedly) for himself and gave her the air (if you'll pardon the expression)—he married her off to a bigot, a philistine, the worst kind of scoundrel, who tormented the life out of her. And, while still young, only twenty-two, Haia-Etel passed away.

Now our Rachel was as close as could be to Haia-Etel, and they loved each other very much. One Sabbath afternoon, the two of them had been sitting together at a window, coiffured and wearing their Sabbath best, as is proper. Rachel, as usual, was singing her songs, and Haia-Etel was listening. The song went:

Ah, you're going away,
Ah, you're going away,
And you're leaving me behind! . . .

309

"Rachel, my dear, Rachel, my sweet!" said Haia-Etel. "Sing it again!"

"Again?" Rachel asked in surprise. "Well, I can start all over again, if you like."

Ah, you're going away,
Ah, you're going away,
And you're leaving mee bee-hiiiind! . . .

All at once, Rachel saw the orphan cover her face with her hands, her shoulders were heaving. Rachel stopped singing when she heard her sob.

"Goodness gracious, Haia-Etel! You're crying!? Why in the world are you crying? What's wrong, tell me, Haia-Etel? Why are you crying so suddenly?"

"Oh, Rachel dear!" she answered with a sob. "Oh, Rachel dear. That song, that song of yours!"

"My song? What's the matter with it? Why is it making you cry like that?"

"Oh, Rachel, don't ask, don't ask a bitter heart! There's a fire burning in me! An infernal blaze, right here, can't you see!"

And Haia-Etel pointed at her own heart, and Rachel looked at her, amazed and confused.

"Why are you looking at me like that, Rachel? You don't understand, you can't feel what's in me. My heart is so heavy, I'm so miserable, so devastated, I have such awful troubles—I really have to tell you everything . . . everything!"

And Haia-Etel told Rachel a story, a sad story, an ordinary story, that occurs so frequently among Jews, but still a very sad story—about how her Uncle Leyb had treated her so hideously, and most of all, that wicked woman, her aunt, and if it weren't for their young son, Benjamin, she would have run away long ago or else thrown herself into the river. Benjamin was her only consolation in the world, they had grown up together, he was like a brother to her, a blood brother—but now he had gone away, leaving her with all her cares and woes, as though he were a stranger, a total stranger.

"I don't understand, Haia-Etel. Why would anyone be so grief-stricken if their very own brother had gone away, and he isn't even a real brother!"

"Oh, Rachel. You don't know how close I felt to him, how much a part of me he was, really, just like my own brother, even more than my own brother, I tell you! Whenever I saw Benjamin, there was a light in front of my eyes, and when he went away. . . ."

"Benjamin *had* to go away, Haia-Etel. He got married!"

"Oh, Rachel darling, don't say that, I can't hear it. The word 'married' tears my heart out! When I hear someone say 'Benjamin got married,' then I don't feel like living anymore. You just don't know, Rachel. And I hope you never ever know anything like this. . . . Why are you looking at me like that? Benjamin promised, he swore he would marry me."

"But then why *didn't* he marry you, Haia-Etel?"

"You're like a child, Rachel. How can you ask? He probably wasn't destined for me. He was probably meant for *her!*"

"But he swore he'd marry *you.*"

"So what! He was getting ready to tell his father, he kept putting it off day after day. He was afraid of him—you know what Uncle Leyb is like—until they arranged the engagement with her. And when I tried to talk to him about it, he told me the wedding was still a long way off, he'd be able to talk to his father—and so the months went by and the years, until the day came, that awful day, the most wretched day in my life. . . . I was at the wedding myself, I saw everything with my own eyes, everything, I watched him put the ring on her finger, I heard him say the things a bridegroom has to say. . . . The cantor and choristers were singing, and Benjamin looked at the ground to avoid my eyes—but I know he saw me. . . . Oh, Rachel! How can I go on living? How can I endure it?"

"If that's the way he is, Haia-Etel, then he's a big liar and absolutely worthless."

"No, don't say that, Rachel. You don't know Benjamin. You don't know how wonderful he is, you don't know what a good heart he has! . . . It's all Uncle Leyb's fault—that monster! My father's blood upon his head, oh God, oh God!"

"Goodness, he's really gotten to you, Haia-Etel!"

"Gotten to me?! I'm dying, I'm at the end of my rope—and you say he's *gotten* to me!"

"Well, and what about *her*, Haia-Etel? Is she pretty?"

"Who?"

"Benjamin's wife."

Haia-Etel turned crimson at these words, and then pallid, and then all sorts of colors. Rachel couldn't understand why her friend didn't answer. But she did sense that she mustn't repeat the question. "She's probably uncomfortable, so she's not saying anything, she's upset, she doesn't want to talk about it. . . ."

Some time later, Rachel saw her friend at a wedding, at Haia-Etel's own wedding. She was a bride like all brides, she sat the way a bride ought to sit, kept silent, walked to the canopy, put her wig on the next day, had a wan face, a brooding look, she didn't seem cheerful. . . . But so what, it didn't matter: That's the way a bride has to be. What is she supposed to do? Dance a jig? . . .

Who could tell what was on her mind, in her heart? A Jewish woman's heart is a secret, a big secret. A box, a closed box, and it's not proper for any man to peek inside, it's not really very respectful. . . .

AND ONCE AGAIN RACHEL

At Haia-Etel's wedding, Rachel wondered just what was going on in the bride's heart. Rachel didn't talk about this to anyone. But she was intelligent enough to realize—and her heart even sensed—that her friend was far from feeling her best as she sat there with her destined groom, a total stranger, while her own Benjamin was off somewhere with his wife. Rachel very much wanted to ask Haia-Etel if she had heard from Benjamin—how was he, had he written? But upon going to her and gazing into her wan face and hearing her sigh over and over again, Rachel didn't have the heart to bring him up.

We can imagine that this was the first time in her life that

Rachel thought about such things. Perhaps one real fact in life can arouse a lot more thoughts and a lot more feelings than ten good books. Of course, Rachel was a simple Jewish girl, quite artless, but she wasn't stupid. Why shouldn't her native intelligence manage to grasp something? She certainly knew nothing of heroes, of novels, romances, but she did have a pure heart, a pure Jewish heart. So why shouldn't she be able to feel another person's sorrows, another person's sufferings? Haia-Etel and her Jewish romance caused Rachel to suddenly grow a few years older.

At the time, Rachel was also engaged to be married, and she heard so much praise about her fiancé Moyshe-Mendel and all his virtues that she considered herself the luckiest girl in the world.

"My oh my, aren't you lucky!" she heard on all sides.

"A treasure! A windfall! Isaak-Naphtali is a rich man, the finest man in Mazepevke, and he has a son, his only child, and what a boy! A jewel, I tell you!"

And Moyshe-Mendel really was a fine boy and could appeal to anyone. He was good, lively, he had a talmudic mind, he knew the Bible inside out. Furthermore, his penmanship was excellent, he had mastered several scripts, so that the whole town marveled at his writing, and even Mottl Shpraiz, the "girls' scribe" in Skvirre, saddled his red nose with a pair of spectacles, perused the bridegroom's handwriting with the eyes of a mayven, and admitted that the boy had a golden hand, and if he kept practicing until he got perfect, he would, God willing, be able to write.

Rachel seldom talked with her fiancé, for where was he and where was she? It's quite a way from Mazepevke to Skvirre, and all in all they met only once, and for only a couple of hours to boot, and in a whole bunch of people to boot, and with the groom-to-be in one room and the bride-to-be in another room—to boot. Still, they did exchange letters almost every week for a whole year, until the wedding. Admittedly, Mottl Shpraiz (why should we deny it?) played a large part in the correspondence. For since the boy's letters were in three languages—Hebrew, Russian, and German—Mottl Shpraiz had to make sure the bride was not put to shame. And in order to demonstrate quite plainly that any graduate of Mottl's school had something on the ball (which couldn't be said about other scribes), Mottl saw to it that the bride's letters contained a fourth language, French, or rather French characters, in which Mottl was utterly proficient. Altogether, one may say that the groom and the bride played their writing game throughout a year, and they stopped only when the real preparations began for the wedding.

The wedding went off like all Jewish weddings. The bride's side didn't act quite properly, they weren't quite genteel, rather Jewish. . . . And the groom's side pouted and chaffed a bit and called the father-in-law a pig behind his back, which he fully deserved. But so what, it didn't matter: They had a drink, as people do; they made up again; the bride took leave of all her near and dear; they accompanied her till just beyond the town; they hugged, they kissed; they wept; they were sending away a daughter—and she was being taken away, to live with her in-laws.

AND ONCE AGAIN RACHEL

There, with her in-laws, a new world began for Rachel. Everyone liked her instantly, the daughter-in-law, and the only daughter-in-law, and a lovely, intelligent daughter-in-law. And they doted on her, indulged her, they wouldn't allow a speck of dust on her chair. And the most doting of all was Dvosse-Malke, who was delirious at her good fortune and ready to lay down her life for Rachel. It was always "Rachel dear!" and "Rachel dear!" whenever there was a fat piece of meat, a juicy bone, a tasty morsel—always "Rachel dear!" No sooner would Rachel open her eyes in the morning than—aha!—the pitcher of chicory stood on the table. And Dvosse-Malke, who was actually a very busy person, a market woman—Dvosse-Malke would scurry about, making sure her daughter-in-law got everything the moment she needed it.

"Oh, please don't go to all this trouble, mother-in-law."

"No trouble at all. Drink, Rachel dear! Eat, Rachel dear!"

Another time, the mother-in-law came dashing home from the market up in arms, she burst into the kitchen, yelling at the hired help, cursing and scolding violently as though someone were murdering her.

"What's wrong, mother-in-law?" asked Rachel.

"I thought you were awake ages ago—and the milk is still standing there, boiling and boiling! Dammit, may the maid boil and steam! And I have to run around like a chicken without a head! The store's mobbed, God preserve us! And he, my dear husband, just stands there with his hands behind his back like some in-law at a wedding! I begged him to take home these two fresh bagels! In case you're hungry—eat them, Rachel darling, they're good bagels, I always get my bagels from Leytsikhe, I refuse to get them anywhere else, not for a king's ransom—May God help her, the poor thing, what a horrible time that drunkard of a husband gives her! How can such a monster exist on God's earth?!—I just don't understand it. . . . He's just an embarrassment to the father, may he rest in peace. . . . Yes, now what was I saying? Oh, I'm in such a dither! Wait, here she comes, our great beauty—the maid! Where've you been all day?!"

And out came a new series of screams and curses about Rachel's milk, about Rachel's chicory, about Rachel's breakfast—in other words, the whole house whirled around Rachel. Even the father-in-law, who was always preoccupied with himself and his business dealings, constantly looked in on her, asked after her.

All this wooing and worship were actually very unpleasant for Rachel and made her uncomfortable. And to tell the truth, Rachel wasn't as fond of them as they were fond of her.

When we say "they," we mean her father-in-law and mother-in-law, of course. We're not including Moyshe-Mendel, the chief personage, for the relationship between the young people couldn't actually be called good or bad. They never talked very much with one another, and they really couldn't talk: A young man like Moyshe-Mendel can't just sit down at home, right smack in the middle of the day, and talk to his wife. And in the evening, if they did happen to be alone in a room, it never lasted for more than a minute. Either Isaak-Naphtali dropped in to see how they were, or else Dvosse-Malke brought in a pitcher, or a cup, or a glass, or a bowl.

"Just try it, Rachel dear, for curiosity's sake, and have a taste of these preserves."

"Goodness, mother-in-law. I've tasted these preserves a hundred times already!"

"C'mon, child, what are you talking about! You've never even laid eyes on these preserves!"

And Rachel had yet another taste of the preserves, which were already coming out of her ears.

"Gracious me, Rachel darling, you're just wasting away. How can you eat so little! I just don't see what keeps you alive! Goodness gracious me! If anyone from Skvirre sees you, they'll curse the dickens out of me! 'A fine mother-in-law! May she rot!' That's what they'll say! 'A fine way to feed a daughter-in-law! Hanging's too good for such a mother-in-law!' Please, just eat something for my sake!"

"Please don't, mother-in-law. I've had enough, really, I've had quite enough."

"Please, just as a favor to me, daughter. You can do a favor for your mother-in-law once in a while. Pretend I'm your mother! Just take a teensy bit, and don't be so mean to me!"

And Rachel choked down a teensy bit more, and she had more than enough, she was fed up with this life of hers, even though she knew they were loyal to her, completely devoted, and if she had wanted the blue of the sky, they would get it for her. Could there be any excuse? If Rachel had a wish, it had to come true!

However, a human being's not an ox, not a goose, content just to be well-fed. A human being can't get much pleasure from having people run after him all the time, everywhere, worshiping the very ground he treads on, always at his heels, eyeing his every last morsel, every last sip, standing over him when he sits down, sitting over him when he sleeps—in a word, clutching his entire life in their hands and not leaving anything up to him. . . .

That was Rachel's dismal situation at the time this story takes place. Rachel didn't even have someone she could complain to. Her parents thought she was happy, and their letters to her were always full of pride, joy, and blessings to God for all He had done for them. And her letters to them were also filled with "blessings and success," with "joy and pleasure," with "Blessed Be His Name," and with "knock on wood," and they always ended with "happiness and joy," and "joyous hearts, *amen selah!*"

Deep in her heart, she bore a grudge against Moyshe-Mendel because he kept far away from her and acted kind of superior to her, not like her equal, as is the custom of a young Jewish man, a gem! He can't go down to his wife's level, it doesn't seem right to him, it's unpleasant. . . . But in his heart of hearts, Moyshe-Mendel didn't dislike her, on the contrary, he was devoted to her, very devoted, quite naively so, in fact. Once, Rachel was quite ill and spent a few days in bed. Moyshe-Mendel never left her side, he moaned, he worried, he exhausted his strength.

"The poor thing!" he said to his mother, and there were tears in his eyes. "We've got to call the doctor or the healer. I can't stand this, she's burning up! The poor thing!"

By the third day, Rachel got better. Moyshe-Mendel never left her side, and, sitting there, by her pillow, he now had a chance to talk a bit with his dear, lovely Rachel. To tell the truth, both of them wanted to talk. Moyshe-Mendel sat very close to her, so close that her lovely face, wrapped in a white cloth, was almost in his hands. . . . Rachel raised her blue eyes to Moyshe-Mendel and waited for him to say something. Moyshe-Mendel looked down. But when she turned her head towards the window, he looked at her, and when she looked at him, he turned his head towards the window. And so they kept glancing at each other for a long while without speaking. This was the first time after a whole year of marriage that the couple had a chance to talk in private, but they couldn't quite arrange it, they didn't know how to start. Rachel, being the woman, had the right to wait until *he* spoke, and Moyshe-Mendel, being a fine young man, waited until *she* spoke—and meanwhile, both kept silent, exchanging glances.

"What is it, Moyshe-Mendel?"

"What do you mean what is it?"

"Why are you staring?"

"Who's staring?"

"You're staring."

"I'm staring?"

317

"Well, who *is* staring?"

Rachel turned to the wall, and Moyshe-Mendel began chewing on his beard, gazing at Rachel for a long, long time, and sighing, until she turned her head and caught him gazing and sighing.

"What is it, Moyshe-Mendel?"

"What do you mean what is it?"

"Why are you sighing?"

"Who's sighing?"

"You're sighing."

"I'm sighing?"

"Well, who *is* sighing?"

And again they fell silent. Moyshe-Mendel moved even closer, cleared his throat, and tried to begin:

"Listen, Rachel, about what you said—"

The door burst open and in ran Dvosse-Malke with a clamor:

"For goodness' sake! Didn't I *know* the turkeys would smash my china?! He got a yen for turkeys—just like that! All at once! . . . How're you feeling, Rachel? You know what? I think you've got a fever. I can tell. Didn't I warn you not to stand outdoors without a scarf! Don't ever stand outdoors without a scarf! I sent for Kussiel the healer again. Isaak-Naphtali went himself."

"Why bother, mother-in-law? It'll pass, I'm getting over it. I'm going through a transition now."

"With you, everything's a transition. A fine transition! Come, come, child, just listen to yourself! I'll have to sit down here for a while. . . ."

And Dvosse-Malke pushed a chair over to the bed and sat down.

"You know what, Momma?" Moyshe-Mendel suddenly exclaimed. "Why don't you go to the store? I'll sit with her."

And his eyes met Rachel's eyes, and he could read in them: "Oh, Moyshe-Mendel, you've hit the nail on the head!"

"Are you kidding?!" replied Dvosse-Malke and moved closer to the bed. "Go to the store?! What's the big loss? Those huge amounts I take in?! My worst enemies can have them! With all my heart! Listen, Moyshe-Mendel, why don't you go to my bedroom and take a nap on your Papa's bed! You haven't slept all night, you know!"

And that was how they lived, the happy but shackled couple, they had room and board, but never a moment to themselves, they were always under the wings of the good parents, the devoted parents-in-law. And neither the husband nor the wife grumbled, neither complained to the other. Moyshe-Mendel just kept on: He would look into a holy book, do a bit in his father's business, he had his buddies with whom he sometimes had a good time in the synagogue or the market. In a word, Moyshe-Mendel just kept living.

But Rachel didn't live at all. She ate and drank, she tasted her mother-in-law's preserves twenty times a day, never did a lick of work, never got together with other people, since Isaak-Naphtali's daughter-in-law can't associate with "just anyone," and "just anyone" is not going to associate with Isaak-Naphtali's daughter-in-law, for "just anyone" considers himself much finer, wealthier, and more genteel than Isaak-Naphtali, and Isaak-Naphtali considers himself wealthier and more genteel than all the householders in Mazepevke—and so time stretched on for Rachel, as in a prison: eating again, sleeping again, a cup of coffee again, a dear mother-in-law with preserves again, and so on and so on, a whole long year.

RACHEL SINGS SONGS

That was our Rachel's situation when we saw her at the wedding of Haym ben-Tsion's daughter, at the veiling lunch, standing outside by the door, gazing at the Mazepevke marketplace with its stores, market women, the wagon with the lumbering oxen and the peasant boy with the broad hat.

That was our lovely Rachel's situation at the time she first heard that entrancing music of Stempeniu's.

Rachel loved listening to music—oh, how she loved it! It had always given her so much pleasure! Whenever she heard someone singing or playing a new song, she instantly took it over and sang it in her lovely, mellow voice. Her parents would beam with joy and say: "She's got a man's head. What bad luck that she was born a woman, otherwise—she would have set the world on fire. . . ."

Her parents apparently did understand that there was some kind of ability in their daughter, something that nowadays we call "talent." But in those days, Rachel's parents assumed that her ability to take over and sing a tune was in her head because she had a man's head. Among us Jews, the head plays the most important role, more than all the two hundred forty-eight parts put together. A head, a fine little head! That's the crowning glory for us! But, be that as it may, Rachel sang like a free bird until fifteen or sixteen. Wherever she heard a cantorial piece, or a Hassidic chant, or a musician's melody, anything whatsoever, Rachel would sing it again in her own pure voice, which was a delight to hear. . . . But the moment she became engaged, her mother told her:

"Enough, daughter, no more twittering! You'll be living with your in-laws, and just imagine what kind of impression you'll make if you suddenly start chirping away! It's not respectable!"

Rachel, of course, understood that it wasn't proper, so she obeyed, and stopped singing. . . . But she didn't really stop altogether, for sometimes a crooning would burst from her of its own accord, out of habit, apparently, and how could she help it if the singing went on by itself? . . . When you see where the water's coming from, you can block it, but if you don't see, if you don't know—then what can you do? . . . However, not only when she was engaged, but even after the wedding, she would sometimes forget herself, forget what she was, and she would burst out singing as in the past, let herself go as she used to do when she was a girl. She would forget that her mother-in-law was in the room, listening to every word she sang:

Oh there, oh right there,
In that very spot,
Two doves are standing, a pair!
Cooing a lot, and kissing a lot,
And how could they care?
Cooing a lot, and kissing a lot. . . .

"Oh, goodness me! Oh, what am I doing?" Rachel cried out and pulled herself together upon catching sight of her mother-in-law.

"Now, now, it doesn't matter!" her mother-in-law calmed her down, pretending not to notice, sniffing and peering into a jar of preserves. "You know, Rachel, I'm worried the gooseberries won't turn out. I had the same rotten luck a year ago: eight quarts of preserves went bad on me. . . ."

And needless to say, Rachel would never have sung in Moyshe-Mendel's presence for anything in the world: it would have been very silly and awfully unpleasant—opening her mouth right in front of her husband and singing. . . . Perhaps Moyshe-Mendel wouldn't have minded, he might have been very interested. He had heard her crooning a few times and he knew that she had an angel's voice. But how would he have looked to himself if he suddenly sat down in his own home—and listened to his wife singing songs? A fine thing for a respectable young man! If he happened to hear her by chance—then okay. . . . And it did happen, but very seldom. At such times, Moyshe-Mendel would stop, all ears, and then cough as though he were only just arriving, and enter the room as though nothing had happened. . . .

Rachel spent an entire year like that, all alone, among good and loyal people, who were utterly devoted to her; and you can't say that her life was good, and you can't say that her life was bad. She felt alien with her relatives, solitary in her family, deserted among good, loyal people. Sitting morosely over her work, some piece of embroidery, Rachel would hum to herself out of habit, and all at once her heart would ache, and she would yearn for the place where she had spent her childhood.

Flying, flying,
The golden birds,
Over all the seas,
Say hello,
You golden birds,
To my mother dear!
Flying, flying,

321

The golden birds,
Over all the rivers,
Say hello,
You golden birds,
To my father dear. . . .

Dvosse-Malke often liked to tiptoe in and eavesdrop on her singing daughter-in-law.

"What's wrong, Rachel, are you homesick?"

"Oh, no, mother-in-law. . . . I'm just humming," answered Rachel, smiling and wiping her tears.

RACHEL RECEIVES THE GOOD LETTER

We left Rachel in the middle of the veiling lunch, standing by the door and staring at the huge marketplace of the town of Mazepevke. She was deep in her thoughts, which we spoke about earlier. However, her thoughts were quickly interrupted by our bold friend Stempeniu.

This fine fellow, who had an eye on Rachel, noticed her leaving the table. He waited a bit and then went out after her. Stopping by the door, he started a conversation about his town, Mazepevke, and her town, Skvirre. He knew her town very well, all its little bridges, all its fine sights, like the palm of his hand, as they say. And he also talked to her about the city of Yehupets, he had heard she'd been there once. Rachel only replied to every tenth word.

"How come," Stempeniu asked her, "how come nobody ever sees you takin' a walk, not even on *Shabbes* or holidays? You've been livin' here for almost a year, more 'n a year, and no one ever sees you on Berditchev Street. You live so far away, at the end of town, I didn't even know you were here. . . . I only found out yesterday when I saw you. . . . I wanted to rap with you a little yesterday, but I couldn't. . . . You know what these Jewish towns are like. You start to talk, and soon everyone else is talkin' about you. . . . Listen, just go for a walk on Saturday afternoon on Berditchev Street. . . . The whole town's out there. . . . Positively, you hear? Positively, Saturday afternoon, on Berditchev Street!"

Rachel didn't have time to answer, because her devoted mother-in-law Dvosse-Malke had noticed she wasn't at the table. She went to look for her, and when she found her standing outside by the door with Stempeniu, she was a bit surprised at first: "Why is she suddenly standing there with him?" However, Stempeniu, who was generally rather cunning and knew what to do in such cases, instantly turned to Dvosse-Malke:

"We're talking about the wedding, the rebbe's wedding in Skvirre. . . . Your daughter-in-law was still a child back then, when I played at the rebbe's wedding. She doesn't remember it at all. . . ."

"Of course not. How is she supposed to remember?" Dvosse-Malke replied. "But I remember it very well. I was there with my husband, and we spent the night outdoors because the town was so jammed."

"Jammed?" Stempeniu went on. "I can tell you a lot more." And he launched into a lengthy conversation with Dvosse-Malke about different things, smooth-talking his way out of the predicament. And meanwhile, Rachel excused herself and went back indoors to the bride. We've already said that Stempeniu had a way with words, and we have to tell you about another quality of his: He could talk with elderly women, chatter glibly, wind them around his little finger—he had a tongue in his head, and he spoke like an angel. There's an old saying: "An educated witch is worse than a born witch." When it came to glibness, Stempeniu was a sage. He had been to a good school, as we shall see.

"He's got his nerve," Rachel thought to herself. "Ordering me to be on Berditchev Street on Saturday afternoon—positively! Positively? He won't have it any other way? What an idea! Only a musician could talk like that!"

These were the dark thoughts with which Rachel came back in to the wedding. And when the dear Holy Sabbath came, and her in-laws and also Moyshe-Mendel lay down for their naps to take a bit of Sabbath pleasure from their sweet sleep—which Jews have thought the world of since time immemorial—Rachel, as usual, sat down alone at the window and stared out into the street, humming a song to herself. There, on the street, as on every Sabbath, she saw girls with freshly washed hair, with blue ribbons in their braids, with red, yellow, green dresses, with gloves, and with shiny-new, squeaky shoes. They were going out for their "promenade" on Berditchev Street. They wanted to show off their red or blue ribbons, their red, yellow, green dresses. They wanted to have a far look, in passing, as is our custom, at the boys, at the handsome boys in cloth coats, long trousers, and with shiny vizors on their Sabbath caps. The girls would then modestly lower their eyes, and their cheeks would turn crimson with embarrassment, and their hearts. . . . In short, they were going to live it up!

Rachel knew all about it. Why shouldn't she? After all, she herself had once been a girl with red and blue ribbons in her braids, and she herself once went strolling down the promenade with a bunch of girls on a Sabbath afternoon. But now?

Rachel looked around. Everybody was fast asleep and snoring heartily. Everybody! She was the only one sitting there, as though among dead people, as though among real corpses. She leaned her head on her hands, deep in thought, and remembered an old song she used to sing when she was a girl:

All alone,
As lonesome as a stone,
No one to talk to,
Only myself alone,
As lonesome as a stone,
No one to talk to—

"Good Shabbes!"
Rachel lifted her head and saw—Stempeniu.
"I said: Good Shabbes!"
"What's this? What's he doing here?" Rachel was about to ask and move away from the window.
"A good Sabbath to you too!" she replied, turning as red as a beet.
"You didn't listen to me, you didn't go out to Berditchev

Street . . . ? I kept lookin' for you for nothin'. . . . Well, I. . . .
that is to say. . . . Well, just read this!"

And Stempeniu handed Rachel a folded leaf of paper and
quickly vanished from sight.

Rachel held the sheet of paper for a long, long time, not
knowing what to do with it, not understanding what it was, what
it meant. . . . Once her initial surprise was gone, she unfolded
what turned out to be a large sheet of music paper, she saw huge
letters, plain Yiddish words with a lot of mistakes:

> My deerest angel in the sky, wen I saw your raydiant
> shape, both my eyes felt raydiant in a raydiant fire with my
> hart, burning with grate love for you my sole wich your
> hevenly eyes have with your raydiant shape drawn to you
> from the verry first, you are my life, the life of my hart my
> soul I cannot sleep I dream for you are the lite in the
> darkness in eyes I love you like my verry owne life for ever I
> wership the groun you wawk on I kiss your lovely eyes from
> farr away
>
> Stempeniu

FROM THE PRINCESS BACK TO THE PRINCE

Now let's leave the princess, as we do in Jewish fairy-
tales, and go back to the prince. We'll turn away from Rachel and
talk about Stempeniu.

Granted, Stempeniu's letter, which is recorded above word for
word, was not all that skillful. But what can you do? Stempeniu
was certainly a hero, a handsome guy, a fine scoundrel, but he
wasn't a writer. Go fight city hall! His father, Beryl the Bassist,
may he rest in peace, saw that Stempeniu wanted to play music
and refused to go to school for love or money, so Beryl decided
to teach him his own trade. He had him try out all the
instruments until the boy remained with the violin, and Beryl the
Bassist, who had other musical children besides Stempeniu,

actually said that Stempeniu had a streak of his grandfather, Shmulik the Trumpeter, who had personally known Paganini. Thus, by the age of twelve, Stempeniu could already man an instrument and play an entire wedding. That was why Beryl the Bassist loved him more than his other children, who went about in rags and tatters, or simply naked and barefoot. And even though Beryl was a martinet and used to pull Stempeniu's ear, or beat him, whip him, thrash him, break every bone in his body, the boy was nevertheless his favorite, his jewel, a gold mine for his old age. Beryl showed his son off to everyone, proudly saying, half in musicians' lingo: "Just look, you bastards, my junior fiddler's gonna make bread for me in my old age. You can bet your bottom ruble."

However, Beryl the Bassist was not fated to have his beloved son with him in his old age. At fifteen, Stempeniu took off with three rubles in his pocket and an old broken fiddle under his arm, and he wandered through the world. He roamed and rambled everywhere, through so many towns and cities, with so many different bands. Stempeniu couldn't hold out anywhere for more than six months. He always had to keep moving, on and on: from Mazepevke to Stepevke, from Stepevke to Korets, from Korets to Balte, from Balte to Old Constantine, and from there to Berditchev, and on and on, until he hit Odessa. And from Odessa, he headed back—roving from shtetl to shtetl, where he could easily play, make a name for himself, enjoy his reputation. And that's what happened. Any place Stempeniu came to, the people had already heard of him. The Jews had found out that a man named Stempeniu was vagabonding through the world, a man whose music was the end of the world. Which explains the stir caused by Stempeniu when he and his group reached that town. For of course, Stempeniu had his own group by the time he was eighteen, and they wandered about, playing only at certain weddings, rich ones. And so, in the course of time, Stempeniu beat all the other bands, for instance the Kanatop Musicians, who were quite renowned, the Smillers, the Vinitsers, the Sharagraders, and so many other famous groups that the world had been listening to.

Naturally Stempeniu didn't win any friends by taking all the plums from the other musicians, who cursed him roundly and wished him the worst. To his face, they patted him on the back; but in their hearts, they hated his guts. Every musician knew deep down that the moment Stempeniu picked up the fiddle, all the other musicians might as well go to bed.

Musicians, you must know, have always loved to exaggerate. They tell an endless wealth of fairy-tales, wondrous stories, legends. Dreadful exaggerations were heard everywhere about Stempeniu, and it was said that his violin came from Paganini himself. When people heard that Stempeniu would be coming with his band, the local musicians would naturally curse their hearts out at him, only to be outdone by their wives, whose curses would have curled the devil's hair.

"All year long, we go hungry, we starve, we borrow, we pawn, we eat our shoeleather, and what happens? The rich man has a wedding, and along comes a demon, the worst devil in the world, Stempeniu, and grabs the food from our mouths. May he rot in hell! . . ."

However, Stempeniu never had any real enemies. He was a good pal. When the wedding was over, he would get together with the local musicians and treat them to a lavish supper, the liquor flowed freely, they had a wild time, everybody got some money, and before Stempeniu left, he handed out presents to all the children. In a word, he was decent and respectable.

"You know," the musicians' wives said to one another afterwards. "You know, there's nothing more precious than a Jewish soul."

But most of all, Stempeniu found favor in the blue or black eyes of the musicians' daughters, the girls he got engaged to everywhere. And when he swore to a musician's daughter that he was madly in love with her, you could have believed him. For the time being, he really was in love with her (musicians usually have beautiful daughters). But the instant Stempeniu left town, his great love was gone with the wind and the smoke. And coming to the next town, he promptly fell in love again with a local musician's daughter, he swore again that he was madly in love with her, that he worshiped the ground she walked on, that he couldn't live without her, he gave her presents when he said good-bye, drove away—and went through the same thing in the next town. . . .

We can't say that most of these affairs turned out all right for the fiancées. . . . True, many of his beloveds quickly forgot all about Stempeniu and married some other musician. But a few of them, very stubborn girls, put so much faith in that scoundrel, really believing he would come back, if not today then tomorrow, if not tomorrow, then the day after—until they finally began languishing and perishing. While Stempeniu was in some darkened room, kissing a musician's daughter, any number of his brides were lying somewhere else face down, weeping over their rotten luck, their beloved had forgotten them, he had deserted them, never giving them a second thought. . . .

These were the unhappy brides that Stempeniu left in nearly every town that he passed through with his band. But you can't win them all. Sometimes your luck doesn't hold out, and it's your turn to weep and wail. Stempeniu's luck ran out on him when he least expected it. He had to get married, though that was the last thing in the world he wanted to do!

STEMPENIU UNEXPECTEDLY GETS MARRIED

One day, Stempeniu and his band arrived in Mazepevke. They played for three weddings in a row together with the town musicians, who argued with him about their rights and swore that if he ignored them, they would take him apart bone by bone. And they would have done a nice job of it if Stempeniu, who had a good heart, hadn't been willing to join forces.

Since there were several days between weddings and Stempeniu had nothing to do in the meantime, he got to know the daughter of Shaike the Fiddler. She was a fine girl of about twenty-two, dark and fat, and he fell madly in love with her in his usual way: He kissed her, hugged her, caressed her, brought her presents, fondled her like a fiancé, and when the time came to leave, the dark-haired girl (Freydel was her name) told him not to delay any longer, but to sign the engagement contract right away, as is the custom. Stempeniu, not used to that sort of thing, shilly-shallied, tried to talk his way out of it, but even the Good Lord couldn't help him now. Freydel was as tough as nails, she grabbed him by the hand and wouldn't let go, and presto!—the betrothal party took place, God bless them! The musicians drank themselves silly toasting the famous bridegroom, and they celebrated three days straight in Shaike the Fiddler's home, until the dear bridegroom and all the dear guests drove off to the next town, and the town after that, and so on.

Needless to say, Stempeniu promptly forgot all about the wedding and the betrothal and the dark-haired girl, and he did business as usual, that is, he had his romances in every town, as he was used to doing. And so he went from town to town with his group, playing at weddings and having a great time! When all at once— Well, nothing lasts forever in this world! Everything comes to an end. And things came to an end for Stempeniu too. Lightning struck him, and thunder. A plague raged into his young life! Just listen to his misfortune:

He was playing at a wedding in some small shtetl, somewhere in the Ukraine, while romancing Hershke the Flutist's daughter (a rather attractive girl), whom he promised to marry—when in burst Mekhtshi the Drummer with the sleepy face. He motioned to Stempeniu and whispered to him:

"Hey, Stempeniu, there's a chick waitin' for you in that house."

"A chick? What chick?"

"A dark chick with green eyes."

And Stempeniu strode over to the house and saw the dark-haired girl, the fiddler's daughter, his fiancée Freydel!

"Why're you staring like that, Stempeniu? Don't you recognize me. Just get a load of him, peeping and eyeing me. It's me, Stempeniu, me: Freydel, your fiancée, Shaike the Fiddler's daughter."

"Ha! Yeah, I know. What'd you think? I know, I know! But how'd ya get here? Where ya comin' from?"

"How I got here? On my legs, Stempeniu, on my legs. I asked directions all the way. I just arrived at Hershke's place. Where am I coming from? From home."

"Well, what's happenin'? When did you leave home?"

"Happening? Nothing much, Stempeniu. No news. When did we leave home? Oh, about six or seven weeks ago. We've been everywhere! Every place we came to, we were told: 'He was here but he's already left.' We barely got on the right track. . . . Well, how are you, Stempeniu?"

"What?! Me? I'm all right. Why not! C'mon, Freydel, let's get away from here," he said to her, seeing that the musicians were starting to gather around them and stare at the dark girl with the black braids and the green eyes.

"Okay, ley's go," Freydel replied.

And Stempeniu put on his jacket, picked up his cane, and went strolling through town with the dark-haired girl. He peered around to make sure no one was in earshot, and then he said to her more vehemently:

"Now, listen, what's this all about?"

"What do you mean: 'What's this all about?' "

"Well, why'd you come here?"

Well, get a load of you, acting like you don't know, like you dropped dead or something!"

"Listen, Freydel," Stempeniu got more emotional. "Listen, Freydel. I don' like no one pullin' stunts like this on me! I asked you: 'What're ya doin' here?' And you start jiving' me!"

Freydel's green eyes flared up at Stempeniu and, tossing her long black braids, she snapped:

"What am I doing here, you wanna know? I've come for you, Stempeniu. At the betrothal party, you said you'd write in two weeks at the latest and let us know about the wedding date. We waited and waited for more than two months, and when we saw we wouldn't be hearing from you, we decided to go and track your ghost down ourselves, and we've been everywhere, to the ends of the earth, and it was only after lots and lots of trouble that God helped us and we—"

"Tell me, Freydel, who's 'we'? You keep saying 'we' went and 'we' came. . . ."

"The two of us. Me and Mom."

"Your Mom." cried Stempeniu, stopping dead in his tracks. "Your mother? What's she doin' here?"

"Stop screaming, Stempeniu! What'd you think? That I'd come

alone. A girl doesn't travel alone. A fine thing! Imagine!"

"Yeah, but what does your old lady have to do with me?" asked Stempeniu, walking back with her.

"She's your future mother-in-law, Stempeniu. Your future mother-in-law. And later on, she's gonna be your present mother-in-law."

"Freydel, do you seriously intend to marry me?"

"And you didn't mean it seriously, Stempeniu?"

"It's off the wall!"

"What's off the wall!"

"Listen, gettin' hitched is the last thing in the world I wanna do."

Freydel halted for a minute and gazed into Stempeniu's eyes. Then she looked all round and finally spoke to Stempeniu very quietly:

"Just you listen to me, Stempeniu! Don't think you've met up with some dumb kid who doesn't know which side her bread is buttered on. I know you very well, Stempeniu! I know all about your carryings-on. You like getting engaged to a different girl every week, but it doesn't matter, you've sowed your wild oats, that's okay. . . . Basically you're all right, you've got a soft heart, you're a good-looking guy, one in a million, you're a wonderful fiddler and you can support a wife—that's why I want you and that why I'm marrying you, on the spot! You can argue all you like, it's no use, you're wasting your time, Stempeniu, believe me. Now bend your head, I want to tell you a secret . . ."

And Freydel, the dark-haired girl, whispered a secret into Stempeniu's ear, and Stempeniu shuddered from head to foot. He stood there like a clay golem, in the middle of the road, unable to open his mouth, to utter a word. And then along came Mekhtshi the Drummer with his red hair, and he told Stempeniu that he was supposed to go to the town Rothschild to talk about a wedding. Stempeniu took leave of Freydel, nodding and sighing:

"I'll see you later, Freydel!"

"You're not kidding you'll see me later!" she replied, happily saying good-bye to her darling fiancé Stempeniu.

All the people who saw Stempeniu at the wedding were astonished at his pale face and his absent look. It just wasn't the

331

old Stempeniu, a better-looking corpse would have been buried posthaste! It was as though someone had whisked away his merriment, his ardor. Yes indeed, Stempeniu saw that his sweet life as a free bird was over, he was sticking his head in a yoke forever and always. Adieu, radiant summer evenings and long strolls outside of town with musicians' daughters! Adieu, long, delicious braids, undone hair, huge, black eyes! Adieu, silvery moon! . . .

Naturally, Stempeniu fought a bit, he struggled like a fish in a net, with his last strength, using any means he could, but it was about as useful as applying leeches to a corpse. Freydel and her mother stuck to him like those ghosts that come in a dream at night, dragging you off to face the music in the heavenly court of justice. . . . And he was scared to death of his future mother-in-law, who knotted up her black maw as though with a piece of string, but her face blazed as though she were all set to pounce on Stempeniu any minute like a ferocious cat and scratch both his eyes out—if it weren't for Freydel who kept holding her back.

"Leave him alone, Mama, you'll spoil everything. Just watch him, but don't say anything, keep your eye on him so he doesn't escape. It'll be all right, Mama, Stempeniu is mine, he's mine! . . "

SAMSON PUTS HIS HEAD IN DELILAH'S LAP

Freydel put down her foot and got her way: She married Stempeniu according to the law of Moses and Israel, and once she got her hands on him, she really took him in hand. She got a little help from her Mama, who was finally seeing the proud and joyful day when she became a mother-in-law, and Stempeniu had a taste of hell and he was not disappointed. The newlyweds moved to Mazepevke, and Stempeniu settled down there with his band, a resident, in one place.

"It's over, Stempeniu, no more wandering around! Your traveling days are done, Stempeniu, done!" said Freydel to her husband, who was all hers now, and she did whatever she wanted to with him—or else!

After the wedding, another life began for Stempeniu, a brand-new life. He had been a spirited bachelor, but no sooner was he married and in Freydel's hands than he lost all his strength, all his courage, all his brilliance. At home, Stempeniu had no say whatsoever.

"Just remember, your business is the band and weddings. What do you need money for, silly?" That's what Freydel would say, taking every last kopek he ever earned.

Freydel was the picture of avarice. She had grown up in a very poor family and had almost never set eyes on a kopek. As a girl, she hardly ever got a ribbon or a comb, and then only with bitter tears. She went barefoot till the age of fifteen, acted as nanny to the younger children, and got more than her share of slaps from her mother as well as her father, Shaike the Fiddler, who was a drinking man. She ate next to nothing, she dressed to match her bare feet and it was only on Purim that a few kopeks came her way, for delivering Purim presents to other people's homes. She would stash those kopeks deep in her bosom, so that her Mama wouldn't trick her out of them, and she slept with her hoard until Passover, when she bought herself a ribbon or a comb. And that was Freydel's life until she reached eighteen, when she suddenly grew into a tall, a lovely, a healthy girl—ready for marriage! When Freydel got engaged to Stempeniu, she herself didn't realize how lucky she was. Only her mother, who did realize it, argued away at her, setting her straight: She ought to know that her fiancé was making a mint, but that he was a rather frivolous sort, and he spent money like it grew on trees, she shouldn't let him get away with murder, she had to keep him under her thumb, the way her mama did with her papa, Shaike the Fiddler. . . .

When Freydel married Stempeniu, she didn't forget her mother's advice; little by little, and cleverly, she taught her husband the meaning of the word "wife," she explained that a husband can have no secrets from his wife, a wife is not an outsider, she's not a mistress, no, she's his flesh and blood, she is him and he is her. In a word, he had to know, he had to *feel* that he had a wife. . . .

When Freydel began running her own household and kept seeing new rubles that Stempeniu earned so often, she pounced on them like a starving man spotting food. But she didn't enjoy the money. Freydel was worried that they might be penniless from one day to the next, her husband might not earn money later on, God forbid. So she made herself a little pouch and began saving kopek after kopek.

"What are you hidin'?" asked Stempeniu, noticing her movements.

"Curiosity killed the cat. Don't get any gray hairs over it, Stempeniu!" Freydel answered with a smile, and kept doing what she had to, skimping, scrimping, scanting at the market, the store, the butcher's, serving just barely enough for lunch, often not eating or drinking enough, scraping together ruble after ruble. Gradually, when she had gotten together a tidy little sum, she started lending money on security and charging interest. The first time, it just happened, it was an accident, a neighbor had asked to borrow some money, and Freydel did her the favor. Why not? And then, when she saw that the money was growing, and that one ruble became two in the course of time, she began doing business with her small capital, until she simply became a "usurer" with all the trimmings and all the stuffings of this profession, which a lot of our rich people indulge in (this is just between you and me) and don't really dislike at all. . . .

How peculiar! Where did Freydel get her lust for hoarding money? Not from her papa, Shaike the Fiddler, nor could she have seen the like among any of the renowned musicians. Where will you find anyone comparable to musicians, who never turn over a kopek and who spend money like water. Jewish musicians—especially in those days—were like Gypsies, a special tribe, with a special jargon, and with special ways of their own. They always had a good time, it was always Purim for them, life was merry, lively, they fiddled, frolicked, fooled around, worked, carried on, played wild pranks, talked about cheery things. . . . When they came home to their wives, they joked, gobbled up beans and dumplings or else tightened their belts, but they were always romping, dancing, frisking, going to bed hungry, borrowing money the next day, pawning their pillows, redeeming them and then pawning them all over again. The daughters of musicians were usually joyous and frivolous creatures themselves, there were no veils on their hair or their lives. . . . In a word, the musicians lived in paradise, with all the virtues and faults of paradise. . . . And in such an eden, who would ever dream of worrying about tomorrow?

Naturally, Freydel's papa was no tearful sort. Shaike the Fiddler was as poor as a synagogue mouse, but a jolly and jovial mouse, and whenever he earned a ruble he caroused it away in the twinkling of an eye, as they say. And Freydel's mama liked to live well, that is to say, eat well. They hardly had a shirt to their names, but as long as there was a pillow to be pawned they always ate. "All our good luck goes straight to our bellies. . . . How does the old proverb go? 'It's better to deal with the baker than the doctor.' Eat, drink and be merry!" That's what she'd say, Freydel's mama, who was a spendthrift even for a musician's wife.

So how did Freydel get to be the way she was? Where did she get her stinginess? Perhaps it came from want, from always being penniless in her parents' home. Or maybe it was natural with her. Maybe a stingy soul had gone astray into the musician's family and been reincarnated as Freydel.

Whatever it was, Freydel made weird grimaces, sweated, and frothed even if she only *talked* about money.

All the musicians' wives were jealous of her. "What luck!" they said in chorus.

But there was one way in which God neglected Freydel: He gave her no children. And who knows, perhaps that too was why she was utterly devoted, body and soul, to money—because the finest pleasure, the joy of children, was denied her. Generally, we see that the wives whom God has not blessed with children are nasty women, they lack the goodness, the softness of their sex. Such women can love only themselves.

And that's the sort of woman Freydel was. But it can't be said that she hated Stempeniu. Why should she? A handsome man, a paragon, a rare violinist—one in a million, and—this was the nitty-gritty—a good provider, a gold mine!

"My Stempeniu," Freydel boasted to her friends, "my Stempeniu—when he plays a note on the strings, out comes a ruble, two notes and it's two rubles, three notes—and it's three rubles. You understand?"

As far as rubles went, Stempeniu was the very opposite: money meant nothing to him. He'd play at a wedding, stuff his pockets with cash, and—before you knew it, not a kopek was left. If he had something, he gave, he shared, he lent. If he had nothing, he borrowed. In this way, Stempeniu was an artist. All he cared about was the band—present something new, perform an operatic piece, contract for a wedding, do the wedding, playing as God commanded, so that Jews licked their fingers—it was no mere scraping.

There were two things that Stempeniu loved more than anything in the world: himself and the violin. He was busy with himself all the time: bedecking and bedizening himself, curling his hair—in a word, making himself a "bachelor," as Freydel so cuttingly put it, and he would then forget all about the violin.

But when he picked up his violin, he forgot all about himself and the rest of the world. If ever he was overcome with melancholy, he would take his violin, chain the door, and then play his own fantasies for three or four hours at a time, he fiddled anything that drifted into his mind. Now he would pour himself out in a lament, so dolefully, so dismally, and softer and softer. And then he would suddenly lose his temper and play louder and louder, until all at once, something like a sigh tore from the depths of his heart, and the blaze went down a bit, and his anger died out, and soft melodies, dear, sweet songs, growing sadder and sadder, came pouring out endlessly, and then he would become a little cheerier, livelier. . . . Of course, that didn't happen often, the mood didn't sweep him up all the time, but once he was lost in his violin, there was no possibility of yanking him away. Stempeniu's imagination seethed and settled like a source—the more, the fresher.

A person with feeling, with a soul, could not possibly have heard enough of this free music, which cannot be committed to paper. It sounded like an entreaty to the Lord of the Universe from a bitter heart, a prayer to God for mercy, for compassion, the sort of prayer that has to be, that must be accepted up there, at God's Throne. . . . It is said that the Rebbe of Rizhin had his own orchestra, which played while he intoned the praises of Him Who Lives Eternally. That was truly a thought from a great man, an idea from a lofty poetic soul.

"Oh that bitch, Fat Kaile, may she drop dead, the dirty slob. She's paid me the interest for last week, and for this week she says she can't pay me till after Sabbath!"

That was the type of conversation with which Freydel welcomed Stempeniu when he came out of his room after playing, he was still ablaze, his black eyes were shining. That was the fire in his eyes that was so attractive. The fire would flare seldom, and when his eyes met Freydel's, the fire vanished.

When Stempeniu came home after playing a wedding, Freydel would greet him with a smile, fawning on him like a kitten:

"What do you need money for, Stempeniu?" Freydel would say, shaking out all his pockets. "What good is it? What don't you have? You've got everything you need, you're not hungry, God forbid, and you don't go naked, and when you need a couple of kopeks, don't I give them to you? Why don't you let me have the money? It'll be safe with me. Just give it to me, give it to me!"

And Stempeniu stood there like a child being punished, and Freydel twisted him around her little finger, he was like putty in her hands. Ah! What's happened to you, Stempeniu? How can such a nobody like Freydel dance on your head, and you let her lead you around by the nose, like Samson putting his head into his beloved Delilah's lap? . . . Ugh! Stempeniu, what a shame, what a terrible shame!

ALL IS NOT LOST

Poor, poor Stempeniu! . . .

But it's not quite what you think. You don't have to feel all that sorry for our hero. He may not have had much say in his home and he certainly didn't wear the pants there. But to make up for it, he had his world, a world of his own, which had nothing whatsoever to do with Freydel. In his world, Stempeniu was a king, and, as we shall see, he was very happy there.

First of all, he spent half the day rehearsing, that is to say, playing the new numbers over and over again with the band; they would kid around, listen to the jester's quips, and laugh at

337

Mekhtshi the Drummer, whom the jester liked to tease. Then they would tell one another stories about some wedding or other. For every Jewish wedding has its story. At one wedding, the bridegroom dug in his heels, and, come hell or high water, he refused to go to the wedding canopy until they paid out the dowry ruble by ruble, right then and there. At another place, the bride wept so much that she fainted dead away and they could barely revive her—and all the while the jester kept cracking jokes. At a third wedding, a fine thing happened: After the dinner, when it was time to dance—And the musicians burst out laughing, like cannonfire.

"What are you guys carrying on about? Just get a load of their tomfoolery!" Freydel shouted from her room.

"Don't let it bother you!" Stempeniu replied arrogantly. "Haven't I told you a hundred times to keep your nose out of our business!"

And at that moment, Stempeniu felt like the master of the house, a true sultan in his home.

The rest of the time Stempeniu spent dressing, grooming, caring for his clothes, polishing his boots to make them shine like mirrors, combing his hair so stylishly, curling his lovely, black curls, smoothing his white dickey, and then he picked up his cane, a cane with a small knob, a fig carved out of ivory, and he donned a broad, black cap with a shiny vizor pulled down to the eyes. Tilting his head so that the curls were spread on his shoulders, Stempeniu went and took a walk through the town. He had his friends here, whom he would meet, and strolling past the shops, he greeted the young wives, the shopkeepers. The women flushed, they remembered they had been girls once and they had known Stempeniu back then. . . . Those were the days. . . . And now? Who thought about it now? . . .

But still, you can find such young wives nowadays, and especially girls who stand talking to Stempeniu for a long time at the door, talking, chatting about this and that, laughing. . . .

Naturally, such things can't just happen like that, a neighbor sees them and she goes and tells another, a third one, the rumor begins, and when Jewish tongues wag about you, you'll never hear the end of it.

"What's all this gossip about, Stempeniu? Have you done it again?"

"Done what again, Freydel?"

"Done what again?! . . . How can you ask! Everyone's gossiping about you. We're the talk of the town."

"I don't know what you want from me, Freydel."

"What I want from you? I want you to change your old habits. . . . It's about time! Wherever there's a young wife or girl in town, you have to get to know her and stop to talk to her for three whole hours—you just can't get your fill!"

"Oh? Are you possibly referring to the fact that I was talking to Esther?"

"Oh, of course, Esther, what could be wrong with talking to Esther?! What is she anyway, a holy saint or something?!"

"I was speaking to her about a business matter."

"You and your business matters. . . . I know you, Stempeniu!"

"Well, you oughtta know about it. Her father wants to have the wedding in Yehupets, that's a crazy whim of his. Well, I ran into Esther, so I discussed the matter with her. Wouldn't it be a drag if I let a wedding like that slip away from me?"

"How did he ever hit upon Yehupets, the lunatic!" asked Freydel, and her green eyes lit up with the fire that always flashed in them whenever she sniffed money. . . .

"How can you ask questions about a lunatic?" replied Stempeniu, escaping the matter unscathed.

And that's how matters were taken care of, that matter and all matters. Stempeniu had a sharp mind and he knew how to get around Freydel.

Out of town, when Stempeniu went traveling with his band, he was, of course, even more successful. There he had, as the saying goes, "a kosher pot and a kosher spoon"—he could do whatever he wanted to, and when Stempeniu came to some shtetl to play a wedding, he just didn't feel like leaving it anymore. There he had "matters" upon "matters," cheerful ones and dismal ones without end. In short, that was a special world for Stempeniu, his very own world, which Freydel was not allowed to enter for anything in the world, even though she very much wanted to. She actually tried to bribe Mekhtshi the Drummer, but it didn't work. Here, in

339

his world, Stempeniu was a new man, totally different from the Stempeniu in Freydel's house.

STEMPENIU STARTS FALLING IN LOVE

In his own world, Rachel began playing an important role for him, the most important role in his life. We can believe him when he says that his letter to her, which we saw earlier, was quite serious and truthful, for he fell in love with Rachel the moment he set eyes on her at the wedding in Haym ben-Tsion's house.

Stempeniu didn't write the letter immediately. It took a few days for the fire that Rachel's blue eyes kindled in his heart to burn forth, blaze up until he couldn't hold back anymore, he locked himself up in his room, and there, where he wrote his music, and with the same pen and on the same lined music paper, he wrote that letter.

Stempeniu sweated a bit over the letter. Writing was a chore for him, he had never learned how to write anywhere, just on his own. So it was really no wonder that he had a hard time.

Stempeniu carried the letter around for a few days, he couldn't find a way of giving it to Rachel. Mekhtshi the Drummer was a good messenger for such letters when they were out of town, but here, with Freydel around, Mekhtshi was a dangerous postman to use. Stempeniu could hardly wait for the Sabbath, he got all dolled up like a young girl, he put on a high hat in the latest fashion of the times, and went out to Berditchev Road, as on every Sabbath, to take a walk, calculating that Rachel would probably be there. But he was wrong: All the young wives, all the girls were strolling about, sneaking glances at Stempeniu, smiling and turning crimson—they were all there, only Rachel wasn't there! The letter he had written gave him no peace. He felt drawn to her more and more strongly.

"I ought to try and go there, to the street where Isaak-Naphtali lives, maybe I'll find her. . . ." Those were Stempeniu's thoughts, and so he slowly walked towards the window, where Rachel was sitting deep in her thoughts, singing that little song:

All alone,
As lonesome as a stone,
No one to talk to,
Only myself alone,
As lonesome as a stone,
No one to talk to—

At first, when she suddenly heard the "Good Shabbes" and saw Stempeniu in front of her, she thought it was a dream (she had already seen Stempeniu in several of her dreams. . . .). But when she unfolded the small slip of music paper and read Stempeniu's letter, she stood up, looked through the window, and said to herself:

"He's lucky he went away. I would have played some music for him that he'd never forget! Oh, that Stempeniu! . . ."

She clutched the letter and was about to hurl it out the window, but then she faltered, read through it again, rolled it up the way you roll up a scroll, and put it in her pocket.

Rachel's anger kept getting bigger and stronger, she just wanted to see him alone and ask him privately: What was the meaning of this? What was he up to? How dare he write her a note like that! Just who did he think he was anyway? And who did he think *she* was? . . . She began pondering ways of meeting him in some place where no one could overhear them, and she finally hit upon something.

A CORAL NECKLACE FROM FREYDEL

"Listen, mother-in-law, if it's not too expensive, I'd really like to have a necklace of coral beads. Good heavy coral."

"Well, how often have I told you: Just go over to Freydel and pick out whatever your heart desires. If you like, we'll go right

341

now. For my sake, she won't charge you much."

Our dark-haired Freydel, who lent money on interest and took security, mostly coral, had gradually, almost for fun, started dealing in the coral itself, on the side, she bought it very cheap from her debtors and then offered it much cheaper than any coral vendors, and her moonlighting grew and grew until she was actually doing business with all the dealers in Berditchev and Brody. Everyone in Mazepevke knew that you could get a decent string of coral from Freydel, Stempeniu's wife Freydel.

Miraculous! Where did Freydel get her sales talent, her way of dealing with the customers, her ability to talk them into buying? When Dvosse-Malke and her daughter-in-law stepped into her house, Freydel welcomed them with open arms:

"Hello, hello! How are you, Dvosse-Malke? You know, I've had my eye on you for a long time?"

"On me? How come, Freydel?"

"How come, you ask? Why, a year ago, you brought a gem into your home—and that was that! You should have come here with your daughter-in-law at some point and picked out something for her. Why, I tell you, Dvosse-Malke, it's a crying shame!"

"You're so right, Freydel darling, but it's not my fault. What can I do if my daughter-in-law doesn't want coral, no matter how much I beg her?"

"Now that's a new one on me! What do you mean she doesn't want coral? With you, she doesn't want, but with me she *will* want, don't worry!"

And Freydel quickly opened a huge green chest, and began pulling out one set of coral beads after another, placing them in front of the customers, talking all the while and uttering all sorts of good wishes and compliments like a true businesswoman.

"Just look, Dvosse-Malke, if you take my word for it, you'll have your daughter-in-law buy this string of beads, may you and I be as pure as these beads. Why they're pure Orleans beads! Just try them on, if you please, on your throat, that's right. Oh, I'm absolutely envious, they look so beautiful on your white throat! Wear them in good health and may God grant that your mother-in-law can buy five strings of such big pearls a year from now. Oh, how wonderfully they dress your face! Tell me, Dvosse-

Malke, you're a jewelry mayven, what's your opinion? It should only happen to me, by God!"

With these words, Freydel pulled a mirror out of the chest and held it up in front of Rachel, Freydel's green eyes glittered with pride and joy, and she had worked up a sweat with all her talking and swearing and wishing.

"And is your Stempeniu working hard?" Dvosse-Malke asked, pointing to the room where rare and sweet sounds were coming from.

"Yes, he's playing," Freydel replied and began showing other strings of coral, all kinds, and meanwhile she and Dvosse-Malke got into a long conversation, which is what happens when two shopkeepers get together and talk shop.

Rachel sat on the side, not listening to their conversation. Rachel heard another conversation, another voice, other words, that could be heard from Stempeniu's violin, words that went straight to her heart, and she stood up only when the violin stopped playing and Stempeniu appeared in the doorway. Their eyes met and both he and she turned a fiery red. . . . Stempeniu halted at the door, unsure of what to do next. And as she looked at him, Rachel told her mother-in-law that it was time to go home. Dvosse-Malke gasped and wrung her hands:

"Oh, for goodness' sake! Just look at how long we've been talking! Well, Freydel, what are you going to charge me for the beads. You can't ask too much from me, Freydel. You've got to be straight with me!"

"As straight as a ramrod! Listen, Dvosse-Malke, let me choke on the first food I eat if I tell you a lie! Sossi wanted to force eighteen rubles on me for the beads, may the Good Lord preserve me and my husband! What can I do? I hesitated—Sossi is Sossi, and you're Dvosse-Malke. I'll give them to you for fifteen rubles, and believe me, I swear on my grandmother's grave, I'm not earning a kopek on them, as God is my witness!"

"Well, fifteen is fifteen, I'll give you twelve, Freydel, twelve rubles in cash."

"Oh, the Lord preserve us, Dvosse-Malke, don't haggle!" shouted Freydel heatedly, grabbing Dvosse-Malke's hands as if they were about to dance a jig.

In that moment, Rachel and Stempeniu could quickly exchange a few words.

"I want to tell you something, Stempeniu."

"I want to tell you something too, Rachel."

"You already did tell me something."

"When?"

"In the letter."

"It wasn't much."

"It was too much."

"No, it wasn't even one one-hundredth."

"You're wrong."

"I swear by my life, I'm dying! Where can I meet you?"

"I don't know where we can meet."

"In the evening?"

"Where?"

"On Monastery Street."

"When?"

"Saturday night. You can go out on the other side to Monastery Garden."

"I can't, I won't."

"You have to, Rachel. Please, just come out for one minute! Be there, I'll wait for you, on Saturday night, for God's sake, Rachel. . . ."

"I won't come."

"You will come, Rachel, you will come! . . ."

"Well, daughter," called Dvosse-Malke. "Come on, let's go home. We barely got it for fourteen rubles. Why, I didn't realize you were such an expert businesswoman, Freydel!"

"Oh, Dvosse-Malke, God preserve you, you're a hard bargainer, upon my word! Good day to you and stay well! Wear the necklace in the best of health! Use it in the best of health! May it last forever, and may you live even longer!"

"She can go on crutches, the bitch, the way she haggled me to death!" said Freydel to Stempeniu, closing the door behind them. "And that daughter-in-law, the white heifer, she just sits there and keeps her mouth shut. She looks about as good in that coral as a pig! . . ."

CORAL AGAIN

When Rachel came home with her coral necklace, her mother-in-law took her over to the father-in-law, smiling so happily as though she had won God knows what.

"What do you say to these beads, Isaak-Naphtali? A bargain, honestly, a fantastic bargain!"

Isaak-Naphtali went up to Rachel, took a hard look, like a real expert, sniffed, and then asked:

"What did you pay for them?"

"See if you can guess, you're a businessman, so to speak. Well, c'mon, try and guess," said Dvosse-Malke with a smile.

"I can't tell whether they were expensive or cheap."

"If I say it's a bargain, silly, then it's a bargain, a real steal! Believe me, I did enough dickering and haggling with that cheating bitch, that musician's wife, may she drop dead! Oh boy, can she ever bargain, she's a real market woman. The devil only knows where and when she got her training! And what a mouth she's got, an acid tongue, pure filth, and when she talks to a customer, she foams like boiling milk—I hope she kicks the bucket, that lousy bitch! . . . Well, cat got your tongue, Isaak-Naphtali? C'mon, let's hear your expert opinion, what do you think the coral should cost?"

"What this coral should cost?" repeated Isaak-Napthli, stroking his beard. "Now, let's see, these beads should cost, about, well about—Wait, I'll tell you exactly how much, I don't want to make a mistake—a bargain, you say, a bargain? Well, if it's a bargain, then you paid no less than five and a half rubles, but it's worth a full seven."

"Asshole!" Dvosse-Malke shot out like a cannon, and Isaak-Naphtali quaked and stepped aside. "You asshole! You shithead! A coral necklace like this—five and a half rubles? You crazy idiot! A deaf mute wouldn't have said that in a year! Don't you have eyes in your head? Take a good look, you big moron!"

345

And Dvosse-Malke grabbed Rachel's hand, pulled her over to her father-in-law, pushed up Rachel's head, and showed Isaak-Naphtali the bargain, while spouting insults and curses. Poor Isaak-Naphtali sniffed and blinked, afraid to say a word. Until God took pity on him and in walked Moyshe-Mendel with his cane, he was coming from the marketplace—and now he began estimating the price of the beads on Rachel's lovely white throat and he guessed they must have cost in the neighborhood of three rubles. . . . Dvosse-Malke blazed up in such fury that she practically burst out crying like a little child, she was grief-stricken that no one understood what a big bargain she had gotten and perhaps she was heart-broken that Stempeniu's wife had so grossly deceived her.

"And you call yourself a businessman?!" she shouted at Moyshe-Mendel. "You're as big an expert as your father! Three rubles, sonny-boy? Why not less?!"

"Because they're not worth more, they're very plain beads. I've seen coral beads in my time, Mama. You can believe me, I've seen really valuable coral necklaces. . . ."

All day long, the three of them argued and bickered about the coral necklace.

"You'd give me a lot more pleasure if you shot a bullet into my heart," screamed Dvosse-Malke, "rather than saying 'five and a half' to me! Okay, let her cheat me, the bitch, I hope she gets the plague—no one's ever cheated me!—Fine, I hope God strikes her dead, her and that Stempeniu of hers. But why pour salt into my wounds and say 'five and a half' to me? You and your goddamn 'five and a half'! I hope she gets five and a half dozen boils on her body and five and a half fevers in her liver! I swear, I'm going to get my money and my blood back from her, like from a dog's teeth! You can believe me! But how can you torment me with 'five and a half'!"

The whole scene was so unpleasant for our Rachel that she took the coral beads from her throat and hid them deep, deep down in a chest, intending never to wear them again as long as she lived. The thing that annoyed our Rachel most was that Moyshe-Mendel was so absorbed in fighting with his mother over the beads that he didn't even come over to Rachel as he should have done, as is right and proper, to say: "Wear them in good health." They had led her around by the hand all day and peered at her necklace as if inspecting a cow, everyone stepped over to her, pushed up her head, touched the beads—and ignored her completely. . . . Rachel, who was not nasty or bad-tempered by nature, was furious at everybody all day long, and especially at Moyshe-Mendel. This fine fellow thoroughly enjoyed his lunch and then trotted off to synagogue. And since there was a party there that evening to celebrate the completion of the study of a talmudic tractate, Moyshe-Mendel remained from after evening prayers until dawn, as he did quite often.

Rachel felt altogether ill and angry. Her face blazed like an infernal fire, her head was splitting, her ears were buzzing and whistling. She didn't understand what was wrong with her. . . . At suppertime, she couldn't eat a bite. Naturally, Dvosse-Malke nagged her to eat more, to drink more—but it was no use. Rachel went to her room with red eyes, quickly undressed, lay down in her bed, and then all at once, a flood of tears burst from her eyes—hot, burning tears, and so many, so many.

A HARD NIGHT

Why did Rachel weep? She didn't know why herself, and she didn't even feel she was weeping. For a long time, her heart had been heavy, very heavy, and suddenly it was soaked through, it overflowed, it poured out its tears. Rachel, as we've already said, felt that she was lonesome, that she was lacking something, that something was missing, but what it was she didn't know and couldn't know. Rachel knew perfectly well that her parents had married her off, gotten her off their backs. The term "off their backs" is enough to show how separated people get: children from parents and parents from children. The term "off their backs" can often be heard among us Jews, in almost every family. The term "off their backs" is a terrible shame, an insult to

347

our entire nation, which boasts of being so compassionate. . . . Most of all, Rachel was annoyed my Moyshe-Mendel, by his behavior and his actions towards her. Rachel understood what part she played for her gem of a husband with her beauty and kindness, with her virtue and loyalty. Rachel saw what she meant to him. . . .

And lately, Rachel had been especially upset, confused, bewildered. What she had endured with Stempeniu was no trifle. Rachel, pious Rachel, who had never swerved from her Jewish way of life by even a gnat's eyelash, who had never transgressed even the most insignificant rule of all the laws for Jewish women, Rachel, a Jewish wife immersed in the Yiddish Bible—thinking about another man, receiving a letter from him, meeting with him—and she didn't resist. On the contrary, she felt so drawn to him, not with a bad thought, God forbid, but just like that, to see him and hear him play the violin.

Oh, his music, his music! Rachel would have been willing to give up food and sleep forever so long as she could hear Stempeniu, hear him and . . . see him! His eyes, when they gazed, they warmed, they caressed, they pampered. . . . Oh, his eyes!

Rachel grabbed her head with both hands and listened to her temples beating, her heart beating, and her soul yearned, yearned. She didn't know what was happening to her. She pulled the quilt up over her head and saw her old friend Haia-Etel, may she rest in peace. Rachel remembered that story of Haia-Etel and Benjamin, and a frost ran through her body. She pushed the quilt away and suddenly she heard a very familiar melody, a familiar sound of a familiar violin. Rachel thought she was imagining it, but the music came nearer and nearer, it was the kind of music they play to escort the in-laws home after a wedding. Rachel had already heard and recognized what was being played, she also realized that it was Stempeniu playing away on the violin, and she had no doubts that it was Stempeniu accompanying the in-laws home after the wedding dinner. But what was he doing here? There was no wedding on this street tonight and there were no in-laws here! What could it mean? But the drum and the cymbal came nearer and nearer. The whole band was playing with a vengeance, but more clearly than anything else she could hear Stempeniu's violin, for its sweet melody, its tender song were subduing all the other instruments.

Rachel couldn't lie still. She leaped out of bed, strode over to the window, opened it, and leaned way, way out.

Rachel hadn't seen such a night for a long time. The moon was strolling in the middle of the sky and it was surrounded by millions of stars—diamonds twinkling and glistening. The air was warm, soft, and fresh. No breeze whatsoever, so that the high poplars looming in the big Monastery Garden stood tall and erect like sentries on guard. No leaf stirred. But seldom, very seldom, a lovely scent of fragrant herbs came wafting from there, and it was very welcome in Mazepevke, which had a different smell during the day. . . .

And this wonderful night was so fitting for our lovely Rachel, pure, virtuous, beautiful Rachel with her long, white throat, and the rich blond hair lying scattered upon it. (Ah, could Rachel have thought at such a time that the moon and the author of this novel could see her own hair, without the marriage wig?) Her eyes were no less blue or pure than the pure, blue heavens, and her lovely, radiant face was no less beautiful than the lovely, radiant night. But Rachel's thoughts were elsewhere: Her mind was where the strange music could be heard and her heart was where Stempeniu's violin was.

The musicians were playing so sadly, as though they had only just buried someone, put him in the ground. For us, a joyous occasion comes out as weeping, and fun and pleasure make us shed tears. . . . Even gloomier was the music at midnight, when all the world was sound asleep and only a tiny group of Jews were celebrating with a dismal tune as they came home from the wedding dinner with lowered heads: What was it? Had parents gotten a child off their backs—please excuse me—taken care of a child, for goodness' sake—well, all right. . . . In this quiet, lovely summer night, you could hear Stempeniu's violin more clearly than ever, it grieved the heart, it drew the soul, it sapped your life's blood—and Rachel stood half-naked at the window, listening. She wanted to flee from there, close the window and flee, but she was shackled to the spot as if in irons, as if held by a magnet. She gazed and she listened so earnestly as though she weren't hearing his violin, as though she could hear him talking to her, pleading, begging, weeping. . . . And not only Rachel was listening to those beautiful melodies from Stempeniu's violin in the radiant summer night: The moon and the stars, the soft, fresh air, all nature and all her creatures awoke from their slumber and got up for a moment to find out what the strange singing was at midnight, what those sounds were at midnight.

The nocturnal chorister, the tardy nightingale in Monastery Garden, upon hearing that music, rolled up his sleeves and tried to show off his prowess as he likes to do; but now, in late summer, he couldn't sing more beautifully than Stempeniu's violin, for the poor bird had lost his voice at the end of spring, and all that remained was a screech, the kind that rises from a cantor's throat after the Days of Awe—if you'll forgive the blasphemous comparison. . . . The rooster, that screamer, heard the playing of the musicians and, thinking it was already dawn, stepped down from his perch, flapped his wings, mumbled his morning prayers, let out his usual cockadoodledoo with a cantorial cantillation, and then went back to his rest, furious that he had been bothered for nothing. . . . Even the dogs, the hounds, far away, on Monastery Street, at first began barking and howling, as is their custom, upon hearing the Jewish musicians in the middle of the night, and then they fell silent and looked for places to sleep. Even the cow, Dvosse-Malke's chestnut cow, stopped chewing her cud near the house, perked up her ears, and let out a deep moan from her belly, like a sinful Jew. And the neighbor's two goats got so excited that they sprang up from the ground and changed places, menacing each other with their horns. In short, all things and creatures came alive, showing that they could hear the music in that warm, silent, radiant, magical summer night.

At the same time, our virtuous Rachel was standing at the window as though shackled in irons. She stood there, riveted, wonder-struck, in utter confusion. "Oh, what a night! Oh God, what a night this is!" She stood there, absorbing it with all her senses. She swallowed mouthfuls of the fresh air. She was totally spellbound. She gazed at the blue sky and remembered those summer nights when she was a girl, sitting in front of the house, gazing up at the white moonbeams while playing jacks and singing that old song:

The moon is shining through the night,
And Pearl is sitting by the door,
Sighing and moaning through the night,
Alas, her heart is so sore!
Sighing and moaning through the night,
Alas, her heart is so sore!

She had sung the song in those bygone days, never understanding it, and now she did understand it, not fully, but she understood something and felt it. She felt that something was tugging at her, pulling her outside, into the open air. She felt hemmed in here, hot and ill, ill! . . . Rachel remembered another song that she used to sing as a girl, during summers, outside by the door.

I stand on the shore
And I can't come to you,
Oh you call me from afar—
But I can't swim to you.
Oh, you call me from afar,
But I can't swim to you!

"From afar?" But he was so close now! He was right there, Stempeniu, with his violin, his long hair, his black, burning, fiery eyes, which were always staring at her and warming her with their glow, with their fire. And at that moment, she yearned to be near him forever, to be near him and listen to him playing forever, and see his beautiful eyes forever. . . . But there was one thing Rachel didn't understand: How had he come here, Stempeniu, at midnight, with his violin?

How had Stempeniu come here with the in-laws? She simply couldn't understand, no matter how hard she thought about it. Rachel remembered that there had been a wedding somewhere near the synagogue. How had the in-laws gotten here? She understood the mystery only when she saw them very close by, almost at her house, the musicians and the in-laws. She solved the riddle only when she saw Stempeniu halting right at her house, right next to her window, and starting to play more freshly, more ardently. Now Rachel understood what Stempeniu had done: He had taken along the whole crew, all the in-laws, all the guests, from a dozen streets away, past her window, and for whom? At first, it was very pleasurable for her, and her heart was so joyful that it almost sprang from her breast. And willy-nilly, Rachel burst into such merry laughter that she was frightened by her own voice, she looked at herself standing there half-naked, her throat bare, without her marriage wig—and she hastily jumped away from the window, slammed it shut, and threw herself into the bed.

"Oh God, oh God!" thought Rachel. "The things you can do if you don't notice where you are! Standing naked in the middle of the night, at the window, in front of a crowd of men, thinking about such vain, silly things, having such ugly thoughts about someone like Stempeniu. . . . And Stempeniu—leading a whole congregation of Jews along a dozen streets—for what, for whom? It takes a lot of nerve to do a thing like that! . . . Where does he get such nerve? . . . I have to ask him. He has to stop doing that! He's making me miserable! . . . I have to have it out with him once and for all. What's that old saying: 'It's better to let off steam right away!'. . . He tells me a fairy-tale: Lovey-dovey! 'Very respectable I swear, Saturday night,' he says, 'on Monastery Street,' that's where he'll make his intentions clear. . . . I wish it were Saturday night already so I could hear what it's all about. Of course I'll go, why should I be scared? Scared of whom? Jews should only be scared of God! . . . It's a disaster, it's an evil spell. . . . There are good reasons why people tell all those stories. . . . But what does he want from me, what does he want? And who's to blame if not me? You mustn't give someone else even your little finger. . . . If Moyshe-Mendel were here now, I'd tell him everything. But where is he? Does he ever listen to me? What does he care if I'm miserable, if I'm in agony? . . . Oh, I ought to pray. It's no good not praying! . . .

"For Thy Redemption I hope, oh Lord,
I hope, oh Lord, for Thy Redemption,
Oh Lord, for Thy Redemption I hope."

Rachel buried herself deep, deep into the pillows, covered herself up with the quilt so as not to hear the musicians, and prayed out loud: "For Thy Redemption I hope, oh Lord." But they came sneaking in through the window, the sweet songs of Stempeniu's violin, growing softer and fainter and farther away. And Rachel prayed:

"For Thy Redemption I hope, oh Lord.
I hope, oh Lord, for Thy Redemption,
Oh Lord, for Thy Redemption I hope. . . ."

And Stempeniu's violin was almost inaudible in the distance. And the last sounds were dying out. And Rachel's eyes gradually closed, and her lips were whispering, almost inaudibly:

"For Thy Redemption. . . .
I hope . . . for Thy Redemption. . . .
. . . I hope. . . ."

And Rachel fell asleep.

Rachel fell asleep and she dreamt that Stempeniu was putting a string of coral around her neck. . . . On one side stood her father-in-law in his prayer shawl and prayer thongs, and Freydel was hitting and smacking him for all she was worth. . . . Moyshe-Mendel was dead-drunk, he was straddling a poker, making crazy faces, and Stempeniu was putting a string of coral around her neck. . . . On the other side stood Haia-Etel in her Sabbath best, decked out like a princess, smiling so joyously, so sweetly, and lighting many candles.

"What are you doing, Haia-Etel?" asked Rachel. "Why are you lighting so many candles?"

"How can you ask," Haia-Etel answered, laughing. "It's the Eve

353

of Sabbath, it's time to light the candles and say the blessing! . . ."

Rachel looked at the candles burning brightly and shining, and Stempeniu was putting a string of coral around her neck. . . . He stood next to her, so close that she could hear him breathing. He stood there gazing straight into her eyes, warming her with his stare. Rachel was happy, she laughed and sang, and Stempeniu was putting a string of coral around her neck.

Suddenly, the candles went out. Haia-Etel and everyone and everything vanished. It was pitch-black and icy cold, like a cellar, like a grave. . . . The wind whistled and blasted, and a singing could be heard, a gloomy singing: a violin was playing, once again a familiar violin. Stempeniu's violin. Stempeniu himself wasn't there, but his violin could be heard, yet it was so sad, so gloomy, like the *ne'ilah*, the last prayer on Yom Kippur. And there was the sound of weeping and sobbing. It was Haia-Etel crying for her youth, which had sped by so quickly, like a dream, crying for her darling Benjamin, who had left her for someone else, forgetting Haia-Etel, forgetting. . . .

"Oh, Mama!" screamed Rachel and woke up, turned over on her other side, fell asleep, and dreamt again, all kinds of dreams. She was bewildered all night long, and she thought she could feel Stempeniu next to her, putting a string of coral around her neck. . . . Then Haia-Etel returned with black candles, crying, mourning, reading prayers out loud: "Almighty Father in heaven, powerful God, Lord of all lords, King of all kings, who art only God from eternity to eternity! May our ardent prayers reach Thee and be granted by Thee. Hear the prayers of the pure souls who stand before Thy Throne of Glory and plead to Thee on our behalf and for the living on the earth, who are as full of sins as a pomegranate is full of seeds, and our fore-fathers. . . ."

Haia-Etel spoke the prayers out loud. She wept, she grieved, she lamented—and she disappeared.

A FIRE IS KINDLED

In the town of Mazepevke, there is a monastery, which, they say, was built by Mazepa. A high, white stone wall surrounds the monastery on all four sides and occupies three-quarters of the town. On one side of the wall, there are shops in niches, and on the other side, deep cellars, where, they say, the highwaymen hid all their weapons, and where apples and all kinds of goods are now stored. The third side of the wall is overgrown with brambles and guarded by tall poplars and other trees, beyond the wall, in the big Monastery Garden. The fourth side of the wall is bare and smooth, crumbling in many spots and losing clay and bricks, so that for many years it's been in need of repair. Facing it there are houses and cabins, yards and patches, both Jewish and Christian, and the narrow street running between the bare wall of the monastery and the houses is called Monastery Street.

There, on Monastery Street, in a corner where the trees begin, our lovers had their first rendezvous: Rachel and Stempeniu.

Readers, who are used to "highly interesting" modern romances, have suffered enough from this novel, which has had no tearful scenes, no assignations. No one has shot himself, no one has poisoned himself, we have met no counts or marquis. We keep seeing only ordinary people, musicians and everyday Jewish women. These readers must be looking forward to Saturday night, they are waiting for a piquant and titillating scene on Monastery Street. . . . But I have to say in advance that their expectations are useless. There won't be any piquant and titillating scenes because our Rachel hasn't come here for any sinful purpose, God forbid, she hasn't come here like a debauched woman hurrying to kiss her lover in the darkness, heaven forfend! Rachel only wanted to ask him how he, Stempeniu the

355

Musician, had the nerve, the chutzbah, to write a letter to her, Isaak-Naphtali's daughter-in-law, Moyshe-Mendel's wife, and *such* a letter to boot! . . .

"I have to give him a piece of my mind!" she thought to herself. "I have to make it clear to him once and for all! What's the old saying?—'It's better to let off steam right away. . . .' "

This thought did not come to her suddenly. Rachel had had a whole week's time and even more, all day Saturday, to think it over and, oh me, oh my, what things she had thought in that one day! What a terrible struggle she had had with her temptation. . . . No, the word "temptation" isn't proper here at all. How did she, a Jewish wife, who had never read novels and never known about romances, except for the story that her friend Haia-Etel had told her (may she rest in peace), the story we talked about earlier—how did Rachel come to feel temptation, love? Nonsense! If she were still unmarried, it would be different. She'd be—how can we put it?—a free bird, her hair still uncovered, an independent person. But she was a young wife, and an extremely pious wife at that, and of an excellent family! She was enraged at herself, a blazing fire, and she could find no rest. First she lay down on her bed, but then she felt all stirred up like a feverish invalid, who feels sick at heart and bored to death—he only wants to dash out into the world. . . . Rachel got up and went over to the *Tsene Rene,* the Yiddish Bible version for women. She opened up in the middle of Genesis and—how odd! Her eyes fixed on the verses: "And Dinah the daughter of Leah which she bare unto Jacob, went out to see the daughters of the land. And when Shechem the son of Hamor the Hivite . . . saw her, he took her, and lay with her, and defiled her. And his soul clave unto Dinah. Now the Bkhai writes: 'Shechem talked her into it. . . .' "

Rachel gazed at her *Tsene Rene,* which her mother-in-law had given her when she was still engaged, and little by little she began forgetting that she was sitting with the Bible, and her thoughts wafted over to him, to Stempeniu, to Monastery Street, under the trees, where he had promised to wait for her. . . . And no sooner did Stempeniu enter her thoughts than she felt drawn to him, like a magnet, and she didn't understand what was happening.

"I only want to ask him what he wants from me and why he's bothering me."

And now Rachel remembered her friend Haia-Etel, may she rest in peace, and the way she had suffered because of her Benjamin. . . . But Haia-Etel was related to Benjamin and she was only a girl, while she, Rachel, was a married woman, a "matron" (oh dear, what a harsh word for a Jewish woman). And he—who was he? A musician! What business did he have with her? Who did he think he was anyway writing letters to her! That no-account fiddler! That brazen good-for-nothing!

"Come hell or high water," she decided. "Come hell or high water, I have to tell him. Why should I be afraid of him? I'll meet him, I'll go there, it won't matter—nobody'll see me. I'll just dash over for a minute, it's not far, it's just across the way. . . ."

And Rachel looked through the open window into Monastery Street and saw the trees, the high poplars, standing proudly, and she heard the birds singing so beautifully from the garden. And her thoughts wafted over to the place where she would see him and talk to him privately, within an hour or even less. And she felt her heart pounding and struggling and (the truth, we have to tell the truth!) the minutes were long for her—she could hardly wait, if only it were night. Her father-in-law and her husband would come back from synagogue and perform the ceremony closing the Sabbath, her mother-in-law would change her clothes and start carrying on about the samovar and the borsht for the final Sabbath meal—and that's when Rachel would slip into her shawl and walk slowly, towards the door, step outside, just as if she were going for a stroll—who would take a second look at her? Until she came there, where. . . . Oh, her body trembled, her cheeks burned, and her heart—oh, her heart! It practically leaped out of her body, and she felt more and more drawn to that place, and that was all she could think about. She saw nothing before her eyes, only the trees of Monastery Garden, only Stempeniu with his blazing eyes. She heard nothing, only the lovely singing of the birds in the garden, and that godlike playing of—Stempeniu. At this point, Rachel·was totally absorbed in one thought—to get there, to Stempeniu, be there, with Stempeniu, and nothing in the world could have held her back. . . .

THE FIRE BURNS AND THEN GOES OUT

And as for Stempeniu, no sooner was it night than he sent his band out to the *zmires,* the traditional pre-wedding party, where the girls get together with the bride and dance. Then he took the violin under his arm so that Freydel would think he was going to the wedding. But once he left the house, he handed the instrument to Mekhtshi and then he sped to Monastery Street, and he paced up and down in the shade of the trees, stopping every minute to see if Rachel was coming, beautiful Rachel. He never doubted for an instant that she would come. His heart told him she would. He had seen it in her eyes when they had met that day, the day she was trying on the coral necklace.

And Stempeniu was not mistaken. Scarcely had fifteen minutes gone by when he caught sight of a woman across the street, floating towards him with a white shawl on her head. She was walking quickly, glancing around on all sides. The white shawl was pulled down almost over her eyes, and her hands were trembling, her teeth chattering, her heart pounding—her entire body shaking. She took a hard look, she halted, she spotted Stempeniu and moved towards him, saying:

"How dare you, sir—let me ask you—"

"Don't use the polite form with me, Rachel, use the familiar form," replied Stempeniu, taking hold of both her hands and staring deep into her eyes. In his eyes, Rachel saw the same glow as in the stars that were gazing down from the dark-blue sky of that beautiful summer night. . . . All the Jews in Mazepevke were concluding the Sabbath, chanting the praises of the prophet Elijah, as was customary, sighing and brooding, worrying about work and business, wishing they could have the luck of the pious man who had met Elijah and greeted him and been greeted by him. The women of Mazepevke removed the veils from their heads, took off their Sabbath garments, their jewelry, and set about their everyday work. In a word, Mazepevke was busy ushering out the dear and holy Sabbath—and it never occurred to anyone that at this very moment, Rachel, the daughter-in-law of Dvosse-Malke, was standing with Stempeniu the Musician on Monastery Street, and that the two of them were talking about things that were anything but Jewish. . . .

Only the blue heavens, the bright stars, which were peering down with their brilliance, only the high poplars in the monastery, only the nocturnal birds in the huge garden, calling to one another in their language—only they could hear and see what was happening; only they knew that on this lovely, magical night, under the monastery trees, in the Christian street—Rachel was standing right next to Stempeniu, in such a different state that she completely forgot who she was and what she was. Here, amid the lovely splendors of nature, Rachel felt as she had never felt in her life. The fear, which had stalked her all the way here, suddenly left her, and she felt as if she'd grown wings and were as free as a bird and could fly, fly. . . . Stempeniu moved closer to her and placed his hands on her shoulders. Rachel shuddered. She wanted to step away but, instead, she looked at Stempeniu, and tears rolled down from her radiant blue eyes.

"Why are you crying, Rachel?" asked Stempeniu, wiping her tears away with his hands.

"Ah, Stempeniu, I feel so good here, next to . . . you . . ." (she shifted to the familiar form) "next to you, Stempeniu! Why am I . . . ? Why can't I be . . . ?"

"Mine? Is that what you want to say? You *are* mine, Rachel, you *are* mine!"

"What do you mean I'm yours, Stempeniu? How can that be?"

"You're mine, my beloved, do you understand, because I'm yours forever, for all time, until the dark grave, I'm yours till death, my darling, my life!"

"Benjamin said the same thing, he swore—and then in the end. . . ."

"Who's Benjamin?" asked Stempeniu, amazed, peering into Rachel's eyes the way you look at a child when it says something utterly silly. "Who are you talking about, my darling?"

"Benjamin, Haia-Etel's cousin. My friend Haia-Etel was an

359

orphan and she had a cousin named Benjamin, and when they were very young, they swore they would get married, he promised her, he swore an oath on his holy word of honor—and in the end, oh, it was so ugly for her, poor Haia-Etel, she died a long time ago, God rest her soul, may she forgive me. . . . But she was crazy about Benjamin, she worshiped the ground he walked on. She told me so herself. . . . I can see her now, I can see her by the window, with me singing songs to her, and she's crying and she keeps saying: 'Oh, don't believe them, you mustn't believe what men tell you! . . .' "

Rachel told about her friend Haia-Etel the orphan, and Stempeniu kissed Rachel's hands, caressed her, looked into her eyes—and Rachel kept talking about Haia-Etel and how she passed away, how she went out like a candle, out of love for her dear Benjamin. . . .

Haia-Etel had been dead for several years, but Rachel remembered her well. She often dreamt about her. Now she felt as if Haia-Etel were standing on the other side of the wall, wearing a shroud and gazing over at Rachel and beckoning to her, pointing at Stempeniu and shaking her head as though to say: "What are you doing? . . ."

"What's the use, Rachel my darling, what's the use of talking and remembering such things, especially at night? Just look at me with your bright, lovely eyes, oh the way they shine and glow like two beautiful diamo—"

Stempeniu hadn't even uttered the last word when Rachel wrested herself loose from his hands with such force that Stempeniu was terrified of her.

"For God's sake, Rachel, what's wrong?"

He tried to take hold of her again, but she wouldn't let him. She trembled and whispered: "Do you see her? She's over there! She's standing there! . . . She's looking at us, at us. . . ."

"Who's standing there? Who's looking at us? What are you talking about, Rachel? My darling, come to me, take my hand. . . ."

"Oh! Leave me alone, Stempeniu, leave me alone." She was using the polite form again. "Can't you see, something white is standing there? Oh, it's her, it's Haia-Etel! Haia-Etel! . . . Oh, leave me alone, leave me alone! . . . How dare you, how dare you! . . . Good night to you! Good night! . . ."

And Rachel vanished in the shade of the trees. Stempeniu saw only the ends of the white shawl fluttering in the wind, looking like two white pinions. That is how a good angel flees, that is how a good dream disappears. . . .

Oh, you Jewish woman, you showed your virtue there and all your purity. Oh, Jewish wife! You showed all your fidelity there, all your devotion!

Upon coming home, Rachel wanted to tell everyone, shout to everyone, where she had been and whom she had met. But she found the entire household sitting around a table with several guests, in front of a huge samovar, and they were all engrossed in talking shop, as Jews usually do, gathering somewhere on Saturday night when the Sabbath is over. After resting for twenty-four hours, you chat a little about business, about the next day's fair, and about various political matters.

"I'm not going to have a booth at the fair," said a fat little man with a dry-goods store. "The fairs can go to hell! I'm fed up with them! Troubles and headaches—that's all you can get out of a fair!"

"Why do you say that?" exclaimed Dvosse-Malke, her hands folded on her chest. "I don't understand why you're so down on fairs, Yudel. Just last week, Lord preserve us, you made a bundle—may it happen to all Jews. Why, you were raking in money all day long!"

"All you talk about is raking in money!" cried Isaak-Naphtali, not looking at his wife as he worked the beads on an abacus.

"And I wouldn't want a worse fair than last Sunday," cried Moyshe-Mendel, checking the accounts. "How can you deny it? I don't understand."

"That's the point," said Yudel, "you just don't want to believe anyone else. When you see ten peasants crowding in and practically carrying away my booth, you call that 'raking in money' and you start resenting it."

"You know what, Yudel?" exclaimed a cross-eyed young man. "Why don't we forget about the county fair. Tomorrow is

361

another day, and we'll have our fill of it then. Let's talk about something else."

And they began talking about important matters: citrons for the Feast of Tabernacles, synagogue problems, and of course war. Everyone talked, everyone smoked, the samovar boiled and steamed and the house was filled with fumes. The oven was hot: borsht and goose breasts were cooking for the last Sabbath meal.

"Where've you been, Rachel?" Dvosse-Malke asked her daughter-in-law.

"Right there . . . on Monastery Street."

"What's it like outside? Nice weather? God preserve the weather for all fairs. . . . What's wrong, dear, you're so pale, do you have a headache? Maybe you should lie down a bit."

At these words, everyone turned around and looked at Rachel's wan face, and it was unanimously decided that she was groggy from the samovar's fumes. Rachel went to her room to lie down, and now the company began talking about fumes and how fumes were no laughing matter, they might seem like nothing, why, they were only smoke—but they could kill a person just like that. And one man related that once, in his grandfather's home— may he rest in peace—the entire household was practically wiped out by fumes. And someone else told a lovely story about how his uncle's entire family was practically poisoned by a kind of fish known as a "sea eel," and they were just barely saved from death. Another man told a very lovely story about a demon, a poltergeist, a wandering ghost, and so on and on . . . until they began talking about death.

"Whatever people talk about, in the end they talk about death!" someone exclaimed.

" 'Elijah the Prophet'—we ought to have a look—'Elijah of Tishbi'—what's my wife doing?—'Elijah of Gilead.'. . ." Moyshe-Mendel suddenly murmured, while singing the "Elijahs" of the Sabbath night. He got up from the table and went to look in on Rachel.

RACHEL GOES BACK TO THE STRAIGHT AND NARROW PATH

"Help! Help!" the company heard a shout from the side room, and they all dashed in and saw Rachel stretched out on the bed, her head thrown back, and Moyshe-Mendel standing next to her, scared out of his wits.

"What's wrong? What's happening? Fainted? Water! Hurry!"

"Water! Water!" everyone shouted and no one moved.

"Oh, goddamn it all!" screamed Dvosse-Malke and got a dipper of water, took a mouthful, and sprayed it on Rachel's face, which was as dead as a tomb.

"Get the doctor!" screamed Moyshe-Mendel in a strange voice.

"The doctor! The doctor!" they all screamed, looking at one another.

"Tie her hands with a handkerchief and squeeze her nose!"

"Her nose! Her nose!" they all screamed and stood where they were.

"That's right, Dvosse-Malke, harder, harder!" the guests spurred her on as she worked with might and main, rubbing, squeezing, pouring water, pulling eyelids—until finally they revived Rachel from her faint and got her to sit up. Rachel looked around groggily and then asked: "Where am I? I'm so hot, so hot! . . ."

"Move away, everybody, give her air!" said Dvosse-Malke and sent the whole company into the living room, while she and Moyshe-Mendel stayed with Rachel, whose eyes were fixed on Moyshe-Mendel.

"What's wrong, daughter, what happened?" the mother-in-law asked.

"What is it, Rachel?" asked Moyshe-Mendel, leaning over her.

"Please ask your mother to leave," Rachel answered softly.

"Mama, please step outside for a moment," said Moyshe-

363

Mendel. He accompanied his mother out of the room and then returned to Rachel's bed.

"Tell me what's wrong," Moyshe-Mendel asked her for the first time with deep love.

"Oh, Moyshe-Mendel, swear you won't tell anybody. . . . Swear it'll remain our secret. . . . Promise you'll forgive me for what I've done to you. . . . If Haia-Etel, Lord rest her soul, hadn't warned me. . . . Oh, if it hadn't been for Haia-Etel. . . . Oh, Moyshe-Mendel, my darling!"

"Just listen to what you're saying, Rachel. You're raving! What do you mean, Haia-Etel?"

"My friend Haia-Etel, may she rest in peace. Haia-Etel the orphan, she's been in the True World for a long time. I've dreamt about her several times. But today, now. . . . Ah, Moyshe-Mendel, bend over to me, nearer, nearer. . . . That's right, I'm scared. . . . I'm sorry for what I've done, oh, how sorry I am!"

And Rachel moved closer to Moyshe-Mendel until she was lying in his arms. The room was dark. Only a single ray of light entered from the door to the living room, and Rachel and Moyshe-Mendel could hardly see each other. Their eyes met and a tiny fire kindled in them, the kind of fire you see when people fall happily in love for the first time, when the heart and not the tongue does all the talking, when people converse with their eyes and not their lips.

"Tell me, Moyshe-Mendel my darling, do you really care for me?"

"How can you ask?" Moyshe-Mendel replied. "You're right in my heart like a—I don't know like what. . . ."

Moyshe-Mendel had no other way of expressing his love for Rachel. But we can believe that he meant it with all his heart, seriously—and perhaps more seriously than the fine fellow who has a greater knack for uttering his feelings in words.

But let's leave them, the happy couple, there in the half-darkened room, where, a year after the wedding, they had their first chance to have a heart-to-heart talk, as they sat there like doves. Things that had been hidden deep down for an entire year suddenly came to the surface like trees on water.

Once Rachel felt a little better, Moyshe-Mendel sat next to her, softly crooning the "Elijahs" under his breath.

"Elijah the Prophet . . . Elijah of Tishbi . . . Elijah of Gilead. . . ."

And Rachel said to him:

"I want to ask you to do something for me, Moyshe-Mendel. Promise you'll do it."

"Well? What is it? Tell me, Rachel, I'll do anything you want me to."

"I think we've lived with your family long enough. You're no longer a student, we've got a little money tucked away, thank goodness—why don't we move to a big city, Yehupets. Once I'm there, among my friends and relatives, and with you—I'll feel as fine as ever. We'll be alone. It's time we stopped living off your family, honestly, I'm so sick and tired of it that I can't enjoy anything. We're like strangers with your family, absolute strangers. . . ."

Moyshe-Mendel sat there, gazing in surprise at Rachel. Then he began rocking and swaying like before, singing his "Elijahs."

"Okay, very good, 'angry man,' it's fine with me. 'Elijah the Prophet' . . . this very week!"

"You'll do it for me, Moyshe-Mendel, won't you?" Rachel said to him with deep love. "We'll be on our own, I'll have my own household, and I'll take care of you like the apple of my eye. Ah, Moyshe-Mendel, you're usually so absent-minded that you never say a kind word! But today you're so different, so different. . . ."

"Elijah the Prophet. . . ." crooned Moyshe-Mendel softly, "Elijah of Tishbi . . . Elijah of Gilead. . . ."

And in the living room, the men were having a different kind of conversation: they were trying to figure out why Isaak-Naphtali's daughter-in-law had suddenly fainted. One man said it was an evil eye, another concluded the opposite, she'd been caught in a draft, and the third one, an elderly Jew with married children, had his own explanation:

"Believe me, I've got three daughters-in-law, I know a thing or two about such matters, I tell you, she's having 'whims.' Isaak-Naphtali, get set for cakes and vodka or a circumcision. Mazel-tov, Dvosse-Malke! Your daughter-in-law—well, well, she'll be all right! Why are you so embarrassed, Dvosse-Malke? Don't worry, it's perfectly kosher. . . . Jews do it all the time. . . ."

Dvosse-Malke was simply melting with delight, she'd been anxiously looking forward to this for a long time.

"Well, well!" she said, pretending to be annoyed. "Cut it out— you and your jokes! I'd better see how the borsht is doing. It's taking longer than usual! . . ."

A YEAR LATER

"A dull story!" says the reader, apparently quite dissatisfied, for he's been raised on those modern romances, where people hang themselves and drown themselves, poison themselves and shoot themselves, or where a heder teacher becomes a count, a serving maid becomes a princess, and a belfer (school assistant) becomes—a dragon. Now can I help it if we have no counts or princesses? We have only ordinary Jewish men and women, Jewish girls and Jewish musicians. . . . But why bother with justifications? By now, the reader can say what he likes. I've brought him this far, and he'll certainly go further with me, he'll want to know what happens in the end and what becomes of Rachel, and what becomes of Stempeniu.

We will now skip a year (what is one year in a human life?) and we will visit Isaak-Naphtali's home for the dinner concluding the Sabbath. And there we find the same people as a year ago, and hear the same conversations as a year ago, with not a hair changed. And everyone keeps talking about the fair, business, profits, children—until the conversation turns to Moyshe-Mendel and Rachel, who live in Yehupets now.

"Dvosse-Malke, show us the letter from the kids in Yehupets," Isaak-Naphtali cried to his wife. "Here, read it Yudel."

"Let him read it!" said Yudel, pointing to the cross-eyed young man.

The cross-eyed man took the letter and read it fluently; the salutation was in Hebrew:

Peace and all good wishes to my beloved Father, the wise, learned, enlightened, and eminent gentleman, the highly esteemed Lord Isaak-Naphtali, son of Moses-Joseph, may he rest in peace. And to my highly honored and pious Mother—

"Stop that!" they all shouted. "Stop that! That's all rhetoric, for God's sake, kid stuff, it's their foolishness! Read the rest, on the other side!"

The cross-eyed man turned the letter over and continued reading its mixture of Yiddish, Hebrew and Russian:

And since you have asked me, Dear Father, to tell you about business and commerce here in Yehupets, I must inform you—

"Oh, so that's what it means!" the company cried happily. "Keep reading, go on!"

I must inform you that dry goods do particularly well here as does haberdashery, though haberdashery does not do as well as dry goods. And groceries likewise do not do badly, no worse than in Mazepevke. Woolens are worth their weight in gold. Sugar, flour, and bran are also a business here, they are exported, and Jews earn tidy sums thereby. In short, Yehupets is a blessed land, the city itself is enormous and worth a visit. It is altogether another world here in Yehupets, you can meet Jews here of whom you would never have dreamt that they were Jews. Paper is also a business here, everything is business here. And Jews frequent the stock exchange, buying and selling all kinds of stocks, and brokers earn money galore.

And my beloved spouse Rachel sends you all her fondest greetings. She writes to you herself below. May the Good Lord grant that we hear good news from you—amen. I must also inform you that the store which I rented is located right on Alexandrovsky Street, and the money I take in is not at all bad, praised be the Lord. My beloved spouse Rachel, long may she live, has already mastered the trade and can already talk to the customers. But I go and buy at the fairs myself. I have credit with merchants in Moscow and Lodz. Dealing with Moscow is not difficult, Moscow sells with a conscience and likes Jewish clients. Even when a businessman goes bankrupt, Moscow helps him out and will not let him fall.

Dwellings are extremely expensive here. For two alcoves and a kitchen—one hundred seventy-five rubles a year, not including wood and water, and everything costs a fortune here. Jews are mostly agents and brokers and there are an enormous number of these Jewish agents and brokers here, and a Jew can thereby earn a respectable ruble. In short, Yehupets is a place to earn one's living. May God give us health and strength and grant that we hear the same from you, which I wish you, I your son, who wishes you peace and happiness in your lives,

Moyshe-Mendel

son of the highly esteemed Isaak-Naphtali of Mazepevke.

My very best to my dear uncle and my dear aunt with all their offspring and their household.

My very best to Reb Yudel with all his offspring and his household.

My very best to the highly esteemed Reb Simkhe-Hersh with all his offspring and his household.

My very best to the highly esteemed Reb Dov-Ber with all his offspring and his household.

My very best to Stisye-Beyle with all her offspring and her household.

Rachel's letter followed, in a Germanicized Yiddish:

I too send greetings to my highly esteemed father-in-law and my dear mother-in-law. I hope you are well. I am in good health, may God preserve me. Also my Yossele greets you and thanks his dear grandmother for the blouse many times. He promises you that God will give life for that and,

God willing, in three or four years he will begin going to heder and, God willing, he will learn eagerly and, God willing, he will be a good Jew, may God grant him a long life, amen. Dear father-in-law, if you could make Yossele a skullcap and a pair of woolen socks, I would be very thankful, for I am very busy in the store, and I do not want to hire a nurse for Yossele, it would not be right. I have only taken on a girl and I pay her four rubles out of my household money, she looks after the baby and pastures the cow—you should see the cow I bought! She gives a whole gallon of milk, excellent milk, and I get cheese and butter from her, thank the Lord. But my dear Moyshe-Mendel has suddenly started hating dairy products. Give him a good talking-to, please, he doesn't take care of himself at all! Yossele is bawling his head off now, the poor thing wants to eat—may I hunger in his place! I will conclude my letter, please send heartiest greetings to all our friends and relatives and please write to us, God willing, and I remain your devoted and well-wishing daughter-in-law, Rachel.

"Well," said Fat Beryl. "My own children should do no worse!"

"You're sinning, Dvosse-Malke, you're sinning!" said Yudel. "I swear, you're sinning!"

"Of course, thank the Good Lord, they're doing well—knock on wood. But I miss her so much—I can't forget her, Yudel, I can't forget her."

And Dvosse-Malke started listing all her daughter-in-law's virtues and all her manners and showed him why she couldn't forget her. Everyone talked, they talked about Yehupets and about business in Yehupets. Then they poured themselves drinks, they toasted, *l'chaim*, holding the cups for a long time, and they wished one another all the luck in the world, and glad tidings for all Jews and salvations and consolations. But then the borsht came to the table, spreading a marvelous fragrance through the house, and the company became merry. They were absorbed in their conversations and forgot all about Moyshe-Mendel and Rachel and the city of Yehupets and all of them together.

369

STEMPENIU HAS A TRUE TASTE OF HELL

But one person could not forget beautiful Rachel.

The reader can guess that we are talking about Stempeniu.

Yes indeed, Stempeniu. Who can possibly depict his great sorrows? Who can feel his heart and grasp his great chagrin?

"How awful!" thought Stempeniu. "How miserable!" thought Stempeniu. "She didn't even remember me, she didn't even say a word, she didn't dash off two lines to me, for politeness' sake: 'So long, I'm leaving!' Dammit, it's awful."

Never had anything like this happened to Stempeniu, although any number and all kinds of things had indeed happened to him, and once—some pretty awful things that ended pretty badly, as we mentioned earlier. Yet he would never have dreamt of such a setback, such a rebuff as he'd gotten from Rachel. Stempeniu, who was so respected in the rabbi's court that even the rabbi's daughters joked around with him, Stempeniu, who was so doted upon by Countess Brerzerzko and all the Polish noblemen that they sent out their carriages for him and spoke French to him— Stempeniu should get a rebuke, and such an awful one at that, from a simple Jewish woman!?

"I really miss her!" Stempeniu admitted to his band "I really and truly miss her and I'd go after her in Yehupets, if it weren't for . . . if it weren't for. . . ." Stempeniu looked around on all sides, and the musicians knew *whom* he was looking for.

The musicians all loved Stempeniu, they simply adored him, they would have gone through hell and high water for him. And as much as they loved Stempeniu, they despised Freydel. They couldn't stand her greed, her stinginess, her foul temper.

"Before he got hitched up," the musicians said to one another, "he didn't give a shit about money, you could get a ruble from him, or even three, or four, and never have to pay him back. But ever since that filthy bitch got her claws into him, he's never got a kopek of his own, no matter what he does. Remember those great

370

dinners we used to have with him and the trips we used to go on! Now, everything's lousy, we ain't got nothin', our bellies swell up like mountains, and we starve our guts out. Not a crust of bread all year long, and all we do is sit around lookin' forward to the weddin' season. You'd think that just for politeness' sake she'd offer a guy a cup of tea occasionally, and maybe even have us over for a meal—may she rot in hell, the bitch!"

"Believe you me, there are times when I feel I'm about to croak from hunger, but I wouldn't eat a crumb of that bitch's bread for any amount of gold in the world!"

"How can he live with her, that snake, that pig?! I would've fed her poison a long time ago or strung her up, I swear on my mother's grave!"

"Oh, Stempeniu, you're up shit's creek and you've been sold down the river!"

That's the way his band spoke about him, they knew all about his problems, they felt his sorrows, even though he never spoke about them to the other musicians.

If Freydel was in the market or busy with her wares and clients, then things were fine: Stempeniu treated the band to cigarettes, they sat around, they kidded around, they exchanged stories about the past, and they rolled cigarettes like there was no tomorrow. But then, in flounced Freydel, everyone was turned off, and they started leaving one by one.

"For God's sake, it's as smoky as a tavern here!" said Freydel, snorting and peering at the packet of tobacco, which was running low. "Smoking like chimneys, it's disgusting! My head's already aching from the fumes! You'll be the death of me! You think there's something virtuous about smoking so much, Stempeniu? Listen to me, Stempeniu darling, stop smoking. Believe me, it'll ruin your health!"

"You don't give a shit about my health, Freydel! Just admit that your heart bleeds for the money I spend on cigarettes! Why put on an act?"

"How can you say such a thing! Who's putting on an act? I only care about his health and he says I'm putting on an act! What a morning! I've haggled my lungs out, I've bargained and dickered, I've eaten my heart out, I didn't take in a kopek, and I've

371

been cursed out like a maid, like a maid, I've been humiliated, I've been trampled on like a piece of dirt—and my corals just lie there and rot! . . ."

"I'd really like to know, Freydel my dear, why you hustle so much and why you're such a tightwad! Do you have a mob of starvin' kids to feed?"

"Get a load of him, the poor shmuck! You should cut your tongue out, that's what you should do! Maybe I carry everything off to my mama, huh, Stempeniu? Or maybe I eat it up myself, I'm such a glutton, right, such a drunkard, right—the whole world oughta watch out for me—huh, Stempeniu? C'mon, look me in the eye, Stempeniu! Huh?"

"Did I say you ate anything up? It's the other way around, I'm only sayin'—"

"You're saying, you're saying—how should I know what you're saying, huh, Stempeniu? You should curse God for saddling you with a spendthrift like me, a spendthrift who turns one kopek into two and thinks about you day and night. C'mon, just tell me, what are you lacking, what don't you have? Cat got your tongue? Why, I'd love to know: What would've become of you and your fiddle if it weren't for me, Stempeniu, if you didn't have me for a wife?"

"Oh for God's sake!"

"Oh for God's sake!? You've already forgotten the way you looked at the wedding—not a shirt to your name, not a single sock without a hole in it, no pillow, no pillowcase, nothing and less than nothing, and you were earning chunks of gold—where did it all go to?"

"Am I supposed to tell what I did with my earnings when I was a bachelor?"

"Ah, that's the trouble with you, Stempeniu, that's your problem! You can't stand hearing the truth about yourself, and you complain if a woman works her fingers to the bone for you, drudges, labors, goes through agony, doesn't even allow herself a crust of bread, and leads a horrible life, and all for whose sake? For him! All for his sake, and do you know for what good deeds? He's sure to put up a golden tombstone for me—oh God in heaven, oh God, oh God!"

372

"What'd I do to you? Who's doing anything to you?"

"What should you do to me? You've done enough to me already! You robbed me of the best years of my life! You took a young child, an innocent girl, you pulled all that sweet talk on me, you promised me golden mountains, oh, what cock-and-bull stories you told me, you liar! If only I'd never met you! I'd have a man worthy of me and I'd never have become Stempeniu's wife—what luck, what marvelous luck I've had!!"

"Well, are you sorry we got hitched, Freydel? There's a rabbi in Mazepevke and a river, which means we can get divorced—"

"What? Is that what you're after? So the cat's out of the bag! You think I don't know that that's what you want? You wanna get rid of me! I know, Stempeniu, I know, you can't pull the wool over my eyes! I'm in your way! What did I ever do to deserve this, Stempeniu? I ask you, for God's sake, tell me what did I do to deserve this? I wanna know too!"

"Oh," replied Stempeniu, waving his hand, he went to his room and took the violin down from the wall.

The violin—that was his comfort, his only friend in the world. With the violin, he could forget his troubles, remember his youth, his freedom, which he had lost forever, forever! So many different people were evoked by the singing of his violin; so many lovely, happy, radiant, images of the past came to him when he began to play; they appeared—and vanished! . . .

Among all the past images, one image touched him more than any other, an image he could not forget: the dear and lovely image of Rachel, her bright face, her blue eyes, her long lashes, her white throat, and her sweet, good smile, for which he would have given anything, anything in the world!

Stempeniu played and played; he played on and on, so that Rachel's ghost would not disappear as always. He only wanted to see her ghost. Even thinking about her was so dear to him, so dear.

Stempeniu played as he had never played before. One can say that in his playing he reached the highest possible level. Anyone who didn't hear him play at that time did not hear anything good.

That's the kind of joy we feel when a bird sings in its cage: The bird is dreaming of green leaves, gorgeous blossoms, open air, a free world, an open world, a great, wide world, and it feels like singing to pour out its bitter heart—and it sings, it weeps, it pours out everything it feels! And we feel joy and delight, we have true pleasure.

"I really miss her so much!" Stempeniu said for the hundredth time to his band. "I miss her like she was my flesh and blood, and I'd go after her in Yehupets if it weren't for. . . ."

And Stempeniu looked around on all sides and saw Freydel dickering with a customer over corals, silk cloths, woolen yarn.

Our Freydel had gradually rigged up a whole shop in her house and had become a genuine businesswoman, on a par with all the other storekeepers in Mazepevke.

Very frequently, she was visited by her mother, Fat Zipporah. Her mother said Shaike missed his daughter very much and had sent his wife to see how Freydel was. But Freydel knew she was lying, there wasn't a crust of bread in her parents' home and her mother had come here to put an end to her fast, to get a bit out of life, to make her stomach stop growling.

"You know what, daughter? Why don't you make those butter rolls, you know, the kind I used to make, pleated and nicely dried out. They're so healthy with a cup of chicory, and with a nice load of butter they're absolute heaven. And for breakfast, fry some goose cracklings with an onion. Papa's always loved that, if you remember that far back. Food is the best medicine."

And Zipporah licked her lips and thought up a new breakfast every day, a new lunch and a new snack and a new dinner—and it can't be said that Freydel was very happy about it. The first week, she more or less put up with it, but the second week, she began getting huffy with her mother, and her mother got huffy with her, until they had an awful fight and they let out all their anger on Stempeniu when he tried to butt in and make peace between his wife and his mother-in-law.

"Mind your own business!" shouted Freydel. "And don't worry, I won't give my mama your legacy. Don't worry, Stempeniu!"

"A fine son-in-law!" said Zipporah with a jab of her tongue. "An ox has a long tongue, but it can't blow a shofar! Decent people treat a mother-in-law like a mother. He can see how my darling daughter treats me! How does the saying go: 'Blow your nose and smear your face'—and he won't even wiggle his tongue! Some man you are, you fiddle-strummer! I just don't understand why he doesn't get fed up with it, Lord in heaven! And what my daughter has to boast about—I'll never know. If you're lucky, then even a bull will have a calf. I've seen creatures like you, I have! Your father-in-law was once a fine fiddler like you, Stempeniu, but he turned out to be a big nothing. What's that old saying? 'A new broom sweeps clean.' You can't get angry at me, Stempeniu, I'm just telling you the plain truth, and even though every dog's the master in his own kennel, I'm not exactly an outsider, you know, I'm your mother-in-law, after all, and if you're going to dine with the devil then you'd better use a long spoon. . . ."

And Zipporah unleashed her tongue and talked a blue streak, as was her custom when she let go. But Stempeniu didn't hear her out. He picked up his violin as he always did when he was in a bad mood—and he forgot all about his wife and his mother-in-law and all his problems. And he only saw Rachel with her blue eyes. . . .

"I miss her, I really and truly miss her!" Stempeniu brooded and tried to think of some way of going to her, of seeing her again, somehow, somewhere. . . .

Idle thoughts! He didn't realize that he would soon be done with his song, that his days were almost gone, he didn't see that his black curls would keep thinning out, that his fiery eyes were gradually losing their glow, that creases were emerging on his white forehead.

Foolish strong man! Don't forget yourself. Can't you see your Delilah, your wife Freydel, at your side? Your Delilah has rocked you, has lulled you in her lap, softly shorn away your long hair and taken away your strength, all your strength, as the other Delilah did to Samson. . . . You've got one comfort left in the world—your violin.

Play, Stempeniu, play your violin! Play, and we will listen. . . ❀

WHEN ALL IS SAID AND DONE

DOVID BERGELSON

I

For four whole years, their engagement kept dragging along in the small town, and it ended in the following way:

She, Gedalye Hurvitz's only child, Miriam, finally sent back the engagement contract and began strolling around with Lipkis, the lame student.

The fiancé's father, *nouveau riche*, tall, and dark-haired, was a refined ignoramus, unlettered in the holy writings, who, at forty-eight, had started praying at the nearby synagogue on weekdays too; he was already extremely wealthy, respectable, and a man of few words. He kept pacing up and down in his room with a cigarette in his mouth, thinking about his three large estates and musing that it might not be proper for him to mention her father's name together with the engagement contract that she had sent back.

And the fiancé's mother, short, very stout, and asthmatic, always hoarse and gasping, like a fattened goose, did not find out about the return of the contract until much later, when coming home from abroad with a sunburnt face and a heavy heart, no healthier than before. In her quiet, melancholy way, she cursed the former fiancée and that awful Marienbad, which had senselessly drained her vital strength. She kept swaying back and forth, rubbing a rheumatic leg, and quietly and pensively complaining

377

that God only knew whether she would live to see her son get married.

And one evening, when the house was full of guests, she caught sight of Miriam and the lame student strolling past the open window. She lost all control and thrust her head outside, yelling after her in a hoarse, breathless voice:

Miriam's father no longer had a kopek to his name! God save us! What was she carousing for anyway, like a dog on a leash, that . . . that . . . !?

And he, the tall and handsome twenty-seven-year-old, couldn't bear it. He scolded his mother right then and there: "Shhh! Shhh! Just look at her!"

He was quiet and forebearing by nature, and greatly respected his taciturn and *nouveau riche* father, he wanted their home to be as quiet and respectable as the houses of the gentry with whom he had been dealing through his father since the age of sixteen. It wasn't pleasant, however, to remain in town and watch Miriam stroll by every evening with the lame student; so his father leased the Bitznev estate for him outside the town, and the son actually moved into the whitewashed manorial cottage nearby, next to the village priest.

Here, in the desolate, quiet countryside, the peasants addressed him as "Sir" and doffed their hats to him. And his two younger sisters, and the hoarse, overly stout mother would often come by, bringing presents, home-baked things. He smiled at his sisters every time because they were being tutored by a student and because they were still meeting "her," even though she had sent back the engagement contract. He would shake hands and ask:

"How are you? How is everything?"

And here in the village, he wanted to pay his mother the same respect that mothers enjoyed in the homes of the gentry, who had their own or rented estates nearby. He remained standing in her presence the whole time, and unable to use either the familiar or the polite form, he kept addressing her in the third person: "Mother may want to have a cup of tea . . . ? Mother may want to lie down a bit . . . ?"

And it was only when she complained about her illness and his still being single, and began cursing that woman who had sent back the engagement contract, that he twisted his face in displeasure and scolded her in an annoyed and respectful tone, just as he used to scold her in an annoyed and respectful tone in his father's house:

"Shhh! Shhh! Just look at her!"

He hardly ever went home except when he had to go on business. While there, he would act quiet and respectable, like an outsider, a very welcome guest, and smile politely at his sisters, or, when a child came running through, he would slowly lift it up and put it on the table, stroke its messy cheeks and smile:

"What are you doing, huh? Running around?"

He spent most of his visit with his father in the small, smoke-drenched office, discussing various business matters, thinking about the dowry—his six thousand and Miriam's three thousand rubles, still on deposit with the old Count of Kashperivka—and fearing that his father would soon start in:

"Yes, and what about the six thousand rubles we deposited with the count . . . what are we going to do about those six thousand rubles we deposited with the old Count of Kashperivka?"

Miriam's father, Gedalye Hurvitz, the absent-minded and aristocratic Torah scholar, whose head always reeled in a commercial atmosphere, had been suffering extreme business difficulties, and his local creditors would spend every afternoon in the marketplace tallying up his holdings behind his back:

"Let's see, he's got five thousand rubles in the Kashperivka woods and three thousand in Zhorzhovke poppy seeds. And what about the mill? How much did he sink into that unlucky Ternov mill last summer?"

He simply couldn't figure out why Hurvitz didn't take the three thousand rubles back from the count; and as he sat in the little smoke-drenched office, all he wanted was for his father to keep smoking his cigarettes in silence, keep pacing up and down for a good long time, and share his thoughts about his ex-fiancée's father:

"He apparently knows his daughter quite well. . . . He apparently still hasn't given up on the marriage."

Late one Sunday evening, when all the rooms were emptily waiting for the rest of the family to return, he sat with his father longer than usual in the dark office. Eventually he heard the younger sister, scarcely back from her walk, removing her corset in the next room and expressing her amazement to someone:

"Did you get a load of Miriam? Can you imagine?"

It was clear that Miriam had run into his sister on the promenade, had stopped her, and asked something, and that was why, here, in the darkened room, his heart suddenly started pounding, and he suddenly forgot what he and his father had been talking about. He must have repeated the same pointless words two or three times, bursting to go into his sister's room and ask her about the meeting; but pulling himself together, he remained sitting in the office, and never got to ask his sister anything. Later on, she, along with the rest of the household, saw him out and watched him climb into his carriage to spend the night at his estate; and as he drove off, he merely smiled at her and nodded too much. He knew that Miriam, escorted by the lame student, was fully capable of going over to his sister on the promenade and unabashedly asking about him, her ex-fiancé:

"How's Velvl getting on? How come we never see him in town?"

Miriam would stop at nothing. Now, for example, just when was it? Just the other day, together with the lame student, she actually had entered the big emporium in the middle of the marketplace, even though she had seen his wagon out front and knew perfectly well that he was inside the store. He was so wrought up that he wanted to get out of there as fast as possible, and he told the storekeeper louder than usual:

"So, let's have the bill ready by Sunday . . . at the very latest by Sunday."

And she just had to stop him right then and there and ask: Did he really think he looked good with that soft, blond little beard he had recently grown?

There, by the shop entrance, the lame student was standing with someone, and, to show he didn't give a damn about Miriam's talking to her ex-fiancé, he exclaimed overly loud:

"Who says a draft can be harmful? Does it say so in the medical books?"

And as for Velvl, the strapping young man, his heart pounded too fast and he thought it best to smile and answer her with a dig:

"Some people like beards, and some don't."

In any event, he made it clear that he had his pride and could stand up for himself. And above all, above all . . . he had done the right thing in loudly asking the shopkeeper again whether he, Velvl, could count on his bill being ready by Sunday.

At least, he had shown her he was a busy man, preoccupied with his estate, and uninterested in her daily chitchat with the lame student.

Afterwards, he was extremely wrought up all the way home, and mused about the harvest. Practically all the grain had shot up on his fields and was already starting to turn green.

The grain didn't look at all bad, and he would be earning a nice sum this year. In winter, when the hard-trodden snow covered the ground, and his silent, deserted farm lay idle and sated, he would buy himself a polished sleigh, also a fur coat with a removable collar, and, driving to town, he would keep running into Miriam, with her student, off to see a friend somewhere.

II

Soon came the days of cutting and gathering the grain, the work on the farm was in full swing, and he didn't even have time to think about driving to town.

Peasants, men and women alike, holding sickles, were deployed all over his fields; and wagons, his own and rented ones, were carting the dried sheaves uphill towards the barn, to the nearby steam engine, which, in between great mounds of straw, had been smoking since the crack of dawn. It whistled every time the boiler ran out of water, and it cheerfully kept threshing the full, dry ears.

All day long, he rode around on his horse, fully occupied, carefully watching the reapers and the farmhands who were

381

cleaning and weighing the grain in the low, dark sheds; and every so often he would drop over to the steam engine and yell at the lazy, smirking peasant girls.

He would get up with the first rays of light almost every morning, and go to sleep at sundown, dropping weary and dusty upon his bed, happy at the warm evening's promise of a clear and lovely day.

He usually slept fully dressed, and dreamed nearly all night long about his own noisy and bustling barn, his own well-appointed home, with her, Miriam, moving about, smiling at the townsmen who had come to buy his grain, sitting down at the boiling samovar, and suggesting:

"Velvl, perhaps the gentlemen will join us for a cup of tea?"

The surrounding air, the big stacks of straw, and the piles of threshed grain seemed to be mutely thinking that all his efforts—hustling around, never getting enough sleep, making money—were somehow closely connected with Miriam and the lame student, who spent all day strolling through town together. His efforts might ultimately lead to important changes, there might be deep regret in Gedalye Hurvitz's home about the broken engagement, and whenever they caught sight of his wagon through the window they would say to one another:

"Velvl just went by, he's got a new pair of horses he just drove by with."

And when the work and the hubbub were finally over, and all the low sheds were crammed with all the threshed grain, he suddenly came to, as if from a dream, looked around, and realized that the hottest summer months were past, and the days were growing markedly shorter and cooler; that he was tired and slept in his clothes too much, slept in them both night and day, awaking at the slightest drizzle that clattered down on his tin roof from the cloudy sky, and lying there groggy and with open eyes, thinking about those beets of his—they were growing . . . growing. . . .

Once, on a Christian holiday, he slept fully dressed all the way through till evening. By the time he awoke, it was already dark and cool outside, and here and there, in some of the village homes, the first night fires were trembling into life. Silence filled the dark air, and only the soft breeze knew mournful stories about the day that had died; it wafted through his open window in the dark, hauntingly, naggingly:

"The day is really gone at last . . . gone at last."

Fully rested and calm, he washed, put on a white collar and white cuffs, slowly drank his tea, and had the wagon hitched up:

"Isn't it about time I drove to town . . . ? Yes indeed, it's time."

He hadn't gone in for quite a while now and really missed it.

Sitting in the wagon, he wondered whether he ought to tell that "coachman" of his to whip the horses on so that he might reach the beginning of Main Street early enough to see Miriam and the lame student among the strolling couples.

Yet he didn't say a word to the "coachman," allowing him to trot "genteelly" and quietly the whole way in. Once, when the man blew up at the right-hand horse and angrily gave it an unnecessary lash, Velvl even upbraided him in the tone of a respectable and practical employer:

"Easy now, easy! We've got all the time in the world."

He was calm, a bit irritated, and sedate, constantly thinking about Miriam and shrugging:

Someone could really think he needed her . . . that he was running after her.

But as he approached town, his heart began pounding with more desire than usual, and he started casting nervous and confused glances at the strolling couples even though it was already fairly dark outside and difficult to recognize a person's face even up close. He was angry at himself for constantly turning his head towards the couples, not wanting to look, and yet looking all the same, and thinking:

"She's not here. . . . Who cares? . . . I'm sure she's not here."

From various corners of the town, small evening fires meditatively peered at his rolling wagon. They reminded him of how much time had gone by since his last visit, increasing his yearning for her, his former fiancée, and making her sad face, which he hadn't seen for so long, dearer and dearer.

He thought to himself:

She had to be sitting there now, in one of those bright houses,

383

sad, silent, and indifferent to the people around her, her blue eyes staring at the lamp.

And if anyone were to mention him, Velvl Boornes, if anyone were to say:

"He'll be making a nice tidy sum this year . . . a nice tidy sum."

—she would briefly tear her sad eyes away from the lamp and ask:

"Who? Velvl Boornes?"

And then she would again gaze sadly into the lamp, gaze long and silently, and no one knew what she was thinking about, and no one knew whether or not she regretted sending back the engagement contract.

Suddenly, near the first houses, someone haled his wagon and shouted:

"Your parents aren't home. They left for the county seat early yesterday morning."

He glanced around and spied a young man, a steward, just a young steward on one of his father's properties, walking out to his home in the country to spend the night.

And he somehow felt insulted that this young man in high boots had stopped him, here on the edge of town, about a trivial matter, that his parents, without letting him know, had gone off early yesterday morning to take care of something at the county seat.

Someone among the strolling couples seemed to pause and laugh at his embarrassment. So he yelled angrily at the steward:

"So what if they're not at home, so what?"

And he immediately poked the "coachman's" back and told him to drive fast, fast. He was wrought up and confused, and all the while, as they drove to the center of town, he kept thinking:

"What a fool that steward is . . . what an idiot he is. . . ."

But, approaching his father's home, which faced the market, he saw that the parlor windows were brightly lit and were peering festively into the night. He suddenly forgot how wrought up he was, and he wondered, amazed:

"Do they have company? . . . What kind of company could they be having?

And he instantly remembered Miriam and glanced over at her

father's house with its dark windows peering out from the opposite street. And he felt his heart begin pounding wildly:

Miriam was capable of anything. She might be visiting his sister.

Slowly, he removed his overcoat in the brightly lit vestibule. He had time, and he even smiled at the old woman, the cook, who came hurrying through the dining room. He was very glad he had smiled. In any event, he had to remain calm and cautious . . . and above all—above all, he mustn't be caught off guard or let anyone notice how glad he was that she had come.

Various voices from the parlor could be heard in the dining room, which he eventually entered. People were arguing about philosophy, and the lame student was also there, trying to outshout everyone else:

"Now wait a second, just how much have the metaphysicians contributed up till now?"

One of Velvl's little brothers happened to come into the dining room from the parlor, saw him, ran over to him, and threw both his arms around Velvl's knees. Velvl lifted him up, set him down on a chair, and began to smile:

"So you're running around, huh? Running around?"

However, the child had left the parlor door open, and Velvl stole occasional glances inside:

Besides Lipkis, there was the city student whom his father had recently brought back to tutor the children; one of his younger sisters was there too, and a large, unfamiliar girl. His sister and the unknown girl were sitting on the soft couch, and they, the students, were standing, confronting one another with burning faces, deeply engrossed in their dispute.

He finally walked in, asked his sister something about their parents' trip, then walked over to the city student, shook his hand, asked respectably how he was, how things were going.

The student, however, was so involved in the argument that he didn't reply at all and kept shouting at Lipkis:

"And what about love? What about every thought that turns into a sensation?"

Here, in his father's parlor, the two students didn't even notice him, they kept arguing all evening about something beyond his ken and actually forgot that he was present. And he had to spend the night there, and, setting out for his estate at nine in the morning, drive through the western end of town, and see:

Miriam, all dressed up, sitting in a carriage for the county seat, waiting for Lipkis, the lame student, near a side-street house, waiting for him cheerfully, and smiling. And he, the lame student. . . .

He came limping to the carriage, hurrying, his face was bewildered and still had traces of soap on it, and he paid no attention to what his mother, the widow, was calling after him from the open door:

"Lippa, please . . . take along your heavy overcoat. . . . Just for me . . . take along your overcoat."

Velvl drove back to his estate, he was all wrought up, and he resolved:

From now on he would go to town very seldom . . . just as seldom as possible. . . .

III

And he started going to town very seldom, just as seldom as possible.

He even said to an agent who proposed sending him buyers for the remaining grain:

"The merchants can just as easily come to my place. . . . I don't throw people out, after all."

And as he spoke these words, he was convinced that the agent would repeat them in his ex-fiancée's home; that eventually the merchants would start coming to his place from town, would come respectfully and genteelly, the same way they came to the gentry in the neighborhood.

Calm and silent, he eagerly went over to his low grain sheds every day and to his outermost fields, where so many peasants, men and women, were deployed, hurriedly digging up his sugar beets; and at night, he lay on his couch all alone in his brightly lit room, thinking about himself, about the money he had earned, and about Miriam, over there in town, moving along in a warm autumn-jacket through the cool, dark streets; he remembered his six thousand rubles and Miriam's three thousand, deposited with the old Count of Kashperivka, and he took pleasure in the new furniture with which he had recently decorated his manorial house.

He'd done the right thing, hadn't he, to throw away three hundred rubles on this new furniture, huh? Yes indeed, he'd done the right thing.

Outside, around his brightly lit house, the night was still and lifeless. A starry, unusually vast sky stretched high above the darkened countryside, which had gone to sleep early; but in the priest's fenced-in yard, the vicious dogs had been barking since early evening, rioting at the slightest sound near or far, or simply opening their jaws, somewhere towards the sleeping village, and balefully filling the cool night air with their sad, startling early-autumn howling.

Around eight o'clock, the dogs would suddenly begin barking more viciously and more murderously, and footsteps, heavy peasant trudging, could be heard near the kitchen door. At this point, lying on his couch, he would raise his head, strain his ears, and start calling towards the open door:

"Alexei? Was there any mail, Alexei?"

He knew there wouldn't be any mail for him outside of the *Stock Exchange Journal,* and yet every evening he would call out the same words to his man, call them out because he liked them and because they made him sound like those refined manor lords with whom he had neighborly dealings.

Then, for a long time, he sat respectably and thoughtfully by the lamp with the blue shade, looking through every page of the *Journal,* which was spread out before him. Coming to passages he didn't understand, he would read them aloud several times, and, most important of all, he would never skip the annuity rates in the stock exchange listings. He already had money of his own, and he could thus buy an annuity any time and, just like the manor lords, keep the certificate locked up in his bureau. There was someone else who kept buying annuities, Nokhem Tarabye, a short little fellow, who was always cheerful and always busy, the same Nokhem Tarabye who lived eighteen kilometers away, near the wealthy sugar refinery, keeping a rich manorial home and educating his children in some big, faraway town. Once, when running into Nokhem Tarabye with some other people, he had even had a chance to show him that he, Velvl Boornes, was no ignoramus, and he managed to ask him out loud and cheerfully:

"Mr. Tarabye, how are the four-percents doing this week? It says in the papers that they hit rock bottom last week."

Tarabye's jaw dropped and he stared at him with his large, lively, and jocular eyes:

What? So he was talking about annuities of all things?

He stood for a while with a look of seeming amazement on his face, and an open mouth, and never answered the question.

And that look of amazement had a much deeper meaning. It was no accident that shortly thereafter, the agent, who often drove by with his horse and buggy, told him:

Honestly, it was really something the way Nokhem Tarabye had just recently praised him, Velvl Boornes, in front of a whole bunch of merchants.

Honestly and truly, it was really something, he had heard it from Nokhem Tarabye's own lips:

"Mark my words: Avrom-Moyshe Boorne's son is turning into a rare young man. I tell you: He's got the makings of a manor lord."

Once, that same Nokhem Tarabye even paid him a great honor. Passing his estate, he drove his new phaeton into the courtyard and cheerfully asked the coachman, Alexei, in Polish:

"Is Mr. Boornes at home?"

It was around four in the afternoon.

Through the window he could see Tarabye hop down from the phaeton. He got very confused, quickly opened the door to the front veranda, which was usually closed, and ushered his visitor in with great decorum.

The short rich aristocratic little man had such sharp and lively eyes, he even noticed the brass plate on the outside of the veranda door and, upon entering the house, he praised him:

"Very good! Very good! That's what life is all about, isn't it?"

And Nokhem Tarabye, as usual, kept chattering on about

himself, his vast business dealings, and his grand style of living; he kept pointing a finger at his hard collar while his hard cuffs slid out of his sleeves, which were a bit short.

Tarabye only needed two or three hundred cords of straw for the ox stables in his sugar refinery, he could mention it once he was back in his phaeton. Meanwhile, he managed to chatter cheerfully, telling about his older son who was employed in a large bank somewhere, about the younger one who was at engineering school, and about his twenty-three-year-old girl, who liked country life so much that she never left home and, consequently, had taken longer in her studies.

That daughter of his had recently said to him:

She wanted to go to Odessa.

To which he replied:

"Go to Odessa."

And after three weeks, she came back from Odessa and showed it to him in black and white, saying:

"You see, Dad, I passed the high-school equivalency exams."

And for a while, the dull head of the twenty-seven-year-old bachelor was filled with such peculiar thoughts about Tarabye's daughter and about his former fiancée. And it seemed to him that her passing the equivalency exams had something to do with him and with Miriam's sending back the engagement contract and strolling about with the student Lipkis; and he felt so small and insignificant, he simply couldn't let things go on in this way, he had to do something.

And now something happened to him that shouldn't have happened to him.

He began getting over-friendly with the goy, the young village schoolteacher who visited the priest's unmarried daughters; he finally invited him over and began taking lessons secretly.

Once he even said to the goy:

"Fractions are such a clever subject . . . a really clever subject."

And the goy, as a joke, went and told everyone what he had said.

Now the priest's daughters always choked with laughter every time they saw him go past their porch. And in town, Miriam once stopped his sisters and said sarcastically:

"Well, your Velvl seems to be trying to get into the university."

389

IV

He met Nokhem Tarabye once again.

It was at the sugar refinery, when he was picking up the money for his sugar beets.

He stood before Tarabye respectfully, like a devoted and bashful pupil, listening to him chatter on cheerfully about recently running into his former fiancée and having a refined conversation with her.

There, in her father's home, before leaving, he had put his arm around her waist in an aristocratic manner, addressed her graciously in Polish, and murmured a few quiet words about him, Velvl:

He had an eligible young man for her, a marvelous young man.

And he winked roguishly at Velvl, and patted him on the back:

He needn't worry about a thing, he could count on Tarabye.

And he even swore to him assuringly that Miriam would make him a wonderful wife.

Velvl was so thankful to the intelligent and cheerful man, thought of him respectfully while driving home, and smiled to himself:

Now *there* was an intelligent man for you . . . now *there* was a sophisticated man for you.

For nearly two weeks, he remained excited and cheerful, pressing too much tea on the agent, who came to him from town, and going to the stable far too often, cheerfully repeating to his driver:

"We've got to get you a new hat, Alexei. Remind me when we go to the county seat."

It was good to spend whole evenings lying on his bed, thinking that Miriam's autumn saque would finally be hanging in the vestibule, imagining how some day, lying on this very same bed, he would answer Miriam:

What? He *minded* her taking the wagon, *minded* her taking it? If she wanted to drive to town, all she had to do was tell the servants to hitch up and drive her in.

He was waiting for something, he was at his wits' end wondering how Tarabye would keep his promise.

Well, Tarabye would soon be visiting in town, no doubt about it, he'd be driving over on business and he'd be sure to drop in on Hurvitz.

But day after day wore on, and Tarabye's phaeton still didn't show up in town.

Miriam was still as solicitous about the lame student as though he were her own brother, she even meddled in his affairs, and argued behind his back:

What? Was he supposed to keep hanging on to his mother's apron strings and keep tutoring the town daughters? What kind of a goal in life was that anyway?

There was nothing new in town, except for the rumors about the old Count of Kashperivka, who was already living abroad with his son-in-law:

The count was going bankrupt for sure, and soon Kashperivka would be taken over by the bank.

His mother frequently wrote him about these rumors, cursing the former fiancée and her father, and constantly nagging:

Six thousand rubles. . . . Was that a trifle? Six thousand rubles, did he realize how much money that was?

And furthermore:

The notes were made out in Gedalye Hurvitz's name after all, and the count didn't know anyone but him.

Without even realizing it himself, he again began sleeping through many of the short, cool October days, filling the air in his quiet, fully furnished house with a heavy, melancholy snoring, and then waking up over and over and recalling:

He was having all sorts of trouble now . . . and nothing would come of thinking about Miriam all the time . . . and mainly, mainly . . . what a fool he'd been to waste all that money on the furniture and the new horses.

Once, later on, here in the country, an unusually warm Sunday drew to a close. The sun, on the edge of the sky, was turning the thatched roofs and the bare trees reddish-gold, and peasants in

391

coarse black coats were standing near the shop in the lonesome Jewish house. The red glow made them feel like happy children, they thought about the grain they had stocked for a plentiful winter, and they smiled at one another:

Isn't it about time we put sheaves of straw around the walls of our houses, huh?

Around that time, one of his father's employees came with the count's notes, woke him up in great excitement, and told him the news:

The old count had come to Kashperivka in the middle of the night, and Gedalye Hurvitz . . . Gedalye Hurvitz had probably rushed over there at the crack of dawn.

Drowsily Velvl hurried over to Kashperivka in his wagon, found the old count all alone in the empty manor house, where the furniture was already packed away; he received the full amount for his notes, which were made out to Gedalye Hurvitz. The old count, assuming that Gedalye Hurvitz had sent him over with the notes, asked him to tell Hurvitz:

He was paying him six thousand rubles in cash, and as for the remaining three thousand . . . he didn't have it at the moment, but he would send him the money from abroad.

And Boornes realized that Hurvitz's three thousand rubles were lost, he felt he was doing a low thing, yet he nodded to the count:

Fine, fine . . . he would tell him.

It was only early in the evening, when his wagon was climbing up the first hill on the way home from Kashperivka, that he recognized Hurvitz's wagon with the peasant boy, the driver, far away; his heart began pounding, and he quickly told his own driver to turn left and take the narrow side road. He was frightened, he couldn't believe it, and, for the first time, he thought about Miriam's father.

Did that mean he had been in the forest since the crack of dawn? . . . Was he only driving to the old Count of Kashperivka now?

And, all along the side road, he kept glancing over at Hurvitz's wagon:

392

The lank, raw-boned horses were, as usual, badly harnessed to the shabby britska, the tethers of the right-hand horse were too short, and so he kept jumping; and the reins of the left-hand horse with the gaping blind eye were too big, so that instead of pulling with his chest he pulled with his shoulders. And, up on the wagon, Gedalye Hurvitz himself was sitting with crossed arms, the bewildered face with the pointed nose and the gold-rimmed glasses looking slightly upward, and the two ends of his beard fluttering left and right.

Boornes felt very sad and frightened, and thought to himself: Was the engagement really over? . . . Absolutely over? . . .

The next morning he got up very early and had the wagon hitched.

It was a cool and cloudy day, and a fine October drizzle kept coming down, starting, stopping, and then coming down again.

All the way into town, his face was angry and very gloomy. He kept thinking about Nokhem Tarabye's proud and unpleasantly taciturn daughter, whom he had once spied at the county seat, and he made up his mind.

She wouldn't want him, Nokhem Tarabye's girl, she definitely wouldn't want him.

The previous night, thinking about Miriam, he had decided: He would drive over to Gedalye Hurvitz's place and give him his share of the money.

He liked his decision so much and wondered what people would say about it, and mainly . . . what Nokhem Tarabye would say about it.

But, arriving at his father's home, and while still in the corridor, he heard shouting from the small office, it was the arbitrator that Gedalye Hurvitz had sent, and his father kept interrupting him with his quiet, boorish argument:

And what if the shoe had been on the other foot?

He stood in the corridor for a while, listening to them arguing.

And he mentally repeated the question:

Was the engagement really over? Was it all said and done?

And for some reason, instead of entering the small office, he walked into the dining room, where his mother was cursing his former fiancée in front of guests. His face instantly became severe and annoyed, and he exclaimed in an irritated and genteel tone of voice:

"Shhh! Just look at her!" ❀

[Part One]

THE KISS

LAMED SHAPIRO

Shachne's hands and feet were trembling, and a foul taste filled his mouth. He was sitting on a chair, and he could hear the wild shouting in the street, the whistling, the shattering of windows, and he felt as if all the crashing, screaming, shattering were inside his head.

The pogrom had begun so abruptly that he didn't even have time to lock up his store. He had dashed home, but there was no one there. Sarah and the children must have gone into hiding somewhere, leaving the bit of silver and the money behind, abandoning the house to its fate. He himself didn't think of hiding, he didn't think of anything. He could only focus on the hollering in the street and the foulness on his tongue.

The noise of the pogrom kept sweeping in and falling back like a fire, and suddenly it surrounded the house on all sides. The windows began to rattle, stones flew into the dining room, and all at once, peasants with sticks and knives were scrambling in through the doors and the windows, mostly young bullies with drunken red faces. Shachne had to do something. He dragged himself from the chair and began crawling under the couch, right in front of the peasants. They roared with laughter.

"What a prick!" one of them said, and grabbed his foot. "Hey you! Get up!" His mind cleared, and he burst into tears like a child.

"Please, boys," he pleaded, "I'll show you where the money is,

395

and the silverware, and everything else, just don't kill me. Why should you kill me? . . . I've got a wife and children. . . .

It didn't help. They took everything, and then beat him, bashing his teeth, his ribs, his belly, fiercely, murderously. He wept and wheedled, and they kept beating him. He knew one of them and begged him for mercy:

"Vasilenko, you know me . . . your father worked on our house. C'mon, didn't I pay him? . . . I gave him a decent wage . . . Vasilenko . . . Vasilenko. . . . Help me! Help me! Save—"

A punch in his chest cut off the wheedling. Two peasant boys plumped down upon him and shoved their knees into his belly. Vasilenko, a small, thin guy with a crooked face and gray eyes, smiled arrogantly and said:

"So what if you paid him! So what! Dad worked, and you paid him. I'd have liked to see you *not* pay him. . . ."

Still, he was pleased that Shachne had turned to him for help, and he told the others:

"Okay, guys, that's enough, let the corpse live. Look, he's practically croaked. . . ."

They slowly pulled away from their victim and started going out, smashing everything that was still whole.

"Well, Shachne, you owe me your life," said Vasilenko to Shachne, who stood before him with a sunken head and a battered face, panting heavily. "If it hadn't been for me, the boys wouldn't have wasted any time. . . ."

He was about to leave, when all at once he had an idea.

"Okay," he held out his hand to Shachne. "Kiss it."

Shachne lifted his bloodshot eyes and gave him a bewildered look. He didn't understand.

Vasilenko's face darkened.

"What! Didn't you hear me? Kiss my hand!"

Two of the guys stopped in the doorway, curious about what was happening. Shachne looked at Vasilenko wordlessly. The peasant's face turned green.

"What!? You Jew-bastard!" He gritted his teeth and gave Shachne a resounding punch in the face. "What are you waiting for? . . . Hey, guys, get over here."

The peasants came closer.

"Okay, get to work on him. If he's such a fuckin' aristocrat, he'll have to kiss my foot. Or else—"

He sat down in a chair. The peasants grabbed Shachne and threw him down at Vasilenko's feet.

"Pull it off!" Vasilenko commanded him, banging the boot in his teeth.

Shachne slowly pulled off the peasant's boot.

"Kiss it!"

They confronted one another: a red, dirty foot reeking of sweat—and a battered face with a long, dark, dignified beard. Somehow the peasants had pretty much ignored the beard, it had only lost a few tufts here and there, but it still bore the full dignity of a respectable Jew. Vasilenko's green, crooked face with its gray eyes was looming over him.

"I told you to kiss it!"

Another punch in the teeth. For an instant, everyone in the room was silent and motionless. Then Shachne bent over, and Vasilenko let out a fearful, piercing shriek. All his toes and a large part of his foot had vanished into Shachne's mouth, and two rows of teeth were buried deep in the filthy, sweaty flesh.

What happened next was like a wild and heavy nightmare.

The peasants started kicking Shachne so violently that his body boomed like an empty barrel. They ripped off clumps of his beard, gouged his eyes out, found his tenderest parts, and tore off chunks of his flesh. His body quaked, fevered, thrashed, and twisted about, and the two rows of teeth locked in deeper and deeper, harder and harder, and inside the foot something cracked, teeth, bones, or both. Vasilenko kept screaming the whole time, wildly, insanely, like a stuck pig.

The peasants had no idea how long the whole thing lasted, they came to their senses only when they saw that Shachne's body was no longer writhing; and when they looked at his face, a shudder ran through their bodies.

The eyeballs were dangling from the bloody holes, huge, round, and sticky. The face was gone. The beard was a mash of wet, bloodstained tangles, and the dead teeth clamping the foot were gaping as in a slaughtered wolf. Vasilenko had tumbled off the chair and was thrashing about on the floor. His body twisted like a snake, and long, hoarse yells came out of his throat. His gray eyes were bulging, dim and glassy.

With a terrified "God help us!" the two peasants dashed out of the house.

The pogrom was still raging through the street, and in the turmoil of shrieks and shouts, no one heard the convulsive scream of the man who was still alive but slowly dying in the corpse's teeth. ✿

JOSEPH SHORR

DOVID BERGELSON

I

In early spring, Jacob-Nathan Vidderpolier, a Talmud instructor in Great Setrenitz, wrote a Hebrew letter to Mokher-Tov in Brashek.

The letter said:

"Could my friend and acquaintance be good enough to write to me in detail about Yeshua-Heshl Rappoport's deceased son-in-law Moyshe Levine, the same Moyshe Levine who, together with Rappoport's wealthy son Avram, inherited the large sugar mill in Brashek, and then passed away a year ago?"

The letter went on:

"I am not unaware that my Lord Mokher-Tov was an intimate of Moyshe Levine's house, yet I know I may rely on the decency of my lord and friend, I believe that he will not lead me astray, God forbid, and that he will tell me the entire truth from within his heart."

Two weeks later, in reply to this letter, he received a postcard filled with minutely written Hebrew. A portion of the card was covered with the long and respectful title, and the language was generally in the same flowery tone employed by Rabshekah, the Assyrian chief officer, a few thousand years earlier when exhorting the Jews on the walls of Jerusalem.

"Why should I not be able to speak the entire truth from within my heart? Could I, after all, hold back anything from my devoted

399

friend? And is there anything to conceal about a beloved and loving man, who always walked in the ways of truth and righteousness?"

Mokher-Tov, however, had always been a firm partisan of the Jewish Enlightenment and of Hebrew, and thus could expertly depict anything in that language. The second half of the card delineated not only Moyshe Levine's life but even his face with its very blond hair, and its bright beard, which grew, not on the cheeks, but directly on the narrow border between the face and the full, white throat. The card also described Moyshe Levine at the time that Yeshua-Heshl Rappoport had brought him back as his son-in-law from abroad:

People could speak of nothing else. They had called him a "gem," and proclaimed him learned enough to "settle rabbinical questions." But he himself had merely smiled at such notions because, in a rather secular manner, he believed in "special providence" and knew many of the German poets by heart.

"And it is quite true," the card continued, "that Moyshe Levine rapidly squandered his fortune, whereupon his wife began quarreling endlessly with him, only because of the money he had squandered, and not, God preserve us, because, as gossip would have it, she had, as a girl, allegedly been in love with a young man from Riga. Well, her father, Yeshua-Heshl Rappoport, was still alive at the time; he was a rugged man, with an open, generous hand, and he liked to do things quickly and in style. So he bestowed a second dowry on Levine and built the lovely estate for him in Brashek, near the sugar refinery, setting him up on condition that the money remain in the firm and that Levine draw payments from the accounting department for the rest of his life."

Jacob-Nathan received this card rather close to Passover.

Having a good deal of free time on his hands, he wrote a second and longer letter to Mokher-Tov, expressing his utter amazement:

"I am absolutely astonished at my lord and friend Mokher-Tov, who is regarded by all as a talmudic scholar. Did not our sages of old say that 'a word to the wise is sufficient'?" Why was it then that Mokher-Tov had not caught his drift and had refrained from writing anything about Moyshe Levine's only daughter, "for whom I have a rather decent prospect?"

Jacob-Nathan never got an answer to this letter. Apparently, Mokher-Tov, the enlightened Jew, was nobody's fool. Jacob-Nathan was adulated by all the rich Jews in Great Setrenitz; Mokher-Tov could honor him with a flowery postcard in Hebrew and yet ignore his major concerns and not feel obliged to indulge in idle chatter about a household with which he had been on intimate terms.

Jacob-Nathan, for his part, held his peace. During Passover Week, when the days turn dry and warm, he felt a sudden urge to consult the Rabbi of Skvirre.

"I have some important matters on my mind," he said. "I will have to consult the Rabbi of Skvirre."

And before leaving, he insisted that it made absolutely no sense to take the railroad.

"Anyone," he said, "who doesn't travel by wagon from Great Setrenitz to Skvirre is simply out of his mind. The train meanders all over the countryside and takes forever."

The road to Skvirre, which winds southward from the large hilly town of Great Setrenitz, has long been narrow and overgrown. Lonesome and crestfallen, it crosses the cheerful railroad tracks and runs on for a while in between the three cobbled streets, which carry the town's cheerful murmurs in all directions. Then, as weary as a wandering beggar, the road drops into the desolate valley, where an old brickyard, a ruinous hulk, stands amid a hodgepodge of bones, the relics of dogs who were shot or died a natural death. Next, cutting through the steppe, the road is accompanied by vast, straight fields, slightly parched, spreading their grayish-green colors far into the distance, and always ready to swear "by that single tree, up on the horizon, leaning over a well, that there is indeed silence in the world."

Jacob-Nathan was driven for the first thirty miles by a Setrenitz drayman, and he arrived in Kozlovve, the tiny, dreary backwoods town, which has been squatting there for years with its back to the undermined loamy mountains, still waiting for the Sabbath, the Monday fair, and a tiding that the Messiah is on the way.

401

From Kozlovve, Jacob-Nathan rode on towards the large and wealthier town of Brashek with its adjacent sugar factory, large water mill, and Polish church. But, since he didn't arrive in Brashek until past noon of the next day and since he couldn't find a drayman from Skvirre, and since, moreover, Mokher-Tov had gone out of town that very morning, Jacob-Nathan got off at the one real inn, which actually belonged to Mokher-Tov and hence was known throughout the area as "Mokher-Tov's inn." He ordered a substantial lunch, washed it down with a bit of strong Passover wine, and then prepared to take an afternoon nap so leisurely, as though he were paying for everything with the coupons from his own two thousand rubles instead of with the interest-free loans he had "sponged" off the Great Setrenitz patricians.

During his after-meal prayer, a tacit interplay occurred between him, the broad-shouldered, middle-aged teacher, and Mokher-Tov's daughter-in-law, who was clearing the table. Every time he scrutinized her with his burning black eyes, she felt a strange chill in her heart; she was even prepared to say that she didn't like that man with his curried pitch-black beard and his Hassidic finery. Yet she went up to his room far too often, and unnecessarily, until she realized she had made a mistake . . . and that it had all been show.

He lay there, Jacob-Nathan, on the daybed, before going to sleep, with a strong Russian cigarette in his mouth, thinking to himself that the warm day outside was lovely, it was really summer, and that both Kozlovve and Brashek had been turning into virtual ghost towns. There wasn't a single follower of the Rabbi of Skvirre to visit in either place. For instance, Haym Vaintroib had left Kozlovve a few years back and settled in Palestine. His rich, whitewashed house had been purchased by some well-to-do shopkeeper, and Vaintroib's thin, blond son, who had once run away from home, was supposedly a famous painter now, somewhere in Paris, or in Berlin. And here in Brashek, Yeshua-Heshl Rappoport's children had rebuilt the large sugar mill they had inherited, and they had filled it with all kinds of accountants and engineers, secular, clean-shaven men.

And, having thought about these matters and smoked his

cigarette down to the last puff, he rolled over on his side; the strong glass of wine, his lack of sleep the previous night, demanded a sound slumber, and his body obeyed. In his profound sleep, he could hear formidable things happening beyond the drawn curtains and the thin walls of the inn; you could have sworn that the whole of Brashek was celebrating some enormous wedding, and that the wedding itself was a rather wealthy and sweeping affair. But a few hours later, he awoke and noticed that Brashek was as calm as ever and that nothing had happened. It was simply that during his nap, Mokher-Tov, the owner of the inn, had come back with his son's horse and buggy after visiting a nobleman for whose forest he was acting as broker. Entering the courtyard, the wheels had banged and clattered against the worn-out boards. Mokher-Tov had knocked on Jacob-Nathan's door a few times, and it had sounded to the sleeping occupant like someone so festively beating a drum.

Mokher-Tov, upon arriving home and learning who was staying in room number three, stood facing his wife for a time, smiling and stroking his dark-gray beard—it mostly grew from his throat, that beard of his, and was usually tucked under to appear a bit smaller. He blew the dust off his octagonal hat, the kind that enlightened Jews wear and that looks like a cantor's cap with a vizor; and then he repeated good-naturedly:
"Really? Really? Jakob-Nathan Vidderpolier . . . ."
And now he buttoned his coat and smiled to himself. He was generally a good-natured man. Once, a boy and girl in Brashek had fallen in love and asked him for help, and he had gone to their parents and talked and talked to them appeasingly, citing evidence from Ibn Ezra and the story of Jacob and Rachel.
He knew Jacob-Nathan from Great Setrenitz, where he himself had once owned a hardware store and associated with the rich. There, it was common knowledge that about eight years ago in some small town, Jacob-Nathan had deserted his poor wife and never sent her anything at all to live on, and yet . . . . "There goes Jacob-Nathan," people would say every time they saw him leaving a wealthy house where he gave Talmud lessons. The rich men would stuff twenty-five-ruble bills as interest-free loans into his

pockets, and they never failed to bring him presents from abroad, a splendid valise or even a silver cigarette case, and by way of justification they would add that some scholar who was translating the Talmud into Russian had been unable to do without his help and had written to him about all the knotty points.

Mokher-Tov laughed at his wife, who didn't know that Jacob-Nathan had remained a follower of the Rabbi of Skvirre to this very day merely to spite the world. The poor woman believed that Jacob-Nathan was really traveling to Skvirre to visit the rabbi, but Mokher-Tov could guess Jacob-Nathan's true reason for taking this trip and even for stopping here in their hotel. Nevertheless he genteelly buttoned his coat and was ready to pay Jacob-Nathan the same respect that he showed all his wealthy guests.

When Mokher-Tov finally knocked again at Jacob-Nathan's door, the guest was already sitting with a freshly washed face by the samovar, which was boiling on the round, one-legged table; the silk fez had slid down deep on the back of his neck. He poured himself some tea, and his black eyes darted quickly towards the door as though he had by no means been expecting a visitor:

"Aah! Reb Mokher-Tov. . . ."

Mokher-Tov walked over with a friendly smile and a bow, repeating the bow when he inquired after the hotel guest's health and was offered a chair.

"Not bad. . . ." was the reply. "Not bad. . . ."

The hotel owner's excitement, his bowed figure, his smile, the way he sat down—it was all so genteel and proper, as though Jacob-Nathan had always been the real and known occupant of this room, the host, and he, Mokher-Tov, were nothing but a casual visitor. Mokher-Tov was so surprised to see this man, who was fawned upon by the richest Jews in Great Setrenitz, that he didn't hear the first few sentences of the monologue, which began with "I" and reminded any listener that the speaker did not like to be interrupted.

"I recognized your Brashek immediately. I've always said: With its new tile rooftops, Brashek always looks as if it's just had a good market day, and everyone's made money, and everyone's in a fine mood."

Mokher-Tov was also bothered by the noise of the leaky boards that he had discovered only yesterday on the one-legged table, even though the top was now covered with a white cloth, and the crack was absolutely invisible. But then he heard Jacob-Nathan's last few words and smiled again and shook his head once more. He remembered the "anonymous gifts" that he was personally collecting here in town for an impoverished cobbler and for a Jewish pauper, and he expressed his thought so genteelly as if desirous of thereby defending his town:

"Nevertheless, there are . . . there are poor people in Brashek."

"*Poor* people?! . . . Hahaha!" Jacob-Nathan was not ashamed to admit that he hated the word *poor*. Didn't Mokher-Tov agree that it was absolutely a four-letter word, and one of the ugliest words in the language? He, Jacob-Nathan, would rather talk about the rich. Just who were the rich Jews in Brashek?

And he inhaled the strong smoke of the freshly lit cigarette and threw his head against the upholstered back of the armchair. He burst out laughing at the notion that there were so few rich Jews in Brashek, and at the same time he demonstrated that he could quite well sit in an armchair. As he brandished the cigarette, it was obvious that his arm was hairy and cuffless, which made it look like the arm of a kosher slaughterer or a rabbi accepting a question on ritual cleanliness. But Jacob-Nathan didn't care. He was already talking about rich men in general and felt that they never tried so hard to be "somebody" and never remained such total "nobodies" as among us Jews. Hahaha! . . . He already saw that Mokher-Tov couldn't endure it.

Mokher-Tov lowered his eyes in embarrassment and shrugged his shoulders skeptically: "Well, as for not enduring it. . . ." All he meant to say was : "Rich Jews have always been big philanthropists . . . . For instance even the Shorrs in Great Setrenitz."

Philanthropists?! . . . No. As far as that went, Jacob-Nathan had always been at loggerheads with the whole world. He practically jumped up and wouldn't let Mokher-Tov finish: "I know some wonderful rich Jews. I knew the grandfather of the Shorrs of Setrenitz."

In his opinion, the grandfather of the Shorrs was nothing but an arrogant fool, as well as a big ignoramus. All his life he'd been trying to ape Yeshua-Heshl Rappoport of Brisk, who had managed enormous sugar refineries in the area. He aped him in everything, even with the sons-in-law he acquired abroad, the large donations he made to charities, and the German governesses he hired for his grandchildren. And just who was he anyway, that Rappoport? Jacob-Nathan could tell him if Mokher-Tov was curious to find out.

Mokher-Tov shook his head. He simply couldn't agree at all. He was about to say something, but Jacob-Nathan wouldn't let him, he was beside himself.

Jacob-Nathan poured out a torrent of abuse against all the rich men who had ever had a name in this area. His fury wouldn't abate, and mainly he kept confusing the Rappoports with the Shorrs.

They were all alike, he shouted, as far as he was concerned they were all alike.

Mokher-Tov smiled and averted his eyes. It was obvious that Jacob-Nathan had a definite motive. And he, Moker-Tov, felt he could tell what that motive was. But if the man did have a purpose in his mind, what was the sense of arguing and proving him wrong?

And finally, when Mokher-Tov stood up, politely took his leave, and was about to go, Jacob-Nathan actually had to buttonhole him for a moment and admit that he had a specific reason for traveling via Brashek: He had once written to him to inquire. . . . He simply had to find out something about Moyshe Levine's daughter.

And now Jacob-Nathan was perplexed at this man, this fool, who wasn't at all surprised and was answering in such a tone as if he had been awaiting this very question for a long time.

"Yes, yes, yes . . . the daughter."

Mokher-Tov, however, was pensively rubbing his finger on the tablecloth. Apparently there were images moving about before his lowered eyes, shapes of the girl and her family. He seemed unable to make up his mind: Should he talk or shouldn't he? He wavered for a long time but then he finally did begin:

406

"The girl isn't even twenty yet, and there's a whole *affair*...."

Mokher-Tov smiled: He didn't mean it in a simple sense. Just recently he had read in a Hebrew book that an affair doesn't necessarily mean that a boy and girl are in love. And his voice became so different, so genteel, as though he were telling about the past, about legendary rabbis.

Everyone knew that her mother, Yeshua-Heshl's daughter, had just gotten married in spring to that man, the one from Riga, and now she was living there with him. The whole Rappoport family was awfully distressed because she hadn't waited at least a year, after her husband's death for the child's sake. And people were once again talking about a love affair, and God knows what. But he, Mokher-Tov, had his own view of the matter: It was quite simple. That man, that is to say, the one from Riga, was supposedly worth three million rubles by now and happened to have remained a bachelor. And she, likewise, wasn't even thirty-nine yet.... And as for the girl, well, the girl had been strongly affected ... strongly affected.

Mokher-Tov thought for a moment and then added: "So she finally had to go abroad."

After musing for a long, long time, Mokher-Tov talked about a few more things, about the whole Rappoport family, who loved the girl, and about her uncle who was acting as her guardian, Yeshua-Heshl's elder son Avram, who lived in Kiev and was said to be very wealthy now; about how the girl had come home before Passover and was now living in Kiev with her uncle Avram, instead of in Brashek.

And when Mokher-Tov finally left, the room was already getting very dark, and the air, heavy with the smoke of many cigarettes, was astir with dead and living shadows....

Suddenly the door opened again and, strangely enough, it wasn't a servant with a lamp, it was Mokher-Tov himself. The room was so dark that he looked like a shadow. He was terribly sorry but he had to tell Jacob-Nathan something, there was one more thing. And he kept apologizing and excusing himself until he finally came to the point.

Just recently, he had been visited by a marriage-broker, well, not really a marriage-broker, just a schoolteacher, who said he had a possibility for Moyshe Levine's daughter, he wanted to talk to Isaac-Mayer Shorr's only son Joseph, who lived in Great Setrenitz, and whose father came from a collateral branch of the Shorrs, supposedly not a very good one, and had recently left him the large flour mill in Setrenitz together with all the houses.

And once again he begged Jacob-Nathan to forgive him. It certainly wasn't his intention to meddle in private matters, God forbid; but he had always been a friend of Moyshe Levine's family and he knew that Issac-Mayer Shorr's only son Joseph had once been Jacob-Nathan's pupil. And he only wanted to say that if Jacob-Nathan also had the same idea as the marriage-broker, then it was very wrong of him, very wrong indeed. . . .

Jacob-Nathan gave him a bewildered stare (it now looked as if the man knew something else about the girl, perhaps he knew whoever it was that she kept visiting abroad, but he absolutely wouldn't let on). There was one thing that Jacob-Nathan couldn't understand, but then the "Vidderpolier" kindled within him. He simply laughed at the Brashek teacher, the marriage-broker, who had no concept of how to propose a match. And then he stood facing Mokher-Tov and tapped his finger on his own chest:

"*I* am leaving Brashek and going straight to Kiev. *I* want to present the match. . . . *I*, Jacob-Nathan Vidderpolier."

II

It was the middle of Passover Week, and Jacob-Nathan Vidderpolier spent the whole day after his conversation walking around the tiny wooden station house eight kilometers from Brashek, watching for the train that would take him to Kiev. He was bored out of his wits from waiting. There was nothing worth seeing around the station. Only one other waiting traveler, a priest, was pacing up and down the large, clean, empty platform, and Jacob-Nathan yawned right in his face and idly scrutinized him from all sides: Some sort of black, tidy, hairy creature in two broad cassocks, one atop the other, and he probably spent a lot of time every day washing and combing that

408

long hair of his, and that's what *they*, the goyim, called a *holy* man, a sort of rabbi, God forbid. Jacob-Nathan shrugged his shoulders and felt sorry for Gentiles.

When the lumbering passenger train finally pulled in, Jacob-Nathan boarded a long whitewashed car filled with clean-shaven secular Jews of various ages, traveling from one big town to the next. He felt solitary among them. They were mostly in white shirtsleeves, making themselves at home with their little tea pots and their food spread out before them, and they were having cheerful conversations with women who seemed like camp followers. They all looked like one big crew traveling incessantly from one big country fair to the next. Jacob-Nathan peered at them cautiously and in amazement. Among these clean-shaven Jews, who were eating bread in the middle of Passover, he was the only Jew wearing a black gaberdine and a silk cap, and able to read the sacred writings. He gingerly sat down with them, striking up a conversation and all the while peering right and left in such astonishment as though about to exclaim:

"Just look! They can talk! . . . They're talking Yiddish, like normal human beings!"

But then it turned out that some of them were from Kiev and actually knew the man to whom he, Jacob-Nathan, had set out on his journey right in the middle of Passover Week. They knew all about Avram Rappoport. He was a Zionist, they knew, and had bought up a lot of land in Palestine. He had sugar mills of his own, worth millions, and his only child was a sculptress, studying at the Academy of Saint Petersburg.

"She's a hunchback, you know."

"What? A hunchback?"

Jacob-Nathan felt depressed. Pensively, he scratched one side-lock:

Avram Rappoport was a Zionist and supposedly worth millions, and his daughter was a sculptress studying at the Academy of Saint Petersburg; it all made Jacob-Nathan doubt whether anything would come of his venture. Being among such terribly rich and liberal Jews had always made him a lot more uncomfortable than being among native goyim. Thus, in Kiev, he spent a

409

few days wandering about, at his wits' end. He was staying with a friend, who was a wealthy follower of the Rabbi of Skvirre, and to whom he complained:

He was burdened with cares, really burdened down. He had thought up a match, had come to Kiev to propose it, and was afraid that he was on a wild-goose chase, that nothing would come of it.

But on the third day, when, because of Passover, he went to pray at the local Hassidic synagogue, he saw something on the East Wall, near the holy ark, a nickle plate with the legend:

"Abraham, son of Joshua-Heshl Rappoport"

He stood by that plate for a long time, perusing the legend over and over again, and then asking an idler whether this was actually "the great" Avram Rappoport. And he felt a deep sense of relief at the thought that Avram Rappoport must surely come here every now and then to pray and that his prayer shawl must be locked up somewhere in the office of the old beadle, who was standing in his own prayer shawl by the reader's pulpit. The idler also told him that Avram Rappoport kept a kosher home; that his father, Yeshua-Heshl, before his death, supposedly made him swear to continue the old man's donations to charity, and to put on his prayer shawl and phylacteries every day; that Avram Rappoport actually went to synagogue every *Heshayne-Rabbe* (when each man's fate for the coming year is sealed in heaven) and waved the palm branches, and, who knows—?

"Maybe he still remembers a page of Talmud!"

There was a rich and genteel congregant here today, marking the anniversary of a death. When prayers were over, he celebrated the completed study of a section of the Talmud. Because of him, Jacob-Nathan was already standing in the group of the men who were celebrating, and he proved that there was a corruption in the text, and that none of the men surrounding him knew the proper meaning, they really weren't very literate. The Jews looked at him respectfully, and they began inquiring:

"Who is that man?"

And then, by the time they were drinking the health of the Rabbi of Great Setrenitz, who was said to be dangerously ill, Jacob-Nathan was already standing in the group, at its center.

Holding the glass of wine in his hand, he glared nastily at a man for interrupting him, and he spoke in such a tone of voice as if the greatest magnates in the whole world were listening.

"*I*," he was saying, "*I* swear to you that the Rabbi of Great Setrenitz is a great scholar and a God-fearing Jew."

That same day, he went over to Avram Rappoport's house again and discovered that he was already back in Russia, there was a telegram from him that he was arriving that night, he had stopped off at one of his sugar mills between Rovno and Brisk. Jacob-Nathan sighed in relief, he had once again started thinking that something would come of his venture. Walking away from Avram Rappoport's home, he looked at the rich and very silent street, there were already light-weight automobiles outside and private light-weight carriages. Not far from Rappoport's front entrance, Jacob-Nathan caught sight of a tall Jew with a crooked, simian forehead, a broad, deeply flattened nose, and some bristly reddish hairs in lieu of a beard and moustache. The Jew asked him with his mournful, authentically Litvak accent:

"Are you a Zionist preacher, too?"

It was clear that he also had to see Rappoport, he had been coming by for some time now without ever finding him at home. Jacob-Nathan moved so close to the preacher that he smelled his bad breath. But it was hard to get any information out of him. The man simply unbuttoned his short threadbare overcoat, from beneath which a greasy and even more threadbare jacket stuck out; he pulled forth a tin box of tobacco and kept answering everything with the very same words, looking at the cigar he was rolling rather than at Jacob-Nathan.

"Well, yes," he was saying, "well, he's hard to find, well, sure . . . ."

On the last evening of Passover, Jacob-Nathan was in the home of the wealthy Hassidic Jew, who was entertaining a relative, a clever and amiable young man of liberal views, employed at the local bank; a young man who was still a bachelor, with nothing to do on a free evening, which was why he had come to his orthodox uncle's home, to while away the evening with clever jokes. Noticing that Jacob-Nathan kept asking how to go about finding Avram Rappoport, the young man told him that Rappoport had a meeting at his, the young man's, bank the next day at twelve noon; the meeting was in the director's office, and it would be easiest to approach Rappoport as he walked down the full length of the bank.

The young man added that Rappoport would be easy to recognize:

"He's of medium height, slightly hunched, and he's got a closely trimmed black beard shaped like a domino."

Jacob-Nathan suddenly leveled his quick black eyes at the smiling young man.

"A closely trimmed black beard?"

"Yes, with a receding hairline and a pale forehead."

The smiling young man still had his eyes down, but when his wealthy and orthodox uncle left the dining room for a while, the young man, in his clever and amiable fashion, got up from his chair and, for the benefit of the youngsters, did an imitation of Avram Rappoport walking down the full length of the bank. He moved slowly, a bit hunched, terrified and tired, like someone skulking along, afraid to be noticed. The right arm was bent, and the thumb was moving as though kneading a wad of wax. And the company roared.

Jacob-Nathan was still sitting at the head of the table, glaring angrily at the clean-shaven young man, who was showing off his wit. Nevertheless, late that evening, he once again conferred with his host, the follower of the Rabbi of Skvirre, and decided to get up very early the next morning, at the crack of dawn.

III

That morning, Avram Rappoport also opened his eyes earlier than usual and saw the heavy furnishings in the dim, comfortable bedroom; he was startled by a reflection in the mirrored door and by the woman asleep in the other bed. Everything around him looked strange. Heavy wardrobes were glaring angrily at one another. The entire house seemed annoyed and unwilling to recognize the master, who hadn't been home for two months.

Drained, debilitated from arriving late at night, Avram Rappoport nevertheless put on his clothes, went into the study, and lifted the blinds. It was a wet, cool summer morning, a morning without sun or sky, promising a wet, cool, twilit day, and during this day Avram Rappoport would have to deal with a few difficult business matters which he had already begun. Out of habit he delayed throwing on his prayer shawl and phylacteries, and out of habit he even skipped the brief morning prayer. Pacing up and down the study, he thought about the many shares he had bought in various sugar mills. Now, all these half-forgotten shares were upsetting and alarming him. The chambermaid came into the study and jabbered something to him, but he didn't understand, so he raised his head and asked her: "What . . . ?"

His mind was already teeming with all the business he had to take care of now that he was back, and it was too difficult to squeeze another thought into his head. A bit later, he was sitting in the electrically lit bathroom, to which the chambermaid had called him and where the barber had been waiting for quite a while. Because the entire house was dozing all around, because the rooms were staring through the wide-open doors in an early-morning mood and in a renewed silent cleanliness, the barber's scissors in the overly warm bathroom seemed so genteel and sacred as though he were using them to tell how dear this head was to the city and to the many people who came to ask for favors. Rappoport sat heavily, and slightly bowed, under the snipping. He was half drowsing, and recalling: that he had a meeting today with the director of the large bank; that at the Zionist conference before Passover, when he was up on the rostrum reading his paper, some foreign professor with a long Assyrian beard had been sitting right in front of him, nodding his head the entire time with an expression that seemed to say:

"That's right, that's right. . . . He's got the bull by the horns."

Now he could so clearly picture the professor's face, but at the same time he was half drowsing and thinking about his Brashek sugar refinery, where there would never be any order because it had been inherited; about the refinery in Great Setrenitz, of which he wanted to be the sole proprietor, with no partners at all; and about his wife, with whom he had always gotten along so well. Last night at the station, when she had stiffly hugged him, he had felt she was holding him closer than ever, and he had thought that the scent hovering around her probably came from the new powder she had gotten abroad last summer. He closed his eyes because of the pungent cologne with which the barber was refreshing his face, and the fiery spots on his cheeks turned beet-red.

Coming out of the bathroom, he thought to himself that the barber had gotten a piece of beard to the left of one of those red spots; and at the same time he felt that the two charitable donations he had made before leaving Palestine may both have been too large. He had to go to his study right away and check whether he had recorded those two contributions. But in the dining room, his wife, a tall, blond woman with a long, worn face, was already sitting at the table. He looked at her. Once, that face had been beautiful, but now it greatly needed powder, and there were red splotches on the forehead and in the corners of the mouth. Because of her husband's arrival, she had gotten up perhaps a whole hour earlier than usual, and she was happy. Underneath the powder, her face looked sleepy, and her entire body was cosily wrapped in the warm shawl.

"Avram," she asked, "are you back?"

And as if pleasantly surprised, she added after a while:

"It's so good to have you back."

Snuggling into the warm shawl, she rested her head on her elbows and smiled up at him for a while. There was an instant when her eyes glowed at him, so tender, and genuinely youthful. She was right at the age when a woman simply no longer interests the men around her and starts binding her still devoted husband more firmly to herself. She could tell him now that the entire house had seemed empty without him, that Sarah Levine, their niece, had been here since before Passover, that Nessi, their daughter, who was studying at the Academy of Saint Petersburg, had recently written that she had a lot of work, which was why she couldn't come home any earlier than this week, and if he were to go abroad again that soon, she, his wife, would not stay here alone, she would go with him. While talking, she poured tea for both of them, each time sticking out a slender, naked elbow from under the shawl. She had to display them boldly, these naked elbows; in any event, they were the one thing about her that had remained young and fresh, as in her girlhood. And Rappoport stood beside her devoted and silent, keeping his hands deep down in the pockets of his jackets, and recalling that he had to go and record something in his study. Whenever his sedate eyes alighted on one of her naked elbows, he remembered that he had once loved her. And whenever his eyes alighted upon her face, he could only think that he had great respect for her; he had to go to his study, but his respect demanded that as long as she was speaking to him, he had to stay here and listen. And he respected her because, although coming from an important family, something she could boast about, she nevertheless always made an effort to show that in any case, her husband's family was no less important. Now she was sitting here next to him, pouring his tea, and talking about inconsequential things; but as a girl, a wealthy orphan, she had gotten one proposal after another from the richest and most important Jews in Russia and abroad. She still liked to figure out the intertwined family tree of all the greatest families, up to the Rothschilds of Frankfurt and the two Jewish barons, and yet now she was terribly happy that her husband had just come home, and she was boasting that she had married him.

From outside the dining room, they kept hearing noises from the front entrance and the frequent ringing of the telephone. From the office, voices inquired whether "Avram Saulovich" would be coming soon. On the other side of the narrow, almost childish little door connecting the study with the small room, the bookkeeper, a young boy, a Zionist, was sitting, and copying from one book into another. He was pleased with the question he was about to ask Rappoport in Hebrew, and so he turned it over in his mind several times:

If Mr. Rappoport had used his local mandate at the congress, then shouldn't the Berlin expenses be entered in the Zionist account?

Rappoport listened to him in the dining room, inattentive, slightly stooped, lowering his head and pacing up and down. He seemed to be thinking about the bookkeeper's question. But he

415

finally halted, not near the bookkeeper, but near his wife; he made a face and asked to have his servants harness the carriage and wait for him at the second entrance. Now he again recalled his meeting with the bank director, the many shares he had bought, and the disorder that could lead to misfortune in the Brashek sugar factory. His wife wanted him to look younger, and so, in the bedroom, she had given him a dinner jacket to wear. But he couldn't remember when he had put it on, and he hadn't heard what his wife was saying. In his overcoat, he slowly and heavily made his way down the stairs leading through a long corridor to the side entrance. But then he paused on one of the steps, lost in thought, remembering that earlier, when leaving the bathroom, he had meant to do something in his study. He couldn't recall what it was, and yet he turned around, trudged up the stairs even slower than he had descended them, ran into the bookkeeper, glanced at him, but said nothing. Back in the study, however, he couldn't remember what he had meant to do, though he did recall something else that he had forgotten. He removed a small memo book from the desk, took it over to the telephone, and called his office manager.

"Yes, I'm back . . . thank you."

Slowly he opened the memo book, poked his nose about in it myopically, and started dictating the new business deals that he had concluded en route.

He put down the receiver. His entire head felt foggy. He couldn't remember anything he wanted to do in the future, and yet deep inside he felt great pleasure at this. Although generally liberal, he nevertheless had a superstitious belief in certain good omens, and such fogginess was one of them. There were good reasons why people talked about his still sending the Rabbi of Great Setrenitz the thousand rubles that his father had always sent him annually. Returning to the front entrance with his foggy mind, he caught sight of several people waiting in the hallway, they were sitting in a row on the red wooden settee, his eyes met the eyes of a Christian and he thought that this was a neighbor who lived in his wing. The Christian stood up and made his request:

He wanted to have a wall in the basement knocked down.

But Rappoport refrained from answering and started down the stairs. The man's request was meant for Rappoport's wife, not for him, and the others who were waiting, the Jews, could take their problems to the bookkeeper.

Outside, near the front entrance, stood the Jew with the Litvak accent, the Zionist preacher, rolling a cigar. Perhaps if he went over to Rappoport, the rich man might listen to him. But by the time he saw the fancy phaeton at the side entrance and held out his hand to stop him, Avram Rappoport was already sitting in his vehicle with his back to him, and the fancy coachman had already pulled in the reins. The two jet-black horses, who had been standing for so long, trembled in alarm, jerked forward, and dashed off with the phaeton towards the fancy carriages and quiet automobiles that were purring back and forth at the far end of the street.

Near the big bank, where Avram Rappoport got down from his phaeton, he recognized old Madame Bernstein's automobile. And suddenly it struck him: He thought of her and her riches, and the hundred thousand rubles with which she had assisted him some five years ago, when he was anything but as rich as now. She had left the hundred thousand rubles with him secretly, for more than a year, and even today she still looked upon him as a protégé. Now she was closely connected with the local Jewish hospital, to which she contributed large amounts every year. The entire staff of the hospital was against her, and she would most likely collar Rappoport here in the bank and bore him with all their feuds. Inside the bank, he saw her from behind at one of the tables. Her upswept hair, elderly and dark gray, stuck out from under her old-fashioned black hat, her arm was linked in the arm of her steady companion, a young and simple woman with the face of a seamstress, and she was peering through a lorgnette at a tall man who was speaking to her with great respect.

Rappoport sidled past to keep her from noticing him. It was a few minutes before twelve, and he had time to listen to a Jewish acquaintance who stopped him on the way. But when he started off again and was just about to reach the director's door, he was stopped by another Jew in Hassidic finery, who introduced himself as Jacob-Nathan Vidderpolier. From the very first moment, Rappoport felt that the man's black gaze was extremely sharp and insolent. He promptly turned his head away to the other side. A moment later, he grimaced slightly in order to register the man's words and comprehend why he was suddenly mentioning Sarah Levine, his sister's only child, who was now visiting him. But, ignoring the match that this man was proposing, Rappoport thought that Vidderpolier looked peculiar with his hat off, wearing only his skull cap over the closely trimmed hair and the long earlocks, he apparently had done the trimming very recently, right here in Kiev. The man was still talking, but now Rappoport heard nothing and understood nothing. He was thinking to himself that he was Yeshua-Heshl Rappoport's eldest son, that he gave to his charities and carefully observed his traditions. His father had always listened to any proposal of a match. Suddenly he remembered that some five years ago, when he was anything but as rich as now, a financial broker had gotten him a substantial loan from the father of this Joseph Shorr. He took out a calling card and handed it to his interlocutor, and then he reached for the doorknob and shrugged his shoulders:

What could he tell him? . . . Who was to say? . . . Why not have the young man come over? . . . Let him come by on Saturday night.

At twelve midnight, it was totally dark in Rappoport's home, except for a light in the bedroom. Ethel Rappoport was already undressed and lying down, and Avram was sitting on the other bed, taking off his shoes. He put them down to the side, those shoes, reflected for a moment, and, without looking at his wife, he smiled.

"Our little Sarah," he said shyly, "has gotten an offer of marriage."

"Sarah!?"

His wife quickly sat up to hear who the prospective suitor was. She wrinkled her forehead, strained her eyes, her entire body stretched out towards her husband.

"Who!? . . . Are you serious? . . . How awful! . . ."

Rappoport slipped under the comforter and fell asleep, while she sank back down in her bed, lying all alone with her exasperation and her sorrow. Just who were they anyway, those Shorrs of Great Setrenitz? Little nobodies! Practically nouveaux riches, not from a very nice place, and they had always lived almost reclusive lives. The Rappoports had smirked at the way the wealthiest of those Shorrs tried to parrot them with their big contributions to charity and the sons-in-law they imported from abroad, and now they were making Sarah an offer . . . . The poor thing, what a pity! Ethel Rappoport, feeling her left eye twitching nervously, was unable to fall asleep. She could see her sister-in-law Hannah right in front of her, see her so near as though she, Ethel, were in Riga and could see Hannah living there with her second husband: A fine business! She hadn't even waited until the first anniversary of her husband's death, she had married the rich bachelor from Riga, whom she had loved as a girl. Now the whole world was gossiping about her love affair, and her daughter Sarah was getting *such* offers!

"The poor thing, what a pity!"

And around eight in the morning, when Avram Rappoport, as usual at that time, opened his eyes, his wife instantly sensed it and, raising her head, she looked over at him.

"Avram," she said, "did you sleep? I couldn't sleep a wink all night long. Didn't you give that filthy man, that . . . matchmaker, a good tongue-lashing? You actually gave him a calling card, to have the boy come here? *Eto vozmutitelno!*" she added in Russian. "It's scandalous."

IV

Meanwhile, Joseph Shorr of Great Setrenitz had already received Jacob-Nathan's first letter, which said that he ought to be prepared and that with God's help:

"The match with Moyshe Levine's daughter is going to work out, God willing!"

People in Great Setrenitz already knew. The morning of the last day of Passover, the men were gossiping about it in synagogue, on the Bench of Honor. They peered over at Joseph Shorr, who was sitting up ahead, in the pew that had once belonged to his recently deceased father; they again observed the new black coat on his sedate and stately figure and the little beard of a wealthy prospective bridegroom, a beard freely wrinkling around his matt, boyish, attractive face; and they said he was rising faster than they could measure, that Joseph Shorr, by God.

"Maybe now he'll get the kind of match that his whole family's been after for years."

Joseph Shorr's thin, half-pious lips barely moved, and every time he fell to thinking, his large, black eyes began to stare with a brand-new velvety sheen, a sheen of long-preserved bachelor-hood about to reach its goal and full of unexpected happiness that comes suddenly and overwhelms all other feelings. Everything around him was like a world of shadows, all a-jumble. And then something else happened.

Minna Mureynes came back to Great Setrenitz. The lovely and intelligent daughter of a wealthy family, she had spent a good long time abroad, turning the heads of all manner of wealthy young bachelors and important men. The day after her return, she ran into Joseph Shorr in the street and instantly noticed the velvety sheen in his black eyes. Her face actually saddened, and she immediately started asking people who he was. The rest was told on the Bench of Honor in synagogue, by the local marriage-broker, a suave gentleman, whom old Mureynes had invited over for the wine blessing on the first day of Passover.

"Minna Mureynes was sitting there," he recounted, "in the dining room, and she wasn't at all well-dressed, her hair was totally disheveled like a Gypsy's, and she was wearing slippers on her bare feet."

She was sitting like that out of laziness, or indifference; after all, she had been abroad for a good long time, and had led a free life there, and she hadn't liked any of the wealthy young bachelors or important men whose heads she had turned. Now she was bantering with the marriage-broker, she smiled, wrapped herself in her shawl, and shouted at the marriage-broker as if he were deaf:

"Get me Joseph Shorr!"

On the other hand, Moyshe Levine's daughter may also have been a rather obvious possibility for Joseph Shorr; after all, he was the youngest and finest of all the proud and very wealthy local Shorrs; the big flour mill he had inherited ground away cheerfully right on the high bank of the deep and narrow river, half a kilometer from town, and all the passing ships had to see how his mill stood out from all the larger and smaller factories around it, endlessly disgorging an insolent black smoke into the clear blue sky; reveling in its own wealth, it shone in the middle of the daylight with its own festive electricity. In addition, right here in the large, hilly town, he had two very wealthy aunts, who refused to socialize with any of the parvenu families in town, and never attended any of their weddings. For their children they had special foreign marriage-brokers who supplied them with matches abroad; and they lived far from the teeming center of town, in two large, overgrown hereditary mansions, which exhaled genteel melancholy and old, gloomy affluence upon infrequent passersby. They were the town's *crème de la crème,* these two aunts, Esther and Hodel, and never permitted anyone in their family to marry into a lesser station. But first of all, there was absolutely no way for Joseph Shorr to claim any descent from that lofty side of the family. His father, Isaac-Mayer Shorr, was a stingy man and a fanatic Hassid, who was infamous for his foul temper, and prideful as well, and whom all the workers at the mill flattered to his face and mimicked behind his back. In his youth, however, he had quarreled with both sisters, Esther and Hodel, about some inheritance matters, and ever since, he had kept hollering that they and their husbands were persecuting him and were his mortal enemies. His first marriage, with a barren woman, had gone poorly; but after her death, though getting on in years, and to spite his family, he married a young woman, a divorcée, who was merely out to "improve herself" with him and get a fine wardrobe; the issue of this marriage-for-spite was he, the genteel and sedate Joseph Shorr, with his genteel and sedate manners and with his fine Jewish and secular knowledge, which he had crammed into himself till the age of twenty-three. Joseph Shorr had a father who was powerful and prideful, who hadn't let his own sisters enter his home for thirty years, and who had

421

suddenly gotten very sentimental just a few hours before his death, had sat up in bed and sobbed so deeply for having lived such an awful life. Joseph Shorr's mother, a young divorcée, had merely been out to "improve herself" and get a fine wardrobe.

Stiff and taciturn, Joseph Shorr might well have had all these considerations on his mind, deep inside himself. Besides, he had already run into Moyshe Levine's daughter once, and it was the first time in his life that he had ever felt a wedding mood in the world. Furthermore, their encounter had been quite unexpected and anything but usual and proper. That was a couple of weeks before Passover, upon Joseph Shorr's return from Warsaw, where he had been visiting his young aunt Reyzel, that same aunt who had never managed to get along with his fanatically Hassidic father, her brother, and who, as a girl, had run away from him and gone to Paris.

No one believed that Aunt Reyzel had a lot of problems, only because she was always running at the mouth about them and about all the important people she knew all over the world. In her youth, she had had a lot of chattery, girlish romances, but in the end she simply found her rich young husband through a marriage-broker. However, her husband was an even bigger chatterbox than she, and nothing in the world could ever surprise him. He personally knew everything and everyone. He was, so to speak, half a world, a sort of God; and Aunt Reyzel suffered. Silently, she had to watch her husband talk Joseph Shorr's ear off and tell their guest all sorts of exaggerated things about himself.

No indeed, Aunt Reyzel wasn't a very happy woman. Joseph Shorr had realized as much during the few brief days he spent in her home. As she brought him to the railroad station, he felt deeply moved. Had he not been raised in Isaac-Mayer Shorr's stiff and taciturn home, he would have taken her hands and said that the important thing is: to suffer quietly and well, so that no human being will ever know. Aunt Reyzel was also deeply moved and filled, as it were, with sacred sisterly emotions. Kissing him, as in his childhood, "on his pure eyes," she choked down her tears; after all, she had found a friend in him, someone she could talk to.

All her life, she said, she had been looking for nothing more than a friend.

But when the train pulled in, she instantly noticed something in one of the windows, her face became as curious as a marriage-broker's, and her eyes were frivolous and feminine and chattery. She smiled too much and too foolishly and whispered to Joseph Shorr that he was lucky:

He was traveling home in the same compartment with a rich and beautiful girl, with Moyshe Levine's daughter.

"With Moyshe Levine's daughter!?"

Joseph Shorr wasn't quite certain who she was. In Great Setrenitz, there was talk that she definitely "had someone" abroad . . . .

"Otherwise she wouldn't be taking all those trips."

And afterwards he felt more and more confused and different from other times, and his eyes were too shiny when he looked at the young, blond girl occupying the seat across from him in the compartment.

"Moyshe Levine's daughter. . . ."

All evening long, the girl lay back with closed eyes, silently pressing her folded hands on her breast, and he stared at her and thought to himself that she probably "had someone" abroad. Now it looked as if all that was left for her to do was doze away and press her folded hands on her breast, and imagine that her one and only, whom she had left abroad, was still leaning his head on her shoulder. . . .

At one point, something happened:

The girl opened her eyes at him, blue, sleepy eyes, which rested on his young, boyish face for a moment, trying to recall something, and then once again becoming indifferent and disappointed. And his heart skipped a beat, and a warm marriage mood, a wave, suddenly washed over his heart and drowned it.

"She's a beautiful girl. . . ."

In the light that came from under the yellow silk shade of the electric lamp, he opened his Hebrew book and tried reading. But eventually he closed it and went out into the corridor. He was annoyed that he had been looking at the book for so long without managing to read any of it. Nor did he like to pretend he was reading. In fact, for minutes at a time, he felt bad about Aunt Reyzel because, he thought, there was so much about her that was "pretentious," and then he struggled with his hereditary family pride that made his blood surge. He didn't want to look at the girl anymore, yet he couldn't remain in the corridor for too long. He stepped back into the compartment and suddenly realized that the electric lamp was shining too brightly. He tiptoed over and switched it off, not for himself, but for her, so that she could sleep. In its stead, another lamp went on in the corner, a high, blue lamp, and it suddenly became clear that the quiet muffled murmur of the heavily rolling train was already fully nocturnal. People were already sleeping throughout the car, but he, Joseph Shorr, still had time. He was sitting all alone deep in his darkened corner, rocking lightly with everything in the car and looking at her:

The girl was lying, as before, with closed eyes, only her hands were under her head with its wavy blond hair. Her feet were gathered under the dress, which covered them down to the tips of the childishly shiny patent-leather slippers, and the black-striped shawl was wrapped around her waist and her innocent girlish shoulders. She was beautiful. And he gazed at her sleepily.

"Moyshe Levine's daughter."

And so, after this encounter with Moyshe Levine's daughter, Joseph Shorr came home feeling like a new man, and slept several nights in a row like a fiddler after a wedding. Slept so lightly, as if the aristocratic girl might come at any moment to knock at his door and say:

"It's a lie. . . . I don't have anyone abroad. . . ."

In addition, the air was full of spring, and the ice was stirring early in the river that flows past the hilly town.

Days wore by in a light frost, carefully listening to detect what the astonished surroundings would think of next. Small, trembling fires were put out earlier; tired of baking matzos and hastily preparing for Passover, the meandering back streets of Great Setrenitz dozed off at twilight. And the early evening, like a long-held breath, silently gaped and silently counted the clatters of the express train crossing over the distant iron bridge. Frightening the abyss underneath, it crumbled the stillness and was already far, far away, rushing back towards the place to which it had brought the young blond girl just a few days ago.

The sunny air was redolent with bridal devotion, with the young girl, with him, the young boy, and other things, entire verses from the Song of Songs. . . . Joseph Shorr went to the big mill he had inherited, and where, even before his father's death, a dozen Jews, *promolchiks* (threshers), as the Russians called them, were milling the grain. Every day, on the way home, cutting diagonally across the large square outside the town, he would run into the very same two girls, two friends, strolling up and down. In their galoshes, they tested the hardness of the snow while gazing at him good-naturedly as he passed by. The girls seemed to be old friends of his, but he knew nothing about it. One of them was Minna Mureynes, the fine young daughter of old Mureynes. Gazing at him, she would tell her friend a secret, every day a new secret. The secret was in the black eyes that followed him for a long way, him, the fine young man, the rich twenty-four-year-old bachelor. But Joseph Shorr also had a secret in his eyes; he would look over at the girls as he passed, unable to decide which of them reminded him more of her, of Moyshe Levine's daughter. . . .

He had no friends to confide in; born and bred in an unfriendly and reclusive family that was not especially popular among the townsfolk or the surrounding neighboring houses, Joseph Shorr had finally left home, he, the taciturn bachelor, stiff and unfriendly somewhere deep inside. Here in town, he seldom even visited his two sacredly wealthy and reclusive old aunts. They liked him so much because he didn't have to ask them for anything and because he was more polite than his father. They never missed an opportunity to praise the "fine young man," and he never visited them.

But one evening, here in Great Setrenitz, on the noisy main street. . . . One evening, he really thought he saw her, Moyshe Levine's daughter. He was walking on one side of the street and she was walking ahead of him on the other side. She was teasing

425

and wordlessly summoning him; she kept halting and looking back at him. But eventually, she turned at a darkened corner and vanished in the dense strolling crowd. Joseph Shorr stopped in his tracks and looked around. In the pressed, late, dusky air, faces were hurrying by, strange and alienated as in a solar eclipse, and his ears were filled with a roaring as of water plunging through the sluice gates of a large, high dam although there was no dam anywhere around Great Setrenitz. What could it mean? Slowly he returned home and spent the entire evening musing that she, Moyshe Levine's daughter, had probably long since reached the place to which she had gone for Passover, from abroad. Perhaps now, in the evening, instead of going anywhere, she was staying at home, perhaps she was ironing a white jacket for Passover. . . .

And the next day, he couldn't control himself anymore, he went off with all his experiences to his one friend, the town rabbi's only son, Itsik, with whom, as a child, in the rabbi's house, he had studied the Shulhan Aruk, the laws and prescriptions of Judaism.

V

The rabbi's large Hassidic court had been waning for several years now. Every room was filled with troublesome secrets, with spite and quarreling. The old, learned rabbi was getting more and more pious from year to year, he didn't know he was dangerously ill, and, as in the past, he inflicted great fasts upon himself behind closed doors. A few years ago, he had stopped accepting petitions and presiding at Sabbath dinners, and he thought he was living on his official salary of three thousand rubles. His enemies, who had always been certain that he wasn't as foolish as he pretended to be, suspected that he had given up those duties simply because "business was bad." And his wife, who wanted to uphold the grandeur of his court without his knowing it, secretly took funds from his former disciples, whether or not they were believers.

Joseph Shorr skulked along through many half-empty unoccupied rooms, afraid that the rabbi's wife would receive him as the child of an old follower and friend and tell him all the family misfortunes.

Then, taciturn and proudly stiff, he sat opposite Itsik in the lonely isolated room where once upon a time they had studied together. In this very room, Itsik had once rigidly held him by the elbows, forcing him to listen to a story similar to the one that Joseph Shorr was now living, a story about a wedding with fiddlers, that had only just taken place in the rabbi's court at the start of the winter evening, and about a girl's perfumed hand which had stiffly snuggled up to him, Itsik, in the dark.

But in the end, nothing came of this visit. Itsik still had a pure-white, pristine neck, and a pristine complexion, the kind that yearns all week long for the Hassidic rabbinical silk clothing it dons on the Sabbath, and he was still as radiant as four years ago when he had been secretly reading Heine, Ahad Ha'am, and Nadson. Just recently, he had returned from abroad with the old rabbi, whom doctors had given up for lost. But that wasn't the important thing, and that wasn't what Itsik was talking about. The important thing was what he had seen while traveling home. Rigidly, powerfully, he clutched Joseph's upper arms with both hands, forcing him to listen to his description of how the express train, which was bringing him and his father home from abroad, had been streaking through the vast free fields of Russia, emitting gloom deep into the dreary twilight, and how he, Itsik, standing all alone in the first-class carriage, had caught sight of a small Jewish village as the train dashed through. The small village was so deserted, as if it were Sabbath and the people were taking their afternoon naps. A pool of mire was shining in front of the houses that faced the rails; a flock of geese were pecking the ground with their bills in an agitated miry yard, and a girl . . . a girl in white came running out of the last, decent-looking house and stopped on the porch, a girl in white. . . .

And apparently Itsik was now in love with that girl. He had dark circles under his eyes and said he had become a chain-smoker because his head . . . his head was "in the clouds. . . ."

Joseph Shorr actually didn't say anything about himself, he sat opposite Itsik, taciturn, watching his face and thinking about him spending whole days at the window, eyeing the white geese who were feeding close by on the grass near the rabbi's mansion. The white geese, Itsik said, reminded him of that village, of "those geese," and especially of the girl, that girl in white. . . .

In Joseph Shorr's opinion, Itsik was lost to the world; he wasn't even doing anything about the Great Setrenitz rabbinate, which would devolve upon him after his father passed away. But how could he, Joseph Shorr, be of any help to him? He was absorbed in his own problems, his own recent experiences: He sat at home and waited.

One afternoon, he received a visit from his former Talmud teacher Jacob-Nathan Vidderpolier. The man simply walked in, quite casually, as though just to drop by, but he remained at the table in his Hassidic finery, unabashedly inquiring at length and in depth about Joseph Shorr's inheritance.

Finally, with utter nonchalance, he confided that he had a possible match for him.

"A match with Moyshe Levine's daughter."

"Moyshe Levine's daughter?"

Joseph Shorr couldn't tell where the idea had originated: with himself, with Jacob-Nathan, or in a letter the man might have received from Joseph's chattery Aunt Reyzel in Warsaw. He didn't particularly believe Jacob-Nathan. A few years ago, the man in Hassidic finery had deserted his poor wife in a little town somewhere and never sent her anything at all to live on. Joseph Shorr sat opposite him, proud, taciturn, and stiff; watching Jacob-Nathan play, as though it were only a piece of paper, with the hundred-ruble note he had just given him for expenses; hearing his visitor repeat the same words a second time:

"Aha . . . aha . . . so the girl goes abroad too often." And then:

"It would be good to find out why she goes abroad so often."

When Jacob-Nathan was gone, Joseph Shorr was still thinking about it. He should have gone back to the rabbi's court to see Itsik and to ask the rabbi's wife about it, because she was closely related on one side to the Rappoports and knew all there was to know about them.

But then, during Passover Week, Jacob-Nathan went off to

Brashek, from where he wrote to Joseph to be ready; God willing, the marriage with Moyshe Levine's daughter would be a sure thing.

"That's *not* the reason she goes abroad so often. . . ."

If things worked out, he would remodel his father's house here in Great Setrenitz. He had been thinking about it for some time. As for the Jew occupying the two stores to the left of the back stairway, he would tell him to look for a new location. The man had filled up the entire entrance with the smell of shoemaking and fresh leather, and besides, everything about the houses reminded Joseph Shorr so strongly of his old, stingy father.

Jacob-Nathan's second letter came to him from Kiev, where the girl was just visiting her uncle Avram Rappoport and where Jacob-Nathan had to hastily summon Joseph by telegram. Apparently they had already been talking about it in Avram Rappoport's home, the girl had also been present and had consented to meet him, perhaps she still remembered him from the time they had shared the train compartment.

After this second letter, Joseph Shorr had a few more suits made and stopped going out altogether; a sudden hermit, he was waiting for Jacob-Nathan's letter. To while away the time, he remained at home, reading books, and he felt as if Moyshe Levine's daughter were standing behind him all the time; as soon as he finished reading a page and grew pensive, she could suddenly say:

"Turn the page, darling!"

He remembered the devoted gaze of her blue mournful eyes, as though he were still in the train compartment, seeing her blue sleepy gaze rise from the pillow, look for an instant at his boyishly young, attractive face and attempt to recall something. . . . He never, even for an instant, stopped devouring the pages of the book he was reading, and he kept thinking about her. It was wrong, very wrong, to take pleasure in the thought of the great fortune she could bring him.

And furthermore:

He, Joseph Shorr, at any rate, was rich enough without her; he had enough money of his own.

One evening, he prepared a bath for himself and stayed in it till late at night. He washed and washed, virtually hallowing himself, and then he put on brand-new, unworn linen. That very same night, he was awoken in bed and was handed Jacob-Nathan's telegram.

Everything was going beautifully, Jacob-Nathan would be waiting for him the day after tomorrow, in the evening, at the railroad station in Kiev.

He remained fairly calm after reading this news. He was standing by the lamp, in his underlinen, with the telegram in his hand, his nostrils were still pale, his breathing was a bit heavier than usual, and he thought to himself: The day after tomorrow is Tuesday.

"A lucky day."

VI

When he set out on his trip, the day smelled of the thin drizzle, of the happy marital morning after a rainy night, a deluge.

A politely silent cabman was respectfully sitting in front of him, nimbly avoiding a whole line of coaches with people in a festive mood, who were hurrying to the nine o'clock train as though to a wedding. The cabman, limberly whipping away, ascended a hill towards the station. A few familiar faces, that Joseph Shorr had seen somewhere or other, went whirling past his eyes, and a hatbox teetered on the driver's seat, threatening to fall at any moment. A pair of female eyes beneath a veil swept curiously over his face and came to rest on his freshly barbered bridegroomish throat and cheeks. Who could that have been? He was so excited with the previous night, with himself, with the happiness in store for him, that he quickly forgot those eyes. A bit later, in the train, it turned out that some other people were traveling to Kiev; old Mureynes, and the fine daughter of his old age; they were in the second compartment, and old Mureynes was carrying on and treating his daughter like a truly chivalrous gentleman.

Well, he was asking her, was she comfortable?

Oh yes, old Mureynes, a secular Jew, with a whole set of wealthy forebears, and with his broad, hunched shoulders, gave no sign whatsoever that his foundry in Great Setrenitz had been doing poorly for three years in a row and was now at a full standstill, with birds nesting in its gigantic chimney. In the train, he and his young daughter were still traveling with every possible convenience, two large foreign suitcases, a big box of chocolates to nibble on the way, and even a special case for cigarettes. He smoked them, one after another, those thick Russian cigarettes, and his gray moustache and the edge of his wide gray beard were already as yellow as the large smoky, amber holder between his lips. The moment he stepped out of his compartment into the long corridor of the railroad car, he instantly lit another cigarette; he almost seemed to be smoking on schedule, as though taking a medicine.

"Tuesday," he said, "is always a lucky day, a lot of people from Great Setrenitz go traveling."

In his great wealthy politeness, he pretended not to know why Joseph Shorr was going to Kiev.

Joseph Shorr was standing at the window in the corridor, gazing out as the train stopped for a few minutes at a time in stations illuminated by fresh sunlight. He made room at the window for old Mureynes, and their conversation soon turned to their home town, to Great Setrenitz. Old Mureynes could still remember both of Joseph Shorr's grandfathers, the paternal and the maternal one; he remembered the days when Great Setrenitz was small and still unpaved.

"Unpaved?"

Joseph Shorr felt that this must have been a very long time ago. He laughed:

"Well, 'four kings were fighting against five others, and one of them was named Chedorlaomer . . . .' "

Deep inside, he felt the pride of the Shorrs stirring: The man had known his grandfathers. All at once, the talking and laughing stopped in the compartment behind old Mureynes, and out came his fine young girl, Minna Mureynes. She paused in the open door of the compartment, holding on to the doorposts with both hands. She stood there for a while, light, airy, about to leap.

431

She gazed at Joseph Shorr and at her father, and she seemed to be contemplating them from afar, to decide whether they fitted together as father-in-law and son-in-law . . . .

And then suddenly she dropped her head and walked over to them with downcast eyes and with the slow humble steps of a pauper.

"Minna Mureynes," she barely murmured, offering Joseph Shorr her hand and peering at him closely.

It was strange to look at her. After all, while abroad, she had turned the heads of the wealthiest and most important young men, and people were saying that some of the important men she knew had chased after her from Germany to Switzerland. But old Mureynes acted as though he didn't notice her and deliberately refused to break off his conversation. In fact, he gave his daughter a paternal stare and told her he was talking about Joseph Shorr's grandfather on his mother's side, Shmuel Rab-Rabi, who had once come down to Great Setrenitz from somewhere deep in Poland, purchased a prominent house and brought huge lime kilns to the area. Old Mureynes really had liked Joseph's grandfather, and he wanted his daughter to know that Shmuel Rab-Rabi had really had an unusually sharp mind.

"He was always smiling, and he had a big blond beard and a good Polish head on his shoulders."

And he was never that busy with his work.

On long summer afternoons he would wander about his mansion in his long dressing gown, it was made of linen with velvet flowers, and he would puff away at his long Polish pipe, and read *Duties of the Heart,* and there was always an intelligent smile around his blue eyes, so that you couldn't tell whether he was reading out of piety or simply out of curiosity, the way you might read a romance.

"A romance?"

Both the fine young daughter and Joseph Shorr liked this description and the two of them laughed.

And old Mureynes looked into their faces and laughed along. Taking deep draws on the thick Russian cigarette, he choked down his laughter deep within. He looked as if he were taking pleasure in making "his children" laugh; but then he caught himself and his face took on a serious cast.

432

"In Great Setrenitz," he went on, "people thought the world of Shmuel Rab-Rabi. A fine mind, they said, a learned Jew, who never talked about his learning. And his family was interesting too. He came here from somewhere deep in Poland, without a wife, all he had was a young daughter, a divorcée, she got married again soon after, to Joseph Shorr's father, and there was also a nine- or ten-year-old boy with curly hair, Jonah was his name, he was a bit mixed up, but he had a good mind, even better than his father Shmuel Rab-Rabi."

And old Mureynes had never forgotten him, that nine-year-old pipsqueak, even today.

He, old Mureynes was considered one of the best chess-players in Great Setrenitz, and little Jonah used to come by and beat him in game after game.

Jonah was still young when he left Great Setrenitz, but old Mureynes, performing a mental feat, figured out that Jonah couldn't be much older now than thirty-two or so.

"Isn't that right?" he asked Joseph Shorr.

It turned out that Minna Mureynes, the fine young daughter, also had a word to say about him. In Berne, she had lived briefly near a small Jewish colony; they were supposed to be the leaders of a political group that had since disbanded. Now one day a young man came to the colony, he had a young face but gray hair. He was known as Jonah, and the colony gave a welcoming party. There was a woman, a Christian, who was so happy to see him that she gave up her room to him.

Minna Mureynes was still gazing at Joseph Shorr with such smiling friendly eyes as though gazing at a desired bridegroom. She didn't know whether the Jonah in Berne was the same one that Joseph Shorr and her father were talking about, but she was happy just the same. She had been able to add a word or two when they were talking about his uncle Jonah.

Suddenly, however, they noticed that Joseph Shorr's face had become stony, and they lapsed into remorseful silence. Joseph Shorr remained wordless, stiffly, stubbornly, a typical Shorr; but perhaps he didn't feel comfortable talking about an uncle who, ever since his childhood, had grown more and more estranged from his entire family and then completely washed his hands of them.

433

They arrived in Kiev at twilight, and through the window they caught sight of a wet, freshly washed station, a cold building with a cold and alien crowd of people on the platform, and the travelers themselves suddenly became cold and alien to one another as they said their good-byes in the railroad car.

Joseph Shorr was all excited again.

He stood with the porter on the platform, waiting and waiting for Jacob-Nathan. But no Jacob-Nathan emerged or came towards him in the terminal. It was getting to be annoying. Old Mureynes and Minna came walking past and they looked back at him. Other travelers from Great Setrenitz went by, and all of them saw him standing and waiting, dressed in brand-new clothes, like a bridegroom.

Finally he took a droshky and rode into the city, to a hotel.

But in the city, he began to have a sneaking suspicion about Jacob-Nathan. Negotiations for the marriage were evidently not going too well. Jacob-Nathan came to the hotel the next morning and sat in Joseph Shorr's room with a mournful expression. He obviously had nothing new to report. Eventually he began chain-smoking and asking Joseph Shorr for a calling card. He said:

"This is what I'm going to do: I'll get this card right over to Rappoport's home; I'll do everything that has to be done."

Joseph Shorr didn't believe him, he looked at him suspiciously, and paced around the room unable to make up his mind. But in the end he did give him a card. Someone from Rappoport's house was supposed to come here in the morning and invite Joseph Shorr to visit them. But Joseph Shorr waited in the hotel for two days and two nights; he was all alone in his expensive room, deeply depressed, at his wits' end from the dreary waiting, and nobody came to him. Furthermore, Jacob-Nathan himself, during those two days and two nights, felt too confused, he only slipped into the hotel for a few minutes at a time, quickly asking as he came in:

"Well? What's new?"

As if the required news weren't going to arrive through him, but, as if he, Jacob-Nathan, were going to receive it here, in Joseph Shorr's hotel room.

At last he showed up, sweaty and worn out, the bearer of

Avram Rappoport's blank card: a large card with oblique golden edges and finely stroked embossed Russian letters, and when it lay on the table it emanated an alien richness, cold and aloof, as though wanting to say:

"Who knows? Perhaps he wasn't all that willing to hand me over; perhaps he was pushed into it."

Joseph Shorr kept pacing up and down the room, almost afraid to touch it. But then he replied;

"Fine, I'll be there Saturday evening."

And there was nothing else he wanted to know about anything happening in Avram Rappoport's home; after all, he was Joseph Shorr, hard, stern, and stiff deep inside himself somewhere. On the Sabbath, he went through the day with the deeply peaceful and nebulous feelings of a rigid and stubborn person, who, in spite of himself, refuses to think about anything.

"It really doesn't matter."

And when he finally awoke from these nebulous feelings, it was already a cool Saturday evening, eerie, mournful, and sluggish. In the quiet coolness of the big city, the sun went down, red, cold and remote, and then a wind started roaming the pallid darkness, blowing and slapping on the high rooftops. Something soulful nestled in the air; after all, a week was gone.

"Where has the week gone to?"

And down below, the life of the metropolis flowed about through the streets; it was noisy and haunting and a-choke with yearning; it was midsummer night, the Vigil of Saint John, Christians were returning home with burning candles in their hands, and all around, the swarms of church bells were sluggishly pealing.

VII

Joseph Shorr was walking along the noisy main thoroughfare, still not knowing if this was the right way to Avram Rappoport's home. He was drowsy and still unwilling to think about anything.

Walking slowly, all alone, and turning at a far corner, he came

435

to a dimly lit theater entrance with two large Russian posters announcing a lecture on a Jewish topic; and with a quiet, timid familiarity hovering about them, a quiet Jewish hideaway in this evening of heavy alien tolling and bright Christian candles openly rummaging through the dark street. There was no one in the theater entrance. It was deserted. And Joseph Shorr, after standing for a moment, went in, simply went in, just like that, out of deep indifference, or a pure stubborn determination to prove to himself that he was calm and taking his time, and not hurrying anywhere. When he paused at the edge of the dimly illuminated auditorium, by the entrance, he suddenly caught sight of rows upon rows of the shoulders of seated listeners, a great many open female jackets with flushed girlish faces, faces that were far too red, peering over at him, the newcomer, scanning his face too sharply with their hot eyes. But in front, on the empty, brightly illuminated stage, a fairly heavy-set student was standing at the pulpit, with a ruddy, oldish face and with brand-new university buttons, wearily wiping his forehead with a white handkerchief. He looked as though he had been drudging all day and was now resting. But when Joseph Shorr strained his ears, he could make out the student's words about the troubles that Jews were having in Russia and in other countries. Everything the student said was true. And everyone was listening with keen interest. But it had so little to do with him, Joseph Shorr, and he was, after all, a stranger among all these people, none of whom knew him. He stood for a while, looking around, and then left the theater.

On the corner of the quiet and wealthy street where Avram Rappoport resided, Joseph Shorr, the stiff and stubborn only child, hesitated for the first time. He stood there for a while, staring.

Across the way, an electric streetlamp, hanging high in the air, was shining coldly; it hung still, but if you gazed at it, it looked as if it were just barely swaying in the wind; it poured cold stillness into the heart of any passerby, and there were very few people passing. Only one man was walking along, on the other side, much taller than Joseph Shorr, clean-shaven, like an actor, with large thick eyebrows and with bags, swollen drowsy bags, under his eyes. Joseph Shorr watched just as the man emerged from the pallid darkness across the way. A moment ago, he hadn't been there, and it looked as though the night had just given birth to him, sudden birth, just like that, just as he was, with his hands thrust deep into the pockets of his short topcoat, and with the haughtiness of solitude in his slightly hunched shoulders. Now he was approaching Avram Rappoport's front entrance; now he was arriving; now he was there.

"Pardon me. . . ."

Two men bumped into one another by the milky glass door at the entrance, which led into a hallway and then up to the first floor. They apologized for having raised their hands at the same time to press the electric buzzer. One of the men was Joseph Shorr; rested from the Sabbath, he couldn't remember when he had made up his mind to walk over to the door; the other man, a Hebrew poet, no longer all that young, who had completely stopped writing two years ago, and who, almost to spite himself, had gotten a job in a local committee, half-social, half-Zionist, which existed almost entirely on Avram Rappoport's contributions. He looked around in such amazement when Joseph Shorr said:

"Pardon me!"

Joseph Shorr was still calm, as well as groggy, and around him, in the comfortable, illuminated, wealthy dining room which he was entering, someone was saying that now, around the big Christian holiday, there was talk, in the city, of a coming pogrom, it was a fact.

"A fact?"

Mrs. Rappoport's reddish face twisted nervously and wearily. She leaned over the table to the person who was speaking, and at the same time, looking out the window, she caught sight of a burning candle that a belated passerby, a Christian, was carefully bringing home.

Not stirring from her place, like a woman after labor, she said: "I asked to have the shades drawn."

And this too was noticed by him, Joseph Shorr. He was already sitting not far from her, Mrs. Rappoport, and he coldly looked around. Not that many people were sitting at the table; but still, about half a dozen were clattering their teaspoons and crumbling

437

their cake in the saucers. Glasses of tea were shining red, and among them a flushed face. A cheerful coloratura laugh floated past his ears, infecting everyone at the table except him, Joseph Shorr. In another moment, it seemed, he would be sorry he had come. And suddenly, he remembered something and felt a great, great excitement in his breast. Every so often, his marital mood would again surge through his heart, and his heart would swell and swell, and his mind would awake from its sleep, and he would think:

"She's right here in this house!"

"Moyshe Levine's daughter!"

At any moment, she might walk in through one of the wide-open doors that looked on from all sides with a bright, cozy festiveness; perhaps, at this very moment, she was dressing somewhere, in her room, in honor of his coming.

Joseph Shorr had been received in Rappoport's home good-naturedly, like all the other guests; they kept introducing him to new people.

But the girl wasn't all that quick about coming from her room.

Every time a new person came in out of the cool night, Joseph Shorr had to bow politely and shake hands politely:

"Joseph Shorr."

He was sitting right across from the Hebrew poet with the clean-shaven face and the swollen bags under his eyes, and had nothing to say to him. Now he was fully awake. He was filled with deep respect for his motive in coming, for himself, for the entire house, and even for the guests who kept entering with smiles on their fresh faces and smelling of the cool night. The guests, however, were all frequent visitors here and, by chance or design, they avoided looking at him; if they did offer him a hand, it was also merely in passing, and they promptly forgot all about him. He watched them having a good time and gathering around Avram Rappoport's daughter, the sculptress, who had only just come home, late Friday night, from Saint Petersburg.

"Nessi!"

"Where's Nessi?!"

Nessi was thin, childishly small, with a congenital pointed

hump between her thin, sharp, bony shoulders. But she no longer looked all that young. There were yellow, oldish spots near her temples. People forgave her for studying in Berne and in the Saint Petersburg Academy only because the poor thing was a hunchback, but they *were* fond of her, they crowded around, stroking her small, pallid hands, the way you stroke the hands of a child. And yet there was somehow more of the adult about her than anyone else here, and her black slanted eyes emanated some kind of sedate good-naturedness, and an entreaty, the entreaty of a person who has long since forgiven life for everything and long since come to terms with everything. She was somewhat estranged from her parents, and no one ever noticed them speaking to her. And yet, while not looking at her, they nevertheless seemed to be constantly thinking of her and of their complaints about her style of life, which was so different from the wealthy manner to which they were accustomed. And now she had come home, as usual, like a stranger, come quietly, with no warning that she was en route, not even a wire. One of the guests was taking extreme pleasure in relating how he had been on the way home last night, so much later than usual, how he had been walking all alone down a deserted street, and then suddenly there she was: Nessi, trundling from the railroad station, all alone, with a bad, nocturnal cabman: the night was cold, the road uphill was a long one, and she had felt sorry for the horse, who was swaying too much with his scrawny croup, she begged the cabman, the old Christian:

"Don't drive them so hard, please, don't."

And Nessi, by chance or design, didn't hear.

Joseph Shorr watched her as she stood next to Madame Koyre, stroking the woman's hair with her small hands and asking about her husband, who was out of town.

Ah, no, she obviously wasn't a bad person, the sculptress, Nessi, but what did it all have to do with him, Joseph Shorr? Rolled up and buttoned up in his new black jacket, he was sitting on his chair at the crowded table and was full of genteel patience. The important thing was that none of the people here should think that he, Joseph Shorr, had noticed anything; he too was of a sufficiently wealthy background and by no means had he come

439

here to learn anything. Somewhere deep inside, he was just as evenly barbered and cleanly soaped as on the outside; it was as if, were he to move, something in his newness would creak. And in all his newness and genteelness, he was ready to devote himself to the conversation thesë people would have with him. This would have to be a conversation pertaining only to him, to his coming here; he peered about for the host and the hostess, but the host wasn't present, and the hostess, as if by design, never looked at him:

"Madame Koyre! . . ."

She wanted the young woman to sit closer to her and was vexed because her words were vanishing in the cheerful tumult.

"Madame Koyre! . . ."

At last, Madame Koyre's fine nostrils quivered and her thin, transparent face began to flush, she started smiling and edging close to Mrs. Rappoport. Madame Koyre was the daughter of an old Hebrew writer. Everyone knew that in his youth her father had been rather wealthy and had never depended on anyone else, which is why they all were practically melting in their enormous respect and their love for her. Now he had already been sick for two years and was staying in Switzerland. There was talk that Avram Rappoport was supporting him with his own or with community money, but there were a few people who didn't know about it and were still making flattering remarks about him, even behind his back. Some elderly visitor in glasses, with long hair and hunched shoulders under his threadbare jacket, looking as if he had once been a government-approved rabbi in a big city, came out of the study, speaking Hebrew with Avram Rappoport, and, as they entered, he terminated his long conversation:

"And so, let me tell you, the journal cannot otherwise survive."

He had obviously been doing some long, hard work with Avram Rappoport in the study and had been talking away at him for a long time. Now he wearily drank his glass of tea at the table and relaxed. He peered professorially over his glasses and asked the young woman, Madame Koyre, whether an item he had lately read in a Hebrew newspaper was true:

Her father, he had read, was feeling better and was thinking of coming back to Russia fairly soon.

And at the same time, Avram Rappoport, the host of the house, having been left alone, was still standing by himself not far from the table, as though forgotten. A bit stooped and lost in thought, he stood there; and it was impossible to tell what he was thinking: about what the old man had been drumming into him for hours in the study; about the alien glass of tea, which had been drained, and in which his eyes were now buried; or perhaps even about himself, about his enormous business dealings, which had nothing to do with anyone in the room. Someone spoke to him, and so he turned around in surprise, listening with a surly face to the rumors about a pogrom, and then he wandered across the room, like a grouchy in-law, distant and lonesome among all these people who had come to entertain him. All at once, he recalled something, looked around at the table, and halted:

"Wait . . . that's him, the young man from Great Setrenitz, the one who's here to have a look at Sarah."

He felt guilty:

After all, Sarah had smiled upon hearing that he would be coming to see her, she had gone off for the whole evening with a friend who carried greetings from abroad, that blond young fellow who was so terribly happy because a number of news-papers and magazines had suddenly been informing the world of his existence. His name was Joel Vaintroib.

Avram Rappoport's eyes twinkled; he sat down on the empty chair behind Joseph Shorr, leaning his head on his hands. He scrutinized Joseph Shorr's freshly barbered throat and neck with such great interest as though to determine something:

That's what a young rich bachelor looks like nowadays when girls don't even want him to see them. . . .

In great sympathy, he leaned over, hugging the back of his chair, and began a conversation with him.

What? He wasn't running his flour mill himself? It was still leased out to others?

Joseph Shorr's tone of voice changed. All at once he felt that his time was come. Out of great respect for his lofty host, he answered the question a good deal louder than usual. He didn't think he could make a go of the mill by himself all that soon. Right after Pentecost, when the lease would be up, he intended to make repairs.

441

"Overall repairs."

He was still shifting his chair around so as not to be talking to Avram Rappoport from the side, and he didn't feel very good because he had just said something stupid:

He explained that besides all the repairs, he was thinking about replacing the sheet-iron chimney with a brick chimney. But now something *happened,* and Avram Rappoport left him alone for a moment. All the people at the table sprang up and went towards the newly arrived guest, and Joseph Shorr looked over and immediately recognized him. It was the ruddy student with the oldish face and the brand-new university buttons, the lecturer at the theater. Joseph Shorr watched the other guests flocking around the newcomer, eagerly asking about his lecture, and the student answered tersely, almost reluctantly. And suddenly, Joseph Shorr forgot about the student and the lecture, about himself, and about the stupid things he had been saying a bit earlier. His eyes veered:

No one was left at the table except for Mrs. Rappoport and young Madame Koyre, and the two of them moved even closer together as though by tacit understanding. Mrs. Rappoport whispered something in Madame Koyre's ear, and Madame Koyre listened with great interest; she didn't stop smiling, and her blue, blood-rimmed eyes were staring at him, Joseph Shorr. It was obvious: they were whispering about him. His hereditary family pride stiffened in him, and the blood of the Shorrs, *his* blood, shot into his face. Just behind his back, someone mentioned the name of Moyshe Levine's daughter; it was the ruddy student. He wasn't standing very far from Joseph Shorr at the table, but he hardly noticed him. He was still absently absorbed in his lecture and, absently, he took hold of someone else's teaspoon.

"Where is Sarah?" he asked quietly, looking down at the spoon.

It became clear: she had gone off somewhere for the entire evening.

"What?" he asked, slightly bewildered, while Avram Rappoport turned around to him, Joseph Shorr, and started speaking once more.

He still had pallid nostrils, and his breathing was heavier than

442

usual, but deep inside he was once again stiff and hard. He walked about the room with Avram Rappoport, who led him into the adjoining room, the vast white parlor. Who could tell? Perhaps Avram Rappoport had a specific reason for taking him there; perhaps he wanted to see him in private and tell him something.

VIII

But even in the vast white parlor, he didn't succeed in remaining alone with Rappoport.

The shades were down and the lustres were sparkling clean. Mute shadows were drowsing between dark, distant mirrors. Chairs in white slipcovers were trustfully nestling against the snug, cozy walls, and the soft, endless, black carpet, the old friend of this home, stretched underfoot day after day, waiting patiently for festive occasions. The room was dusky, but a bit further, by the tiny, bright-red glow in the far corner, which was illuminated by the red light, something was going on. There were about six or seven people, sunk deeply into the low, matching armchairs; they all looked weary, stony, and pensive, as though being photographed, and they were listening to Nessi Rappoport defending her friend Vaintroib, the young painter, against nasty comments. She was speaking softly, Nessi was, very softly: she didn't want to offend anyone. And she smiled good-naturedly, as if the others were saying foolish things, then she modestly lowered her long, long lashes.

"No, my dear friends," she said, "you have no idea. . . ."

In her lap, Nessi was holding an embroidered case of yellow silk.

Her thin, childishly tiny hands were pulling out the reproductions, one after another, paintings by her friend, the young artist, and her audience was looking at them one after another, and then putting them down, one after another.

One painting showed four blind horses. The important thing,

443

however, wasn't the horses themselves, but the story the viewer was reminded of:

Once upon a time, somewhere in a small backwater shtetl, dreary summer afternoons are wearing on, and the endless sunny hours bore everyone to death. A rooster is always crowing there, more gloomily than anywhere else; a father, wealthy and stubborn, lives there, unhappier than any other father if, upon awaking from his afternoon nap, he finds that his boy still hasn't gone back to heder after lunch. He has a heavy tongue:

"C'mon, boy, get to school," he shouts at his lazy little son, "what's gonna become of you?"

But the boy has been sick of school for so long now, sick of the rabbi and the other pupils, who endlessly keep repeating the tedious biblical portion after Passover; he is leaning against the painted fence in front of his father's house, he is utterly crestfallen. "What a lazy good-for-nothing," he remembers.

And overhead, old, spreading acacias are murmuring in front of the windows, supporting his thought:

"A good-for-nothing? Yes indeed, a good-for-nothing."

He wanders behind his father's house and watches the flies buzzing around filthy places. He roams through the alleys of the shtetl and stops for a long while at the back door of the shtetl's big treadmill, where they are grinding millet. He stands and watches: Four blind horses are ceaselessly stomping on the enormous wheel of the treadmill and clambering up; they are very nearly falling, and they think they are climbing a dangerously high mountain. They are climbing to heaven. They strain their necks forward, flaring their nostrils, widening out their blind eyes, and yet they remain in the same place.

And it was this little boy who, later on, did a painting of those blind horses. Now he was an adult; but once, he had to run away from home with a meager sum, a few hundred rubles of his father's. He was back from abroad now, a renowned painter, and he was painting; he painted the hilly town of Great Setrenitz, and newspapers were writing about him, and Nessi was saying that he was a great man, a truly great painter:

"There are," she said, "fortunate people in the world."

Someone pointed an expert finger at the farthest of the four blind horses, the black one with the deep, sunken spine. Someone else sluggishly dragged his myopic eyes across the snarls hanging over the blind eyes and the hooves, and then, as sluggishly, emitted a hearty snort.

"Jewish horses. . . ."

Joseph Shorr had another look at the picture; he again forgot that Avram Rappoport was no longer in the parlor, and he again felt crestfallen; he had to admit to himself:

He was absolutely inexperienced in such things.

The kinds of things that were being discussed in Avram Rappoport's house had never been talked about in his father's home or in the home of his two rich aunts. In order to grasp the point of the debate, he changed places and sat down on a chair closer to the others, leaning his head towards them in a Hassidic manner. He listened attentively, but then it turned out that the conversation wasn't all that deep. It was fairly dominated by the ruddy student with the oldish face and the brand-new buttons, who was sitting here in the parlor across from Nessi. A bit earlier, someone had asked him about some articles he had published pertaining to Zionism, and now, more earnest than anyone else, he was sitting deep in the low easy-chair and absolutely refused to agree with Nessi that her friend, the young painter Vaintroib, was a great man:

No, Nessi would have to forgive him, but he had a rule that a great man is a *substance*.

"A substance?"

Off in the corner, the Hebrew poet, the taciturn man with the swollen bags under his eyes, stopped rocking for a moment in his high rocking chair and stared with the surprised face of a mute. But the student didn't even look around at him.

"And another thing," he said, "people pounce upon a midget and make him out to be a giant."

The student knew Vaintroib personally. In Saint Petersburg, just before Passover, when he had taken one of his last major exams and was heading home, he had shared a compartment with a friend of his, an interesting girl, and who should be sitting in the same compartment but the young painter himself, Vaintroib, on the way home, and he had acted just like a small-town dummy, a pseudo-intellectual, a clod.

The student was so angry at all the intellectual Jewish families

445

in Saint Petersburg, who had talked about nothing but that Vaintroib before Passover, and he was angry at all the female students who had gone running to see him. But why was he so hotly talking about the fact that Nessi and all the newspapers were praising Vaintroib? In itself it was a terrible insult to him, the ruddy and not very young student. . . .

Joseph Shorr looked him in the face but didn't understand. And suddenly someone interrupted the student, and the conversation made some other things clear:

Apparently, the young painter was in town; Nessi knew him fairly well, and he had been coming to see her rather frequently, here in Avram Rappoport's home.

And something else became clear:

Tonight, he, Vaintroib, had gone off for the entire evening with her—Moyshe Levine's daughter.

Joseph Shorr's heart almost died, it died for a moment, and that was that. But he quickly regained his senses and barely twisted his lips, he was so annoyed at himself and at what had bothered him:

After all, he, Joseph Shorr, was no more than a guest here, this was the first time in his life he was spending an evening here, why should he care about Moyshe Levine's daughter?

And to keep from thinking about her, he made an effort, leaning his head once more in a Hassidic manner and listening attentively. The ruddy student was talking again, about traveling in that train compartment with his friend all the way from Saint Petersburg, and how Vaintroib had constantly been eating the girl's oranges and her chocolate, and never once stopped talking about himself.

But now Joseph Shorr had to make more of an effort to get the story straight in his mind:

The student had started home for Passover. . . .

The student had then, perhaps not by chance, traveled from Saint Petersburg together with a girl he knew. Perhaps, before leaving, he had spent a day or two waiting for her. He was sitting at her side in the compartment, close and snug, and wanted to clarify a few things for her.

446

Ah yes, the ruddy student, no doubt he was always able to make things clear, and who knows? Perhaps the things he wanted to clarify for the girl were closely related to the one or two articles he had published about Zionism. But the blond young fellow, Vaintroib, the painter, who had long blond hair and wore a velvet jacket, and was sitting opposite them—he constantly broke in with idle chitchat and wouldn't let them carry on their conversation; he kept swaying back and forth, rocking his legs and clicking his tongue.

"Tsk, tsk, tsk!" He made fun of the girl's parti-colored scarf, "such fine colors. . . ." He kept looking straight in the girl's face, while eating her chocolate and her oranges, and acting like a happy young fiddler accustomed to great successes at weddings, and he never stopped talking about himself.

He, Joel Vaintroib, was going home again after many long years, he was going back to the little shtetl of Kozlovve, near Great Setrenitz, and people there always called him Yoylik, just plain Yoylik. He once had a father back home, who was partly a follower of the Rabbi of Skvirre, and partly a Zionist, and his father had finally moved to Palestine, after selling his rich whitewashed house to a well-to-do shopkeeper. The house had old acacias in front of the eight-paned windows with yellow frames, and out in the grassy yard, next to the trees, there were three rocks growing, big ones, with sharp points. Now he, Joel Vaintroib, simply couldn't forget all these things. Old acacias in front of the window and, out in the yard, three big, sharp rocks. He would often wake up at night and start painting them, those very rocks. He could remember every notch in them, every rung. And then, for a long while, he would be unable to fall asleep and he would muse, he would lie with closed eyes and see Kozlovve: He was sitting there all alone on the porch steps of the house with the closed shutters that concealed the shopkeeper's sleeping family. He sat there in the middle of the night, on the steps of the house, listening to the old acacias murmuring deep, deep in the night, the same trees that once, in summertime, had heard his father always shouting: "You lazy good-for-nothing . . . !"

"No," the old acacias were murmuring to him now, "you've

accomplished something, Yoylik, you're not a good-for-nothing."

Now he was returning, he had already wired the shopkeeper that he wanted to buy back his father's house.

The student really didn't know when to stop, he talked on and on, telling how that Vaintroib had gotten on everyone's nerves in the train compartment.

Never, said the student, had he heard anyone babble on like that; never had he met anyone so stupidly in love with himself, with his own breath.

But by now, nearly all the people who had been around the student were gone. He was talking, but no one cared, no one was listening.

Joseph Shorr gazed at the childishly small girl, Nessi, who was still sitting, sad and lonesome, by the tiny, bright-red fire, and no one went over to her. She was pitiful to look at.

He remembered:

She had come back home, only last night, like a stranger.

"Please," she had begged the coachman, "don't drive so fast!"

And now she looked so unhappy here, in her father's house, and it was hard to tell what she was thinking: Perhaps she was still musing about the young painter, Vaintroib; after all, she herself had been talking so much about him all through the evening. And perhaps she no longer remembered a rather sad story about herself, the hunchbacked sculptress, an unfortunate story that had taken place so very quietly:

"A wealthy and powerful man, a father, had a child born to him, a simple, deprived Jewish child. . . ."

In order to show her his warm feelings, Joseph Shorr bowed and started a conversation with her.

"It would be interesting to know: How old is he, that painter Vaintroib?"

"How old?"

At the sound of his voice, Nessi, lost in thought, felt her long, long eyelashes tremble; and in her slanted eyes, her normal good-naturedness and her entreaty quickened.

"How old is Vaintroib?" she said. "I don't know, my dear fellow, he's still young, very young."

448

And again Nessi sank back into something and became pensive. Joseph Shorr was so grateful that she had called him her "dear fellow."

Well, and what about her? he asked. She was a sculptress, after all; why didn't she talk about her own work?

Nessi apparently didn't care about herself at all.

"Ahh?" she said. "No, my dear fellow. I'm nothing but a simple craftsman. That's one thing I know."

She wasn't offended at his question, she spoke as softly with him as with an equal. He was so grateful that he was even willing to forget what had happened to him this evening, he was willing to sit with her a bit longer and ask:

How come . . .? How come she thought so?

But all around them, most of the people had already left, it was getting rather late.

The last guests said good-night.

Outside, by the front entrance, two men were standing, the Hebrew poet and the ruddy student, and they were much more familiar and straightforward in their conversation now than earlier in the parlor; they were thinking of going somewhere. As for him, Joseph Shorr, here too they didn't look around, they didn't notice him, as though a cat were going by. What could they have thought about him? What could anyone have thought about his visit this evening in Avram Rappoport's house? The point was that no one here had thought anything about him. Inside himself, Joseph Shorr felt a deep, convulsive hurt of insult; he walked away.

At the corner of the quiet and wealthy street, not far from the electric streetlight, which was hanging high in the air, he ran into Moyshe Levine's daughter with the young painter Vaintroib, who was seeing her home. There was a moment when they were level with one another, and she cast a glance at him from up close as though suddenly recalling where she had once seen him and failing to understand what he was doing here, now, at the stroke of twelve.

Joseph Shorr once again saw her eyes, intelligent blue eyes, which were trying to remember something as they gazed at him,

449

and a mouth, severely shut, a straight line, strongly reminiscent of something, so near, and intimate. Joseph Shorr couldn't remember his mother. He was four when she died; but who knows? Perhaps his mother had the same kind of mouth, and perhaps that was why he felt so attracted to it. He could feel his heart crack, but he still didn't know whether she had recognized him or not. And suddenly, within him, the proud heir quickened, the only son, who had grown up in Great Setrenitz, in Isaac-Mayer Shorr's secluded, aristocratic home. At least, back in Great Setrenitz, he didn't feel so crestfallen and frustrated as he did at this very moment. Back there he still had his inherited property, two houses of his own, and his big mill. . . .

Behind his back, he could hear him laughing, the young painter Vaintroib. He was telling something to the beautiful girl whom he was seeing home, and he laughed with great pleasure. But it scarcely concerned Joseph Shorr. He walked with quick steps, thinking about the houses he owned in Great Setrenitz and the mill he had inherited:

"Yes indeed, my big mill, that's worth something too."❧

A TALE OF A GOAT
Y. M. WEISSENBERG

"Now look, Gittl, darling," said one sister to the other, both of them old women with hairy warts on their chins, and with mouths as sunken as graves, except that one sister was somewhat better off in her old age. And she was the one who was complaining: "Now look. You can see there's only a tiny piece of soft bread on my table, I soaked it in water just so my teeth can manage it, and since I can't give you what you need, all I can do is advise you to go panhandling, no one will turn you down. . . ."

"Now look, Beyle, darling," the other sister replied, "God's will be done, but I can't go begging, I can make it through the day somehow or other—but at night . . . . Sister, darling, do put me up, just give me a place behind the oven to rest my head. I'll lie on my shawl, just so long as I have a roof over my head."

"I know how stubborn you can be," said the wealthier sister, "but just look for yourself, the rain leaks in over there." She pointed at the spot where, just a short while ago, she had knocked over a cup of water, and the floor was still wet.

The poorer sister sighed, sighed again, and barely staggered out of the house, both her hands clutching the jambs, she hadn't had a crumb of food for three days now, and, having no place to stay, she lay down in the street, and died a pure and honorable death.

Now when a person dies in the street, charitable people are profoundly touched, and so her fellow Jews donated a shroud and four cubits of earth under a tree in the cemetery.

451

Behind the bier came several women, including the sister, and, six feet away from the house, they threw coins into the poor box which Abraham the beadle was brandishing as he walked in front of the bier, calling out in Hebrew: "Charity delivereth from death." They eulogized her warmly, saying she had been a pure and righteous woman, and had never in all her life taken anything from anyone (which is the highest praise you can bestow on a person), and they hoped that good angels would welcome her with open arms. And then the women all returned to their respective homes, had a cup of water handed out to them at their front doors—and they washed their hands (according to custom) of the whole business.

But God sits up in the sky and looks down at the earth. And thereby hangs a tale:

A farmer owned a sassy little goat, who ran amuck in his rye field, whereupon the farmer, nothing daunted, tied her up and put her in a wagon, and when market day came round, he drove off to bring her to the butchers in town.

Upon arriving, however, the farmer went into the tavern to liquor up a bit—and the goat remained lying in the wagon, waiting, for one hour, two hours, and still the farmer didn't show up. She took stock of the situation, ripped away the plaited straw, and, getting up on her skinny little legs and shaking her beard, she pranced off the wagon.

That was that.

Now the marketplace was full of wagons, and horses standing backward between the shafts, with their heads in the wagons and their collars down by the wheels—and the goat lost her way.

She wandered about, leaping over the wagons with an idiotic and frightened look, and with a heartrending "baa-baa," so that the horses kept snorting with flared nostrils and stiffened ears as they peered at the white, wild, bearded creature who was prancing about in between the wagons.

Evening. The wagons had all driven away. Yellow droppings were scattered over the deserted marketplace. The goat came to a halt: Where to now? Night was coming on—and, exasperated, she started dashing around the wall of the market shops, baaing and baaing—and her wailing floated so pitifully through the still

452

twilight of the marketplace that only God could have come to her rescue.

Meanwhile a small light started shining through a window. It was in the home of the wealthy sister, who was observing the traditional seven days of mourning for the poor sister, and, what with being old and having to observe a wake, she had lit her lamp earlier than anyone else around the market.

Now when the goat saw the tiny glow through the windowpane, she remembered that her owner often went to the barn at night carrying a burning lantern, so she assumed that this was her home, and she made a beeline toward it.

She promptly realized she had made a slight mistake. She saw a door with a glass pane, which the barn didn't have. And because she didn't understand what was going on, and yet did need a place to stay, she pranced into the covered porch.

Once inside, she found a staircase leading to the attic—gaped up the steps and slowly started climbing.

At the top, she came upon a bundle of dried pea stalks right in the corner under the shingle roof, she nestled down in them to rest her legs after a day of running around.

The pea stalks had been prepared by the lady of the house for a rainy day, just like a ball of wool in her trunk, although she hadn't torn a thing for the past ten years because she always walked very slowly and gingerly, with the spectacles on her nose attached to her ears by a string.

Late at night. The door and the shutter were already fastened, a tiny night light was burning in the room, shedding a ruddy glow on the walls—and the rich sister was already lying under her featherbed with a kerchief knotted round her head.

All at once, there was a rustling in the attic, and the sister perked up her ears. . . . She hadn't imagined it, something had really and truly rustled—and her blood turned to ice. What could it be, she wondered, and tried to bury her head under the covers, but the harder she tried, the more she felt she had to perk up her ears, and the more she perked up her ears, the more clearly she heard the rustling.

"That's bad," she thought to herself; ever since her sister's death, a fear had been haunting the place.

453

And climbing out of bed, she turned up the lamp, took a stack of sacred books, together with her husband's prayer shawl (he'd been dead for some thirty years), and, placing them around herself like a barricade, she slipped into her bed again. God's will be done! What could she do, her sister was trying to get back at her.

Meanwhile, the attic had gotten too cold for the goat, and so she quietly came down the stairs, and the old woman fearfully listened to the horror creeping along.

There was a shove at the door and the old woman jumped up with trembling eyes: "Sister, darling, what do you want from me?"

The goat stopped dead in her tracks for a minute, and the old woman with the little lamp in her hand stood quaking in the middle of the room, peering and peering.

And she saw a big white eye with a gaping lid ogling through the peephole in the shutter, whereupon she collapsed in the middle of the room with the little lamp in her hand and died too.

Well, if a person dies, you have to think about burying him. The neighbors dislodged a brick from her oven and found enough money to pay for a shroud and a small plot, and the women spent a whole day at her windows, eulogizing her with shaking lips: What a pure and decent person she'd been, what a good person she'd been, what a good soul she had had—why, the poor thing had died of a broken heart over her dead sister.

Which was all well and good, so long as she got buried within the prescribed twenty-four-hour period; that night they were already carrying her bier. All around it, the members of the burial society, and, in front, Abraham the beadle with the poor box in one hand and the lantern in the other.

But the goat hadn't forgotten that her owner used to go to the barn with a burning lantern, and she started bounding toward the bier, dashed along in front of it, and she kept stopping every so often, peeking up goatishly at the mourners—and then dashing on.

The mourners could plainly smell a rat, the goat was bedeviled, a dybbuk, and so they did their best not to look toward her as she pranced along.

May God preserve us. Demons have been known to prance

along. Nevertheless, on they went to the cemetery, God's will be done, and they halted with the bier at the open grave. But the goat was already peering out from the trees as they shone the lantern by a mound of sand, and, peering over, she recalled the way her owner had once buried potatoes on an autumn night, he had also lit up a mound of sand, and her heart, albeit a nannygoat's heart, became anxious, and her eye peered out, doubly huge, from the trees, especially because she hadn't had a bite to eat since she'd left the farm.

And later, when the mourners were gone, she kicked up the grave and plowed her horns through the sand; but her labor was useless, she couldn't find a thing. So, in deep misery, she stepped into a rabbi's tomb and went to bed without any supper.

Morning, the grave-digger took one look at the fresh grave—something terrible had happened. He dashed over to the burial society to announce the news.

The town was terror-stricken, they realized what it was all about: At night, a goat prances toward the bier, and in the morning they find the grave all messed up.

Women in childbed were terrified, a quiet commotion spread through the town, a deep, secret terror, and it was decided that the rabbi and the town worthies were to go to God's acre: first of all, to tell her that she had to realize she was dead and ought to be resting in peace. And secondly, to recite a couple of psalms over her grave and release her soul from the demon that had pranced toward her bier that night, gloating over his victim.

The rabbi put on his gaberdine and his high fur hat, the town worthies their velvet hats, and off they went.

And as they went off, the handworkers put aside their work, the cobbler his hammer, the tailor his scissors, and they jumped into their coats and dashed along.

They did all they could for her soul, but during the recital of the psalms, Tsivye, the blind woman who recites prayers for the dead in the cemetery, and two other matrons climbed into the rabbi's tomb to ask him to intercede on their behalf, and the moment they saw the goat lying under the railings they jumped up screaming and, with outflung hands, dashed over to the congregation.

And the Lord's congregation was scared out of its wits, a panic broke out—and it was decided that the rabbi, on behalf of the entire congregation, was to go and order the goat out of there and assign her a place in the desert where no human beings ever pass, or else under a bridge somewhere.

The rabbi inspected the tassels of his prayer shawl, then he and the entire crowd surrounded the tomb, and he knocked at the door.

"Get out of there," he told the goat, softly and sedately. "It is I who order you to do so, I, the insignificant Samuel, Rabbi of the Holy Congregation in the name of the Community . . . and you are to leave only through the single hole at the peak of the roof so as not to injure anyone, God forbid."

And the crowd stood with mouths agape and ears perked, and waited for the rabbi's will to be done—only the goat didn't feel like budging. So the rabbi grabbed his cane, intending to use it the way the old Rabbi of Kotzko (may he rest in peace) used to deal with dybbuks. The goat panicked, and, with pointed horns, charged straight into the rabbi's beard and knocked him head over heels in his gaberdine, and the whole congregation, the hosts of the Lord, jumped up and dashed into town, gaggling like a flock of geese. And the townsfolk began locking their doors and shutters: The demon was on the loose! And they all hid inside their homes. The town became a tomb, and the goat started roaming the deserted streets unmolested with her head held high.

Since then, a lot of water has flowed over the dam, grass has covered the marketplace, and whole gardens of moss the roof-tops—the townspeople are still hiding behind their shutters, and even if some extraordinary visitor were to come into town, not one of them would dream of opening the door to him. ❧

PART FOUR
WAR, REVOLUTION, DESTRUCTION

The nineteenth century had brought social and political ferment, especially with Marxism, Zionism, and various reformist and revolutionary movements in Eastern Europe. Jewish life, and Yiddish literature, took up these energies in various creative ways. Father/son conflicts, running a scale from tender (as in Peretz Markish's *Generations*) to violent, became a staple in Jewish writings. Workers and artisans became heroes, often political fighters—in contrast to traditional views, which had either scorned them as inferior to the intellectual, rabbinical, and wealthy strata, or idealized them as the true bearers of piety, simplicity, and holiness.

Similarly, the Jewish underworld took its bows in fiction, but rather nervously, since both writers and readers didn't care to dwell on this shady facet.

In "The Draft," Fishel Bimko develops caricatures into gutsy satire: the gap between the soft wealthy classes and the tough proletarian roustabouts. Military conscription was indeed a terror for Jews, who were hardly popular in Christian armies. Furthermore, Orthodox Jews would be cut off from study, kosher food, and most other aspects of religious life.

However, modern war affected civilian life far more devastatingly. Avrom Reyzen's "Acquiring a Graveyard," with its tender irony, sketches one such aspect of World War I in the Jewish Pale of Settlement in Tsarist Russia.

In the wake of the Great War came the Russian Revolution and

457

its utopian promises. The ambiguity of this period was both satirically and mystically exposed in Moyshe Kulbak's novel *Monday*. Borrowing expressionist techniques of exaltation, juxtaposition, exaggeration, and collective characters like the Mass, he contrasted and interwove Jewish and Communist Messianism. Kulbak uses the traditional notion of the *lamed-vovniks*, the secret saints, usually to be found among the simplest and most ordinary Jews. His main figure is an outsider, a mystic and intellectual, who has no place in the revolutionary society—thereby incarnating the qualms that many Jews, especially the religious and the intellectual ones, felt about the revolutionary movements and the coming Socialist world.

The utopias never came. Jewish culture was persecuted in the Soviet system as in the Fascist countries. And then World War II brought the worst destruction in Jewish history.

Dealing with the horrors of the Nazi period is an impossible task for most writers, especially Jews, because most literature is unequal to the events, and there is danger of cheapening those events with self-pity, sentimentality, and even martyriological idealization of the victims. An effective way of coping with these problems is reached in Der Nister's "Meyer Landshaft." Der Nister had previously written mystical fantasies and fairy tales. But settling in the Soviet Union during the twenties, committing himself to socialism, and forced to abandon his previous work by censorship, he turned to a more realistic mode. Like most other Yiddish writers in the Soviet Union, he was killed in the anti-Yiddish purges of 1948–52. In his story "Meyer Landshaft," he chose, wisely, to dwell on the psychology of the victims, on the sense of loss, rather than the physical horrors themselves. Forming an iron-clad defense against cheap emotions and sentimentality, he uses long, seemingly rambling, highly rhetorical periods, sentences that seem as undecided as Meyer Landshaft himself, taking a long, long time to reach any resolution. The distanciation created by the style, the cunning alienation effect, force us to deal with the psychology of individuals—something difficult to do amid collective annihilation.

GENERATIONS
PERETZ MARKISH

Mendel the Miller had his own opinion about the descent of man. He believed that God had created man in His own image, just as his father, his grandfather, and his great-grandfather had believed.

His son could go right ahead and say that human beings are descended from apes—that didn't prevent Mendel the Miller from calling him in after the Friday evening dinner, and, having tucked his shirt up over his head, grinning and teasing him:

"I don't know what the apes do, my son, but you're going to rub your papa's back with vinegar in honor of the Sabbath and obey the commandment to honor your parents! Well?!"

That was the way he did things, Mendel.

Once a week, half a glass of castor oil; and every week a backrub with vinegar. Not because he had any pains in his stomach or his ribs, but just for fun. For the sake of order and economy.

And when Ezra, his learned son, had given him a sound backrub with vinegar—and with a smile—the miller would turn around, content with his rubbed-down flesh and his warmed-up bones, and say in sheer delight:

"Rub, rub, Ezra. An ape, you say? Don't spare your hands, my son, right there, in the side, that's it! That's a fine summing-up of the world—a little on the spine, Ezra. So according to your accounts, Adam must have been—don't rub so hard—an ape? Ha? What's that you say, my Aristotle, an ape?"

As for his own descent, Mendel only had to look at the cemetery. There he saw a long line of generations from the shtetl back to the kingdom of David's dynasty. All the shtetl Jews saw their pedigrees in those old gravestones with rubbed-out stars of David and rubbed-off inscriptions, stones hunching over the grass that covered the graves, the rotten bones of forebears. And whenever Mendel walked out of town and unwillingly saw the slaughterhouses to the right of the cemetery, he would turn his head. He hated them, the wet, slippery crates with the damp smell of flayed carcass. He hated the butchers with their wanton sons, always striding about with rods in their hands, as though forever hunting someone to drive along. And he constantly felt as if one of them were about to sic an angry bull on him and shout from a distance:

"Watch it, Mendel, you're lost in thought!"

A good part of the road approaching these greasy, slippery slaughterhouses was scattered with rotting horns and hooves; green, paunchy flies and stray dogs were having the time of their lives.

Mendel also knew that to the left of the cemetery there was a teeming swarm of tanneries, yellow pits overflowing with frothy lye. It seemed to Mendel as if there were always a stifling yellow rainfall there. Deep pits with acrid smells of tannery fluids. And the pits were belching up yellow and green foam. Swollen, speckled hides were soaking in them, like hairy horse blankets.

Here, Mendel knew, Zalman the Trustee, that worried man, might come along, or a couple of dressers, or even the owner himself, Mr. Berman.

But the last person Mendel would have expected to run into was his son Ezra, the university student with the gold buttons, who had come home to visit for a few weeks.

When Mendel spotted Ezra in the distance with Beryl the Convict, he decided to walk on by as though he hadn't seen them. But he couldn't stand it, and he called to him across the road:

"Didn't you see, Ezra? They didn't come by train."

"What train?" answered Beryl the Convict.

Mendel didn't want to hear what Beryl had to say. He wanted to ask his Ezra:

Weren't there better places to take a walk outside of town? And couldn't he find any better friends in town?

But instead, he asked:

"Well, Ezra, didn't you see Mottl's horses either?"

And when Ezra shook his head from afar, Mendel turned back angrily, and all the way home he babbled to himself:

"Convicts . . . . Apes . . . . Fine friends he gets for himself! . . ."

And he didn't even notice that his annoyance quickly carried him back to town and deposited him at his house.

Entering his home after such an unexpected encounter with Ezra, he did not take off his coat; instead, he whirled around furiously. He combed all the corners, looking for something to let out his bitterness on and to give him an excuse for hurrying back.

First of all, he got up on a chair next to the clock and began turning the hands. He kept turning them until the clock started ringing with such a staccato groaning that Mendel himself got panicky and began shouting through the house:

"I'd like to know who's been fooling with my clock. Who's been turning the hands for entire days so that the clock stops every minute?"

"What's going on with the clock again?" His wife ran in from the kitchen. "What's wrong?"

"Quiet! Can't you hear me counting? Quiet! . . . Forty-five, forty-seven . . . . Shush! Shush! Just look, you can't say a word in this house! Her and that son of hers, you can't say anything to them! They attack you on the spot. For absolutely nothing!"

"What's wrong, Mendel? You're not all there today! What are you yelling about? Just look, look!—Down from the clock and on your son . . . ."

" 'Just look, look'!" Mendel mimicked her. "No one's allowed to say anything to them! The mother and the son! Next you'll be saying that people come from monkeys, ha? You won't say it?"

"What? Monkeys?" his wife broke in. "Ha? Did you say monkeys?"

"No, turkeys!"

"Mendel! What's come over you all of a sudden?" she asked, terrified.

"C'mon! Stop nagging me, Fradl, I didn't say anything! I didn't say anything about monkeys. So leave me alone! I just can't get a word in edgewise around here! They attack me on the spot!"

He left the clock ringing and ran out of the house. He didn't notice that he was moving towards the synagogue.

Opposite the high church with the blue dome, the little wooden synagogue looked as if it were wearing shingle rags and sinking into the earth. It stood there, stooping, hunched, its crooked back carrying the women's section with the tiny windows the way you carry a paralytic. Inside, the atmosphere was stale. It smelled of grease, of wax, of parchment, and of gingerbread and vodka.

Every Sabbath, Jewish grocers and shopkeepers and paupers came here with prayer books and prayer shawls to store up a meager bit of heaven and find out the latest news and edicts.

Between two lines of shops, a road ran through the entire shtetl until the railroad station. The marketplace was engraved in the road like an old, ravaged talisman. And Jews drove along this path to do business and walked along this path to synagogue and strode along this path to the station and traveled off to America. And they were carried back along this path to the cemetery, where gravestones with rubbed-off inscriptions guarded the rotten bones of forebears in their Jewish tribe.

There, in the graveyard, shtetl centuries lay open as in a chronicle of generations.

People were born, people died.

People wept at weddings, they wept at funerals, and they just wept for no special reason.

But when cholera was raging through the town, Mendel's father, old Hersh, had hired musicians to play in the streets. He hurried around, encouraging the band:

"Play, you guys! Play! Don't look to the side! Play! It's a remedy, Jews. It's good for the sick and it's bad for the devil. Play!"

The band marched through town, playing for the calamity. On one side—the musicians; on the other side—the black box. And thus the corpses were accompanied to the graveyard by musicians.

Now Ezra was walking down the same street. He went around

at night with a gang of young men, carrying a red flag in his bosom, and the townsfolk couldn't fall asleep because of the songs coming fearfully from behind the town wall.

And Jews openly said to Ezra's father:

"Mendel, your Ezra with his apes—he's going to bring a calamity to the town! You'll see, Mendel! Just remember, Mendel!"

Once, when a bullet thundered over the dome of the town church, the old dry-goods man, Sender, washed his hands and said a blessing.

But the next day, peasants from the surrounding countryside came running with sticks, crowbars, axes, and with the priest, and they yelled and crossed themselves:

"You goddamn Jews! Goddamn Jews are shooting at God!"

The constable was already visiting the Jewish shops and taking money from the shopkeepers. And after every coin that he counted in Mendel's home, he touched his saber and dully twisted his ears:

"It's going to slice! We're gonna slice your guts out, all you Jewboys!"

"Shooting?!"

At the constable's words, Mendel's throat went dry. He barely managed to whisper:

"It was thunder, Your Grace, thunder from the sky!"

Mendel's wife, Fradl, was weeping in the kitchen, and every so often she murmured into the other room:

"Mendel, give him some more, Mendel, give him some more and make him stop talking like that, Mendel!"

Mendel, counting out the silver rubles for the constable, kept glaring in her direction, saying in Yiddish:

"I'll talk to you later, Fradl, when the angel of death is gone. But leave me alone for now, Fradl, leave me be. Can't you see the angel of death is still here. Let me puke out my heart, Fradl. Leave me be!"

Ezra wasn't at home. He had gone to Beryl's at the crack of dawn and then to the gardens. Two men were waiting there. Mottl, the typesetter, and Levin, the dresser in Berman's tannery.

Ezra looked all around and then exclaimed:

463

"Beryl, you go on to work. You don't know from nothing. Running away would be worse. There's no place to hide. And it'll soon look suspicious. One man can drive off in the wagon. That'll be Mottl. I'll stay. You go to work. If they arrest us, then remember what we have to do, brothers. It's better to die than say even one word. Enough. Let's get going. Each man in a different direction."

They listened, intent and prepared. And as they left, only Beryl clenched his fist and said:

"Look, guys! Petro the Policeman is gonna leave the smithy with a red-hot poker in his mouth, but not with me, goddamn it!"

Beryl had always liked the work. He felt depressed when he had none. If they needed to poke out a burgher's eye or smash his rib, Beryl wouldn't let anyone else at him. He did it himself. And he would paste up leaflets in the most dangerous places.

"What's the big deal," he would tell his gang, "sticking up a leaflet in Berman's tannery? You have to stick one up on the constable's wall. In the chancellery. On his mailbox, so he can read it every morning. Goddamn it!" One for the constable and the other sewn in his cap. Now he was looking forward to meeting Petro the Policeman.

But Petro was already waiting in the home of Eli-Leyzer the Blacksmith.

And as soon as Beryl had rolled up his sleeves and stationed himself at the anvil, Petro crept up from behind with a gun and barked:

"Hands up!"

Turning his head, Beryl saw the black hole of a revolver up against his mouth and heard Petro's command:

"Well? Are you gonna come peacefully?"

And so, with his sleeves rolled up on his brawny arms, Beryl walked through the town, arriving at the cooler. Petro's pointed revolver showed him the way, and half the town ran up and followed at their heels.

It was a morning in early autumn. Shopkeepers stood by their shops, their hands tucked into their sleeves; and with warm vapor emerging from their mouths, they asked one another:

"Him! Really? Beryl? That motherfucker! And they said . . . .

464

You can't believe anybody." Beryl didn't see the town again for four years. By then, they had nicknamed him Beryl the Convict.

When he returned to town after four years of hard labor, he couldn't find any of the old gang. All he did find was his old cap in the attic. He ripped it open and pulled out a leaflet which he had sewn in before his departure. The leaflet had been awaiting him for four years. He pulled it out, gazed at it, gazed and then said:

"Literature!"

After four years of hard labor, he started calling leaflets "literature," the shtetl now depressed him more than hard labor had. He hung out with the dressers until Ezra came back to town. Ezra with the student buttons. And they got together at a secret meeting of the tanners. The meeting renewed Beryl's desire to paste up leaflets and beat up burghers.

Nevertheless, when Petro the Policeman had walked Beryl through town in his rolled-up sleeves, old Sender had peered through the window and shaken his beard:

"Let him live like that, the bastard, let him live like that—if he's the one! We know who shot at the church, don't we!?"

And the town dogcatcher was having a drink in Pearl's tavern, and he swore to the town that he would catch all the Jews on his hook.

"Like this!" he kept saying with a wave of his hands as though he had caught them on his instrument. "Like this! All of them! Like dogs!"

The shtetl was crisscrossed with ditches and drains. Time and events flowed away in them along with the rainwater. The ditches were spanned by small wooden bridges, almost like litter planks, like poor Jewish biers. The edges of the ditches were lined with brambles and tangly-bearded prickles. The squashed horizons around the shtetl were constantly astir with the muffled tumult of unfinished weddings, sobs at the seatings and veilings of brides, terminated quadrilles and other dances. There was always a smell of funerals, the echo of Mosikl the Gravedigger's cry: "Charity delivereth from death!" And no roosters crowed there. They always mourned someone from the crooked fences and perches.

465

From every roof, from every wall you could feel a misfortune that had already happened or was about to happen.

At the crack of dawn, burly slaughterers drove the heads to the slaughterhouse. The more elegant cattle turned up their noses, refusing to join the herd.

When the slaughterers trudged back with warm forequarters on their shoulders, Jews were already returning from synagogue, and tanners had already long been tanning in Berman's tannery. And the marketplace smelled of a riot caused by Vasil the Fireman, who had stolen a pack of tobacco from a poor shop. And Mendel the Miller was already at the station, waiting for a freight train.

That was how a day went.

In the evening, when Mendel came home, bristling with old Sender's pinpricks about today's kids, he strode over to his Ezra and circled him like a quiet, devoted animal, finally asking:

"Do you need anything at the station, huh, Ezra? I'm going early in the morning, I am. Don't you need anything, Ezra?"

He went to the station, poor Mendel. Went to the station every day. Trudging to the station, he had left Egypt forty-eight times in his life, wandered through the desert forty-eight times, and entered the land of his holy forebears just as often. And yet he remained at the station. In early years, his son Ezra, had joined him on these magnificent voyages when he was still very young. The little travel companion joined his father on these voyages until he went on one alone. His own voyage. All by himself. No longer in the desert. And certainly not to the land of his forebears. He went to a big town, where every stone cried out in poverty and hunger, throwing cripples and children out like cats.

Together with his father, he did the final reckoning of Pharaoh's Ten Plagues on his fingers and felt that the Plagues were raging somewhere near him, all around.

He saw them every day:

Yellow, rusty Jews with beards like rags. They smelled of lye even at a great distance. Their faces were withered and faded as though they had been struck by the hail of the Ten Plagues.

But Ezra already knew that this hail did not come from God—it came from Jonah Berman, the owner of the tanneries, where

Jews labored from early in the morning till late at night.

Jonah Berman's tanning factory with its lye pits gaped at the shtetl Jews with the same assurance as the graveyard:

"Sooner or later you'll come here!"

One spring, after Passover, when Ezra found out that his friend Beryl had been taken from heder and apprenticed to Eli-Leyzer the Blacksmith, he felt utterly dejected. It was as if Beryl would no longer be his friend. And he resented the fact that Beryl would be standing in Eli-Leyzer's smithy with the bellows, push up his sleeves, and hold fire in his hands, so that the entire shtetl would be scared of him. And every Sabbath, he would stroll out to the highway and do whatever he felt like.

"If he's a blacksmith, who's he gonna be afraid of?"

Ezra had said to his father at that time:

"Papa, how much longer do I have to go to heder? Why can't you take me out too?

"What?! Are you an orphan or something?!" his father promptly asked.

"But what about Beryl?"

"Take an example from Shloyme Senders. You can't compare yourself to Beryl! He knows what he has to already, he's a great scholar. But you've still got a bit to learn. You'll still have a chance to drive goats through the streets. Don't worry. There's time."

However, since they wouldn't send him there, he kept going to Eli-Leyzer's smithy to see Beryl.

Tears welled up in his eyes the first time he saw Beryl at the bellows.

There he stood, Beryl, pulling the wire on Eli-Leyzer's bellows. And every puff sent a crackling shower of sparks in all directions. And Beryl seemed to be holding his arm and his head in the midst of the shower of sparks. He had no fear whatsoever. He turned over the coals that were red on one side. He turned them over as if they were nuts, and not coals. And from puff to puff, they grew more and more luminous. And the fire became paler and whiter, and the iron rod, which Eli-Leyzer held in the long reddening pincers as in the long red bill of a crane—Ezra could almost feel the iron rod in his own hand, as it became softer and softer, melting like gold. Any minute now, Eli-Leyzer would yank

467

it out and start kneading it with a hammer. He would knead it like golden dough. He would twist it back and then twist it forth, until it got darker, and then he would thrust it back into the fire, and Beryl would keep on working the bellows.

If only he could bang the hammer just once, he thought to himself, just one single time!

Ezra couldn't stand it. He marched over to Beryl and murmured to him softly so that Eli-Leyzer couldn't hear:

"Beryl, here's a kopek, Beryl. Just let me pull on the bellows a little. C'mon, just one pull, Beryl!"

Ezra gave him a pleading stare, envious of the little bit of smoke on Beryl's nose, under his lip, and on his sides. Beryl looked like a real blacksmith, especially because of his smoky nose and upper lip. He swiftly pocketed the kopek, grabbed Ezra's hand, and together they quickly pulled the wire of the bellows until Ezra's father Mendel came along, saying in the distance:

"Eli-Leyzer, you could probably get along without my Ezra at your bellows, don't you think? There are enough blacksmiths in town without him."

And he signaled to Ezra:

"Come on home, sonny-boy, c'mon! You wanna become a blacksmith, God willing! You like some nice professions, thank the Lord! God willing, you'll end up as a ragamuffin! With God's help!"

Whenever Ezra walked past the smithy and caught sight of Beryl helping to shoe a horse, he could hear him from far away shouting self-importantly to the horse: "Foot! Foot!"

And when Beryl caught sight of Ezra, he started shouting even louder:

"Your foot, motherfucker, your foot!"

Ezra's head began to spin, he walked around the horse on one side, then the other. He peered under the horse's belly and saw Beryl holding nails in his mouth and stroking the horse's legs. Horseshoes were lying to the side. New ones. Fresh from being cooled in water. They were still blue, like the horse's eyes, the color of vaporous plums just off the tree. But there was nothing Ezra could do here. He walked and walked around and then had to go away.

468

The peasant glanced at him, and Ezra could hear the whistling of his whip in that glance alone.

If it weren't for the peasant, thought Ezra, he would have shouted, like Beryl, at the entire shtetl:

"Your foot, motherfucker, your foot!"

That year, the Red Sea parted for the last time for Ezra. Pharaoh's chariots went under for the last time, and so did Mendel's control over him. That year, after the high holidays, the fog that always hovered around the railroad station was torn open, and Ezra went far, far away. And Mendel still didn't get any further than the station. To the station every day, and back from the station every day.

Now he was standing next to his son, who was on a visit, and he asked Ezra:

"Do you need anything at the station, Ezra, huh? I'm going there early in the morning. Don't you need anything?"

And since Ezra had nothing for his father to take along to the station, Mendel came closer to his son and spoke softly to him with feigned regret:

"Nothing? Nothing at all?"

At the same time, he sneaked a sidelong glance at the skull that Ezra had brought back from the city and that was now perching on the table. He glanced at the skull to see where the teeth ended, and where the nose and eyes were; and, without raising his head, he blurted out, concealing his distrust:

"Well, what do you say? You say people are descended from apes? Huh? Well, okay, let it be apes!"

Ezra patted the miller on his back and burst into a loving grin:

"Oh, Papa, Papa!"

But Mendel the Miller looked at the walls that were hung with effigies of great tsaddiks and cried out to his son:

"Are you trying to tell me, Ezra, that Abraham came from a monkey? No? You're not saying it?"

And soon Mendel trudged off to the railroad station. The miller felt gloomy. He knew every single peasant hut along the way. Every single head of peasant cattle. He recognized the fettered horses scattered on both sides of the field. In their boredom, they were sticking their nostrils into the sparse grass, that was too lazy to grow. There were the slaughterhouses. There were the tanneries. And there was the cemetery.

And windmills waved at one another with their skinny, useless arms. They were plowing the air and plowing through the winds and plowing up the entire countryside. The fields were silent, and silent was the only road that sprawled crooked over the hunchbacked hills and the valleys. Silently, the road carried twelve looming league-posts with black and white stripes—silently it carried them together with Mendel the Miller from the shtetl to the railroad station. ❀

(Chapter One)

THE DRAFT

FISHEL BIMKO

In the springtime, right after Passover, with the first gentle rays of the summer sun, a new worry afflicts all the little Jewish towns: the draft. The gang of Jewish roustabouts starts in, rubbing out and crossing out the list of the draftees who have to report this year: talmudic mannikins, pale, puny adolescents, and the better class of artisans, who croak for genteel marriages (God help them if the draft is breathing down their necks). They, the gang of roustabouts, libertines, who tie on the community feedbag all year long—they join forces with the goyim early on: thieves, pickpockets, butcher scamps—they're needed as ornaments in families to scare off all the fine people; first of all, they're to milk their benefactors dry, and especially, they're supposed to protect the town, to keep it from being harmed, God forbid, by those goddamn peasants, those bastards, who hit town in the fall and can easily make a shambles of the place; and the roustabouts aren't offering their services for the love of Jews, to keep a Jewish shop intact—oh no, they don't give a shit—they're doing it out of hatred for their enemies, they want to smash a peasant's jaw so that he'll remember for the rest of his life:

THE DRAFT!

Right after Passover, when the lame goy from town hall had handed out all the cheery notices to all the young men who had to report for physicals this year, the homes of the soft, worn-out boys were visited by a new worry; the fathers got new creases in their foreheads and planned to get rabbinical advice as though

471

they were about to embark on a long voyage; and mothers began moaning, and talking with a Days of Awe intonation, trying to find, in between two words, an ancestral merit from under the ground, to redeem their sons from the goyim's hands. . . .

Berel the Lout, one of those roustabouts, who had gotten a notice but couldn't read it so well and wanted to know what they wanted from him, suddenly had an idea, he clapped his forehead: "Aha!" and, as proud as a pregnant peacock, he went off to Leyzer's tavern.

"Ah, Leyzer? . . . What did I tell you? . . . Did you forget? . . . Ah? . . ."

And after guzzling his fill, downing a few mugs of beer, he became extremely cheerful and, as was his habit, he launched into a half-drunken heart-to-heart talk with himself.

"Can you imagine! . . . Every year I thought: Now I'm up, now I'm up. . . . But they forgot all about me, they didn't want me. . . . Ha. . . . Ha. . . ."

In the evening, he went around to all the other draftees on the same list, boys near their reckoning, and he started encouraging them, reminding them what they had to do this year to get control of the town and become its real masters.

"Oh, those peasants, those goyim!" he screamed, with blood-shot eyes, clenching his fists. "We'll teach them to destroy the town . . . . Trying to be big cheeses . . . . I'll fix their wagon. . . ."

In the evening, around prayer time, he crashed into the synagogue and lumbered over to Avrom Makhels, a rich man, who had a dozen houses and mills, and who also had a good heart, and, most important of all, he had a kid who was going to get hitched this year, and so Berel said to him in a tearful voice:

He, Berel the Lout—if he had to go off and serve, he'd still be Berel the Lout; and if you're a good soldier, then the fire won't burn you anyway; you get a ribbon and sometimes two, and you don't have to worry about the liquor either, but the main thing, well, he didn't have the money to go away. . . .

And he swore:

He should only make it safe and sound, do his hitch in the service and come home safe and sound, and he was sure that

Avrom Makhels' boy would remain at home . . . . Avrom Makhels apparently caught the drift of his sermon and slipped him some money to make him hold his tongue, passed it to him secretly, so that no one could see, and he also assured him:

If things really got to that pass, then he'd make sure that Berel had everything he needed to go off: shirts, pants, buttons, brushes—anything a soldier needed he'd be sure to have for his knapsack, and even money, too, cold cash . . . .

So Berel left the synagogue, slurped down a few more steins of beer at the first tavern along the way, to make up for the sobering blast of the wind, and then he rolled down the street, dead-drunk, barely able to keep on his feet. As luck would have it, who should come along but a recruit, one of those soft adolescents, a mama's boy, newly married, a delicate thing, all skin and bones, pale and scrawny, and Berel the Lout smacked him on the shoulder with all his strength, and burst into uproarious laughter:

"Get a load of the soldier, one of the boys . . . . Hahahaha! . . . A soldier . . . . Hahahaha!"

And he began ordering him around:

"Leeeeeft—MARCH! DOUBLE TIME!"

The young man stood there bewildered. The first smack had sent the glasses zooming from his nose; but then he looked around and saw who it was, that mock brigand, and the fear of God left him, but he was so embarrassed in front of the people clustering around him that he turned as red as a young girl getting her first kiss. And to get rid of his harasser, he said:

"For God's sake, already, it's not the end of the world! . . . If you have to go, then you have to go. The law's the law—that's what the Talmud says!"

Berel the Lout got a kick out of the heroic soldier-boy, and threw his arms around him, hugging and kissing him . . . . The young man tried to struggle free, but Berel kept obstructing him with his big, burly, rocking body and waving his hands so close to the boy's face that he had to twist back his head to keep from getting a bop on the nose, and this chutzbah made Berel so furious that he screamed:

"What?! . . . You want Berel the Lout to suffer for you and all you stuck-up bastards, you pigs, who wear galoshes on your aristocratic feet even in the summer and who eat meat for dinner even on a plain Wednesday? . . ."

And he grabbed the boy's lapels and shook him for all he was worth, and when the young man saw that he was in for it, he writhed out of Berel's hands, scooted into a doorway, and vanished. . . .

Berel stood there alone, cursing. His anger gradually waned, but he still waved his arms drunkenly at the passersby, and with tears in his eyes, he poured out his heart to them:

He, Berel the Lout, was going off to serve in the army and—that would be the end of Berel, the town could already forget Berel, he was off to the war: shooting . . . stabbing . . . killing. . . .

And he burst out crying as though certain that: He was off to battle tomorrow, and would never come home again.

The summer slipped off unnoticed. Berel had stopped working right away, he loafed around, and women were right when they said: It was a miracle he didn't go crazy. But where did such a guy get food—his face showed no sign of hardship, God forbid.

And the answer:

He was a recruit; a recruit lives off the community. Avrom Makhels, Sholem Yankels, Borukh Moyshes, all such Jews with houses, sawmills, refineries—there were lots of them in town; and if they didn't have all that much money, stuffing their bellies—they all had sons facing the draft, and the quota had to be filled.

And he, Berel, knew what was happening with all these recruits: which of them had gone away and—where he had gone . . . and—what he had done there.

At first, he was alone; gradually, in the course of time, he started getting visitors; one of them, Shmuel the Beanpole, who had started to walk—actually, he had always walked, and on his legs he was as tall as Og, King of Bashan, a long drink of water—but he was walking now for other reasons; because of varicose veins on his calves. And for that reason, doctors supposedly once told him to wear rubber stockings, but Shmuel the Beanpole was no fop, he wouldn't let himself be talked into such rubbish.

So he and his father battled away. His father would tell him: "Listen, Shmuel, do what you're told!" And Shmuel: "Leave me alone!" Lately, just before induction, the "fop" had sobered up and gone about the thing on a grand scale, walking his legs off, hoping he'd flunk the physical.

Shmuel the Beanpole had gotten Berel as a partner; the two of them plodded and plodded along, but Berel couldn't understand why the Beanpole took him down back streets and deserted roads, until. . . . He caught him in the act, and with a cheerful smile, as was his wont—he slapped him on the back.

"You rat. You wanna stay home too? So who's gonna go? Reuben, the widow's boy, her only son, that shlemiel, so that the army'll trample on him like a worm?"

And someone else joined them in the course of time: Little Borekh. Everyone knew he'd get out of the draft. But no one minded, because they thought of him as the kid in the gang. And once Berel held him between his knees and teased him with the solicitous affection of a father:

"Well, Borekh, you've got a hernia on the right side, God should only do you a favor and give you one on the left side— then you'll be divinely privileged to wear a truss on both sides, so they'll kick you out of the army twice."

By early autumn, you can smell the Draft Board in the air; along with the Days of Awe mood, there's a special Draft Board mood. A cold wind blows, yellow leaves come pouring from the trees, chestnuts fall and splinter to pieces, and gangs of recruits march through the streets, they've already quit their jobs, and they go about with canes in their hands like holiday strollers, but without that feeling of good cheer in their hearts.

And if someone asks them:

"What's all this walking around gonna get you?"

They shrug, they frown half-gloomily, knitting their brows, as if to say:

"What can we do? We don't know whose turn it'll be tomorrow."

And in the synagogues, the little one-room hovels or the big houses of study, you can see a lot more young men, hanging around to say another prayer or two, even at twilight, and deep into the September night, which is longer than an ordinary summer night; some of them sit there, studying the holy words with profound ardor, chanting, rocking, swaying, bending creased and worried faces over open Talmuds, and looking as though they were pouring out their bitter hearts:

"These are such great days. Oh, Father, Father, and when else can we beg you: Please help us to stay at home!"

One boy, with burning black eyes—for a while he stopped chanting the holy words, though rocking on with his scrawny, God-fearing little face, with his curly earlocks bobbing over his cheeks; and a deep sigh tore loose from his skinny, hollow chest:

"Oh, Father, Father, do not cast me among the goyim. Do not let me be wrested away from the religion of my fathers, from the Torah. Help me, Father, help me, send me salvation."

Near the stove, plain, uneducated workers were sitting, almost abashed, and praying from the prayer books; they had stopped shaving, and their beards looked grimy, they frowned, they devoured the psalms, and one of them spoke in the silence like a woman reciting a prayer for the dead:

"We cannot study the Torah, but we are still your Jews; we keep the Sabbath, we know about the Days of Awe, look upon that as our merits; do not let us be scattered, do not let us eat non-kosher food, do not let us profane the Sabbath and the holidays, God forbid. . . ."

In those days, the younger generation split in two: One half, the soft pantywaists, who could be kneaded like clay figures— they went to synagogue to pray. And the other half, with Berel the Lout at their head, the roustabouts, they went to Leyzer's tavern. The crowd was made up of tough tailor lads, apprentices, who couldn't read or write, and who had always regarded the military as "bullshit."

"We'll get used to it soon enough . . . . Sewing tunics . . . making boots . . . baking bread—who cares? . . . And the three years'll be up before you know it. We'll bring back a few hundred rubles, we'll see the world, and that'll help us make a decent match. Thirty-six months—that's nothing . . . . So—live it up, boys, live it up like there's no tomorrow!"

Along came a policeman, they linked arms with him and took

him to Leyzer's tavern, and they drank him under the table. Then Berel the Lout put him on top of the table and asked him to dance a kazatska. The policeman could barely keep his eyes open, the booze started boiling inside him, and when the onlookers, all glassy-eyed, began whistling through their fingers, he thought: "It's Easter in the barracks, fellows! Bang those drums!" And he tucked in his coattails and launched into a jig. He kicked up his heels and wedged his hand into his ribs, and he danced. Rivers of sweat came pouring from his face, his hair stuck to his forehead, he turned as red as a lobster and—he kept on and on until he totally forgot that he was among Jewish recruits, that he was in Leyzer's tavern; he pulled out the naked sword from its sheath, waved it over their heads, and screamed in his hoarse, drunken throat:

"Hey, Jews . . . we're gonna slaughter all of you!"

The crowd was in an uproar; only Berel the Lout kept his head. He deftly and adroitly slipped the sword out of the policeman's hand and smashed his fist so hard into his gut that it boomed like a barrel.

"You goddamn pig, you shouldn't show yourself among human beings; go fuck yourself!"

The policeman—flying down to the floor like a child's ball and looking as though he'd guzzled down a whole glass of vodka at one swoop, started begging, pleading, weeping:

"No . . . . I swear— . . . . I didn't mean it. . . ."

The crowd was yelling and shouting and they wanted to settle his hash for him.

"Rip off his epaulettes!"

"Smash his sword!"

Only Berel the Lout took his part:

"Leave him alone, boys. We don't have to do anything to him."

He put him on his feet, wiped the sweat off his face with his handkerchief, and even defended him:

"What do you want from him? It ain't him, it's the liquor talkin'. He's got a good heart, the goy. Leave him be. He's got an old lady at home and seven brats. . . ."

The crowd was seized with pity for the policeman, they chipped in a few kopeks for attacking him, they tied them up in his shirt so he wouldn't lose them; Shmuel the Beanpole and Little Borekh started walking him out, they led him into the street respectfully and honorably, and after them came the entire crowd. . . .

Outside, they stopped to think:

"What are we gonna do with him?"

The crowd screamed:

"Throw him away!"

"Leave him in the street!"

Berel the Lout said: "The poor guy!"

Someone in the crowd yelled: "Shove it up his ass!"

And Berel: "He's got an old lady and seven brats at home."

Someone cried:

"Take him home!"

"Take him home!"

Little Borekh played a prank, he yelled into the man's ear with his womanish voice:

"Where d'ya live?"

The policeman shook his head a little and tried to stand up straight, the crowd laughed, roared . . . . Finally, they all hit the road, singing and whistling, the policeman flew into the air, he hovered aloft—when they came to the town limits, they halted, they looked around, they gaped.

"Where's his hat?"

The policeman was gone.

The escorts stood there and shrugged:

"Where the hell is he?"

"What'd ya do with him?" Berel shouted angrily.

Someone said:

"He must have given us the slip!"

The crowd laughed.

"Find him!" shouted Berel.

The crowd thundered:

"Fuck him!"

"Go to hell!"

"Find him!" Berel shouted angrily over their voices.

No one paid any attention; they all ran back to town and knocked on the windows of the wealthy boys:

"You sleepin'?"

"Get your ass outa bed!"

"Time to say your prayers!"

"Get to synagogue!"

And they stayed up all night, as though watching over a new-born baby-boy during the ritual night before its circumcision.

By the Days of Awe, all the recruits were at home. Thus, normally, they came home, not at any fixed time, but mostly for a holiday, and they managed to get back to town before Rosh Hashanah.

"C'mon: It's Rosh Hashanah! We'll go to synagogue too. We just have to . . . well . . . we have to have a look . . . find out what's happening . . . ."

And on Rosh Hashanah and Yom Kippur, they were all in synagogue. They held the little prayer books in their hands—but whether they were really praying wasn't all that certain . . . . The old men mumbled: "There's a draft board for them every year. If only they knew they were Jews and realized they have to pray. . . ."

And Berel the Lout very personally made an effort, and he stood in the antechamber of the synagogue throughout Yom Kippur with a ravenous stomach—he was fasting; at every "I have sinned," when he saw them beating their breasts, he beat his own breast too.

The morning after Yom Kippur, when the deadline of heavenly terrors was past, everything went back to its normal trot. They rousted through the streets all night long, yelling and screaming and getting drunk like it was going out of style.

Berel the Lout was his same old self. Wherever there was a trial, he was the judge; wherever there was a party or a funeral, he was the leader; and if he said it was day, then it was day . . . .

He was outraged at a few sons of rich families who had refused to pay him a ransom, and he swore: They would all have to go and serve with him in the same outfit; even if they bound up their heads and their ears, even if they crammed cotton into their shoes, and even if they didn't have a tooth to their names—it wouldn't help the motherfuckers a bit. . . .

479

On the Feast of the Torah, he and his whole gang went back to synagogue, all of them dead-drunk; Berel could barely crawl up to the reading platform, he clambered on all fours, banged his fist on the pulpit, and heaved into a long sermon:

Well, you see, since he and his whole gang were going to boot camp, and everyone knew about it—well, then they ought to be allowed to carry the Torah scrolls around the platform, as Jews always do on this feast, to celebrate the completed reading cycle of the year.

Well, what they had coming to them—they got! They were honored with the Torah scrolls, and the cantor started off with them around the platform, squealing in his squeaky voice: "He who helpeth the poor!" And the entire synagogue rolled in the aisles. . . .

The boys turned crimson, they were furious! It was humiliating! It wouldn't have taken much to make them throw away the Torah scrolls—with guys like that, you never know what's going to happen next . . . . And they might have beaten the shit out of the administrator and the cantor.

That night, they got even with the town for what had been done to them; they smashed all the tabernacles set up for the holiday, they tore off the wings and dragged them away with the walls and the red-fir branches and scattered them to the four winds. . . .❀

ACQUIRING A GRAVEYARD

AVROM REYZEN

The tiny Jewish town was isolated from the rest of the world. Only rare echoes came straying here from the cities or even the large towns. No one needed the little shtetl, and it needed no one. It got along all on its own. With potatoes from its own fields, flour from its own windmill, and meat from its own sheep. As for clothing, Leybe the Tailor was a genius at his trade, and he sewed for both women and men. True, the material was brought in from the city, but this was done by Yankel, who was practically the only storekeeper in town; once a year, he would travel to the state capital to buy various goods. But Yankel was a quiet man. You didn't have to hawk your wares in the shtetl. And he was so quiet about his trip that it almost seemed like a secret: Every year, he would vanish for two days with no sign of life, and when he came back, only a few people, not all, would find out where he'd been. The curious ones would pounce upon him:

"Yankel, what's happening out in the world?"

But Yankel had nothing to say. To his way of thinking, there was nothing to tell—everything was trivial! Once though, when they really cornered him and he felt he had to tell them something, he smirked, stroked his black beard, and replied:

"It's like, well, say—a hundred shtetls rolled into one. Altogether, it's a hundred times bigger than our little town, so how can you be surprised at the hubbub!"

And that was the only news that the townsfolk, Jews of course, ever received from the big world, once in a blue moon.

481

But while they never knew about real life (though they imagined they were having a fine time!), they also never knew about real death. Because of the tiny number of people, the "mortality rate" (as the statisticians phrase it) was generally very low, close to zero, and so the town had no graveyard of its own. The few old people there were diehards, they kept on living, on and on. The townsfolk even bore a grudge against Hendel the Bagel-baker, who was so old that no one could remember his age. People would count and count, always getting mixed up. And there was nothing you could do but start all over again! . . . Now one old man did finally get around to dying. But after thinking it over, he slipped off to Palestine. Once there, he actually died six months later, but it took the town any number of years to find out. Old Hendel was the one who told them. He broke the news with a smile, one weekday evening in synagogue:

"Didya hear about old Henekh? . . . He up and died!"

And the men simply couldn't understand, and decided this miracle was somehow connected with Palestine . . . . They were sure that if he hadn't left town, he would even have outlived old Hendel. On the other hand, they were jealous, for if you're buried in the Diaspora, the Angel of Death comes to your grave and pounds your corpse into dust and ashes, and Henekh, by coming to rest in the Holy Land, was spared this fate.

What with the old people so stubbornly refusing to die, it is quite understandable why a corpse was such a rarity in town! Now the middle-aged people were less stubborn, and every now and then, one of them, a man or a woman, would fall dangerously ill. But with no doctor around, the patient would be taken to the next town, which was slightly bigger, and there he would usually die, and be buried in the local cemetery.

And thus, the little shtetl had no graveyard of its own.

Strolling around on a Sabbath or a holiday, some of the philosophically inclined burghers would talk about the town's lack of a graveyard. And even on a weekday, someone or other would come out with:

"And what about a graveyard?"

Only the elderly people kept tactfully silent about this defect, but those who were in their middle years or even quite young harped on it, insisting it was a matter of life and death. . . .

The community bigwigs even called a town meeting, and this important issue was hotly debated. Old Hendel himself showed up at one session. He did most of the talking and pointed out that for now a graveyard was still unnecessary. There was no hurry. . . .

The younger people, who fully believed that there *is* such a thing as death in the world, and that a human being has to die sooner or later, were resolutely in favor of a graveyard. One of them, Chaim the Carpenter, even drew up a plan of the site and the layout. But, since nobody died for a long while after the meeting, people forgot about the graveyard issue.

And that was how things stood for years and years.

Till the war broke out.

Before the war was even officially declared, soldiers appeared in town, from our own emperor's army. Our own countrymen. Yankel the Storekeeper was certain he'd do good business: Soldiers, he had once heard, do a lot of buying. But these soldiers were of a different kidney. They did walk off with a lot of stuff, but they wouldn't pay, and you could argue with them till doomsday. So Yankel hit upon the idea of shutting down his store: Let them think it was a holiday! Whereupon they opened it up themselves and took the few left-over wares they needed. Then they went to Yankel:

"Who do you think you are closing your store to military men!"

And one of them stuck his rifle up against Yankel's chest.

Yankel was sure the soldier was joking, the man wouldn't actually go and shoot someone for such stuff and nonsense.

And Yankel's face lit up with a good-natured smile, as if to say:

"C'mon now! Would you shoot one of your own countrymen? Wait till the enemy comes! You'll have enough work on your hands then!"

But the soldier took the smile as an insult, and soon Yankel was lying stretched out in front of his store, wide-eyed and gaping, as if bowled over by the whole business! . . .

And so the little town found itself face to face with death.

Even Old Hendel now realized that a graveyard is an important matter, and that there is indeed such a thing as death.

483

A few days after that, the soldiers began searching for spies. Mottl the Butcher, who was bringing two oxen from a nearby village, was thought to be a provider for the enemy army. Forty-eight hours later, he was publicly hanged.

Next, the enemy army arrived. The battle took place behind the shtetl.

The shrapnel and the bullets flew over the shtetl like hail. The Jews took cover wherever they could.

But their hiding places were of little use. After three days of battle, the Jews had twelve casualties.

They could never have imagined so many corpses. Being new to such matters, they tried to awaken the bodies as though they were asleep. But none of them got up—they were dead.

Now the graveyard had at last become an urgent matter.

Even Old Hendel, who once again had managed to slip away from death, freely admitted:

"Yes, now we've got to have a graveyard! . . . This is just the right time! . . ."

But one of the younger men waved him off:

"The whole town's become a graveyard! . . ."

MONDAY

MOYSHE KULBAK

Mordecai Marcus as a Man

In the revolutionary town, there lived a teacher of Hebrew, a quiet man—Mordecai Marcus. He lived in a garret, all alone, and he often had time to sit up all night, poring over thick volumes, till the next morning. He would sit there, quietly thinking about the way of the world.

In a dark corner of his room, there was an old ramshackle sofa; he would lie on it all evening long, with a cigarette in his mouth, dreaming sleepily and brooding so hard that sometimes his head would start buzzing.

No one in town seemed to know him, and even his father forgot all about him, so that he could live quietly up in his garret, enjoying his meditations. But, as is known, he did have one friend, a woman—Miss Gnesye, who would often come up for a few hours, conversing genteelly in the quiet garret. And Mordecai Marcus, as is known, would tell her his deepest thoughts.

He opened himself up to her.

Miss Gnesye, a tall, thin woman, would quietly enter the garret and say "good evening" with a smile; and Mordecai Marcus would jump up and promptly take her to the table by the window, and their genteel conversation would promptly begin. Miss Gnesye would sit there, leaning on the table, with her umbrella in her hand, her feet in white stockings, she held her

485

shoes, with their very high heels, at an angle, the way a dog holds its tail, and she would listen and listen.

She was straight out of a book, Miss Gnesye was.

Mordecai Marcus enjoyed talking to her about all kinds of sublime things; but, remaining alone afterwards, he would get to thinking. And he was angry for talking too much. He stretched out on the sofa and he mused and mulled so long and so hard that you could have touched his thoughts with your hands.

And now Mordecai Marcus was happy.

He had a habit, Mordecai Marcus, remaining from his youth. On Monday, a simple day, he would sit down at the window, lean on his elbows, and stare into the street below, at the poor people begging from door to door, in accordance with Jewish custom, and he would observe them, the pale beggars, with a strange, dull trembling in his mind. That was the way you look at the priests in the temple when they perform the benediction. He watched people silently doing a sacred labor for which he was still inadequate.

"Pure poverty is an exaltation," he thought.

And Mordecai Marcus, peering down from his attic at the street, the revolutionary street, grew fond of the two little old ladies wrapped in shawls with knots in back, appearing every Monday and Thursday at the thresholds of houses; they were stooped, like short mushrooms cropping out of the soil. He peered after them, and there was something he didn't understand.

Something that was really quite clear to everyone else.

And Mordecai Marcus kept thinking.

Once, on an uneasy day for the town, he lay there, all snuggled up under an old coat, wool-gathering, when all at once he heard gunfire.

There were quick, orderly shots outside.

He walked over to the window, leaned out—there was no one there, but a head was slowly and cautiously jutting through a front door and peering down the length of the street. Mordecai Marcus asked the head:

"Sir, what is that shooting?"

"Who knows! They shot—and they're shooting."

So Mordecai Marcus closed the window and resolved not to go out for a good, long while—the attic would be peaceful.

And from then on, he sat in his garret, Mordecai Marcus did, he fixed tea by himself, drank it with bread, and peered into a book. But he always kept his little Bible open to the Book of Job, there on the table, he would thrust his thick eyes into it and beam with joy:

"They lifted up their eyes afar off and knew him not, so they lifted up their voices . . . and they rent every one his mantle, and they sprinkled ashes upon their heads towards heaven . . . . And they sat with him upon the ground. . . ."

And thus he lived up there in the garret, in peace and quiet joy—Mordecai Marcus.

THE GREAT BEAR AND THE REVOLUTION

That night, the Great Bear was looming in the sky.

The revolutionary town had been growing higher and deeper. The mass crowding the marketplace and the parade grounds moved further down into the side streets, as though a darkness were spreading its arms and legs.

The town was silent.

The meager starlight shone upon the mass of shoulders, disheveled beards of the porters' unions, thick moustaches of the metal-workers, and in the back somewhere between brick walls— the skinny needle-trade.

Flags waved in the pure hush.

And it stood there, the mass, concealed, in the heavy grip of the town streets, and it listened carefully.

A fresh frost passed through, empty and deserted, like the cold thought of the mass, which was thinking, bare and naked. Sheeplike whites of eyes gaped from their deep sockets, far, far into the night, with a secret amazement, and one man lived the life of the next, one pulse silently overflowed into the next pulse, whining from within, as from a buried cave.

487

A member of the Jewish Labor Alliance was wandering around, he had come late, and he was running every which way.

"Where's the Alliance comrades? Where's the Alliance?"

And he got lost in the darkness. And the Bear hovered aloft and with a cool silver thread he wove a pure silence over the darkness.

Mordecai Marcus was standing there, squeezed into his tight summer coat, his head tilted, watching the noble course of the stars, and he thought to himself that there was quiet and disquiet in the world.

And at the other end of the marketplace, far away, a voice yelled something.

The mass barely stirred, and suddenly it screamed, as though from beyond the tombstone; hearts turned over, and no one, no one, knew that it was here:

REVOLUTION!

The first thing that crept into the city was an armored car, rumbling about, cold and dark, a monstrous freak, bearing a red flag.

Riders in bast shoes came galloping on famished nags.

Chinese horsemen.

Shepherds arrived with rifles.

And up on the platform, where torches were blazing, stood a scraggy man with a black beard, he was pale in the night, and he quickly explained his revolutionary position.

The day was starting to dawn.

The rigid mass was exhaling a thin frost of daybreak. It gaped at the platform, where now a small clean-shaven speaker was standing, with large framed glasses. He stood there motionless, unstirring, and his blank voice spoke a command, which the mass instantly decided to obey.

A breeze fluttered through the wide banners over the square, revealing houses with posters of blazing cities. House by house. And in the gray twilight, the rectangular red everywhere disturbed the peace and the world, and it was terrifying, like spilled blood:

REVOLUTION!

Mordecai Marcus the revolutionary was swept along in the throng of his party. He slowly moved up the hilly street, stopped, gazed thoughtfully and absorbed the cold grayness of the strange dawning. Something very important was brooding in him, but he didn't know what.

In the distance, through the fog, he could see the mountain slope behind the town. A few workers with turned-up collars ran along the street, hurrying home. And down below, at the door of Dr. Bitshkovsky, the Jewish physician, a swaggering horseman sprang down from his mount, it was probably Bitshkovsky's son Misha, who had ridden back with the Red Army. Snatches of songs came wafting from the marketplace: Something was afoot there too, and yet there was something eerie about this little side street.

Mordecai Marcus walked faster. He hurried over the tiny bridge, which vacantly echoed his footsteps, and then he struck across the fields towards the mountain slope. Thick moustaches of metal-workers whisked past his eyes, like the freezing sparrows that fluttered slowly out of their nests.

And heavy, polished stars were shining low over his head.

He was sitting alone on the hill, leaning against a rock with his red hands, and he stared, silent and hidden. He was lost in thought. He had come a long way without a thought in his head. A darkness was pressing upon him, trying to dissolve. He stood up and suddenly it seemed to him as if this bowing hill had moved far out into a pure world, where there were no more people. His disembodied thought was floating around, he was absorbing the entire universe and staring, staring, not just with his eyes, but with the shining crystal of his soul. He was staring at the Great Bear in the sky.

And by the time Mordecai Marcus came down from the hill, the darkness had become clear to him, the hairy darkness that had woven into his soul.

There was something now that he understood.

With a light, buoyant step, he walked through the streets and

489

turned up towards the synagogue courtyard, where the charity hospital was located. It was dawn when he entered it, with a tiding that no one seemed to understand, but the poor people in the charity hospital welcomed him like an old friend.

That's how the story went afterwards.

He spent several days with these paupers, speaking to them feverishly and continuously, and they clustered around him. They listened to him for a long time, and no one answered. A peculiar thing, but it is known that Mordecai Marcus had no faith in mankind, he cursed society, and he bitterly ridiculed the Sabbath, while strongly praising Monday, the simple day, when the poor go begging from house to house.

JUDAH

The town came to a halt, like an unwound clock that has stopped ticking. A long, slanting rain was drizzling down, and the bloated clouds hung so thick along the buildings that they blotted out the sky.

A Jew was hugging a wall, and he was a sorry sight, he looked as if he would stand there for the rest of his life.

The burgher trudged around, utterly senile, with his trousers rolled up and his hat shoved down, waving his cane, waving his cane . . . . And the eye of the Revolutionary Committee glared at him, cautious and angry.

In these cool days, the crosses and high towers of the town were rigid, with a strange, naked indifference, and they claimed that everything was all the same to them, and no matter what happened—it would not surprise them.

On the telegraph wires across from the row of stores, a dead cat was hanging, head down, its fur fading in the rain, and none of the burghers was in the marketplace to take down the carcass.

From time to time, small detachments of gray soldiers marched through at a revolutionary pace down to their barracks.

● ● ●

490

One store was open. Judah, the scraggy grocer, was sitting in his store, with one sleeve tucked in the other, dozing, right by the porch. Inside, in the high flour-covered store, a heavy sack of oats was hunched over on a counter, and on the shelf stood a jar, encrusted with fly droppings and containing candy from before the war.

Judah's business had been going down, but he wasn't much of a hustler, and he just didn't care.

A little girl was running, running across the marketplace, barefoot, with a skinny braid, she ran right into his store and asked in a high-pitched voice:

"Gimme a kerenka's worth of candy, but no moldy stuff."

However, Judah wouldn't get up now.

Not when he had made up his mind to rest. He looked askance at the little girl. He scratched his head and told her to come back, maybe, maybe some other time.

But when the little girl insisted, he flared up:

"A little girl shouldn't eat candy . . . . It's a waste of money, it's no good for you, ugh!"

And he remained seated on his log, one sleeve tucked into the other; he thought about his bad habit of sitting in the store, and, half asleep, he felt as if the store had replaced his dead wife, who had passed away some thirty years ago.

The long drizzle gathering in the crumpled hat began running down his nose and his grimy beard, which was composed of several blond hairs.

He sat there, gazing drowsily at the town, which was blanketed in the heavy charge of clouds like a rectangular box without an exit, and silent people were walking about on long, emaciated legs.

He sat and he sat, Judah did, fast asleep.

The day waned.

The city waned, melancholy, into night, and Judah was still asleep. Along came a mutilated soldier, with only one ear, walking by like a beaten dog. He halted, stared at the shop-keeper, and spit into his collar.

Judah awoke, scratched himself, and went back to sleep.

And it was only late at night that he heard an uproar in the marketplace. A man with strong hands had grabbed hold of his lapels and was shaking him hard. He awoke. A bunch of men were standing in the darkness of the street. A pale young man, surrounded by soldiers, was staring at him, Judah, talking continuously and motioning at him.

"Who's he?" asked Judah.

"Your son Mordecai, God help us!"

"What's wrong?"

"Nothing. He's being taken to jail."

"What? C'mon, Mordecai, why are they taking you to jail?"

But Mordecai Marcus had already been marched away from the market square. Judah futilely gazed at the empty space where Mordecai had been standing. Judah's question was answered by a stranger, a Jew, who was terribly angry.

"You're a fool, you shopkeeper!"

The Jew spoke these words, spat, and stomped away. And the marketplace was silent again. Gray and deserted and Monday-like. Judah peered to see if anyone was coming, but not a living soul appeared in the marketplace.

It was only afterwards that a straw hat emerged from below, and then—an umbrella and a pair of white stockings and black shoes.

Miss Gnesye had run out in the middle of the night to see if she could do anything.

STESYE AND GNESYE

The two little old women that Mordecai Marcus had stared at through the window!

Two old women, whose job was to measure the ground of the cemetery with cotton thread for candle wicks, Stesye and Gnesye (another Gnesye), wrapped in shawls with knots in the back, their faces scrawny, with old, small elbows sticking out, and spectacles perching on their faces, the strings drawn back behind their ears.

492

Two psalm-readers, as gray as dogs, Stesye and Gnesye, who went begging from house to house every Monday.

Two old women, quietly sitting at the thresholds, cursing and blessing with their sunken mouths.

Stesye and Gnesye lived in the ablution chamber of the graveyard, peering through the tiny window day by day, watching a bird fly past or a grass haulm growing.

And at night, they slept: Stesye on the oven, Gnesye on the plank bed, covered with a fur and a cloth.

And they murmured in their sleep, lying there, lying there, like two wax candles.

And in the middle of the night, Stesye would sometimes awake. She rubbed the dry crevices, her eyes, and she asked:

"Gnesye, Gnesye! Are you asleep?"

Gnesye replied: "No. What about you, Stesye?"

"Me neither."

They climbed out of their beds, washed their hands, knotted on their shawls, and slowly took the death thread out of the box.

Then they opened the low, heavy door of the ablution chamber and went out into the grounds of the cemetery.

Stars were shining.

Stesye took one end of the thread and walked far ahead, and Gnesye held the ball of yarn behind her, unwinding and unwinding, and thus they measured the ground.

Thus they measured.

The white thread drew through the darkness, it rolled and blew into the wind, it rolled up into the air, longer and longer, until it had tied itself around all the crosses and the high towers of the town. It enmeshed the stars. And it spun, and wove, and enmeshed the whole town in a death thread.

THE SKINNY STORK

The next morning, in the hilly marketplace, which sloped downward, the two white stockings and the black high-

493

heeled shoes appeared, still reeling about and clattering, and the umbrella helped them along.

Miss Gnesye. She was looking for someone to intercede. She was going to old Dr. Bitshkovsky, a respectable "person" from the "past," an old friend of Marcus' (who was his daughter's tutor). Miss Gnesye made a racket.

An old servant opened the door, but since it was a personal matter, he asked her to be so good as to wait.

Miss Gnesye, clutching her umbrella, sat down angrily, opposite a wall with a sunset over a quiet lake; its name was "Sundown." In the inner rooms, a flute was playing, and people were laughing there.

Who could be laughing in the gray, dark rooms of the old doctor's house?

The flute-playing, however, came nearer, it was approaching the door. In he walked, the doctor himself, pot-bellied, myopic, with a short, red beard, he was blowing on his flute and rocking his head in time to the music. He walked over to Miss Gnesye:

"Can I help you?"

Miss Gnesye stood up:

"I am a good friend of Mr. Marcus'."

"Your fiancé?"

"No. Just a friend, Doctor. Excuse me for barging in on you like this, but something dreadful has happened. Mr. Marcus has been accused of agitation. They say he is the leader of the poor people in town!"

"Whose leader!" The doctor gaped into her face myopically.

"The poor people."

"Really?"

"Yes."

The doctor smiled broadly into his flute:

"Dear me! A tricky fellow!"

"We do sympathize with the Communist idea, Marcus and I. However, his weltanschauung does not permit him to accept the Party platform in toto. Where is Freedom of Speech? Equality? Fraternity?—The great shibboleth of the French Revolution, which quickened the spirits of all progressive men, beginning with Rousseau, Voltaire, and ending with the great Tolstoy, who,

494

in my opinion, is the most important artist of our time!"

"Very true. And so?"

But all at once, Miss Gnesye felt that it wasn't she speaking. She had actually meant to say something else. Something had spoken out of her involuntarily. She felt miserable, she blushed—and as a result she got totally confused:

"Read the *Divine Comedy*, written by the deft hand of the brilliant Italian. Read Calderon, Racine. Read the divine Shakespeare—the concept of liberty was the be-all and end-all of their creativity. Ah, it is only in the land of our Pushkin—"

"Are you through?" asked the doctor.

And Miss Gnesye broke off, almost in tears. And at that very moment, some hearty guffaws resounded from the next room. The doctor glared at her askance, but after taking a good look, he began calming her:

"It doesn't matter, you wanted to show off a bit . . . . It worked."

And he paced back and forth, pensive, and then opened the door for her into the inner rooms. She stepped into a shadowy dining room smelling of medicines; on the floor there were dusty pictures in heavy frames, leaning against the walls; drapes lined with embroidered fringes were drenched in dust.

Drawers hanging out.

Sheets of music scattered over the chairs.

Someone was standing, silent and hidden, near the small white stove—the mutilated soldier, the same soldier who would go over to Judah the grocer from time to time and spit into the sleeping man's collar. There was talk among the townspeople that Bitshkovsky's elder son had been affected mentally by the war.

The doctor's small, sickly daughter was sitting at the piano. She was absorbed in picking something out on the keys and didn't even look around when the others came in.

And Misha, Dr. Bitshkovsky's younger son, freshly washed and combed, in a gray military shirt, was sitting at the table, drinking coffee, and joking around with a young girl, round, buxom, with cropped black hair, she was half-lying on the couch, her feet tucked underneath her, and she was the one who was laughing and not listening.

495

The doctor presented Miss Gnesye, who was standing in the center of the room, bewildered, with red spots on her cheeks, not quite grasping whom she was supposed to address. The doctor was trying to help her and, with the flute in his hand, he communicated Miss Gnesye's request to Misha. Misha burst out laughing (not at Gnesye, not at Gnesye!). The doctor began slapping his back.

"My friend, my friend, Red jackasses are already sitting in your government offices, all of them the same." And he wheeled and strode over to the piano, where Lena was impatiently waiting for him. He smiled at her and, as though suddenly remembering, he quickly began gathering the sheet music scattered on the chairs.

They all looked at him in silence.

"Why don't we play 'Aase's Death,' Lena?"

Lena nodded, and the doctor stood absorbed by the side of the piano, as if Miss Gnesye simply weren't there. It wasn't long before he dropped his thick lashes over his eyes, stuck out his belly with the heavy chain dangling on it, and quietly and neatly blew a full scale on the long, white flute. He appeared to be very happy with the instrument.

Misha stood up, pulled his shirt out over the leather belt, and very quietly asked something, apparently addressing her, Miss Gnesye:

"And how did it happen so suddenly? He's such a quiet person, isn't he?"

She merely shrugged nervously.

"And where's he being held?"

Poor Miss Gnesye launched into another blue streak:

"With this case, one may fittingly say that, in our Russia, the treatment of the individual has, in its barbarity, outdone the dark Middle Ages, when the clergy with its sterile scholasticism controlled men's minds. Forgive me, my honored friend, but in its breadth of power, the dictatorship of the Communist Party has gone far beyond the times of the Roman Caesars."

"Stop it, he doesn't read books, stop it!" the doctor begged her, and the mutilated soldier, who had kept calm all the while, glowered at Miss Gnesye with turbid, bulging eyes. He walked off with broad strides, grumbled under his breath, spit, and left the room in a surly mood.

Miss Gnesye's pulse stopped, and Misha turned around, gazing after the soldier. He stared at the closed door for a long time, then he began entering the addresses she gave him in his memo book, and then he decided to see her to the door as quickly as possible; and she, ancient and helpless, Miss Gnesye, sat there, belaboring herself for acting like such a fool in front of others. All she really wanted to do was express her protest clearly and simply, and why did it have to come out so confused? Why?! And now they were playing "Aase's Death." Lena was hunched awkwardly over the keyboard. Miss Gnesye noticed immediately, and she thought to herself: "Yet no one's laughing."

The doctor was stroking his flute like velvet and, contrary to custom, he danced to each beat, with his face twisting into such awful grimaces that one felt like laughing. Yet his melody came out so pure and mellow and transparent. . . .

Alas, alas, tears were coming from her eyes. The music hurt her, hurt her, and Miss Gnesye wept.

She was weeping because it was obvious that a woman was dying in the song and didn't realize it. And no one told her. And now they could already hear that purified hush preceding death. . . .

Alas, alas. . . .

"What is death, Dr. Bitshkovsky? What is life?"

The doctor peered at her through a crack between his lids. Perhaps he had misheard her question, or else he was laughing at her again for trying to act refined. Ultimately, it was all the same to her. When one stands at the farthest edge, where the world ends and the holy crystal begins—all people are equal. She had gone away now, Aase, with an alder-wood cane in her hand, gone across the crystal fields, and suddenly the earth peeled away from her, like a shell.

She blended into the radiant purity, Aase.

And dying was not such a bad thing in this world.

————No one was visible in the white street. Miss Gnesye stepped off the porch. Chestnut trees had shot out their rosy candlesticks in the night, and they stiffened in the strong radiance. The sky was glowing blue, all soaked with sunlight. Miss

Gnesye, with her white and black legs, oh so silently reeled up the street.

But then she halted at the gate.

The mutilated soldier was standing there, lazy and foolish, as if for no particular reason, and he was staring at her. She felt a coldness under her skin, but she didn't look around as she stepped off the pavement. The soldier walked over to her, casually. All at once he grabbed her arms and pulled the bewildered woman into the yard. Miss Gnesye let out a cold, wild squawk like a duck.

She was all disheveled as he dragged her over to the nettle bushes in the corner of the yard. He began flogging and whipping her bared abdomen with the nettles.

The wrinkled, parchment-like body writhed dreadfully in his hands, and the legs, in old garters, kicked about desperately like the blades of a ship's propeller. A hoarse, wild howling shot from her chest as though she were having a fit.

The soldier, with foam on his mouth, tore off the nettles one by one and stuck the leaves to her body:

"You skinny stork! . . . You mangy mouse!

"You slimy toad!

"You smelly, stinking skunk! . . . You motherfuckin' bitch!"

The old doctor, all disheveled, came running out the back door. He saw the naked calves struggling out of the bushes, and, in total confusion, he grabbed at the windows and began pounding on the frames:

"Misha! Misha!"

The soldier let go, threw her into the bushes, and, guffawing and foaming, he whirled about and leaped over the fence. Misha came dashing out with a gun. He ran after the soldier, jumping over the fence. He fired. And again an irksome laughter echoed from the other side of the courtyard.

AN ENEMY! AN ENEMY!

The poor women Stesye and Gnesye had a dream towards the end of the night: They had been inducted into the army. They clambered down from their oven beds, terrified and naked, like featherless chickens, shaking their heads, and then they immediately began knotting and tying up their kerchiefs. They took hold of their canes and left the ablution chamber. The Jewish judge would interpret their dream for them.

Day was dawning.

Stars hung by the low, heavy door, they were so large that you could touch them with your hands.

Stesye and Gnesye sat down in the darkness on the threshold of the ablution chamber, their strength was gone, they tucked the shawls back from their old ears and listened hard, far away.

Somewhere, divisions of soldiers were actually marching, one-two, one-two. . . .

Behind the town, on the round hills, the enemy legionnaires had been stationed since dawn, black and gray, slender, edged with red ribbon.

Blue bullets were banging and pouring like rain from the clouds.

The enemy crept in from the mountains, strong waves ceaselessly flooding towards the town, drawn into the gullet of the streets.

Something turned underfoot.

From the door, where once a cautious head had appeared, dashed a gigantic Jew, with a rumpled, fiery beard: A man reeled off through the streets, flailing his arms like broken wings, and yelling darkly at the bolted shutters:

"Illumination! Jews, it's a pogrom! Illumination!"

All that could be heard was a weeping from inside the houses, but no one came out to him. He dashed away, his fiery beard fluttering, from one street to the next, as though the bullets weren't hitting him, and his dull shriek kept piercing, warning from afar:

"Illumination! Jews! Why are you silent?! Illumination!"

The Red horsemen came riding out, led by an old officer, snuffing around strangely in the air with his gray, thick moustache. All at once, they started galloping downhill, their heads jutting out from the horses, and the red and gray linings of their coats fluttered up in the wind.

"Goddamn you!"

A grenade sighed through the air and plopped into the river. It exploded and spluttered in the water like a rocket.

The small wooden bridge arose and its pieces flew over the fields.

Misha came flying past on a scraggy horse, stopped at the bridge, leaped across the water, and caught up with his Red division far beyond the stream, where the slender legioneers were already lying at the gates. The squadron broke through the enemy line, left it behind, and, wheeling to the left, the men galloped over the living plaited fences and dashed across the fields into the dusty mountains.

In town, the men were fighting on foot.

They lay in the entrances. Quietly rolling cigarettes. Quietly loading the rifles, shooting randomly into the streets, as if bored.

And all at once—

A dash of horses, dust, marching soldiers, and terrible gunfire. And suddenly, for an instant, another huge silence. It was fearful. A machine gun stitched the night, rattled like sand on tin.

There was action in the entrances. Quietly, a crucial matter was being handled, something that no one was meant to observe.

A revolver—a young, cocky fellow let out a bang, emptying himself like a toddler on a pot.

A hush.

The naked streets became empty and clean.

A mangy dog trotted through, with his tail between his legs, running, running, in one direction, driven from somewhere. A dull, full resounding crash came from far away, muffled as if in cotton, and a dull echo accompanied it through the town.

The windows rattled.

Men on foot, like a herd of cattle, clutching their rifles, in tandem, came running uphill, none of them injured. They poured over the marketplace, the rifles argued, curt and smoky and flaming, with the clatter of the gunlocks in the hands. And the machine gun, very near, very near, began rattling again. . . .

"Bourgeoisie! Bourgeoisie!"——— It stuck its watery head out of some attic, stuck it out over the town, it moved its eyelids heavily and gritted its teeth of American gold. And then drew its head, slowly, cautiously, back into the attic.

Machine guns were grinding, grinding, grinding,

The mutilated soldier came down from the porch, he listened hard, and then moved along the houses to the fields, from which the town could hear the grenades.

Revolvers barked like puppies.

And machine guns cautiously pecked, pecked, banged, and stitched in a familiar way, like sewing machines.

"Long live the Red Army!"

THE FIRST MOONLIT NIGHT

In the round mountains behind the town, new corpses were sprawling about, long bodies with bent knees and eyes bulging at the sky.

The mountains marveled coldly in the windless moonlight.

The tired light could be heard running over the cold victims in the silence.

The fields were dreaming, as if sanctified, in the pure stillness.

The mutilated soldier was walking through the mountains. He halted, a fat shadow, by the corpses, and turned them over, and the moonlight poured softly from his hands.

A snake slithered through the grass.

No rustle.

No stirring.

501

A hush.

A deeper hush.

A death thread wound into the sky, curled over the fields and forests, white and still. It spun, long, long, and wove around the dark corpses on the field like a cool strip of dew.

The mutilated soldier sat down heavily on the slope, hugged the mountain, and remained stuck to it, like a lizard on a rock.

MORDECAI MARCUS AS AN ARTIST

The rectangular piece of lead was now hanging by the side of the prison with a crisscross of iron bars. It was the only soft space in the walls, and eyes came upon it to rest from the darkness.

Mordecai Marcus sat on the plank bed with his legs hanging down, dangling underneath; he was thinking. The entire prison was thinking slowly: A quiet man is well off, living with pure Being in the world.

And Mordecai Marcus smiled with tears in his eyes at the somber happiness that had come to him unawaited from the cold, bare walls.

"Think no thoughts. Be still, like water, and you will enjoy clear Being."

He cautiously touched the cold walls, and smiled at the idea that they had left him here all alone with his body in these four walls.

A pureness ran through the blue window into the darkness of the prison, as from a fresh well. He absorbed the cool blueness and kept thinking, thinking: That had been a state of trance, the day he had spent with the beggars, preaching poverty to them. That was it, a state of trance, which would certainly never come back; and now, he, Mordecai Marcus, was just an ordinary Hebrew teacher again, stuck in jail for no reason:

"But why do I so dismally love those people? And why do I

desire to *be* like that, not the least bit active, the way the moon exists, though it doesn't *do* anything?

"Maybe there's another corner in the world where you can fall in accidentally, and you really do exist, but no one knows about it.

"We who never laugh: we who smile with tears in our eyes—when were we ever purified? And why do we have such good fortune for nothing? And why should we so profoundly enjoy sorrow, while some people go about languishing, trying to torment themselves but unable to do so. And they decay when they do nothing, don't they?"

He got off the bed and put the chair next to the table, which was chained to the wall, and climbed up on it. What was going on over there, on the other side?

The river flowed right next to the prison, blue, bluishly sad, like him, the Hebrew teacher. But further on, the countryside was glowing in the sun: The mountains around the town were smoking, they were covered with black-gray soldiers on foot and on horseback: Dust eddied over the roads. Wherever the earth had a rent, people tumbled over, rolled over in the quagmire with their faces up, and then in the mud, and they stayed like that. Dull thuds washed past like huge waves. The soldiers came down from the mountains in thick troops, vanished in the eddying dust on the roads, and it seemed as if they would never emerge.

Mordecai Marcus jumped down breathlessly from the table, absorbed in something that suddenly drifted before his eyes.

"Ah, people sit and torment themselves for years and years, and cannot fathom the secret of the world. They sit somewhere in the darkness, no one talking to anyone else, and they wait. All at once, someone comes and says:

" 'Listen, there's nothing for you to wait for. Listen, you saints, you've been saints all these years for nothing—nothing exists!' "

He was overjoyed at this, Mordecai Marcus.

"Now that's a tribute—and that's a reward for saintliness!"

And he ran to the bed with a warm writhing in his heart, and took out a notebook from the head of the cot, and a pencil dangled on a string from the notebook. He quickly sat down at the table:

503

"Nothing exists, you idlers, you who have waited so long!
"NOTHING EXISTS!"

And for years and years now, they've been sitting there, hidden, those ten old idlers in the little synagogue, sitting and listening in silence. The ten small shadows barely stir in the deep darkness. The sky is wedged in the tiny windows like a blue chunk of ice. It breathes coldly into the mountains and, terrified, it embraces their exhausted bodies.

Alas, it is hard to speak, and useless, for the tongues lie dry in the mouths like leaves of clay. Once, while dying, the silent one, Zachariah, promised he would come back from there and reveal what is reality in the worlds and what is illusion in the worlds. So they sit there, hairy and bearded, their heads sunken into their shoulders, and they wait for him, the somber messenger.

No one comes.

Stars shoot past the window—a sign that something *is* happening all around, and that the worlds are still in motion.

The little saintly men started shaking with enthusiasm, each in his corner, none looking at the others, each forcing himself not to speak a word. But Gimpel of Zhamut couldn't hold out, he began murmuring softly to himself:

"Ah, you can all see the error from the very first. Man was given the sense of vision. He can see the colors of the world, but he doesn't know where there is a God in the world. He was given the sense of hearing. He can hear sounds and harmonies around him, but he thinks that the world itself is a harmony. He has a sense of touch, he feels himself and he feels the world, he touches two worlds and has no conception of either. Now that he has all five senses, he can comprehend the secret of Creation differently. But is it the pure world? Is it? Isn't it an illusion?"

And the synagogue grew silent: the eternal light burned in its glass case, like a soul. They seemed to be in the pure world, where the outer shells had fallen away. But all at once, Shmaye of White Russia jumped out of his dark corner and, waving his fists, he shouted bitterly:

"Listen! I don't agree with the sharp minds, and I renounce my intelligence altogether. A child is born without a mind: What does it mean? It means that I am taking in with the mind in *this* world. How in the world can I use an instrument made of water to scoop up water?"

And Beryl of Luninetz, who was lying with his head against the pulpit and whose open chest glared with the paleness of a dying man—he also started to talk, singing to himself with closed eyes:

"Oh, I understand you, God, with my skin and with the tips of my fingers: Take me into your home and draw the soul from my life, pull it out like a splinter from flesh. Why in the world should I have a soul? Oh, God?"

And the synagogue was hushed again, all were peering with closed eyes. It was the hush that has no breath. But now, Avrom the Faster stole out from behind the stove, barefoot, sleepy, his unbuttoned coat revealing his bare skin. Coming to Beryl, he halted and stared at his languishing face, his head against the pulpit, his pale nose bright in the darkness. Avrom smirked into his filthy goat's beard, and scratching himself with relish, he said:

"Beryl, I won't do anything in this world. After all, trees blossom without doing anything. Children grow without doing anything. I'll sing like a bird, and I'll feel good. I'll eat like a crow, and I'll be full. Provide for me like the dog and the raven, oh, dear God! I feel fine with a coat, and even finer without one. I feel fine with a woman, and really fine without one! Oh dear God! Dear God!"

And thus, bareskinned, he strode through the dark synagogue, rubbing his hands in joy and tearfully singing his hymn of praise to the world. He walked through the door and listened for the coming of the man who would put an end to all doubts. The anteroom was filled with a dreadful hush. Avrom held his tongue and stole back behind the stove. In the darkness they could hear someone weeping bitterly in his corner. Someone had realized all at once that the torment of the cold worlds had washed up to the last shore of the soul and that no answer exists. A lectern crashed upon the floor. Gimpel of Zhamut stood up trembling; his heart was full of madness, he flung out his arms.

"I tell you, all of you, that I will soon curse God!"

No one moved. The eyes, turned inward, were silent. Each man, petrified, lay in his darkness, wherever he was. Gimpel sat down, fainting, powerless to do anything, but still haunted by the yearning: "Oh dear God! We cannot wait any longer."

And then came a soft knock at the door. Barely audible. No one moved. The knocking went on. They sat breathlessly staring at the door.

"Open up!"

And all at once, they leaped from their corners, ran breathlessly to the entrance. The eternal light flickered in its alcove. They clustered together, staring, staring. Hush! Slowly the door opened, the heavy door. Zachariah came in, covered with snow, wearing a long fur coat, with a rope around his hips. Holding a lantern in his hands, he turned his cold eyes upon the holy men.

Zachariah remained silent.

And Avrom the Faster, who stood closest to him, began tugging at his sleeve:

"Well, Zachariah?"

And Zachariah replied:

"I have come to tell you, brethren that *nothing exists.*"

"What?"

"Nothing exists there. No one came to meet me, neither God nor anyone with a view of God. I went across the waste fields from one world to the next. I did not find anyone. Everything is waste and wild. Brethren, I tell you, the living are far better off than the dead."

. . . They asked no more. Each man returned silently to his place, his dark corner. There he packed his things together and softly stole out from the synagogue.

And they never saw one another again, the ten shamefaced holy men.

He felt better, as though a heavy, troublesome darkness had trickled out of his soul. He stood in the middle of the room, with his eyes shut, listening to what was happening inside himself. It was as if someone had stirred up a nest that should have been forgotten; and beyond the door, the stiff, hard tread of the sentry echoed through the air.

It seemed to be late at night.

Overhead, off to the side, the pensive moon poured through

the rectangular stretch of blue, like a soft, quiet chant from another world. The prisoner climbed onto the table, stood up, and peered through the window:

The distant mountains loomed astonished in the windless light of the moon. Corpses with folded knees were scattered across the mountains, and someone was walking through the mountains, pulling the bodies over and trampling on them.

Mordecai Marcus turned away, gingerly climbed down, and stretched out on the plank bed, lost in thought. His head lay back, and he began to ponder, as is customary, as was customary with him.

And after long weeks, a few people came into his cell, acting friendly. They liked him. And Mordecai Marcus picked up his bundle and walked out. He halted in the bare, dim passageway. He actually had nothing to do in town, and he turned to his judge, the kind, pudgy student:

"I couldn't stay in prison voluntarily?"

"Oh, no!"

"No?"

And at the door, he turned to the judge once more with the face of a doomed man. He held out his soft, white, pudgy hand and said with a smile:

"You understand, I was in a state of trance, I'm certain it won't come back. But once again I can sense that they will come to me, they will *have* to come to me, the poor. Do you understand?"

It was a bit too hard to understand.

THE MASS

Out soared a gray bird, it pulled low several times over the fields and let out a dark squawk. Then it took off again clumsily, not towards the sky, but far, far across the meadows to the edge of the turbid plain. The thin, twisting river suddenly

507

became hard and blue; a storm was coming. A long, brown cloud crept out from the side, and with hot, hanging tatters it slowly drifted across the scraggy trees. Suddenly a wind swept through the countryside. It tore back the branches of the oaks, and it pounced upon the young alders, twisting and bending them to the earth. The cloud, hot and disheveled, began to embrace everything. It emitted charged pieces, that drifted down and clung to the bushes, the ditches, and the holes in the riverbanks. A sharp, jagged flash of lightning cracked forth. The forest in back gaped open for an instant with a wet fearful gullet that was stuffed with old leaves, moss, and fallen trees. A peal of thunder crashed into it, and the gullet closed. Then the broad thunder was bound and carried off on a heavy wagon. Thick drops started springing and banging on the leaves. And it began. . . .

The proletariat tightened its belt around its belly, and at eight o'clock it went to the municipal theater. It came in a mass. Its waves filled the orchestra, the balconies, and the gallery, until the entire auditorium smelled of boots, bodies, and fur. And the proletariat got ready to listen and listen.

All that could be seen on stage, between bright, heavy curtains and red tables, was a sparkling silver bell, just a bell.

And the depth of the theater was dark.

The proletariat heavily shifted its thousand heads, scattered above and below, and it whispered heavily, heavily, like a wind soughing through trees.

And behold, the skinny burgher also came in. As quietly as grass, he slipped into a corner, from where his hobnail eyes blinked into the darkness. And someone else came into the throng, the tall, black-bearded Jew, who had once been glued to a wall, a pitiful sight, for he had looked as if he would stand there for the rest of his life. And the crowd became still in the darkness.

Mass came into being.

It peered cautiously, the mass, with its myriad eyes, someone might want to harm it, injure it. It writhed with its men in the corridors of the municipal theater, and its arms, long and hairy and trembling, were tensed against the barriers. The black-bearded Jew was sitting somewhere, pale, his knees quaking, like someone who suddenly feels death. But he couldn't stir a limb in the darkness here.

Hush and hush.

The mass, for some reason, felt sorry for itself, sweetly sorry. It wanted to weep for its sorrows. And heads bent down. And some had tears in their eyes. But the mass unexpectedly felt deeply happy, and gave vent to its happiness high up in the gallery, laughing and laughing.

"Hey you, comrade! . . . What's so funny?"

The mass flared up, it stamped its feet. Its eyes filled with bloodthirsty madness. It had been tricked, and now it wanted revenge. The whites of eyes glared, like jewels flashing back and forth in the dark. But. But it quickly calmed down, the mass. It instantly smiled a foolish smile, like a moron who understands nothing.

Comrades clambered on the stage. The mass glared and glowered at comrades in leather jackets, in boots, and with beards. Misha, wearing his full cavalry uniform, sat down right by the bell. He gazed nervously at the others, who were slowly sitting down on the tables, the benches, crossing their legs, and with cold smiles on their lips, they sent piercing glances into the darkness, where it, the mass, was sitting. And the auditorium became more and more quiet, more and more nervous.

Misha got up, straight and stiff, with a wanly lit face bending towards it, the mass, and he began. He spoke to it:

"You, mass. . . ."

He spoke in a staccato tone, the words rattling out like pieces of steel. Like gunshots. The mass lapped it up. It lowered its myriad shock of hair. And it sat there, the mass, like a sheep.

Ah, all at once it had respect for him. He might lose his temper, Misha. And Misha did lose his temper, but not at the dark, cryptic, toiling mass. He exhorted it:

"You are exhorted, mass! . . ."

And it listened with all its hard, hairy ears. Encoiled, like worms in bark. He screamed, the peasant who had come to town for the council of deputies; but the mass gulped him in, and he vanished in its darkness. Low foreheads dripped sweat into eyes; eyes crept about like glowworms in a forest.

509

Misha stopped talking. Suddenly. He sat down again. The mass roared out, dull and all around, as though the shouts were coming from the walls. The mass roared from all its mouths, and its hands tangled together below, ceaselessly, and its joy burst and echoed from the darkness:

"Revolution! Revolution!"

And hush.

Then he walked over to the table with measured steps, the short man, the speaker with the large, rimmed glasses. Once, at night, he had powerfully commanded the mass on the parade grounds. Comrade R. He halted cold, lifted his clean-shaven face, and crossed his arms on his chest. Comrade R. waited. His heavy eyeballs peered through his glasses like blue ice. He waited, and a thin, fine coldness passed through the dark. The mass fell silent, panting.

"Comrade, hear your answer to the bourgeoisie."

And he paused.

"Comrade, you say: 'I stand with a knife in my hand, and you stand with a knife in your hand. This is class struggle! Yet you are shoulder meat and I am hindquarter meat. But look, mine will win. Bourgeoisie, you skulk around and around like a thief in the night, and I come to confront you, I stand against you! Strike! You refuse. Why do you refuse?

" 'Look. You have soft hands, and mine are hard and hairy; that's why your head is bald and mine is covered with hair. You are a general and I am a common soldier. You go to war and I die. You love and I am jealous. You eat and I pay. I refuse! This is class struggle. I stand with a knife in my hand and you stand with a knife in your hand.' "

And he stopped, fell silent, turned into rock, and he merely stood there. The darkness looked like a damp cave in which someone was writing in phosphorous letters, writing something that had to be immortalized. The space was suffocating. Fists clenched in laps, like stones, blood was filled with a dark boiling. Because someone with long, blue fingers was seeking and choking the thousand hairy throats of the mass. And it ground its numb teeth and remained silent.

"You say: 'Who are you, bourgeoisie, what makes you think

you are my equal? I found the rivers. I built the cities. I put up factories. I laid roads. I spanned bridges. I sent out trains. I sailed the oceans. I dug in the earth. I plowed, planted, sowed, weeded. And you? Who are you? What makes you think you are my equal? Just look: What I built, you guarded. What I brought, you collected. What I labored for, you took. I refuse! This is class struggle! I stand with a knife in my hand and you stand with a knife in your hand.' "

And then, from among the seats, a hard, heavy hand calmly arose, there, where the scrawny, black-bearded Jew was sitting. No one saw it. It carefully grabbed his long neck from behind and pressed him down, slowly, slowly, under the chairs. There, little by little, scarcely noticeable, it gripped his neck and throat, pressing his nose to the floor. And the eyes of the mass hung on the bright stage. The Jew thrust out his tongue, which was as hard as a board. His sticklike legs sprawled out under the chairs. The hand calmly pulled back again. It lay heavily on the barrier, trembling slightly.

" 'The mass! Who went out into the desert and erected the pyramids? Who drained the swamps of Babylon? Whom did Hannibal lead to Rome? Who built London? Paris? Berlin? Moscow? Who marched with Napoleon to conquer the world? Who fenced-in Russia? Who pounded out her roads? Who caressed her, the dear mother? I! And now I refuse! This is class struggle! I stand with a knife in my hand and you stand with a knife in your hand!' "

And he stepped down with his cold, measured little paces. And the auditorium was hushed, like a well.

GUESTS, CONVERSATIONS, WEEPING, ETC.

Mordecai Marcus sat at the garret window as quiet as a dove. Mordecai Marcus sat there, leaning on his elbow, and not thinking. The thoughts he had suddenly had months ago, like couriers from his soul, announcing that something had hap-

511

pened to his soul, they had not been detained. And now his soul would have to come forth itself. But there was only stillness inside him. Stillness as in a house from which the tenants had moved long ago.

"Oh, what is it?"

He felt drowsy. He paused here, where apparently he had to gather himself and get across as mightily as he could; otherwise he, Mordecai Marcus, would perish.

"And what's happening out in the world?" asked Mordecai Marcus drowsily.

"Probably nothing."

"Certainly."

He looked around.

Out on the stairs, someone was laughing loud and playfully. The old wooden steps groaned under feet that appeared to be taking several at a time. Mordecai Marcus stood up. The door banged open, and in dashed the young girl, the plump, buxom girl who had been in the Bitshkovsky house when Miss Gnesye had been visiting. She held a bouquet of lilacs. Misha came in after her, calm and smiling. And Mordecai Marcus stood in the middle of the room, embarrassed and confused, glancing around the tiny space, which looked like a spider web waiting for flies. He was smiling. The laughing girl ran over and held out her soft small hand:

"My name is Sonia. I've heard a lot about you. . . ."

She gave him a friendly nudge, and then ran gracefully to the tiny windows, opened them, and puffed the dust away from the frames:

"Do you have a pitcher? A small pitcher?"

He smiled. He shrugged his shoulders.

She found a clay cup in a corner, filled it with water from the pail, put in the bouquet, and placed the cup with the dark-blooded lilacs on the table.

Misha examined the garret, walked through it, and was happy at seeing Marcus confused by the visit. He walked over to the table, where a book was lying, and he bent over it:

"Job? Aha, the Book of Job?!" he turned to Marcus.

"Yes," said Marcus, puzzled.

And Misha brought the small Bible closer to his face. He started testing his earlier knowledge of Hebrew.

"Hmm . . . . 'They lifted up their eyes afar off and knew him not, so they lifted up their voices and wept; and they rent each one his mantle, and sprinkled ashes upon their heads toward heaven. So they sat down with him upon the ground seven days and seven nights, and none spake a word unto him, for they saw that his grief was very great . . . .' You see! I still haven't forgotten it!"

And Sonia burst out laughing.

"But . . . but there's a revolution taking place in the world!"

"Fine. They say there's a revolution."

" 'They say!' What do you mean: 'They say!' And you don't know?"

Misha stared at him with his strong, black eyes.

Marcus reddened slightly. He didn't answer. Sonia, who had already cleaned up the entire room, came over and sat down on Misha's lap. She hugged him, rocked on his knees, and then asked Marcus softly and coyly:

"Were you ever in love, Marcus?"

He looked up at her earnestly and replied:

"No."

"Never at all?"

"No."

"Then I'll take back the lilacs. . . ."

She sprang up with a laugh, danced through the room, and went over to the window, not the lilacs. She gazed out at the two narrow little streets that crossed down below.

"I don't know, Misha. I don't understand anything." Marcus was getting excited. "I'm absolutely not interested. I'll try to wait and see what happens. I feel that I'm altogether out of place here. I'll see. Why should I take your position, which is alien to me?"

And they fell silent.

Suddenly, he seemed to change, and he moved over to Misha:

"You know what? I like it this way. I like someone who lies by the stove and doesn't do anything and doesn't need anything. Did you feel sorry for me when you found me in this garret? You thought to yourself: 'A lonely man, this Marcus.' But. . . . But I like it. You have no idea how much I like it. Well . . . this gloominess, for which I'm always right. And perhaps people even ought to envy me, Misha, because I'm the happiest man in town. You smile?"

"No. I'm not smiling."

"The bourgeoisie can have all my property. So can the proletariat. What do I have from my property? You don't know how good it is to be poor and go begging from house to house."

Both remained silent.

"When I was a little boy, I remember following the beggars. I was delighted by the linen bags, the tattered coats, and I thought: 'When I grow up, I'll definitely go begging from house to house.' You know?! Because a poor man doesn't make such an issue of mankind. He doesn't care whether there are any people in the world."

"Well? And how will it end?"

"You mean suicide? No. A thousand times no. How can you think such a thing? I love life with every fiber of my body. I love the world, just like a calf. And that's why I don't need anything. That's why I'm never late. And that's why I sit here in this room, brooding over myself, as though I were brooding over a rare vase, to keep it from breaking."

Sonia called from the window, randomly:

"But you said you didn't love anyone."

Mordecai turned to her. She was leaning out into the street, dangling her legs at him. Mordecai Marcus calmly stood up. He calmly walked over to the bookshelf. There, he took down a dusty religious book bound in black, he opened it and began to read with his big, myopic eyes. Sonia gazed at him in strange curiosity.

" ' "Behold, thy mother and thy brethren are standing outside and they wish to speak with thee." He, however, answered the man who had spoken to him: "Who is my mother and who are my brethren?" And he pointed to his disciples and said: "These are my mother and my brethren." ' But you know," Marcus went on, speaking to both visitors, "you know, he made a mistake.

514

There exists a great love for existence, for the world, a cruel love that shatters man. And the man who comes upon it unexpectedly—he cannot love anyone."

"You're peculiar people," said Misha. "You talk, and I understand nothing. You yourself think you're the happiest man. You want to go begging and you can't. My father is happy too. He has a flute. At night he sits in his underwear and plays by candlelight until dawn . . . . I don't understand what's happening with you people . . . . You spoke to me, Marcus, and I didn't understand."

"And you, what do you say?" asked Marcus, embarrassed.

"Me?"

"Yes."

"I never thought about saying anything . . . . I act. I clean the horse. I receive orders, I obey." He turned away.

"Misha? Hey, Misha?"

Someone was yelling up to the window. Sonia hurried over and peered down into the street. Lena had arrived with that short man, Comrade R. In his soft hat and horn-rimmed glasses, he stood there, hunched, morose, smoking an English pipe, and he craned his long neck towards the garret.

"Oh, Comrade R."

Misha strode over to the window. Laughing, he invited him up. Told him how to reach the garret. Comrade R. smiled and started up, showing Lena the way.

And with tiny, very rigid steps, he entered the garret, and his cold blue eyeballs peered over the glasses at Marcus:

"A comrade?"

He held out his hand to Marcus.

"No."

"Who?"

"My friend. A counterrevolutionary, no less."

"Well?"

Comrade R. sat down at the table with the pipe in his mouth.

"This counterrevolutionary has spoken his piece, and now he's asking what we have to say. Our 'metaphysics.' " Misha was half joking.

"Hm . . . . Can I have a glass of water?"

515

Sonia brought him a glass of water. He drained it at one swallow, peered curiously around the room, and stood up.

"Well, shall we go?"

And Marcus felt too big for the room. He wandered clumsily among them, and they appeared to be saying good-bye. Comrade R. halted before him, eyed him up and down, and offered him a thin, hard, long hand:

"And we, comrade, are merely . . . merely revolutionaries. . . ."

He took a very, very friendly leave. Mordecai Marcus remained behind the door, his feelings astir. Without realizing it, he ambled around the room several times. And, confused and pondering, he stopped at the table.

Slowly he bent over and lowered his head into the bloody lilacs. Suddenly, he burst out crying. He felt empty and gloomy. He didn't know what to do next. It made no sense to hang around here aimlessly. And, unaware of what he was doing, he walked over to the wall and lit the tiny, smoky lamp that perched on the shelf, gray and covered with spider webs.

Outside, the dusk was thickening into night.

Mordecai opened the Book of Job. With his other hand, he picked up the lamp and, taking soft, cautious steps, he left the room.

His face was wet with tears and very pale. It was as though he were going to lament the destruction of the world.

The dark, narrow street lay empty and naked.

He stepped off the sidewalk, held the lamp aloft, and in a hoarse voice he tearfully began reciting from Job.

At first he felt alarmed at what he was doing, but all at once he felt strength coming from somewhere, and he strode along, chanting and lamenting. He threw back his head, stretched out his arms to heaven with his smoky lamp, and wept bitterly.

People appeared in the doorways—they thought it was a funeral.

Terrified faces peered from the windows, shouts rang out, and people followed, not understanding what was happening. People followed him.

516

Street after street.

And, till late at night, he wandered about, like a sleepwalker through the town.

In the morning, Miss Gnesye brought him to his garret, he was half-conscious, more dead than alive. Silent. She sat with him throughout the day, talking to him, trying all she could to get him awake, and he lay on the little sofa, cold, staring at her with motionless eyes, never saying a word.'

MONDAY

"Oh . . . oh . . . !"

It was Monday, the ordinary day, when the poor go begging from house to house. This time, they went out in hordes through the revolutionary town. The Jew with the fiery beard, the one who had marched through town in the time of danger, shouting "Illumination!", now strode at their head, carrying a huge bag on his shoulders and a birch staff in his hand. He looked like Moses leading the Jews out of Egypt.

They crowded through the narrow little streets, in between the dark, skew houses with the twisted cornices. Through the heavy gates, they crept into the courtyards, sticking out long, spindly arms to the windows:

"Give us alms, give us alms!"

And slices of bread came tumbling down, tattered shoes, patchwork clothes, even though no one was at the windows up there. In the foggy streets, the hunchbacks hovered and loomed through prayer-worn coats. Craning necks were bound with blue veins and scab behind caps that were tugged down over eyes.

Avrom the Faster, barefoot, with his coat on his filthy naked body, splayed his arms and legs, like a spider under a roof, and Stesye and Gnesye, wrapped up in their shawls with the large knots in back, plodded after him, clutching the elderwood sticks, and chewing or praying with their toothless mouths.

These hordes crept out into the empty marketplace, they

halted at a yellow building, stretching their arms towards a high balcony, and the women screamed:

"Commissar! Revolutionary Commissar! Food!!"

And the balcony, lined with little flowers, blossomed before their hot, dirty eyes like a garden plot, but it was quiet up there, and no one responded.

"Commissar! Food! Otherwise we'll starve to death!"

And then Sonia appeared at the window. Laughing, she threw down a crumpled wad of paper right into Stesye's kerchief. The beggars knelt. The beggars thanked their benefactress, turned around, and trudged on. The Jew with the fiery beard kept marching, and the hordes cheerfully ran and hobbled after him. Oh, holy Monday! Avrom tearfully burst into song, he flung out his hairy arms and sprang about like a goat:

Oh God, oh God,
I don't want to do anything in the world.
The trees blossom without doing anything.
The children grow without doing anything.
I'll sing like a bird, and I'll feel good,
I'll eat like a raven, and be full.
Provide for me, oh God, as you provide for the dog and the raven!
I feel fine with a coat,
And even better without one.
I feel fine with a woman
And even better without one. . . .
Oh God, oh God!

And the beggars wrung their hands on their shoulders, thrust out their humps, and hopped about, laughing and weeping. And they shone with the deep, dismal joy of the world. Their fiery tangled beards were blazing, boots without soles rose in the air, and crutches rattled like castanets:

"Why doesn't the sun shine brighter on Mondays and Thursdays?"

"Why is there no music in the streets?"

"We don't want a Sabbath, we don't need a Sabbath, we are weekday Jews!"

And like a herd of swine they came back into the gray streets,

singing and weeping. Up on the illuminated stories, the people
tore gold rings from their fingers, the husbands bit the earrings
off their wives' ears and threw them out the windows. But the
beggars didn't pick them up for they were radiant with the dark,
evil joy. The Jew led them, he fearfully lifted his legs over the
streets and they followed him. They blissfully wrapped themselves in their rags and guffawed tearfully in their hearts. And
they halted at the corner of the two streets, where the garret
stuck out above them like a dovecote. All the hosts arrived, lined
up, and, staring at the garret, they shouted:

"Come down, you noble Jew! Come down, you anointed
pauper!"

"Oh, come out!"

The windows in the garret opened up. And they appeared
there: Miss Gnesye and he—Mordecai Marcus. He stood there
without a jacket, a pale figure with trembling lips. The beggars
below were heaped and huddled together like a sprawling corpse.

"Speak to us, great pauper!"

"Comfort us, blessèd man!"

Miss Gnesye looked as wan as a queen, and now they were
bringing the king out to his people. She stared at them with
lowered eyelids. And they too remained silent. And he, Mordecai
Marcus, gazed at the people. He saw flat bodies, round legs. He
saw noses that lay like chunks of wood on the sides of faces; eyes
twisted up towards foreheads. And hunchbacks, and hobblers,
and syphilitics, and epileptics. And he was enraptured, and tears
welled up in his eyes. And he flung out his arms to them:

"Jews, today is a holiday! Who says that the poor are poor and
the outcasts miserable? You, with your pouches on your backs,
you gray weekday Jews—you stand at the source of the world.

"But not the happy are unhappy, and he who has—has
nothing.

"I have seen blood and water—and the water is more peaceful.
I have seen a sheep and a slaughterer, and the sheep is more
holy.

"You are the waters of the world, and the thirsty will come to
you and drink.

"Oh! Who loses his chains? He who has put them on. But you
are like the earth, which is fenced but never fenced in. And you

519

are like the earth, which does nothing and never laughs.

"Behold, what source is bottomless? The source of grief. I have seen. I have seen merrymakers, and they made merry and stopped, and those who grieve—refuse.

"Praise be unto you whose fate is dark, who eat during the day, like horses, from a bag, and sleep like them at night, with open eyes.

"And praise be unto desolation, of which the birds also sing."

The beggars stood in the street below and they wept. Tears of sweet sorrow poured into beards. It was really Monday, the day of salvation.

"They throw gold to us from the windows, and we do not take it!

"Earrings with ears. . . .

"Ah! Why do you need gold? You need *nothing!* A messenger has come to us from *there,* and he has announced that *nothing* exists. But we do not believe him, for we do not seek, we do not ask anything of him.

"Our prayer is heeded without our praying, and our work is done without our working.

"Behold, there exists a great prayer that is prayed not with the lips, and that no one hears, and that prayer is the holiest.

"A field does not pray that grass grow from it, but a naked rock that wants no grass.

"The rock says its prayer, and the heavens crack asunder in dread, for why is it praying? What does it want? It wants nothing.

"I will sing to the deaf, for I shall not be heard. I will pray to you, but you shall not exist at all.

"Behold!" he pointed at Miss Gnesye. "A woman was whipped in broad daylight, a woman was dishonored, and she is praying the prayer of nothingness. She was whipped with nettles on her bare womb, and she was thereby sanctified. Behold!"

The beggars, as though insane, stretched out their rigid wooden arms to her and knelt down in the mire for Miss Gnesye, shouting to her and screaming to her:

"You holy virgin, praises unto you!"

"Praises unto you, happy virgin, for he has done woe unto you!"

And Miss Gnesye glared at them, and she was covered with a warm sweat. Never had she looked so bold and proud as now when her huge disgrace was revealed to all the world. She wanted to open her parched lips and tell about the evil that had been done to her in bright daylight, and how that had elevated her. But that very same instant, the beggars apparently forgot all about her. They lay down in the mire, undid their pouches, and began hungrily devouring the pieces of bread. Paupers! Paupers! Avrom the Faster wandered among them through the darkness, one sleeve tucked into the other. He did not eat, for he had already died once. And the garret too became pitch-black.

ANOTHER! . . . ANOTHER! . . .

In the evening rooms, there hung a long ray of dust and light from the sun, that was sinking somewhere in the mountains.

Lena, alone in the corner of the echoing room, was playing a haunting piece on the piano; she held her heavy head towards the window, through which the light was trickling. In the darkness, her wan face loomed wearily with its thick, mannish nose, which was too harsh for her features.

Lena, oh Lena.

Who lived like an old woman, and whose thoughts quivered unclear, unclear, like a child's.

And thus she was twofold lost.

And thus she never had any friends here, nor did she like the adults. Lena.

The old doctor, her father, was her friend. And she laughed only when he told jokes. The two of them would go strolling in the evening, outside town, and sometimes, while strolling, her father, would complain to her that he felt "as lonely as a raven" here, he didn't care for life in this world at all, and Lena would comfort him:

"It's all right, Papa, don't worry . . . ."

521

And then, back home, she hunched gloomily over the key-board again, playing "Aase's Death," a piece that both of them loved with a holy and mysterious love.

"Aase's Death."

White blossoms of snow drifted through the dark rooms. They floated, pale and sparkling, and then faded by themselves without any death.

The yellow column of light slanting through the room became yellower, dimmer.

Lena's silhouette stood out in the darkness, and the white fingers roving softly across the keys.

Stillness.

Someone was treading through the inner rooms, striding back and forth. It was the mutilated soldier, who for some time now had been unable to find any rest.

And he kept talking to himself out loud.

No one was in the house, but Lena was used to him.

The mutilated soldier shuffled his feet at the door. And now he came in.

Now.

He didn't look around. He evidently came in to get something. The heavy sideboard with the wooden birds on its doors loomed up before his eyes. He pulled out the drawers, opened the doors, and groped about for something.

"What are you looking for?"

He didn't answer. He didn't feel like talking to her, apparently. He was shifting things from one place to another.

And finally—he went over to the couch, stretched out with his face down, and remained there.

Lena turned her face to the wall and stared at him lying there, ragged and barefoot, his soles filthy, and Lena thought that he was probably sad and gloomy. But now he got up:

"Lena?"

"Yes?"

"Do you remember my name?"

"Lyonik."

"Well, what do you think? Does the name fit?"

"Not now."

He twisted around and sat up on the couch:

"Why?"

"I don't know. A Lyonik ought to be handsomer, younger. . . ."

"Well, don't you think I'm handsome?"

Lena held her tongue.

"You won't say?"

Quiet and fearful, she looked around and began answering:

"You've only got one ear, and your face is so colorless . . . ."

"Why do I only have one ear?"

"Were you wounded?"

"I don't know."

And Lena almost burst into tears. He gazed at her for a moment and then stretched out on the couch again. She gave him a sidelong glance, wrapped herself up in her shawl, and sat there silent, motionless. He asked:

"Do you smoke?"

"No."

"I know you don't smoke. And now I want to ask you this: Do you talk?"

She remained silent.

"You ought to talk, because we're silent. We're really as mute as stones. Do you know why? Because we don't have our language. And we don't cry. Do you know why? Because everyone, everyone is crying. But listen, you." He sat up again. "Could there possibly not be any reward for the deeds? Oh, Lena, Lena, my darling Lena, I just can't believe it. Listen, Lena, you precious jewel, try to understand me. I was lying in a forest at night, a forest of fir trees, alone in my hole, and I was listening, and I learned something very important. I can hoot like an owl. No one can imitate it, I'm the only one. Hooooo . . . . Hoooooo . . . . I want to become smaller than my elbow, I want my face covered with feathers, then I can perch all alone on a roof. Hooooo . . . . Hoooooo . . . . When you hear an owl screeching, then you know that bad things are very near: Hooooo, hoooo, hoooo!"

Lena, sitting with her head upon the back of the chair, thrust her fingers into both ears, and his screeching gnawed at her throat like rotten teeth. He took heart, got up from the couch with his arms akimbo, and began speaking momentously, in a deep bass:

"You've heard: Cain supposedly killed his brother. So he has to suffer the punishment. But where is Cain? Why can't we see him—anywhere? And where is the sign on his brow? Nowhere!" He spread his arms. "Do you know why? Because the victim likewise took it upon himself to bear the mark of Cain. Yes, my child. When you go to sleep, he comes to me, naked and dark, with a long beard. Cain talks to me and questions me. Just listen to what Cain asks me: 'Why didn't you wrap up your ear in paper and take it home?' Hoooo, hoooo, hoooo! My child, it is very painful, for I long for my ear. I loved it so much when it hung right here, and I can still see how well it adorned me. Listen! Do you hear me or not? I order you to answer me!"

"Well?"

"Do you hear?"

"Yes!"

"Do you think a girl would kiss me now?"

She remained silent.

"Answer me!"

"I don't know."

"You do know! Answer."

"No."

He sat down on the couch, musing and staring with bovine eyes, and he motioned to her with his finger:

"Come here!"

Lena wrapped herself tighter in her shawl and didn't answer.

"Come here! Right now! Come on!"

And when she stood before him, pale and trembling, he screamed in a frenzy:

"Kiss me!"

The disgust rose up in her throat, but she took hold of herself, leaned over, and gave him a kiss.

"Right here in my ear!"

"Okay!"

"Another!

"Another!!

"Another!!!

"Another and another, till death!!!!"

His teeth clenched, he grabbed her and threw her on the couch. Lena writhed like a mouse; but then she suddenly understood, and mutely she threw herself upon his head, bent down, elusive, calculating, and all at once she bit him in the throat. He flung and twisted himself lengthwise, like a long worm. And his hands grabbed her, he wrenched his body to fall on the floor, but she wouldn't let go. Silent, silent, she lay upon him, coiled, like a leech in a shell, gnawing with a frenzied sweetness on the bleeding throat. And her eyes bulged out as though hanging from her forehead.

That night, the old doctor turned a shade grayer, and he did not play his flute.

A MATCHMAKER

And up in the garret, the room really did look like a dovecote. There was even a fur hat on the floor, stuffed with water and barley.

Apparently, Mordecai Marcus had once raised a chicken.

Cobwebs covered everything, even the bookshelves and the few bare pictures on the walls, and a coolness wafted through the room, silent and constant, as though there were openings in the walls.

It was hard to explain why Mordecai Marcus' room had such a birdlike atmosphere. Perhaps it was haunted by the soul of a fowl, that could only live in this way.

And it was dark and cool here.

Miss Gnesye was still sitting next to him on the sofa, and he, Mordecai Marcus, was still lying there, gaping with cold, fixed eyes, not saying a word, and Miss Gnesye felt desperate.

"Has he gone mute altogether?"

But then he slowly propped himself up on his elbows and

525

gazed long and strangely at the closed windows, that let in a turbid and ugly evening, and, with no strength left, he fell back on the bed. He took a faint breath and seemed to give her the slightest of smiles.

"What?" Miss Gnesye leaned over to him.

"Nothing."

"What do you mean 'Nothing'?" she cheerfully repeated.

"I've gotten through, my dear friend."

She folded her hands in her lap, understanding nothing, answering nothing.

"Do you know what I'm like now?" he softly asked.

"What? Well, tell me. What are you like?" she bent over him.

"I am like a river now. Yes, a river whose water has flowed away. The bed lies clean and still, and no one disturbs it. Do you know what that means, my dear friend?" He propped himself up again.

She looked at him, frightened, and then said:

"No, I don't know."

"It means that I have won, dear friend. I have won and carried out my pure truth."

Miss Gnesye nodded.

"Ah, I would rather not do anything in the world. Not move a finger. And I tell you, it is a great joy when a man attains such a consciousness. Now I shall be everywhere, everywhere, because now I will merely be a witness to what happens. Do you understand?"

But she remained silent.

"I sanctified myself today as a poor man, my dear friend. I finished with the human race, I put it down next to me. The question now is: Should I not die too? I wonder."

And he propped himself up and stared at Miss Gnesye, and his nose, which was very white, stood out in the darkness, sharp and jutting.

Out by the staircase, someone shuffled at the closed door. They looked over curiously and waited. The door opened very, very gradually, and in walked, very slowly, Judah, angular and silent. He paused at the threshold for he couldn't come any further into a home. And he crossed his arms on his abdomen like two pieces of wood, and stood there, silent, with his head hanging.

Then he took a few sidelong steps, toward the sofa; and giving Mordecai a sidelong look, he drawled:

"And what will be the end of it, Mottl?"

Mordecai stared and didn't understand, and Judah began inching around the sofa with tiny steps, he looked at the wall and said:

"I'm a father, after all. A father has to be concerned about his children. Do you hear what I'm saying? Enough of this debauchery!"

And he stopped, he stared into Miss Gnesye's eyes, looked at her carefully, looked her over, and then, pointing at her, he said:

"Do you hear what I'm saying to you? . . . There's a girl sitting here . . . . A decent girl . . . . Take her and marry her! . . . How long is your debauchery going to last, I ask you? . . . Tell me! And you, Miss, you ought to stop carrying on with boys . . . . I don't understand these respectable fathers. . . ."

Miss Gnesye brought her knees together, she dropped her head modestly on her breast and turned pale. And Mordecai Marcus was very embarrassed. He put his legs on the floor and, in his confusion, he adjusted his tie, which had twisted over his shoulder. And he gave his father a pleading stare; if only he would stop. But Judah wasn't finished.

THE SECOND MOONLIT NIGHT

It was a moonlit night. The cool sky was turning silver, far off in the blueness. The crosses and towers of the town looked stiller and longer. The dark hand paused on the face of the town clock. Pale, pale figures left the houses to look at the sky. Judah awoke, sitting by the sack of oats; gradually he dozed off again, but strangely, with fixed, open eyes. The town lay mute, as in a frozen crack of lightning. A head drifted up in the sky. It hovered in the blueness with closed blond lashes, and the

527

large, naked skull shone brightly in the moonlight. A death thread arose, curled far and long across the sky, and twisted in a weave around the neck. The head floated among the crosses and towers of the town, and all at once it halted, opened its lifeless watery eyes above the town, and peered, peered. The bright, mild blueness washed over the head softly, poured over it like holy water, and the head stirred, cold, in the stillness.

And far.

And still.

Still . . . .

MORDECAI MARCUS SHEDS LIGHT ON CONFUSED NOTIONS AND THE PHILOSOPHY OF THE SUBHUMAN . . . .

It was evening in the park, it was good to think under an ancient spreading oak. Mordecai Marcus was sitting with his legs crossed, calmly, like Buddha, gazing pensively at Miss Gnesye, who was sitting nearby on a bench, writing something in the sand with her little umbrella.

Mordecai Marcus stared at Miss Gnesye, thinking that there was such a thing as joy in the world, and that thought, which is the pure activity of mankind, is fruitful only when it is still and clear like an afternoon in the fields.

The thick, violet shadow of the tree lay across the narrow path, which looked as if it were strewn with golden coins.

The park was deserted, and not a leaf stirred on a tree.

Mordecai Marcus turned to Miss Gnesye and began to talk:

"My dear friend, have you ever thought about the nature of knowledge?"

Miss Gnesye stopped writing and prepared to listen.

"Isn't it the moment when the innermost person within us sees the existence of the world? Which is why I feel that people do not need to philosophize if they believe their senses and their intelligence. Metaphysics is the highest degree of art. It has to

528

slake the thirst of those who want to live together with existence. My dear friend, the act of knowing means stripping oneself of the traditional notion of 'human being' and becoming existence, and thus the value of knowledge lies not in uncovering hidden reality, but in the very process of knowing. Knowledge is religion, religion. . . ."

Miss Gnesye, absorbed in thought and craning her long neck, looked holy, like a Madonna. She was gazing at him, Marcus, smiling devotedly and nodding to everything he said, and he, Mordecai Marcus, was speaking because thoughts had ripened in him and were dropping like ripe apples from a tree:

"My dear friend, first the thinkers separated the object from the subject in order to permit philosophizing. The subject was given the power of a second world, which was strong and closed off. And starting from this double aspect in regard to the world and man, the philosophers proceeded to construct systems in which two forces struggle bitterly for control. Sometimes the object won out, and then we were led to the primal source of *matter,* from which the mind, the spirit were said to derive. And then again, the subject won out, and idealism would flourish. Mind and matter are hence two concepts that are mutually exclusive. And thus, my dear friend, man separated himself from himself, the bearer of the mind, as a contradiction to the world. A world that cannot exist without that contradiction. Man separated himself from existence and began leading and guiding it. For thousands of years, my dear friend, we have been reeling with our minds and our tongues until, alas, we have gotten all tangled up in our thoughts, unable to extricate ourselves. But I want to tell you not to divide the one notion of existence into two mutually contradictory attributes. And if philosophizing must thereby come to a halt, that does not mean that we will be cut off from pure knowledge. We shall know the world altogether without philosophizing, my dear friend."

"How can we?" Miss Gnesye asked, alarmed at her own question.

"Allow me, please. We must first distinguish between two other notions. You have heard the term 'struggle for existence'?"

"Yes."

"Well, that comprises the notion of struggle for existence and yet another notion—existence itself. These two concepts were confused, leading us to incorrect knowledge. We accepted the struggle for existence as existence itself, activity as life, work as being. You can see, dear friend, that a historical conception of reality was declared to be reality per se."

Mordecai Marcus adjusted his tie, which had been slipping more and more towards his shoulder, and then he went on:

"This error derives, in my opinion, from the moralist, who is disquieted by the struggle and tries to rationalize it along with his other absolute truths of good and evil" (and why was Mordecai so ironic about good and evil?). "The metaphysician, however, for whom there only exists one need, knowledge, is disquieted, not by the struggle, but by existence in and of itself. And subsequently, you will see," he pointed a long finger at her, "how Nietzsche, the moralist and metaphysician, was confused, and unable, because of his ethical feelings, to draw the ultimate consequences from his metaphysics." And a new thought came to him. "But one cannot neglect another factor in these notions: In the struggle for existence, our intelligence is the weapon. We cannot do without it, just as a cat cannot do without her nails; but, my friend, the cat does exist. She feels her being in the world not when she is tearing apart her prey, but in those moments of passivity, when she is warming herself in the sun.

"You see, you see. In that case, existence fully excludes activity. Do you know why? Because being means: knowing oneself to be in the world. And knowing means: yielding to reality. Struggle, however, means separating oneself, secluding oneself, activity of something against something. And just as the intelligence is a device used by man in the struggle, it is not a device of knowledge. Intelligence builds, and knowledge does not wish to build, it does not want to add anything. Not even concepts. We thereby come to irrational knowledge, and now I have to call your attention to Bergson, who also went out on this path. He went astray, however, because of his cautiousness, because he always wanted to look behind him and see the road back. Analytical intelligence, in his opinion, does not penetrate the essence of the given, and only intuition radiates through the object. But it is questionable, dear friend, it is questionable whether intuition can bring us to the essence of things. Who knows: Perhaps if Bergson were to focus his innermost gaze on his own consciousness at a moment when it was really inactive, he might, in the end, find *passivity* after all in the incessant, flowing stream.

"But listen, dear friend, and you will find a contradiction in his conception. For Bergson's very application of the 'innermost gaze' is sufficiently indicative of activity. It proves that the moment was full of activity, and he even says that pure knowledge occurs in a moment when 'I am not active.' He contradicted himself by trying to leave behind a minimum of activity. And alas (he regretted it), he came so close to the hidden secret of life, and in the end, he himself shut the door and did not cross the threshold."

And the violet park was hushed. Miss Gnesye trained the sparkling whites of her eyes on Marcus and admired him, admired the acute, knowing mind of the man sitting there so quietly while the gold came pouring from his lips. She felt a sudden warmth in her heart. A sudden warmth from a thought that writhed through her like a silver minnow pulled out of water. She recalled the way Judah had demanded that Marcus get married. It dawned on her now that Mordecai Marcus was the only man fit to be her husband. *He and no one else.* She turned crimson, and started wiping and cooling her face with her handkerchief. But Mordecai Marcus didn't notice.

"We know, hence, that pure Being is the opposite of activity. Any kind of activity is rejected by the mind so that we may attain absolute existence. But then again, when we reject the mind, we remain alone with the body, and perhaps the body is the source of our knowledge. Truly, the passive body, which does not build, does not create, is closer to Being in that it does not separate from it. I have already mentioned Nietzsche. He was the first to dwell on the worth of the body, but he comprehended it as a value and not as an absolute. Perhaps because Nietzsche was more of a moralist, the problem of values had a higher significance for him than knowledge. But it *is* clear, that he *did* grapple all his life with the body, which creates without creating or doing, and he did want to substitute it for the mind. 'I am still and altogether body, and nothing but body; and the soul is merely a name for something that is enclosed in the body.' Yes indeed. But instead of proclaiming the body to be the bearer of cognition as the sole expression of eternal pure Being, he merely overestimated values, and that was all.

"My dear friend, you asked earlier how we can gain cognition of the world without philosophizing. But just think: What do the pure metaphysicians want, what do we want? We want cognition of the absolute, we want to be thoroughly permeated with the absolute. For them, it is an addition of new concepts; for us, it is necessary to point out the *certitude* of cognition, but we shall not thereby in any way achieve a *positive* addition to our knowledge. The attainment of the ultimate reality has to occur in *negation*. Oh, dear friend, the process of cognition takes place not through an active, positive activity, but through *non*-thinking when our body frees itself of the mind.

"Haven't you ever noticed, my friend, the way your mind stops suddenly and you cease living for an instant? That blank is counted in your lifetime, but you can assure us that during the blank you did not think, you did something passive, nothing active. That is the instant of *negation*, when we see the most important thing, the ultimate secret of the world. The mind paused for an instant, and during that momentary inactivity the body was incapable of separating itself from the cosmos, it vanished in the unicity of the world, like a finiteness in an infinity; the self negated itself totally and became world, the human world.

"My dear friend," he spoke a bit too loud and his eyes were moist, moist. "I know a man named Avrom the Faster, he goes through the world, from house to house, and he softly croons a song to himself, and then he keeps silent. He is the noblest person I have ever met. He bears within himself a quiet, dreadful inkling of the world, and his blood is always too heavy for him. And I do not know, dear friend, why he feels that there are no human beings and that only God roams about here on the mountains and the waters."

And throughout the park, the rosy lanes wound between the

trees, like thoughts of the earth. The sun was setting. And not far off, in a deserted pond, a thin squirt of water came dashing from a pile of rocks, slowly bubbling in the rosy silence. Miss Gnesye sat there, deeply confused by her bashful feelings for Marcus, and she didn't look at him and wouldn't speak, fearing she might burst into tears. And there was no one else in the park. Mordecai Marcus sat on the bench, fixing his moist eyes on the setting sun.

"And there he is: the subhuman, the world-human, whom you never see outside the world, and outside of whom you never see the world."

And in a still, hoarse voice, he began reciting some ancient poem from an ancient book.

> *"They look at him and they see him not;*
> *His name is: Straight.*
> *They listen for him and they hear him not;*
> *His name is: Torment.*
> *They go after him but they cannot embrace him;*
> *His name is: Small.*
> *His above is not brighter and his below is not dimmer.*
> *Endlessly delighting—*
> *They cannot name him.*
> *He goes back to non-Being.*
> *That is what is form without form*
> *And what is image without image.*
> *Coming towards him, they see not his face.*
> *And looking back, they cannot see his other side."*

Marcus fell silent, but then he heard Miss Gnesye next to him. He looked around and saw her weeping, her head was sunken, the handkerchief at her eyes barely twitched with her shoulders. He was astonished. Very tenderly, he leaned over to her:

"Are the things I presented to you so very sad?"

But Miss Gnesye unexpectedly leaned her head on his chest. She wept bitterly, and through her bitter weeping, Marcus heard her voice clearly pleading, pleading:

"Mordecai, I love you . . . I can't stand it anymore, Mordecai. . . ."

533

He turned crimson from head to toe, became fully flustered, like a child, and was so confused that he didn't know what to answer.

No betrothal came about that day.

SOCIETY

In the evening, a thin, yellow crack of lightning sliced through the sky like a diamond. The burghers, startled and dazzled, ran screaming into their homes and locked their shutters. (What is a burgher without shutters?) Judah, who was sitting next to the sack of oats in his shop, awoke comfortably, and then gradually and miraculously dozed off again—with rigid open eyes.

Lightning flashed.

The long phosphorous fires rambled across the sky as under a cold, blue glass, and in the stillness they looked like screams that only the eyes can perceive.

The edge of a tattered cloud came dragging from behind the mountains. It crept heavily, the cloud, emerged from the mountains, gray and smoldering, and it breathed hot over the town, exhaled black, rolling balls from its innards.

The crosses and the high towers of the town loomed frozen in the dark stillness.

They waited.

Lightning split the sky! For a sudden instant, the holiness of another world shone blue. And all at once, a thunder burst forth, banging and banging as though it had gotten caught and tumbled down without hitting its mark.

Pitch-black.

Among the clouds in the sky, a head came drifting out. It swayed through them with closed blond lashes. Softly, softly, it glided from one cloud to the next, and the skull, cold and naked, shone in the lightning.

The doctor's old servant, his collar thrust up, ran down from the porch and hurriedly starting closing the shutters; he yelled angrily into the house for someone to help him.

A few thick drops splashed down from the sky, clattering loudly on the tin roofs like fingers; and then stopped. All at once a peal of thunder boomed nearby. The burgher's head tumbled over among the clouds and vanished. The rain gushed down in curtains of water. The wind scattered it about, lifted and flung the shiny metallic water across the streets, across the disheveled trees.

No electricity was burning.

Some guests had gathered in the doctor's dining room, and now candles were lit. The emaciated faces were barely visible in the darkness. Comrade R., his legs crossed, was half reclining on the davenport, smoking his pipe. Mordecai Marcus sat at the table, pale and worn out. He held the cane in his hand and just stared at the walls, at the ceiling, at the tip of his nose. On the other side of the table, Misha was rolling cigarettes. He blew into the tiny tubes and nodded in absorption every time he finished a cigarette. And Miss Gnesye was also there, in her attire, sitting in the dark corner, by the bookcase (Miss Gnesye loved books!). And all evening long, she had been hanging on Mordecai's every word. Sonia was also in the room, she too had grieved today. And a tall broad-shouldered man was there, the head of the tanners' union, he had kept silent all night, sitting with his finger on his chin.

In the darkness outside, the rain kept wailing, and its long wet hands groped along the houses.

The company was hushed. Comrade R. snorted, murmuring something to himself, the way a man who is asleep sometimes does when bad dreams come to him.

"Some rain, huh?"

"Yes."

And they were hushed again.

Lena came in from the next room, silent, terrified, and the old doctor came after her, leaned over and whispered something to her.

Ever since that incident, the doctor had never spoken aloud to

535

her; they only whispered to one another, or used signs.

Misha looked over at Lena, and, as though not noticing anything, he kept rolling his cigarettes. The doctor lost his bearings. Ever since that incident, the doctor often lost his bearings and stopped in his tracks. But then he immediately found his bearings, and, somewhat too fast, he walked over to the piano and lit a candle. Lena calmly, calmly sat down with her back to the others and slowly opened the lid of the piano. He brought over a score and made a sign to ask whether this was the one she meant, and she nodded: "Yes!"

A flash of lightning flickered in the cracks of the shutters. The union head turned to the windows and then looked to see what the others were saying, but no one seemed to care. So he kept on sitting there, calmly.

"It's gloomy here, isn't it?" Comrade R. blew out a puff of smoke.

"Yes, yes, comrade. It's gloomy even in times of social revolution—!" But the doctor broke off and bent over to whisper something to Lena.

Comrade R.'s pipe released smoke rings, which swayed in the air, and he kept snorting as though asleep. He riveted his framed eyes on the candle flame, and rested, rested in his way, lying there with his head on the pillow of the davenport.

The flute hurriedly withdrew.

And the doctor now realized that Marcus was also in the room. He turned, shaking his head and humming:

"Mottl, Mottl, you're getting senile!"

He looked at Mordecai Marcus, who was sitting on the chair as calm as before, staring at the doctor's bowed back. Mordecai Marcus didn't know what to say to the doctor. Comrade R. scanned him with the blue frost of his eyes, cudgeled his brain to recall something, and then, as though in his sleep, he pointed a finger at him:

"And what about your 'metaphysics'?"

Mordecai Marcus stared and felt very lazy, and his "metaphysics" was apparently too clear for him to talk about it. His small eyes shifted to Misha, as though he wanted to ask his advice—and Misha kept rolling his cigarettes, smiling at him:

536

"Nothing."

"But . . . but . . .?"

"It's a philosophy of negation," Miss Gnesye suddenly blurted out from her corner, and somewhere in the darkness, the blood must have shot into her face.

"What?" Comrade R. put his hand to his ear.

Mordecai Marcus leaned over to answer in Miss Gnesye's stead: "Negation. Negation. Like an act of cognition. We feel that man attains cognition of the world not through a positive process of thinking, but through non-thinking, at the very moment when the mind is separated from the body, the time we call 'negation.' "

"Hmmm. . . ."

"We believe that society has to be built on that feeling of the world. Yes, we love the poor who have nothing to give, those who go begging from house to house with their pouches on their backs."

"Because a pauper's soul is lodged in your body," Comrade R. threw in spitefully.

"Yes, yes!" Mordecai Marcus all at once became animated. "I think so too. Did you notice it as well? Really? Do I really have the soul of a subhuman?"

Comrade R. kept silent.

And a thin crack of lightning flashed through the shutters, instantly followed by a nearby boom of thunder.

Misha stood up, swept the tobacco together with his hands, and said, smiling:

"There really is something beautiful about poor people. I once saw an old beggar with a pouch on his back, he was by a door . . . . A true Father Abraham."

"But, my dear friend," the doctor interrupted, "Father Abraham didn't go begging from house to house, he merely made his way from tent to tent."

Lena looked up at her father and smiled, he responded happily and asked her with a sign whether she was ready to play.

Certainly.

"Aase's Death."

Sonia emerged from the weary corner as though the darkness impeded her hearing. She stood at the piano, numb and gray as a sparrow, and she listened with her eyes as well. Outside, the rains flooded in broad waves; the walls and roofs were dripping melodies and water.

And Comrade R. sprawled there, thinking: "Why did Aase die so easily? She floated across, as on a soft little boat, into the light, and why did she smile so naively and mildly, the old woman? Does life end far away with a melody?"

And Comrade R. had a different image: They would come to him with a scythe, a rusty scythe, for he wouldn't give in, and it wouldn't be easy, for him or for them. . . .

He spit on the floor and, with his cap over his eyes, he sank back into the davenport. He let out a snort.

The doctor, with his waistcoat unbuttoned on his heavy belly, shook himself and with his tiny moist eyes he glanced at each person to see whether they were listening, and he was terribly thankful that they were all moved and listening with lowered heads, and "flickering."

He thought about that very word: "flickering."

But the most enthusiastic of all was—the doctor himself, in the middle of the music, he yelled towards the davenport:

"Music! Give us music in the streets! . . . That would be something! . . . Then we'd give you the power . . . . Not before. . . ."

But how could anyone reply to the doctor? He was already bending over and whispering something to Lena. No one dared to say anything. They all held their tongues. All at once, Misha stood up, as though having decided something extremely important, and he took the doctor aside:

"And where is he?"

"Who?"

"He."

"Why all of a sudden? . . . I don't know." The doctor tried to move away, but then he cheerfully added:

"He's in the stable somewhere, in the stable."

Misha exuberantly turned away, whistling. And the doctor hurried back to his flute.

But again something curious happened, stirring everyone up, although for no good reason.

Mordecai Marcus got to his feet, panic-stricken and deathly pale. His voice was barely audible, but he managed to say clearly:

"My friends, it appears that I shall die during the next few days. Excuse my fright, please, it came so unexpectedly for me too. But look," he turned to Miss Gnesye, "at that time we thought I might not need to! . . . ."

And he quickly walked over to the door and took his hat from the hook and, standing at the threshold, he turned to the others, who were still seated as though not grasping what was happening.

"Please forgive me for alarming you . . . . Please excuse me, my friends! Please! . . ." And he took a deep bow by way of begging their pardon.

Miss Gnesye got to her feet, she cried to him, like a hen, but that was all. The broad-shouldered union leader took her in his arms and carried the sobbing woman over to the davenport.

JUDAH

A rectangle of sparse light from a window lay on the pavement of the narrow street. Shutters were drawn everywhere.

Misha came trudging through the dead street late at night. The heavy echo of his footsteps rang through the stillness with the iron thud of his boots on the ground. He stopped at the window:

A gray, naked, square house. Inside, on the wall, hung an old clock with flowers on its face. One big hand was moving around on it—a jerk, and then it moved, a leap, and it moved again.

Underneath the clock, as though nailed to the wall, Judah was standing, asleep. He stood with lowered eyelashes, his sleeves tucked into one another, and the long wire of the pendulum moved with great difficulty behind his disheveled cap.

There were no chairs. A table covered with an old oilcloth filled the entire room. The cloth had once been painted with the same flowers as the clock face. A herring lay stretched out in a chipped narrow plate on the table. A long, skinny herring. Next to it, a candle was burning in a Sabbath holder.

Misha tore his eyes away from the window. He felt a pang of regret.

MISHA DOES WHAT HE HAS TO, AND MORDECAI DOES WHAT HE HAS TO. . . .

Only a wan face peered suspiciously through a window. It was noticeable. And on a porch, the famished burgher was sitting and smiling. A brown horseman in a sheepskin cap galloped away and disappeared a moment later in the dust behind the town.

Something was beginning to happen in the revolutionary town.

There are water worms that lie in wood on the bottom of rivers. Sometimes they stick out their long hairs from their homes and look and listen, but in a time of danger all that remains of them is the cold wood lying in the slime.

The mass, the panic-stricken mass!

It peered from an attic, from behind a fence; but it wasn't there; it looked and listened; its eyes roved here and there among the legs; but it wasn't there.

No one saw the mass.

A man was shot in silence, and on the edge of town, behind a stove, a heart was writhing. It saw the bullet coming out and going in and perforating the skull. The mass needed no ears—it heard. And it needed no eyes—it saw. And if someone died, the death was done to *it*, the mass. The mass maintained a cruel silence, for it was a secret. A scream tore out—and the mass muffled it. Blood—and it covered it. And through the walls, from street to street, from one house to the next, it announced:

"Quiet! Quiet! Don't talk loud! . . ."

Mordecai Marcus lay on the ruined sofa, a blanket drawn over his head, and only his long legs sticking out. He lay there sick and weak, and listening, for that was the mass's order. And he heard and saw, saw blood pouring everywhere. From far away, there echoed the compressed tread of battalions. The air smelled of wild foreign flesh, and eyes darted about.

Misha dashed back home with a rifle on his shoulder. The town was already banging and chirping with machine guns, but they were so orderly, so calm, so quiet. (A town is never so quiet as when a battle takes place in it.) Misha ran through the dark, somber rooms, but there was no one there. The doctor and Lena had apparently left in time. Misha opened the closets, threw the clothes on the floor, and hurriedly packed together a small bundle for himself. It was only now that he noticed a canary in a cage inside his father's bedroom. A lump of sugar lay between the wires, and the little bird thrust out its body and hungrily nibbled the food. From time to time, the windows rattled with the gunfire. Misha clambered up, took down the birdcage, and put it on the floor, by the window.

Someone called him from the yard, apparently waiting, waiting for him there, but he was in no hurry. Within him, the same darkness was awakening as in the dark, somber rooms. The heavy oaken beds, one of which had been standing there fully made ever since his mother died, and the dusty shadows of the solid wardrobes and dressers were all around him, hauntingly alive. He felt them like a second body, a doppelganger, that had to separate from him now, and he felt pangs of regret.

Slowly he walked over and opened the door to the dining room; the same dark, dusty stillness; but something, something moved in the corner. He thrust his head in and suddenly he saw: riding on a chair, near the stove, his brother Lyonik, looking as though he had been waiting for him. He stopped, put his hands on the back of the chair and gawked into space with rigid open eyes. Their eyes met, halted, and both of them endured the long, silent, wild gaze. But apparently they did speak, for Lyonik burst into nasty, irksome, disrespectful guffaws, and Misha slowly took the rifle from his shoulder. Misha deliberately touched the safety catch, and kept staring, staring at his brother's mutilated face. Lyonik spread his palms on the back of the chair, leaned his chin on his hands, and waited.

"Well???"

541

A shot flared out.

Through the smoke, Misha managed to see the chair topple, legs tumbling behind it, and he could clearly hear the gushing of blood, the plopping of heavy drops on the floor. But there was no scream, no scream at all.

Silence.

He cautiously left the dining room, closed the French doors, and listened. Silence everywhere. Quickly, he picked up the bundle, peered around again, and then dashed out through the back door.

Sonia was waiting in the yard. She was standing by the wall, dressed in a leather jacket and carrying a rucksack on her narrow shoulders; he ran over without looking at her and gave her his pack, she lifted her pale, narrow chin, wanted to ask him what had happened inside, but he wouldn't let her, he was in a hurry. He gave her a rapid kiss, pointed to the end of the yard, and started leading her by the hand. He escorted her out through the broken fence, into the fields, gave her another kiss, and told her to get out of town as quickly as possible. He himself went back to the gate, cautiously opened it wide, and sprang into the street.

The enemy was lying between the thick walls of gates. Single heads, like 'walnuts, right on the ground, emerged from the gutters every so often and then were instantly dragged back. He moved, step by step, along the walls, his entire body listening all around, and he shot, and he shot . . . . And all at once, a great joy seized hold of him, he had never known anything like it before: *"I am doing what is mine to do!"*

A powerful light shone from him, he could almost touch it with his fingers. He felt more important than the town; the fate of all these people and these streets was in his hands. And never had he known this strength of his before: his heart beat broad and deep inside him, he carried it in his breast like a petard. Fires lit up in the doorways, and he strode towards them and past them, with his rifle, which kept discharging, almost of its own accord. Never before had he felt every muscle of his body in this way, and now he loved it so much, this tense body of his, which he bore along as if it were cast in bronze. And now he suddenly understood what being *human* meant. The courage bounded from him, and with such a force that he could feel his head soaring from his shoulders, and he saw his head in front of him, and he grinned at it:

"I am doing what is mine to do!"

On the telephone wires hung the old mangy carcass of the dead cat; the eyes, on thin, tiny arteries, dangled around the rotten head, and inside, in the open belly, it was black and hollow.

Ah, Comrade! Comrade! Why didn't the order come in time to take the cat down from the telegraph wires? And now it was too late. No one was left in the streets. Somewhere by a wall, stood a rifle. And a boot was sprawling in the middle of the gutter. . . .

In a hunched, narrow street, near a machine gun, lay Misha, stretched out in the mud, aiming dead-true, and carefully pulling out the cartridge belt behind him. There, at the end of the street, the enemy flung himself into the entranceways and lay there, surrounded by rocks, pieces of wood, slats broken off from fences, a gate, a trough, and Misha kept smoking cigarettes that lay next to him, scattered on the ground. His watch also lay before him on the ground.

It was a turbid evening, the clouds rolled through the street, gray and dry, merely to make the world ugly. And everything was superfluous. Misha shot into the town, apparently to spite someone, for it really made no sense lying in some unimportant side street and firing full-blast at no one. He looked around. He knew the place very well, but he couldn't recollect why. The tiny garrets bent over him, meager and crooked, with black windows, like fainted heads. And now he remembered, he raised his eyes, looked for that window, and shouted up:

"Marcus! Hey, Marcus!"

Up in the garret, behind the window frame, Marcus' head appeared, with a terribly long, white nose, which followed him hideously; he peered down, very grave and pale. Misha smiled up at him, and Marcus cautiously responded with a shake of his head, which might also have signified regret. They didn't speak. And everything was clear. Marcus was troubled because Misha was lying there all alone, amid the enemy. And he actually wanted to warn him, but it was obviously too late.

From the intersecting street came sudden shouts; windows

543

shattered. Marcus stuck out his head and, flustered, he began yelling wildly and waving his hands:

"Misha! Hey, Misha! They're surrounding us! Misha! They're surrounding us!"

Misha sprang to his feet. He grabbed the watch from the ground and ran straight, straight, down the street. On the tiny sidewalk, which twisted like a skinny worm along the crooked street, he vanished among the houses, and Marcus didn't see anyone emerge to chase after him.

He took a breath. His hands trembled. He barely managed to close the window, drag himself to his sofa, and collapse upon it with no strength left in him. Lying there, he listened to the coursing of his blood, which didn't have the patience to move in his arteries, and was stuck everywhere, in every corner of his body. And his head just lay there, alien and heavy, like a piece of wood, worn out, no use to anyone anymore.

Gunfire. There was gunfire below, right by the house. Marcus turned over, sat up, propped on one side, and pressing his head into the wall with all his might:

They were coming to him.

But now there was a hush, the stillness was so naked and open that one could hear what was happening behind all things. It was impossible for him to believe that he would die now, now, when all were still surviving, and even Misha, who had earned death, he thought, had also run away.

There.

Someone seemed to be coming to him up the stairs. He quickly pulled the quilt over his head and held his breath. Maybe it was just his imagination. Someone was coming. Coming. *Coming!*

The door opened. A wind blasted in, and a muffled shriek. And then they pulled him off the sofa; broad, flat faces, wedged on neckless shoulders, moved about the room, as though released from a cage. They yelled. He didn't answer, and suddenly he felt utterly calm. The table was already upside down, the clothes scattered every which way, and the books flung across the floor, and he walked among them with a smile on his face. For it was clear that it was all a mistake. They spoke to him, and he didn't know, he didn't know anything:

"No," he said, "I don't know. . . ."

And then they hit him with something, right in the pit of his stomach; he was still peering around and smiling. Strange, it didn't hurt at all. But now he would certainly follow any of their orders. He undressed, stood there in his shirt, barefoot, he covered his knees with his hands and pressed them together because he was cold.

They ordered him to go down to the courtyard. It was a little too cold, he smiled. But he went. And there they beat him again, just a few punches, and not in the pit of his stomach anymore, but in his head. Avrom the Faster emerged before his eyes, standing there in the courtyard, by a wall, his coat on his bare flesh. And Avrom gazed at him with tears in his filthy eyes, and he seemed to be comforting him, that was how it had to be, for there was no such thing as a reward. And he also saw the other small saintly men, somewhere on the horizon, about to take their lives, with their very own hands. Behind him, there was a cold brick wall. He felt it from behind, turned, and realized all at once that he had been put against it to be shot, and suddenly he spoke, very clear, and angry:

"Gentlemen, I don't want this. . . ."

But then there was gunfire, and something scratched his armpit. He slowly sank down on the earth and breathed lightly at having gotten off so easily.

THE SMALL SAINTLY MEN ARE BACK AGAIN

The deceived men, the small saintly men, were still wandering about the world. Only Beryl of Luninetz went to the edge of a forest and hanged himself from a strong tree. He had long since rotted there, and he looked like a scarecrow hung up to drive the birds away from the area. Gimpel of Zhamut went back to his native town, five hundred miles away, to find his wife and sin with her during her menstruation. But he scarcely had any strength left at his arrival, and he discovered that she had

545

died long ago and not a trace of her was left.

To the small saintly men, the sky looked like rusty iron that weighs down upon the back, to be carried without payment and without breath. And thus, wherever one of them sat, he refused to stand up, for it wasn't worth the trouble. And Shmaye of White Russia, who stood with a tucked-in beard and a stretching hand, remained standing, petrified, forever and ever, till the end of time.

MORDECAI MARCUS SAYS HIS PRAYERS

The revolutionary town, which was wedged in the mountains, was quiet again. Crosses and high towers were drenched in shiny pink, craning like the necks of geese, and all the wide rooftops in the surrounding area were covered with thin mists like dreams. The streets were hushed. The old staircases, the cornices, and the houses, whose wide bricks were crumbling from the bullets, looked as though a storm had passed over them. The river, the mountains, and the forests all around gazed bluishly at the calm that had been restored to the town. It was dawn, pure and festive.

At the hospital, all the beds were filled. Mordecai Marcus was lying apart, in a large white room. His hair was washed, his skin was pale, he had on glistening linen such as he had never worn in all his life. He lay in the bed, propped up on white pillows, dazzlingly clean and staring at his own body, which seemed useless to him now, and he smiled blissfully. Through the wide, shiny windows, the sun was glowing. The patient was thinking slowly, and his thoughts today were clear, transparent, and silent, silent, like sheep.

The hospital physician walked in. Mordecai Marcus smiled at him, and he couldn't understand why the freshly washed physician eyed him so earnestly, why he felt his pulse and shook his head, as though pitying him. On the blackboard over the bed, his name was written in white chalk:

"Mordecai Judeyevitsh Marcus."

And he thought to himself that they had correctly guessed the spelling. The physician leaned over and asked softly, almost casually, whether he wanted to convey anything to his friends.

No. What did he have to leave them?

There was no way of telling. The patient had lost too much blood. . . .

"Well?"

Who knew what could happen, even though he was steadily improving.

"Oh? . . . You're talking about *that?*"

"Yes."

And now Marcus understood. His eyes suddenly kindled with a sacred and nebulous grief. He settled back slowly on the pillow, his head fell to the side, he started breathing heavily. Now, for the first time, he felt how weak he was. He was seized with a huge longing for the world and it struck him as terribly unfair that people have to die. Now he felt it, so naked, so open. He wept. The sun shone on his white bed, gathering only where he lay— shone and broke over him in thin, fine rays, and he felt sorry that he had to leave it for others. But suddenly, unexpectedly, his sadness ebbed, as though his blood had flowed off somewhere. He slowly opened his eyes. The light shone on him like a white, warm wing that had passed over him, leaving a sweet grief of waning, a blend of misery and joy, as though he had been saved from a danger. He smiled mournfully at the physician:

"It's really not the way people imagine it."

Marcus told him to tell his near and dear that he wanted to talk to them before the end. He wanted to talk now that everything had become clear to him; perhaps it could be instructive for his friends, helpful for living in this world. And he remained alone in the bare whiteness of the room, which shone festively and with a funereal joy before his eyes.

In the thick darkness of the room, shadows were floating. Heavy heads were visible—Marcus' friends, who had gathered to make their farewells. The old doctor and Lena sat right at his bedside as though carved from the same stone, gray, faded, not stirring at all. At the foot of the bed, Miss Gnesye sat like a stick. From her black shoes, her white stockings shone through the

547

darkness. Her eyes blinked, and from time to time she wiped her face with a handkerchief. Reb Judah was also there, he was standing against the wall, off to the side, his hands tucked in his sleeves, and he was doing something with his sheeplike eyes, which he had been given to look at the world. He was waiting and not waiting, but he didn't understand why he was needed here. And there were also several bearded Jews with very blue noses and long arms that dangled at their sides down to the earth. The Jews had come from the charity hospital, where once Mordecai Marcus had lived among them. On either side of the door stood Stesye and Gnesye, like gray birds, like mutes who could only part and close their lips—as a sign of life. It was dark around the one burning candle, and the room smelled of old bodies, which people carry about as corpses until their strength runs out. All the visitors silently lowered their eyes, sweetly grieving, probably for themselves, and perhaps for him.

Marcus opened his eyes. They all looked at him, with gaping mouths, waited for him to speak, but he merely gazed at them calmly, moved his eyes from one person to the next, and he appeared to be smiling, an affectionate smile, from a stranger, far away, far far away. He wanted to push himself up on the pillows, everyone noticed. The doctor rose, gave him a hand, but then sat down again on his chair with a lowered head, not looking at anyone. Mordecai Marcus began in a very low, barely audible voice:

"You see, my friends, I am going home. I have walked for many years under a good star, which warded off all evil from me while others suffered and died. I loved sadness, just as you love your mothers, but now I am afraid that my sadness will stop and I will dry up like a tree growing out of rocks. But perhaps my fears are groundless, for I can already hear a faraway singing on the other side of the sky, and where there is singing, there is also sadness and happiness, probably, for the new arrival.

"I know that you are sitting here and thinking: 'If a man has lived, what did he want?' I wanted not to disappear and that was why I didn't do anything. Only human beings act, and I know that there are none in the world. We want nothing, we do nothing, we demand nothing.

548

"You have heard it said that Job cursed God. But how could he, who did not act, curse God? He came as far as the final crystal door, and it is the cruel, strong, cold dazzlement of the world that people call—cursing. My friends, you were happy when you saw him sitting barefoot on the earth, with ashes on his head. Why did you rejoice at his misfortune? Probably because there is joy and sadness and because there is happiness and torment.

"Look, I am going home and I am taking this Book of Job along. Perhaps I won't find anyone there, and I will have to sit down again on the earth there and start all over again."

Suddenly, Miss Gnesye began shaking on the bed. She began rocking as on hinges, and at first no one could tell whether she was about to cry or laugh. A cawing, as of a crow, came from her mouth. And she fell upon Mordecai's legs, throwing out her long arms like the blades of a windmill. The visitors realized it was her way of crying, and they watched to see what would come of it. But nothing came of it. She screamed and wept, wept without tears, as women can sometimes weep.

Mordecai Marcus drew a breath and opened his turbid eyes, where the whites were already mixing with the pupils. He tried to smile, but it didn't work:

"My friends, there is a still joy in wanting nothing. You have come to a cold wall that freezes vast and dark before the eyes; you lean against it, and how sweet is the sadness of reaching nothing and wanting nothing. Buddha wanted nothing, but he did not believe in sadness, and so melancholy secretly shone forth from him. However, I believe, and therefore I say: Praise be unto you, sadness, who have accompanied me to the very last step into the grave. You have warmed my soul with your meek eyes, when I have wept with the delightful misery within me and with the yearning for nothing. Praise for the excess of dark bliss in my life, which I always sated with singing in my soul and I never hungered for solace from elsewhere.

"What did I want, my friends?—Not a reward. Do with me, I said, as You do with Your fields and I will pray. I will pray, but do not listen, for I do not want my prayer to reach You.

"Behold, I lay in my garret at night as in my body, and I heard the world of myself, and I prayed to no one. Something like long silvery hair wafted from the moonlit sky, and I prayed with a singing to no one. For I did believe, my friends, I believed in the stars, in the Milky Ways and in the light that pours from human beings. I believed in all worlds, and especially in the cold sadness that breathes from all things and all people."

They leaned over the bed, barely catching his final words:

" . . . In the radiance, I saw another light, a brighter one. It was the figure of the pauper. He was coming quietly, even though I wasn't waiting for him. And when he showed me his wounds, I laughed, and it hurt me that his wounds were healing. Behold, I do not desire any reward, and every wound is dear to me. Come, I will tear open your wounds, so that they never shall heal, for I do not desire any reward . . . . Oh, it is getting darker and darker. I can only hear the song of the white donkey in the darkness. Where is it wandering without a rider? . . . The bag is hanging from him and the old flask, but *he* is not here . . . . Woe is me . . . . Woe is me. . . ."

And what happened next—nobody knows. ✤

MEYER LANDSHAFT

DER NISTER

A FRAGMENT ABOUT AN INCIDENT IN
TODAY'S OCCUPIED POLAND

I

It was a few days after they marched in . . . . There
were rumors that the town *Kommandant* had already summoned
the Jewish community elders, empowering them to carry out all
orders and commands that the occupying force would issue
specifically for the Jewish population.

In Meyer Landshaft's home, as in all Jewish homes, the family
was utterly distraught. Meyer Landshaft—an unusual sort of
Polish-Jewish businessman, a man of few words, well-versed in
the holy texts and of a good family, a good stock, and a pious
man as well; whose piety, however, never prevented him, in his
younger days or now, in his early fifties, from looking into books
by Luzzato, by Nakhman Krokhmal, and even by non-Jews,
authors whom he knew rather well, for instance Klopstock or
Schiller; this Meyer Landshaft—a tallish man, with a large, wide,
blond beard, with blondish eyebrows over grayish eyes, that
peered out from between his lashes like silent lakes surrounded
by reeds; this Meyer Landshaft, whose tidy clothing alone
required everyone in his presence to remain more quiet than at
home and which, whenever he came in either from the street or

551

from another room to someone waiting for him, compelled that person to straighten up respectfully; this Meyer Landshaft, who, in all situations, even terribly difficult ones, for example, when a child was sick or some other trouble was afflicting the house, never showed the slightest change in his face, because his inner faith would not permit him to doubt or lose his conviction that even the worst predicament would be happily resolved; this Meyer Landshaft, who now, after reading his fill of newspaper stories about what the new occupiers had done, first with the Jews in their own country, and especially after attacking Poland, when people found out what they were doing with Jews in the Polish towns and shtetls that they had conquered and subjugated—now, when this Meyer Landshaft, like so many others, had failed to leave town after the enemy's sudden entrance before anyone could even think about whether or not to stay—now, even this Meyer Landshaft felt he was caught in a trap, and he began to forsake his normal rule—of believing that things would get better. . . .

You could see this in his grayish eyes, peering out from between his lashes, as though struck by a powerful tempest that gathers in even the quietest lakes, surrounded by reeds; you could tell by his nervous, staccato answers if you asked him anything upon his returns from town, where he went, not to do business—buying or selling—but merely to get the latest news, to hear what people were saying about the things they were so terrified of . . . . And as for his wife Hanna-Gitl, who had always gone along with him, hand in hand, always so greatly honored him, loved him, and hung on his every word, ready to satisfy his every wish, even forestall his wishes—whenever she asked: "What are people saying in town? What's the latest news?" he would answer: "Nothing, nothing . . . . No talk, no news . . . ." And he would look away, avoiding her eyes, and turn and do things in the house, the kind of things you do before moving from a house or going on a trip, when you're confused and don't quite know what you're about.

He was not behaving now as he usually did in the past, when, unless he was taking a meal or dealing with people, he would always be seen holding a book in his right hand, tilting it slightly,

552

a bit myopically, towards his right eye and the right side of his face, and peering into it. But not now. His mind wasn't on books now. And if at some point he did manage, for a brief instant, to emerge from the personal anxieties that had attacked him, Meyer Landshaft, like all the Jewish inhabitants in the town, he used that instant to walk about, isolated, sharing his thoughts with no one, walk from wall to wall and from corner to corner in the room, twisting his hands when no one was watching, and constantly whispering the Hebrew phrase: "Oh Lord, art Thou hastening Thy destruction?" That is to say: Had God really, heaven forbid, decided to end everything and wipe out the Jews? . . .

But no, he didn't even have time for that because chiefly and above all he was busy worrying about himself and his family, over whose heads he saw the hovering sword . . . . But there again his mind focused on no one in the family—not himself, who was as imperiled as any of them, not his wife Hanna-Gitl, who had always gone along with him, hand in hand, always hung on his every word, ready to satisfy his every wish, even forestall his wishes; not his married sons and daughters and their spouses and children, his grandchildren—no, his mind focused on no one— when he hunted for air and an escape from the cage he was caught in, that is to say, the various rumors, each more horrifying, that came to his ears—no, his mind focused on no one so much as his youngest daughter, his baby, Vittl, or Wanda in Polish, as they called her in high school, where she was studying and about to graduate.

II

She had long, delicate fingers, Wanda, the sign of a highly refined ancestry, and perhaps also the sign of a late birth to parents who had already borne many children before her, the very last. She differed from all the other children in her great resemblance to her father, in her fine, quiet, well-mannered ways—while the other children were more like the mother, Hanna-Gitl, who was not from such a lofty background and

553

whose uneducated father, it was said, had paid a tidy sum to get a son-in-law like Meyer Landshaft.

She was also her father's favorite because she was the baby and also because the father saw her somewhat as a reflection of himself, and even though he outwardly didn't show her more affection than the other children, everyone in the house nevertheless viewed her as an exception, to whom the father gave more, if not in words then with quiet, loving eyes, that he rested on her from time to time.

Naturally, neither the mother nor even the children were jealous of her, on the contrary—to their father's exceptional love they added their own, and they weren't jealous when their father allowed her to do something that the other children weren't allowed to do: go to the Polish high school, where, incidentally, they got the priest, the religion teacher, to excuse her from classes on Saturdays, since she worked hard enough to do everything she had to during the week.

In short, Wanda: an exception at home, and also among her friends, with whom she was very retiring, very moral—an effigy of her father's behavior, which was well-known both in the family and in the town. All the businessmen, all her girl friends said that Wanda would never put up with a free word from any of the boys, her fellow classmates, never put up with foolish liberties from them. And furthermore: She even concealed and drew in her girlish form as though ashamed, as though regretful that she hadn't been born in armor.

And now she, Vittl/Wanda, the slim, blond seventeen-year-old creature, with a great measure of childhood innocence, which peered from her eyes, thoughtful eyes that were covered with a thin, thin veil of dreaming, she weighed heaviest on her father's mind, caused him the worst anxiety, because she was in the greatest danger—of being noticed by them, appealing to those whom she shouldn't, absolutely mustn't appeal to under any circumstances.

Now her father's eyes rested on her very often, and if someone addressed him on any important matter, he would turn away in the middle of the conversation and look at her, as though fearful of losing her, of losing sight of her.

Why? Because, aside from the rumors about the fine things that the new occupiers had already done in all the places they had reached earlier, and about the same things they had already started in the town where Meyer Landshaft lived—aside from all those things, which were already horrible enough, Meyer Landshaft, like other involved fathers, had heard a rumor that made him tremble: a rumor about certain houses where young women were brought: unmarried girls, young wives, for the shameful pleasure of the officers or the ordinary soldiers. . . .

Soon, it was no longer a rumor. It was told with all certainty that the Jewish administration had already received a clear order to contribute a number of Jewish women for that shame. They were still keeping it a secret, not leaking any details to the greater public, thinking they could appeal to the occupiers and get them to rescind the edict. But it didn't work. And now the Jews were already trudging about, devastated, and among them, and, as we can imagine, more devastated than anyone, Meyer Landshaft, who looked so dazed, who never uttered a word, but who could be seen twisting his fingers quietly . . . . That was one thing. And the second: In the morning, in the evening, at night, if someone had listened to his prayers to heaven, he would have heard only one desire, expressed in the words of a biblical verse that was not in any prayer: "The eagle hath no fear of any predatory fowl, for she flieth higher; but she feareth the huntsmen, so she carrieth her eaglets above and not below herself, saying: 'It is better for the arrow to pierce me than my children.' " And that was what Meyer Landshaft wished: "Better me than my children"—meaning Wanda.

III

In his great bewilderment, Meyer Landshaft stopped associating with other people, he remained at home for days on end, and just to keep his mind occupied with something, anything, he began sharpening the kitchen knives, which he normally did only on Fridays, for the Sabbath—an old custom of his.

"What's this all of a sudden?" asked Hanna-Gitl and also the older children, seeing him do this unusual chore in the middle of the week.

"Nothing . . . . Just . . . ." he answered, not looking in their faces, as during the past few days when anyone spoke to him. And in their great respect and esteem, neither Hanna-Gitl nor the children asked him anything further, realizing why he was occupying his mind with such useless things and why he was so sparing of words and answers.

Sitting there, sharpening the knives, he most certainly had no thoughts, except perhaps only about what he, as a knowledgeable man, had once read, namely, that in hard times, similar to these, hard times for the nation, fathers had once been forced to execute their own children—like strangers: to kill them in order to prevent them from falling into the hands of others . . . . He didn't know how that had been done, or what had happened to the "compassionate father" (for it is written in Psalms: "As a father hath compassion upon his children, so hath the Lord compassion upon them that fear Him"). But as in those earlier times—he thought to himself—compassion is the most merciless thing of all, which a man has to tear out and destroy in himself.

He must have trembled at that thought . . . . But he trembled even harder when, sitting at the table, doing his sharpening, he suddenly heard his doorbell ring, and he was certain it wasn't a familiar hand, which they would surely have recognized, but some alien hand, which pressed the button hard and long, letting the bell quaver, urgent and demanding.

It must be either a mailman, a telegraph boy, in a hurry, or members of the occupation force, who demand an instant response, an instant admission, with no respect for the people whose bell they are ringing.

Meyer Landshaft was so alarmed by the ringing that he made an awkward movement and cut his hand, and blood began running from the cut. But he noticed neither the cut nor the blood. He then heard one of the family hurrying to the door and opening it. And from the silence of the opening and the encounter with him, or with them who had rung, Meyer Landshaft concluded that these were certainly no ordinary visitors crossing the threshold and entering his home.

From the corridor leading to the dining room, where Meyer Landshaft was sitting, he could hear the thud of military feet, heavy-soled boots, and the surprised silence of his family—and, as it turned out, the frightened encounter of the person who had let them in was palpable through all the rooms.

The family came and gathered in the dining room, where they felt the soldiers would come first, the first room visible from the corridor, without a door. And that was what happened. The entire family was at home, as generally on all those days that were ruled by the physiognomy of the occupying force, still undefined for the non-Jewish population, but already very sharply defined for the Jewish population, who felt forsaken and three-quarters condemned.

Meyer Landshaft's entire family, pale, frightened, collected in the dining room. And no sooner had they come in, no sooner had the soldiers marched in, than all of them, both the soldiers and Meyer Landshaft's family, watched Meyer Landshaft, as though he had been expecting this, get up from his chair, as pale as the others, and, seeing them all gathered in the room, he suddenly had only one word to blurt out: "Wanda," which meant that of all his family Wanda was to come over and stand at his side.

IV

"*Hände hoch!* Hands up!" came a second voice, louder than Meyer Landshaft's, the voice of the officer commanding the squad, and right after that order, the same officer shouted again: "Get in a row! Men and women separate! And nobody try to move!"

They obeyed. Silently. Meyer Landshaft saw the men in the house line up to his left, his sons and sons-in-law; and to his right, the women, with Wanda closest to him, after he had called her over, when the soldiers had appeared, and next to Wanda—his wife, and next to his wife—his daughters and daughters-in-law.

The commanding officer, a lieutenant, at first glared silently at the file of people to make sure that it was orderly and that they had obeyed him properly and that no one moved . . . . *In Ordnung!* Then he turned to some man, not a military person, who had marched in with the soldiers—an administrative official, empowered by the Jewish elders, and forced by the occupiers to come along to all the Jewish homes, like now to Meyer Landshaft's home, and to do what they demanded of him: this time for some kind of registration that the occupiers considered necessary.

"*Zähl!* Count!" the lieutenant ordered the man. "Wait! No!" He changed his mind after glancing at the row of men and then the row of women, fixing his delighted gaze on Wanda, and dwelling on her for a long time.

Any of the family who still had some wits about them in their terror at this degrading ceremony could see that the lieutenant, the commander of the squad, was more drunk than sober. And they noticed this in his dangling blue eyes, which were shiny and seemed virtually to be floating in grease, and they noticed this too in his uncertain movements, his precarious equilibrium.

He began counting from the left row, the men, pointing a finger into each chest: one, two three, until he came to the chest of Meyer Landshaft himself, who, like all the others, was holding up his hands, but who was turning his head, not to the row of men at his left, but to Wanda, who was at his right.

The lieutenant, before passing on with his finger to the line of women, remained in front of Meyer Landshaft for a while. Then he stretched his counting hand to Wanda, peering with a silly grin at what his finger had so lightly grazed—Wanda's breasts, as though he were sticking his finger in honey that he was about to lick.

A cry came from Meyer Landshaft—from him, the man of few words, who had never in his life said a loud word to anyone, and who probably wasn't even capable of saying a loud word.

"*Hände weg!* Hands off!" came from Meyer Landshaft's mouth, a strict order, which made all the others, except for him, lower their hands in terror, forgetting that they had to hold them up, according to the lieutenant's order.

"What?!" The lieutenant almost didn't understand who was

meant by that disrespectful, threatening cry—he, he himself, the *Herr Offizier,* was supposed to remove his unclean hands from that which was not for him and from which he was to remain far away.

"What?!" he roared, glaring at Meyer Landshaft and taking a few steps back from where he was standing, in order to have a better look at that man from the distance. "What did he say? What did he dare to say to a German officer?"

And he glared drunkenly at Meyer Landshaft through half-closed eyes and saw him standing with his hands up and with blood running from one hand into his sleeve.

"Blood!?" he roared again, as though viewing it on his own hand, as though his own hand had been wounded. "What's that blood?" he shouted, peering around the room suspiciously, at all the people, as though, before his arrival, they had planned some evil and sharpened some kind of weapon, thereby wounding themselves.

Really: He glanced at the table and saw knives and a whetstone, which apparently someone, before his arrival, had held in his hands and prepared for a suspicious use—so it seemed to the officer.

"Who did this, who was sharpening knives?" the lieutenant asked, pointing at the knives on the table.

"I was!" replied Meyer Landshaft, and the others sensed a great satisfaction in his reply, apparently because the knives were averting the lieutenant's eyes from the girl whom he had just noticed and at whom he had so pleasurably thrust his honeyed finger.

It took a few seconds for the lieutenant to figure out how to act . . . . (Incidentally, we ought to say that these things happened back then, when the occupiers had not unloosed their right hand to carry out their plans for Jews in those areas they had only just invaded and gained control of, they were still keeping within certain, almost legal bounds—not like now, at the time we are writing, when such a lieutenant would not have hesitated with a man like Meyer Landshaft, killing him on the spot, without a second thought, for the least word he didn't care for, like any Jew, guilty or not, like a rat carrying the plague: to be wiped out. . . .)

V

"Arrest him!" screamed the lieutenant as soon as he realized what had to be done. "Arrest this bloodthirsty Jew, who sharpens knives to use against us!" he screamed to the soldiers accompanying him.

"Oh, no," Meyer Landshaft's daughter, Wanda, suddenly stepped out of the line . . . . And, modest as her behavior may have been with her own people, the students at school, whom she had never permitted a free word, or the least hint about herself, as a member of the female sex, she now, however, in the moment of danger for her father, who was obviously as dear to her as she to him—she, never giving voice to her feelings, but carrying them in girlish concealment, just as her father carried his love for her in his gazes . . . . Modest as Wanda's behavior may have been previously, when she never exploited her ability to attract men, she now, however, coming to the lieutenant and trying to save her father from the terrible situation caused by his powerful stance against the lieutenant—she now, suddenly—who knows how?—played up that ability, peculiar to all women at certain moments, when they have to charm someone and attain something for their charm. . . .

"Oh, no, Herr Lieutenant," she said, behaving like an adult for her family, this first time in her life—for the members of the household, for her father and mother. She was inspired with fluent speech, and lowering her eyes in her normal modesty, as whenever she faced a strange man, and then raising her eyes to this strange man, she said, with a smile that she had acquired from somewhere:

"Oh, no, Herr Lieutenant, it's a mistake. Those aren't knives for the occupiers. My father isn't like that. It's a custom here, my father always does it on Friday for the Sabbath, and now there's no business because of the confusion in town, and so he's started doing it during the week, you can look at them, Herr Lieutenant, they're ordinary kitchen knives."

And with lowered eyes, Wanda just barely smiled and continued to play up that ability which was supposed to make the man she was talking to, the lieutenant, forget the insult he had gotten from her father, who had told him to remove the hands with which he had taken indecent liberties . . . . She stepped over to her father and caressed him affectionately to demonstrate his innocence, vouching for it with her proximity, and to risk her life for him, that is to say, for the business of the knives, which, as the Herr Lieutenant could see, was really a bagatelle, not worth wasting any breath on.

Wanda was successful. They could see small fires, mixed with small shadows, in the lieutenant's eyes, as he looked at her, first when she stepped out of the line, and then when she stood opposite him, defending her father, and especially afterwards, when, upon finishing her defense, she tenderly went over to her father and gently caressed him.

The somewhat drunken lieutenant was giving in, and the situation was almost, almost resolved: If Wanda had just said a few more words about her father in that same defending tone, and if her father, Meyer Landshaft, had silently continued to let her defend him, then, almost, almost, the lieutenant would have forgotten all his anger and taken back his order to arrest Meyer Landshaft.

But that wasn't what happened. Because the moment Wanda affectionately joined her father, and he, the father, saw the devices she, his Wanda, was using to woo the lieutenant's favor and avert his anger from him; when he saw the manner in which Wanda wanted to save him, he pushed her away, and, just as the lieutenant, for Wanda's vouching and for her sake, was about to free the father of any suspicions and not accuse him of anything else—at that moment, Meyer Landshaft, his reason incomprehensible, suddenly stepped out of the line, and, even more suddenly and unexpectedly, he said something absurd and repeated the same words he had spoken earlier, when the lieutenant had asked the people: "Who was sharpening knives?" and he, Meyer Landshaft had spoken up in front of everyone, had taken the blame and said: "I was!"

"I was!" he now repeated the same words: "I was!"—as though trying to remind the lieutenant that no one else, only he, Meyer had said it, and that he was standing by what he had said, refusing to back off from it, unrepenting, not accepting any efforts by anyone to intercede on his behalf with the lieutenant, not even his daughter Wanda, whom he loved so much.

"What?!" cried the lieutenant, utterly amazed, upon seeing Meyer Landshaft's defiance and gazing at him as though he had just caught sight of him appearing out of nowhere. He couldn't believe his ears when hearing the man who had been on the verge of release from his predicament, and who had now, for no reason whatsoever, as the lieutenant assumed, brought back his predicament and taken it upon himself. It was as though a man with a healthy, innocent head had slipped it into a hangman's noose.

"Meyer!" his wife, Hanna-Gitl, cried in terror and amazement, upon seeing her husband, for the first time in his life, committing such a senseless act, as now, saying something that could endanger both him and all the others, God forbid.

"What's he doing?!" These words were blurted out reluctantly and with great but concealed fear by the Jewish administration official (who had witnessed the entire scene) when he heard Meyer Landshaft's defiant words, which virtually sealed his doom, drawing the misfortune upon himself, the reason being incomprehensible: It could have been resolved happily, in the best way, which seldom happens in such cases.

"What's he doing?" said the administration man to himself, turning away, unable to look at Meyer or his senseless act. "Criminal," he said almost aloud, "suicide" (the latter in Hebrew), at a loss to grasp what was happening in that man, who didn't understand the whole thing, who didn't understand the simple facts of life in dealing with authorities, especially such authorities, when they suspect you of something, even some foolish act, which can become very serious, and which you have to clear yourself of—and not only was that man not defending himself, but he was refusing the possibility of help from his daughter, who very nearly could have pulled him out of the pitfall.

Those were the thoughts of the administration man, and those were likewise the thoughts of Meyer's wife, Hanna-Gitl, and likewise of all the other people in the household, who, looking at him, were stunned and speechless, unable to comprehend why he was drawing the calamity on like a beloved piece of clothing.

But Meyer Landshaft himself did understand and he had a reason and justification for his deed, being unwilling to allow the lieutenant's amorous eyes to fall upon Wanda, seeing how the lieutenant was leering at her and sizing her up and delightedly resting his insolent, gaping, filthy officer's eyes on every part of her. . . .

VI

"Arrest him!" shouted the furious lieutenant at the soldiers after Meyer Landshaft had aroused his anger a second time, even making him forget about Wanda, whom he had only just been leering at with such desire, and whom, had he only been permitted to approach her even slightly, he would have exonerated of any suspicions and accusations.

"Arrest him!" the lieutenant said, harsh, resolute, no longer eyeing Wanda, doing his officer's duty—to wipe away the open enemy, this Jew, who was sharpening knives to use against the occupiers.

"Please don't, *Herr Offizier!*" begged first Hanna-Gitl, then her and Meyer Landshaft's older children, then Wanda, who said to the lieutenant: "Take me, Herr Lieutenant, take me instead of him!"

"Arrest him!" the lieutenant commanded for the third time, ignoring, refusing to see, all the people who were surrounding him with their entreaties.

They seized him, Meyer Landshaft . . . . Wanda and also the other children tried to accompany him to the *Kommandantur,* running alongside him the whole time, refusing to leave him. But when they were approaching that destination—the high, broad building the length of a block—and they came to a glass entrance, which was flung wide open by a sentry to let the soldiers in, and finally, after the children had stood out on the sidewalk, for a long time, opposite that building, waiting for him to come back out, and he did not appear, they despaired of seeing him released today and they went to do the kind of things you do in cases like that: look for some way to intercede, run to find help from the Jewish administration and private individuals, Jews and non-Jews, from whom they believed they could get assistance.

A foolish act . . . . One would think offhand, a trifle . . . . But the very fact that Meyer Landshaft was taken to the *Kommandantur* and accused of defying the authorities, even worse, sharpening knives in broad daylight, something a man like him does not normally do; that very fact alone and the lieutenant's testimony, confirming that when he found him sharpening knives and asked him what he was doing, the Jew had not denied anything, on the contrary, he had even defiantly retorted that he was indeed doing that—that alone and all that was enough for the authorities to deal earnestly with Meyer Landshaft and hand him over immediately to a certain interrogator, to whom he was led in a secret room, out of the way, in the huge, dense *Kommandantur* building.

The interrogator was a tall, aristocratic-looking man with deeply pitted cheeks indicative of sinful nights and years of revelry, and now a severe, a stubbornly taciturn man, with a sidelong glare, like a rooster, and a monocle in his eye. It cannot be said that Meyer Landshaft was dreadfully tortured there. But just the isolated and out-of-the-way room in the long, hollow corridor of the *Kommandantur* building, the taciturn demeanor and sidelong glare of the interrogator, whose one eye looked like that of an old sick golden eagle with a bad conscience—those things alone were enough for Meyer Landshaft, a man of few words, a scholar from a fine background, who had never had any dealings with government authorities, and who had never found himself having to be interrogated, especially by such an interrogator—those things alone were enough for him to feel from the very start that he was in some division of hell. . . .

True, at first he had tried to act free and unrestrained in front of the interrogator, being alone here and out of the danger that had only just faced his Wanda at home . . . . The so-called accusation was something he regarded as trivial, something he could easily upset and invalidate. Coming before the interrogator, he mustered his skimpy knowledge, gathered from the books in the language that the interrogator used as he addressed him now—Meyer Landshaft was hoping, both modestly and also a little boastfully, to show that he, the interrogator, was dealing not with just anybody, but with a man who was not only eminent in town, but who was also well-versed in the works of a Klopstock, a Spielhagen, a Schiller, so that he, the interrogator, could understand that such knowledge, such experience were obviously enough of a guaranty and could serve as something of a protection against any kind of misinterpretation, any sort of suspicion. . . .

The interrogator eyed him indifferently. He allowed him to have his say and virtually let him believe that everything he, Meyer Landshaft, said was being taken at its full face value—as proof of his innocence, and that the lieutenant who had brought him here had apparently made a mistake, suspecting a man who was above suspicion.

The interrogator listened to everything he said, he gazed at him, taciturn, as though counting every word, until the very last, which made Meyer Landshaft think they would even apologize to him, give him back his freedom, as a man who had truly been brought here for nothing, here, where he didn't belong.

That was what he thought, and then all at once the interrogator stood up from his chair and forced Meyer Landshaft—who didn't know why—likewise to stand up and face him, and Meyer sensed in the last minute that the interrogator's action did not bode good. Really. . . .

It cannot be said that even now the interrogator's behavior towards Meyer Landshaft was like that of all the occupier's interrogators, according to the normal practice, after an interrogation. He was not thrown into a side room for certain Gestapo men to "work him over": by ordering him to climb up on a table and sit down on a chair there and then knocking the chair out from under him so that he would fall and break his back; he was not beaten with a rubber truncheon; nor was he punched in the chin, the teeth, and forced to push back his head, further and further, until his neck was on the verge of breaking.

No, this time the interrogator did it alone, unassisted, and not all that harshly . . . . He merely walked over to Meyer, quietly, wordlessly, and as Meyer stood before him, surprised and already frightened, the interrogator grabbed Meyer's beard with both hands and suddenly and hastily pulled and tore it, so that the interrogator's hands clutched two dense tangles of hair, and Meyer Landshaft's cheeks, with a meager remainder of tufts, looked like a stubble field after the harvest—that was all.

"Go away!" said the tall, aristocratic-looking interrogator to Meyer Landshaft, gazing at the victim like a sick golden eagle and with a bad conscience. "Go away. That's what you get for the knives you were sharpening, as you say, for your filthy Jewish sabbath. Go about your business, and if we need you, we'll call you, with your plucked face."

VII

He left . . . . But if any of his family or friends would have encountered him as he trudged home from the *Kommandantur*, they would most certainly not have recognized him: He had changed too much between the time of his arrival there and his departure, both because most of the hair was gone from his beard and because his normal silence was so intensified that his tallish stature and his silent and pensive walk almost made him look like the famous mournful knight, as he is depicted, that is to say, like a man who has burned out inwardly and now looks like the chimney of what once was his house.

Upon his arrival home, he was spared any questions about what had happened, they saw without asking, and they immediately understood his dissembled and unspoken intention: to remain alone in his isolated room until the shame was gone and until the hair had grown back in his beard.

They never went into the room, none of them, except for Hanna-Gitl, his wife, to bring him food and take care of him, and even she, when she went in, during the first few hours and even the first few days, she couldn't draw a single word out of him. Apparently, the pull on the outside had torn something from inside him. He remained mute. And the only thing that maintained him, strengthened him, and comforted him in his isolation was, perhaps, the thought that by taking upon himself the shame of the *Kommandantur* and that interrogator with the pitted cheeks, with the long legs, and the monocle—by taking upon himself the shame of feeling the pull by that man's hands, he, Meyer Landshaft, had actually saved the honor of his child, Wanda, who was on the verge of being violated far more horribly than he.

"Thank God," he must have thought whenever Hanna-Gitl came in to him and he asked her: "Is there any news in town, what are people saying, and . . . . How is Wanda?" That was always his last question, as he withdrew into his isolation again, refusing to show himself to the world, to other people, without his normal stately appearance.

But even this solace did not last long: The lieutenant had had a good reason for coming to his home with his soldiers that time. They had registered many women in many Jewish and Gentile homes, except pregnant women and those who were nursing babies, and in Meyer Landshaft's home, they registered Wanda in the list . . . . The way they did this and the way they took the women for unspeakable, shameful things is another story, which is unparalleled in the chronicles of evil that the world is familiar with. The way children were torn from homes, the way they were jammed into freight cars, with only a tiny grated window at the top of one side; the number that was stuffed into one car, the way they were collected at the railroad station, with no parents, no relatives allowed to come and say good-bye to them; and the way the jammed trains with these prisoners lumbered out of the stations; and how many tears, sobs, and quiet swoons could be heard from the sealed railroad cars, through the tiny grated windows—there is no need to say anything further about these things, what we know is enough.

We have to imagine what went on in all these homes when children crossed the parental threshold for the first time, never to come back again; and if they were to come, it would probably be better if neither side were to experience it, not the children and not those to whom they were dear.

We have to imagine what went on in the home of Meyer Landshaft—with everyone, with Hanna-Gitl, with the older children, with the sisters and brothers, not to mention—Wanda herself, but more than anyone else, the father, Meyer Landshaft.

567

He, Meyer, during all the days when they prepared Wanda for the journey (according to regulations, the women had to take along shoes, clothing, and food for several days, as though going to some kind of work), when occasional cries could be heard in the home, a cry from one and then from someone else in the house, letting go in hysterical outbursts; during all those days, Meyer Landshaft did not appear. Not even on the last day, not even at the last hour, nor in the last few minutes, when Wanda was saying good-bye to everyone, accompanied by wild sobs from her mother, Hanna-Gitl, as well as from her brothers, sisters, and other relatives—not even when Wanda went up to her father's door, and her voice, among all the cries in the house, could be heard pleading: "Daddy, open up, I want to say good-bye to you"—not even then did Meyer Landshaft open the door, or throw his arms around Wanda. During the first few moments, he remained silent, then he said: "No, daughter, I can't." Not out of cruelty, to be sure, but because he simply didn't have the heart. Standing at the door, Wanda seemed to hear a weeping, which accompanied her and afflicted her for a long time en route—the weeping of a man lamenting not only his own doom, but the doom of an entire world.

Wanda couldn't endure it and she left . . . . But that evening, at the station, when the train was transferred to a distant line and when several of the prisoners, unaccompanied by anyone, stood in the car where Wanda was, stood under the high window, which they could barely reach, saying good-bye, with their last looks, to their home, from which they were being torn away—at that time, Wanda, like others, also stretched her head to that little window. . . . She wasn't thinking of anyone then, not even her mother, whose last loving kisses she could still feel on her jacket, right by her breast, when her mother, upon saying good-bye, had wept into her breast, burying her face there for a long time, unable to tear herself away—no, not the mother, she was thinking of no one else, only her father, imagining him behind the locked door, as he stood and listened to her pleading, the pleading of his youngest child, his baby, Wanda, and he did not have the heart to open the door, to come out and take a final look at her.

And there was warfare among all kings.

And the whole earth collapsed.

And nothing was left of the demons.

They became nothing.

Amen.

—Rabbi Nakhman

BOOKS BY JOACHIM NEUGROSCHEL

Anthologies:
Yenne Velt: Great Works of Jewish Fantasy and the Occult
The Shtetl: A Creative Anthology of Jewish Life in Eastern Europe

Translations:
Alfred Jarry: *Absolute Love*
Reiner Kunze: *The Wonderful Years*
Ilya Ehrenburg: *The Life of the Automobile*
Paul Celan: *Speech Grille*
Hans Magnus Enzensberger: *Mausoleum*
Miodrag Pavlovich: *The Conqueror in Constantinople*
Racine: *Phaedra, Andromache*
Molière: *The Learned Ladies, The Misanthrope, Tartuffe*
Anton Chekhov: *The Marriage Proposal*
Edmond Rostand: *The Romantics*
Richard Huelsenbeck: *Memoirs of a Dada Drummer*
Jean Arp: *Arp on Arp*
Jean Dubuffet: *Writings*
Andreas Franzke: *Dubuffet*
Ivo Frenzel: *Nietzsche*
Franz Wiedmann: *Hegel*

571

Manes Sperber: *Man and His Deeds*
Hugo Friedrich: *The Structure of Modern Poetry*
André Thirion: *Revolutionaries without Revolution*
Fischer-Dieskau: *Wagner and Nietzsche*
Anonymous: *The Book of Bahir*
Martin Buber: *Selections from "Der Jude"*
Liliana Betti: *Federico Fellini*
Elias Canetti: *The Province of Humanity, The Conscience of Words, The Ear Witness*
Dolf Sternberger: *Panorama of the Nineteenth Century*
Dieter Wellershof: *The Shadowy Border*

Translations into German:
Robert Murphy: *Diplomat among Warriors*
Norberg-Schultz: *Intentions in Architecture*